BUILDING A HEALTHY CULTURE

Building a Healthy Culture

Strategies for an American Renaissance

Edited by

DON EBERLY

Foreword by U.S. Senator Sam Brownback

William B. Eerdmans Publishing Company
Grand Rapids, Michigan / Cambridge, U.K.

Wm. B. Eerdmans Publishing Co.
255 Jefferson Ave. S.E., Grand Rapids, Michigan 49503 /
P.O. Box 163, Cambridge CB3 9PU U.K.

Printed in the United States of America

06 05 04 03 02 01 7 6 5 4 3 2 1

Library of Congress Cataloging-in-Publication Data

Building a healthy culture: strategies for an American renaissance /
edited by Don Eberly; foreword by Sam Brownback.
p. cm.
Include bibliographical references.
ISBN 0-8028-4918-0 (alk. paper)
1. United States — Cultural policy. 2. United States — Civilization — 1970-
3. Politics and culture — United States. 4. United States — Social conditions — 1980-

E169.12.B785 2001
973.92 — dc21

2001019358

www.eerdmans.com

In publishing this work,
Hudson Institute
gratefully acknowledges generous support from

Mr. Paul J. Klaassen
Chairman of the Board and CEO
Sunrise Assisted Living
&
The Klaassen Family Foundation

The JM Foundation

and

The W. H. Brady Foundation

Contents

III. STRATEGIES FOR CULTURAL RENEWAL

Mass Social Movements: Essays by Movement Organizers and Scholars

Reform of Professions and Elite Fields

Foreword

U.S. SENATOR SAM BROWNBACK

In many ways, it is the best of times. Over the past several decades we have made extraordinary progress. Medical advances and high-tech innovations have changed and lengthened our lives. New doors of opportunity have been opened to those historically denied entrance. Economic growth is exceeded only by investor optimism. The cold war is over, and communism has fallen.

And yet, the last few decades have also ushered in a vague sense of unease, a belief that, as a society, we have lost ground morally, spiritually, and culturally. Horrific crimes are committed by children still in grade school. Neighborhood ties are growing thinner and fraying. Families are breaking down and marriages are breaking up at unprecedented rates. Our popular culture is awash in violence and vulgarity, with movies, television programming, music, and games that glamorize killing garnering both commercial success and critical acclaim. Civic participation is falling and public cynicism toward government rising. Even the ordinary interactions of everyday life — driving to work, running errands, shopping — seem more likely to expose us to road rage, incivility, and customer disservice. There is a sense that our society has grown meaner, ruder, and more alienated.

Indeed, poll after poll, and survey after survey, show both an optimism in America's economy and an anxiety over its moral direction. A large majority of Americans believe that our nation is on the wrong track morally and culturally — and that the state of our society is the most important issue we face. Having faced, and triumphed over, so many great external challenges, America's great challenge for the new decade and new century is an internal one: the renewal and reinvigoration of its cultural institutions.

It is hard to overstate the importance or the magnitude of this challenge. We are at a cultural crossroads: the weight of the academic, aesthetic, social, and civil institutions that have sunk into relativism is approaching critical mass. The traditional guardians of the true, the good, and the beautiful have abandoned their posts. Indeed, many of America's premiere universities now question the notion of truth, numerous elite fine-arts institutions discard (or even disdain) standards of beauty, and some mainline religious institutions deny the existence of absolutes of good and evil.

This is not to suggest that all of America's social and cultural institutions are corrupt or that the corrupt are beyond reach. Far from it. Americans are an innovative and reform-minded people, and our nation has great capacity for renewal. It does mean, however, that the ideas promoted through many of our most influential culture-shaping institutions are themselves inimical to a healthy culture and a civil society — and, ultimately, to democratic governance.

It is no exaggeration to say that reforming these institutions is essential to preserving both a civil society and a free and democratic nation. A healthy democracy requires self-government on the part of its citizens; self-government requires virtue, self-restraint, and adherence to a moral code beyond the letter of the law. If we do not cultivate the latter, we will not keep the former. As Samuel Adams, one of the more libertarian patriots, said: "A general dissolution of principles and manners will more surely overthrow the liberties of America than the whole force of the common enemy."

Because self-governance can only be cultivated, not coerced, it has been the work of culture-shaping institutions to encourage and equip individuals and groups to, on one hand, exercise self-restraint and self-discipline, and, on the other, show concern and compassion for others. The frailty of cultural institutions, therefore, cannot be compensated for by increasing the power and reach of government. The work of cultivating virtue is one of moral suasion, not of legislation. The Senate could pass a law tomorrow requiring that we all love one another (there would, of course, be a few dissenters), but even if it passed with a large margin, was signed at a lavish Rose Garden ceremony, and won the almost universal acclaim of press and pundits, little would change. Law is a teacher, but it cannot effectively mold character. Without vigorous and vibrant cultural institutions, the development of democratic character will not occur.

Against this backdrop the entertainment culture has grown in power and pervasiveness. Harvard University professor Robert Putnam posited that the biggest reason more of us are "bowling alone" — detached from other people and organizations — is that television and other forms of electronic entertainment have supplanted human interaction and affiliations. And, indeed, adults and children alike are spending more time watching television, listening to popular music, playing video games, and surfing the Internet. Certainly, there are positive and edifying programs, games, and songs, but much of popular culture became popular not by aiming to uplift, but by appealing to the darker side of human nature. Thus, as children today are given less time by parents and other responsible adults, and are more vulnerable to negative messages, examples, and images as a result, popular culture is inundating them with precisely those things.

Indeed, much of popular culture can be parasitic, eating away at the civic virtues necessary to sustain democratic freedoms. Hence we have advertising campaigns that urge consumers to "Be your own rock," "break the rules," and even "hock a loogie at life"; pornographers who cast themselves as first amendment protectors; and shoot-em-up video games that tout their ability to blur the lines between fantasy and reality even as they simulate murder. At the very time when self-restraint is so needed, the purveyors of our popular culture send a markedly different message: that liberty is license, and that if is not exercised to its maximum — no matter how offensive, distasteful, or vicious that is — it is in danger of being lost. Ironically, in their bid to "celebrate" freedom, they undermine it, by destroying the moral underpinnings of democratic governance and citizenship. As C. S. Lewis noted in *The Abolition of Man:*

> All the time — such is the tragi-comedy of our situation — we continue to clamour for those very qualities we are rendering impossible. You can hardly open a periodical without coming across the statement that what our civilization needs is more "drive" or "dynamism" or self sacrifice, or creativity. In a sort of ghastly simplicity we remove the organ and demand the function. We make men without chests and expect of them virtue and enterprise. We laugh at honor and are shocked to find traitors in our midst. We castrate and bid the geldings be fruitful.

If we are to renew our culture, we must restore the culture-shaping, value-making institutions. Clearly, we have a lot of work to do. *Building a Healthy Culture: Strategies for an American Renaissance* helps us get started with this work. It is a practical manual, as well as a strategic guide, for renewing, revitalizing, and reclaiming the culture-shaping institutions that mold and influence our lives. It takes up its task in several ways.

First, it provides a dispassionate analysis of the state of our culture-forming institutions, and of their impact, influence, and function. It gives due weight to the fine arts, acknowledging that stories, songs, and pictures do more to shape American life than laws, and, for this reason, are of unheralded importance. Second, it spotlights innovative and effective emerging social movements that are now in the process of working their way through various institutions.

The social entrepreneurs and movements highlighted in this book are not only sources of encouragement, they are a glimpse into America's unrealized potential. It is important to identify and recognize these emerging movements, not only to celebrate them, but to bring them to attention so that others may replicate them. By honoring their victories, we hope to sow the ground for many more such movements.

Ultimately, our greatness as a nation depends more on what happens in America's communities than in America's Capitol. What goes on in our families, churches, schools, and neighborhoods is a far more important indicator of our national character and civil health than what goes in on the corridors of Congress. Congress reflects America. Communities *make* America. The march through the institutions will be a long march; no quick fix will do, no shortcuts exist. Reform cannot and does not occur without dedicated reformers, energized social movements, strategic plans, and a coherent philosophy. The creative and innovative capacity of the American people is, I believe, unparalleled anywhere in the world. The United States is, and may long remain, the world's leading cultural exporter. To ensure that these cultural exports take our nation in the right direction requires the strategic thinking and committed efforts of dedicated, thoughtful individuals in every sphere of cultural life.

Appealing to conscience and reason takes time, patience, and persistence, and offers few short-term political benefits. But it is the best way to keep citizens involved, society civil, and our culture healthy.

Introduction: The Moral and Intellectual Framework

DON EBERLY

Imagine a world in which TV producers got together and announced that they would compete for audience share without resorting to prime-time programming that was completely unfit for children. Imagine corporate marketing executives collectively deciding to withhold sponsorship of offensive programming. Imagine a world in which parents could guide their children through grocery store checkout lines stocked with magazines relating the wonders of sex — within marriage.

Imagine that new technological hurdles to gaining access to Internet porn were suddenly developed, which, though not blocking it from the determined minority, would relegate it once again to the back alleys of society. Imagine an entire season of new film releases that were both huge commercial successes and blockbusters in their creative power, but didn't expose thirteen year olds to repeated sexual scenes. Imagine MTV suddenly presenting programming for kids that traded the cynical and seductive for hopeful images of a society filled with meaning and opportunity, where everyone was committed to service to humanity, and where the dream of finding love that lasts forever was real. Imagine an outburst of fresh support for making the popular culture friendly toward marriage and family.

Should such a cultural scenario suddenly unfold, there would almost certainly be an outburst of national pride and optimism about the future the likes of which the nation has never before witnessed. If we take public opinion polls seriously, Americans possess a deep longing for a new wave of action to elevate cultural standards.

The Situation in America Today

There is a profound irony in America's current circumstances. Were it not for the continued coarsening of the culture, America would be both the most materially successful and the healthiest society ever to have existed. America, in many ways, is a picture of health. It is enjoying the longest economic boom in peacetime history. Many of its worst social indicators, such as youth crime, teen pregnancy, and divorce, appear to have stabilized somewhat recently. Cities once thought to be nearly uninhabitable have a renewed sense of order and decorum. It appears that many Americans are reacting to the social chaos of the past several decades with a new search for community, stability, and order. Trend observers notice a deep longing for more enduring relationships, particularly within the family. New social movements are raising the prospects of renewal in areas of marriage and fatherhood.

Moreover, in numerous private and public concerns, America is caught up in a health craze. A casual survey of the popular culture confirms that health is in. Healthy air and water. A healthy diet. Healthy bodies. Women's health. Men's health. When it comes to the health of the natural ecology or the human body, it seems that society will spare no effort. In fact, in an otherwise value-free culture, the most strident forms of officially supported intolerance are now directed toward environmental or physical pollutants. In the public campaign against drugs and, increasingly, against tobacco, for example, the standard is described as "zero tolerance" — such is the craving for health.

In stark contrast to this powerful quest for physical and ecological health, America's cultural environment — its film, television, and popular music — has, to an unprecedented degree, become spiritually unhealthy and morally toxic. In an otherwise health-preoccupied society, popular culture is defying the trends. In fact, the coarsening culture not only stands alone as a negative trend but may also be nullifying the transforming potential of other more positive social trends such as the reduction in teen pregnancy. It appears likely that negative trends in popular culture are impeding what would otherwise be a full-fledged social recovery.

The Necessity for This Volume

That rather remarkable paradox provides the stimulus for this book. This entire volume is about culture — the state of American culture, why culture matters, and what can be done to promote what will be called cultural health. What is being offered in this book will certainly not solve the cultural problem overnight. The objective is to start the process of recovery by addressing what may be the core problem — the lack of any meaningful discussion of long-term strategies to permeate and recover the culture.

Thus far, much of the response of Americans concerned about cultural corruption has been to expect more from politics. Large percentages of morally concerned citizens wrongly believe that the problems of moral license, sexual promiscuity, and divorce, and the loss of shame, shock, and manners, can somehow be corrected predominantly through political organizing. The basic remedy being suggested in this volume, by contrast, is to promote cultural renewal by cultural means: to replace bad culture with good culture. Cultural problems require cultural solutions.

Many of those who don't turn to politics to solve cultural problems resort to simplistic and increasingly ineffective cultural protests. Cultural protest does little to change reality in a marketplace of ideas and values that is shaped increasingly by proliferating electronic media outlets. When all is said and done, a lot has been said and almost nothing has been done about the culture.

Another major emphasis of cultural reforms has been to suggest that the answer to the cultural problem is simply better parenting and more parental protections. Many cultural reformers have been urging the general public, especially parents, to adopt smart consumption controls in the form of more V-chips, better rating systems, and more effective "net nannies." Up to a point, there is much merit in parents building controls into their family's culture-consuming habits. What more and more parents are concluding, however, is that good parenting is not enough when it comes to the culture.

And they are right. It is a mistake to think we can compensate for cultural ruin through a new generation of super-parents. Most parents feel powerless and helpless in the face of forces that are both invading the home and pervading the world beyond. Parents find it next to impossible, for example, to ensure that the rules they attempt to enforce in their own homes regarding cultural products like videos and computer games are enforced in locations outside the home. Moreover, they are intimidated by the thought of appearing prudish in the eyes of their kids, their kids' friends, or other parents.

It is naïve to think that we will conquer the problem of culture by merely insisting that parents build even thicker and higher hedges of protection around their families. This would require a degree of isolation that the vast majority of parents are incapable of or unwilling to carry out. This is not only naïve: it is wrong. As David Blankenhorn, president of the Institute for American Values, has put it: "parenting should not require a heroic struggle against the world beyond." A good society should not impose that scale of burden on parents.

Even though there is an important place for all of these measures, they are not enough, and at some basic level they wrongly absolve the producers of cultural pollution of their responsibility.

The Purpose and Scope of This Volume

The thesis of this volume is that much of the moral and social breakdown in America is being fueled by cultural influences, whether the influence of popular culture or of defective elites across numerous professions and fields, and that the great challenge for this generation is to both think more seriously about culture and develop initiatives and reform movements within cultural sectors. The book does not merely detail the current state of cultural decay in America, therefore; its contributors take the hopeful position that our culture can in fact be improved, and the book focuses on models for reform, both historical and contemporary, many of which use voluntary associations to address a specific social or moral problem. The volume raises doubts about recent attempts to confront cultural degradation through partisan politics, and recommends as an alternative strategies for "remoralization" within cultural spheres.

The essays in the first section of the book, "The Imperative of Building a Healthy Culture," focus on the ramifications of cultural decay, not only for individuals and families, but for society as a whole and even for our democratic system of government. The second section, "Historical Models for Cultural Transformation," discusses transforming public movements and figures of the past, which provide insight for us as we seek cultural renewal today. Finally, in "Strategies for Cultural Renewal," organizers and scholars of numerous reform movements today — in areas ranging from courtship to community revitalization to journalism — describe the work currently being done and the work that still needs to be done to revitalize our culture.

The Claims of This Volume and Its Call for a Cultural Debate

This volume is dedicated to the proposition that the maintenance of a healthy culture is an integral part of defending and preserving a free society. The contributors to the book argue that culture, though generated by private individuals and corporations operating within the framework of freedom, has real consequences not only for the health and well-being of individuals, but for society generally, and for the very freedoms that make cultural openness possible in the first place. It is the thesis of this book that it is increasingly the culture that is the preeminent force of history, helping to shape the attitudes and choices of the young, the overall ethical tone of society, and even America's role in the world.

This volume argues that America needs a great debate about its cultural health; that far greater responsibility for national well-being must be accepted by America's cultural elite; and that among culturally concerned Americans, far greater priority must be given to generating new cultural reform movements and to training a new generation of leaders who will make it the purpose of their lives to revitalize critical aspects of culture. It is furthermore believed that a thoroughgoing American renaissance is not in store unless all Americans of good faith work harder at finding solutions to our ever-coarsening culture.

For those who fear that cultural renewal is mainly about turning back the clock, it should be pointed out that a full-fledged debate about cultural health need not be a journey of nostalgia. Much of the cultural debate to date has focused on time periods, for example the merits of the 1950s compared to the 1960s. Although there are important insights to be gained by carefully evaluating these periods, such discussion largely misses the point. America will not be returning to a previous period. And most people acknowledge that earlier periods were too discriminatory, too closed, and too restrictive.

The debate now is about what kind of society we intend to build as we move into the future, and we believe this should be one which embraces important principles from the past, but which is nevertheless geared toward advancing collective and individual health in the context of today's economically dynamic and technologically advanced world. Nostalgia or reaction has never guided great reform movements. Such reforms were not inspired by a call to return to a previous age as much as they were guided by principles appropriated from the past and effectively applied to present circumstances.

If the debate is not about nostalgia, neither is it about partisanship. Too many of the occasions for cultural debate have taken place in a highly partisan context, such as the presidential impeachment trial — a situation which may serve the objectives of the moment but rarely generates lasting attention to, much less solutions for, the nation's cultural conditions. Another example is the episodic fashion in which cultural issues suddenly surface in presidential campaigns, only to recede from discussion as rapidly as they appeared. Promoting cultural health is not a partisan project for the added reason that it is not primarily about passing laws. Cultural health can't be achieved by simply replacing one partisan majority with another. Any debate that merely appropriates cultural issues to serve immediate partisan objectives will be seen for what it is.

In short, the nation needs a genuine debate: one that is broad and deep, sustained over a period of time, and focused on cultural health — what it is, and how we can achieve it. The authors believe that there is such a thing as a healthy culture, one which maximizes the potential for human happiness and flourishing, reduces social conflict and human suffering, and creates an environment where families are protected and children are granted normal childhoods characterized by unhurried innocence. The authors are also hopeful about America's capacity for self-renewal. While current cultural conditions are lamentable, new movements can be created with resources, energy, and organizing skill to replace our unhealthy culture with one that is healthier.

It must be acknowledged up front that, to some degree, the pursuit of a healthy culture does carry an implied disapproval of unhealthy cultural expressions and choices. The mainstreaming of pornography, the celebration of sex outside of marriage, the embracing of bizarre and offensive art, the granting of cultural space to those seeking legitimacy for alternative family forms, and a host of expressions that not many years ago would have been widely regarded as aberrant are all examples of values and ideologies that are fundamentally harmful to cultural health. Clearly, one cannot address the need for cultural health without suggesting the need for greater voluntary restraints on expressive freedoms, and limits on behaviors that are manifestly harmful to children, families, and the perpetuation of a healthy social order.

Facing the Skeptics

Anyone seeking to advance cultural renewal must be prepared to face a range of skeptics as well as outright resistance. Many of the same leaders who can be counted on to volunteer for health crusades when the issue is physical or ecological health react to the idea of promoting cultural health with wariness, resignation, or outright hostility. Other skeptics argue that "culture is too big and too amorphous to change." A few stiffly resist the idea that cultural health has any relationship to personal or social well-being. Even if it can be shown that it does, these skeptics will attempt to deflect the issue by invoking the first amendment, the presumption being that the matter is thereby entirely settled.

As recently as forty years ago, when today's baby boomers were in elementary school, it was widely assumed that certain basic values would be observed everywhere and by all. Those exercising power over the nation's moral ethos from their positions of leadership, especially those responsible for the domain of popular culture, were understood to bear a unique responsibility to serve the public good. Only a few at the fringes of society questioned the need to preserve the moral tone of society against a natural drift toward license.

While many readily acknowledge that it would be nice if cultural elites still considered themselves the voluntary guardians of at least minimal agreed-upon standards, the suggestion is rarely voiced, so great is the fear of being portrayed as repressive or intolerant. The most powerful resistance to asserting higher cultural standards comes in the form of an aggressive ideological case for tolerance.

Today, tolerance is thought of by many as of far greater importance than judging a person's character, no matter how defective a given person's character may be. It is presented as not only the preeminent American value but also a value that stands above rational argument. As a secular principle, it is essentially theological in character in the minds of those who most readily invoke it. Tolerance is presented as a cardinal virtue, non-arguable and absolute in a universe that is otherwise thought of as lacking moral grounding. The price of being tolerant, the tolerance dogmatists will argue, is steering clear of moral judgments altogether, except of course when such judgments are needed to resist those calling for a cultural cleanup.

Closely aligned with the dogmatism of tolerance is the deconstructionism of the postmodern Left, which contests the very premise that there are universal standards of what is good, true, or beautiful, arguing that such concepts are nothing more than cultural constructions. To the postmodernists, notions of truth are entirely self-derived and individually fashioned. Asserting that there might be universal standards of beauty is considered culturally arrogant.

Aiding and abetting the cultural libertarians, however unwittingly, are the economic libertarians, who can be heard essentially validating the pro-tolerance position of the Left, although for different purposes. Making choices is entirely up to the individual consumer operating in the open market, they argue. If something on television or radio offends, the answer, we are told, is simple: change the channel. This is a vision of culture as consisting of no more than millions of private transactions involving individual consumers and the producers of products. Culture is about private matters, and of no legitimate public concern.

What business, the skeptic will ask, does an individual have suggesting that curbs be placed on cultural expressions, however voluntary and non-censorious those curbs might be on what another private individual consumes? The result: morality is strictly a personal and private matter. There is no widely accepted concept of public virtue, and no means to enforce such a principle even if it did exist. People are expected to police their own lives and to somehow find the means to dodge the toxic elements that invade their space from all directions. Advancing public morality is for busybodies.

Finally, there is on the cultural Right a deepening sense of alienation from the dominant culture in America and a growing tendency to withdraw support and participation. Among religious conservatives especially there is a deeply pessimistic outlook that views culture as having slid too far and thus as being beyond redemption. The only answer, these skeptics assert, is withdrawing entirely from the main institutions of society into moral enclaves. To this constituency, the images of cultural renaissance presented in my opening paragraphs would be dismissed as beyond imagining, even utopian.

The Debate Is about Freedom and Its Responsible Use

Although some use the cultural debate to divide and polarize the nation, the discussion of America's basic values must include participants from across the social and political spectrum because, at its core, this discussion is about America and our ever-changing idea of freedom. Any debate about the culture is in reality a debate about the meaning, scope, requirements, and boundaries of freedom. The contributors to this volume take the view that freedom is fragile if it is not defended through the continued cultivation of virtue and responsibility.

The Founding Fathers appear to have taken for granted that each succeeding generation would work to preserve the virtue-generating institutions upon which a well-ordered free society depends. Today, the debate about culture is taking place in the context of both dramatically weakened social institutions (what some have called mediating institutions) such as the family and neighborhood, and the rise to unprecedented influence of the popular, or mass, culture. These are things that the Founders could not have fully anticipated.

The debate over the state of American culture is not a contest between political conservatives and political liberals as much as it is a debate, transcending party politics, about competing conceptions of freedom. One need not be an ideological conservative or a member of a particular party or religion to join in advocating cultural responsibility. Liberals such as the late John Gardner and Christopher Lasch, and Robert Bellah, the principal author of *Habits of the Heart,* as well as many other intellectuals operating on the Left, have decried the civic destructiveness of America's growing cultural excesses.

Each of the political parties and ideologies operating in America today has its libertarian wing, committed to a concept of freedom that is absolute, countenances no limits, and believes that there is no such thing as a universal conception of morality, truth, or "the good." According to the libertarian school, every choice belongs to private individuals and to no one else. Competing for acceptance with the libertarian schools is what we will call a "civic" conception of freedom, which speaks directly and centrally to the responsibility that both producers and consumers of culture must be called upon to exercise. Again, this debate is predominantly about matters that transcend the state and that cut through partisan and ideological coalitions. In effect, this is a debate about first things.

Culture Counts

America finds itself at the dawn of a new century enjoying unprecedented prosperity, awe-inspiring technological might, and unchallenged military supremacy, yet weakened internally and embarrassed abroad by an increasingly debauched culture. America is a highly accomplished world superpower, but it is slowly ceasing to be a great civilization. The world admires our entrepreneurial energy and constitutional system, but increasingly resists American cultural influence.

My first reminder of this came when speaking several years ago to some of the top organizers and intellectuals of the democratic reform movement within the People's Republic of China. The topic of the talk was the role of character in a free society. I stressed how important it was for democratic societies to inculcate values conducive to individual self-governance, and that it was especially important to develop character-shaping institutions. These Chinese democratic reformers were quick to challenge my assumption that imparting character to their people was a responsibility borne by them alone. In a technologically interconnected world, they insisted, it is our hedonistic American culture that is increasingly corrupting character the world over. These Chinese democrats pointed out that each new step their society took to create greater openness was met with a flood of American cultural programming.

This is the point made so powerfully by former White House National Security Advisor Brzezinski in his essay, where he warns that in spite of America's unmatched economic and military dominance in the world, the global relevance of America's political message could be "vitiated by the growing tendency to infuse the inner content of liberal democracy" with a lifestyle he describes as a "permissive cornucopia." Brzezinski doubts that a global power not guided by a "globally relevant set of values" can exercise predominance for long.

In other words, a nation with the most powerful weapons can issue commands, but it is powerless to compel genuine moral respect, which is the most essential ingredient of true statecraft. Brzezinski states in *Out of Control* that unless there is some deliberate effort "to reestablish the centrality of some moral criteria for the exercise of self-control over gratification as an end in itself, the phase of American preponderance may not last long, despite the absence of any self-evident replacement," and he calls for "a prolonged process of cultural self-reexamination and philosophical reevaluation."[1]

If history is any guide, our economic and military greatness combined with our moral and cultural disintegration could put us on tenuous ground. Time may prove the idea of American exceptionalism — the notion that the U.S. stands above the laws of history — to indeed be a myth, and one grounded in the worst form of hubris. It should be clear by now that prosperity is not by itself the basis of national greatness, and can even contribute to a loosening of

1. Zbigniew Brzezinski, *Out of Control* (New York: Scribners, 1993), pp. xiii, 22.

cultural and social standards. Nations can advance economically and regress culturally. As British philosopher Eric Voegelin has stated: "A civilization can, indeed, advance and decline at the same time — but not forever. There is a limit toward which this ambiguous process moves."[2] Unless Americans confront their cultural condition, America could, like great civilizations that came before, face widening debauchery and social disintegration.

The role culture plays in maintaining the nation-state is frequently ignored. From cultural debauchery always flow cynicism, demoralization, and a general sense of weariness in defending the nation's most elementary ideals. The late novelist Walker Percy captured his concern for America, saying he felt he was witnessing a nation "with all of its great strength and beauty and freedom gradually subside into decay through default and be defeated," not, he said, by outside adversaries, but from within "from weariness, boredom, cynicism, greed, and in the endless helplessness of its great problems."

America certainly continues to show signs of dynamism and health, and one could even argue that her social immune system is finally coming alive, as is evidenced by the mild stabilization in recent years of some social pathologies. But all Americans should heed the warning that contained within our current cultural condition are genuine seeds of potential long-term social erosion, if our response is one of indifference.

Freedom Requires Social Health

In the American system of ordered liberty, democracy is dependent for its health upon conditions that are more or less social or cultural in nature, as Mary Ann Glendon argues in her essay. The Founding Fathers conceived of a system consisting of three spheres: the political or law-making sector, the economic sector, and the socio-cultural sector. Freedom, to be durable, requires maintaining more than vibrant political institutions and a robust market economy; it depends upon character-shaping social and cultural institutions. In short, a free society requires that each generation perpetuate through cultural institutions a widely shared sense of responsibility, mutual sacrifice, and commitment to the common good. Self-government, which is the essence of freedom, depends upon qualities of self-control that are transmitted culturally from generation to generation.

George Washington argued repeatedly that a free republic could not be maintained without a virtuous people. For the nation's founder, individual mo-

2. Eric Voegelin, *The New Science of Politics* (Chicago: The University of Chicago Press, 1952), p. 132.

rality was not merely a private matter. It was the very foundation of liberty, as liberty was then understood. Liberty was not an abstract principle. It had substantive content and requirements. Thus, liberty would prosper if it were surrounded by moral and cultural health. "The foundations of our national policy," said Washington, "will be laid in the pure and immutable principles of private morality." "Private virtue and morality is a necessary spring of popular government."

The culture bears a heavy responsibility to preserve a democratic society. Cultural institutions are, in fact, the seedbeds of public virtue upon which a healthy political order depends. A British political philosopher, Michael Oakeshott, has stated,

> Political activity may have given us Magna Carta and the Bill of Rights, but it did not give us the contents of these documents, which came from a stratum of social thought far too deep to be influenced by the actions of politicians. A political system presupposes a civilization; it has a function to perform in regard to that civilization, but it is a function mainly of protection and to a minor degree of merely mechanical interpretation and expression.[3]

The Founders had a clear sense that democracy was not merely about ballots and procedures; it would rest upon sturdy character and well-practiced democratic habits. A society in which great numbers of people vote yet lack the disposition for democratic society, are defiant of social norms, and are intent for the most part on gratifying their wants, will be just as disordered a society as one in which few bothered to vote. In a free society, it is cultural institutions that bear a heavy responsibility to shape moral norms — or mores — minimizing society's reliance on the law and state regulation.

In sum, sustaining freedom requires preserving institutions that shape character (especially families and communities), real social and cultural authority, and a widespread acceptance of responsibility. These are not being sustained today, when each of the institutions that supply the social capital upon which American democracy depends has faced erosion, in some cases perilous erosion. Primary institutions such as the family are fraying (slightly less than half of all children born today will reach the age of eighteen without having their lives disrupted by a rupture in the family) and civic institutions such as neighborhoods are thinning out.

3. Michael Oakeshott, *Religion, Politics and the Moral Life*, ed. Timothy Fuller (New Haven: Yale University Press, 1993), p. 93.

What Exactly Is the Culture?

Even the most elementary task in a discussion of culture, namely attempting to define it, to explain how it is shaped, or to establish its boundaries, is likely to generate skepticism if not hostility among some. These individuals will be quick to challenge the idea that there is such a thing as a unified American or western culture, except perhaps its core democratic values of liberty and equality. In fact, those very liberal political values will likely be invoked to raise doubts about the legitimacy of asserting a particular set of cultural values in what is now a hyper-pluralistic society, home to people from every cultural and ethnic background. In a land that prizes liberty, it will be argued, people must be free to develop their own conception of reality, choose their own lifestyles, and weave together their own worldviews. America is about millions of private choices made by autonomous individuals and little else.

It strikes some as odd to imagine the culture as an instrument of social governance, but it is. In contrast to the direct regulatory powers of the state, culture can be said to govern human affairs "lightly." A healthy culture will take the time to establish boundaries around the individual and to grant or deny permission in accordance with broadly understood and accepted moral standards in society. It will also seek to elevate and ennoble. Positive cultural influences can compel people to do one thing and not another. Civic duty, for example, is an American cultural norm. It barely exists in many other nations, including the European democracies out of which America was born.

The full dimensions of what we call culture can hardly be captured in a short description. The term itself implies something held in common — as Webster puts it, "an integrated pattern of human behavior that includes thought, speech, action, and artifacts." The traditional view is that culture's purpose is to regulate and order our lives through informal and non-coercive means — through social regulations such as manners and moral norms.

At its most abstract level, culture consists of the ideas, values, attitudes, and myths by which we order our lives and which are broadly reflected in the works of our minds and hands. Culture is our souls' writ large; it mirrors what we value and love. It embodies the basic ideas, attitudes, beliefs, and habits of a people. These attitudes and beliefs are continually shaped and reshaped by powerful cultural institutions, at both the elite and popular levels.

Culture is a huge sphere, difficult to describe, much less analyze, and even harder to reform. At the elite level, it is shaped through numerous fields such as philosophy, art, literature, education, and science, and then transmitted through thousands of channels of expression in the vast domains of human communication and reflected in daily life in speech, myths, rites, rituals, and beliefs. This realm of high culture includes important elite professions such as law, medicine, and journalism, which exert tremendous influence over the course of the culture.

The realm of popular culture includes entertainment, film and television, popular books and magazines, theater, the vast arena of technological communications, publishing, advertising, and much of the private market itself. One could argue that there is also a political domain of culture, where great conflicts over values and lifestyles such as abortion, gender issues, the family, pornography, political correctness, and multiculturalism are fought.

Differentiating culture from other major realms of life (such as the economic, legal, political, and religious) is in itself difficult. Culture both affects and is affected by the institutions of the nation, the state, and civil society, but it is not interchangeable with them.

America's Cultural Condition

The contributors to this volume are well aware that discussion of America's cultural problems can quickly degenerate into an attitude of "declinism," which insists that our current conditions are part of an inexorable, downhill slide. The view presented here is that much is actually well with America, that America has proven again and again a remarkable capacity to confront its problems, and that positive change can come to the sphere of popular culture just as it has already begun coming to some of the social indicators. The case for cultural pessimism grows less certain when the many examples of renewal movements are taken into account. Even if only those discussed in this book are considered, it becomes clear that cultures can and do improve in response to well-orchestrated movements aimed at reform.

Ultimately, Americans will consider an alternative cultural direction for the same reason they regularly consider lifestyle changes: the life-enhancing possibilities offered. Midge Decter, a leading New York cultural critic, states: "You should bear in mind that what you would urge upon your fellow Americans is not just what is necessary for a decent national culture but what will make their own lives richer and better." Efforts to reform the culture, she says, will "not just help to clean up the culture but will actually make it pleasing and cheering to people."[4]

Because the contributors to this volume hold an optimistic outlook, they have gone out of their way to avoid repetitiously citing evidence of bleak cultural conditions. That said, it must be acknowledged that if corrective action is to be organized, there must first be an understanding of the nature

4. Quoted from a private letter to the editor.

and scope of the problem. Few people within the mainstream of public debate will deny that American culture seems to have lost its way. It is a culture that no longer prefers the healthy and that which is conducive to strong families to the unhealthy. It is a culture that is all too indifferent to its toxic effects on children.

There are some who will nevertheless ask what it is the contributors to this volume are concerned about. Sam Karnick, editor of *American Outlook,* the policy journal of the Hudson Institute, offers this fairly comprehensive survey of our cultural landscape:

> American culture has become a slum of vulgar language, strife between the sexes, grotesque clothing and hairstyles, sexual indecency, annoying telephone solicitations, loutish TV talk shows, crude movies and music, putrid "shock radio," sordid politics, rowdy audiences in movies and sporting events, discourteous and dangerous driving, jostling in checkout lines, and the kind of general meanness that escalates to domestic abuse, verbal and physical assaults, and even murders. The lively arts appear distinctly moribund and corrosive. Movies are gratuitously violent, TV is grotesquely oversexed, popular music is cacophonous and vulgar, literature is barely literate, paintings are ugly and incomprehensible, the legitimate theater has become agitprop for sexual license, video games are increasingly gruesome and occultic, and so on.[5]

"And so on," indeed. All of these things, and more, that daily bombard our senses are surface ripples produced by deeper currents far below the surface of our culture. P. A. Sorokin, the famous Harvard sociologist who wrote about an emerging crisis in the culture in the 1940s, described a cultural virus invading all of society's "main sectors," including "art and science, philosophy and religion, law and morals, manners and mores; in the forms of social, political, and economic organization, including the nature of the family and marriage — in brief, it is a crisis involving almost the whole way of life, thought and conduct of western society."[6]

If the purpose of culture is to order and govern our lives in accordance with broadly shared values, then our culture no longer functions as a culture. Its purpose is no longer to order, but to grant emancipation from the very idea of moral norms. The popular worldview of our time consists of near-religious faith in the sacredness of the autonomous sovereign self. If the job of culture is to elevate the human condition and to guard against human excesses, our cul-

5. Sam T. Karnick, "The Everything Culture," *American Outlook,* Summer 1999, p. 8.
6. P. A. Sorokin, *The Crisis of Our Age* (New York: E. P. Dutton, 1943), p. 17.

ture is clearly failing. American society is fast becoming morally normless, which is tantamount to saying that it is steadily ceasing to be a society at all.

The importance of culture's role in humanizing society should not be underestimated; culture has the ability to elevate and ennoble, a role particularly important in shaping the lives of children. Former school principal Peter Gibbon captured the loss of a humanizing culture in the lives of children when he said, "I am terrified that our children are not being raised by exemplar lives and confident schools; nor by high culture, vigilant communities, families, churches, and temples, but rather by an all enveloping enemy culture interested in amusement, titillation and consumerism."[7] In other words, the culture, according to this school principal, has lost its positive, humanizing influence.

As noted above, the introduction of toxic threats into our land and lakes or the human body is regularly confronted with indignation. When it comes to the introduction of toxins into the moral ecology of the nation, however, American society has broadened the range of behaviors deemed acceptable further perhaps than any previous society. This loosening of taboos is illustrated most profoundly in the trendy deconstructionism of high culture and the sexual preoccupation of popular culture. To suggest that there be a norm in the area of human sexuality or marriage, for example, often produces stiff resistance, notwithstanding the fact that healthier cultural standards would make life dramatically better for society's most vulnerable members, children. The current trajectory of the culture, however, is to eradicate the few remaining obstacles to maximum personal freedom, a phenomenon that Patrick Moynihan has described as "defining deviancy down." There are very few personal acts that anyone can still publicly assert to be morally wrong. Only the most elementary taboos — child or spousal abuse, incest, genocide, and bigotry — remain.

When we talk of cultural failure, it is usually in reference to the loss of this norm-setting function. The very idea of culture implies the existence of curbs, or what Bill Bennett calls "cultural guardrails." The term "culture" conveys a tightening, not a loosening; it implies the search for stability, not disintegration. A culture that serves simply to loosen and not to restrain ceases to be a culture at all. The term itself becomes an oxymoron.

Some defend the idea of culture as a free-for-all as a necessary step in providing widening freedoms for the individual. There are those who can imagine as natural only a cultural trajectory providing more and more openness, not less. They argue that important new freedoms for the individual could not have been won without the relaxation of cultural checks, such as those of tradition,

7. Peter H. Gibbon, "In Search of Heroes," *Newsweek*, 18 January 1993, p. 9.

custom, or religion. Others accept that cultural standards have worsened, but deny that people are actually harmed by our deteriorating culture. A significant minority refuse to accept that any idea or image is inherently harmful or injurious to society. Representatives of the entertainment industry, for example, regularly try to debunk the overwhelming empirical evidence that television violence produces violence in children. When the evidence that cultural pollutants do real harm proves impossible to refute, they shrug it off as simply one of the prices we pay for freedom. In other words, that which is socially regressive is sold as human progress.

The Increasing Power of Culture

The many issues having to do with culture and its influence on American life are not merely private matters, as was noted earlier. Few would deny that popular culture is now exercising unprecedented influences over the values of the nation, for good or bad. The chief job of every civilization is to take narcissistic infants and turn them into self-regulating and other-regarding adults. Defenders of democracy cannot be indifferent to the values that are being inculcated, nor should they ignore whether that job is being performed by parents, schools, neighborhoods, or, as is increasingly the case, the popular culture.

The Increased Role of Culture in Socialization

Popular culture has become Americans' primary source of information, attitudes, and beliefs, starting at the earliest of ages. The growing dominance of popular culture in socializing the young today represents uncharted territory, even for a society as open as America. In fact, what is unprecedented in our experience, and what is perhaps revolutionary in the human race, is the power that popular culture now has to compete with, if not entirely supplant, other forms of authority — parental, educational, religious, and political.

It is this phenomenon — the power of an omnipresent entertainment and information media culture to displace more personal influences — that is a new reality for democratic society, and one that deserves heightened attention. Whereas parents, priests, and pedagogues once presided over the socialization of the young, this process is now dominated by television, film, music, cyberspace, and the celebrity culture of sports and entertainment. It is popular culture that largely informs our basic understanding of society, our public life, our obligations to each other, and even the nature of the American experiment. Studies show that large majorities of kids can name a particular rock group but can't identify the most elementary aspects of America's history or constitutional system.

If the Founding Fathers could have anticipated this phenomenon, it seems certain that it would not have escaped their comment. The constitutional framers, along with such early observers as Alexis de Tocqueville, commented extensively on the role "mores" (by which they meant essentially social customs) played in preserving the democratic order. Tocqueville, the foremost observer and analyst of American democratic society, marveled at how well Americans performed this socialization task, to which he attributed our democratic system's success. Were he writing *Democracy in America* today, he would undoubtedly describe at some length the place of the Internet, "walkmans," computer games, and television in the lives of many Americans.

While it must be acknowledged that there is much good to be found within mass cultural programming, the dominant impulse of popular culture today does not appear to be aimed at guiding the young toward adult responsibility. Much of the music, film, and television consumed by youth tends to present life as a permanent state of youthful play, characterized by self-indulgence and mass-amusement, tendencies that are antithetical to democratic life if not countered by other influences.

Culture as the Engine of Social Breakdown

Charles Krauthammer argues in this volume that the single greatest shaper of wants and values "is not government, but culture," and that mass culture has been "vastly underappreciate[d]" as an engine of social breakdown. Elsewhere, he writes: "Never before in history have the purveyors of a degraded, almost totally uncensored culture had direct, unmediated access to the minds of society's young. An adolescent plugged into a Walkman playing 'gangsta rap' represents a revolutionary social phenomenon: youthful consciousness almost literally hardwired to the most extreme and corrupting influences."[8]

At least for a brief moment, the tragic shooting in Littleton, Colorado, caused Americans to focus on what might be called the "social ecology" that now shapes our lives, beliefs, and values. Many openly questioned whether the violence perpetrated by Eric Harris, the self-described philosopher who had a web page dedicated to his hate-filled ideology, was the isolated work of a psychopathic killer or whether his actions might have been nourished by a cultural environment that is now toxic and fundamentally corrupting to character.

8. Charles Krauthammer, "A Social Conservative Credo," *The Public Interest,* Fall 1995, p. 17.

Our growing violence and inhumanity in America is due in large measure to the decline in authority of those basic formative institutions combined with the rise of a popular culture that has not accepted this sense of collective responsibility for inculcating democratic character. Those who stand in positions of power within the mass culture have been on the receiving end of a massive transfer of power. It is fair to ask how they have reacted to this vast increase.

There are great numbers of conscientious people who make their living in music, entertainment, and film who would agree with the analysis presented here. Many producers of popular culture, however, view themselves not as citizens with a responsibility to help generate social health, but merely as capitalists seeking to profit by responding to the desires of consumers. Their ethic seems to be: whatever someone wants, no matter how debased, we have a right and even an obligation to produce it.

Many find the very idea of sharing responsibility for "civilizing the young" laughable. That's not the role of entertainment, they will say. The role of entertainment is to challenge and to stretch standards. "Break the rules!," "Have no fear!," "Be yourself!," are the common themes within mainstream cultural programming, designed to discredit traditional forms of authority such as parents.

As many will correctly observe, there is nothing particularly new about the young finding new ways to subvert the authority of parents and teachers. Every generation of American youth has revolted in its own way against established rules and moral norms, and every generation of adults has concluded that standards are collapsing. People say, "remember our shock at the first appearance of Elvis's gyrations on stage," or, if they're old enough, they recall the public's reaction to new forms of "lewd" dancing that emerged in the 1920s.

Unfortunately, this reasoning, while partly sound, only encourages the worst kind of cultural relativism and spreads a sense of futility among those who would seek to clean up the culture. Such reasoning reflects our loss of the capacity — and more importantly of willingness — to think critically enough about these things to distinguish between that which is merely new and trendy but nevertheless socially harmless, and that which can turn an alienated youth operating at the margins of society into a genuine sociopath. The refusal among the thinking classes to distinguish between Elvis's hips and that which graphically portrays the simultaneous rape, hacking, and dismemberment of women represents a form of cultural dysfunction in itself.

Ironically, this cultural relativism also leaves kids with fewer and fewer socially harmless ways to challenge the status quo represented by their parents. When a society has lost its capacity for shock, even in response to the most debased behavior or the violent and misogynistic rantings of some rappers, youth are forced to find ever more extreme ways to shape their identities and make a statement about their independence. What happens when such things as tattoos, body piercing, or male earrings instantly become mainstreamed as they have recently, even adopted by adults? Is it possible that Eric Harris and Dylan Klebold turned to a fascination with Hitler and death because nothing else socially provocative enough for them to build an identity around remained?

In rebutting a challenge to this cultural relativism, defenders of corrupt culture often resort to the ultimate conversation stopper: the First Amendment. While there is a dire need for a fresh debate about the First Amendment, what often passes for a discussion of it is nothing of the kind and involves no serious debate about the constitution. When defenders of the entertainment industry invoke the First Amendment, they are rarely even referring to a constitutional right to expression, a right acknowledged by all. Often what they are saying is, "what I am free to produce, I have an obligation to produce." In other words, if someone wants degraded or extreme material, they feel an obligation to produce it lest a right to expression go unexercised and hence potentially become compromised. In other words, a freedom not exercised is a freedom denied, or even a freedom threatened.

In fact, it is this expansive and irresponsible view of freedom that could very well lead in time to the erosion of freedom. Perhaps the best example of this is the draconian steps schools have had to take in the wake of Littleton against anyone suspected of being capable of committing a crime. The irresponsible use of freedom by some can quickly erode the state of freedom for all, including rights of privacy, expression, and association.

The Costs of Cultural Nihilism to Individuals and to Society

The increasing relativism of American popular culture is related to its increasing nihilism. Traditional values and beliefs are no longer revered and many no longer even believe that any objective or absolute moral truth exists. The consequences of such nihilism are numerous and grave.

Loss of Social Cohesion

Cultural nihilism can have real consequences for the social order of a free society. John Gardner, the late founder of Common Cause who spent most of his years fighting the corruption of the electoral and lawmaking processes, frequently noted the central role that shared values play in a democratic system by providing social glue. "There has to be some core of shared values," said Gardner. "Of all of the ingredients of community this is the most important.

Values may be reflected in written laws and rules, in a shared framework of meaning, in unwritten customs, in a shared vision of what constitutes the common good and the future."[9] As Gardner pointed out, democracy does not need only a sound lawmaking process; it depends for its existence on social cohesion grounded in shared values.

"A shared framework of meaning," "unwritten customs," and "a shared vision of what constitutes the common good"? These concepts are steadily extinguished in a nihilistic culture. The language of "shared" and "common" signifies so little that it is rarely used, and, when it is, it generates ridicule among many. Gardner presented the consequences of this phenomenon in stark terms. "[W]ithout the continuity of shared values," he said, "freedom cannot survive."[10]

The culture bears a heavy responsibility to transmit a society's core principles and ideals from generation to generation. Nations are said to live by their myths. Americans, for example, have traditionally thought of their country as a great "melting pot." When a culture caters instead to individuals and promotes an entirely privatized concept of the good, one can expect a steady erosion of unifying social beliefs and norms.

More important still is the role of culture in sustaining deeper beliefs regarding the nature of man and the transcendent foundations of freedom. It is these foundational principles that find little encouragement within academia today, especially in particular fields, and are often scoffed at as antiquated in public debate — a worrisome fact given that the cultural revolution of the 1960s and '70s showed that cultural movements have it within their power to erode social cohesion and the public legitimacy of institutions. Freedom requires a transcendent grounding. When the Supreme Court declared in 1992 that "central to personal dignity and autonomy is the right to define one's own concept of existence, of meaning, of the universe, and of the mystery of human life,"[11] America's highest judicial body validated the basic idea of cultural relativism.

Presumably this right to define one's own concept of reality and the universe does not extend to denying the dignity and autonomy of other human beings, although this is not stated and one can question whether it is ensured under such a system. The court case invited Americans to become metaphysical nomads, free to roam about, either embracing or rejecting common notions of meaning and purpose, and to repudiate if they choose the foundations of the very liberty that makes possible their freedom to think and choose.

9. John W. Gardner, *Building Community* (San Francisco: The Independent Sector, September 1991), p. 16.

10. Gardner, *Building Community*, p. 16.

11. *Planned Parenthood v. Casey*, 1992.

The rise of popular culture coincides with, indeed it has precipitated, the collapse of those older belief patterns grounded in a balanced and ordered freedom. The older culture, which went perhaps too far in producing stoic self-denial, has been traded in for a culture that has gone to an even greater extreme in its pursuit of self-realization and sensuality. America is in the midst of a process of cultural disestablishment, in which the ideals and symbols that once animated our collective consciousness are disintegrating, without a viable candidate for replacement waiting in the wings.

In this new culture, each person gets to write his own rules based essentially on feelings and perceptions. There are no universal principles, only personal opinions and desires. There are no proven or privileged values to guide collective decision-making, only a vast universe of differing personal tastes. There is no concept of justice to prompt common action, only self-advancing individuals.

Thus at a deeper and more important level, cultural decay is about the collapse of cultural coherence and authority, whereby, as British sociologist Os Guinness puts it, the "beliefs, ideals, and values that once defined America have lost their compelling and restraining power."[12] The United States is witnessing the disappearance of a coherent and widely shared cultural narrative that binds citizens together in common enterprise. Even the nature and scope of rights — so highly prized by advocates of cultural openness — becomes confused and conflicted.

When society is severed from its original underpinnings of faith and culture, citizens lose the basis for a common life together, and society fragments. This new American culture, rather than requiring self-restraint and social obligation as the price of freedom, demands nothing of the individual and everything for him.

Psychological Disorientation and Stress

A common theme of cultural analysis has been the uprooting and alienating influences of modern and postmodern culture. What emerges is a picture of the individual radically ungrounded in anything except the self and severed from such sources of moral meaning as family, religion, custom, and even place. Robert Bellah puts it this way: "In the absence of any objectifiable criteria of right and wrong, good or evil, the self and its feelings become our only moral guide."[13] The individual carries the full burden of knowing his own wants and desires.

12. Os Guinness, *The American Hour* (New York: Free Press, 1993), p. 20.

13. Robert Bellah et al., *Habits of the Heart: Individualism and Commitment in American Life* (New York: Harper and Row, 1985), p. 65.

Ironically, modern philosophy and psychotherapy's notion of the unencumbered self, with freedom to enjoy all of life through psychological perceptions and feelings, carries with it enormous psychological burdens. According to Bellah, the American understanding of the autonomy of the self places the entire burden of "one's own deepest self-definition" not on tradition or community, but rather on "one's own individual choice." Most of us, he says, imagine an "autonomous self, existing independently, entirely outside any tradition or community."[14]

William Van Wishard, a futurist and cultural critic who has written extensively on the shifting makeup of America's core beliefs and psychological orientation, describes a major psychological and spiritual reorientation that has been underway in America, first among a "small creative" minority of artists and intellectuals and more recently among the general public. He describes a "breakup of the inner images of wholeness" which has given rise to widespread anxiety and alienation. "What we are talking about," he says, "is the loss of a viable, all-encompassing collective myth that, historically, has provided the individual and society with defined values and offered answers to the ultimate questions of existence."

Some counter by pointing to the widening interest in spirituality in American society as evidence of a healthy search for meaning and coherence. Van Wishard, however, replies that "it is little comfort to point to the public opinion polls showing what percentage of Americans believes in a deity." The true measure of a nation's spiritual condition, he says, "is not found in such polls; rather it's found in the quality of a nation's culture. A culture is to a nation what dreams are to the individual — an expression of its inner psychic life."

Van Wishard describes the function of culture historically "to cultivate the higher attributes of life, to encourage wholeness of personality, and to link the individual with some transcendent reality." Today, however, "[o]ur inner moorings have been loosened," Van Wishard states. Such a culture, one "which becomes disconnected from its transcendent roots," also becomes "dysfunctional."[15]

The availability of widely accepted psychological symbols connecting aspirations to roots is an essential ingredient of cultural wellness and national cohesion. In the West, this sense of psychological coherence was for years, to a considerable degree, supplied by Judaism and Christianity, but many believe the undergirding power of the Judeo-Christian worldview is steadily receding.

14. Bellah, *Habits of the Heart,* p. 65.

15. Van Wishard quotes in all three paragraphs are taken from "Technology, Myth and a New Role for Humanity," an unpublished speech by William Van Wishard.

Václav Havel has tied the loss of inner psychological symbols of wholeness and a sense of moral transcendence to a deepening fissure between faith and the culture. Havel asserts that "people have ceased to respect any so-called metaphysical values." He added: "We live in the first atheistic civilization in human history," one that "proudly asserts that man is capable of knowing everything, describing everything, and doing everything." Humanity has, in turn, lost a "sense of humility and responsibility, a relationship to the world as a whole, to its metaphysical order, to the miracle of creation."[16]

Dehumanization

Culture, as that term is normally understood, cannot be merely man-made. It must be rooted in ideas, myths, stories, and religious beliefs that transcend man. Today's culture, largely stripped of its transcendent dimension, is therefore premised upon a self-contradiction: a culture that elevates individual autonomy and boundlessly glorifies the human personality, unrefined by faith or reason, is a culture that ultimately degrades man.

Another consequence, therefore, of replacing that which is ennobling and elevating in human culture with that which is banal, course, and prurient is the increased desensitization of human beings toward the moral worth and dignity of others. When senseless acts of violence and degradation become the standard fare of popular culture, people are slowly conditioned to accept a cheapened view of humanity and of human possibilities. This is not humanism, but its negation.

Sadly, it is all too easy to make peace with the vulgar and the vicious when one is surrounded by it. The ancient philosopher Cicero captured it this way: "If we are forced at every hour, to watch or listen to horrible events, this constant stream of ghastly impressions will deprive even the most delicate among us of all respect for humanity." No longer a matter of purely partisan interest, the cheapening of culture and human worth is raising profound questions regarding the ethical course of the nation. Individuals ranging from Pope John Paul II to Holocaust survivor Elie Wiesel deliver a common message: a society that celebrates debauchery and treats human beings in a utilitarian fashion as objects of material and sexual gratification is a society in the process of disintegration.

The greatest achievements of the human race in areas of art, music, and literature have come as man transcended materialistic bounds. In other words, true humanism requires transcending man. This is what P. A. Sorokin had in mind when he said that a culture grounded entirely in a naturalistic world

16. Address by Václav Havel, Harvard University, Cambridge, 8 June 1995.

lacking transcendent moorings and meaning is a "sensate culture," leading not to man's elevation, but to his degradation. He described as the central self-contradiction of our culture the fact that it is simultaneously "a culture of man's glorification and man's degradation." On the one hand, he says, "it boundlessly glorifies man and extols manmade culture and society," while on the other "it utterly degrades the human being. . . ."

In this culture, Sorokin continues, the final arbiter of what is good and just is not transcendent truth, but feelings and sensations. Values become completely utilitarian. There are no universal principles, only private preferences, opinions, and tastes. In the sensate culture where the individual is the only sovereign, legitimate social authority erodes and interpersonal trust crumbles. Vast realms of activity once considered voluntary and consensual come under the purview of the law. Fragile families and dysfunctional individuals fall under the custodial care of government agencies and caseworkers. All roads lead to the courts. Power trumps morality.[17]

Boredom and Ennui

Aimlessness and boredom, or what Hilton Kramer calls "complacent nihilism," are not the ingredients of a healthy culture or a great nation. In a society increasingly dominated by the massive superstructure of popular culture, it falls largely to the institutions of culture and civil society to cultivate what Alexis de Tocqueville called the "habits of the heart." When this function breaks down, institutions of the state are called upon to do things for which they are ill prepared, which only produces a deepening frustration among the people. It has been suggested throughout this introduction that cultural nihilism can weaken democracy, even breed contempt for it. While those serving in the political arena should do their utmost to avoid encouraging distrust, it is not the job of the state to confront these things.

Cultural nihilism ultimately corrodes democracy, robbing it of its spiritual dynamism and social vitality. How can democracy be healthy when the culture generates among the young contempt for public institutions and distrust toward those who have volunteered to serve their country? Can a culture that promotes self-indulgence and materialism also produce a willingness among the people to make sacrifices should the nation be called upon to defend itself or its allies in war? Will the next generation be inclined to restore communities through increased civic participation when, as pollster George Gallup Jr. puts it, "the very idea of a good person is ridiculed"?

17. Sorokin, *The Crisis of Our Age,* p. 242.

Cultural nihilism generates a widespread sense of weariness and dissatisfaction. Democracy requires vibrant civic institutions and an ample supply of citizens whose hearts have been captured to serve purposes larger than themselves. It simply does not flourish in the midst of cynicism, heartlessness, and boredom. Yet these are the attitudes that are projected and affirmed in much of the popular culture reaching American youth. Cultural critic Eugene Peterson says that "the enormous entertainment industry in our land is a sign of the depletion of joy in our culture. Society is a bored, gluttonous king employing a court jester to divert it after an overindulged meal." Gone is our own imagination, our individual creativity or our gifts of service to the world, our willingness to defend our system. Instead, says Peterson, "we buy the vitality of another's imagination to divert and enliven our own poor lives."[18]

Eric Cohen, editor of *The Public Interest,* describes well the boredom and frustration of our time in the passage that follows. He suggests that our times are especially susceptible to

> maladies of the soul: debased irony and cynicism, which reduce life to absurdity; a therapeutic ethic, which deifies the self and devalues virtue and transcendence; the revolutionary spirit, which denies the fact of human limitation or rebels against all tradition and restraint; and, most common, the life of the bourgeois egoist, who is decent and practical but spiritually unsatisfied.

The modern citizen, says Cohen, is a drifter — homeless, cut off from things which are stable and binding, "divorced from tradition, nature, and the old responsibility of upholding the family name." The drifter "does what advertisers tell him or what his urges urge him. He has sex when it's convenient but never falls in love. His parents are divorced or distant and his home life is dominated by the anxious extremes of yelling and silence."

Continues Cohen:

> The moral drifter has no responsibilities, no hope, and no purpose. He is free from all commitments and tries not to concern himself with the perilous questions of life and death. He is a stranger, a tourist, and an indifferent observer. He is the television watcher, the apathetic consumer, the college student who stares blankly for four years from the back of the classroom, waiting he says for real life to begin.

18. Eugene Peterson, *A Long Obedience in the Same Direction* (Downers Grove, Ill.: InterVarsity Press, 1980).

"When it comes to politics, culture and morality," says Cohen, the drifter "is tolerant by default." "He does not judge others because he is unwilling, afraid, or unable to judge himself. He focuses almost entirely on himself, and yet he is, at bottom, ambivalent about himself, holding no strong opinions one way or another." Cohen continues:

> To the drifter, everything is at best a game, a joke, and an ironic play. If he is not entirely humorless, the sadness of the drifter is softened by easy pleasures, repackaged humor, and childish naughtiness. He sits for hours in front of the television, remote control in hand, flipping from station to station, sitcom to sitcom, with nothing in particular to watch and nothing in particular to do. He is not horribly sad, but he is bound by nothing, loves nothing, and reveres nothing.[19]

This is not a culture that nourishes a hunger for imagination, wonder, awe, or gratitude. Public educators, the vast majority of whom still believe that our education crisis is attributable solely to such things as classroom size and poor teacher training and pay, might consider how this culture discourages interest in the life of the mind. Pastors and priests, who are witnessing the youth disappear from their congregations, might consider that this culture does little to nourish the soul or generate interest among the young in spiritual matters. Those who lament youth violence but can think of little to do about it except perhaps regulate guns must realize that this is a culture which, at least among those operating at the margins of society, incubates killers. Cohen captures the irony: "The same nation that mourns over the mayhem at Littleton chuckles at the pop nihilism that comes out of Hollywood — and sees no contradiction."[20]

The Destruction of Intimacy; the Loss of Mystery

Few aspects of American culture more completely fit the description of complacent nihilism than the current public preoccupation with sex. What was once a culture of almost stoic self-denial, erring (most would acknowledge) on the side of restraint, has become a culture single-mindedly committed to the pursuit of sensuality.

Popular culture contributes to this new tendency by encouraging everyone to ignore the rules, especially social norms having to do with sex. Calvin Klein projects sexualized images of youth as "people who do only what they

19. Eric Cohen, "To Wonder Again," *First Things,* May 2000, p. 23.
20. Cohen, "To Wonder Again," p. 25.

want to do"; Saab sells cars by telling us to "peel off inhibitions." The search for new sexual frontiers may well be the most dominant theme in American popular culture today. No one can deny that sex is one of the most powerful and important forces in the human experience, but this is precisely why it must be protected and preserved for maximum enjoyment through widely accepted sexual mores. Sex is far too important to debauch.

While American culture once encouraged people to repress thoughts and behaviors that were regarded as aberrant, now, says James Wilcott, "the problem is the opposite; getting people to put a cork in it." "What was once impossible to accomplish has become impossible to stop."[21] Even our deepest secrets, "our once hidden shames," are now routinely exposed by popular culture.

To think of sex as powerful and beautiful but nevertheless a thing to be enjoyed in private is to be considered repressed. Nevertheless, as Wendy Shalit, who is attempting to re-popularize "modesty" for the sake of preserving what is sacred and beautiful, asserts: "compunction is not a dysfunction." Reacting to the naked appearance of supermodel Cindy Crawford on the cover of *W Magazine,* Shalit observes: "Cindy Crawford declares that she is 'comfortable with her body' and shows it to the whole world. But there is good reason to protect the private realm and keep sex sacred: not because you are ashamed but, on the contrary, because you want to reveal yourself only to the one who loves you."

In other words, that which is truly beautiful and which moves us most deeply should not be entirely unveiled except under certain conditions. A culture that gives sexual expression free rein is one that will get plenty of sex combined with a scarcity of genuine, enduring love. The late Russell Kirk described a sexually normless society as "loveless desolation."

The impact of our culture's out-of-control sexuality on children and families is quite obvious and need not be addressed here. But what has received little attention is the impact of sexual license on the power and enjoyment of sex itself. By merging genuine human sexuality with essentially a debased, pornographic conception of genital activity — what is termed "hooking up" on college campuses — the culture is increasingly producing a loveless, soulless sex that strips sex of its mystical power. It may come as a great shock to those who have pursued sexual emancipation in the culture to be informed that they, not the self-denying Victorians, have come close to destroying sex in all of its mystery and beauty, but the evidence suggests that this is so.

In an article entitled "Put Sex Back in the Home and Close the Door," *Washington Post* writer Donna Britt states that "few would willingly return to TV married couples sleeping in twin beds and female stars remaining screen virgins well into their thirties." But, she asks, "is it good to go from pretending

21. James Wilcott, "Dating Your Dad," *The New Republic,* 31 March 1997, p. 32.

sex doesn't exist to pretending little else does?" Britt describes the frustrations of being a mother in a society in which porn has "gone mainstream" and is sold in the marketplace via the theme "relax, it's just sex."[22] "Pretending sex is as simple and healthy as flossing one's teeth minimizes its life-altering side effects, including pregnancy, abortion, and HIV," writes Britt. And besides, she asks, why would anyone want to floss in public? Most lamentable, she adds, is that when the "air of secrecy and specialness is gone," there are "life and spirit-threatening consequences."[23]

In other words, sex has been demystified. The sexuality commonly presented today is devoid of all but the most base eroticism and centers not on the infinite possibilities of romantic and spiritual union but on exploring the finite and exhaustible world of physical anatomy. Today's sex is a reductionist sex centered on maximizing the release of bodily passion while starving the souls of men and women alike of transcendence. Ours is a world in which physical intercourse — of any kind, combination, location, or frequency — exists in plenty, while the achievement of genuine human intimacy, trust, and vulnerability is, for many of the sexually active, elusive.

This is sex, in other words, that is not even remotely sexy. It is the rushed release of pent up bodily hungers. The purveyors of a sexually hyperactive mind-set have created a culture that no longer seeks to capture the mind and imagination around the tender, trust-winning wooing of a romantic lover, what was once called "courtship." It is a culture in which male-female sexual coupling involves a relationship that is almost always tenuous and subject to abrupt rupture, and, frequently, filled with pain and remorse as well.

Sources of Cultural Disintegration

Changing Means of Cultural Transmission

If the moral substance of culture has been altered, the institutions that transmit cultural values have undergone equally dramatic change. Holding a culture in common becomes infinitely more difficult when all modes of living, thinking, and communicating become subordinated to some form of new information technology. A culture transmitted directly through technology rather than mediated through real institutions is a culture that will lose its cohesion.

Prior to the past century, there was no such thing as popular culture. The

22. Donna Britt, "Put Sex Back in the Home and Close the Door," *Washington Post,* 28 March 2000.

23. Britt, "Put Sex Back."

technological revolution in the twentieth century changed that. Culture and society have practically become subsidiaries of the technological structure that presides over our modern modes of communicating and living. No longer do the rhythms of daily life in face-to-face communities establish our social habits — chat rooms in cyberspace fill the void. As a result, the individual is no longer bound in any meaningful way to the moral instruction of religious or moral authorities. He or she independently receives information and values from an infinite variety of sources — whether legitimate and authoritative or not — unmediated by moral mentors. The morally authoritative institutions that previously carried out mediating functions are rendered impotent. Whereas culture was once contained and community was bounded, today we have what could be called the "surfing sovereign": each man, woman, and child with a personal web site, all mouse-clicking their way along the cosmos of unlimited ideas, ideologies, religions, and lifestyles, designing a worldview out of the crazy quilt patches of cyberspace. Every taste, interest, and ideology has its own platform.

Not all are convinced society will end up without local rootedness in this new environment. William J. Mitchel, dean of the School of Architecture at MIT and author of *E-topia,* says the new digital order "will not turn us all into rootless, laptop-toting, cell-phoning nomads. Far from it. Most of us will want more or less permanent places of our own." In fact, he says, living our lives in digitally dispersed communication "may make many of us yearn, more than ever, for places to rub shoulders, to be part of community."[24]

Moreover, there can be no doubt that technology has had numerous positive effects. In education, commerce, and even in culture, technology is often employed for the good. It can, in fact, contribute in some ways to stronger communities. It can be employed to strengthen groups and associations, and technological advancements can lead to less mobility and rootlessness in society, as people are able to keep in touch across large distances.

But while technology can reduce disconnectedness, it also transports the entire universe of information and ideas to the individual. Technology makes man an omniscient observer and vicarious participant in the whole expanse of human experience. Instead of "familiar bonds of place," says columnist Neil Peirce, we find ourselves "dealing with a far-flung world of loose-knit configurations of electronically mediated meeting places."[25]

It is fair to question whether an individual will ever again be able to yield

24. William J. Mitchel, quoted in Robert Samuelson, "And the Limits of Wealth," *Washington Post,* 10 May 2000.

25. Neil Peirce, "What Will Urban Life Be Like in a Digitalized Age?" *Washington Post,* 5 December 1999.

the same degree of allegiance to a particular community, culture, or worldview when a whole world consciousness continuously crowds in on him. Community is not virtual; it is real. It involves real face-to-face relationships in real institutions like churches, fraternal associations, and volunteer groups. The virtual community does not care for the poor, does not raise children, and probably does little to create generous citizens. These tasks are accomplished by real communities.

Technology also collapses boundaries. It eliminates the distance of time and space between vice and virtue, which have always been in conflict but never before thrived within milliseconds of each other. The red-light district was far less menacing to society when it was located in a remote place, where it was hard to get to, where it was easily detected, and where conditions were unpleasantly seedy. Now it exists at the command of a mouse or remote control, all in the comfort and anonymity of our own homes. Censorship, if it ever was the answer, becomes progressively less viable in this environment. Moreover, the presumption of self-censorship that once existed among the purveyors of popular culture is gone, and the technological means for effective censorship have largely vanished.

While community, which has always rebounded because of the social nature of man, will almost certainly survive these most recent challenges, and may actually become stronger as a bulwark against the alienating aspects of mass society, what happens to the popular culture is anyone's guess. The challenge of restoring a common culture, with proper boundaries and controls, has been rendered dramatically more difficult, if not impossible, by new technologies. Many ask at what level of society, and by what means, can common culture, even at the most basic levels, be restored? The cultural air we breathe carries a concept of reality in which there are no fixed reference points. Whatever values and opinions we hold today face permutations tomorrow. This is what futurists mean when they announce that "technology will destroy culture" — not merely a particular culture, but the very possibility of culture.

The personally empowering but socially disabling nature of modern technology has received extensive discussion in some academic quarters, but, like the substantive content of culture, it has been given too little weight in the popular debate over civil society and culture.

Revolt of Elites

If culture has been transformed by the means through which cultural beliefs are transmitted, it has also been consciously challenged from within by philosophical movements, especially at the elite level. One of the main reasons the culture is difficult for many to comprehend and even harder to effectively change is because much of what we call "the culture" comes to us from professions and industries that are remote to average Americans. It is from the commanding heights of the fine-arts industries — film, television, music, art, publishing, theater — and from within scores of other elite professions that the moral ethos of society is largely set. Much of the cultural change that has come to America has come about by what the late Christopher Lasch called, in a book by that title, a "revolt of the elites." Lasch describes "an aristocracy of brains" — a broad group of influential elites ranging from lawyers to journalists to investment brokers — who worship their own technological expertise, science, and rationality, disdaining the traditional habits of people linked to community, family, religion, and country.

This elite, according to Lasch, is "in revolt" against "middle America," which it views as "technologically backward, politically reactionary, repressive in its sexual morality, middlebrow in its tastes, smug and complacent, dull and dowdy." When it comes to loyalty to traditional American values, the new aristocracy, he says, is "in transit."[26]

Communitarian Robert Bellah describes a cultural transformation of American life so complete that ordinary people now speak in a different "voice" from the institutional leaders around them.[27] Similarly, University of Virginia sociologist James Davison Hunter, author of *Culture Wars,* argues that Americans are now locked in a heated contest over "different systems of moral understanding." Conflicts go beyond single divisive issues to deeper moral and philosophical concepts.

The institutional elite are frequently categorized as "progressive," meaning secular, rationalistic, and anti-traditional. The "progressive" cultural coalition described by Hunter does not look favorably upon re-moralization, with its commitment to recovering enduring moral precepts. Progressives frequently focus on alternative notions like diversity and tolerance, which are usually advocated as a means of guarding against moral judgments.

Gertrude Himmelfarb advances an analysis similar to that of Lasch, Bellah, and Davison in a book entitled *One Nation, Two Cultures,* in which she describes the contradictory tendencies in American culture at the dawn of this new century. Himmelfarb maintains that the contradictory tendencies within the culture coincide with a deep divide between what remains of a traditional society that still subscribes to the old "bourgeois" ethos and an "ad-

26. Daniel J. Silver, "The Revolt of the Elites and the Betrayal of Democracy," a review of the book of the same name by Christopher Lasch, in *The American Spectator,* May 1995, p. 72.

27. Bellah, *Habits of the Heart,* p. 65.

versary culture" represented predominantly by "bohemians" in the elite ranks of society.

At one end of the spectrum, says Himmelfarb, is "what sociologists call elite culture," which statistics confirm is more morally permissive and socially progressive than the public at large. At the opposite end of the spectrum is what remains of traditional culture (those prepared to define family and moral values along conventional lines), or what can now be understood as a genuine counterculture — what she calls "the dissident culture." To clarify, she says that the "two cultures" are "neither monolithic nor static." "Nor are they totally separate and distinct." But the gap between progressive elites and the non-elite public exists, and explains "the peculiar, almost schizoid nature of our present condition: the evidence of moral disarray on the one hand and of a religious-moral revival on the other."[28]

This minority, she says, is perennially on the defensive, not because it lacks grassroots numbers in society, but because its elites

> cannot begin to match, in numbers or influence, those who occupy the commanding heights of the dominant culture: professors presiding over the multitude of young people who attend their lectures, read their books, and have to pass their exams; journalists who determine what information, and what "spins" on that information, come to the public; television and movie producers who provide the images and values that shape the popular culture; cultural entrepreneurs who are ingenious in creating and marketing ever more sensational and provocative products.[29]

The moralists have been further rendered powerless by the success with which cultural elites have "democratized and popularized" many of the attitudes once confined to bohemian circles.

Unhealthy culture proves difficult to transform, therefore, because it is shaped predominantly by elites who have power far out of proportion to their numbers, who are not accountable to the general public, and who are not easily affected by grassroots opposition. Many who seek to promote cultural health are prone to organizing these grassroots movements, on the assumption that all that is needed is a certain amount of protest from the people — the consumers — against the producers of culture. But the problems of American culture, as we have seen, have mostly to do with a cultural elite that has lost its way, and they will not be corrected simply by organizing boycotts and protests. Such an

28. Gertrude Himmelfarb, *One Nation, Two Cultures* (New York: Alfred A. Knopf, 1999), p. 119.

29. Himmelfarb, *One Nation*, p. 126.

approach has limited impact, and, as a long-term strategy, it is largely misguided.

As Himmelfarb notes, "An occasional boycott by religious conservatives can hardly counteract the cumulative, pervasive effect of the dominant culture."[30]

Impulse toward Liberation

The dominant impulse within popular culture has perhaps been to emancipate individuals from what were portrayed as stultifying, repressive cultural norms. Conventional moral norms, indeed the very idea of a norm, imply certain boundaries in the public realm where our common life is developed. Cultural nihilism, operating in the service of individual emancipation, necessarily destroys these boundaries between the private and the public. In the name of openness, it exposes, often in great detail, those functions of body and mind that were once universally considered too private and secret, if not shameful, to expose. Privacy, which once served as a protective container for matters considered personal, has instead become aligned with a movement to publicly legitimate private choices.

The impulse toward liberation is neither neutral nor benign in its effects on America's social institutions. Alan Ehrenhalt, author of *The Lost City,* concludes that while "there may be a welter of confused values" operating in society today, "there is one point on which all Americans speak with unity and unmistakable clarity." We have, he says, become "emancipated from social authority as we once used to know it."[31] This quest for emancipation from social authority "has meant the erosion of standards of conduct and civility, visible mostly in the schools where teachers who dare to discipline pupils risk a profane response." The problem in locating all authority in the individual, according to Ehrenhalt, is that it clashes directly "with the obligations and social norms that held families and communities together in earlier years."[32]

When art and entertainment strive to emancipate the individual from constraints, society increasingly becomes conditioned to resist conventional moral and cultural tastes. Reverence for history, the wisdom of the ages, and moral customs is replaced by a spirit of perpetual creation and reinvention with a preference for the untried and unconventional. This is the society of unim-

30. Himmelfarb, *One Nation,* p. 126.

31. Alan Ehrenhalt, "Learning from the Fifties," *Wilson Quarterly,* Summer 1995, p. 8.

32. Ehrenhalt, "Learning from the Fifties," p. 25.

peded freedom imagined by Rousseau when he made his famous statement "Man is born free, but he is everywhere in chains." Rousseau's society is supposed to be a "happy sanctuary," free of responsibilities, disappointments, or limits, where life is lived in a natural and childlike way, with each person seeking to live in accordance with his native or natural impulses, no matter how base.

In this culture, the individual is guided by a youthful spirit of cultivation in a world of few rules, rather than following the natural developmental process toward the demands of adulthood. What emerges is a culture shaped by adults who refuse to accept the requirements, moral or intellectual, of adulthood. Robert Bly describes the dominant demographic today as "a sibling society" that seeks liberation from repressive paternalism by giving way freely to impulse, thereby regressing back to childhood. This is a society in which adults no longer advance higher ideals, and in which many adults are comfortable emulating adolescents, paying deference to the always shifting attitudes and trends of youth culture. A culture dominated by adolescent thinking is essentially narcissistic.

Moving beyond adolescence requires making judgments about one's own conduct as well as the conduct of others, seeking to improve one's own character, and accepting natural limits. Rochelle Gurstein, author of *The Repeal of Reticence,* illustrates the difficulty of making these judgments in a society that has judged such activity to be wrong. To ask adults in a society, especially those in cultural authority, to "occasionally raise above a puerile, sniggering adolescent level," she writes, "is evidence of snobbery, or, worse yet, of attempting to inculcate middle-class or 'highbrow' values in others." To raise objections to free expression or individual choice, "no matter how graphically violent, sexually explicit, perverse or morbid — is to invite the epithet 'puritan.'"[33]

Gurstein argues that modern expressive liberalism has broken down because it can "no longer discriminate between the essential circulation of ideas, which is the cornerstone of liberal democracy, and the commercial exploitation of news, entertainment, and sex as commodities." Likewise, this modern form of liberalism "can no longer distinguish between the expression of unorthodox ideas in the pursuit of truth, which is the lifeblood of art, and the desire to publicize anything that springs to mind in the name of artistic genius." In other words, the restraint and appropriate inhibitions necessary to preserve a good society have become intolerable to the cultural avant-garde. Any shared notion of the true, the beautiful, or the good has been lost. In fact, according to Gurstein, it is no longer possible to converse in an older language of love and

33. Rochelle Gurstein, *The Repeal of Reticence* (New York: Hill and Wang, 1996), p. 5.

beauty. Such discussion, she says, is seen as "evasive, sentimental, platitudinous, or naïve." To be bound by a restricted view of the good is to be inauthentic and not truly free.[34]

We have witnessed the defeat of what Gurstein calls "the party of reticence" in the twentieth century. With that defeat, our "faculties of taste and judgment — along with the sense of the sacred and the shameful — have all become utterly vacant." Without faculties of taste and judgment, "it is now clear that disputes about the character of our common world can only be trivial, if not altogether meaningless."[35]

The "Creative Destructionism" of the Market

Any discussion of the culture, to be fair and realistic, must confront the role that is played by the economic market in loosening social and cultural standards. If technology has played a role in weakening the traditional boundaries of community and culture, so too has the emergence of an uprooting mass consumerism and a market-dominated society.

The question of whether or not a dynamic free market system weakens the social order is an age-old debate. Although the market system is now widely accepted as the favored economic system on both moral and practical grounds, markets are not without their effects on the social order, as most will acknowledge. They have a restless, uprooting, and relentless effect on society and culture.

A culture dominated solely by the market principle awakens permissive attitudes toward consumption, amusement, and immediate gratification. Columnist and political philosopher George Will describes those who are oblivious to the impact of the market on settled morality as people who "see no contradiction between the cultural phenomena they deplore and the capitalist culture they promise to intensify; no connection between the multiplying evidence of self-indulgence and national decadence, and the unsleeping pursuit of ever more immediate, intense and grand material gratifications."[36]

The idealization of markets as the soul arbiter of human relationships and values can easily produce an instrumental means of reasoning. Writing in 1942, the prominent economist Joseph Schumpeter suggested that the driving entrepreneurial spirit would undermine both the bourgeois ethos and the tra-

34. Gurstein, *Repeal of Reticence*, p. 5.

35. Gurstein, *Repeal of Reticence*, p. 5.

36. George Will, quoted in Mark Henrie, "Rethinking American Conservatism in the 1990s: The Struggle Against Homogenization," *The Intercollegiate Review*, Spring 1993, p. 37.

ditional institutions that sustained it.[37] Thus the social and cultural system that gave rise to capitalism itself became the victim of the process of "creative destruction." Said Schumpeter, "Capitalism creates a critical frame of mind which, after having destroyed the moral authority of so many other institutions, in the end turns against its own."[38]

Schumpeter merely continued a debate begun by no less a figure than Adam Smith about the impact of prosperity on the moral health of a nation. Smith described "two different schemes or systems of morality," one essentially held by the working classes and the other by elites.

> In every civilized society; in every society where the distinction of ranks has once been completely established, there have always been two different schemes or systems of morality current at the same time; of which the one may be called strict or austere; the other the liberal, or, if you will, the loose system. The former is generally admired and revered by the common people: the latter is commonly more esteemed and adopted by what are called people of fashion.[39]

By people of fashion, Smith meant essentially those having financial power in society. Those occupying this station in life were more given to the vices of "luxury," to "the pursuit of pleasure," "to some degree of intemperance," and to "the breach of chastity." While the common folk tend to abhor and detest such laxity, Smith said, among people of fashion and luxury the vices are "treated indulgently." The reason for this was quite simple. Smith explained that the prosperous could financially sustain the consequences of overindulgence, while the poor knew that such a lifestyle would produce quick ruin.

Gertrude Himmelfarb maintains that "much of the social history of modern times can be written in terms of the rise and fall, the permutations and combinations, of these two systems."[40] The struggle between morality and economics is a recurring pattern of American experience. Smith understood that those who generate wealth and those who seek to promote a more elevating, civilized culture are not always the same people. Economic prosperity is no predictor of social progress, nor is the rise of a large class of successful business owners a predictor of greater concern about cultural or moral health. The cycles of history also suggest that times of economic prosperity coincide with a loosening of social standards, whereas periods of economic deprivation pro-

37. Himmelfarb, *One Nation,* p. 12.
38. Joseph Schumpeter, quoted in Himmelfarb, *One Nation,* p. 12.
39. Adam Smith, quoted in Himmelfarb, *One Nation,* p. 3.
40. Himmelfarb, *One Nation,* p. 4.

duce a bracing up of standards. Abundance, says Robert Samuelson, "gives us more freedom." With material abundance "we are increasingly liberated to 'be ourselves,' but self-expression can slip into self-indulgence, sometimes self-destruction."[41] Few will volunteer to forfeit hard-won economic prosperity, but for those who seek cultural rebirth, the power of "creative destructionism" in contributing to cultural excesses must be acknowledged.

It is one thing to accept this creative destructionism as inevitable, unavoidable, and necessary for a greater good, to acknowledge the trade-offs that come with it, and to work to ameliorate its effects. It is disingenuous, however, for market advocates not to acknowledge that the dynamics of market capitalism can uproot traditional community bonds and loosen cultural standards.

Cultural Strategies: The Task for the Twenty-first Century

If it is correct, as this book argues, that America's weaknesses lie predominantly in the cultural sphere, that political solutions to cultural problems are neither effective nor appropriate, and that the answer is therefore developing new initiatives around the social movement model, then the remaining questions are few: Why are these reform movements not being organized with greater imagination and determination today? Why is the same intellectual power and organizing energy not being brought to cultural recovery that was recently directed to stopping totalitarianism abroad or an out-of-control welfare state at home? And how is it that so many have come to excuse the purveyors of cultural pollution of their most elementary duties of citizenship? When corporations pollute the air, society does not recommend that people, on their own initiative, purchase gas masks, as though it is strictly a private matter involving individual consumers. It is the pollution itself that is declared to be bad. We mount up to resist the polluter, and we demand that emissions be cut. That is precisely what we must do in the area of popular culture.

The alternative to cultural protest, super-parenting, and a host of other "demand side" measures is cultural recovery, advanced through movements aimed at permeation, replacement, and renewal. Throughout American history, large-scale social movements were organized to bring badly needed corrections to American society by moving out and permeating that society in strategic ways. In the nineteenth century, numerous initiatives working for moral uplift, temperance, private charity, cultural reform, and the restoration of social standards were organized within American society. In other words, social problems were confronted through social, not merely political, movements.

41. Samuelson, "And the Limits of Wealth."

There is no shortcut here. We must fix American problems the American way. At times of social breakdown and cultural loosening in the past, leaders and citizens joined together to promote responsibility movements through the key sectors of society. Yes, private responsibility on the part of consumers will matter. Strengthening the family, especially by confronting father absence and divorce, will certainly help, as will boosting the resolve of parents to protect their children from harmful values. Families will play an important role in pushing back against the power of popular culture. But, alone, their efforts will not be enough. We will need big ideas as well as specific plans. It is with that in mind that the contributors to this volume offer their words of analysis, challenge, and hope.

I. THE IMPERATIVE OF BUILDING A HEALTHY CULTURE

The Cultural Underpinnings of America's Democratic Experiment

MARY ANN GLENDON

If history teaches us anything, it is that constitutional democracy cannot be taken for granted. There are conditions that are more, or less, favorable to liberty, self-government, and the rule of law, and those conditions involve the character and competence of citizens and public servants. But character and competence have conditions, too, residing in nurture and education. The American version of the democratic experiment leaves it primarily up to families, schools, religious groups, and a host of communities of memory and mutual aid to promote the republican virtues of self-restraint, respect for others, and sturdy independence of mind — and to transmit them from one generation to the next. Thus, the deteriorating health of these groups has grave implications for a regime of ordered liberty.

The stakes are high, for as Alexis de Tocqueville pointed out long ago, if democratic nations should fail "in imparting to all citizens those ideas and sentiments which first prepare them for freedom and then allow them to enjoy it, there will be no independence left for anybody."[1] The American Founders, like Tocqueville, simply took for granted that the requisite habits and beliefs would be taught and transmitted mainly within families and the institutions that surrounded and supported them. The young United States seemed blessed with an

---

The assistance of Michael O'Shea, Harvard Law School Class of 2001, is gratefully acknowledged.

1. Alexis de Tocqueville, *Democracy in America* , transl. George Lawrence, ed. J. P. Mayer (Garden City, N.Y.: Doubleday, 1969), p. 315.

abundance of social, as well as natural, resources. Today, however, families, neighborhoods, religious groups, and communities are showing signs of exceptional stress. We have begun to realize that we cannot indefinitely consume our social capital without replenishing it.

What lends particular poignancy to the present situation is that — as with the natural environment — many threats to the social environment are the by-products of genuine improvements in the general standard of living — technological advances, social welfare programs, and increased opportunities for individual fulfillment. The crucial question is this: How can we preserve and pursue the social, economic, and political goods of a democratic republic without eroding its cultural foundations? This essay traces some key shifts in the relation between democracy and its culture-forming institutions and argues for a more "ecological" approach to politics.

Democracy and Culture at the Dawn of the Democratic Era

Democracy generally connotes a range of *political structures* through which popular consent may be expressed and related freedoms (especially of speech and association) may be protected. But it is important to keep in mind that democracy is also a set of *ideas* about equality, freedom, and popular sovereignty that have transformed the political and social landscape of the world. Those ideas came to the fore, and modern democracy was born, in the struggle to replace hereditary monarchies with representative governments. In France, that struggle involved an all-out attack on culture-forming institutions — a move that, paradoxically, endangered democracy. Under the slogan "there are no rights except those of individuals and the State," French revolutionaries targeted not only the feudal statuses of the Old Regime, but also the Church, the craft guilds, and many aspects of family organization. They saw civil society as a bastion of inequality, a source of oppression to individuals, and a competitor with the state for the loyalty of citizens.[2] One consequence of that revolutionary zeal to abolish the old *corps intermédiaires* between citizen and state was that "civil society" became a major subject in continental European political thought throughout the nineteenth century. Tocqueville, Hegel, Marx, Durkheim, and others wrote at length about what the relations were, or should be, among individuals, the institutions of civil society, and the state.

Tocqueville, in particular, speculated about what might ensue if the institutions of civil society, once regarded as too powerful, became too weak. He

2. Marcel Waline, *L'individualisme et le droit* (Paris: Domat Monchrestien, 1945), p. 323.

pointed out that, with the increasing centralization of political power, the very same groups that had once seemed to stifle individual development and to obstruct national consolidation might turn out to be essential bulwarks of personal freedom and to provide useful checks on majoritarian rule.[3] He speculated further that growing individualism, together with excessive preoccupation with material comfort, might weaken democracies from within by rendering their inhabitants susceptible to new forms of tyranny. "Habits form in freedom," he warned, "that may one day become fatal to that freedom."[4] As the bonds of family, religion, and craft fraternities loosened, he feared that men would become feverishly intent on making money or dangerously dependent on "a powerful stranger called the government."[5] That state of affairs, he surmised, could foster the emergence of new forms of despotism:

> Far from trying to counteract such tendencies, despotism encourages them, depriving the governed of any sense of solidarity and interdependence, of good-neighborly feelings and desires to further the welfare of the community at large. It immures them, so to speak, each in his private life and, taking advantage of the tendency they already have to keep apart, it estranges them still more.[6]

Tocqueville was no reactionary. He was convinced that nothing could halt the advance of the democratic principle. Indeed, he described himself as "constantly preoccupied by a single thought: the thought of the approaching irresistible and universal spread of democracy throughout the world."[7] The only question, so far as he was concerned, was whether it would produce free democratic republics or tyrannies in democratic form. His book on American democracy (an instant best-seller that went through twelve editions by 1848) urged Europeans not to resist the inevitable, but rather to work with all their might to assure that freedom was preserved in the coming regimes. From his observations in the United States he was persuaded that everything depended on whether the citizens possessed the habits and attitudes needed to sustain liberty within democracy. To those who shared that way of thinking, civil society — as the locus of the groups in which the requisite habits and attitudes are formed — became a matter of crucial political importance.

Though the cultural foundations of democracy were of great interest to

3. Tocqueville, *Democracy in America,* p. 506.
4. Tocqueville, *Democracy in America,* p. 254.
5. Tocqueville, *Democracy in America,* p. 301.
6. Alexis de Tocqueville, *The Old Regime and the French Revolution* (New York: Doubleday Anchor, 1955), xiii.
7. Tocqueville, *Democracy in America,* p. xiii.

many nineteenth-century continental thinkers, matters were different in the United States. At the time of the American Revolution, land ownership was more evenly distributed than anywhere in Europe, and most Americans lived in self-governing towns and cities. About four-fifths of the (non-slave) population were independent farmers, small businessmen, and artisans.[8] The American insurgents had no interest in radically restructuring society; their aim was to achieve independence from England. Strictly speaking, theirs was a secession rather than a revolution. As soon as they were free of the colonial yoke, the Founders concentrated on producing an ingenious design for a republic with democratic elements, a Constitution with vertical and horizontal separations of powers, and a system of checks and balances. The design was for a *federal* system that would leave authority over matters that immediately touched the lives of citizens mainly in the hands of state and local governments. Except for the Founders' concern to control the power of "factions" (special interests),[9] civil society received relatively little attention in American political thought until the twentieth century — when it became apparent that large corporations were acquiring sovereign-like power and that many of the mediating structures of civil society were in distress.[10]

The chief interest of the American experiment, in Tocqueville's view, was not that it was a model for any other nation to copy, but rather that it afforded concrete evidence that the benefits of democracy need not be purchased at the price of liberty. To those of his readers who were fearful that democracy meant mob rule (tyranny by the majority), he said: "American laws and mores are not the only ones that would suit democratic peoples, but the Americans have shown that we need not despair of regulating democracy by means of laws and mores *(les moeurs)*."[11]

What did Tocqueville mean when he wrote of "regulating" democracy by laws and mores? He described with admiration how the American Constitution and federal system provided structural checks on pure majoritarianism. But he saw the small self-governing townships of New England as furnishing an

8. Robert Heilbroner, "Reflections — Boom and Crash," *The New Yorker,* 28 August 1978, pp. 52, 68.

9. James Madison, *The Federalist Papers,* Nos. 10 and 51.

10. The work that sparked interest in the study of civil society in the United States was Robert Nisbet's *The Quest for Community* (New York: Oxford University Press, 1953). Recent works of note include: Robert Bellah et al., *Habits of the Heart: Individualism and Commitment in American Life* (Berkeley: University of California Press, 1985); Amitai Etzioni, *An Immodest Agenda* (New York: McGraw-Hill, 1983); Nathan Glazer, *The Limits of Social Policy* (Cambridge: Harvard University Press, 1988); and Council on Civil Society, *A Call for Civil Society* (New York: Institute for American Values, 1999).

11. Tocqueville, *Democracy in America,* p. 311.

equally important kind of check, an internal check within the citizenry itself. By affording many opportunities for participation in government, they permitted citizens to acquire "clear, practical ideas about the nature of their duties and the extent of their rights."[12] "Local institutions are to liberty," he wrote, "what primary schools are to science; they put it within the people's reach; they teach people to appreciate its peaceful enjoyment and accustom them to make use of it. Without local institutions a nation may give itself a free government, but it has not got the spirit of liberty."[13]

The French visitor was even more impressed by the vigor and variety of the *social* groups that stood between the individual and government. He saw a country where most men, women, and children lived on farms or were engaged in running a family business (both forms of livelihood involving intense cooperation among the participants). These families — the first and most important teachers of the republican virtues of self-restraint and respect for others — were surrounded by a myriad of religious, civic, and social associations. Those latter groups provided settings where "every man is daily reminded of the need of meeting his fellow men, of hearing what they have to say, of exchanging ideas, and coming to an agreement as to the conduct of their common interests."[14]

Thus, though he had high praise for the Constitution of the United States, he insisted repeatedly that the success of the American version of the democratic experiment was due less to the laws created by the people than to their culture or, as he put it, their "mores" — the widely shared habits and beliefs that constituted the true and invisible constitution of the republic.[15] "Laws," he wrote, "are always unsteady when unsupported by mores; mores are the only tough and durable power in a nation."[16] (In this respect, he was reminding his contemporaries of older classical and biblical traditions that stressed the importance of "laws written on the heart.") The Athenian Stranger in Plato's *Laws* says of unwritten customs:

> We can neither call these things laws, nor yet leave them unmentioned . . . for they are the bonds of the whole state, and . . . if they are rightly ordered and made habitual, shield and preserve the . . . written law; but if they depart from right and fall into disorder, then they are like the props of builders which slip away out of their place and cause a universal ruin — one part

12. Tocqueville, *Democracy in America,* p. 70.
13. Tocqueville, *Democracy in America,* p. 63.
14. Tocqueville, *Old Regime,* p. xiv.
15. Tocqueville, *Democracy in America,* p. 308.
16. Tocqueville, *Democracy in America,* p. 274.

> drags another down, and the fair superstructure falls because the old foundations are undermined.[17]

Both laws and mores in America were, Tocqueville discerned, undergirded by the influence of religion. "Religion," he wrote, "is considered as the guardian of mores, and mores are regarded as the guarantee of the laws and pledge for the maintenance of freedom itself."[18] His message was clear — culture is prior to politics and law, and religion is at the heart of culture. The health of the structures of civil society would be decisive in determining whether future citizens of emerging democracies would enjoy equality in liberty or endure equality in servitude.

Democracy and Culture in the Industrial Era

As Tocqueville predicted, the democratic principle spread. In the latter half of the nineteenth century, it showed its strength in the legislatures of the industrialized republics. Universal (male) suffrage brought a steady increase in legislation aimed both at improving conditions in factories and tenements and at establishing rudimentary protections for the poor and unemployed. In Europe, this legislation laid an early foundation for modern "social" democracies. In the United States, however, the Supreme Court, in its first vigorous exercise of the power of judicial review, held many of these laws unconstitutional as violations of property rights and freedom of contract. In Russia, revolution set in motion a chain of events that simultaneously foreclosed the development of democracy there for nearly a century and corroded the substance of civil society.

Meanwhile, the Industrial Revolution was producing four momentous transformations in civil society. It would be hard to say which of these related changes was more consequential for the future — (1) the movement of most remunerative work outside the home, (2) the rise of large market actors whose power rivaled that of governments,[19] (3) the bureaucratization of both political and economic structures,[20] and (4) the development of mass communications.

Much has been written about political implications of the latter three developments, but over time the transformation of family life that took place

17. Plato, *The Laws,* 793b, c.

18. Tocqueville, *Democracy in America,* p. 47.

19. A. A. Berle and Gardiner Means, *The Modern Corporation and Private Property* (New York: Macmillan, 1934); Morris Cohen, "Property and Sovereignty," *Cornell Law Quarterly,* vol. 13 (1927): 8.

20. Max Weber, *Economy and Society* (Berkeley: University of California Press, 1978).

when most men became wage earners was to have political consequences too. The separation of home and work ushered in a wholly new way of life — that modern phenomenon known as the homemaker–breadwinner family. It represented an advance over the age-old family division of labor in farming and fishing villages: if the man's salary was large enough, his transition to wage work brought relief for his wife and children from the hard life of the family farm or other family enterprise. But this new sort of family turned out to be less secure for women and children. Their economic welfare now depended entirely on the husband and father, while he was no longer so dependent on them. The divorce rate began slowly to climb. A telling shift took place in child custody law: as children became liabilities — in the economic sense — rather than much-needed assets, the traditional legal presumption in favor of fathers was replaced by a presumption in favor of maternal custody.

Tocqueville saw the expansion of business enterprise, even in its early phase, as posing a new threat of minority tyranny. He noted that the rising entrepreneurial class, unlike the aristocracies of old, did not seem to feel obliged by custom to come to the aid of its servants or to relieve their distress:

> The industrial aristocracy of our day, when it has impoverished and brutalized the men it uses, abandons them in time of crisis to public charity to feed them. . . . I think that generally speaking the manufacturing aristocracy which we see rising before our eyes is one of the hardest that have appeared on earth. . . . [T]he friends of democracy should keep their eyes anxiously fixed in that direction. For if ever again permanent inequality of conditions and aristocracy make their way into the world, it will have been by that door that they entered.[21]

By the early twentieth century, it was apparent — even to friends of capitalism — that large market actors had acquired a great deal of influence over the political process and everyday life.[22] In a 1927 essay, Morris Cohen, an American philosopher later associated with the political thought of Franklin Roosevelt's New Deal, suggested that the powers of large property owners over persons who were not economically independent approached what historically had constituted political sovereignty. "It may well be," Cohen wrote, "that compulsion in the economic as well as the political realm is necessary for civilized life. But we must not overlook the actual fact that dominion over things is also dominion over our fellow human beings."[23]

21. Tocqueville, *Democracy in America,* pp. 557-58.
22. Berle and Means, *The Modern Corporation,* pp. 352-57.
23. Cohen, "Property and Sovereignty," p. 8.

The centralization and bureaucratization of government meant that politics and economic life were increasingly dominated by large, impersonal organizations. The family home came to be regarded by many as a "haven in a heartless world."[24] That haven, however, was coming under siege.

Democracy and the Free Market Advance: The Cultural Supports Falter

In the aftermath of World War II, the democratic principle again extended its reach. New nations emerged with constitutions in democratic form, and, together with mature republics, pledged themselves in the Universal Declaration of Human Rights to the goal of realizing "better standards of life in larger freedom."[25] To the demands that democracy itself places on civic competence and character, many countries added the demands of the welfare state. The countries that embarked on these ambitious ventures seemingly took for granted that civil society would continue to supply the habits and attitudes required by democracy, the economy, and the expanding welfare system. Meanwhile, however, the institutions upon which republics had traditionally relied to foster republican virtues and to moderate greed were falling into considerable disarray.

Nowhere is this more apparent than in the case of the family. Even the farsighted Tocqueville did not foresee how deeply the ideas of equality and individual liberty — and even the market ethos — would affect relations among family members. He understood that tyranny could be accomplished softly, working on the mind rather than the body, but he could not have imagined the technological revolution that would put immense culture-shaping power in the hands of the media. Confident that "democracy loosens social ties, but it tightens natural ones," he believed that "orderly and peaceful" homes could be depended upon to produce self-reliant citizens who knew how to respect others, to compromise differences, and to restrain their own tendencies toward selfishness.[26] Habits acquired in the home would provide the foundation for developing further skills of communal living in other sites such as schools, workplaces, and towns. Women, as the first and main teachers of children, were key to the whole system:

> There have never been free societies without mores, and . . . it is woman who shapes these mores. Therefore everything which has a bearing on the

24. Christopher Lasch, *Haven in a Heartless World: The Family Besieged* (New York: Basic Books, 1977).

25. Preamble, Universal Declaration of Human Rights (1948).

26. Tocqueville, *Democracy in America,* pp. 89, 291.

status of women, their habits, and their thoughts is, in my view, of great political importance.[27]

Who could have foreseen the series of turbulent changes that, beginning in the mid-1960s, shook up the roles of the sexes, transformed family life, and wrought havoc with the cultural foundations of democratic republics? The sexual revolution and sudden shifts in birth rates, marriage rates, and divorce rates caught professional demographers everywhere by surprise. In 1985, French demographer Louis Roussel summed up the developments of the preceding two decades:

> What we have seen between 1965 and the present, among the billion or so people who inhabit the industrialized nations, is . . . a general upheaval across the whole set of demographic indicators, a phenomenon rare in the history of populations. In barely twenty years, the birth rate and the marriage rate have tumbled, while divorces and illegitimate births have increased rapidly. All these changes have been substantial, with increases or decreases of more than fifty percent. They have also been sudden, since the process of change has only lasted about fifteen years. And they have been general, because all industrialized countries have been affected beginning around 1965.[28]

Several other developments also had serious implications for society's seedbeds of character and competence: an unprecedented proportion of mothers of young children were working outside the home; an unprecedented proportion of children were spending all or part of their childhood in fatherless homes; institutions outside the home were playing an ever-greater role in the formation of children; the mass media were gaining ever-more direct access to children; and no society had yet come up with an adequate replacement for the unpaid labor of women. The societies affected had, in fact, embarked on a vast social experiment.

At about the same time, there were signs of disturbance in schools, neighborhoods, churches, and community and workplace associations — institutions that traditionally depended on families for support, and that in turn served as important resources for families. That was no coincidence. Not only had urbanization and geographic mobility taken their toll, but many of the in-

27. Tocqueville, *Democracy in America*, p. 590.

28. Louis Roussel, "Démographie: deux décennies de mutations dans les pays industrialisés," in *Family, State, and Individual Economic Security*, ed. M.-T. Meulders-Klein and J. Eekelaar (Brussels: Story Scientia, 1988), vol. I, pp. 27-28.

stitutions of civil society had relied heavily on women who were now in short supply as volunteers and caregivers.

The movement of most women into the workforce deprived many groups of unpaid staffers, removed the informal law enforcement system (the "eyes and ears") from many neighborhoods, and precipitated a caretaking crisis. The traditional pool of family caretakers for the very young, the disabled, and the frail elderly was drying up, with no real replacement in sight — an ominous development for the most vulnerable members of society. The extent of the crisis can be appreciated when one takes account of the fact that the proportion of the population that cannot be self-sufficient (very young children, the ill, and the frail elderly) has hardly changed in the past hundred years.[29] The *composition* of that population has shifted (with fewer children and more elderly in the mix than a century ago), but their *proportion* to the whole has remained relatively steady.

In the late 1980s, the rates of demographic change slowed in the more affluent democracies. At present, they seem to have stabilized, but at new high or low levels, leaving a set of problems that no society has ever before had to confront on such a scale. In the United States, for example, divorce and nonmarital births have brought about a situation where between a fifth and a quarter of young children currently live in single-parent homes, and over half spend at least part of their childhood in such households. Women head the great majority of these homes, and their economic circumstances are precarious: nearly half of all female-headed families with children under six live in poverty. The schools, churches, youth groups, neighborhoods, and so on that once provided assistance to such families in times of distress are in trouble too. They not only served as reinforcements for, but also depended on, families, neighborhoods, and each other for personnel and reinforcement.

The developing nations are following a similar trajectory, but at an accelerated pace. Many are simultaneously undergoing democratization, industrialization, urbanization, and the separation of home and business. In the 1990s, the world passed through a largely unremarked watershed: for the first time in human history, a majority of the earth's inhabitants no longer lived in small farming and fishing villages.[30]

Whatever else may be said about these new conditions, they have impaired civil society's capacity for fostering the habits and practices that make for democratic citizenship. As an insightful journalist observed, we are experiencing a

29. Mary Ann Glendon, *The New Family and the New Property* (Toronto: Butterworths, 1981), p. 90.

30. See generally Richard Critchfield, *Villages* (New York: Doubleday, 1983).

> fraying of the net of connections between people at many critical intersections. . . . Each fraying connection accelerates the others. A break in one connection, such as attachment to a stable community, puts pressure on other connections: marriage, the relationship between parents and children, religious affiliation, a feeling of connection with the past — even citizenship, that sense of membership in a large community which grows best when it is grounded in membership in a small one.[31]

Observers across the political spectrum have expressed concern about the implications of these developments for the quality of the workforce, the fate of the social security system, and the incidence of crime and delinquency. Less attention has been paid, however, to the *political* implications — the likely effect upon the world's democratic experiments of the simultaneous weakening of child-raising families and their surrounding and supporting institutions. Not only have the main institutions that fostered non-market values in society become weaker, but values promoted by the market and the media seem to be penetrating the very capillaries of civil society.

Surely Tocqueville would have asked: Where will modern republics find men and women with a grasp of the skills of governing and a willingness to use them for the general welfare? Where will your sons and daughters learn to view others with respect and concern, rather than to regard them as objects, means, or obstacles? What will cause most men and women to keep their promises, to limit consumption, to stick with a family member in sickness and health, to spend time with their children, to answer their country's call for service, to reach out to the unfortunate, to moderate their own demands on loved ones, neighbors, and the polity? Where will a state based on the rule of law find citizens and statesmen capable of devising just laws and then abiding by them?

The findings of recent surveys of the political attitudes of young Americans are disquieting. In 1999, over a third of high school seniors failed a national civics test administered by the U.S. Department of Education, and only 9 percent were able to give two reasons why it is important to be involved in the self-government of democratic society.[32] Another study found a sense of the importance of civic participation almost entirely lacking:

> Consistent with the priority they place on personal happiness, young people reveal notions . . . that emphasize freedom and license almost to the complete exclusion of service or participation. Although they clearly appre-

31. William Pfaff, "Talk of the Town," *The New Yorker,* 30 August 1976, p. 22.

32. Chris Hedges, "35 percent of High School Seniors Fail National Civics Test," *New York Times,* 21 November 1999, p. 16.

ciate the democratic freedoms that, in their view, make theirs the "best country in the world to live in," they fail to perceive a need to reciprocate by exercising the duties and responsibilities of good citizenship."[33]

When asked to describe what makes a good citizen, only 12 percent mentioned voting. Fewer than a quarter said that they considered it important to help their community to be a better place. When asked what makes America special, only 7 percent mentioned that the United States was a democracy. Such attitudes cannot be dismissed simply as a function of immaturity, for a comparison with earlier public opinion data revealed that the 1990 cohort knew less about civics, cared less, and voted less than young people at any time over the preceding five decades.[34]

The Ecology of Freedom in the Era of Globalization

At first glance, democracy appears triumphant at the dawn of the twenty-first century.[35] Republics in democratic form have spread across Eastern Europe and Latin America and into many parts of Asia and Africa. A majority of the world's countries, over a hundred nations, now call themselves democratic, though "democratizing" would be a more accurate term in some cases.[36] Scholars tell us that democracies are disinclined to go to war with one another, and that no famine has ever occurred in a democracy.[37] Democratic principles and ideas are increasingly urged upon, and have been adopted by, many institutions of civil society.

But governments in democratic form can mask an undemocratic reality. The future of the world's democratic experiments appears clouded by several overlapping developments.

1. In the first place, there has been a certain *atrophy of the democratic elements in modern republics. The centralization of government* has drawn deci-

33. People for the American Way, *Democracy's Next Generation* (Washington: People for the American Way, 1989), p. 27.

34. Michael Oreskes, "Profiles of Today's Youth: They Couldn't Care Less," *New York Times,* 28 June 1990, pp. A1, D21.

35. Francis Fukuyama, *The End of History and the Last Man* (New York: Free Press, 1992).

36. Barbara Crossette, "Globally, Majority Rules," *New York Times,* 4 August 1996, sec. 4, p. 1; Fareed Zakaria, "The Rise of Illiberal Democracy," *Foreign Affairs* (November-December 1997).

37. Fukuyama, *The End of History;* Amartya Kumar Sen, *Development as Freedom* (New York: Knopf, 1999).

sion-making power away from local governments that once served as "schools for citizenship" and afforded average citizens the opportunity to participate in public life. *Globalization* has drained power from the nation-state. Non-representative *special interest groups* and lobbies often play the decisive role in shaping legislation and administrative action.[38] A development in some countries which could spread to supra-national tribunals is the *overly ambitious exercise of judicial power* to invalidate popular legislation, as well as to use hyper-individualistic interpretations of rights to undermine the institutions of civil society. All in all, it is increasingly difficult for most men and women in today's democratic regimes to have a say in framing the conditions under which they live, work, and raise their children.

2. As discussed above, democratic experiments are also threatened by *the decline of their seedbeds of civic virtue.* Character and competence do not emerge on command. They are acquired only through habitual practice. Those habits will be either sustained or undermined by the settings in which people live, work, and play. Democracies therefore cannot afford to ignore nurture and education or the social and political institutions where the qualities and skills that make for good citizenship and statesmanship are developed and transmitted from one generation to the next.

3. Third, the megastructures of civil society have acquired such power as to raise *the spectre of new forms of oligarchy.* In terms of economic resources and ability to shape policy and events, the influence of some market actors, foundations, and special interest organizations exceeds that of many nation-states. Indeed, nation-states have limited power to affect the large economic forces that shape the lives of their citizens. The status and security of most people are increasingly dependent upon large corporate employers or government. In the United States, for example, only about 10 percent of the working population is self-employed, about a third works for large firms, and about a fifth for federal, state, or local governments.[39] Routines of family life have been adjusted to conform to the demands and timetables of the economy. The general standard of living has risen in many places, but at the same time disparities have widened between rich and poor. Troubling questions arise: Has "emancipation" from the oppressive aspects of older ways of life merely afforded men and women the opportunity to develop their talents to fit the needs of the market? Have women been freed from one set of rigidly bounded roles only to become unisex hominids whose family life must regularly be subordinated to the demands of the workplace?

38. In the United States, for example, political campaigns of both major parties are financed primarily by big business. Leslie Wayne, "Business Is Biggest Campaign Spender, Study Says," *New York Times,* 18 October 1996, p. 1.

39. Heilbroner, "Reflections," p. 68; Glendon, *The New Family,* p. 156.

And what will the new oligarchs be like, if the democratic elements in modern republics should one day become mere empty forms? The men and women who hold key positions in governments, political parties, corporations, mass media, and foundations are often quite remote from the concerns of the average citizen. Strong ties to persons and places, religious beliefs, attachment to tradition, and even family life are apt to be less important to those at the top than to the men and women whose lives they affect. Decision-makers already have tended to be rather free in adopting measures that undermine the delicate communities on which others depend for practical and emotional support — as witness the organization of work and schooling, the planning of cities, and programs for public assistance, all of which are too frequently designed without considering the impact on families and neighborhoods.[40]

If that were not cause enough for concern, modern mass media render the problem of "soft tyranny," identified by Tocqueville, more acute than in his day. Modern tyrannies, he predicted, would prefer the kind of power that acts upon the will, rather than the crude use of force. Unlike ancient despots who frequently resorted to physical oppression, new forms of despotism would "leave the body alone and go straight for the soul" — to the point that "even desires are changed."[41]

4. *Materialism, extreme individualism, and hedonism* have taken their toll — and perhaps have even set the stage for regimes where individual liberty will be lost or confined to matters that distract from politics. As Tocqueville wrote, "What can even public opinion do when not even a score of people are held together by any common bond, when there is no man, no family, no body, no class and no free association which can represent public opinion and set it in motion? When each citizen being equally impotent, poor, and dissociated cannot oppose his individual weakness to the organized force of the government?"[42] In a country which permits its fonts of public virtues to run dry, he warned, there would be "subjects" but no "citizens."[43] One wonders: Is the unlimited sexual liberty so relentlessly promoted on all fronts today a kind of consolation prize for the loss of real liberty in the political and economic sphere? A kind of latter-day bread and circuses?

40. Robert E. Rodes Jr., "Greatness Thrust Upon Them: Class Biases in American Law," 1983 *American Journal of Jurisprudence*, pp. 1, 6. See also Wilson Carey McWilliams, "American Pluralism: The Old Order Passeth," in *The Americans, 1976: An Inquiry into Fundamental Concepts of Man Underlying Various U.S. Institutions*, ed. Irving Kristol and Paul Weaver (Lexington, Mass.: Lexington Books, 1976), pp. 293, 315.

41. Tocqueville, *Democracy in America*, pp. 255, 434-35.

42. Tocqueville, *Democracy in America*, p. 314.

43. Tocqueville, *Democracy in America*, pp. 93-94.

5. Finally, there is the corrosive effect on the polity of a *spreading lack of confidence that there are any common truths* to which men and women of different backgrounds and cultures can appeal. Many serious twentieth-century thinkers argue that tyrannies, old and new, whether majoritarian or of minorities, are rooted in nihilism.[44] Hannah Arendt, for example, wrote: "The ideal subject of totalitarian rule is not the convinced Nazi or the convinced Communist, but people for whom the distinction between fact and fiction (i.e., the reality of experience) and the distinction between true and false (i.e., the standards of thought) no longer exist."[45] Pope John Paul II, reflecting on the experience of totalitarianism in Eastern Europe, put it this way:

> Totalitarianism arises out of a denial of truth in the objective sense. If there is no transcendent truth, in obedience to which man achieves his full identity, then there is no sure principle for guaranteeing just relations between people. Their self-interest as a class, group, or nation would inevitably set them in opposition to one another. If one does not acknowledge transcendent truth, then the force of power takes over, and each person tends to make full use of the means at his disposal in order to impose his own interests or his own opinion, with no regard for the rights of others.[46]

In view of the atrophy of democratic participation, the disarray among the small structures of civil society, the menace of oligarchy, and the spread of materialism, hyper-individualism, and popular relativism, what can one say about the prospects for "renewing American culture"?

Whither Democracy and the Social Environment?

At the dawn of the democratic era, it seemed to Tocqueville that the irresistible advance of democracy was leading to only two possible outcomes — democratic freedom or democratic tyranny.[47] Today, with the democratic nation-state and its cultural supports weakened, the market seems to be about where democracy was then. The market is both a set of institutions and a powerful idea, fate-laden and irresistible, with the potential to improve the lives of men

44. *Veritatis Splendor,* n. 99; *Centesimus Annus,* n. 44. See also, Michael Novak, "Truth and Liberty: The Present Crisis in Our Culture," *Review of Politics,* vol. 59 (1997): 1.

45. Hannah Arendt, *The Origins of Totalitarianism* (New York: Meridian, 1958), p. 474.

46. *Centesimus Annus,* n. 44.

47. Tocqueville, *Democracy in America,* p. xiv (1848 Preface).

and women everywhere or to subject them to new forms of tyranny. The great challenge is to shift probabilities in the first direction.

This overview of democracy's ever-changing relationship to its cultural supports suggests four tentative conclusions: (1) For the benefits of democratic society and the free market to be realized and their destructive potential minimized, the explosive energies of free politics and free economics must be disciplined and directed by a vibrant moral culture.[48] (2) The moral culture depends, in turn, on the health of society's main culture-forming institutions. (3) Paradoxically, liberal democracy and free markets pose threats, not only to each other, but to the seedbeds of the very qualities and institutions both need in order to remain free and function well. (4) The corrective may lie in another paradox: democratic states and free markets may need to refrain from imposing their own values indiscriminately on all the institutions of civil society. They may even need, for their own good, to be actively solicitous of groups and structures whose main loyalty is not to the state and whose highest values are not efficiency, productivity, or individualism.

Could law and policy help to revitalize, or at least avoid further harm to, families and other fragile institutions upon which political freedom and economic vitality depend? Unfortunately, we do not know very much about how to encourage, or even how to avoid damage to, the social systems that both undergird and buffer the free market and the democratic polity. In fact, we probably know even less about the dynamics of social environments than we do about natural environments.

One thing we have learned through trial-and-error is that intervention, even with the most benign motives, can have unintended and harmful consequences. In an address to the French National Assembly, anthropologist Claude Levi-Strauss called attention to the endangered state of social environments, but cautioned at the same time against regulatory hubris. Two hundred years after the French Revolution attacked civil society, he told the legislators that the task now was to restore civil society:

> Notwithstanding Rousseau, who wanted to abolish any partial society in the state, a certain restoration of partial societies offers a final chance of providing ailing freedoms with a little health and vigor. Unhappily, it is not up to the legislator to bring Western societies back up the slope down which they have been slipping. . . . But the legislator can at least be attentive to the reversal of this trend, signs of which are discernible here and there; he can encourage it in its unforeseeable manifestations, however incongruous and even shocking they may sometimes seem. In any case, the legislator

48. See George Weigel, "The Priority of Culture," *The Pilot,* 7 June 1996, p. 11.

should do nothing that might nip such reversal in the bud, or once it asserts itself, prevent it from following its course.[49]

Evidence is accumulating that the idea of "regulating" complex social systems (in the sense of controlling their development or ensuring desired outcomes) is an illusion.[50] Interventions can shift probabilities, but often in unanticipated ways. Prudence thus suggests proceeding modestly, preferring local experiments and small-scale pilots to broad, standardized, top-down programs. Often, the principle of "do no harm" will be the best guide. At a minimum, that would require attention to the ways in which governmental or business policies may be undermining fragile social structures, or discouraging persons who devote time and effort to the nurture of future citizens.

Conclusion

Is there reason to hope that the fine texture of civil society can be reinvigorated? One close observer of changes in the political capillaries of democracies finds hope in the fact that many kinds of micro-governments are spontaneously emerging at the neighborhood and community level in Europe and the United States. George Liebmann, whose three densely-packed monographs on civil society deserve to be better known,[51] has studied the emergence of such phenomena as *woonerven* (residential street control regimes) in The Netherlands, neighborhood councils in the Nordic countries, local law enforcement in the twenty-five thousand communes of France, and business improvement districts and residential community associations in the United States. He has found that many of these groups have evolved from small, spontaneous cooperative endeavors into responsive and effective "sub-local" governments. Though some of these associations are controversial, Liebmann contends that they are spreading and are likely to spread further, in reaction to the centralization and bureaucratization that have dominated political and social life for

49. Claude Lévi-Strauss, "Reflections on Liberty," in *The View from Afar* (New York: Basic Books, 1985), p. 288.

50. See, for example, Mitchell Waldrop, *Complexity: The Emerging Science at the Edge of Order and Chaos* (New York: Touchstone, 1992); Michael Novak, "Hayek: Practitioner of Social Justice 'Properly Understood'" (lecture delivered at the University of Chicago, 28 October 1999).

51. George Liebmann, *The Little Platoons: Sub-Local Governments in Modern History* (Westport, Conn.: Praeger, 1995); *The Gallows in the Grove: Civil Society in American Law* (Westport, Conn.: Praeger, 1997); *Solving Problems Without Large Governments* (Westport, Conn.: Praeger, 1999).

most of the century. They may be the "schools for citizenship" of the twenty-first century.

At the national level, another encouraging sign is experimentation with the delivery of social services such as education, health care, and childcare through smaller seedbed institutions (religious groups, workplace associations) rather than state-run bureaucracies.[52] Yet another positive development is increasing interest in the principle of subsidiarity: the idea that no social task should be performed at a higher level or by a larger institution than can perform that task adequately. The editor of a journal that follows such developments predicts that the most important political issues in the twenty-first century will be either global or local:

> Problems are migrating up and down all over government, in search of the appropriate place for solution. . . . Citizens are essentially looking for two forms of public authority: intimate ones in their community that can deal with their needs in a humane way, and regional ones big enough to impose some order and stability on economic life. The governments they have are mostly too remote and bureaucratic for the first job and too small and weak for the second one.[53]

Ultimately, what will be decisive for democracy and the free market alike is not the seedbeds of civil society (which can produce weeds as well as flowers), but the seed itself. The seed is the human person, uniquely individual yet inescapably social; a creature of unruly passions who nevertheless possesses a certain ability, individually and collectively, to create and abide by systems of moral and juridical norms.

52. Peter L. Berger and Richard John Neuhaus, *To Empower People: From State to Civil Society* (Washington, D.C.: American Enterprise Institute, 1996).

53. Alan Ehrenhalt, "Demanding the Right Size Government," *New York Times,* 4 October 1999, p. A33.

The Culture's Impact on World Affairs

ZBIGNIEW BRZEZINSKI

The decisive development of our era has been the victory of the West in the protracted, forty-year-long Cold War. That victory, of America over Russia, brought to an end the bipolar struggle for domination over world politics. But while the United States is now without a peer, with none of its rivals capable of replacing its comprehensive power, America's domestic dilemmas inhibit the physical scope of its power and impede the translation of that power into acknowledged global authority.

The Century of Organized Insanity

Twentieth-century politics, dominated by the rise of totalitarian movements, deserves to be described as the politics of organized insanity. That insanity not only produced unparalleled bloodshed, but also involved the most ambitious attempt in mankind's history to establish total control over both the internal and the external condition of the human being itself. The failed attempt to create coercive utopias — that is, heavens on earth — on the basis of dogmatic designs of truly cosmic brazenness perverted the rational and idealistic impulses unleashed in Europe some two hundred years ago by the French Revolution.

The failure of these totalitarian experiments coincided with the political awakening of mankind on a truly global scale. This coincidence means that the liberal democratic framework, now associated with both the French and American revolutions, is potentially applicable on a worldwide basis, thereby creating the basis for a possible worldwide political consensus. Disintegrative forces globally at work, however, may still prove more potent than integrative forces. The global relevance of the West's political message may be vitiated by the growing tendency in the advanced world to infuse the inner content of liberal democracy with a lifestyle that I define as permissive cornucopia. The priority given to individual self-gratification, combined with the growing capacity of the human being to reshape itself through genetic and other forms of scientific self-alteration (with neither subject to moral restraint), tends to create a condition in which little self-control is exercised over the desire to consume and to tinker with the self. In contrast, outside the richer West much of human life is still dominated by fundamental concerns with survival rather than with conspicuous consumption. These divergent trends undermine and inhibit global consensus and enhance the dangers inherent in a deepening global cleavage.

A Global Power for How Long?

Today, the United States stands as the only truly global power. But it does so in a setting in which traditional international politics are being transformed into global politics — politics that are becoming, under the influence of modern communications and increasing economic interpenetration, an extended process, obliterating the distinction between the domestic and the international. Inherent in this is the potential for the emergence of a genuine global community. The question arises whether a global power that is not guided by a globally relevant set of values can for long exercise that predominance. To be sure, American power is real, and, in fact, it is unlikely to be challenged in the foreseeable future by any of its potential rivals. Neither Japan nor Europe is likely to displace America. In that sense, the U.S. global position is historically unique. Nevertheless, unless there is a deliberate effort to reestablish some moral criteria for the exercise of self-control over gratification as an end in itself, the phase of American dominance may not last long, despite the absence of any self-evident replacement.

In fact, although a single and increasingly interdependent global political process is emerging, America's difficulty in exercising effective global authority within it — because of inner weaknesses derived more from cultural than from economic causes — could produce a situation of intensifying global instability. A great deal depends on how the West reacts to the disappearance of the communist ideological challenge. Will the values of the pluralistic and free-market societies strike a viable balance between individual desire for material self-enhancement and the need to infuse into life an awareness of its transcendental dimensions? The dilemma was posed well by Nobel laureate Czeslaw Milosz, who wrote the following in mid-1991:

> The erosion of the religious imagination is, in my view, the core of twentieth-century thought; and it is what has lent our age its apocalyptic features. But the dissolution of totalitarian movements by no means suggests that a fundamental change has taken place in this regard. It is enough to look at the prosperous and well-fed sector of humanity in the countries of the West to become convinced that the concept of a religiously ordered cosmos is disintegrating also under the impact of science and technology, and that if people, especially among the younger generations, still have a strong need for faith, it is a homeless, groping faith that does not necessarily turn to Christianity.

The warning expressed by Milosz points to the historic danger that the discredited meta-myths of the coercive utopia might be followed by the spiritual emptiness of a permissive cornucopia. The word "cornucopia" is derived from the mythological horn that suckled the god Zeus. It has the miraculous capacity to become full of whatever its owner desires. Hence, the term "permissive cornucopia" is an accurate one for a society in which everything is permitted and everything can be had.

There are grounds for serious and legitimate concern that in the advanced, rich, and politically democratic societies, cornucopian permissiveness is increasingly dominating and defining both the content and the goals of individual existence. The notion of a "permissive cornucopia" involves essentially a society in which a progressive decline in the centrality of moral criteria is matched by heightened preoccupation with material and sensual self-gratification. Unlike a coercive utopia, a permissive cornucopia does not envisage a timeless state of societal bliss for the redeemed, but focuses largely on the immediate satisfaction of individual desires, in a setting in which individual and collective hedonism become the dominant motives for behavior. The combination of the erosion of moral criteria in defining personal conduct and the emphasis on material goods results in both permissiveness on the level of action and material greed on the level of motivation.

To be sure, the philosophical and cultural content of the West is in flux, and perhaps it is too severe a judgment to define it as a permissive cornucopia. Many exceptions can be made. Suffice it to say that if the predominant culture and philosophical outlook of the West do in fact reflect values that justify the cornucopian appellation, concern is justified regarding the long-term viability of "Western civilization" and, especially, its ability to provide a meaningful message to the politically awakened world in the post-utopian phase.

ZBIGNIEW BRZEZINSKI

The Principal Definer of Morality

A society in which self-gratification is the norm is also a society in which there are no longer any criteria for making moral judgments. One feels entitled to have what one wants, whether or not one is worthy. Moral judgments become dispensable. There is no need to differentiate between "right" and "wrong." For pragmatic reasons of social order, the critical distinction is made between what is "legal" and "illegal"; thus legal procedure, especially the court system, substitutes for morality and for the church as the principal definer of that morality. Religion as the internalized guide to individual conduct is replaced by the legal system, which defines the external limits of the impermissible but not the immoral.

One can call this new outlook, in which external rules guide conduct and social interaction, "procedural morality." It differs fundamentally from a morality that is internalized, personal, and inclined to make distinctions between "right" and "wrong." Moreover, procedural morality, if it stands by itself, creates a condition in which more than just a few are tempted to test the limits of the permissible — "to try to get away with it" — because no absolute inner moral restraint is operational. Individuals first judge how effective, or ineffective, the procedural system of restraint is, and then act accordingly.

Under ideal circumstances, procedural morality and inner morality would be mutually reinforcing in a democracy. The delicate balance between them would rest on the social acceptance of the sovereignty of judicial procedures and on the state's acceptance of the desirability of social institutions dedicated to the reinforcement of internal, personal morality. In the past, that latter role was largely played by organized religion. But in modern society, both politics and economics conspire to create a culture inimical to the preservation of a social domain reserved for the religious. An increasingly permissive culture, exploiting the principle of the separation of church and state, squeezes out the religious factor without substituting for it any secular "categorical imperatives," thereby transforming the inner moral code into a vacuum.

The moral vacuum defines the essential meaning of the notion of spiritual emptiness — an emptiness which appears to be increasingly pervasive in much of "Western civilization." It is a striking paradox that the greatest victory for the proposition "God is dead" has occurred not in the Marxist-dominated states, which politically propagated atheism, but in Western liberal democratic societies, which have culturally nurtured moral apathy. It is in these states that religion has ceased to be a major social force, and this condition has arisen not because officially propagated atheism won the day over religion, but because of the corrosive effects of cultural indifference to anything but the immediately and materially satisfying dimensions of life.

Television's Role in Defining Freedom and the Good Life

Two other issues of major importance are pertinent here: the definition of freedom and the definition of the good life. The first pertains to the meaning of citizenship and the second to the essence of the human being. In a society that culturally emphasizes the maximization of individual satisfactions and the minimization of moral restraints, civic freedom tends to be elevated to a self-validating absolute. In other words, civic freedom is divorced from a notion of civic responsibility. Traditionally, ever since the French and American revolutions, the notion of freedom has been defined in the context of citizenship: that is to say, individual rights have been defined within a sociopolitical setting. For these responsibilities to be voluntarily shouldered, however, genuine motivation is required, which in turn calls for an inner spirit that prompts the willingness to serve, to sacrifice, and to exercise self-restraint.

If patriotic citizenship was once the framework for the definition of civic freedom within a democratic society, that definition is in jeopardy today. Increasingly, freedom is defined as the accumulation of rights and entitlements as well as license for any form of self-expression and gratification. The notion of self-imposed or socially expected service to society has become unfashionable. Thus, in effect, personal freedom has become the absence of restraint, except in cases of legally defined threats to someone else's physical or material well-being.

The gradual redefinition of freedom, away from the notion of responsible civic freedom and toward the notion of licentious personal liberty, both contributes to and is reinforced by ongoing trends in mass media. On the whole, the values conveyed by the media repeatedly manifest what justifiably might be called moral corruption and cultural decadence. Television is a particularly serious offender in this respect. It is now the primary purveyor of mass culture, and, through its combination of the audio and the visual, a compelling one. Today, for much of the world — and especially for the young — television is the most important instrument for both socialization and education. In that respect, it is rapidly replacing the roles traditionally played by the family, the church, and the school.

Television gives the young viewer a first glimpse of the outside world. It sets the standards for what are to be considered achievement, fulfillment, good taste, and proper conduct. It conditions desires, defines aspirations and expectations, and draws a line between acceptable and unacceptable behavior. With audiences around the world increasingly glued to television sets, there is nothing comparable, even in the era of enforced religious orthodoxy or at the high point of totalitarian indoctrination, to the cultural and philosophical conditioning that television exercises on viewers.

The content of American and West European television is not all undesirable, of course; some of it is even good. But Gresham's Law applies not only to good and bad money; it applies also to programming that is exclusively dependent on advertising and audience appeal. The sad fact is that the television producers who are cultural pornographers have a competitive advantage over those who are not. The net result is that Western television has become more and more inclined to the sensual, sexual, and sensational. To the extent that any values can be extrapolated from television programming, they clearly extol self-gratification, normalize intense violence and brutality, encourage sexual promiscuity through example and stimulated peer pressures, and pander to the worst public instincts.

As the predominant purveyor of mass culture, it is this medium that has become predominant in shaping the national culture and its basic beliefs. As James B. Twitchell observes in his incisive *Carnival Culture: The Trashing of Taste in America,* American TV has become "a medium whose input is so profound and so resolutely banal that it has almost single-handedly removed vulgarity from modern culture by making it the norm." The result is a mass culture driven by profiteers who exploit the hunger for vulgarity, pornography, and even barbarism. Such supremacy of decadence and hedonism in a culture cannot help but have a demoralizing effect on the values of society, undermining and eroding once deeply felt beliefs. It is no exaggeration to say that Hollywood movie and TV producers have become cultural subverters who — cynically exploiting the shield offered by the First Amendment — are propagating a self-destructive social ethic.

Television thus not only alters our conception of freedom, it also influences our view of the good life. Increasingly, the meaning of "the good life" is defined by television as instant self-gratification and the acquisition of goods. The utopian fanatic is in this fashion replaced by the insatiable consumer. In the age of awareness of massive human inequity and deprivation, it is politically and morally disturbing to calculate how much of Western consumption is unnecessary, driven only by artificially stimulated desires for the latest fads, fashions, gimmicks, and toys. Moreover, consumption derived from artificially induced desire and not from need is increasingly a middle-class phenomenon, not just confined to the very rich.

Democracy may be the West's most important contribution to the world, but it is a vessel that has to be filled with content. The democratic political process, the constitutional system, the sovereignty of law, are all peerless guarantees for the preservation and enhancement of individual rights and of human potential. But democracy by itself does not provide the answers to the dilemmas of social existence and especially to the definition of the good life. That role is played by culture and philosophy, which together generate the values that motivate and shape social behavior.

Science, Technology, and Self-alteration

The concern already expressed — namely, that a meaningful social model for the politically awakened globe cannot emanate from a permissive society — is accentuated by the diverse impact of modern science on the global human condition. In the technologically and economically advanced parts of the world, science and technology are dramatically enhancing the human capacity not only for self-gratification but also for self-alteration.

The most important political effect of technological innovation has been to create social intimacy on the global scale — overcoming time and distance. But that new intimacy both combines and collides at the same time. In much of the world, the daily struggle for survival by the acutely impoverished masses now occurs in the context of an intense awareness of a totally contrasting lifestyle on the part of its own elites as well as of the cornucopian West (with which the elites of the poor countries identify themselves and which they aspire to imitate). As a result, the gap between enhanced expectations and actual capabilities may have never been as great as it is today.

Furthermore, in the advanced world science increasingly creates a dynamic toward human self-engineering which may soon become as uncontrolled as the dynamic of self-gratification. In fact, self-alteration is in part self-gratification. In the absence of any deliberately defined criteria of choice, self-alteration may become as massive as the technological and scientific onslaught on the natural environment that is already occurring. The ecological movement, in response to that assault, has been seeking to define some criteria of self-restraint so as to preserve the organic balance between humanity and nature and prevent the mindless destruction, in the name of human control, of that connection. An analogous dilemma is now surfacing with regard to human self-alteration. Inherent in the illusion of enhanced human self-control through science is the surfacing of urgent questions of ultimate importance: What is the human being? What is the irreducible and essential quality of human authenticity?

These issues are likely to become dominant questions in the advanced countries within the next several decades. The Industrial Revolution has led in this century to the temptation and the belief that social engineering, based on a dogmatic ideology, can produce collective well-being within arrogantly coercive utopias, but this is an illusion.

The United States: The Catalytic Nation

History teaches that a superpower cannot long remain dominant unless it projects — with a measure of self-righteous confidence — a message of worldwide relevance. That was the experience of, for example, Rome, France, and Great Britain. Moreover, unless that message is derived from an inner moral code of its own, defining a shared standard of conduct as an example for others, national self-righteousness can degenerate into national vanity, devoid of wider appeal. It will eventually be rejected by others, as was the case with the Soviet empire. This is why the internal dynamics, not only economic but especially cultural, of contemporary America are so directly relevant to America's capacity to influence constructively the thrust of global change.

Changes in the character of international politics, changes that increasingly blur the traditional distinctions between international and domestic politics, further magnify the relevance of America's domestic condition to America's global standing. Appreciation of the nature and implications of that change are the necessary points of departure for an assessment of America's own staying power as the world's preeminent state as well as an assessment of the possibility of a rival emerging to challenge America's position.

The rise of America during the twentieth century coincided with the crisis and then collapse of the relatively conservative world order, based on a hierarchy of sovereign states. Indeed, by the end of the century the once-evocative concept of exclusive state sovereignty had been displaced by the much more popular notion of inclusive international interdependence. This shift in emphasis reflected the surfacing of the new global political process, with its blurring of the distinction between the truly foreign and the exclusively domestic.

Within this global process, it is America that today is the genuinely catalytic nation — the object of admiration, resentment, and imitation among other nations, and, even more important, the nation with the greatest immediate impact on the social mores of other nations. America dominates the global chatter, the global perceptions, and the global educational interactions. At any one point more than 500,000 foreign students (with close to 200,000 of them from Asia) are studying in the United States (which is several times more than are in any other host country). It has been estimated that more than 80 percent of the global transmission and processing of data originates from America, that more than 50 percent of the worldwide film viewing (and an even greater percentage of TV sitcoms) involves American-made productions. No nation comes even remotely close to the United States in the dissemination of television programming abroad. (In recent years, the UK and France have been in second place, but though each country traditionally has had worldwide cultural aspirations, their respective sales have amounted to less than 15 percent of the total American export hours.) Every continent is affected (some would say, infected) by the images and values that American television programs project. This condition has prompted frequent foreign charges that American "cultural imperialism" has become a threat to indigenous cultural diversity.

Moreover, America is, in fact, itself a global society in microcosm. Its open multiculturalism — with New York, a semi-European metropolis; Miami, a quasi-Latin American city; and Los Angeles, rapidly becoming an extension of the Orient — reinforces the organic links between America and the rest of the world. Even America's urban racial turbulence mirrors the more unsettled social and philosophical condition of the world at large, while internal American trends are not only the objects of foreign fascination but are perceived as forecasts — for good or bad — of their own futures.

The consequence of this condition produces a paradox: America today is the only state that possesses all the decisive attributes of a global superpower, yet, at the same time, it is shaping a new pattern of global politics, the inherent characteristic of which is not only the progressive dilution of the sovereign integrity of the nation-state but also the reduction in the capacity of a superstate to exercise decisive global power.

In effect, America's global preeminence reinforces and even generates the conditions that prompt its increasing global impotence. It is a striking fact that the power of the United States in the world is analogous to that of the U.S. president in coping with America's various domestic, and especially racial or urban, problems. The president is expected by many to be able to act decisively, though in fact his power is limited not only constitutionally but also by the very complexity of the problems that he confronts, and especially by the democratization that galvanizes more and more demanding constituencies. Their entitlements become their rights, and expanding rights inherently become obstacles to the exercise of power.

A similar condition prevails worldwide. Global political problems are simultaneously socioeconomic, environmental, and even philosophical. It is therefore harder and harder to find clearly defined answers for them, and they are less and less susceptible to military power emanating from a single political center.

Global political dilemmas, which are heavily influenced by cultural and philosophical factors, cannot be quickly remedied by a few specific prescriptions. Indeed, it must be recognized that the expectation of instant solutions to complex and deeply-rooted problems is itself a characteristic of our modern age, with its mind-set heavily conditioned by ideological expectations and technological capabilities. These have induced a reductionist mode of thought, with an inclination to evade sensitive moral and attitudinal problems by imposing on them doctrinal or technical solutions. The needed correction will not come from a catalog of policy recommendations. It can only emerge as a consequence of a new historical tide that induces a change both in values and in conduct; it can only come out of a prolonged process of cultural self-reexamination and philosophical reevaluation, which over time will influence the political outlook of both the West and the non-Western world. That process can be encouraged by an enlightened dialogue, but it cannot be politically imposed. In the course of any such process, the West will have to shed its parochial blinders to its own cultural malaise, not only because its spiritual emptiness deprives it of the ability to empathize, but also because it would be physically impossible to duplicate on a global scale the West's consumerist society, with its limitless appetite for self-gratification beyond personal need.

The marked decline of the nuclear family as the basic social unit aggravates the cultural-philosophical malaise of contemporary America. That decline is the direct product of changing social values, as reflected in and propagated by the mass media. Family implies structure, responsibility, and restraint. The very requirements of good family life work against the grain of uninhibited hedonism, for they impose the obligations of sacrifice, loyalty, and trust. In contrast, the weakening of family ties makes the individual more susceptible to fads, fashions, and thus also to an increasingly fluid inner faith which, before long, becomes transformed into a self-serving justification for egocentrism. All of this is inimical to the perpetuation of enduring principles, not to mention a shared criteria of self-denial.

Conclusion

American global leadership, and especially American authority, is thus bound to become more dependent on what actually transpires within America — on how America responds to a set of tangible and intangible challenges. The response to the tangible challenges will probably be of decisive importance in defining America's relationship to its economically powerful rivals, especially Europe and Japan. The response to the intangible ones will be even more decisively important in shaping America's broader capacity to exercise genuine global authority — that is, to transform its power into leadership that commands moral legitimacy.

America's continued global preeminence depends on the social and philosophic dimensions of America's condition — which are no less important than economic factors in determining America's global role — and these are, unfortunately, ominous. These factors influence the perception of America by the rest of the world, thereby either enhancing or constraining the role that America is able to play as the catalyst of global change. For this reason, the biggest danger to America today is posed by the intractability of America's social problems and by the values that increasingly dominate America's culture and spirit.

America clearly needs a period of philosophical introspection and of cultural self-critique. It must come to grips with the realization that a relativist hedonism as the basic guide to life offers no firm social moorings, and that a community which partakes of no shared absolute certainties but which instead puts a premium on individual self-satisfaction is a community threatened by dissolution.

The Culture's Impact on Social Pathologies

CHARLES KRAUTHAMMER

It was an axiom of the conservative movement that swept Washington in the 1990s that the growth in the size and power of the welfare state is a primary cause of the decline of society's mediating institutions — voluntary associations, local governments, church, and above all, the family, the single most important instrument of social cohesion and values transmission. The operating assumption was that the nanny state, whether by design or inadvertence, had taken over the family.

Welfare policy, for example, creates social chaos by means of governmental incentives that are almost comically perverse. Every teenage girl in the country is told the following: have a child, make sure it is born out of wedlock, make sure you have no job or prospects, and Washington will then guarantee you a monthly check, free medical care, and years of free job training and child care. After thirty-five years of this, the illegitimacy rate went from 5 percent to 30 percent. Surprise.

Liberals were confounded by the fact that the great expansion of their social programs coincided with the dramatic rise of most every index of social breakdown — divorce, illegitimacy, violence, crime, drug abuse, suicide, untreated mental illness (disguised as homelessness). Lacking any new theory to explain this unfortunate association, they continue to prescribe the only therapy their worldview allows: more social programs.

In his 1995 State of the Union Address, President Bill Clinton embraced a Charles Murray premise when he declared that "the epidemic of teen pregnancies and births where there is not marriage" is "our most serious social problem." His conclusions, however, were distinctly un-Murray-like — yet another federal program. After driver's education and drug education, we shall now have pregnancy education — a few minutes of classroom time to urge young girls and boys not to do precisely what the entire welfare system allowed, indeed encouraged, them to do: indulge in irresponsible childbearing.

The Limits of Structural Reform

The conservative response was equally clear: not a new government intervention to mitigate the catastrophic consequences of the old intervention, but withdrawal of government intervention in the first place. The contraction of the welfare state was the single most important theme of the conservative revolution. It imbued practically every item on the Republicans' political agenda. And it promised a rosy future: Pare back the welfare state and the mediating institutions will once again have the space to flower, reclaiming their rightful place at the center of a revitalized civil society.

It was a rosy scenario, and unlikely to materialize. Social disintegration is not a reversible chemical reaction. It is far easier to reduce a complex, cohesive social structure to its barest elements of atomized individuals and fractured families than to reassemble those atoms and fractions into a new whole. Institutions so displaced and broken, particularly the family, may not be capable of spontaneous reintegration.

This is not to say that one should flinch from trying. But in, say, abolishing the current welfare entitlement, one should not assume that this in and of itself will solve the conundrum of intergenerational illegitimacy. Abolition may be the first step, because without it there is no way back from where we are. But it is only a first step. And, if it is the only step, the policy reforms will fail.

That is the case because looking at the effect of government on society is too limited an analysis. The intrusions and expropriations of the welfare state have, generally speaking, created the sustaining conditions that allow the breakdown of families and other mediating institutions. They establish a structure that underwrites self-destructive and anti-social behavior. But they do not *create* the wants and the values that find their expression in such behavior. The epidemic of teen pregnancy, for example, is fueled by the desire of boys for predatory and casual sex, the acquiescence (often encouragement) of girls, and the contempt of both for the bourgeois norm of settled, married parenthood. Where do these attitudes come from? The welfare check permits their realization. But it hardly creates them. What does?

Cultural Causes of Decay

The single greatest shaper of these wants and values is not government but culture. Mass culture is a very recent phenomenon. As an engine of social breakdown, those who might be called structural conservatives vastly underappreciate it. Those who believe, for example, that changing the tax structure of the inner city (through enterprise zones) will effect a radical transformation of its social dynamics are missing the larger reality. Never in history have the purveyors of a degraded, almost totally uncensored culture had direct, unmediated access to the minds of society's young. An adolescent plugged into a Walkman playing "gangsta-rap" represents a revolutionary social phenomenon: youthful consciousness almost literally hardwired to the most extreme and corrupting cultural influences.

Two hundred years ago these influences might have reached a thin layer of the upper class, a class well insulated by education, the social code, and sheer wealth from the more baleful consequences of cultural decay. Today these influences reach everyone. Particularly vulnerable are those in communities where the authority structure has disintegrated because of absent or incompetent parents and where there is no power or money or codes to mediate the culture's influence or cushion its effects. In such a milieu in particular — and everywhere to some extent — mass culture rules. The results are plain to see.

We have, for example, a quarter century of psychological research on the relationship between exposure to television violence and aggressive behavior. To quote Leonard Eron, a longtime student of media and its psychological effects, on the question of the relation between television and increased violence, "the scientific debate is over." One could, of course, have done without the social science and simply reasoned, as Irving Kristol said in the early 1970s, that if the unquestionably held view that good art can elevate is true, then it must be equally true that bad art can degrade.

The defenders of the culture argue that their art merely reflects already existing social changes. One could, for the sake of argument, concede that point and still note that, by constantly validating and confirming disintegratory social trends, these cultural purveyors are legitimizing them and establishing a feedback system that only serves to reinforce, amplify, and accelerate the chaos.

Mainstream films aimed at young people, for example, specialize not just in glorifying violence but in trivializing it. Cruelty as camp is a staple of the PG13 movie. MTV is a festival of misogyny, a sourcebook on the degradation and objectification of women. And ordinary prime-time television is a laboratory of "alternative lifestyles." It has been pointed out, for example, that the typical sitcom family (with one or two notable exceptions) is what in the 1950s was called a broken home. And these homes — *Murphy Brown's*, most famously —

are not generally depicted as unfortunate accommodations to the sadder consequences of social disintegration but as self-affirming choices worthy of not just admiration but celebration. What is forgotten about the *Murphy Brown* episode is that real, live television anchors from NBC, CBS, ABC, and CNN went on the show to toast Murphy's motherhood.

Dan Quayle's attack on the breezy, brazen amorality at play here restarted the current national debate about the cultural causes of social decay. Even the most established liberal voices have been coming to grudging acknowledgment of the fact that much of the rampant deviancy in society is learned, and learned mostly from the mass media. The National Commission on Children, for example, acknowledged that "pervasive images of crime, violence, and sexuality expose children and youth to situations and problems that often conflict with the common values of our society," and even ceded that "the media, especially television," might actually be "a cause" of "our society's serious problems."

The Medicalization of Vice

Liberals have a serious difficulty dealing with this reality, however. It is hard for them to say the obvious: our culture's art is bad, its messages morally wrong. Why? Because having promoted "value-free" education and a self-validating moral relativism, they have forfeited the language of morality.

Accordingly, they have had to resort to a substitute language: medicine. Medicalized morality has the advantage of appearing both authoritative and value-free. Liberalism can now address the problem of cultural decay thus: We cannot say what's right or wrong, good or bad, but we can say what is harmful. Hence, sexual promiscuity is to be eschewed not because it is wrong but because it is "risky," a risk to limb and life, as are drug abuse and the like. The right sex is safe sex. Teen violence is a "public health emergency." And the man to lead the fight against teen pregnancy is a doctor, the Surgeon General. He did such a good job with smoking. Why not with sex?

To be sure, some liberals have so rejected the connection between morality and social breakdown that they are reluctant to apply even the smoking model to allegedly immoral behavior. President Clinton's first Surgeon General, Joycelyn Elders, was so sanguine about teen sex that she wanted it taught. ("We've taught children in driver's ed. what to do in the front seat of a car but not what to do in the back seat of the car.") She was so reconciled to drug use that she spoke favorably of legalization. But she was, at the same time, a ferocious enemy of tobacco. She was quite reconciled to kids having sex in the back seat of a car, it seems, so long as they did not light up afterward.

But such views are no longer politically sustainable, even in a Democratic administration. The new recognition that teen pregnancy and illegitimacy are social pathologies in need of a campaign to change behavior and attitudes is an advance; but, by assigning the job to doctors, by framing the issue in terms of public health, by confusing morality with hygiene, the point is missed.

Yes, the victims of teen violence, promiscuity, drug abuse, and suicide end up in the emergency room. But so do the victims of hurricanes and war. Hurricanes and war are many things, but they are not medical problems. Neither are teen violence, promiscuity, drug abuse, suicide, and the other indices of social decay. Moreover, when you appeal to the vulnerable young to avoid these behaviors on the purely self-regarding health grounds that they are risking damage to themselves, you are preaching to a constituency that is not apt to buy your cost-benefit calculations.

Virtue's Return

The medicalization of vice — the campaigns for safe this and safe that — has gone as far as it can go, and that is not very far. The result is that we are seeing a "remoralization," if not of society, at least of language. Encouraged by such books as William Bennett's *The Book of Virtues,* Gertrude Himmelfarb's *The De-Moralization of Society,* and James Q. Wilson's *The Moral Sense,* the frank use of the old-fashioned language of virtue is making a comeback.

Establishment discourse has been forced to readmit moral categories into the debate about social decay and deviancy. The change is visible and rapid. One can almost chart it by comparing the reception accorded Dan Quayle's 1992 assault on *Murphy Brown* and that given Bob Dole's on Time Warner and Hollywood just three years later. The establishment media pummeled Quayle. The response to Dole was: Why aren't the Democrats saying this too?

This represents a significant advance in two respects. First, it legitimizes the use of frankly moral language in public discourse. Second, it legitimizes the deployment of the language against the purveyors of culture and the holding of them to certain standards of decency.

This engagement in the cultural war is a necessary complement to the "structural" conservatives' attempts to rein in the welfare state. Reining in the state creates civil space open to new influences. But the cultural agenda — and particularly the attempt to force the mass media to clean up their act and later their message — will crucially determine what gets to fill that space.

In the Absence of Religion

But even that will not be enough. Culture wars, however satisfying and necessary, are not sufficient. If there is to be a remoralization of society, it will have to occur at the level not just of supply but of demand. Getting the culture producers to limit the toxicity of their products will not be that difficult. Even without overt government censorship, political and popular pressure are quite capable of inducing the culture creators to self-censorship.

In a free-market society, however, such supply-side changes are not enough. The failure of the war on drugs should have taught us that. The producers of culture may accede temporarily to political demands for self-censorship out of fear or regard for public relations. But a more enduring change in the cultural market, as in any other, awaits a fundamental change in demand. The customer has to stop buying the stuff.

And where does that change come from? We now leave the realm of governmental reform and media self-censorship and enter entirely new territory, religious territory. Irving Kristol has written about the current and coming religious revival as an echo of earlier Great Awakenings. There certainly is a religious revival under way, and it does establish a basis for a most fundamental reversal of social decay. But I have my doubts about the firmness and permanence of this *fin de siècle* awakening.

This is an age of advancing science and material abundance. Science and abundance offer invitations to skepticism and pleasure that are hard to refuse. It is difficult for me to believe that, in such an era, a self-abnegating religious revival will prevail.

I hope I am wrong. It is the task of the political strategist, however, to prepare for the possibility that the Great Awakening is not at hand. In which case the arrest of social decay, the revitalization of civil society, is a far more difficult and chancy proposition. It must then depend upon the more coercive and less reliable agency of politics — a politics crucially capable of articulating cultural with structural reform. Neither alone will suffice.

The Culture: "Upstream" from Politics

WILLIAM B. WICHTERMAN

Political interest in America's worsening cultural conditions has grown in recent years. Some have even characterized the polarized political debate over moral values as a "culture war," which indeed it often appears to be. The rise to majority status of the Republican Party in the United States Congress in the 1994 elections was made possible in part by a constituency and an agenda that took dead aim at America's cultural conditions.

I write not only as a cultural conservative, but also as one who served as a congressional staff member in the midst of this convulsive political period in Congress. Over the past decades, a series of unexamined assumptions has settled in the consciousness of many of my fellow conservatives. (Although liberals have clung to mythologies of their own, my focus is on cultural conservatives.) Republicans' perceived[1] performance in Congress, simultaneously alienating "mainstream" citizens and disappointing the conservative core constituency, is prompting cultural conservatives to reexamine their assumptions.

The conventional wisdom of many cultural conservatives runs something like this: Our nation is in decline largely due to a series of public policy mandates, especially those handed down by the courts. These mandates have undermined the founding principles of our country and the institutions of society. Since the

1. I say "perceived" because many of Republicans' legislative actions have been widely misreported by the media. From school lunch funding to the proposed ban on partial birth abortions, the media has regularly failed to accurately portray what is being proposed.

culture wars began through government, so the argument goes, they can and must be won through government. Whether it is the abortion license, no-fault divorce, school prayer, special legal protections for homosexuals, or pornography, many cultural conservatives believe they must elect a conservative majority and appoint conservative judges to reverse the nation's moral corruption.

In contrast, I believe that the cause of America's moral degradation is not political but cultural. While cultural conservatives bemoan judicial activism that reinterprets the plain meaning of the written Constitution, they forget that the courts are only finishing on parchment a job already begun in the hearts of the American people. A sound cultural constitution that values the good, the true, and the beautiful, and that seeks to suppress perverse inclinations, has been subverted by our rejection of transcendent truth, and the interpretation of the written Constitution has reflected that change. Transcendence has been erased from the paper only as it has drained from our culture. Politics is largely an expression of culture.

Many cultural conservatives have difficulty believing this since they have been steeped in the doctrine that politics is the root of America's cultural decay, rather than its flower. This belief has led them to overlook more influential shapers of culture, and misled them into believing that conservative governance could have prevented cultural debasement. The truth, as social commentator Don Eberly has rightly noted, is that "politics is downstream from the culture."

Cultural conservatives concerned about moral erosion have spent much of their energy working for change in the political sphere, and too little energy working in the cultural sphere. Economic liberals have tried the same tactics with similar results.[2] This has been a profound mistake, not because politics plays no role in shaping the nation, but because its role is less important than that of other culture-shaping institutions: the family, academia, journalism, religion, entertainment, literature, and the fine arts.

The Framers of the Constitution understood the primacy of culture and founded a government intended to reflect the higher elements of a generally virtuous populace. As American culture continues its slide away from belief in transcendent truth, the Framers' constitutional order is slowly being replaced by an increasingly democratic legislature, reflecting the appetites of the majority. Even the judiciary, the branch most associated with leading the nation against the majority, largely reflects social changes already underway.

The task before cultural conservatives is to renew the culture, thereby re-

2. In the twentieth century, liberals tried to institute economic centralized planning. By the end of the century, it was becoming clear that their attempts were falling short. It has proven impossible for statist economic policies to be sustained as the culture exalted higher still individualism and liberty.

storing an operative acknowledgment of transcendent truth. Without this renewal, the unwritten constitution of the culture will continue to deny transcendence and degrade morals, and our society will keep on sliding into the moral abyss. And since government is, in Plato's phrase, the soul writ large, this degradation cannot help but find expression in the state.

The Unwritten Constitution of the Culture

That the culture is in a steady decline, if not a virtual free fall, has been amply demonstrated by numerous commentators, including William Bennett, William Raspberry, and Robert Bork. One only has to surf network television, browse through a Blockbuster video store, attend an academic conference or "professional" wrestling bout, or walk through an art museum to witness the cultural toxicity. Fatherlessness, abortion-on-demand, random violence, drug abuse, rampant extra-marital sex, debasing manners, and general incivility all point to a nation headed to moral oblivion.[3] The corruption of popular culture is led by the framers of the unwritten constitution, those individuals and institutions that shape the mores and habits of the heart. I posit that CNN's Ted Turner and Hollywood movie producer Oliver Stone have a far greater impact on culture than the entire U.S. Senate.

It is important to note that it is not just political conservatives who are concerned about cultural ill health. There are many Americans of all political stripes who decry teen pregnancy, violent videos, the collapse of marriage, and the vulgarity of prime-time television. Although they may differ with conservative Republican legislative prescriptions, they join in the chorus of dissenting voices decrying the direction of American culture, and we must not overlook their participation in cultural renewal.

The primary spiritual illness afflicting the culture is the loss of an active belief in absolute truth that transcends the immanent realm or present temporal world. Transcendence, as it will be used here, refers to belief in absolute truth grounded in a reality larger than the collection of temporal events and experiences forming everyday life. C. S. Lewis refers to belief in transcendence or "the Tao" as "the doctrine of objective value, the belief that certain attitudes are really true, and others really false, to the kind of thing the universe is and the kind of things we are."[4] This is not to say that cultures rooted in transcendent

3. While some of these downward trends have turned the corner in recent years, the historic trajectory has been grim and cause for celebration is premature.

4. C. S. Lewis, *The Abolition of Man* (New York: Macmillan Publishing Co., Inc., 1947), 29.

truth are immune to social decay. Indeed, the content of this belief in transcendent truth is very important. Nonetheless, it is the eroding of belief in transcendence and the rise of subjectivism[5] that is at the core of the American culture's declining health.

At first glance, the rejection of transcendence by Americans is not readily apparent from the evidence. According to the Barna Report,[6] 95 percent of Americans still believe in God; 68 percent agree God is the all-powerful, all-knowing, perfect creator of the universe who rules the world today; 84 percent believe Jesus was God or the Son of God; and 43 percent attended church in the last week. On the other hand, 72 percent of adult Americans believe that "There is no such thing as absolute truth; two people could define truth in totally conflicting ways, but both could still be correct" — and this includes 62 percent of born-again Christians and 42 percent of Evangelical Christians.[7] In other words, a significant percentage of Americans have inherited a theistic world from previous generations but they have "syncretized" it with the cultural elite's relativism, holding fundamentally incompatible ideas and affirming both simultaneously. The so-called moral majority is at best a schizophrenic majority, both embracing a transcendent God of the universe and rejecting the very basis of that belief.

James Davison Hunter's portrait of America as a deeply divided people, locked in a culture war with one another, does not seem to comport with the operational subjectivism of most Americans. Closer to the mark may be Alan Wolfe's *One Nation, After All.* Wolfe argues that there is no culture war because the middle class does not believe in most things strongly enough to want to impose them on others. While he agrees that America's elites are engaged in cultural conflict, he finds that America's middle class has found a common creed in a nonjudgmentalism that trumps morality. Thus, when the Supreme Court hands down decisions overturning state restrictions on abortion and Internet obscenity, bans student-led prayer in official school functions, and mandates legal authority to enact special rights for homosexuals as a protected class, Americans register their disapproval in opinion polls, but not at the polling booth. Where the Court's decisions should provoke legislative and electoral resistance, the public shrugs. For many supposedly theistic Americans, their morality has no legs.

It would be wrong to say that American culture has completely rejected transcendent truth. To be sure, there is much in American society that is still

5. "Subjectivism" means that all truth is relative and is defined by the individual.

6. Website (www.barna.org) under "Research Archives," "Beliefs: general religious, heaven and hell, and theological."

7. George Barna, *Virtual America* (Ventura, Calif.: Regal, 1994).

rooted in a notion of objective right and wrong. The overall trajectory of American culture, however, is cause for great alarm.

The Power of the Unwritten Constitution over the Written Constitution

Some will argue that the American form of government is not so easily changed or its Constitution so easily amended that this cultural degradation will find expression in the wise government of the people. The true genius of the American Experiment, they say, lies in its insightful structuring of checks and balances among the branches of government, not in the character of its citizens. The Framers recognized the limitation of trusting in human goodness to establish good government and overcame that obstacle through their clever drafting of the Constitution.

This attempt to privatize morality and pretend that it has no effect on government does not work. In time, the unwritten constitution of the culture does rewrite the constitution on paper. In his book *The Revenge of Conscience,* J. Budziszewski writes that "every country gets the government it deserves: one cannot expect liberty, justice, or concern for the common good where knaves rule a rabble. . . . The single greatest problem of politics is simply this: How can we make government promote the common good when there is so little virtue to be found?"[8] Attempts to recover a correct rendering of the Constitution solely through the appointment of strict constructionists to the high court, while laudable and important in their own right, overlook the greater influence of popular culture on judicial decision-making.

The restoration of just policies must be preceded by the rediscovery of transcendent truth in the unwritten constitution our culture creates. Robert Bork notes that "The tyrannies of political correctness and multiculturalism will not be ejected from the universities by any number of conservative victories at the polls. Modern liberals captured the government and its bureaucracies because they captured the culture. Conservative political victories will always be tenuous and fragile unless conservatives recapture the culture."[9]

It would certainly be a mistake to think of politics as nothing but a reflection of culture. Law is a teacher, and politics is one of the culture-shaping institutions. Legal sanctions do help to inform and guide the conscience of a nation.

8. J. Budziszewski, *The Revenge of Conscience: Politics and the Fall of Man* (Dallas: Spence Publishing, 1999), pp. 55-56.

9. Robert H. Bork, *Slouching Towards Gomorrah: Modern Liberalism and American Decline* (New York: Regan Books, 1996), p. 339.

Everything from tax policy to health insurance law plays a role in shaping culture. My own active political involvement underscores this conviction. The mobilization of voters, the distribution of voter guides, congressional hearings, petition drives, phone banking, and fundraising are integral to a healthy republic. There is every indication that increased political activity by citizens concerned about cultural renewal would have a positive impact on government actions. With declining rates of voting, organized political activity is unquestionably effective in shaping government policies. Therefore, calls to abandon the political realm are both wrong-headed and irresponsible.

But the tendency for many Americans is to overstate the importance of politics in shaping culture. When compared with Hollywood, academia, media, or the family, politics plays a relatively minor role in forming culture. Political life, while it may appear to be at the vanguard of a society, is more like the infantry. Politics stands at the front lines, but is directed from the rear by the culture. Its prominence in the place of battle may deceptively suggest that the battle rages there. That we mark our history by various government actions like the New Deal, the Great Society programs, *Roe v. Wade,* and the 1994 Republican congressional takeover might suggest that law and politics lead our society. On the contrary, notes philosopher Michael Oakeshott, politics protects a particular social order, but it does not lead or guide it. The Magna Carta and the Bill of Rights only *seem* to emerge from the political order. In fact, their content is written by a "stratum of social thought far too deep to be influenced by the actions of politicians."[10] Oakeshott continues: "A political system presupposes a civilization; it has a function to perform in regard to that civilization, but it is a function mainly of protection and to a minor degree of merely mechanical interpretation and expression." The animating genius of any political system is far behind the lines of the visible political battle, calling the shots like a general.

Edmund Burke wrote that "manners are more important than laws," and Plato wrote, "Give me the songs of a nation, and it matters not who writes its laws." Consider what animates most individuals: literature, religion, entertainment, and music. Individuals rarely change their lives based on a political speech or a government act. An individual may be inspired to work for a political candidate who reflects what he finds most important in preserving or creating a certain kind of culture. But, more often than not, it is the cultural consensus that precedes the political expression.

10. Michael Oakeshott, *Religion, Politics, and the Moral Life,* ed. Timothy Fuller (New Haven: Yale University Press, 1993), p. 93.

The American Framers' Reliance on Culture

The Framers of the United States Constitution believed that a republic could be maintained only with a healthy culture as its foundation. Although the Framers did not specifically use the word "culture," their concern for republican virtues among the citizens was another way of saying the same thing. John Witherspoon, signer of the Declaration of Independence and professor and president of the College of New Jersey (later Princeton University), who was dubbed the "great teacher of the American Revolution," said:

> Nothing is more certain than that a general profligacy and corruption of manners make a people ripe for destruction. A good form of government may hold the rotten materials together for some time, but beyond a certain pitch, even the best constitution will be ineffectual, and slavery must ensue. On the other hand, when the manners of a nation are pure, when true religion and eternal principles maintain their vigour, the attempts of the most powerful enemies to oppress them are commonly baffled and disappointed.[11]

George Washington said in his Farewell Address of 1796 that "Of all the dispositions and habits which lead to political prosperity, Religion and morality are indispensable supports."[12] Likewise, Gouverneur Morris, drafter of the U.S. Constitution and the ambassador to France during the French Revolution, wrote, "[The French] want an American Constitution with the exception of a king instead of a President, without reflecting that they have no American citizens to uphold that constitution."[13] It was the constitution written on the heart of the American citizenry that made the difference between France and the United States. "While the law allows the American people to do everything," wrote Alexis de Tocqueville, "there are things which religion prevents them from imagining and forbids them to dare. . . ."[14]

If the brilliance of the American government lay solely in its Constitu-

11. John Witherspoon, "The Dominion of Providence Over the Passions of Men: A Sermon Preached at Princeton on May 17, 1776," in *Political Sermons of the American Founding Era (1730-1805),* ed. Ellis Sandoz (Indianapolis: Liberty Press, 1991), p. 553.

12. George Washington's Farewell Address of 19 September 1796, in Matthew Spalding and Patrick Garrity, *A Sacred Union of Citizens* (Lanham, Md.: Rowman and Littlefield, Inc., 1996), p. 183.

13. Gouverneur Morris, letter of 10 July 1789 to William Carmichael, in *The Life and Writings of Gouverneur Morris,* vol. 2, ed. Jared Sparks (Gray and Bowen, 1832), p. 75.

14. Alexis de Tocqueville, *Democracy in America,* in *Political Thought in America,* ed. Michael B. Levy (Chicago: The Dorsey Press, 1988), p. 295.

tion, there would be no reason to worry about the unwritten constitution of its citizens. The Framers, however, believed that government is "the greatest [as in "truest"] of all reflections on human nature. . . . If men were angels, no government would be necessary."[15] Even with the careful thought behind the founding document, the brilliance lay not in the Constitution as an abstract document divorced from the spiritual and cultural state of a people, but as a document which reflected the highest, truest, and best in the American people at that point in history. Benjamin Franklin responded to the wife of the mayor of Philadelphia, who asked what the Constitutional Convention had crafted, by saying, "My dear lady, we have given to you a republic — if you can keep it."[16] His reply demonstrates that the Framers knew that the durability of the new nation would reside not primarily with the superior design of the government but with the enduring character of the nation's culture.

A Republic, Not a Democracy, to Reflect the Will

Although a healthy culture was necessary for the maintenance of a healthy polity, it alone was not sufficient. The Framers consciously intended to construct a democratic *republic* that would be an expression of the people's higher selves as manifested in the will, and an inhibitor of the lower self, manifested in the passions. Political theorist Claes Ryn writes that the higher self "refers to that in our being which pulls us in the direction of our own true humanity, that is, towards the realization of our highest potential as defined by a universally valid standard."[17] The lower self is moved by human appetites and is guided less by conscience and more by short-term self-interest. The will affirms transcendence, and the passions reject it.

From this desire to accentuate the healthy elements of culture, the Framers consciously chose not to establish a democracy. In fact, the word "democracy" does not even appear in the U.S. Constitution. Americans have largely lost the ability to distinguish between democracy and the democratic *republic* established by the Framers, and would be surprised to read the harsh words the Framers had for democracy. James Madison warned, "Democracies

15. James Madison, *The Federalist Papers,* No. 51.

16. Taken from "America's Bill of Rights at 200 Years," by former Chief Justice Warren E. Burger, printed in *Presidential Studies Quarterly,* vol. XXI, no. 3 (Summer 1991): 457.

17. Claes Ryn, *Democracy and the Ethical Life* (Washington, D.C.: The Catholic University of America Press, 1990), p. 62. This book is essential reading for individuals interested in the relationship between culture and politics. Dr. Ryn's works, Plato's *Republic,* and Eric Voegelin's series of works, *Order and History,* have been the most important influences in crafting my thesis.

have ever been spectacles of turbulence and contention."[18] Fisher Ames, author of the House of Representatives' language for the First Amendment, said, "The known propensity of a democracy is to licentiousness which the ambitious call, and ignorant believe, to be liberty."[19] According to Gouverneur Morris, "Democracy [is] savage and wild."[20] "A simple democracy . . . is one of the greatest of evils," inveighed Benjamin Rush, signer of the Declaration of Independence.[21] John Witherspoon warned that "Pure democracy cannot subsist long nor be carried far into the departments of state — it is very subject to caprice and the madness of popular rage."[22]

Instead, the Framers sought to establish a democratic republic in which the immutable law of the universe, rather than the nominal majority, was more likely to find expression in government. They hoped to impede the majority's passion from expressing itself in government and to ensure that the majority's will, which the Framers insisted must be grounded in an affirmation of transcendent truth, would find its voice. Theirs was a popular government whose majoritarian elements, while not absent, would be softened by representation, divided government, and constitutional authority.

Because the Framers believed that humanity was corrupt,[23] they relied, in part, on representation rather than on plebiscite. Representation was not an unfortunate byproduct of a large nation, destined to waste away once the means of more direct democracy were achieved. Even supposing that electronic technology had been available to the new nation, permitting online voting, referenda, and polling data, the Framers would have chosen representation. They believed representation would serve as a check on the passions of the majority. This check was designed not only to protect minorities, but also to protect the majority from its

18. James Madison, *The Federalist Papers,* No. 10.

19. Fisher Ames, "The Dangers of American Liberty" (February 1805) in *Works of Fisher Ames* (Boston: T. B. Wait & Co., 1809), p. 384.

20. Gouverneur Morris, *An Oration Delivered on Wednesday, June 29, 1814, at the Request of a Number of Citizens of New-York, in Celebration of the Recent Deliverance of Europe from the Yoke of Military Despotism* (New York: Van Winkle and Wiley, 1814), p. 22.

21. Benjamin Rush, letter to John Adams on 21 July 1789, in *The Letters of Benjamin Rush,* vol. 1, ed. L. H. Butterfield (Princeton: Princeton University Press for the American Philosophical Society, 1951), p. 523.

22. John Witherspoon, *The Works of John Witherspoon* (Edinburgh: J. Ogle, 1815), vol. VII, p. 101, Lecture 12 on Civil Society.

23. Consistent with the Judeo-Christian worldview in which they were grounded, the Framers believed that humanity had fallen short of what God intended it to be. This "Fall" (to use the biblical idea) from God's intentions and his original creation does not mean that humanity is as bad as it could be, or that it can never rise above the worst proclivities of the heart. But it does mean that the whole self (reason, will, emotions, etc.) is subject to sin and self-deception.

lower self. Representatives were to "refine and enlarge the public views by passing them through the medium of a chosen body of citizens, whose wisdom may best discern the true interest of their country . . . ."[24] While supporters of majority rule abhor the notion that representatives would do anything other than directly transmit the majority opinions of their constituents, the Framers relied on representatives as one way of thwarting the majority's sometimes flawed judgment.

To inhibit majorities, the Framers also relied on checks and balances among the branches of government. They distrusted governmental power not only because of its ability for an elite few to oppress the majority, but also because of the ability of the majority to oppress a minority. They sought to establish a system in which a bicameral legislature,[25] a chief executive wielding a veto pen, and an independent judiciary would be in constant tension with one another. This complicated structure ensured that quick action by the government, especially in domestic affairs, would be difficult to achieve without an overwhelming and sustained consensus. The government was deliberately hobbled with inefficiencies and duplication in order to thwart the passions of transient majority opinion. It is no wonder that this complicated structure is anathema to majoritarian enthusiasts, who are frustrated by the inability of the voters to quickly and easily force government action.

The third check on popular wishes was intended to be the most difficult of all to surmount. The Constitution, the literal embodiment of the enduring will of the people, was crafted to express the people's higher and more virtuous aims, and was intended to be "a mirror for the national conscience."[26] It was ratified by near unanimity, ensuring that it reflected the clear consensus of the people. The Constitution codified the principles by which justice would be sought.[27] As Ryn writes, "The constitutional norm serves as a constant reminder of the contrast between the values endorsed by the people in its better moments, when it looks at politics in the perspective of the moral end, and the imperfect, sometimes degrading practice of day-to-day politics."[28]

To ensure that the Constitution reflected the enduring will of the people,

24. Madison, *The Federalist Papers,* No. 10.

25. Interestingly, Reform Party Governor Jesse Ventura of Minnesota, a noted populist, advocates the elimination of the bicameral legislature in the states, since it impedes the instant expression of the majority. But he maintains that it is still important in the federal legislature to ensure that smaller states' rights are not trampled upon by larger states.

26. René de Visme Williamson, *Independence and Involvement: A Christian Reorientation in Political Science* (Baton Rouge: Louisiana State University Press, 1964), pp. 126-27.

27. Proceduralists expect the majority to define justice, but the Framers expected the complicated republic to approximate the pre-existing justice which transcends time and place. Consistent with natural law theory, the Framers assumed that justice existed, and it was the role of a healthy government to approximate that law.

28. Ryn, *Democracy,* p. 199.

instead of their temporal passions, the Framers made certain that it would only be passed after much deliberation. The value of deliberation stands at the heart of the process enacted by the Framers. Unlike the majoritarian theory which views deliberation as an unnecessary impediment to expressing the public voice, the Framers' view of deliberation was rooted in their desire to approximate transcendent justice. If transcendent truth exists, and humans are corruptible and self-interested, as the Framers believed, then deliberation is necessary to *reveal* truth. The Constitution could be ratified only after approval by the supermajority of both chambers and the affirmation of three-fourths of the state legislatures, and the deliberation required to accomplish this was intended to establish the fundamental principles by which the republic would function.

Once the Constitution was enacted, the Framers intended the Supreme Court to safeguard the enduring principles of the Constitution, or the higher self of the people. Although a simple majority vote in the legislature was enough to enact our passions, the Court was designed to defend the people's higher will by checking their baser passions. If the passions of a majority sought to overcome the Constitution's will as defended by the Court, a constitutional amendment was required — an almost insurmountable barrier to any but the most enduring of our designs. The idea of an unelected body serving for life, independently interpreting the U.S. Constitution to ensure that the majority does not override fundamental principles, expressed the Framers' belief that higher principles should not easily be cast aside.

The cultural antecedents for the establishment and ratification of the U.S. Constitution were the acknowledgment of transcendent justice and truth, humanity's corruptibility, and the importance of empowering the will and mitigating the passions. Out of this worldview was born the Framers' democratic republic in which numerical majorities were inhibited through representatives, a divided government of checks and balances, and a Constitution affirmed by a supermajority.

Rousseau's Democracy of Passions

The Framers' constrained and inhibited popular government stands in stark contrast to the majoritarian democracy advocated by individuals with a more rosy view of human nature. For them, representative government is a poor excuse for a more robust democracy of the people with fewer undemocratic elements. The basis of their beliefs is easily traceable to the influential eighteenth-century political theorist Jean Jacques Rousseau, who rejected representation and constitutionalism as illegitimate expressions of the people's interests.

Because Rousseau believed that the only true democracy was the direct vote of the entire popular assembly of all adults, he regarded representative democracy as an oxymoron[29] and viewed representation as a form of enslavement. The only time citizens of a representative democracy are free, he argued, is on Election Day when they cast their votes for their representatives.[30] Rousseau also rejected any constitutional limitations on the direct expression of the people's desires. A law passed last year could not be binding for this year's citizens, who are subject only to the current majority.

Undergirding Rousseau's rejection of representation and constitutional limits was his belief in the innate goodness of humanity. In a well-constituted state where the goodness of nature rules, "good sense, justice, and integrity" belong to everyone equally. Therefore, the general assembly will inevitably reflect that goodness in its laws. The natural passions and appetites are the very sources of goodness in humanity. Virtue is spontaneous, natural, and within the grasp of anyone at any time; it is not the result of arduous self-discipline. Decisions made by the popular assembly should be nearly unanimous, since justice is achieved not by "long debates, dissensions, and tumult," but by harmony and agreement.[31] Deliberation only signifies that humanity's natural inclinations are being corrupted by reason, according to Rousseau.

Rousseau's distrust of the anti-majoritarian character of the U.S. Constitution finds modern expression in prominent political theorists such as Robert Dahl. Dahl contends that the Framers, while nobly seeking to defend civil rights, erroneously constructed a government "adverse to the majority principle, and in that sense to democracy."[32] In effect, the Constitution, argues Dahl, favors privileged minorities and thwarts the wishes of the majority at every turn. In their effort to protect inalienable rights, the Framers undermined democratic procedures by favoring elite minorities. In the place of the constitutional democracy established to reflect transcendent justice, Dahl puts forward a procedural democracy.[33] In a procedural democracy, fair procedures take precedence over particular ends; justice is *defined* by the orderly democratic process. There is no concern about whether the decisions of that process are right or wrong, since they are "correct," by definition.[34]

29. Jean-Jacques Rousseau, *On the Social Contract,* in *The Basic Political Writings,* trans. Donald A. Cress (Indianapolis: Hackett Publishing, 1987), p. 198.

30. Rousseau, *On the Social Contract,* p. 154.

31. Rousseau, *On the Social Contract,* p. 205.

32. Robert Dahl, "On Removing Certain Impediments to Democracy in the United States," *Political Science Quarterly* (Spring 1977), p. 5.

33. For an excellent exposition of the difference between procedural and republican democracy, see Michael Sandel, *Democracy's Discontent* (Cambridge, Mass.: Harvard University Press, 1996).

34. In the seventeenth century's *Leviathan,* Thomas Hobbes also entrusted the

Rousseau and Dahl demonstrate the implications for the American Experiment of a rejection of transcendent truth. Their common view of humanity's natural goodness led them to advocate government that encourages uninhibited majorities, government in which appetites find greater and more immediate political expression. The more popular culture adopts the basic outline of their worldview, the more their models for governance will be accepted by the populace.

The Erosion of the Framers' Republic

It is striking to note how different was the Framers' understanding of the democratic republic they created from that envisioned by Rousseau and touted by today's cultural leaders. Where majoritarians seek direct rule, the Framers preferred representation. Where majoritarians eschew all constitutional limits on the people assembled, the Framers relied on a constitution affirmed by a supermajority to constrain the will of the simple majority. Where majoritarians believe that all values are morally equal and that virtue was that which comes naturally, the Framers believed that humanity was corrupted, that virtue was cultivated through self-discipline, and that elected individuals of superior wisdom should interpret the long-term interests of the people. Where majoritarians are contemptuous of deliberation and reason, the Framers believed that deliberation was necessary to attain wisdom. Where majoritarians and proceduralists eschew any limits on the popular opinion and want a more efficient governmental mechanism to reflect that view, the Framers built a system intended to foil hastiness and express the will rather than the passions. The unwritten constitution of the Framers' culture produced a written constitution in stark contrast to that envisioned by majoritarian proponents.

Given that Americans are increasingly adopting a subjectivist worldview and retreating from the Framers' fundamental belief in transcendence, it is not surprising that the structure of our government is beginning to look more like Rousseau's ideal and less like the Framers' model. This brings us to a specific examination of how the unwritten constitution of the culture is rewriting American government.

---

power of defining justice to the state, making him a forerunner of the postmodern rejection of transcendent justice. Although he entrusted all power to the sovereign ruler while proceduralists entrust it to the people, both insist that justice is only what the state defines it to be, and nothing more.

The House: Democracy on the Rise

The Framers, while not enthusiasts for democracy, were intent on establishing popular government in which the ultimate authority for decision-making lay with the people. It is commonly known that they established a bicameral legislature to reflect the tension between the larger and the smaller states. What is less recognized, however, is that this bicameral structure also reflected the Framers' understanding of the self as divided between the will and the passions.

The Framers recognized the need for the more immediate expressions of the people's passions in the House of Representatives. With their two-year terms and smaller constituencies, House members were intended to be in closer touch with the short-term views of the numerical majority than was the Senate. Furthermore, the more rigid rules of the House were supposed to ensure that the majority party would have tight control over what bills were debated, the timing of their consideration, and what amendments would be considered. This framework ensures that numerical majorities are better able to act on the immediate interests of the majority of the American people.

As popular culture gradually accepts the notion that all values are of equal worth, that absolute truth does not exist, and that the cult of the self replaces theism, however, the internal structure of the House has become more democratized than was intended by the Framers. The Framers had envisioned strong House leadership guiding the body, but the centralized power has been drained away from the Speaker to committee chairs and rank-and-file members. The post-Watergate reforms have increased the number of subcommittees and the power of their chairs to control the House.[35]

Individual members of Congress have also become more firmly tied to the wishes of the majority within their congressional districts. Advances in electronic communications and media coverage, the competitive nature of House races, the advent of polling, and improved transportation have aided Representatives in keeping in closer contact with their constituents. E-mails, blast faxes, lobbying groups, C-SPAN, and nonstop media coverage ensure that interested constituents can monitor the progress (or regress) of their individual concerns and provide daily input to the Congress. These technological changes, combined with the cultural demand for more direct democracy, have heightened the responsiveness of House members to their constituents.

Ironically, Americans feel increasingly disconnected from their government. There is a widespread belief that the Congress is more attuned to the

35. The Republican takeover of 1994 has returned some power to the House leadership. However, Speaker Newt Gingrich's consolidation of power is slowly being reversed by his successor, Speaker Dennis Hastert.

agendas of special interest groups than to the constituency at home. In fact, just the opposite is true. Members of Congress carefully watch polling data to guarantee that their votes reflect the majority within their constituency and constantly track constituent concerns to ensure they are "in touch." Representatives live in closer communication with their constituents and are more responsive to their concerns than at any point in American history.

The Senate: Losing Its Resistance

If the House was to be the hot tea, the Senate was to be the saucer to cool it. It was to take a longer, more deliberative view, reflecting the more long-term will. Whereas House members were to be in closer touch with voters due to their shorter electoral terms, Senators were given six years between elections, providing them greater leeway to make decisions that might conflict with the short-term majority interests in their states. Furthermore, only one-third of the Senate is up for election every two years, further insulating it from fleeting passions. Senators also represent entire states, diminishing their ability to reflect a more confined majority in a smaller congressional district. Their election by the state legislature further insulated them from momentary majorities. And the ability of the Senators to filibuster legislation by controlling the debate indefinitely and preventing a vote was a powerful check on the majority's passions. The Framers intended that the Senate, while still a body representing citizens, would be several steps removed from the people.

Once again, it is clear that culture has shaped politics. The rise of subjectivism and its subsequent demand that ostensibly benign human nature be given rein in immediate popular expression has resulted in the erosion of some of the more reflective elements of the Senate. The constitutional amendment ratified in 1913 to provide for the direct election of Senators, instead of their indirect election by the state legislatures, was an expression of the people's desire to have greater direct control over their Senators. Likewise, the ability of a single Senator to filibuster has been gradually eroded by the growing strength of cloture voting.[36]

36. Although the filibuster was not an invention of the Framers, it was created by Senate rules in 1806. From 1806 until 1917, there was no means to end debate. Not until 1917 did the Senate adopt Rule 22, permitting a vote on cloture upon the petition of sixteen Senators. If two-thirds of the Senators present and voting approved shutting off debate, cloture was invoked. In 1975, Rule 22 was strengthened to allow just three-fifths of the entire membership (sixty Senators) to stop unlimited debate. Even then, another thirty hours of debate was permitted to proceed.

The Executive Branch: Institutionally Strong, but Weak in Character

Unlike the Congress, where majoritarian reforms are slowing eroding the ability of the legislature to act independently, the executive branch is not losing its ability to override temporal majorities. When the Framers established the presidency, they recognized that government needs the ability to lead decisively, especially in times of crisis. The President's veto power, another way the Framers placed a check on the majority, remains inviolate.

Although the institution of the presidency is basically sound, it is the character of its office holders that is reflecting the cultural predilection for majoritarianism. Take, for instance, President Bill Clinton's reliance on polling to guide policy decision-making. When the news first broke in January 1998 that the President of the United States had an affair with a White House intern, President Clinton commissioned political consultant Dick Morris to conduct a poll. According to Morris, the poll showed that Americans would forgive adultery, but would not abide perjury or suborned perjury. The President allegedly replied that he would "just have to win then."[37] Well-documented sources have demonstrated a similar reliance on polling in military actions and domestic policy-making.[38]

Although the presidency retains its institutional strength, the means of its election, the Electoral College, is under attack. Many Americans no longer understand the need for an Electoral College. They fail to see the need for a second body to interpret or restrain the immediate vote of the people as expressed in a national election. Whereas the Framers intended electors from each of the states to be people of wisdom who would be a potential check on an unwise decision of a national majority, the public views electors as an anachronistic and anti-democratic restraint on the people. Providing the electors do not override the majority's wishes, the Electoral College will continue to be tolerated, if only because removing it would require the almost impossible process of a constitutional amendment.

I should note that it is not my intent to prescribe constitutional or governmental reforms to stem the cultural tide of moral degradation. In fact, such governmental reforms could not possibly redirect culture if it were not willing to be so directed. For instance, bringing back the indirect election of the Senate, strengthening the filibuster, or reinvigorating the strength of the House Speaker

37. Interestingly, the poll results did not comport with the ultimate willingness of the American people to retain a President who they believed did, in fact, lie under oath.

38. See Dick Morris, *Behind the Oval Office: Getting Reelected Against All Odds* (Los Angeles: Renaissance Books, 1999).

would have little, if any, impact on the restoration of just government. The point is that the government's evolution reflects the culture's premium on democracy as the cure for American ills. Preference for direct democracy emanates from the loss of a belief that Representatives are to pursue justice. Representatives and senators are now seen as mere conduits for expressing their constituents' desires. The constitution of the heart reinterprets the Constitution and concretely changes the process of American governance.

Yet it is in the Supreme Court, the body designed to be least subject to the passions of the majority, where the public's operational rejection of transcendent truth is most fully expressed.

Leadership in the Courts: Reflecting and Accelerating Social Degradation

Cultural conservatives have come to see the judicial branch as the chief enemy of well-ordered government. Repeatedly the courts have seemed to thwart the wishes of the majority on issues such as flag burning, abortion, school prayer, homosexual rights, and pornography. In each case, national polls have indicated that a majority of the nation has stood for more conservative principles than those handed down by the Court. The symposium in the journal *First Things* on the Court's usurpation of popular government[39] struck a responsive chord among many cultural conservatives. But the symposium ignored that the Court is heading where the culture is already leading, and where the cultural gatekeeping institutions have already arrived.

Roe v. Wade: Joining the Sexual Revolution

Take, for instance, the first item in the social conservative indictment against the corrosive influence of the federal government, the Supreme Court's 1973 ruling in *Roe v. Wade.* In the pre–*Roe v. Wade* era, the thinking goes, abortion in America was almost always illegal, in many cases unsafe, and above all rare. *Roe* constituted a sudden and dramatic change, not just in the theory of abortion, but in its practice. The Court legitimated a practice, say conservatives, and breached a philosophical wall that released the abortion plague on a mostly pro-life American culture. Thus came the revolution, which quickly resulted in an annual abortion rate in excess of one million per year, rising as high as 1.6

39. See Richard John Neuhaus, ed., "The End of Democracy? The Judicial Usurpation of Politics," *First Things,* November 1996, pp. 18-42.

million in the late 1980s. Absent the Court's decision, the argument continues, the legal abortion rate would have remained very low.

Not surprisingly, the true story of abortion in America is quite different. In 1972, just prior to *Roe,* nearly 600,000 *legal* abortions were performed in the United States. In fact, the national abortion rate had actually increased faster *before* the High Court's actions (see Figure 1 on p. 94).[40] Eighteen states had liberalized their abortion laws in the five years before *Roe.* California, New York, Washington, Alaska, and Hawaii had a largely unlimited abortion license. Seventy-five leading national organizations had endorsed repeal of all abortion restrictions from 1967-1972, including twenty-eight religious and twenty-one medical groups — even the YWCA had joined in.[41] National surveys conducted before and after the landmark abortion decisions demonstrate a conflicted public opinion. On the one hand, in the year leading up to the January 1973 decision, national polls found that 64 percent of Americans believed that abortion should be decided solely by a woman and her physician.[42] On the other hand, most Americans believed that it is against God's will to destroy any human life, especially that of an unborn baby (63 percent in March 1973), and that no one's life, including an unborn child's, should be taken without permission (55 percent in March 1973).[43] The public's loyalties were torn between belief in transcendent truth and subjectivism.

Even if conservatives had held a majority on the Court, upholding instead the states' ability to prohibit or restrict abortions, I argue the abortion rate still would have continued to grow. In fact, the abortion rate probably would have climbed to at least one million per year even without *Roe,* and more likely higher still. Pro-choice citizens would have been ignited to mobilize to change more state laws, and pro-life Americans would have rested on their victory in the Supreme Court. With 70 percent of the population living within a two-hour drive of a state with an abortion license, access to elective abortion would have remained high.[44]

The loss of respect for life, rooted in the sexual revolution of the 1960s,

40. Gerald N. Rosenberg, *The Hollow Hope: Can Courts Bring About Social Change?* (Chicago: The University of Chicago Press, 1991), p. 184. I am indebted to Rosenberg's work in shaping my understanding of the limits of Court action in effecting cultural change. While an obvious proponent of the cultural changes, Rosenberg adeptly demonstrates that the Court is powerless to start change and can, at best, only encourage its continuation. Absent a broader social movement for the change in question, the Court's power is sharply muted.

41. Rosenberg, *The Hollow Hope,* p. 184.

42. Gallup, June 1972.

43. Louis and Harris Associates, March 1973.

44. Michael Barone, *Our Country: The Shaping of America from Roosevelt to Reagan* (New York: The Free Press, 1990), p. 756, n. 14.

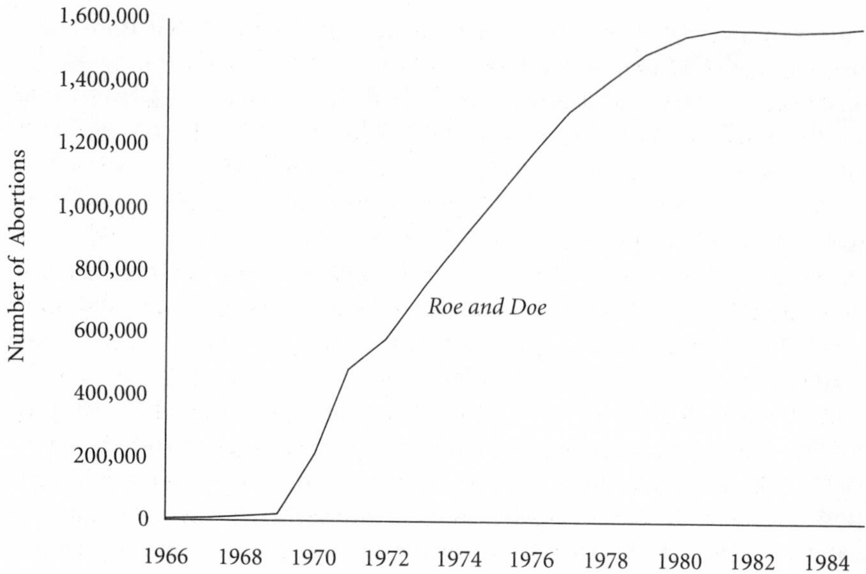

Figure 1. Legal Abortions in the United States, 1966-1985

Source: Gerald N. Rosenberg, *The Hollow Hope: Can Courts Bring About Social Change?* (Chicago: University of Chicago Press, 1991), p. 179.

was already sown in the culture before the Supreme Court ever took up the issue. The de-linking of sex and family ties had been unable to sever the unwanted product of the sexual encounter. The culture was quickly embracing the Pill as the first defense against childbirth, but a backstop was needed for "unintended pregnancies." Elective abortion-on-demand completed the sexual revolution, and the Court ratified that cultural decision. But the unwritten constitution of American culture had to be amended before the Court was able to act. The Court was simply joining the cultural revolution already well underway.

Romer v. Evans: Ratifying the Culture's View of Sex

In 1996, by a six to three majority, the Court ruled unconstitutional Colorado's Amendment 2 to the state constitution, which had prohibited state and local jurisdictions from adding "sexual orientation" to minority protection statutes. Amendment 2 had been drafted after Denver, Boulder, Aspen, and Aurora enacted laws adding "sexual orientation" to the list of protected civil rights, giving homosexuals a means to use civil rights laws in discrimination claims. The

Court majority ruled that the Amendment violated the Equal Protection Clause of the Fourteenth Amendment because the state could not prove a "rational basis" or "legitimate legislative end" for denying homosexuals "the possibility of protection across the board." The Court's opinion said that Colorado's sole reason for Amendment 2 was "animus" toward homosexuals.

One reason that resistance to the decision has been pusillanimous, at best, lies in the conflicted views of the public toward homosexuality. On the one hand, a slim majority of 52 percent of Americans believe that homosexual behavior should be considered an acceptable lifestyle (44 percent believe it should not).[45] On the other hand, 65 percent believe that homosexuals should be allowed to serve in the armed forces (and a plurality of 48 percent believe they should be able to serve openly), 60 percent believe they should be hired as teachers, and 53 percent as clergy.[46] Fifty-seven percent disagree with the statement that homosexuals should not be guaranteed protection from discrimination,[47] and 64 percent of Americans disagree with the statement that homosexual behavior should be against the law.[48] A majority of Americans (51 percent) believe that landlords should have to rent to homosexuals even if they are morally opposed to homosexuality.[49] Thus, the nation is steadily embracing homosexuality as an acceptable way of life.

The cultural predicate for Americans' growing acceptance of homosexuality lies in the growing assumption that sex is merely a physical act devoid of any other significance. Reduction of the meaning of sex combined with the simultaneous exaltation of sex as the highest experience available to humanity thins any deeper meaning in human existence. The culture is both stripping transcendence from sexuality and affirming it as the highest temporal experience.[50] These growing cultural dogmas lead logically to the *Romer* decision. Other judicial decisions cannot lag far behind, including the extension of marriage to homosexual couples and, possibly, polygamous arrangements.

Furthermore, Americans' overriding fear of judgmentalism prevents them from "imposing their morality on others." Tolerance has been enthroned as the value against which all others must yield. While Americans retain an older view of sexuality as a transcendent spiritual bond with myriad social implications, many Americans are unable or unwilling to implement the public

45. Gallup Poll, 9 February 1999.

46. Gallup Poll, 24 November 1996.

47. ABC News/Washington Post Poll, 5 August 1996.

48. Center for Survey Research, University of Virginia, 14 April 1996.

49. Center for Survey Research, University of Virginia, 14 April 1996.

50. Philosopher Eric Voegelin's thesis that gnostic cultures immanentize transcendence applies well to the emerging postmodern view of sexuality. Eric Voegelin, *The New Science of Politics* (Chicago: University of Chicago Press, 1952).

implications of this view. They have accepted the cultural judgment that such views are best left in the privacy of one's bedroom, and not imposed on the secular populace.

Romer did not lead the culture to a fulsome embrace of homosexuality, but simply joined the revolution in sexual mores already underway. While the public retains a superficial reticence to federal civil rights protections for homosexuals, it has already adopted the subjectivist assumptions that paved the way for the Court's decision. *Romer* is the inexorable conclusion to be drawn from the cultural privatization of sexuality, as well as the creed of nonjudgmentalism.

The Expulsion of School Prayer: Reflecting the Privatization of Religion

Because of its decisions *Engel v. Vitale* (1962) and *Abington School District v. Schempp* (1963), which expelled official prayer and Bible reading from the public schools, the Court has been blamed for the decline in public morality and charged with overriding the public will. On closer examination, it becomes obvious that the Court was simply acting on the growing rejection of transcendence and the privatization of religion in the culture.

As in the abortion case, the Court's actions in *Engel* and *Abington* were not unprecedented. Prior to 1962, nine states had already prohibited both state-sponsored prayer and Bible reading, although most of these prohibitions were the result of judicial actions.[51] Another twelve states had no provisions regarding Bible reading, and twenty-three states had no provisions regarding prayer. Within the states lacking any requirement or prohibition, it is possible that many local jurisdictions had already banned both practices. A 1960 survey of school superintendents revealed that only 42 percent reported that devotional Bible reading was conducted in *any* schools of their system.[52] It is therefore possible that far less than 42 percent of all *classrooms* had Bible reading. Unfortunately, no data is available as to how many superintendents permitted officially sponsored prayer within their schools. It is likely, however, that the Supreme Court's decisions had no effect on a significant number of schools that

51. Of the nine states with prohibitions on both Bible reading and prayer in public schools, only Arizona had passed legislation to bring about these prohibitions. Alaska's State Board of Education had promulgated regulations to do the same. In California, Louisiana, and Wyoming, the State Attorney General had prohibited both, and court decisions had banned them in Illinois, Nebraska, Washington, and Wisconsin.

52. R. B. Dierenfield, "The Impact of the Supreme Court Decisions on Religion in Public Schools," *Religious Education* (September-October 1967), p. 448.

were already in compliance with the Court's actions.[53] At a minimum, the Court did not overturn a universal practice in American schools, and more likely ratified a trend already underway.

A cursory examination of the Court's decisions does seem to confirm cultural conservatives' belief that the Court overrode the majority's wishes. Public disapproval of the Court's actions in *Engel* and *Abington* has hovered around 70 percent for more than three decades. Instead of reflecting the broader culture, the Court appears to have changed American culture. If that analysis is accurate, however, it fails to account for the inability of the majority to use the constitutional mechanisms to overrule the Court. Presidents of both parties have continued to put forward, and the Senate, in Republican or Democratic control, has continued to confirm, justices who are unwilling to overturn the rulings. Attempts by the legislature to amend the Constitution to allow school prayer have failed to generate much beyond simple majorities, and support seems to be losing steam over the years. In 1971, the House fell twenty-eight votes short of the necessary two-thirds majority. The amendment did not get another vote for seventeen years, when it fell forty-four votes short. Thus, the amendment is losing ground even under a Republican Congress influenced by the rise of the Religious Right, which had been largely silent in the 1960s and 1970s. Efforts in the Senate have been similarly ineffective.[54]

That most of the cultural gatekeeping institutions, including many mainstream religious institutions,[55] supported the *Engel* and *Abington* decisions when they were first issued only partially accounts for the majority's failure to overturn the decisions. A more complete explanation rests in the weak will of the majority and in its operational rejection of transcendence through its privatization of religious faith. The relegation of religion to a filler of gaps in sci-

53. It is interesting to note that compliance with the Court's decisions has been slow and remains incomplete today. In 1972, one-quarter of schools in the South still offered prayer over the public address system and/or at morning assemblies. Anecdotal evidence suggests that thirty-six years after the Court's ban, this practice continues in isolated southern communities, often uncontested by the ACLU. This active defiance may account for part of the public's acquiescence.

54. The Senate voted on a constitutional amendment on school prayer in 1966, voting 49-37 in favor, nine votes short of the necessary two-thirds majority. In 1970, the amendment was successfully added to the Equal Rights Amendment by a 50-20 two-thirds vote, though this was perceived as a killer amendment to the ERA, not as an affirmation of school prayer. Finally, in 1984, the Senate voted to table one version of a constitutional amendment 81-15, and voted for another 56-44, falling eleven votes short.

55. Including the National Council of Churches, the Synagogue Council of America, the United Presbyterian Church, the Baptist Joint Committee on Public Affairs, the Methodist Church, the Episcopal Church, the Union of American Hebrew Congregations, the Seventh Day Adventists, and others.

entific knowledge and Americans' growing confidence in science as the arbiter of all truth enfeebled the majority's attempt to defend religious expression in the public schools. The Court had simply followed the public's logic in expelling religion from the schools. The public was left with a sense that this was too extreme, but it had lost the paradigm to support its view. The majority had abandoned the very weapons necessary to attack the Court's judgment that the public square must remain neutral on religious questions. It is unlikely that an America of an earlier era would have failed to overturn *Engel* and *Abington*. The Court's decisions are truly a reflection of the culture, if only of the culture's inability to resist the Court's logic.

While it is true that the Court has overstepped its constitutional mandate and misinterpreted the original meaning of the Constitution in the case of abortion, federal civil rights enforcement for homosexuals, and school prayer, its decisions are largely consistent with the popular culture's fundamental assumptions. Where the public is not yet in agreement with those decisions, the erosion of their older worldview rooted in transcendent truth and the subsequent adoption of a subjectivist worldview prevent them from mounting an effective defense. The Court is fanning the passions of the majority by handing down decisions consistent with the majority's evolving assumptions.

As has already been noted, government does play a role, albeit a lesser one, in shaping the culture. This is especially evident in the Court's decisions. It has already been demonstrated that the Court was largely reflecting the culture and joining movements already underway in it, but, on the other hand, the Court did help to shape the culture by accelerating the pace of those social movements. Where the public is divided — in a schizophrenic fashion more than in a cultural war — between the vestiges of the older worldview rooted in transcendence and the newfound subjectivism, the Court has reinforced the latter and negated the former.

Although the Framers had intended the Court to be a check on the majority's passions, it has become an accelerator of those passions. Where weak political majorities in various states had prohibited abortion, the Court has denied this expression of belief in transcendence, instead affirming the public's more subjectivist inclinations for sex without consequences. Where a majority in Colorado had decided against granting homosexuals special legal protections, the Court has affirmed sexuality without boundaries as a constitutional right. Where the majority has sought to acknowledge God in the public schools, the Court has affirmed a religiously denuded public square. Time and again, the Court has come down on the baser side of the public's divided self, affirming subjectivism, licentiousness, and passion, and denying the people's remaining belief in transcendence. It has fueled the public's growing passions and checked the public's enervating will.

Since the Framers made it very difficult to amend the Constitution or overrule the Court, the effect of these injurious rulings is akin to the accelerator of a car being stuck to the floor. The Court is encouraging the public to "obey its thirst" and "just do it." It is not as though the majority is left without a brake to stop the passions. But with the accelerator stuck to the floor, using a brake is next to useless. The very mechanisms designed to protect the will from the passions, such as the three-quarters supermajority for a constitutional amendment, now protect the passions, in the form of Supreme Court precedents, from the will. With this inversion of the assumptions that undergirded the old constitutional order, the majority is called upon to enact a supermajority to check its passions — a supermajority that is perilously difficult to obtain in any age, but especially when the majority's will is already eroding.

Renewing the Culture from Within: Recovering Transcendence

Although politics is relatively ineffective at shaping the culture, its role is not unimportant. The law is a teacher that can help recover belief in transcendence. Abandonment of the political sphere would be detrimental to efforts for cultural renewal.

But politics is not enough. For too long, cultural conservatives intent on transforming the nation have focused almost exclusively on the political realm. It is the cultural fields, however, long overgrown with tares from decades of conservative neglect and liberal domination, which need to be plowed and resown. Cultural conservatives must learn, or relearn, that it is the unwritten constitution of culture that shapes the written constitution of a nation.

It is worth noting that once one understands the primacy of culture and joins in the effort to renew it according to transcendent standards, the question of one's political label becomes less important. A healthy culture is about lifting up the good, the true, and the beautiful. These are not ideological categories. There is plenty of common ground for cultural renewal among individuals who differ on the particular role law should play. For instance, some citizens may join in the cultural fight against social pathologies, even though they oppose legal restrictions on those pathologies. This applies to abortion, violent prime-time television, pornography, divorce, and many other social maladies. This is not to say that the policy differences are inconsequential. But renewal can be furthered even without political agreement, again, because culture trumps politics.

Notable efforts are underway to reclaim the culture. Within every gatekeeping institution, bold and courageous scholars, actors, journalists, and artists are challenging their colleagues to re-think their faulty assumptions. Cultural conservatives are beginning to renew their involvement in popular entertainment, journalism, and the arts. There are encouraging signs that Americans concerned about cultural decline are forming "beachheads" to renew culture.

But much more needs to be done, and great gains will only come with sacrifice. Restoration will take time. The degradation did not occur overnight, but began with modernity's denial of transcendence. Cultural conservatives must dedicate themselves to a decades-long work in the culture. If these efforts fail and the culture continues on its present course, the implications for the nation are grave. As the vestiges of the older transcendence are jettisoned, government will continue to reflect and accelerate the passions of the people, and the tyranny of the majority will grow. The infantry of politics cannot help but respond to the cultural generals in the rear.

Conclusion

Because politics is downstream from the culture and the *polis* is the soul writ large, the culture, as the source of political order, must be renewed so that politics can play its hand. Well-ordered government in the absence of a culture grounded in transcendence is unsustainable in the long run.

The Framers' reliance on a healthy culture and their careful formation of a government that reflects the more noble aspects of that culture gave America a good start. It was only as the unwritten constitution of the culture rejected transcendence and embraced subjectivism that the government mirrored the slide away from truth. The rise of majoritarianism in the legislature is one result. In the judiciary, the subjectivist passions of the culture are being fanned by a Court effectively negating the remaining belief in transcendence. The public is unable to resist the decisions of the Court, which is only tracking the culture's logic. The Framers' cautious republic slowly transforms itself into Rousseau's democracy of passions.

Tocqueville recognized that America could not long survive and thrive without a reliance on transcendent truth, especially a religious faith:

> Despotism may be able to do without faith, but freedom cannot. Religion is much more needed in the republic they advocate than in the monarchy they attack, and in democratic republics most of all. How could society escape destruction if, when political ties are relaxed, moral ties are not tightened? And what can be done with a people master of itself if it is not subject to God?[56]

56. Toqueville, *Democracy in America,* p. 296.

With Americans increasingly turning away from the belief in transcendent truth necessary to sustain just governance, the American experiment is imperiled.

Thankfully, there is cause for hope. A belief in transcendence, though weakened by subjectivism, remains in the culture. Its reanimation is not impossible, especially when one surveys the looming alternative in the despair and disorder of relativism. Tragedies like that at Columbine High School may be catalysts, causing Americans to recoil from the false hope offered by the subjectivist worldview. With a ready alternative in transcendent truth still recognizable beneath the gathering dust of cultural decline, despair is premature.

And, with plenty to do in the cultural vineyards, despair is counterproductive. For it is in culture that we can amend the constitution of the heart, and thereby protect, preserve, and strengthen the American Experiment.

The Homogenization of Culture

KENNETH A. MYERS

On a recent visit to a local grocery store, I passed by the magazine rack. Such a place is not the source of most of my reading material, but I stopped long enough to check out some titles. I noticed that *Jane,* a magazine pitched to adolescents, carried a feature on "summer clothes sexier than going naked." Another teen publication, *ym* ("young and modern"), was distributed with a free booklet: "your 8-page school-year love horoscope." The issue also ran an article "love at first sight — what makes him fall?" Though I did not even glance at the articles in question, I doubt the girls who purchase such magazines are likely to gain wisdom about love or about their own identities.

Meanwhile, *American Woman,* a periodical for older but not necessarily more mature readers, teased shoppers seeking fresh produce or gingersnaps: "Discover his private pleasure zones and drive him wild with desire! sexual ecstasy: naughty tricks that *always* work." The magazine also contained a quiz: "How do you rate in bed?" Then there were the fan magazines, one carrying a cover shot of gender nightmare Marilyn Manson; the computer game magazines, several extolling heavy doses of virtual violence and imaginary sex; and the venerable *Rolling Stone* — once the saucy bad boy of newsstands — now, given the raucous competition, looking rather conservative, with a cover photograph of Madonna less provocative than most celebrity photographs from the 1940s.

At the checkout counter, I was greeted with the usual assembly of lurid tabloids and soap opera magazines, each with promises of predictably provocative and pitifully tawdry trash. The cover of *Redbook* featured a photograph of Harrison Ford juxtaposed with screaming headlines in large type heralding an inside feature revealing "46 things to do to a naked man." One might safely assume that "Tell him to get dressed or get out" was not numbered among the suggestions.

These may not be the worst examples of magazine covers parents and children see regularly in public; most city newsstands and bookstores display magazines even more blatant in their commitment to radical liberation. But the matter-of-factness of such display in a family neighborhood *grocery* store, for all passing eyes to see, is a profoundly disturbing fact of life in early twenty-first century America. Certainly *ym* or *Jane* are nowhere near 2 Live Crew in morally destructive megatonnage. Nor do *Redbook* and its ilk rate with the disgusting lyrics in rap music, degrading dialogue in television shows, and detestable violence in movies. Yet the question arises: does not our culture invite the extremities of celebrity vulgarists and blasphemers because it is so blasé about the everyday desensitizing by enticements such as "naughty tricks that *always* work" and "summer clothes sexier than going naked" displayed in the same aisle as Betty Crocker and Mrs. Butterworth?

Whatever the connection between the two, Protestant theologian David F. Wells pulls no punches in his astute assessment of our cultural situation:

> The moral hedges that surrounded our collective life have been trampled down. That is the paramount truth. What once was sublimated is now, in all of its raw and often violent nature, spewed forth in the name of liberty or self-expression. What once had to be private is now paraded publicly for the gallery of voyeurs. The virtues of the old privacy, such as reticence and modesty, are looked upon today as maladies. What was once unseemly is now commonplace.[1]

Perhaps no class of American citizens feels the consequences of cultural regress more forcefully than parents, many of whom believe that popular culture is the most powerful force behind this decline. A 1995 *New York Times* poll indicated that Americans blame television more than any single factor for teenage sex and violence.[2] So parents and other authority figures, quite naturally, try to restrict children's access or exposure to some "artifacts" of popular culture. Or they may patronize only "sanitized" artifacts of popular culture, whether G-rated movies and television programming or rock music whose lyrics have been cleaned up or attached to a good cause.

1. David F. Wells, *No Place for Truth; or, Whatever Happened to Evangelical Theology?* (Grand Rapids: Eerdmans, 1993), p. 168.

2. Elizabeth Kolbert, "American Despair of Popular Culture," *New York Times*, 20 August 1995, Section 2.

Consider how schools, public and private, have within a generation moved from virtually ignoring popular culture to blessing it. Dana Mack, in *The Assault on Parenthood: How Our Culture Undermines the Family,* writes:

> In a misguided effort to make school "relevant" to children's lives outside of school, educators often bring popular culture into the classroom in the form of literature, music and social instruction. In fourth grade, for example, my own child was assigned to write a "rap" poem as part of her language-arts program. Not surprisingly, children take this emphasis on popular culture as an endorsement and end up clinging to the tastes of the marketplace rather than expanding their horizons toward more sophisticated work with a longer shelf life.[3]

Mack notes that "even in affluent suburban schools, arts education is based far more on contemporary models taken from popular culture than on historical models of high art or folk culture."[4]

With blessings from schools, churches, and other historically normative institutions, popular culture is assumed to be a perfectly normal attribute of life. But let the buyer (or parent) beware: popular culture as known today is a complete novelty in human history. Its very nature, not simply its content, coupled with its role in American life, poses great challenges to the work of families in shaping the moral character of children.

The Function of Culture

Historically, culture has had an intrinsically moral dimension. Borrowing from T. S. Eliot, David F. Wells defines culture as "the set of values, the network of beliefs that are institutionalized in a people's collective life and that govern their behavior. Culture, then, is the outward discipline in which inherited meanings and morality, beliefs and ways of behaving are preserved."[5]

Since they communicate moral content from one generation to the next, and because human beings are inherently in need of correction and guidance, cultures have always been mechanisms of restraint. Cultural institutions, traditions, and artifacts developed as means of encouraging members of a society to respect its taboos, to obey its laws, and to become the sort of persons whose

3. Dana Mack, *The Assault on Parenthood: How Our Culture Undermines the Family* (New York: Simon and Schuster, 1997), p. 218.

4. Mack, *The Assault on Parenthood,* p. 218.

5. Wells, *No Place for Truth,* p. 167.

characters served the common good by conforming to a view of the good that the society held in common. In theological terms, cultures are thus instruments of common grace or natural law that keep people from doing everything that they want to do. Cultures are by nature communal — not individualistic — and deliberately intergenerational; cultural artifacts are ways of handing down to the coming generation the commitments and beliefs of the passing generation. Culture by its nature transmits morals, and families by their nature transmit culture. Those two laws of social life seem to have been at work throughout history around the world.

The family, of course, has been the key. As T. S. Eliot has argued, "the primary vehicle for the transmission of culture is the family."[6] Even as forces seek to redefine it, the family remains "a constant expectation for all humanity, past, present, and future."[7] Families, with the aid and support of other cultural institutions, such as church and school, have the primary responsibility of teaching moral principles to the young, not only by establishing the content of morality in their minds, but by instilling a love for the true and the good in their hearts. This affective role, a critical component of moral instruction, explains why stories and songs are central cultural expressions. The stories we love, and the songs we delight in singing and hearing, are the mechanisms whereby we, as parents and children, commit ourselves to virtue.

Since the time of Sigmund Freud, however, the normative and restraining role of culture has been turned inside out. As sociologist Philip Rieff documents in *The Triumph of the Therapeutic,* cultures and specifically cultural institutions in the West have increasingly been redefined as instruments of *liberation* rather than of restraint. Since repression is now presumed to be a bad thing, the commonweal is best served, ironically, without any notion of the common good that cultural institutions formerly enforced. Empowering people to be all that they can be, to express all that they feel, and to obtain all that they desire is now seen to be the proper function of cultural institutions, including the family. As Wells puts it: "The external discipline of the culture is now denied in the name of the emancipated self."[8] This helps explain why unprecedented allusions to orgasms greet customers at the supermarket checkout line.

The transition from culture to its complete opposite, what some have termed anti-culture or postculturalism, has not happened overnight, but was reinforced in the latter half of the twentieth century by all forms of popular cul-

6. T. S. Eliot, "Notes towards the Definition of Culture," in *Christianity and Culture* (New York: Harcourt Brace Jovanovich, 1968), p. 121.

7. Allan C. Carlson, *From Cottage to Workstation: The Family's Search for Social Harmony in the Industrial Age* (San Francisco: Ignatius Press, 1993), p. 5.

8. Wells, *No Place for Truth,* p. 167.

ture, whether sanitized or not. The net result has reaped a far weaker family unit, particularly in its historic role as preserver and transmitter of morals.

The Loss of the Local

Some critics and historians argue that popular culture is nothing new, that Shakespeare was the popular culture of his day. That is not quite true. Prior to the invention of modern technologies of communications and travel, all culture was *local* culture. Music, dances, stories, visual representation, and sports all originated from and were sustained by people who were neighbors, who shared large enough amounts of time and small enough amounts of space to build some kind of knowledge of and affection for each other. Since culture was "produced and consumed" locally, the values communicated through cultural forms were values of the local community. Moral notions that did not fit "community standards" were not publicly tolerated.

In contrast, most of our cultural life is now defined by distant strangers; today's popular culture is mass-mediated culture. As such, the moral dynamic of cultural activity has changed radically. We have moved from being creators and participants in culture to being simply its consumers. Culture is now a commodity — something we buy, "put on," or appropriate. It has become a matter of fashion or taste rather than something we receive, a legacy with permanent worth.

The extent to which mass mediators of culture were able to disturb its local mediation was restrained until the 1960s. Neighborhoods still maintained their own standards, churches did not feel compelled to emulate television and popular music, and ethnic groups still transmitted some notion of identity that predated the products of mass media. But that local, religious, and ethnic independence is rapidly waning. Partly because of aggressive efforts in the name of free speech and partly because of the carelessness of a generation raised on television, the centrality of local life in the shaping of culture has given way to mass-produced culture from Hollywood, New York, and Nashville.

Television, the dominant medium of popular culture, has been central to the transition from local to mass-mediated culture. By weaning children from local (specifically parental) authority, television reflects the dynamics of mass-mediated culture in general.

Prior to the advent of television, parents were the principal agents in establishing a trajectory for their children's intellectual and moral development. Writing in 1964, sociologists Oscar Ritchie and Marvin Koller argued that the home is the child's "small world" where the "family serves as a screen to the culture of its society and selects only those portions that it deems worthy of attention."[9] In this traditional pattern, the family is supplemented in its role by friends of the family, whose visits bring reports from the outside world that have different perspectives, but ones likely to be consonant with that of the parents. "As a person who lives outside the child's home, the guest functions as a transmitter, bringing into the world of the child new ideas and information, and new and different opportunities for vicarious participation in the outside world."[10]

This gentle and sensitive portrait of childhood seems painfully anachronistic today. The family is not the dominant "screen" in the lives of many children, who are given huge daily doses of television almost from birth. Rather than interacting with parents, extended family members, and neighbors, children increasingly interact with 100,000 watts of whatever network executives and cable companies think can make children buy more candy, toys, or designer clothes.

That children watch television in such a quantity may be more significant than *what* they see. As Joshua Meyrowitz argues, television profoundly alters the moral relationship between parents and children:

> Children who have television sets now have outside perspectives from which to judge and evaluate family rituals, beliefs, and religious practices. Parents could once easily mold their young children's upbringing by speaking and reading to children only about those things they wished their children to be exposed to, but today's parents must battle with thousands of competing images and ideas over which they have little direct control. . . . Unable to read, very young children were once limited to the few sources of information available to them within and around the home: paintings, illustrations, views from a window, and what adults said and read to them. Television, however, now escorts children across the globe even before they have permission to cross the street.[11]

Whether or not the worldview children receive from television conforms to their parents' worldview does not really matter. Parents are simply no longer the dominant sources of moral instruction, thereby weakening their role and changing the perception that children have of parental authority long before they are even able to think about such things.

A subtle way television weakens parental authority, according to Meyro-

9. Oscar Ritchie and Marvin Koller, *Sociology of Childhood* (New York: Appleton-Century-Crofts, 1964), pp. 86, 109.

10. Ritchie and Koller, *Sociology of Childhood,* p. 103.

11. Joshua Meyrowitz, *No Sense of Place: The Impact of Electronic Media on Social Behavior* (New York: Oxford University Press, 1985), p. 238.

witz, is by exposing "the backstage life" of adults to children. Even family-oriented shows like *Father Knows Best* or *Leave It to Beaver* reveal the behavior of adults when children are not around, including ways parents talk about their children. Meyrowitz says its *content* is less significant than the revelation of the backstage's very *existence:*

> As a result of such views of adulthood, children may become suspicious of adults and more unwilling to accept all that adults do or say at face value. Conversely, adults may feel "exposed" by television and, in the long run, it may no longer seem to make as much sense to try to keep certain things hidden from children.[12]

In addition, popular culture has been able to interfere with local culture and the moral unity of communities by exploiting generational differences. By creating product lines that are intended to define adolescent identity as a deliberate rejection of parental expectations, the producers of popular culture have successfully entrenched the notion of a relatively new concept, youth culture. Our system of education does not help either, segregating young people from adults as well as from other children outside a narrow age range, not to mention from infants and the elderly. This tendency is even unwittingly encouraged by many churches — the very institutions that should be the most vigilant in demonstrating that all ages dwell in unity, but which often celebrate the idea of youth culture as something divinely ordained.

Given that culture rightly understood is an intergenerational system of communicating moral convictions, the very phrase "youth culture" should be seen as a contradiction in terms. Not only does age segregation weaken the family's ability to pursue the cultural task of moral transmission, the glorification of the present at the expense of honoring the past and preparing for the future works against the task of sustaining a rich idea of what family is. Among other things, it weakens that understanding of the family as an intergenerational entity which T. S. Eliot believed played a vital culture-shaping role:

> When I speak of the family, I have in mind a bond which embraces a longer period of time than this [that is, the living members of a nuclear family]: a piety toward the dead, however obscure, and a solicitude for the unborn, however remote. Unless this reverence for past and future is cultivated in the home, it can never be more than a verbal convention in the community.[13]

12. Meyrowitz, *No Sense of Place,* p. 249.
13. Eliot, "Notes towards the Definition of Culture," p. 116.

The Loss of Moral Authority

Another way popular culture interferes with the local and family mediation of culture is by undercutting the very notion of any properly recognized authority. Children have always challenged parental authority with the time-honored complaint: "But Johnny's mom lets him do it." While a child may not understand the moral reasoning, he is essentially arguing that since other authority figures have looser standards, more stringent standards cannot be justified. On the other hand, a common and worthy parental response is: "I'm not Johnny's mom." That response presumes the parent is the duly constituted authority here, giving her the right to establish local or family standards.

Another way of responding is to observe: "*We* don't do that sort of thing." The first person plural pronoun in the subject of that sentence suggests that the child belongs to a moral community, at least as large as the family, with certain received standards. To the degree parents are able to help children identify with that *we,* they can effectively transmit moral convictions, enabling a child to know he should not do such-and-such because it would not be fitting with his religious identity, or because it would give his family a bad name, or because it would poorly represent his hometown. Without this sense of "binding address," moral identity is left undefined and open; moral authority does not seem compelling.

By encouraging young people to become fans of whatever is regarded as trendy or hip each week, popular culture makes a morally recognizable *we* especially difficult to maintain. Television, in particular, undermines efforts of parents or other authority figures to establish terms of propriety in several ways. The immediacy of the medium and the easy-going, chumminess of television personalities make formalities of any kind seem alien; everyone is on a first-name basis. Its programming is equally problematic. By publicly displaying private behavior, television implicitly legitimizes virtually any behavior in any setting. Joshua Meyrowitz believes this leads to the elimination of the idea of moral and social taboos:

> Any topic on any popular situation comedy, talk show, news program, or advertisement — be it death, homosexuality, abortion, male strippers, sex-change operations, political scandals, incest, rape, jock itch, or bras that "lift and separate" — can be spoken about the next day in school, over dinner, or on a date, not only because everyone knows about such subjects, but also because everyone knows that everyone knows, and everyone knows that everyone knows that everyone knows. In fact, it almost seems strange *not* to talk and write about such things. The public and all-inclusive nature

> of television has a tendency to collapse formerly distinct situations into one. In a society shaped by the segregated situations of print, people may secretly discuss taboo topics, but with television, the very notion of "taboo" is lost.[14]

Television, of course, is not really all-inclusive. It actually presents a rather narrow range of experiences and personalities. But it gives the impression of being "all things considered," with the result that those aspects of existence not explored by television come to be regarded as more marginal to human experience than they might be otherwise.

Nor does television communicate moral accountability the way literature does. According to Meyrowitz,

> A child's book is, in a sense, a "guest" in the house. It makes a "social entrance"; that is, it comes through the door and remains under at least nominal parental authority. As a physical object it must be stored somewhere in the house and it can be discarded. The child's television set, in contrast, is like a new doorway [in]to the home. Through it come many welcome and unwelcome visitors: schoolteachers, Presidents, salesmen, police officers, prostitutes, friends, and strangers.[15]

All these factors profoundly affect the ability of families to be schools of character. By weakening children's consciousness of moral accountability to parents and by distressing the prescriptive power of parents, popular culture establishes its own artifacts and celebrities as sources of moral understanding, creating a moral system that has only one commandment: Fulfill thyself.

The Loss of Tradition

The shift from understanding culture as a legacy to be received (on its terms) to a titillation to be consumed (on my terms) has another consequence: the loss of tradition. That may not initially sound so bad; Americans love innovation, change, and progress. Yet cultural conservatives may need to consider to what extent the traditional values they covet can be sustained without tradition, and especially without a more conscious effort to connect with the past. As Edward Shils, a prominent sociologist, wisely warns: "A family which incorporates into itself little of the past, and, of that which it does incorporate, little of high qual-

14. Meyrowitz, *No Sense of Place*, p. 92.
15. Meyrowitz, *No Sense of Place*, p. 245.

ity — not all of the past was of equal quality — deadens its offspring; it leaves them with a scanty set of categories and beliefs which are not easily extended or elaborated."[16]

While he does not mention popular culture explicitly, Shils believes the family's ability to connect with the past has been weakened by parents who are reluctant to impose their beliefs on their children and who neglect the hard work of mediating tradition to them because of other preoccupations. Cultural transmission is further weakened among single-parents who lack a needed spouse to reinforce family standards. All these factors "make the stream of tradition narrower and shallower." The phenomenon, writes Shils, resembles the aftermath of war which displaces parents from each other and from their children: "The offspring are left to define their own standards; this means the acceptance of the norms of their most imposing coevals."[17]

By eliminating a sense of cultural legacy, popular culture weakens or destroys the sense of a permanent moral order in creation. One function of traditional culture is to transmit this sense of moral order, with the implication that each person is obligated to discern and obey the laws of Nature and of Nature's God. The modern sensibility, embodied so fully in popular culture, is that reality is something each individual invents. No moral order exists in the nature of things, only *my* will and *my* desires.

Traditional cultures work by a sense of prescription. The traditional order is given the benefit of the doubt, not the burden of proof. Living with the habit of submitting to the received order (unless it is perceived to be in violation of some natural law) cultivates a much greater sympathy to belief in moral absolutes. In contrast, the regime of popular culture — in which one *must* do one's *own* thing — makes relativism much more plausible. In fact, the sort of aculturalism that popular culture encourages seems to prescribe relativism.

Not only does it prescribe a state of flux, but popular culture also ends up filling the vacuum left by the abandonment of old ways. According to sociologist Daniel Bell:

> A society in rapid change inevitably produces confusions about appropriate modes of behavior, taste, and dress. A socially mobile person has no ready guide for acquiring new knowledge on how to live "better" than before, and his guides become the movies, television, and advertising. In this respect, advertising begins to play a more subtle role in changing habits than in stimulating wants. . . . Though at first the changes were primarily in manners, dress, taste, and food habits, sooner or later they begin to affect

16. Edward Shils, *Tradition* (Chicago: University of Chicago Press, 1981), pp. 172f.
17. Shils, *Tradition,* p. 173.

> more basic patterns: the structure of authority in the family, the role of children and young adults as independent consumers in the society, the pattern of morals, and the different meanings of achievement in the society.[18]

The Loss of Moral Seriousness

A final criticism of popular culture is its superficiality. Not only is the content of popular culture often trite, but the forms in which it is presented discourage depth, reflection, and moral seriousness. As media critic Todd Gitlin describes it, television encourages the sensibility of being "flat and happy." Because the pace of television is relentless and because slick production values are more important than content, glibness rules:

> On TV both children and adults speak with an unprecedented glibness. Thanks to the wonders of editing, no one on television is ever at a loss for words or photogenic signs of emotion. . . . Hesitancy, silence, awkwardness are absent from TV's repertory of behaviors, except in sitcoms or made-for-TV movies where boy meets girl. Yet outside TV, awkwardness and hesitancy often characterize the beginning, and each further development, of interiority, of a person's internal life. On TV, however, speech is stripped down, designed to move. The one-liner, developed for ads, is the premium style. TV's common currency consists of slogans and mockery. Situation comedies and morning shows are in particular obsessed with the jokey comeback. The put-down is the universal linkage among television's cast of live and recorded characters. A free-floating hostility mirrors, and also inspires, the equivalent conversational style among the young who grow up in this habitat.[19]

Gitlin quotes fellow critic Mark Crispin Miller who has observed that this knowingly snide attitude is so widespread and automatic that it deserves to be called "the hipness unto death." Earnestness is out, attitude is all, and the development of character that was once the proper goal of cultural life is thus stunted if not exterminated. What remains stands in vivid contrast to the kind of moral imagination that Russell Kirk claims is an essential prerequisite to cultural health:

18. Daniel Bell, *The Cultural Contradictions of Capitalism* (New York: Basic Books, 1996), pp. 68f.

19. Todd Gitlin, "Flat and Happy," *The Wilson Quarterly* (Autumn 1993), p. 53.

> One thing we can do is this: to refrain from choking up the springs of the moral imagination. If we stifle the sense of wonder, no wonders will occur among us; and if wondrous remedies are lacking, then indeed the words of doom written on the sky will become as the laws of the Medes and the Persians, ineluctable.[20]

True Entertainment

In the 1950s, Martha Wolfenstein foresaw the cumulative effect of popular culture: entire generations who have a need to be constantly entertained. In her telling essay, "The Emergence of a Fun Morality," the sociologist discerned signs of a new morality displacing an emphasis on goodness. A preoccupation with goodness was, after all, demanding, and interfered with self-fulfillment. But fun morality makes its own demands, since not having fun becomes an occasion for anxiety. Wolfenstein writes: "Whereas gratification of forbidden impulses traditionally aroused guilt, failure to have fun now lowers one's self-esteem."[21] Ironically, many parents, teachers, and religious leaders who today might share Wolfenstein's concerns at face value often appear more worried about being a fun person than about being a good person. As products of this new cultural climate, they assume their roles of moral authority with the same inverted sense of what is moral.

For these reasons, the moral condition of American society under the regime of popular culture is a serious and radical problem for which no simple solutions exist. One step in addressing the problem might be to define the proper role of entertainment in society, in the family, and in the life of the individual. The Oxford English Dictionary lists the root meaning of the verb *entertain* as: "To keep in a certain state or condition; to keep in a certain frame of mind; to maintain a state of things; to maintain in existence." That original meaning remains surprisingly accurate, as in the television program, *Entertainment Tonight.* The only difference is the state, condition, or frame of mind being sustained by modern entertainment.

The condition of our times is one of disorder and relentless, boundless change. Most entertainment serves to render Americans sympathetic to that condition, undisturbed by the losses, and impressed by the pomp and show of bogus "progress." The frame of mind encouraged by modern entertainment is

20. Russell Kirk, *The Wise Men Know What Wicked Things Are Written on the Sky* (Washington, D.C.: Regnery Gateway, 1987), p. 128.

21. Martha Wolfenstein, "The Emergence of a Fun Morality," in *Mass Leisure,* ed. Eric Larrabee and Rolf Meyerson (Glencoe, Ill.: The Free Press, 1958), p. 86.

one which is suspicious of any legacy or inheritance, and which is committed to the assertion of the sovereignty of the self. It is a mentality that evokes a mood of restlessness and blocks out the reflection necessary for acknowledging its disease and then seeking a remedy. It is a sensibility rooted only in the present, ignoring the past, indifferent to the future.

In the Christian tradition, the Church (the bride of the One who Was and Is and Shall Be) is called to entertain herself with past and future matters: with millennia-long memories of her sovereign and suffering Lord and of her own rich history of loving and obeying him; and with visions of a distant yet certain glory in a time beyond time. The present is where people of faith are called to obey, but it only makes sense when triangulated within the history and future of redemption, from creation to consummation.

Conversely, the forms of worldly entertainment are marvelously suited to its content. Thanks to mass media, we are sovereign and isolated consumers of entertainment, seeking temporary amnesia from the unhappiness and disappointment of reality. To imagine entertainment that is radically different, truer to its root sense, and that engages participants in a mutually edifying service of sustaining love is possible. But that sort of entertainment requires serious attention to the recovery of local culture and how the shape of shared life together might recover a richer sort of entertainment.

Poet-farmer Wendell Berry's description of families entertaining one another in his essay, "The Work of Local Culture," describes entertainment in the root sense of the word. In Berry's view, the sharing of memories, not the pursuit of forgetting, maintains a people in its existence. Cultural conservatives therefore should be as concerned about the *form* of entertainment as its content. Our social and cultural disorder does not simply spring from the fact that R-rated movies outnumber G-rated movies. It issues equally from parents who are more likely to take or send their children to the movies than tell them stories. Our society suffers not from being over-entertained, but from not being *truly* entertained. Whether we can recover depends to the extent we attend, not just to the words, but to the way the song is being sung.

The Moral Grounds for Advancing Cultural Health: Whose Standards?

CHRISTOPHER WOLFE

Despite its vast material prosperity, twentieth-century America faces a deep crisis, which is at root a struggle for the soul of America. Over the course of decades, there has been a loss of understanding of the principles of the original American public philosophy. This loss of understanding is closely tied to a radical shift in thinking among the most influential intellectuals in America — and those whose views they affect substantially, such as the elite media — away from the political theory on which the United States was founded. This "progressive" vanguard rejects the more classical and religious elements of the original American public philosophy, especially its roots in the "natural law" tradition broadly conceived, which served to "leaven" or "balance" its more modern or liberal elements.

As with nature, culture abhors a vacuum. In place of the earlier understanding (sometimes called classical liberalism) which informed and sustained the American order, an increasing number of people in both elite and popular culture have embraced a new "liberal" ideology of personal autonomy, in which "rights" are exalted and duties downplayed. According to this new ideology, public policy is to be "neutral" on questions regarding the human good. The popularization of this view has resulted in the decline of those mediating institutions, such as the family and organized religion, that typically have fostered some positive conception of what it means to be a good human being. This in turn has contributed to the deterioration of the culture, reflected in the numbing proliferation of social pathologies.

The negative trajectory of American culture raises serious questions about the viability of contemporary liberalism as the nation's dominant public philosophy. The inability of this system of thought to address the symptoms of cultural disintegration indicates the existence of problems which are not superficial, but systemic. It reveals the fact that contemporary liberalism — "purified" of all non-liberal, pre-modern elements — is unable to provide a sustainable basis of social order.

To ensure the moral and philosophical vigor of the American experiment, it is necessary to recover an understanding of liberalism that willingly accommodates key philosophical and ethical principles that contemporary liberal intellectual elites have abandoned. In particular, we must revive the natural law foundations of the American public philosophy, which alone are able to provide a solid basis for the ideals that define American civilization. The well-being, perhaps even the preservation, of our cherished tradition of ordered liberty is at stake.

The Public Philosophy

While political communities are not persons, they are moral entities, and thus can be said, in a metaphorical sense, to have lives of their own. The decisions a nation makes about how to act as a political community reflect a certain understanding of politics and of human life more generally. The complex web of assumptions, beliefs, and convictions that make up this understanding can be described as a nation's "public philosophy."

A public philosophy gives intelligible form to the way of life of a people, shaped as it is by its political constitution, broadly understood. Terms such as "regime" or "politeia" emphasize the comprehensive character of a society; "public philosophy" focuses on the efforts to articulate that character.

The Functions of a Public Philosophy

A public philosophy serves various purposes. Most importantly, it provides a framework for common discourse, for fellow citizens talking with each other. In so doing, it facilitates decision-making by the political community. A public philosophy also provides the touchstone of "legitimacy," the sense that a particular undertaking — or, more broadly, the set of undertakings — of a government is within acceptable bounds of political morality.

But the functions of a public philosophy include more than merely "political" purposes, defined narrowly. Ultimately, a public philosophy serves an important metaphysical purpose: it helps to explain "us" to ourselves and to others, and to explain the universe to us.

The Articulation and Transmission of a Public Philosophy

Given the difficulty of determining with precision the content of a nation's public philosophy, it will come as no surprise that there are many and varied — even conflicting — means by which a public philosophy is articulated and transmitted. Among these means, there is a *prima facie* case for the priority of solemn or important public documents in the life of a nation — e.g., the Magna Carta in England, the Declaration of the Rights of Man in France, the Declaration of Independence and the Constitution in the United States.

Public officials, and especially the Chief of State, also play an important part in the articulation of the public philosophy — think of Washington's Farewell Address, Lincoln's Gettysburg Address, or presidential inaugural addresses generally.

The unusually powerful position of the United States Supreme Court gives it a unique role in articulating the fundamental principles of the nation. To cite an early example, Chief Justice John Marshall was instrumental in articulating a national understanding of the Union in the first part of the nineteenth century. In our own time, the Court's role has become a source of controversy, as the Court has in some cases become an instrument of political interests espousing the contemporary ideology of personal autonomy.

Other "public" figures, though they are not government officials, may play an important role in the development and transmission of a public philosophy. A good example in recent times is Martin Luther King Jr. In this same category are certain "publicists" or "public intellectuals." Writing in newspapers, magazines, and books, their undertaking is precisely to help shape public opinion through their commentary on current events. Examples of influential public intellectuals include Walter Lippmann, Irving Kristol, and George Will.

The writers and artists of a nation tend to have influence less on short-term interpretations of events and more on the enduring purposes of the society and various aspects of national character. In America, one thinks particularly of nineteenth-century figures such as Irving and Cooper, Hawthorne and Emerson, Stowe and Thoreau, Melville and Whitman, Twain and James. Twentieth-century figures include F. Scott Fitzgerald, William Faulkner, the Southern Agrarian writers, Norman Mailer, and Saul Bellow.

Shifting to the institutional means by which America's public philosophy is transmitted, education and the means of social communication — that is, the media — loom large. The expansion of higher education since World War II has had a substantial impact in reshaping the nation's public philosophy. It has dramatically increased the cultural influence of college professors (especially those at elite institutions), whose scholarship has the greatest impact on other intellectuals and on teachers at smaller schools. Because intellectuals generally tend to be more critical of traditional symbols and heroes, and less tolerant of the "myths" and dogmas of society's "civil religion," this has had the effect of weakening traditional loyalties and attachments among the young, and of encouraging a critical attitude toward authority and received wisdom.

The unprecedented expansion of the means of social communication over the past half-century has also had an impact on the character of the nation's public philosophy. While newspapers have declined, there has been a proliferation of electronic media: television, motion pictures, and popular music. Through these various media, the influence of popular culture has increased exponentially, helping to reshape the public philosophy in profound ways.

Qualifications

This all too brief description of a public philosophy requires qualification at several points. For one thing, the "implicitness" of a public philosophy means that it is not easily identifiable and is quite often not particularly coherent. Also, the leading ideas of a public philosophy are always subject to challenge and change, especially as the various material and intellectual circumstances of society change. There is constant competition to shape the public philosophy, to pose as its authoritative expositor, and often only time will tell which one among competing expressions more truly reflected the nation's public philosophy. Finally, it is more than possible to have competing "strands" of a public philosophy, enduring over long periods of history, in continuing tension with each other, waxing or waning as circumstances encourage or discourage them.

Contemporary Liberalism

Recent controversies in American political life, especially the deeply divisive "culture war" issues, suggest that there is great uncertainty about fundamental aspects of American public philosophy. New Deal liberalism, by the end of the 1960s, seemed unable to deal with a host of new issues that were dividing the nation. Perhaps nowhere was this more obvious than in the ongoing public controversy over various Supreme Court decisions regarding crime (defendants' rights and the death penalty), race (busing and affirmative action), religion (school prayer and parochial school aid), representation (apportionment), and sex (gender discrimination, obscenity, and abortion). Many Court decisions seemed to reflect a new, expansive liberalism, and a powerful statement of this new liberalism emerged in contemporary academic discussions of political philosophy. While this new liberalism quickly became influential among the intelligentsia, it also provoked controversy (theoretical and political) and stimulated a variety of powerful critiques.

Background to the Current Debate

Contemporary liberal political theory is in a state of confusion. The shape of the current debate among political theorists has been deeply influenced by John Rawls's treatise *A Theory of Justice* (1971), somewhat revised and amplified in his *Political Liberalism* (1992).[1] Rawls has attempted to resurrect social contract theory and to give it a more egalitarian form, drawing on Kant to provide a foundation for liberal rights stronger than what utilitarian moral theory can offer. A particularly important element of Rawlsian political theory has been the requirement that government be "neutral" on questions about the human good.

Rawls's neutrality requirement seems to fit in well with and reinforce what has historically been an important aspect of modern liberalism: the so-called "harm principle." This principle, in the famous words of British philosopher John Stuart Mill, holds that "the sole end for which mankind are warranted, individually or collectively, in interfering with the liberty of action of any of their number is self-protection. . . . The only purpose for which power can be rightfully exercised over any member of a civilized community, against his will, is to prevent harm to others. His own good, either physical or moral, is not a sufficient warrant."[2]

Put another way, this principle says that government, in general, may not regulate "self-regarding" action, but only "other-regarding" action. The responsibility of government, according to this view, is simply to protect rights; it should not concern itself with the quality of people's lives, as long as they do not interfere with others. While there are considerable differences over what constitutes "self-regarding" and "other-regarding" actions, the tendency among modern liberal thinkers has been to move more and more toward the relatively direct and tangible effects on others as a requirement for government coercion or even more informal social pressures.

Rawls's work had significant influence in constitutional theory — for ex-

1. John Rawls, *A Theory of Justice* (Cambridge, Mass.: Harvard University Press, 1971), and *Political Liberalism* (New York: Columbia University Press, 1992). For a good summary of Rawls, see Michael Pakaluk, "The Liberalism of John Rawls: A Brief Exposition," in *Liberalism at the Crossroads: An Introduction to Contemporary Liberal Political Theory and Its Critics*, ed. Christopher Wolfe and John Hittinger (Lanham, Md.: Rowman and Littlefield, 1994).

2. John Stuart Mill, *On Liberty* (Chicago: Henry Regnery Co. 1955), p. 13.

ample, in the work of Ronald Dworkin.[3] But Rawls was only one of many liberals — philosophers and constitutional theorists — who provided new defenses for liberalism's increasing tendency to pursue "neutrality" with respect to the question of the human good. Others in this category included Bruce Ackerman, David A. J. Richards, and (in a somewhat different way) Robert Nozick.[4]

The interest in providing more solid theoretical foundations for neutrality and the harm principle coincided with an expanding influence of those principles in American law. While there certainly remain pockets of American law that do not square well with the harm principle, they are for the most part embattled holdovers from an earlier era. Even in areas where limits on adult private consensual activity remain (e.g., drugs and pornography), it is noteworthy that the defenders of legal regulation often consider it necessary to cast their argument in terms of the direct harm to others arising from such activity.

The Critique of Rawls

But Rawls's and other neutral (or "antiperfectionist") versions of liberalism have been subjected to powerful critiques from several different directions, by thinkers such as Michael Sandel, Alasdair MacIntyre, and various members of the critical legal studies movement, who have in common a rejection of liberal individualism.[5] Sandel argues that Rawls's attempt to strip individuals in the "original position" of any personal commitments — that is, to remove them entirely from any social context — represents a destruction of personhood itself, since persons are, in an important sense, constituted by their commitments. MacIntyre has found that the descent of contemporary philosophy into "emotivism," with its denial of objective knowledge of the human good, leads not only to a philosophical dead end, but also to various social pathologies. Roberto Unger criticizes liberalism on the grounds that its epistemology and psychology make practical rationality (and hence the possibility of its neutral

3. See, for example, Ronald Dworkin, *Taking Rights Seriously* (Cambridge, Mass: Harvard University Press, 1977), especially ch. 6.

4. See Bruce Ackerman, *Social Justice in the Liberal State* (New Haven, Conn.: Yale University Press, 1980); David A. J. Richards, *Toleration and the Constitution* (New York: Oxford University Press, 1986); and Robert Nozick, *Anarchy, State, and Utopia* (New York: Basic Books, 1974).

5. See Michael Sandel, *Liberalism and the Limits of Justice* (Cambridge: Cambridge University Press, 1982); Alasdair MacIntyre, *After Virtue,* 2nd ed. (Notre Dame: University of Notre Dame Press, 1984), especially pp. 246-52. For a description of a critical legal studies thinker and his critique of liberalism, see Russell Hittinger, "Roberto Unger: Liberalism and 'Superliberalism,'" in *Liberalism at the Crossroads,* ed. Wolfe and Hittinger.

legal principles) impossible. All these critics, and many more, deny the possibility of liberal neutrality and ascertain in liberal theorists such as Rawls some substantive theory of the human good.

There have been various responses to the perception that Rawls's project was unsuccessful. One response has been to admit the impossibility of theoretical victory (strictly speaking, perhaps, the impossibility of theory) and defend liberalism on pragmatic grounds, as Richard Rorty has.[6] Another response has been simply to jettison liberalism altogether, opting for the radical program of "critique is all there is," the approach of critical legal studies scholars such as Mark Tushnet.[7]

An even more interesting response has been to deny that liberalism as such is necessarily hostile to a common public notion of the human good and to put forward a form of liberal "perfectionism" (from different perspectives, e.g., those of Joseph Raz and William Galston).[8] According to this view, liberalism has been "hijacked" in recent years by antiperfectionists, and it is necessary to restore an older and sounder view of liberalism that recognized — indeed, was based upon — liberalism's superior ability to foster human goods.

Rawls himself, of course, undertook in *Political Liberalism* a response to some of the criticisms of his original project, especially the charge that he had slipped into a comprehensive philosophical liberalism in *A Theory of Justice,* thereby forsaking a genuine liberal neutrality. He attempted to clarify his account of "political" liberalism and developed the key concept of "public reason," which set the parameters for public discussion in a liberal society. But critics found Rawls's notion of public reason either too narrow to be defensible or too broad to be useful.[9]

6. See Richard Rorty, *Contingency, Irony, and Solidarity* (Cambridge: Cambridge University Press, 1989) and *Achieving Our Country* (Cambridge, Mass.: Harvard University Press, 1998). See also Gerard Bradley, "Inescapably a Liberal: Richard Rorty as Social Theorist," in *Liberalism at the Crossroads,* ed. Wolfe and Hittinger.

7. Mark Tushnet, *Red, White, and Blue: A Critical Analysis of Constitutional Law* (Cambridge, Mass.: Harvard University Press, 1988). See also Christopher Wolfe, "Grand Theories and Ambiguous Republican Critique: Tushnet on Constitutional Law," in *Law and Social Inquiry (Journal of the American Bar Foundation)*, vol. 15, no. 4 (Fall 1990): 831-76.

8. See Joseph Raz, *The Morality of Freedom* (Oxford: Clarendon Press, 1986); William Galston, *Liberal Purposes* (Cambridge: Cambridge University Press, 1991). See also Robert George, "The Unorthodox Liberalism of Joseph Raz," and J. Brian Benestad, "William Galston's Defense of Liberalism: Forging Unity Amid Diversity," in *Liberalism at the Crossroads,* ed. Wolfe and Hittinger.

9. See, for example, Robert P. George and Christopher Wolfe, eds., *Natural Law and Public Reason* (Washington, D.C.: Georgetown University Press, 2000).

"Completing" Liberalism

I would like to propose a response that could be considered a variant of the position taken by liberal "perfectionists." Antiperfectionists such as David A. J. Richards look back on earlier liberal thinkers (such as Locke, Kant, and Rousseau) and see in them the seeds, the "incomplete" forms, of their own more "purified" and consistent liberalism.[10] I think they are correct to see in classical liberalism certain principles that a "purified" liberal theory would have great difficulty accounting for. I differ from contemporary liberals in thinking that liberalism cannot flourish without the very principles they wish to winnow out. The more sober classical liberalism wisely did not absolutize its principles of liberty and equality, implicitly recognizing the need to balance them with principles inherited from earlier, non-liberal societies. Two different examples of such principles would be a realist epistemology (or theory of human knowledge) and natural intermediary institutions, especially church and family.

Enlightenment epistemologies that classical liberals such as Locke and Kant embraced ended up cutting modern thinkers off from the real world — in other words, from everything but our perceptions of it. (Tocqueville argued that it is not accidental that this form of thinking flourishes in a democratic age.) The long evolution of this "anti-realist" epistemology leaves us in the twenty-first century with theories of interpretation (especially in various forms of deconstructionism) which — if carried to their logical conclusions — make any knowledge of reality or communication about it impossible. But for how long how can a system of liberal rights flourish in a world without "truth"? It is worth remembering, after all, that the founders of American government established this order on certain "truths" described as "self-evident."

Besides eliminating the basis of objective moral truths, enlightenment thinking has come to give central place to individual autonomy, to the right of individuals to determine their actions without regard to social context. One result of this emphasis has been the emergence of a form of individualism that views intermediary institutions as purely voluntary associations. This perspective is deeply problematic, for if churches and families are viewed as merely human creations, established for reasons of convenience and alterable or even revocable at human will, then their capacity to flourish and sustain satisfying human communities is endangered. This is illustrated by the weakening of religious communities in our own time, especially the "mainline" groups most sympathetic to dominant liberal theory. (Interestingly, it may also appear in those forms of religion which seem to be growing in influence, especially evangelical Protestantism; this type of Protestantism stresses doctrinal perma-

10. David A. J. Richards, "Rights and Autonomy," *Ethics*, vol. 92 (1981): 3-20.

nence, but its organization and structure — especially over time — are more variable and voluntaristic in character.)

It is plausible that the influence of liberal individualism is also a factor in the alarming disintegration of marriage and the family. Because of either family breakdown, in the form of widespread divorce, or nonformation of families, in the case of widespread illegitimacy, a very large proportion of children in our society will not experience the benefits of being raised in a stable, two-parent family. While there are undoubtedly many factors that contribute to these current family patterns, the underlying tendency of liberal societies to emphasize rights rather than duties and the individual rather than communities seems likely to be among them.[11]

The decline of strong "natural" communities and institutions, in addition to undercutting personal human happiness, creates serious difficulties for the transmission of those qualities that together make up "civic virtue." In addition, such decline poses the danger, as Tocqueville argued, that liberal democracies will leave an increasingly isolated individual confronting an increasingly powerful state.[12] Liberal democracy, then, has always needed certain prerequisites that it is unable in itself to provide, prerequisites derived in large part from the natural law and natural right traditions which figured so prominently in classical and medieval thought. In other words, it has been precisely the "incompleteness" of liberalism — its willingness to coexist with principles it inherited from earlier, non-liberal political thought — that has made it successful. Intellectuals in modern liberal polities such as America have forgotten this fact, and thereby, in aiming to "purify" liberalism, may wound it deeply.

Natural Law

"Antiperfectionist liberalism" of the Rawls variety may still constitute the center of gravity among intellectual elites today, but it is a decidedly embattled orthodoxy that is having difficulty offering compelling responses to its critics. This circumstance provides an opportunity for genuine alternative views to join the conversation about America's public philosophy. The alternative that I believe is most adequate, but unfortunately very underrepresented in current conversation, is the natural law tradition.

There are, frankly, a number of problems with arguing for "natural law"

11. See Christopher Wolfe, ed., *The Family, Civil Society, and the State* (Lanham, Md.: Rowman and Littlefield, 1998).

12. Alexis de Tocqueville, *Democracy in America* (New York: Alfred A. Knopf, 1945), especially vol. II, bk. 4.

as the necessary foundation of the American public philosophy. One is the common identification of natural law thought with a particular religion, namely, Roman Catholicism. If natural law were, in fact, a "sectarian" doctrine, it would be unlikely to serve effectively as a basis for American public philosophy. Let me make clear from the outset that "natural law," as I will be using the term, is not to be understood as a sectarian theological doctrine, nor is it tied to any particular religion. Insofar as it has any theological element, it is a "natural theology," similar in many ways to that of the Declaration of Independence, which says that people are endowed with rights by their Creator.

A second problem is the occasional confusion of "natural law" with two other forms of thought that are (in varying degrees) quite different. First, there is the Aristotelian tradition of "natural right" thinking, which has much in common with traditional (Thomistic) natural law (especially when the latter is removed from its original context of revealed theology). Perhaps most important in this tradition is the recognition of a natural order that includes certain objective and intelligible human goods, which are the foundation for ethical norms that can be known by practical reason. Second, there is the modern "natural rights" tradition of Hobbes and Locke, which is profoundly different from the earlier natural right and natural law traditions, in that it takes its orientation not from a standard of human excellence (virtue), but from what is held to be the most basic desire of men, the desire for self-preservation.[13]

In general, when employing the term "natural law" in the context of discussions of public philosophy, I use the term in a rather broad sense, as embracing both the natural right tradition of classical political philosophy and the natural law tradition specifically associated with medieval Christian thought (but not the Lockean natural rights tradition). I use the term "natural law" to cover both for several reasons. First, it simplifies my presentation, because it is awkward always to be saying "natural right and natural law traditions," especially when there is so much similarity in their content. Second, I prefer to use the term "natural law" because I do think that, on the relatively limited number of issues that differentiate the two traditions, the natural law tradition is superior. In particular, natural law is associated with a natural theology that provides a more credible framework for natural law ethics, both in itself and in the context of the American political tradition.

A final problem with using the term "natural law" is the recent development of a "new natural law theory," different in important respects from traditional Thomistic natural law theory. Germain Grisez, John Finnis, and others have been developing this new theory, which they claim is partly a removal of

13. See Leo Strauss, *Natural Right and History* (Chicago: University of Chicago Press, 1953).

certain distortions of Thomas's natural law teaching, and partly an improvement upon it. The key difference between the old and new natural law theories is that the former depends on, while the latter eschews, traditional formulations of ontology and teleology as essential components of ethical theory. For purposes of this paper, I have sought to avoid taking sides on this complicated and important debate. What I hope to do here, at least for the time being, is to state the basic elements of natural law theory in a way that both sides can accept.[14]

Natural Law Principles for a Public Philosophy

What are the essential elements of natural law theory, which I contend provide a better grounding for the American public philosophy than that provided by anti-perfectionist liberalism? Let me suggest the following.

1. Human beings naturally know that they ought to pursue good and avoid evil.
2. This directive to pursue good and avoid evil implies that we ought to act according to reason — that is, according to practical wisdom.
3. A corollary to the principle that we should act according to reason is that obtaining pleasure is never a sufficient reason for performing an action — the activity that gives pleasure must be judged by our reason to be good.
4. Acting according to reason means acting for the sake of certain human goods, and we naturally know certain basic human goods (though corrupt customs can obscure or distort this knowledge). This is true despite the pluralism of beliefs or comprehensive views in modern societies. This knowledge, it should be noted, is not always an "articulate" knowledge, but it is nonetheless genuine.
5. Among the basic human goods are these: life (a good which we share with other animate beings); marriage and offspring (the two-in-one-flesh communion of husband and wife that provides the ordinary context for the birth and education of children); friendship and community; knowledge (especially knowledge of the most important things, the truth about reality); and religion (harmony with the transcendent source of being and meaning, God).

14. Good introductions to the contending positions are Ralph McInerny, *Ethica Thomistica: The Moral Philosophy of Thomas Aquinas* (Washington, D.C.: Catholic University of America Press, 1997), and John Finnis, *Fundamentals of Ethics* (Washington, D.C.: Georgetown University Press, 1983).

6. All good human actions are justified as pursuits of some genuine human good; actions are evil either because the object of the act is evil, or the motive is evil, or it is done in the wrong circumstances.
7. The moral basis of the basic human goods can be elaborated, and in doing so we recognize the outlines of certain classic moral commands, such as the Golden Rule, that ends do not justify the means, and the Ten Commandments (which include worship God, honor parents, and do not murder, steal, commit adultery, or lie).
8. Because of the diversity of human goods and of the ways of achieving goods (not all of which can be pursued at the same time), universal moral principles regarding particular acts are typically formulated in negative terms. That is, we can more often state in universal terms what human beings ought not to do than what they ought to do, though there are some examples of the latter, typically at higher levels of generality.
9. As we elaborate moral principles in more detail and consider their application to concrete circumstances, they are more difficult to know and the directives for action are less likely to be universal. For example, in general, borrowed goods should be returned to their owners, but not a borrowed gun to an owner with murderous intentions. Nonetheless, there are still some exceptionless moral norms, e.g., do not directly kill the innocent, do not torture people.
10. Virtues are stable dispositions of the will, ordinarily acquired by repeated actions, that enable us to choose the good more easily and consistently (and vices are similar dispositions to make bad choices). Virtues, by keeping the will focused properly on the good, help us to avoid distortions in our grasping and choosing of the concrete good. Chief among the moral virtues is prudence, whereby we make judgments about how to achieve the good in particular circumstances.
11. Human laws should serve the common good.
12. Human laws derive their justice — and people have an obligation to obey them — because of their derivation from the natural law: either as directly entailed by the commands of the natural law or as particular (though not necessary) means to achieve the common good.
13. Because the common good is profoundly affected by the character of the citizens of the community, human law has an appropriate (though limited) role to play in fostering virtue (habitual orientation to choose good and avoid evil) and discouraging vice.
14. Prudence dictates, however, that human law should encourage virtue and discourage vice particularly in those matters that involve the good of the community more directly and by directives that most people in a particular society are capable of living by.

15. When government acts to pursue the common good, it ought to do so in a way that encourages the citizens to develop their own capacities and talents, a goal which is itself a crucial element of the common good. This is accomplished more effectually if government respects the principle of subsidiarity, namely that functions ought to be performed by the lowest level of human community that can perform the functions adequately.[15]

While these principles are sketchy, and some are deliberately vague on certain key issues, they provide at least a general framework for understanding the content of the natural law.

Natural law is a key element of an adequate American public philosophy because it provides solid grounding for confident knowledge of fundamental moral and political principles, such as those required to nurture a stable family as the elementary unit or cell of society. In this way, natural law provides the American regime with sound principles by which it can establish and protect "liberty under law," or, in Justice Benjamin Cardozo's famous phrase, "ordered liberty."[16]

Natural Law and Public Philosophy

Let me indicate briefly the outlines of a public philosophy derived from natural law. (Inevitably, the "links" explaining the movement from the principles of natural law described above to the elements of public philosophy outlined below will be largely missing. I can only say for now that it is possible to provide the substance of these links.)

The Foundational Principle: The Dignity of the Human Person

The most fundamental principle of a public philosophy, on which all others ought to rest, is the dignity of the human person. This dignity has solid foundations both in revelation and reason. Biblical traditions emphasize the fact that man was created "in the image and likeness of God." Natural law philosophy stresses that all human beings have intellect and free will, the capacities to know the truth and to love and choose the good.

15. See Christopher Wolfe, "Subsidiarity: The 'Other' Ground of Limited Government," in *Catholicism, Liberalism, and Communitarianism: The Catholic Intellectual Tradition and the Moral Foundations of Democracy,* ed. Gerard V. Bradley, Kenneth L. Grasso, and Robert P. Hunt (Lanham, Md.: Rowman and Littlefield, 1995).

16. *Palko v. Connecticut* 302 U.S. 319, 325 (1938).

These capacities, the sources of human dignity, are not always lived up to, of course. Part of the "philosophical anthropology" at the foundation of a public philosophy, in fact, must be the recognition of the capacity of human beings to act either in accordance with or contrary to the source of their dignity, especially by misusing their intelligence and freedom to do wrong. Nonetheless, each human being remains *capable* of acting freely to attain the good, and therefore never definitively forfeits human dignity.

The Origins and End of Government: The Common Good

The purpose of government is to serve the common good of the political community, which comprehends the intellectual, moral, and physical well-being of the people. The common good must be understood in light of the goods toward which human persons are inclined by nature, in all their diversity and richness. The benefits involved in the common good should be shared in by all, but it is not merely the sum total of individual goods (as the "common good" of a family or a sports team transcends the individual talents and activities of its members).

Government is "natural," rather than "artificial," since it spontaneously flows from lesser communities as an essential means for achieving the common good. (In this regard, a natural law public philosophy follows Blackstone's Aristotelian account of the origins of government rather than Locke's.)

This overall account leaves open the question of how government should be *particularly* constructed (the form of government) in order to achieve its objective. That will depend to a considerable degree on the particular character and circumstances of a nation.

The Legitimate Scope of Government: Limited Government

There are many important limits on the scope of legitimate government action.[17] First are the restraints of the moral law itself, for example not to lie, steal, or murder. (Applying these principles in the political world is not always easy, but the separation of politics from morality is unacceptable.) Among the moral limits on government would be included the obligation to respect the con-

17. An interesting discussion of limited government in contemporary natural law theory can be found in John Finnis's "Is Natural Law Theory Compatible with Limited Government?" in *Natural Law, Liberalism, and Morality,* ed. Robert George (Oxford: Oxford University Press, 1996).

sciences of the citizens, so that religious liberty is a fundamental principle of just governments. (There are still, of course, just limits to religiously-motivated *actions,* even when they are based on conscience.) Such a view of religious liberty is perfectly compatible with the notion that there is a fundamental duty to pursue the truth about God and to act in accordance with it. In fact, that duty is precisely the basis of the right.

A second set of limits is made up of those which flow from the importance of government "fostering" the common good and the development of its citizens, which precludes government *substituting* for their initiative and own efforts to achieve goods. This principle, known as subsidiarity, entails an appropriate decentralization of government functions, one form of which is American federalism. (The same principle would also impel state governments to leave to localities functions which they are capable of handling adequately, and governments in general to leave functions to voluntary associations and to families.)

Political Authority

Political authority is natural, and those who exercise political power legitimately, acting within their proper powers and in the pursuit of the common good, should be respected and obeyed.

In a well-founded and well-developed polity, the people should have a share in rule, and, in a democratic republic such as the United States, consent of the governed should involve not only the general character of the Constitution, but some form of regular accountability of public officials to the citizenry. A desire to limit the potential abuse of government prudently leads Americans to embrace the principle of separation of powers, which provides for different parts of government, often selected in different ways, with different legitimate powers, to provide a wholesome check on political power in general.

The obligation to obey the law is derived not merely from popular will, but from the duty and right of government to foster the common good. (This is one way of saying that the demands of the common good bind "the people" in their collective capacity, as much as they bind public officials themselves.) Even when government falls short of successfully attaining this goal, the importance of political stability normally calls for citizens to obey the laws. But there are limits to the obligatory character of law, in particular when laws command citizens to do things that are morally evil.

Citizenship

A nation must have some principles and rules that determine who will be citizens. The presumption ought to be that all adults residing permanently in a nation who are willing and able to accept the responsibilities of citizenship should be able to become citizens. (These responsibilities presume some preparation in the form of education regarding the principles and history of the nation.) It is also necessary to establish rules determining who will be permitted to reside in the nation — in particular, rules regarding immigration. Those rules consider whether the integration of potential immigrants will advance or impede the common good. Again, the presumption ought to be in favor of generous willingness to welcome others.

Political and Personal Rights of Citizens and Persons

Always very central to the American public philosophy has been the importance of rights, both political and personal. The right of citizens to life and personal liberty is elementary. Freedom of speech, freedom of religion, freedom of association, and certain rights regarding legal procedure were enshrined in the Constitution, and have generally been broadened over time. These rights are derived from the goods toward which human beings are naturally inclined, as means to ends, and it is in light of those goods that reasonable limits on and regulation of rights is appropriate.

The Relation of the Political Community to Other Communities: Civil Society

Besides the relationship of the general government to states given in the principle of federalism, government has important rights and duties vis-a-vis other forms of community. It should provide support for and encouragement to the "cell" of society, the family, which should have a privileged place in the legal and social structure of society. The stability of marriage should be supported by a strong legal bond. Parental rights in the upbringing and education of children should be recognized as primary. Interventions by government into family life are sometimes justified, however, when the essential well-being of a family member is threatened.

Society should encourage and facilitate the formation of voluntary associations, since they contribute greatly to the goods of friendship and individual development that are part of the common good.

"Natural" groups in society, such as ethnic or racial groups, and their individual members should be protected from invidious discrimination and assured of equal participation in the political community. (The extent to which the political community will formally acknowledge political rights for groups will vary with the character and circumstances of the given nation.) Their right to maintain their language and culture should be protected, as itself a contribution to the common good, by means consistent with the common good. (This may require measures to prevent a kind of group isolationism that could create social divisions and unrest; one example of such a measure would be a requirement to learn the country's major language[s]).

Different economic and occupational groups (business and labor, manufacture and commerce and agriculture, professions and services) should have the right to organize and participate in political and social life. Their pursuit of their own self-interest ought to be consonant with a fundamental commitment to the common good (just as the common good should not be considered to be merely a majority or aggregate good, but must consider the good of all the citizens).

The Economic System and the Rights and Duties of Property

The importance of property rights is and has always been an essential element of both natural law theory and the American public philosophy. Indeed, in the founding era in particular, many would have said that the protection of property (broadly understood) was *the* great function of government. It is impossible to maintain the security and independence, the self-rule and self-reliance, of republican citizens in the absence of private property.

The public philosophy has always recognized, however, that property carries with it certain social responsibilities, in varying degrees. One way of looking at this matter is to understand that property provides human beings with the means to pursue the goods toward which they are inclined, and that, in some sense, all the resources of the world exist in order to facilitate the development of all human beings. Accordingly, a just economic system will attempt to make available to everyone in society the resources needed to act well. This entails certain obligations (which can be enforced by political authority, where appropriate) on the part of those who have more than enough property to meet their needs, in a world where many people, through no fault of their own, lack the necessary resources for self-development, and often even the most elementary necessities of life.

Another element of the economic life of a nation is the fundamental human activity of work. By work, human beings provide for the support of themselves and their families, develop their own talents and abilities, and make a contribution to the common good of the community. The political community should foster an economic system that provides effectively for the employment of its citizens. Those who have the power and responsibility to shape workplaces should keep in mind the priority of persons over things, so that the production or provision of goods and services is harmonized as well as possible with the growth and development of those who work. (Among other things, this suggests that economic activities ought to be regarded as cooperative undertakings, with due respect for the rights and responsibilities of all participants.)

Education

Among the most important aspects of the common good is education. Education ranges from the basics (reading, writing, and arithmetic) and skills necessary for employment, to the political education necessary for the proper fulfillment of our duties and rights as citizens, to general moral, intellectual, and spiritual development.

Precisely because education has such broad contours, it is often a subject of great controversy, especially in a pluralistic society. Moreover, there are potential conflicts among those who have significant roles in education, including parents, teachers, the political community, and religious communities. Parental rights to direct the education of children are fundamental, but the political community has legitimate interests and an important role in facilitating the efforts of parents to educate their children, whether by means of public schools or (where possible) by supporting private educational initiatives of parents.

Culture and Entertainment

Issues of culture play an important part in the life of a nation (and indeed may be thought of as an important form of "education" beyond basic schooling). Institutions of higher education will have a great impact here, as will a multitude of cultural institutions and activities, such as those involving music and art. And in modern democratic communities, "popular culture," as found in, for example, television, radio, and movies, may constitute a significant part of the "common" life of the community. Especially given the greatly increased leisure time available to citizens under modern economic conditions, entertainment must be regarded as a very important part of the national life, with great import for the common good. While, in general, cultural activities will arise as the free initiatives of groups and individuals in society, there is room for public promotion of culture and also for public restrictions on elements that debase the culture (e.g., pornography).

The Shared Understanding of the Community Regarding Its History

One of the sources of community is a shared understanding of a nation's past life. This constitutes a kind of "collective memory" of the political community. Indeed, education in the nation's political principles, and the "handing on" of the traditions that have been constitutive of a given nation's ideals and culture, are important requirements for maintaining a "common" life. This education should foster a proper pride in the nation's distinctive path in pursuing the common good, but it can and should recognize occasions on which it has not lived up to its ideals and responsibilities. (For example, an education in American history will recognize the ideals of liberty under law and equal rights and the distinctive contribution of American political life to self-government, while acknowledging that it took great effort and many years to achieve civil rights for black Americans).

Not surprisingly, the effort to define the public philosophy at any given time is often fought out through competing visions of the history of the nation and their relation to present debates. The lens through which a people looks at its past will often shape its present and future.

The Relation of the Nation to Other Peoples and the World

As to its guiding principles, the foreign policy of a nation ought not to choose between (much less oscillate between) an idealism unattached to national interest and a realism devoid of concern for what might be called the "international common good" and the good of other nations. Its primary aim should always be to provide for the independence, security, and well-being (as essential constituents of the common good) of the nation itself. But this legitimate and appropriate focus on national self-interest does not mean that the nation is exempt from important moral considerations similar to those that govern the actions of individuals. In particular, nations must conform to certain fundamental moral norms — for example, not waging an unjust war against another nation even when it is in the self-interest of the nation to do so — and they ought even to be willing to act benevolently for the good of other nations when such action would achieve important goods for other nations or people without excessive costs for the acting nation. No doubt, application of these principles is frequently difficult (what constitutes an "excessive cost," for example?), but that is often the case in the lives of individuals too.

Relations among nations ought to be regulated according to just principles. In principle, it would seem desirable that, where the common good of nations requires coordinated activity, this activity be regulated by principles that are clearly established and stable — by *juridical* principles, therefore. Given the great differences among nations and peoples, however, any international order would have to place great emphasis on subsidiarity.

Moreover, a candid recognition of the depths of differences among different peoples, cultures, and political systems in the world today, as well as a prudent concern for the dangers of political power exercised over large portions of the globe, would also counsel caution in international juridical undertakings and reliance on relationships of voluntary cooperation to cover many areas of common concern.

The Relation of the Polity to the Transcendent Order

Religious freedom is an important principle of political morality, and in a pluralistic society, religious establishments are neither possible nor desirable, but this does not require so strict a notion of establishment as to preclude public recognition of God and his providence, which is, in fact, legitimate and desirable. Traditionally, Americans have recognized the existence of God and his providence — particularly his providence in regard to this nation — by such symbols as Thanksgiving Day proclamations, the use of "In God We Trust" on coins, the inclusion of "under God" in the Pledge of Allegiance, and religious invocations at public events.[18] Recognition of God, of course, does not require a nation to claim or believe that its activity is based on any special, divine authority.

Such recognition of God and his providence has several justifications. First, the subordination of political life to a higher order and the dependence of communities on God for many blessings are "true," and therefore society, which has benefited from that providence, ought in justice to recognize it. Second, natural theology is both true and "useful" as the essential foundation for other important elements of the public philosophy. Perhaps most important,

18. Unfortunately, this kind of recognition of religion has become suspect under modern Supreme Court doctrine. See *Everson v. Board of Education* 330 U.S. 1 (1947) and *Abington School District v. Schempp* 374 U.S. 203 (1963). Justice Brennan's concurrence in *Schempp* tries to distinguish some of these practices from the public school prayer struck down in the case, but the distinction is unpersuasive, except to the extent that these practices are not regarded as serious ones.

the recognition of God as the author of Creation provides the most solid ground for the dignity of all human persons and their "inalienable rights." Those rights can be viewed as important sources of moral limits on the action of government and other citizens.

It is important to recognize the limits of a public philosophy. The above principles should not be expected to resolve all or even most of the vast number of particular questions that arise in the life of a political community, which must always be governed by prudence. Nonetheless, they help to guide and shape the discussion of such prudential questions, and especially help to set the bounds within which the discussion occurs.

Conclusion

The effort to recover the natural law basis of the American experiment is not simply a "restorationist" project. We should not pretend that either traditional notions of the content of natural law or the particular public philosophy on which the United States was founded were completely adequate. Both intrinsic limitations and the changes of circumstances over time may require creative efforts to see more clearly the right content of natural law and to reformulate the original American public philosophy, to improve it and render it adequate to the exigencies of our own time.

For example, traditional expressions of natural law doctrine sometimes failed to see the full scope and implications of the fundamental right of religious liberty, a shortcoming that contributed greatly to doubts about the adequacy of natural law doctrine and to the movement toward modern liberalism. Likewise, the original American regime needed the changes brought about by the Reconstruction Amendments and eventually by public policy to eliminate the unfortunate toleration of slavery, and subsequently of other forms of racism that were incompatible with the basic principles of our public philosophy — though this still leaves us with important questions about, for example, affirmative action. In addition, earlier notions of extremely limited government and very broad property rights might have called for some modification, partly because of changes in our economic circumstances over time — leaving us with the difficult task of defining appropriately a wider scope of government, while at the same time recognizing the need for new limits as well.

But the need to grow in our understanding of the implications of natural law theory and of the principles of America's public philosophy is quite different from an effort to radically replace past principles and to establish American political life on fundamentally different principles. What our national life needs is not the rejection of traditional natural law theory and the original American public philosophy, but their refinement, in order to provide the best possible vision of civic purposes for our modern pluralistic community. This will require us to resist calls (especially those rooted in anti-perfectionist liberal theory) to abandon the effort to re-articulate or forge anew common ideals regarding what is good for human beings, as individuals and communities, and to identify how that good ought to be pursued. It will require us to engage in an ongoing, often difficult, conversation about what our purposes as a nation are.

II. HISTORICAL MODELS FOR CULTURAL TRANSFORMATION

Victorian England: The Charity Aid Society

GERTRUDE HIMMELFARB

England was a "model to the nations" long before America took on that role. It was the first nation to develop a sustained system of parliamentary government. It was the first nation to become industrialized. It was the first nation to institute a public, legal, compulsory system of relief, long before industrialism had taken effect. It was the first nation to experience the problems that arose from such a system of relief and to seek solutions to them. It was the first nation to develop, alongside public relief, an extensive system of private charity. And it was the first nation to try to coordinate public relief and private charity in accord with a conscious and well-formulated set of principles.

England's Poor Laws

This system of relief, known as the Poor Laws, dates back to Elizabethan times. As codified in 1598 and 1601, the laws were both punitive and positive, designed to curb the "sturdy beggars" who roamed the countryside as well as provide relief for the "impotent" — alms and almshouses for the sick and aged, apprenticeship for children, and workhouses for the "able-bodied." Although the laws were binding on the entire country, they were administered by local parishes and supported by "poor rates" levied by local authorities. In the course of

Parts of this essay were adapted from my book *Poverty and Compassion: The Moral Imagination of the Late Victorians* (New York: Knopf, 1991).

the following two centuries, in different parts of the country and under the stress of different circumstances, this system was enforced with varying degrees of rigor and latitude. By the end of the eighteenth century, as a result of the hardships arising from industrialization and exacerbated by the Napoleonic wars, the poor laws were vastly expanded. Under the name of the "Speenhamland system," relief was often supplemented by "rates in aid of wages" — family allowances, in effect, for laborers whose earnings fell below a standard determined by the price of bread and the size of the family. The result was not only a considerable increase in the poor rates but also serious dislocations and rigidities in the economy. (Workers receiving these allowances, for example, were reluctant to leave their parish and seek employment in factories and towns.)

Tocqueville's Critique

More serious than the economic ill-effects of the poor laws were the social: the reduction of the laboring poor to the status of paupers — the "pauperization" and "demoralization" of the poor. This is the theme of a brilliant but little-known *Memoir on Pauperism* written by Alexis de Tocqueville following his visit to England in 1833.

> When one crosses the various countries of Europe [the *Memoir* opens], one is struck by a very extraordinary and apparently inexplicable sight. The countries appearing to be the most impoverished are those which in reality account for the fewest indigents, and among the peoples most admired for their opulence, one part of the population is obliged to rely on the gifts of the other in order to live.[1]

The most opulent country, of course, was England, and because it was in that advanced state of civilization, it was both able and willing to come to the aid of the unfortunate. Thus "one-sixth of the inhabitants of this flourishing kingdom live at the expense of public charity."[2]

In one sense, Tocqueville concedes, this is admirable. It is a "moving and elevating sight" to contemplate a society where the wealthy are willing to give of their riches in order to allow others the basic necessities.[3] This exercise of compassion, however, has unanticipated and undesirable results. By guaranteeing

1. Alexis de Tocqueville, *Memoir on Pauperism*, trans. Seymour Drescher, ed. Gertrude Himmelfarb (Chicago: Ivan R. Dee, 1997), p. 37.
2. Tocqueville, *Memoir*, p. 38.
3. Tocqueville, *Memoir*, p. 51.

the basic means of subsistence, it reduces the only incentives for work, which are the need to live and the desire to improve the conditions of life. The provision of relief as a legal right has other paradoxical effects. "There is something great and virile in the idea of right which removes from any request its suppliant character, and places the one who claims it on the same level as the one who grants it." But this particular right, so far from elevating the supplicant, debases him. In other countries, where the poor are dependent upon individual charity, they are obliged to recognize their inferiority, but only "secretly and temporarily." Here, where they have to inscribe themselves on the poor rolls, they acknowledge their inferiority publicly. "What is the achievement of this right if not a notarized manifestation of misery, of weakness, of misconduct on the part of its recipient?"[4]

Public relief also has the unfortunate result of exacerbating the divisions between the rich and the poor by breaking the "moral ties" between them. Where private charity creates a moral bond between giver and recipient, public relief dissolves that bond. "Legal charity," in effect, continues the alms "but removes its morality." The rich resent having their money taken from them without consulting them, and the poor are ungrateful for what is given them as a matter of right and dissatisfied because it is never sufficient. Thus the two classes degenerate into "two rival nations."[5]

These arguments, however, did not entirely preclude public relief. Tocqueville granted that such relief should be available for special groups (infants and the aged, the sick and insane) and under special circumstances (as spontaneous, temporary measures in times of calamity). But these exceptions would not imply a legal right to relief or any "permanent, regular, administrative system of relief," for any such system would only breed more miseries than it could cure.[6] Beneficence, Tocqueville observed, is "the most natural, the most beautiful, and the most holy of virtues." But even the best of principles may have its defects.

> I think that beneficence must be a manly and reasoned virtue, not a weak and unreflecting inclination. It is necessary to do what is most useful to the receiver, not what pleases the giver, to do what best serves the welfare of the majority, not what rescues the few. I can conceive of beneficence only in this way. Any other way it is still a sublime instinct, but it no longer seems to me worthy of the name of virtue.[7]

4. Tocqueville, *Memoir,* p. 59.
5. Tocqueville, *Memoir,* p. 60.
6. Tocqueville, *Memoir,* p. 70.
7. Tocqueville, *Memoir,* p. 69.

The Poor Laws Amended

Instead of abolishing the poor laws, as Tocqueville recommended, England amended them. (His essay played no part in the debate that preceded the passage of the New Poor Law in 1834; it was published only the following year, and in France, not England.) What was decisive in that debate was the Royal Commission Report issued earlier in 1834. The new law, however, was not entirely in keeping with the Report. Nor was the law consistently implemented and enforced in subsequent decades. Yet the principles of both the Report and the law set the tone and terms of public discourse for the whole of the Victorian period. These principles remain pertinent and instructive today, in America as in England.

The basic problem of the old poor law, the preface to the Report announced, was "the mischievous ambiguity of the word *poor*."[8] The name "poor law" was itself a misnomer, for it perpetuated the confusion between the laboring, independent poor and the indigent, the paupers. Thus the first task of reform was to establish the "distinction between the poor and the indigent" and to place "the indigent alone within the province of the law."[9] And within the class of paupers, a further distinction was necessary, between the "impotent" and the "able-bodied." The former, the aged and sick, were not affected by the new law. They would continue to receive "outdoor relief" in whatever form was appropriate — money, food, medical services, housing — and if they chose to enter a workhouse that would be entirely voluntary on their part. It was the able-bodied who were the proper subjects of the new law. They could receive relief in certain cases and under certain conditions; anything else would be "repugnant to the common sentiments of mankind."[10] But the cases would be those of "extreme necessity" and under conditions that would maintain the distinction between pauper and poor, thus discouraging the laboring poor from sinking to the level of pauperism.

"The first and most essential" means of implementing that distinction was the principle of "less-eligibility": the requirement that the conditions of the able-bodied pauper be less eligible — that is, less desirable, favorable, agreeable — than those of the "lowest class" of the laboring poor.[11] Unlike the system of family allowances, which attempted to establish an objective standard of need

8. *Report from His Majesty's Commissioners for Inquiring into the Administration and Practical Operation of the Poor Laws* (London, 1834), p. 156. (For a fuller account of the Report and the poor laws, see Gertrude Himmelfarb, *The Idea of Poverty: England in the Early Industrial Age* [New York: Knopf, 1983], pp. 147-68.)

9. *Report,* p. vi.

10. *Report,* p. 127.

11. *Report,* p. 127.

for poor and pauper alike, the only standard implied by the principle of less-eligibility was that the relief given to the able-bodied pauper be more meager or more onerous than the wages of labor. Derived from this principle was the most famous (infamous, in some circles, then and even more today) feature of the Report: that relief for the able-bodied and their families be given within the confines of the workhouse, except for medical relief which could be given "outdoors."

What was new about this proposal was not the workhouse itself; that institution was as old as the old poor law. What was new was the use of the workhouse in carrying out the principle of less-eligibility, for within the workhouse the pauper was literally, physically, separated from the independent laborer. The physical conditions within the workhouse need not be inferior to those of the poorest laborer in his cottage; they might even be better. The principle of less-eligibility was satisfied by the very fact of confinement within the workhouse — the stigma attached to it as much as the deprivation of liberty. The "workhouse test" had the additional advantage of being a "self-acting test," obviating any cumbersome "merit test" ("means test," as it was later to be called).[12] Magistrates did not have to judge the neediness of an applicant, since his willingness to receive relief within the workhouse was sufficient evidence of need.

Just as the old poor law had been inconsistently applied, so was the new. Indeed, from the outset the New Poor Law was more lenient than the Royal Commission Report. Outdoor relief was not "disallowed"; it was only "regulated." As a result, many able-bodied paupers continued to receive relief outside the workhouse. And the workhouses themselves varied greatly, depending upon the resources of the parish and the disposition of the local officials. Although many were overcrowded and unsanitary, even by the standards of the day, the newest were sometimes called, not entirely ironically, "pauper palaces."

Yet the principles and distinctions enunciated in the Report, like those in Tocqueville's *Memoir*, continued to govern social thought and policy at least until the end of the century. And the purposes of both were the same: to prevent the "pauperization" of the laboring poor, while satisfying the basic needs of the indigent.

Public Relief Stimulates Charity

It is this background of public relief that helps explain the unique character of private charity in Victorian England. Public relief, contrary to the expectations of many people, did not displace or diminish private charity. On the contrary, it

12. *Report*, p. 148.

seemed to have the paradoxical effect of stimulating charity. In *Democracy in America,* Tocqueville presents the United States as the voluntaristic society par excellence. Yet that distinction surely belongs to England. As early as 1739, a *History of London* by William Maitland detailed the numerous charity schools, hospitals, almshouses, and philanthropic societies that flourished in the metropolis. "As opulency and riches are the result of commerce," he observed, "so are learning, hospitality and charity the effects thereof."[13] When the second edition appeared only seventeen years later, the section on charities had to be greatly expanded to take account of the many new institutions that had been founded in that brief period.

The fervor for good works and worthy causes became even more pronounced in the latter part of the eighteenth century and throughout the nineteenth. "This is the age of societies," the young Thomas Babington Macaulay sarcastically noted. "There is scarcely one Englishman in ten who has not belonged to some association for distributing books, or for prosecuting them; for sending invalids to the hospital, or beggars to the treadmill; for giving plate to the rich, or blankets to the poor."[14] A generation later Sir James Stephen was moved to a similar observation: "Ours is the age of societies. For the redress of every oppression that is done under the sun, there is a public meeting. For the cure of every sorrow by which our land or our race can be visited, there are patrons, vice-presidents and secretaries. For the diffusion of every blessing of which mankind can partake in common, there is a committee."[15] By the latter half of the nineteenth century, there were about seven hundred philanthropic societies in London alone. The combined cost of relief and charity in the metropolis, according to one contemporary estimate, came to seven million pounds annually — a sum sufficient, it was calculated, to keep one in eight inhabitants of the city in idleness.[16]

In January 1879, when the weather conspired with the economy to produce one of the worst winters of the period, Henry James reflected on the social temper of his newly adopted country. He was impressed by the gigantic poor relief system which was "so characteristic a feature of English civilisation" and which was now being supplemented by equally huge sums from private charity. He was also impressed by the scientific way that charity was distributed.

13. William Maitland, *The History of London: from its Foundations by the Romans, to the Present Time* (London: Samuel Richardson, 1739), p. 635.

14. Quoted in Ford K. Brown, *Fathers of the Victorians: The Age of Wilberforce* (Cambridge: Cambridge University Press, 1961), p. 317.

15. Quoted in Brown, *Fathers,* p. 317.

16. For a fuller account of nineteenth-century philanthropy, see Gertrude Himmelfarb, *Poverty and Compassion: The Moral Imagination of the Late Victorians* (New York: Knopf, 1991).

> There is nothing more striking in England than the success with which an "appeal" is always made. Whatever the season or whatever the cause, there always appears to be enough money and enough benevolence in the country to respond to it in sufficient measure — a remarkable fact when one remembers that there is never a moment of the year when the custom of "appealing" intermits. Equally striking perhaps is the perfection to which the science of distributing charity has been raised — the way it has been analysed and organised and made one of the exact sciences.[17]

The Charity Organisation Society

It was ten years earlier that "benevolence" had been raised to an "exact science," for it was then that the Charity Organisation Society was founded, originally and very briefly under the ungainly name of the London Society for Organising Charitable Relief and Repressing Mendicity. This was not another charitable society of the kind so prevalent in England. Indeed, it was because of the proliferation of these societies that the COS (as it soon became known) was founded, not to add to their numbers but to coordinate and rationalize them — to make "benevolence," as was ambitiously said, a "science." Within a year there were a dozen COS district committees and by 1872 three dozen. By the end of the decade it had established itself as the premier charitable organization in London and had become the model for similar societies in America as well as in England.

The longtime secretary of the COS, Charles Stewart Loch (who held that office from 1875 to 1914), commented on the apparent paradox in its title.

> At first sight the words Charity and Organisation seem to be a contradiction in terms. Charity is free, fervent, impulsive. Organisation implies order and method, sacrifice for a common end, self-restraint. There is a kind of wildness in the enthusiasm of charity. But organisation and its kindred words suggest the quietness of gradual growth, the social results of a circumspect sobriety, a balanced and temperate progress.[18]

If Loch's rhetoric suggests a partiality for "organisation" over "charity," for "order" over "wildness," his intention was to integrate both, to preserve "the

17. Henry James, "An English New Year," in *English Hours* (Boston: Houghton Mifflin, 1905), p. 271.

18. Judith Fido, "The Charity Organisation Society and Social Casework in London 1869-1900," in *Social Control in Nineteenth Century Britain*, ed. A. P. Donajgrodski (London: Croom Helm, 1977), pp. 211-12.

quickness and discretion and even the secretness of personal charity" and at the same time "by union and cooperation to improve the condition of the poor." So far from being contradictory, he insisted, charity and organization were logically and practically complementary. Charity was the end or "motive" of the society; organization its means or "force."[19]

The COS did not, in fact, have the power to organize other charitable societies or even to serve as a clearinghouse for them; it was only another voluntary body with the same legal status as the others. It did, however, aspire to be *primus inter pares.* Thus it undertook to keep a register of local charities and their beneficiaries, to inspect and report on other institutions (soup kitchens, model houses, orphanages), and, above all, to investigate applications for relief and make recommendations for assistance. But it could not oblige the other societies to accept its recommendations, or prevent the establishment of new ones such as the Salvation Army, or deter the Lord Mayor from sponsoring yet another Mansion House Fund. Indeed, in spite of its frequent protestations that its function was not to give relief, still less to raise money for relief, many of its district committees did both (which is why it was obliged to repeat those protestations so often). It was more effective in those instances where its members were active in other philanthropic organizations as well as in the Boards of Guardians administering the poor laws. By means of this network they were able to influence the activities of private charities and coordinate them with public relief.

In one sense, the COS may be seen as carrying out the agenda of 1834, the effort to prevent the pauperization and demoralization of the poor. Like the poor law reformers who wanted to discourage "indiscriminate" or "promiscuous" relief, so the charity reformers wanted to discourage similarly indiscriminate or promiscuous charity. And like the poor law reformers who sought to eliminate the "mischievous ambiguity of the word *poor*" by distinguishing between the laboring poor and paupers, so the charity reformers sought to distinguish between the proper recipients of public relief and those of private charity. Poor relief should be given only to the indigent and, in the case of the able-bodied, only in the workhouse. Charity, on the other hand, should be reserved for the "deserving poor" who were not indigent, who were employed and might even have some resources such as savings or possessions (indeed, the latter might be taken as evidence of their being deserving) but who were in need of temporary assistance lest they fall into indigence. If it was the task of the poor law to relieve destitution, it was the task of private charity to prevent destitution by relieving the kind of poverty that might lead to it.

19. C. S. Loch, *Charity Organisation* (London: S. Sonnenschein and Co., 1892), p. 106.

The "Deserving Poor"

This intermediate class of poor, which came within the purview of charity rather than the poor law, was often characterized as the "deserving poor." "Deserving" and "undeserving" were terms used freely by the COS in its early years, in its statements of principle as well as the accounts of individual cases. The "deserving poor" were not assumed to be paragons of virtue; if they were they might not need any assistance (although there were occasions, the COS recognized, when even the most virtuous fell upon bad times). "They do not save, or join clubs, or in any way look forward to the future; they simply spend their earnings as they come; but they are on the whole industrious and sober and possessed of tidy homes."[20] By the same token, not all the recipients of relief were "undeserving"; some were destitute because of illness or old age rather than any fault of character.

By the mid-1880s the term "undeserving," applied to those who were deemed ineligible for charity, began to seem invidious. In 1886 it was altered (in the reports although not in the case studies) to read "not likely to benefit," and two years later to the still more neutral "not assisted." By 1905 the revised edition of the COS's *Principles of Decision* officially abandoned the criterion of "deserving": "The test is not whether the applicant is deserving but whether he is helpable."[21] So far from signifying any change in policy, however, these formulations represented a reaffirmation of principle. Character remained an important criterion for charitable assistance because only those of good character were "helpable." "Charity is a social regenerator," Loch wrote. "We have to use Charity to create the power of self-help. . . . Charity takes account of character,

20. Fido, "The Charity Organisation Society," p. 224.

The COS sometimes exhibited a surprising degree of sympathy and tolerance toward what might have been regarded as moral failings. Helen Bosanquet (who was a member of the council of the COS and a sister-in-law of Charles Bosanquet, its first secretary) wrote an essay on debts among the poor, in which she barely stopped short of commending the poor for resorting to the pawnbroker rather than saving for future contingencies. "Of course," she conceded, "the old-fashioned morality goes in favour of thrift as opposed to credit," but there was much to be said for the familiar adage that the pawnbroker was the "poor man's friend," his salvation in times of need. Pawnbroking was to the poor what credit was to the rich. "Thus the prestige which attaches to credit in the commercial world is fast being transferred to the region of private indebtedness, and as we turn to the poorer classes we find ourselves regarding it as tinged with a curious kind of semi-professional, semi-sentimental benevolence." It was unfortunate, however, she added, that the money obtained from the pawnbroker too often was spent on "boozing, gambling, and wasteful luxuries" (R. I. McKibbin, "Social Class and Social Observation in Edwardian England," *Transactions of the Royal Historical Society,* 1978, p. 180).

21. Beatrice Webb, *My Apprenticeship* (London: Penguin Books, 1971), p. 213.

and selects those cases in which assistance will lead to self-support."[22] The applicants themselves were given to understand this. The first item in the form distributed to them read: "The Society desires to help those persons who are doing all they can to help themselves, and to whom temporary assistance is likely to prove a lasting benefit."[23]

The COS's "poor," its special clients, were needy in a special sense, their need being "temporary," "exceptional," and (for the most part) "causeless." The need had to be temporary rather than chronic if it was to be effectively relieved by the temporary assistance charity could provide. It had to be exceptional rather than ordinary — not the predictable contingencies of life, the brief spells of sickness or slack employment or the incapacity of old age, which should be anticipated and provided for by the individual and collective resources of the poor (friendly societies, for example). And it had to be "causeless" — not caused, that is, by the poor themselves, by drunkenness, slothfulness, or other self-inflicted ills.

In defining the mission of charity, the COS also distinguished the several kinds of unemployment to which the poor were subject. Chronic unemployment should not be relieved by charity, partly because it would be too costly but also because it would discourage the economic and industrial adjustments that were the only solutions to this problem. Nor should periodic (seasonal) unemployment, which was predictable and which the poor should provide for themselves. The unemployment that charity was properly and uniquely qualified to relieve was "exceptional unemployment," the result of trade depressions which could not be anticipated or insured against even by the most provident workers. In practice, of course, these distinctions were not easily or consistently applied. The district committees often approved loans or outright grants to the seasonally unemployed and pensions to the aged. Even so staunch a believer as Sir Charles Trevelyan could be found introducing a resolution in 1878 to give pensions to "deserving chronic" cases; it was not passed because many district committees could not raise the necessary funds. But some did and small pensions were regularly provided by many committees. By 1890 almost seven hundred pensions were being granted, and they absorbed an increasing part of the COS's resources until 1908, when the Old Age Pensions Act made them redundant.

The principle, however, was clear, even if it was sometimes violated. Those who were needy through no fault of their own and whose unfortunate

22. Kathleen Woodroofe, *From Charity to Social Work in England and the United States* (Toronto: University of Toronto Press, 1968), p. 23.

23. W. H. B. Court, *British Economic History, 1870-1914: Commentary and Documents* (Cambridge: Cambridge University Press, 1965), p. 374.

condition was both temporary and unpredictable were the proper beneficiaries of charity. Charity of an "appropriate and adequate" kind (a recurrent phrase in the COS vocabulary) should be given, tailored to specific needs and sufficient for those needs, designed to prevent that lapse into pauperism from which there might be no return. Only such charity, not the poor law or any other means of public relief or public works, could avail in these cases. And only the COS, it believed, was trained to give this discriminating kind of charity.

The "Science" of Social Work: Case Work

The COS claimed to be able to make the proper distinctions and discriminations because it alone acted in accord with the principles of "social science" — "the science," as one of its founders put it, "of doing good and preventing evil."[24] It was in this spirit that it set up an "Enquiry Department" to conduct investigations and collect information which it published in its journals and in reports modeled on the official "Blue Books." It also founded a "School of Sociology" for the training of social workers. The principal technique taught in that school, and the COS's claim to inaugurating the "science" of social work, was the system of casework.

The COS did not originate that system, but it did publicize and use it more systematically than had been done before. Just as an earlier generation of poor-law reformers relied upon the workhouse test to determine those paupers who qualified for parish relief, so the COS used casework to identify those poor for whom it assumed responsibility. This was precisely the "merit test" that the poor-law reformers had abjured — a merit test that went beyond what was later to be called a "means test" because it judged not only the need of assistance but also the ability to profit from that assistance. It was, in effect, a moral as well as financial test.

Casework was not the original emphasis of the COS. In its early years the main function of the district committees (which were coterminous with the poor-law unions) was to keep registers of applicants for charity and relief so as to avoid duplication. Very soon, however, this task became subordinate to the social work conducted by the COS itself, and the registers were then supplemented by detailed case records of the applicants and their families. Special forms and books were devised to record information about each family, its condition and needs, the disposition of the case, and follow-up investigations. Much of the information was obtained from "visitors" — volunteer workers who visited the applicant at home and made inquiries among neighbors, rela-

24. Woodroofe, *From Charity to Social Work,* p. 48.

tives, parish ministers, and school officials to determine the eligibility of the applicant and to monitor his progress and give him counsel.

A later critic of the COS, looking back at it from the vantage point of the welfare state, described its "essential duality": it was "professionally pioneering" in developing the casework techniques that were to become the staples of social work, but "ideologically reactionary" in the individualistic, moralistic ethic that guided it.[25] That duality, however, is in the mind of the historian. For contemporaries the striking fact about the COS was its essential unity of purpose and method. Casework and visiting were the necessary means to achieve its ends: to select those families who qualified for charity, to determine their needs, and to give the charity in the most suitable forms — a grant or loan for the purchase of clothing or coal, tools or merchandise, a sewing machine or mangle, a surgical appliance or stay in a convalescent home. The COS also prided itself on being "rehabilitative" rather than merely "palliative." Visitors were expected to maintain contact with each family and exert the kind of personal influence that helped it become and remain self-supporting.

The family was the unit of casework and the principal concern of the COS. This too has been criticized as inconsistent with the political economy professed by the COS, which made the individual the primary unit. But the principle of individualism, as Victorians understood it, was never intended to belittle or belie the importance of the family, for the primary responsibility of the wage-earning individual was the care of his family. It might also be argued that the very purpose of the COS, the "organization" of charity, was a violation of *laissez-faire* — or even that charity itself was. By this time, however, political economy had been so considerably modified, in theory as well as practice, that only the most dogmatic laissez-faireist would have objected to the kind of charity that was intended to restore the economic independence of the individual and thus of the family. Charles Loch's grandson, who was also the historian of the COS, explained that the Society "implied a sternly individualist philosophy, and paid the poor the compliment of assuming they shared it."[26] He might have added that it also paid them the compliment of assuming that they shared the capacity of acting on that philosophy — of being prudent, temperate, and independent, in the interests of themselves and their families.

25. Derek Fraser, *The Evolution of the British Welfare State: A History of Social Policy since the Industrial Revolution* (London: Macmillan, 1973), p. 121.

26. Charles Loch Mowat, *The Charity Organisation Society, 1869-1913: Its Ideas and Work* (London: Methuen, 1961), p. 38.

Volunteer "Visitors"

Another aspect of casework, the reliance upon volunteer "visitors," was hardly original to the COS, having its roots in the venerable practice of the parish clergyman visiting his flock or the squire's wife making her rounds with baskets of food and clothing. There were even institutions that made visiting their specific mission. The Benevolent or Strangers' Friend Society was founded by the Methodists as early as 1785. In 1828 the Evangelicals established the General Society for Promoting District Visiting; within three years it had 25 district societies, a roster of 573 visitors, and 163,695 visits to its credit. Fifteen years later the Bishop of London organized the Metropolitan Visiting and Relief Association, for the purpose, as its full title put it, of "Promoting the Relief of Destitution, and for Improving the Condition of the Poor, by means of Parochial and District Visiting, under the superintendance and direction of the Bishops and Clergy, through the Agency of Unpaid Visitors, and without reference to religious persuasion." A notable visitor was Charles Dickens's Mrs. Pardiggle, who proudly described herself: "I am a School lady, I am a Visiting lady, I am a Reading lady, I am a Distributing lady; I am on the local Linen Box Committee, and many general Committees."[27] (Mrs. Pardiggle may be better remembered as an associate of Mrs. Jellyby, who was more devoted to the natives of Borrioboola-Gha than to her own family.)

It remained for the COS to secularize and systematize the practice of visiting by making it a "scientific" instrument of charity. Although the visitors were unpaid volunteers, they acquired the status of professionals. It is generally assumed that the mark of professionalization was the payment of visitors — "social workers," as they began to be known in the 1890s. But while the secretary of the COS was paid almost from the beginning, and by the end of the century half the district committees had paid secretaries and in some cases paid supervisors and trainers of the visitors, the visitors themselves remained, for the most part, unpaid volunteers. There was a lively debate on the issue of payment. "Paid officers," some argued, "tend to kill voluntary work."[28] As late as 1912, Violet Butler, an eminent social investigator as well as social worker, explained the psychological rationale for unpaid voluntary work. "We *knew* we were comfortably off and we felt quite guilty. . . . We felt that one ought to be working like other people, like the poorer people, but nobody wanted us, so we preferred to do it *unpaid,* if we could afford to do it unpaid."[29]

27. Charles Dickens, *Bleak House* (New York: Norton, 1977 [1st ed., 1853]), p. 94.

28. Helen Bosanquet, *Social Work in London, 1869-1912* (London: J. Murray, 1914), p. 64.

29. Brian Harrison, "Miss Butler's Oxford Survey," in *Traditions of Social Policy: Essays in Honour of Violet Butler,* ed. A. H. Halsey (Oxford: B. Blackwell, 1976), p. 67.

Whether paid or not, the visitors were expected to abide by professional standards. These determined not only the way they collected information and made recommendations, but also the way they conducted themselves in relation to the poor. From the beginning the COS was sensitive to the charges of condescension and intrusion, of letting loose among the poor a gaggle of Mrs. Pardiggles. In 1870 in its second annual report, it adjured its visitors to behave toward the poor as they would toward their own kind. "Well-to-do strangers should no more knock at the door of a working man without some distinct object or introduction than they should at the door of one in their own rank of life."[30] Helen Bosanquet warned that "inquisitiveness into another person's affairs, and especially intrusion into their home unbidden, is a great offence against social etiquette."[31]

The cultivation of a professional attitude, however, did not imply the kind of "objectivity" that is now identified with professionalism — an impersonality and neutrality that profess to be above moral judgments. Nor did the warnings against inquisitiveness and intrusiveness mean that the visitor was to refrain from inquiring into the habits and character of the applicant or from exerting any influence upon him; on the contrary, these were precisely the missions of the visitor. "The gift," Loch wrote, "avails little; the influence may avail much." Properly exercised, that influence could affect "the thousand and one relations of life."[32]

A Religious Duty

When John Wesley, a century earlier, had enjoined his flock to visit the sick and aid the poor, he had described it as a religious duty that would serve benefactor

30. Harrison, "Miss Butler's," p. 56.

31. Helen Bosanquet, *Rich and Poor* (New York: Garrett Press, 1970 [reprint of 2nd ed., 1898]), p. 120.

In 1905 a manual elaborated on the proper etiquette of knocking: "The first thing to be remembered in knockerless, bell-less regions is that a never-to-be-departed-from etiquette demands that only the hand should be used; and it is desirable that the neighbours should be able to testify that the first two or three taps, at any rate, have been soft and low." And of the use of names: "To call a person 'out of her name' is unpardonable, not to call her by it early and often is scarcely less wounding to her feelings." And of the tone of voice: "In all the preliminary conversation the voice should be carefully lowered. Although the poor commonly speak to one another with what might be considered unnecessary loudness, they resent this tone in their social superiors, not only because it enables inquisitive neighbours to hear too much, but because they know that is not how a lady speaks to a friend" (McKibbin, "Social Class," p. 187).

32. Loch, *Charity Organisation,* pp. 35, 41.

and beneficiary alike; the gift of sustenance was the gift of grace. In the case of the COS that mutuality of purpose was all the more striking because the religious duty itself had been transmuted. The salvation that was now sought carried with it all the passion and authority of religion without the creedal and institutional constraints of a church.

The religious metaphor was pervasive. Reflecting upon his long association with the COS, Charles Loch explained that he had originally been drawn to it by the hope of creating an association of people from different churches and classes who would find in charity "a common purpose and a new unity." That would be "worth anything," for without the interference of the state, "it could renew and discipline the life of the people by a nobler, more devoted, more scientific religious charity. . . . It could help us to realise in society the religion of charity without the sectarianism of religion."[33] Loch's grandson described him as a "natural Christian" rather than an "orthodox churchman,"[34] and while many of his associates in the COS were orthodox churchmen, it was as "natural Christians" that they too functioned in what Loch called the "church of charity."[35] Like all such religious missions, this one was intended to have a redeeming effect on giver and receiver alike. In this case the "giver" was not so much the donor of money as the visitor, who gave a gift — of time, energy, and spirit — that was greater than any mere contribution of money and more satisfying both to the giver and to the receiver. That gift relieved the giver's "consciousness of sin" more effectively than any impersonal monetary transaction might have done. And it more effectively relieved the poverty of the recipient, who obtained the kind of personal help that would enable him to help himself, morally as well as economically.

This was not the gift prescribed by the evangelist: "Give unto everyone that asketh thee." That gift was an end in itself, not so much a means of relieving the needy as a manifestation of the divine spirit, the infinite love of God expressing itself in infinite compassion for man. "Infinite," that is, not measured by need or means, not organized or supervised, but given freely and received freely, without conditions or limits. "When thou doest alms," the Gospel reads, "let not thy left hand know what thy right hand doeth." The COS operated under precisely the opposite dictate. Its "religion of charity" was governed by a "science of charity." And that science required the left hand to know precisely what the right hand was doing, to oblige the giver *not* to give to everyone who asketh.

The COS could appreciate the spiritual intention, if not the practical effects, of the "gift" in its original religious sense. What it could not appreciate

33. Woodroofe, *From Charity to Social Work,* pp. 31-32.

34. Mowat, *The Charity Organisation Society,* p. 67.

35. Woodroofe, *From Charity to Social Work,* p. 32.

was either the intention or the effects of the corrupt version as practiced by a lady bountiful. That was not a self-sacrificing but a self-serving gift, an act of self-indulgence that was more concerned with feeling good than with doing good, and that, in fact, did more harm than good. It was mischievous not only because it was indiscriminate but because it was benevolent in the paternalistic (or, more literally, maternalistic) sense, designed to keep the poor in a state of dependency. Helen Bosanquet quoted one lady bountiful who was upset at the thought that poverty might be "cured," for if it were, "the rich would have no one upon whom to exercise their faculty of benevolence." Another objected to giving the poor the means of becoming self-sufficient because that would make them too independent. "I like them to come to me when they are in difficulties and ask for what they want," this lady explained. Without this "glow of benevolent patronage," Mrs. Bosanquet sarcastically commented, the ladies bountiful of this world would soon lose their interest in the poor.[36]

Shortly after she started work as a visitor in Soho (and long before she took up the cause of Fabianism), Beatrice Potter reflected on some of the anomalies of the new charity. Did it not favor the weak and helpless to the detriment of the stronger and more resourceful? And if this were so, should such considerations have any weight in the face of individual misery? Were "economic facts" as important as the "moral facts" which were the proper concern of charity? And was not the chief of these moral facts "the relationship of giver and receiver" — above all, "the moral effect on the person who receives"? About one thing she was clear: the personal relationship was as important for the giver as for the receiver. "It is distinctly *advantageous to us* to go amongst the poor." And not only because the knowledge and experience of the lives of others would contribute to a better understanding of their problems, but also for one's own character, because "contact with them develops on the whole our finer qualities, disgusting us with our false and worldly application of men and things and educating in us a thoughtful benevolence." This benevolence, to be sure, could take the form of "pharasaical self congratulation." But the real philanthropist was not likely to be guilty of this because he was "far too perplexed at the very '*mixed result*' (even if he can recognize any permanent result) of his work, to feel much pride over it."[37]

The importance of "the relationship of giver and receiver" went beyond the individuals involved in it. In 1870 Charles Trevelyan explained that one of the purposes of the "systematic visitation of the poor" was to narrow the gulf

36. Helen Bosanquet, *Rich and Poor,* pp. 138-39.

37. Beatrice Webb, Mss. of the Diaries, May 18, 1883 (Webb Mss. Collection, London School of Economics). The published version omits an important part of this entry (*The Diary of Beatrice Webb,* ed. Norman and Jeanne MacKenzie [Cambridge, Mass.: Belknap Press, 1982-83], vol. I, p. 85).

between the classes: "to bring back the rich into such close relation with the poor as cannot fail to have a civilising and healing influence, and to knit all classes together in the bonds of mutual help and goodwill."[38] In the mid-1880s, at a time when others, even within the COS, were urging some form of government action to cope with the problem of unemployment, Loch reaffirmed the role of the COS as "a Great Companionship of Charity, West with East, rich with poor, the elder with the younger generation."[39] Later still, in an appeal for volunteers, the COS suggested that the "social" aspect of visiting, even more than the "charitable," was the means by which "class distinctions may be partly effaced."[40] It also saw its network of visitors and committees as a corrective to the unfortunate effects of urbanism, restoring those links that had been broken in the anonymous, impersonal city and forging new bonds of community. It was for this reason among others that the COS urged its visitors to be friendly and "neighbourly," to give charity not as "from strangers to strangers" but as a transaction between people personally known to each other.[41] Only in such a personal relationship would the rich appreciate "the responsibility attaching to wealth and leisure" and the poor have "the comfortable assurance that if the day of exceptional adversity should come, they will not be left to encounter it without a friend."[42]

Modern Skeptics

From the perspective of the welfare state, and even more from that of a socialist society, the theories and practices of the COS — and of Victorian philanthropy in general — may seem naive and inept, woefully inadequate to the problems of poverty and unemployment, and designed rather to alleviate the guilt of the rich than the misery of the poor. Some historians see charity as "conscience money" to atone for "self-conscious guilt-complexes about the possession of wealth"; philanthropy as compensation for some "emotional deficiency" resulting from bereavement, childless marriage, or "internal tension" (presumably sexual); "slumming" as a recreational activity for bored wives and idle spinsters; and philanthropic societies as an outlet for snobbery, social advancement, and professional ambition.[43]

Others invoke the familiar "social control" thesis, in which charity was a

38. Helen Bosanquet, *Social Work*, p. 53.
39. Mowat, *The Charity Organisation Society*, p. 71.
40. Fido, "The Charity Organisation Society," p. 209.
41. Loch, *Charity Organisation*, pp. 61-62.
42. Woodroofe, *From Charity to Social Work*, p. 49.
43. Fraser, *The Evolution of the British Welfare State*, pp. 117-19.

means of pacifying the lower classes and thwarting any serious movement of economic and social reform; visiting was "a cultural assault upon the working-class way of life"; and "moral reformation" was the imposition upon the poor of those "middle-class values," notably "self-help mentality" and "deferred gratification," which would keep them in bondage to the established order. Casework thus became the instrument of social control, the "personalized welfare relationship" transmitting to the poor those alien middle-class ideals, and the continued visitation perpetuating the relationship by continually reminding the applicant of his dependency and obligations. A novel turn of this argument has the COS imposing social control not only upon the recipients of charity but over the donors as well. They too were being regimented, their spontaneous impulses curbed, their contributions used as others saw fit, and their personalities subordinated to a powerful "solidary" system (in Emile Durkheim's sense) that was as much beyond their control as it was beyond the control of the poor.[44]

The idea that Victorian philanthropy was designed to impose upon the poor alien values that violated their indigenous working-class values has disquieting implications. If thrift, prudence, sobriety, industry, cleanliness, and independence were middle-class values, are we to assume that profligacy, imprudence, drunkenness, idleness, dirtiness, and dependency were indigenous working-class values? The COS may well have been guilty of imposing their values upon the poor. But later historians may be doing so as well, attributing to the poor a contempt for "bourgeois" culture more characteristic of intellectuals than of workers aspiring to the material and social benefits associated with that culture. In fact, these middle-class values, epitomized in the words "respectability" and "independence," were hardly the exclusive prerogative of the middle class or even of the "labor aristocracy." If most of the poor could not hope to attain the status of the "respectable artisan" or the "better class of working men" (these too were contemporary terms), the ideals of respectability and independence were no less important to them. They may even have been more important, for the poor knew themselves to be in that precarious condition where the least misstep, the slightest misfortune or imprudence, might reduce them to the status of paupers.

A modern skeptic may also be suspicious of the moral value ascribed to charity in contrast to relief. One historian finds this perverse as well as regressive. "That the giving and accepting of charity (under proper conditions) should be considered an ennobling transaction while state aid was inevitably pauperizing stands in retrospect as one of the more curious articles of faith."[45]

44. Fido, "The Charity Organisation Society," pp. 224, 228, 215-16.

45. David Owen, *English Philanthropy 1660-1960* (Cambridge, Mass.: Belknap Press, 1964), p. 508.

But it may be no more curious than the opinion prevalent today that charity is ignoble while state aid is honorable, reflected in the common view that it is demeaning for elderly parents to be dependent on their families but not demeaning to be dependent on the state.[46] The COS's view of charity was shared by some contemporaries — the philosopher T. H. Green, for example, and the historian and social critic Arnold Toynbee — who had no principled objection to state aid, but who belonged to the COS because they believed charity to be more fitting, less degrading, for the deserving poor than relief. For Green and Toynbee, as for Loch, charity under the proper conditions was salutary, not only for the receiver and the giver but for society as a whole, for it united rich and poor in a common bond of citizenship.

It is not surprising that the word "citizenship" should be so prominent in the vocabulary of the COS. Both Charles Loch and Bernard Bosanquet were students of Green, who made that concept central to his philosophy. Even before the working classes as a whole had been admitted to political citizenship, the COS endowed them, in effect, with something like the status of social citizenship by attributing to them the desire and the capacity for independence. And after they were enfranchised in 1884, the COS thought it all the more important that they cherish the independence that was the true mark of the citizen. (It is significant that one group not enfranchised at this time were paupers; anyone receiving parish relief during the year was not eligible to vote.) In a "world grown democratic," Loch explained, the idea of citizenship took on a new meaning. In the past the state could tolerate a class of dependents. It could no longer do so, for citizenship was inconsistent with dependency.

> The State wants citizens. It cannot afford to have any outcasts or excluded classes, citizens that are not citizens. All are citizens in name; it must see that they are so in reality. It must do its utmost to change the dependent sections of the community into independent [ones]. . . . Accordingly it becomes a duty of the State by some means to prevent pauperism, and of citizens to give their service to the State for that purpose.[47]

46. This view is in fact relatively recent. The repugnance against poor relief was a powerful sentiment in America during the depression of the 1930s, and in some circles well beyond that time. There is still a generation alive that remembers when relief was regarded as shameful, while the assistance of family or friends, church or *Landsmannschaft*, was assumed to be natural and proper. The stigma of relief even affected social security. It took years of education and habituation for social security to become sufficiently differentiated from relief so that those suspicious of public largesse could accept, in good conscience, old age or disability benefits to which they themselves had contributed.

47. Loch, *Charity Organisation*, p. 4.

A New Appreciation of Old Principles

In the course of the twentieth century, almost every tenet of this ethos was abandoned. The "ambiguity of the word *poor*," so far from being regarded as "mischievous," became the basis of social policy. All the means by which the Victorians tried to distinguish between the independent poor and the dependent, between the proper recipients of relief and of charity, were dismissed as invidious and unjust. The idea that any stigma should be attached to the "able-bodied pauper," or that relief should be subject to the principle of "less-eligibility," or that some applicants for charity were more "deserving" or "helpable" than others, or that "indiscriminate," "promiscuous" charity was worse than no charity, or that "visitors" should inquire (within the proper bounds of "etiquette") into the lives of those they were assisting, or that charity was a "gift" for the giver as well as the receiver — these ideas became as archaic as the language in which they were expressed. During most of the twentieth century, social policy was committed to a "value-free" ideology that precluded all such moral criteria and policies.

Or so it was until very recently. Within the last decade or two we have begun to experience a disenchantment with this "progressive" ideology and a new appreciation of some of the old principles and distinctions. We no longer speak of the "pauperization of the poor," but we have come to terms with the reality of a "dysfunctional underclass." No one recommends the revival of the workhouse, but we do seek other ways of implementing the principle of less-eligibility so as to reinforce the incentive to work (by ensuring, for example, that the benefits of welfare not exceed the earnings of labor). We have not abolished the system of welfare, but we have radically reformed it by "devolving" it to the states, thus in effect eliminating welfare as a federally-guaranteed "right" — or, as we now say, "entitlement."

As welfare has come to be problematic, so charity has taken on a new importance. The welfare reform act of 1996, which grants to local communities the "charitable choice" of assigning some aspects of public welfare to religious institutions, has given a new legitimacy and vitality to all private institutions and, more significantly, to "faith-based" ones. We no longer pretend to have anything like a "science of charity," but we are witnessing the resurgence of something very like a "religion of charity." Finally, like the Victorians of old, we are finding that if "the state wants citizens," it cannot afford to have a large dependent class, and if it wants to reduce dependency, it must look to its citizens "to give their service to the state for that purpose."

William Wilberforce

KEVIN BELMONTE

The abolition of the Slave Trade in England, and in our own country, is a memorable exhibition of what may be done by well directed, persevering efforts. The inhuman traffic was sanctioned by custom, defended by argument, and still more powerfully, by a vast monied capital, embarked in the trade. It is not yet fifty years, since this first effort was made, and now the victory is won. Who produced this mighty revolution? A few men at first, lifted up their voice and were reinforced by others, till the immortal work was done.[1]

Lyman Beecher, October 27, 1812

It was the great genius of Wilberforce that he realized that attempts at political reform without at the same time changing the hearts and minds of people were futile. The abolitionists realized they could never succeed in eliminating slavery without addressing the greater problems of cultural malaise and decay.[2]

Charles Colson

1. Lyman Beecher, *A Reformation of Morals Practicable and Indispensable: A Sermon Delivered at New Haven on the Evening of October 27, 1812, by Lyman Beecher, A.M. Pastor of the First Church in Litchfield,* 2nd ed. (Andover, Mass.: Flagg and Gould Printers, 1814).

Beecher's sermon was delivered almost twenty-five years to the day (28 October 1787) that William Wilberforce wrote in his diary: "God Almighty has set before me two great objects, the suppression of the slave trade and the reformation of manners" — a most fitting coincidence.

2. Quoted in William Wilberforce, *A Practical View of Christianity,* ed. Kevin C. Belmonte (Peabody, Mass.: Hendrickson Publishers, 1996), p. xxiv.

Nearly two hundred years ago, Alexis de Tocqueville praised voluntary associations and the way they shaped early American society. He marveled at how Americans of all ages and all stations in life formed associations of many different types and at how they combined to found seminaries, build churches, give fetes, distribute books, and send missionaries to the Antipodes.

Tocqueville might well have been describing Britain during the fifty-year period preceding the start of the Victorian era, a time characterized by historian Ford K. Brown as the "Age of Wilberforce." During this period (1787-1837), and under the leadership of William Wilberforce (1759-1833), Britons formed scores of voluntary societies that produced educational and prison reforms and promoted public health initiatives, shorter working hours, and improved conditions in factories. These societies established lending libraries, soup kitchens, and hospitals, and their exertions resulted in the founding of the Royal Institution of Science, the Society for Bettering the Condition of the Poor, and the Royal Society for the Prevention of Cruelty to Animals.

According to Brown, Wilberforce helped shape the public's willingness to seek reform by example. Brown writes:

> There was probably no . . . benevolent project . . . that was not brought to Wilberforce's attention, and probably not a week of his life passed without appeals for help from private persons he had never heard of. . . . His name was on the subscription lists of some seventy Evangelical Societies, his private charities were constant and there were not many biographies of Evangelical clergymen of the day who needed help that do not mention gifts from him.[3]

Tocqueville's name is widely known today, Wilberforce's is not. Yet it is Wilberforce who has been described as "the single greatest reformer in history." Cultural scholar Os Guinness believes cultural decline of the sort we are seeing today is not necessarily terminal. Pointing to the example of Wilberforce, he asserts that cultures can be turned around. "Wilberforce," he has stated, "was small in stature but towering in significance because of what he achieved, even being referred to as 'the Washington of humanity' while he lived. Wilberforce was a man historians say changed his era. Through his efforts to promote moral renewal, his life gives us an example of how to create the momentum that leads to positive change."[4]

Using Guinness's comments as a guide, it is the purpose of this essay to

3. Ford K. Brown, *Fathers of the Victorians: The Age of Wilberforce* (Cambridge: Cambridge University Press, 1961), p. 70.

4. This quotation comes from a transcription of remarks made by Guinness on 19 November 1998 during a congressional luncheon in Washington, D.C., for newly elected Democratic and Republican members of Congress.

explore how Wilberforce's moral reform successes were informed by what he called "the reformation of manners," and to describe the model for cultural renewal that emerged during the course of Wilberforce's career in politics.

The Anglo-American Heritage of Voluntary Societies and Cultural Renewal Movements

It is not a mistake that Tocqueville's description of voluntary societies in early America so closely resembles the work of the voluntary societies with which Wilberforce was associated in Britain. These two movements share the same heritage. In part, the rise of voluntary societies in Britain directly influenced the rise of such societies in America.

Given this, a good place to begin assessing the lasting significance of the legacy of cultural renewal handed down to us in the life of Wilberforce is with the writings of the great American abolitionist and reformer Lyman Beecher. Beecher (1775-1865) was the father of Harriet Beecher Stowe, the author of the classic anti-slavery novel *Uncle Tom's Cabin.* In a sermon delivered in 1812 titled *A Reformation of Morals Practicable and Indispensable,* Beecher traced the lineage of American voluntary societies to those that arose under Wilberforce's leadership. In addition, he traced the lineage of voluntary societies from Martin Luther to Wilberforce's 1787 founding of the Society for the Reformation of Manners. Beecher wrote that in America, this society "commands . . . respect and gratitude." He then proceeded to cite "facts, more decisive than a thousand arguments, that such reformation as we need is practicable."[5]

To support this contention, Beecher recounted the history of voluntary societies in Britain, noting that the first such society "was established in London, about the year 1697."[6] Similar societies were formed in the American colonies prior to the Revolutionary War, and he described their work as well. Thus, the pursuit of moral and cultural renewal through the work of voluntary societies is a phenomenon that possesses an Anglo-American pedigree.

Wilberforce and the Society for the Reformation of Manners

On October 28, 1787, a twenty-eight-year-old Wilberforce wrote in his diary: "God Almighty has set before me two great objects, the suppression of the slave

5. Beecher, *A Reformation of Morals.*
6. Beecher, *A Reformation of Morals.*

trade and the reformation of manners."[7] It is a great pity that the first of these famous objectives is so much better remembered than the second, for as Lyman Beecher wrote and Wilberforce himself believed, the abolition of the slave trade was but one "memorable exhibition of what may be done by well directed, persevering efforts."

The abolition of the slave trade was in fact directly tied to the work of moral reformation to which Wilberforce also devoted his life. It was not mere happenstance the two objects were combined in his diary entry; the linkage was deliberate and the abolition of the slave trade could not, in his mind, have taken place without a coexistent moral reformation to strengthen the consensus that the British slave trade was a tragic national sin. This linkage between a rise in morality and social reform is not lost on Charles Colson. He recognizes that "it was the great genius of Wilberforce that he realized that attempts at political reform without at the same time changing the hearts and minds of people were futile. The abolitionists realized they could never succeed in eliminating slavery without addressing the greater problems of cultural malaise and decay."[8]

The reformation of manners sought by Wilberforce called for nothing more and nothing less than a change in the hearts and minds of people, one by one. In Wilberforce's case, the first change began with him.

A political prodigy born into a prosperous merchant family, Wilberforce was elected to the House of Commons within days of his twenty-first birthday. He entered political life as an ambitious young man who indulged in the pastimes of high society and sought to establish connections that would further his political career. One of the closest friends of "the boy Prime Minister" William Pitt, he moved in the highest circles of the government.

Wilberforce possessed great political influence and prestige in his own right. In 1784, he stood against the landed aristocratic families in an election that decided the representation of the entire county of York, one of the two most powerful seats in the House of Commons. He scored a stunning political upset, and for the next twenty-eight years served as one of two members of Parliament for York. During the winter of 1785-1786, however, Wilberforce underwent a great change, embracing evangelical Christianity and deepening his devotion to the Church of England. He became an evangelical Anglican. This change was so powerful that it revolutionized Wilberforce's understanding of his call to service in political life. Henceforth, he resolved with God's help to set vigorously about reform.

When seeking to understand the genesis of the reformation of manners, it

7. R. I. and S. Wilberforce, *The Life of William Wilberforce, by his sons, Robert Isaac Wilberforce and Samuel Wilberforce* (London: J. Murray, 1838), vol. 1, p. 149.

8. Quoted in Wilberforce, *A Practical View of Christianity*, p. xxiv.

is vital to remember that Wilberforce did in his day what many are doing in our own: look for historical models that successfully promoted moral reformation and cultural renewal. As early as 1785, Wilberforce had been disturbed by signs of cultural malaise in Britain. As he wrote to his friend Lord Muncaster on August 14, 1785,

> It is not the confusion of parties, and their quarreling and battling in the House of Commons, which makes me despair of the republic . . . but it is the universal corruption and profligacy of the times, which taking its rise amongst the rich and luxurious has now extended its baneful influence and spread its destructive poison through the whole body of the people.[9]

Two years later, Wilberforce began to actively research historical models for moral and cultural renewal. Very quickly, he focused on the proclamations that were issued when a new monarch assumed the throne. He knew, as did most Britons, that a new sovereign always issued a Proclamation "for the encouragement of Piety and Virtue; and for the Preventing of Vice, Profaneness and Immorality." This was most often a mere formality, but Wilberforce discovered that the Proclamation issued by William and Mary in 1692 had been attended with greater success than most issued since that time.[10]

The reason, Wilberforce learned, was that in the 1690s local "Societies for the Reformation of Manners" and "Religious Societies" had been forming about the time that William and Mary's Proclamation was issued. Societies for the Reformation of Manners were formed in greater London to assist magistrates in the detection of crime and the enforcement of criminal laws. Religious Societies worked through personal diplomacy on an individual level to strengthen and renew the moral consensus of the nation.

In 1697, Josiah Woodward, the minister of Popler, traced the history of these events in his book *An Account of the Rise and Progress of the Religious Societies in the City of London . . . And of the Endeavours for Reformation of Manners Which have been made therein.* He wrote: "The Societies for Reformation bent their utmost Endeavours from the first (1) to suppress publick Vice and the Religious Societies endeavour'd (2) chiefly to promote Religion in their own Breasts . . . they have since been eminently instrumental in the Publick Reformation."[11] Looking at American history, historian John G. West has also noted this dual emphasis: "If irreligion and immorality dominated society, it was the

9. R. I. and S. Wilberforce, *The Life of William Wilberforce,* vol. 1, p. 84.

10. John C. Pollock, *Wilberforce* (London: John Constable, 1977), p. 59.

11. Josiah Woodward, *An Account of the Rise and Progress of the Religious Societies in the City of London . . . And of the Endeavours for the Reformation of Manners Which Have been Made Therein,* 2nd ed. (London: Printed by J.D. for the author, 1698), pp. 83-84.

responsibility of Christians themselves to form private reform associations to combat these evils — to convert people and to promote virtue."[12] Wilberforce embraced this dual emphasis and sought to revive it. His sons wrote that this desire "was suggested by Dr. Woodward's *Account of the Rise and Progress of the Religious Societies in the City of London* . . . . Our father proposed to form a similar association, to resist the spread of open immorality."[13]

Wilberforce began his work by endeavoring to infuse his numerous friends with a determination to resist the growing vices of the times. On June 12, 1787, he wrote to his friend William Hey, an eminent surgeon in Leeds, "I am conscious that ours is an infinitely inferior aim, yet surely it is of the utmost consequence, and worthy of the labours of a whole life."[14] Wilberforce also described his concerns about regulating external conduct and changing the hearts of his fellow citizens.

> In our free state . . . it is peculiarly needful to obtain these ends by the agency of some voluntary association; for thus only can those moral principles be guarded, which of old were under the immediate protection of the government. It thus becomes to us, like the ancient censorship, the guardian of the religion and morals of the people. The Attorney-General and Secretary of State, who alone in our country can be thought at all to fill this post, are too much cramped by their political relations to discharge its duties with effect; yet some such official check on vice is absolutely needed.[15]

How did Wilberforce go about promoting moral reformation? He hatched a scheme that to modern ears sounds impossible: he would endeavor to make goodness fashionable among the leadership class. He shared this plan with his friend Beilby Porteus, the Bishop of London. He told Bishop Porteus that he hoped to persuade King George III to re-issue the *Proclamation for the encouragement of Piety and Virtue; and for the Preventing of Vice, Profaneness and Immorality* which had marked his Accession.

Porteus penned an overview of his consultation with Wilberforce in a manuscript book entitled *Occasional Memorandum and Reflexions.* He wrote:

> The design appeared to me to be in the highest degree laudable, and the object of the greatest importance and necessity; but I foresaw great difficulties

12. John G. West Jr., "God and Politics: Lessons from America's Past," The Russell Kirk Memorial Lectures, The Heritage Foundation, Washington, D.C., 25 March 1997, ISSN 0272-115.

13. R. I. and S. Wilberforce, *The Life of William Wilberforce,* vol. 1, p. 131.

14. R. I. and S. Wilberforce, *The Life of William Wilberforce,* vol. 1, p. 130.

15. Quoted in R. I. and S. Wilberforce, *The Life of William Wilberforce,* vol. 1, pp. 131-32.

> in the execution of it unless conducted with great judgment and discretion, especially in the first outset. My advice therefore was to proceed in the beginning cautiously and privately, to mention the Plan in confidence, first of all to the leading men in Church and State, the Archbishop of Canterbury and [Prime Minister] Pitt to engage their concurrence . . . and then by degrees . . . to obtain if possible the assistance of the principal and most respectable characters among the Nobility, Clergy and Gentry in and about London and afterwards throughout the kingdom.[16]

It is again from Porteus's pen that we learn how Wilberforce proceeded to implement his plan. "Mr. Wilberforce . . . took a very active part in this business, and pursued it with indefatigability and perseverance, made private application to such of his friends of the Nobility and other men of consequence."[17]

Wilberforce's biographer, John Pollock, continues the narrative: "Wilberforce secured the entire approbation of Pitt and the Archbishop . . . and communicated the Plan to Queen Charlotte."[18] This plan succeeded admirably, and on May 29, 1787, Wilberforce was able to report to William Hey:

> I trust in a very few days you will hear of a Proclamation being issued for the discouragement of vice, of letters being written by the secretaries of state to the lords-lieutenant, expressing his Majesty's pleasure, that they recommend it to the justices throughout their several counties to be active in the execution of the laws against immoralities, and of a society's being formed in London for the purpose of carrying into effect his Majesty's good and gracious intentions. I have been some time at work, the matter is now I hope brought to a crisis; and the persons with whom I have concerted my measures, are so trusty, temperate, and unobnoxious, that I think I am not indulging a vain expectation in persuading myself that something considerable may be done.
>
> It would give you no little pleasure, could you hear how warmly the Archbishop of Canterbury expresses himself. . . . The interest he takes in the good work does him great credit, and he assures me that one still greater [George III], to whom he has opened the subject in form, and suggested the measures above mentioned, is deeply impressed.[19]

16. Porteus MS (Lambeth) 2013.8, housed in the Bodleian Library, Oxford University.

17. Quoted in Robin Furneaux, *William Wilberforce* (London: Hamish Hamilton, 1974), p. 57.

18. John C. Pollock, *Wilberforce,* p. 59.

19. Quoted in R. I. and S. Wilberforce, *The Life of William Wilberforce,* vol. 1, pp. 132-33.

George III in the years ahead did develop a keen appreciation for Wilberforce's reforming endeavors. "He is a good man," the King later declared, "a good man; I wish they were all like him."[20]

Concluding the narrative, Pollock writes:

> On June 1, 1787 George III gazetted *a Proclamation for the Encouragement of Piety and Virtue*. . . . Few who read it in the newspapers or on walls knew that the moving spirit was Wilberforce the twenty-seven-year-old Member for Yorkshire, without rank or office, but determined to change the moral climate of the age, no less, and thus to reduce serious crime: his motive was humane, not repressive.[21]

"Men of authority and influence may promote the cause of good morals," Wilberforce later wrote.

> Let them in their several stations encourage virtue and discountenance vice in others. Let them enforce the laws by which the wisdom of our forefathers has guarded against the grosser infractions of morals. . . . Let them favour and take part in any plans which may be formed for the advancement of morality. Above all things, let them endeavour to instruct and improve the rising generation.[22]

Looking back on this period and all that followed during the ensuing thirty-four years, Wilberforce wrote in November of 1821:

> It pleased God to diffuse a spirit . . . which began to display its love of God and love of man by the formation of societies of a religious and moral nature, which have already contributed in no small degree to bless almost all nations. . . . The blessings of religious light and of moral improvement have resulted in the growing attention to the education of our people, with societies and institutions for relieving every species of suffering which vice and misery can ever produce among the human race.[23]

As with so many whose lives were transformed during the great evangelical movement that commenced in Britain and America under the Wesleys,

20. Kevin C. Belmonte, ed., *Choice Treasures: A Wilberforce Anthology* (Boston: Riven Oak Press, 1999), p. 25.

21. Pollock, *Wilberforce,* p. 61.

22. Quoted in Wilberforce, *A Practical View of Christianity,* p. 215.

23. In A. M. Wilberforce, ed., *The Private Papers of William Wilberforce* (London: T. Fisher Unwin, 1897), p. 75.

George Whitefield, and the ministry of Jonathan Edwards, Wilberforce's heart was affected first, but this change of heart quickly manifested itself in countless acts of philanthropy. When his list of achievements are borne in mind, his "great change" was perhaps the most significant conversion of the last twenty-five years of the eighteenth century. Wilberforce's reforming endeavors, orchestrated to a large extent through voluntary societies, sought to promote the good society in virtually every aspect of Britain's national life.

Wilberforce's work with and through these voluntary societies anticipates the work of the numerous faith-based charitable organizations that have attracted the notice and admiration of many serving in political life today. Indeed, in some instances (among them Charles Colson's Prison Fellowship), Wilberforce's legacy has afforded the model and inspiration.

Practical Christianity

In the spring of 1797 a dying Edmund Burke derived great comfort from having a friend read to him from a newly published book by Wilberforce, who was an old friend and parliamentary colleague. The book was called *A Practical View of Christianity.* "If I live," Burke said, "I shall thank Wilberforce for sending such a book into the world."[24]

This was a seminal event in history — one that marked the literary convergence of two great reforming minds and saw the mantle of Burke fall upon Wilberforce in a very real way. Earlier, Burke had looked with dismay across the English Channel and seen the French Revolution, as he had predicted it would, degenerate into tyranny and terror. Fearful of such radical cultural decay, he penned his classic *Reflections on the Revolution in France* (1790), a book which was an impassioned plea for cultural renewal rooted in his love of Christianity and Europe's moral tradition. Upon the publication of Burke's *Reflections* Wilberforce read and re-read it, even discussing it on one occasion with a group of friends that included Prime Minister William Pitt, Lord Grenville, and Henry Dundas.

By 1797, Burke and Wilberforce had been friends for many years, and had for a long time made a point of dining together with mutual friends on a semi-regular basis. The two men had much in common. Their devotion to the abolition of the slave trade was one shared ambition. Both had a reverence for Christianity and history, as well as a profound belief in the importance of morality to the welfare of any society. Both were convinced that the sad events in France had resulted in large measure from the rejection of such beliefs. Thus, the pub-

24. Quoted in Robin Furneaux, *William Wilberforce,* p. 152.

lication of Wilberforce's *A Practical View of Christianity* marked the appearance of a book very much in the tradition of Burke's *Reflections. A Practical View,* however, greatly extended Burke's contention that Christianity could play a decisive role in strengthening the moral fabric of a society. What Burke had made a statement of broad principle, Wilberforce set forth in very explicit terms: the Judeo-Christian basis for efforts to promote cultural renewal.

A Practical View was both a blueprint and an apologia for cultural renewal. By 1797, Wilberforce had already been engaged in the work of reform for ten years. During the next thirty-six, he led or collaborated with scores of voluntary societies. The list of these would fill several pages, and focusing on a few of the more important ones will serve our purpose here.

Two organizations merit special emphasis: the British Institution and the Bettering Society. The British Institution was dedicated to "diffusing the knowledge and facilitating the general introduction of useful mechanical inventions and improvements; and for teaching . . . the application of science to the common purposes of life."[25] Wilberforce's involvement in the founding of the British Institution was a direct result of his work in establishing the Bettering Society for the Poor, an organization he helped to found in 1796. Like his Bettering Society colleagues, he believed scientific advancements could improve the lives of his fellow Britons, especially the poor.[26]

The British Institution's most important and enduring claims to fame rest in the many schemes for scientific research it sponsored. Under its auspices, Humphrey Davy was able to perfect his safety lamp and Michael Faraday to discover electromagnetism. Wilberforce's involvement with the work of the British Institution thus stands as a shining example of the good that can result when science is made to serve the purposes of philanthropy.

At the heart of Wilberforce's interest in science was his belief that religion was not "an enemy to the pursuits . . . of learning and of science." He believed scientific inquiry could be a God-honoring pursuit, and maintained that for Christians actuated by the desire "to please God in all . . . thoughts, and words, and actions . . . no calling is proscribed, no pursuit is forbidden, [there is] no science or art . . . which is not reconcilable with this principle."[27]

The story of Wilberforce's involvement in the founding of the Bettering Society is a fascinating one. Four days before Christmas 1796 several reformers met at Wilberforce's home to found the organization, dubbed The Society for Bettering the Condition and Increasing the Comforts of the Poor. The Bettering Society conducted scientific investigations into the problems of pov-

25. Pollock, *Wilberforce,* p. 142.
26. Pollock, *Wilberforce,* p. 141.
27. Quoted in Wilberforce, *A Practical View of Christianity,* p. 202.

erty, and circulated information that could foster relief and improvements in living conditions. One of its most important achievements took place in 1802 when Wilberforce joined forces with Bettering Society vice-president Sir Robert Peel (father of the future Prime Minister) to secure successful passage of the first Factory Act, which limited the excessive working hours and sought to improve the working conditions of Poor-Law apprentice children employed in cotton mills.[28]

In April of 1796, Wilberforce joined hands with Prime Minister Pitt's brother-in-law (E. J. Eliot), Bishop Barrington of Durham, and others in a subscription effort aimed at presenting the parish of St. Marylebone with a soup kitchen. This kitchen had been devised by another loyalist New Englander, Sir Benjamin Thompson, Count Rumford. Oddly, the parish refused the gift. When wartime conditions worsened (Britain was at this time at war with Napoleon's France), Wilberforce and his friends persevered and established what they called "Rumford Eating Houses."[29]

Believing charity for the poor should not be confined to one's home country, Wilberforce was a vice-president of The Friends of Foreigners in Distress, an organization whose distinguished members included a Wilberforce friend who was not a Tory loyalist, John Quincy Adams.[30] Adams greatly respected Wilberforce and was grateful for "opportunities of consulting with him . . . upon subjects so interesting to humanity as those upon which his exertions have been so long and so earnestly employed."[31] The day after voicing this sentiment to Wilberforce in a letter, Adams wrote in his diary: "Wilberforce is one of the party called in derision the Saints, and who under sanctified visors pursue worldly objects with the ardor and perseverance of saints. Wilberforce is at the head of these Saints in Parliament, and is said to possess more personal influence in the House of Commons than any other individual."

The provision of food for the poor was another of Wilberforce's passionate interests. There were many food scarcities throughout his forty-four-year tenure in parliament (1780-1825), and he was very active in relief efforts aimed at ending them. He was particularly concerned for the poor, since food shortages and subsequent price increases hit them hardest.

To this end, he engaged in an important collaboration with the leading agriculturist of the day, Arthur Young (1741-1820). Wilberforce and Young commenced their work together following Young's conversion to evangelical

28. Pollock, *Wilberforce,* p. 142.

29. James Baker, *The Life of Sir Thomas Bernard, Baronet* (London: J. Murray, 1819), p. 13.

30. Brown, *Fathers of the Victorians,* p. 344.

31. This citation from Adams's letter to Wilberforce for 5 June 1817 is taken from the collection of the Adams Family Papers housed at the Massachusetts Historical Society.

Christianity, in which Wilberforce had been instrumental. Following his conversion, Young resolved to do something for the agricultural poor, a matter about which Wilberforce was already "truly and deeply (and every hour more and more) interested."[32]

Circumstances prompted their coming together during the so-called Great Hunger of 1799-1800. Wilberforce was a member of the parliamentary Committee on How to Offset the Scarcity of Grain, or Scarcity Committee, and throughout the period it met he frequently consulted Young. Together they developed a scheme to provide a cheap source of food through the cultivation of potatoes. Unfortunately their plan met with opposition from country gentlemen and landlords who were loath to provide the necessary land. Despite this the Scarcity Committee included their plan among the recommendations finally submitted for implementation. Given the terrible potato famines of the nineteenth century it was probably just as well this plan did not succeed.

Biographer John Pollock reports that much of Wilberforce's power as a philanthropist stemmed from the regularity of his attendance in the House of Commons — this at a time when its chamber was seldom filled. Unless sick, or obliged to be more than twenty miles from London, he was always in his place on the parliamentary benches or seated at a committee table. Because of his faithfulness in this regard, he was able to intervene many times on behalf of the poor when he might otherwise not have been able to do so.[33]

Wilberforce's sons, Robert and Samuel, chronicled their father's private philanthropies on behalf of the poor in their five-volume *The Life of William Wilberforce.* Their list of their father's annual philanthropic subscriptions contains the name of nearly every charitable institution in London and Yorkshire. He also supported a number of individuals, often anonymously. Many of them, his sons assert, "afterwards acquired independence and wealth and were indebted to his support for carrying them through their early struggles."[34] In addition, many young men of promise who were preparing to take Holy Orders received financial support from Wilberforce. Students preparing for other careers received his patronage as well.

Wilberforce's political work had moral power due to his determination to designate a set amount of his annual income for charitable giving. In order to make this amount as high as possible, Wilberforce exercised "self-denial in small things."[35] His sons state that, before his marriage, he was able to give at least one-fourth of his annual income to charitable organizations. Using an in-

32. British Museum Add MSS, 35128.286, Young Papers, Wilberforce to A. Young, n.d.

33. Pollock, *Wilberforce,* p. 142.

34. R. I. and S. Wilberforce, *The Life of William Wilberforce,* vol. 2, p. 305.

35. R. I. and S. Wilberforce, *The Life of William Wilberforce,* vol. 2, p. 303.

complete record for one year during this period (from 1785-1797), they report that £2,000, about £100,000 now, was set aside by their father for charitable purposes.

Wilberforce was devoted to the idea that charity begins in (or near) the home. To one relative, he wrote:

> Never distress yourself, my dear Mary . . . on the ground of my being put to expense on account of yourself, or your near relatives; you give what is more valuable than money — time, thought, serious, active, persevering attention; and as it has pleased God of his good providence to bless me with affluence, and to give me the power, and I hope the heart, to assist those who are less gifted with the good things of this life, how can I employ them more properly than on near relations, and when I strengthen your hands. . . . I am willing to take charge of Charles' education for two or three years.[36]

Wilberforce often gave sums to active clergymen for the purpose of parochial distribution. He visited prisons in London and relieved the financial distress of people imprisoned for debt. Sometimes, members of his family would accompany him to visit prisons. In 1818, his wife and some other friends went with him to hear the prison reformer Elizabeth Fry read from the Bible to female prisoners at Newgate.

On one remarkable occasion, Wilberforce's philanthropy resulted in a victory at sea. Sir Sidney Smith, aware of an officer who was under a heavy burden of debt, spoke to Wilberforce on the young man's behalf. "You know, Wilberforce," Smith stated, "we officers are pinched sometimes, and my charity purse is not very full." "Leave that to me, Sir Sidney," Wilberforce replied. The officer's debt was paid, he was outfitted, and a command was obtained for him. At a later time, this officer engaged an enemy ship, captured it, and was given a promotion. When he returned home, the young officer called on Wilberforce in the uniform of a post captain to thank him.[37]

Wilberforce remained dedicated throughout his political career to education for the poor. He took particular interest and pleasure in educational schemes for indigent or friendless boys who were the sons of dead or ruined clergymen or military officers. One young man whom he aided, Gordon Smith, later became an army doctor. He also founded schools and institutions for the education of the deaf and blind.[38]

36. Cited in R. I. and S. Wilberforce, *The Life of William Wilberforce,* vol. 2, p. 302.
37. R. I. and S. Wilberforce, *The Life of William Wilberforce,* vol. 2, p. 307.
38. Pollock, *Wilberforce,* p. 140.

"Assistance to young men of promise had always been with him a favourite charity," wrote Wilberforce's sons,

> but . . . he gave more than merely money; he made his house the home of one or two youths, the expense of whose education he defrayed; all their holidays were spent with him; and hours of his own time were profusely given to training and furnishing their minds. Nor were the poor forgotten; they were invited to join in his family worship on the Sunday evening, and sought out often in their cottages for instruction and relief.[39]

Wilberforce took a lively interest in the Elland Society, donating £100 per year to it, with the proviso that "my name must not be mentioned." This society, run by his friend Dr. William Hey, was devoted to "catching the colts running wild on Halifax Moor, and cutting their manes and tails, and sending them to college." In addition to this, he often took these young men to his home to arrange for their distribution in proper situations. Pollock reports that Wilberforce took pains to personally place young men under tutors until they were ready for college. He then monitored their progress until they were placed in a curacy, at times sorting out any difficulties between a curate and vicar. He believed that funds spent training clergymen would help to spread the gospel but also aid the poor, since in his mind "such men will always be advocates for them."[40]

"No one," wrote Wilberforce's sons, "ever entered more readily into sterling merit." "We have different forms," Wilberforce said, "assigned to us in the school of life — different gifts imparted. All is not attractive that is good. Iron is useful, though it does not sparkle like the diamond. Gold has not the fragrance of a flower. So different persons have various modes of excellence, and we must have an eye to all."[41]

What then is the essence of Wilberforce's legacy as a reformer? To be sure, his Christian faith commitment translated into scores of philanthropic endeavors that were driven by the engine of voluntary societies. His tireless efforts to secure the abolition of the slave trade and later slavery itself throughout Britain's colonies justly earned him the title of Britain's Great Emancipator. The reasons why he merits being thought of as the greatest reformer of the last five hundred years, however, extend beyond those already stated. The most important aspect of his legacy concerns the power of his moral example. This example, to paraphrase his epitaph in Westminster Abbey, composed by a young

39. R. I. and S. Wilberforce, *The Life of William Wilberforce,* vol. 5, pp. 298-99.

40. Pollock, *Wilberforce,* p. 140.

41. Quoted in R. I. and S. Wilberforce, *The Life of William Wilberforce,* vols. 1-2.

Thomas Babington Macaulay, attests the abiding eloquence of moral life. He touched the hearts and mind of his contemporaries in profound ways. At times he did so individually, as with the Emperor Alexander of Russia or the young men of humble means whose education he supervised late in his life. On other occasions, his moral example had a profound impact on groups of people, as through the writing of *A Practical View of Christianity.*

The lasting significance of Wilberforce's success can be stated in one phrase: he made goodness fashionable. This phrase does not capture the whole story of the reforms that did so much to change British society, however. Wilberforce was profoundly aware that true lasting reform took place in the hearts and minds of individuals, one person at a time. Each of these persons then became agents of change and renewal in their own right. Wherever they found themselves within society — rich, poor, or middle class — and with whatever gifts or talents they had been given, they could and should unite their energies with those of their fellow citizens and follow through on their duty to work toward making the good society. The change in individual hearts and minds was what created the underlying and indispensable moral consensus that informed such a duty.

Pollock has written that Wilberforce's life is proof that a man can change his times, though he cannot do so alone.[42] That observation neatly encapsulates Wilberforce's own beliefs — encapsulates, indeed, his brief but eloquent articulation of the good society:

> If any country were indeed filled with men, each thus diligently discharging the duties of his own station without breaking in upon the rights of others, but on the contrary endeavoring, so far as he might be able, to forward their views and promote their happiness, all would be active and harmonious in the goodly frame of human society. There would be no jarrings, no discord. The whole machine of civil life would work without obstruction or disorder, and the course of its movements would be like the harmony of the heavenly spheres.[43]

It was to this vision that Wilberforce dedicated his life and labors. "Let reform take place in my country, and let it begin with me," is the essence of this citation. Acting in concert with his fellow citizens, whom he urged to join with him, Wilberforce believed that he could do much to bring about the good society.

42. See John C. Pollock, "The Little Abolitionist, William Wilberforce," *Christianity Today,* 21 April 1978, p. 23.

43. Wilberforce, *A Practical View of Christianity,* p. 203.

Four central ideals are set forth in this passage: stewardship, respect for the rights of others (a key concept for a pluralistic society), forwarding the views of others, and the promotion of the happiness of others. It should be remembered that these ideals were not utopian flights of fancy; they produced tangible results and ultimately produced the rich legacy of moral renewal and philanthropy associated with Wilberforce's name. Each of these four ideals is a foundational pillar of Wilberforcian political thought. By themselves they are potent agents of a social ethic, but taken together they achieve the greatest good.

What did stewardship, as defined by Wilberforce, mean? He believed each person was endowed by the Almighty with "means and occasions . . . of improving ourselves, or of promoting the happiness of others." To whom much was given, he believed, much was also required. He concluded: "when summoned to give an account of our stewardship, we shall be called upon to answer for the use we have made . . . of the means of relieving the wants and necessities of our fellow-creatures."[44] It was, then, a sacred duty to use the gift of life well, striving to improve oneself and promote the happiness of others.

For Wilberforce, respect for the rights of others meant the application of the golden rule to every area of life. It informed his abolitionist labor and every other human rights and philanthropic issue with which he was involved. As he wrote: "Let every one . . . regulate his conduct . . . by the golden rule of doing to others as in similar circumstances we would have them do to us; and the path of duty will be clear before him, and I will add, the decision of a legislature would scarcely any longer be doubtful."[45] The golden rule was directly linked to the third of Wilberforce's ideals: forwarding the views of others. In the case of abolition, he defended the human rights of those who had no voice in the British legislature. In his abolitionist writings, he stated directly that it was the golden rule that informed his opposition to the slave trade.

> As to the arguments in favour of the slave trade, deduced from the Holy Scriptures, I am not much disposed to enter into a discussion of them, because I can scarcely believe they are urged seriously. . . . He who can justify the slave trade from the practice of Joseph, might justify concubinage and capricious divorces from that of the patriarchs. With regard to the passages referred to in the New Testament, our blessed Saviour's grand practical rule, of doing to others as we would have them do to us, as it is

44. Wilberforce, *A Practical View of Christianity,* p. 5.

45. William Wilberforce, "The Duty of Great Britain to Disseminate Christianity in India," *The Christian Observer* (May 1812 issue), no. 125, pp. 261-72 of the hardbound edition for the year 1812. Wilberforce wrote this article under the pen name "A Christian."

the shortest, so it is perhaps the best refutation of all such laborious sophistry.[46]

Of these four Wilberforcian ideals, the promotion of the happiness of others is in some respects the most striking one. It neatly turns the Jeffersonian "pursuit of happiness" by each individual for him or herself on its head. Wilberforce is saying that it is when individual citizens promote the happiness of others that they are most truly promoting or pursuing their own. Every individual becomes a powerful agent of social change in this sense, and the power for positive social change is multiplied to the extent that more people pursue, or, more properly, promote, the happiness of others. This fourth ideal is a ringing affirmation of our common humanity and of the ties that bind us together as fellow citizens.

Wilberforce is not saying the individual pursuit of happiness in the Jeffersonian sense is wrong. As indicated above, he readily acknowledged the importance of improving ourselves, which is a pursuit of one's own happiness. He is saying that when it comes to promoting the good society, there should be more to achieving true happiness than the Jeffersonian model affords. In doing so, Wilberforce made an original, uniquely Judeo-Christian, and sadly overlooked contribution to Anglo-American political thought.

The political model bequeathed to us by Wilberforce has additional and important implications for political engagement in modern America. Cultural analyst Don Eberly, reflecting on Wilberforce's public philosophy, has isolated eight of its key components.[47]

- An acknowledgment of the limits of the law absent the reform of manners and morals. The placing of as much priority on changing hearts and minds as on changing laws.
- A recognition of the subordinate relationship of politics to the culture of a nation.
- The organization of grassroots and gatekeeper reform movements operating in elite professions and fields.
- A recognition of the need to transcend ideology to enlist anyone useful on a particular issue, whatever his religious or political creed.

46. See page 223 of Wilberforce's review of the book *A Defense of the Slave Trade, on the Grounds of Humanity, Policy, and Justice,* which originally appeared in the *Edinburgh Review* for October 1804, Issue No. 9. See also R. I. and S. Wilberforce, *The Life of William Wilberforce,* vol 3., p. 194.

47. This list has been distilled from two sources by Don Eberly: *Restoring the Good Society: A New Vision for Politics and Culture* (Grand Rapids: Baker, 1994), and "We're Fighting the Wrong Battle," *Christianity Today,* 6 September 1999, pp. 52-54.

- An understanding that in the past, citizens have reacted to the general disregard for social standards and obligations by organizing society-wide social movements which effectively moved people toward restraint and social obligation.
- A recognition that national character merely reflects individual character — that public policy and personal policy are inseparable.
- A natural skepticism about the reforming possibilities of politics, placing primary emphasis instead on the long-term cultivation of character, culture, and community. A view of politics as downstream from culture, more reflecting it than shaping it.
- A belief that those called to political life are called to serve not in a predominantly Christian nation, but in one that more closely resembles the conditions Paul encountered in Athens. (Paul invoked the literature and philosophy of the times to make his point without imagining a large sympathetic majority standing behind him. Wilberforce wrote and spoke so as to create a broad consensus on the issues of his day. In the modern context, this enables a politician to speak most meaningfully to the diversity of worldviews within a pluralistic society.)

Each of these components of the Wilberforcian model of political engagement has a corollary in his writings or the practices he employed throughout his political career. The first and second of these components, in Wilberforce's mind, were closely linked. He acknowledged the limits of the law absent the reform of manners and morals, and at the same time recognized the subordinate relationship of politics to the culture and moral fabric of a nation. "Why do we make laws to punish men?" Wilberforce wrote. "It is their interest to be upright and virtuous without these laws: but there is a present impulse continually breaking in upon their better judgment; an impulse contrary to their permanent and known interest, which it is not even in the power of all our laws sufficiently to refrain."[48] He also asserted: "The maladies of a state, however they may break out in political effects, will generally be found to arise from moral causes. It is only therefore by carefully studying those causes, that we can hope to detect the true nature of the diseases which afflict the political body, and consequently how best to produce a cure."[49] Thus, in the Wilberforcian paradigm, moral renewal and its kindred form of renewal, cultural renewal, are the first things necessary to perpetuate "the goodly frame of human society." Wilberforce did succeed in securing the abolition of the slave trade, but he did so realizing that without widespread moral reformation that incorporated a

48. Wilberforce, *Choice Treasures,* p. 70.
49. Wilberforce, *Choice Treasures,* p. 59.

sustained public campaign of moral engagement and persuasion, he could not succeed. In other words, laws only go so far. Moral consensus can and should inform the laws of a nation. Likewise, a strong national moral fabric is the best guarantee of the rule of law.

As Eberly noted in his third point, grassroots and gatekeeper reform movements were essential to Wilberforce's public philosophy, and Wilberforce himself was adept at leading initiatives to organize them. When it came to the fight to secure the abolition of the slave trade, Wilberforce circulated petitions and organized county meetings. He did so because of the apathy that prevailed about abolition in the House of Commons. As his sons phrased it, there was an "extremely low ebb of real principle there." Wilberforce believed that "It is on the general impression and feeling of the nation we must rely, rather than on the political conscience of the House of Commons. So let the flame be fanned continually, and may it please God, in whose hands are the hearts of all men, to bless our endeavours."[50]

The genesis of the Society for the Reformation of Manners, described earlier, attests Wilberforce's ability to orchestrate gatekeeper reform movements. Seeking to make goodness fashionable, he sought the concurrence of the leading men in church and state for his plan, namely the Archbishop of Canterbury and Prime Minister Pitt. Their assent was instrumental in securing the approval of George III, and Wilberforce was also successful in obtaining the approval of important members of the nobility, clergy, and gentry in greater London and throughout Britain.

Eberly discerned correctly in Wilberforce's career a willingness to transcend ideology and enlist the help of anyone, regardless of religious or political creed. "Measures, not men," was one of his favorite sayings.[51] Acting on this belief, Wilberforce lent ardent and long-term support to the panopticon prison reform plan of Jeremy Bentham. Bentham's utilitarian philosophy was quite different from Wilberforce's Christian perspective, but it did not preclude the possibility of collaboration or mutual respect. In fact, Bentham's respect for Wilberforce was such that he dedicated an early draft of his *Essays on the Poor Laws* to him.

Wilberforce's career further attests his ability to learn from social movements that had been organized in the past in response to a disregard for social standards and obligations; these initiatives had moved people toward restraint and social obligation, and Wilberforce kept them in mind as he sought his own reforms. His adaptation of the reformation of manners paradigm from 1690s Britain is the prime example of this. As we saw earlier, this component of the

50. R. I. and S. Wilberforce, *The Life of William Wilberforce,* vol. 1, p. 334.
51. R. I. and S. Wilberforce, *The Life of William Wilberforce,* vol. 3, pp. 320.

Wilberforcian model for political engagement was also adopted early in American history by reformers such as Lyman Beecher, who was directly influenced by the example set by Wilberforce and the reformers of the 1690s.

Strange as it might seem, Wilberforce had a natural skepticism about the reforming possibilities of politics. The long-term cultivation of character, he believed, was productive of more sure benefits to society. "The political good we can do is often too small and even doubtful," he asserted. "How often does it happen, that two men, equally wise and well intentioned, recommend two different or even opposite lines of political conduct? Not so in morals. There, happily, as the path leads to superior benefits, so it is far more easily to be ascertained."[52] In this respect, he supported the view of politics as downstream from culture, more reflecting it than shaping it.

Finally, Wilberforce was able to serve effectively in a political climate deeply skeptical about and often hostile to the evangelical Christianity that he espoused. As the apostle Paul did in Athens, Wilberforce invoked the literature and philosophy of the time to make his points. This was a great aid, for example, to his desire to generate recognition and support for the vital role that religion and morality can and should play in society. "The legislators of antiquity," Wilberforce once stated, "made it . . . their deepest study, and primary aim, to preserve from deterioration the public morals."[53] To support this contention he cited, at various times throughout his years in politics, classical and political theorists commonly cited in his day, including Cicero, Locke, Machiavelli, and Montesquieu.

Two citations best express this aspect of Wilberforce's political apologetic. "It is a truth attested by the history of all ages and countries," he wrote, "and established on the authority of all the ablest writers, both ancient and modern, among them Machiavelli and Montesquieu . . . that the religion and morality of a country, especially of every free community, are inseparably connected with its preservation and welfare; that their flourishing or declining state is the sure indication of its tending to prosperity or decay. It has even been expressly laid down, that a people grossly corrupt are incapable of liberty." On another occasion he maintained: "Machiavelli was not considered either as a religious or moral authority, but . . . was eminently distinguished for political knowledge and sagacity. He stated, that 'the rulers of all states, whether kingdoms or common-wealths, should take care that religion should be honoured, and all its ceremonies preserved inviolate, for there was not a more certain symptom of the destruction of states, than a contempt for religion and morals.'"[54]

52. Wilberforce, *Choice Treasures,* p. 30.
53. Wilberforce, *Choice Treasures,* p. 88.
54. Wilberforce, *Choice Treasures,* p. 6.

Conclusion

Though one should not forget the power of Wilberforce's personal moral example and philanthropies, it should also be remembered that he was but one of a vanguard of men and women from all corners of British society that desired and labored diligently to promote moral renewal. In his most reforming labors, Wilberforce acted in concert with the members of the Clapham circle, a brilliant group of men and women who lived and worked together in the village of Clapham in Surrey. Started rather modestly by Wilberforce and his second cousin Henry Thornton in 1792, the work of the Clapham circle continued until Wilberforce's death in 1833.

It was a brilliant circle, counting among its members poet, playwright, and educational reformer Hannah More; abolitionist pioneer Granville Sharp; the gifted lawyer James Stephen; and Zachary Macaulay, father of writer and historian Thomas Babington Macaulay. All had embraced the life-changing faith that had transformed Wilberforce's own life, and sought to love God and promote the happiness of their fellow-creatures as he did. Together these talented men and women constituted a cabinet of philanthropists, led by Wilberforce.

Lyman Beecher's comments regarding Wilberforce and the Clapham circle were cited earlier, but they bear repeating here because Beecher understood so well the elements that led to the great achievements of Wilberforce and his fellow philanthropists — elements that he sought to carry forward in his own work of promoting moral renewal in America.

> The abolition of the Slave Trade in England, and in our own country, is a memorable exhibition of what may be done by well directed, persevering efforts. The inhuman traffic was sanctioned by custom, defended by argument, and still more powerfully, by a vast monied capital, embarked in the trade. It is not yet fifty years, since this first effort was made, and now the victory is won. Who produced this mighty revolution? A few men at first, lifted up their voice and were reinforced by others, till the immortal work was done.

First, Beecher draws attention to the "memorable exhibition of what may be done by well directed, persevering efforts." This is to say that the work of moral renewal, much like fighting a great moral injustice, takes time. The work of abolishing the slave trade, as Beecher points out, took fifty years. In the case of slavery itself, Wilberforce's first inquiries into the human rights abuses associated with it took place in 1780. It was not until 1833, three days before he died, that he learned that slavery was finally going to be abolished by the British Parliament.

Wilberforce commenced the work of promoting moral renewal in 1787. In 1837, four years after he died, Queen Victoria assumed the throne, commencing the era of modern history most associated with moral probity and philanthropy. That the Victorian era was such a time was due in large part to Wilberforce and those who worked together with him. Still, the work took fifty years, two generations, to fully take root in British national life.

Beecher's assertion regarding the "mighty revolution" that was the abolition of the slave trade can be applied with equal accuracy to the work of moral reformation that informed the abolitionist labors. "Who produced this mighty revolution?" Beecher asked. "A few men at first, lifted up their voice and were reinforced by others, till the immortal work was done."

The work of promoting moral renewal is time-intensive. If this sounds discouraging, consider how long the Victorian era endured. Because Wilberforce and his contemporaries labored long and built a solid foundation for moral renewal, the societal benefits continued for many years after their deaths. It may be sobering to reflect that moral renewal is best conducted on a generational timetable. But how else, really, is it to be accomplished?

Wilberforce understood this well. "Men of authority and influence may promote the cause of good morals," he wrote. "Let them in their several stations encourage virtue and discountenance vice in others. Let them enforce the laws by which the wisdom of our forefathers has guarded against the grosser infractions of morals. . . . Let them favour and take part in any plans which may be formed for the advancement of morality. *Above all things, let them endeavour to instruct and improve the rising generation.*"[55]

The work of promoting moral renewal is more properly viewed as a work of preserving, strengthening, and perpetuating a nation's moral consensus. This work should, in this sense, never stop. It has been said that the price of freedom is eternal vigilance; Wilberforce's legacy reminds us that the perpetuation of a moral society requires eternal diligence on the part of the men and women who wish their children to inherit that society.

55. Wilberforce, *A Practical View of Christianity,* p. 215 (italics added).

Nineteenth-Century America

JOHN G. WEST JR.

To American evangelicals, the new century seemed anything but hospitable.[1] Many Americans had stopped going to church. Some openly doubted Christianity, preferring to place their hopes in reason alone rather in than a God who intervenes in human affairs. The nation's cities were turning into havens of crime, promiscuity, and alcoholism. Radical social reformers dotted the landscape, attracting enthusiastic interest, if not outright support. One of the more provocative of the radicals proposed a "Declaration of Mental Independence" denouncing private property, traditional religion, and marriage as *"a trinity of the most monstrous evils that could be combined to inflict mental and physical evil upon man's whole race."*[2]

Even in politics, traditional religion and morality were flouted. Thomas

1. This essay uses "evangelical" in the sense in which it was employed during the period under study. In the 1800s, the term applied to any Protestant group that adhered to traditional Christian doctrines such as the Trinity, salvation by grace, personal sanctification, and the atoning death and bodily resurrection of Christ. The term was not confined to religious groups typified by enthusiasm, populism, and revivalism. Hence, in the nineteenth century, Presbyterians and Episcopalians were regarded as evangelicals just as much as Methodists and Baptists. Non-evangelical groups included Unitarians and Roman Catholics. See Robert Baird, *Religion in America; or An account of the Origin, Relation to the State, and Present Condition of the Evangelical Churches in the United States, with Notices of the Unevangelical Denominations* (New York: Harper and Brothers, 1856), pp. 438-539, 665.

2. Robert Owen, "Oration, Containing a *Declaration of Mental Independence*," in *Robert Owen in the United States,* ed. Oakley C. Johnson (New York: Humanities Press, 1970), p. 70, emphasis in original.

Jefferson, one of the era's most influential presidents, scoffed in private at the miracles of the Bible and historic Christian doctrines such as the Trinity.[3] Another popular chief executive, Andrew Jackson, was the only president in American history who had killed another man in a duel.[4] Yet voters didn't seem to care.

In many ways, the culture wars of America in the early 1800s seem eerily similar to some of the cultural conflicts in America today. Yet most historians wouldn't describe nineteenth-century America as especially secular or amoral. If anything, the period is often held up as the epitome of a Christian America — when Christianity, or at least the Protestant variety of Christianity — was the dominant religion of the state, and when biblical ethics supplied the basis for social relations. Moreover, no criminologist would describe the nineteenth century, at least the second half of it, as awash in crime. In fact, lawlessness went down in the latter half of the nineteenth century — despite urbanization, industrialization, and other factors typically associated with increased crime rates.[5]

What is going on here? Both depictions of nineteenth-century America can't be true. Or can they?

As it turns out, the first part of the nineteenth century *was* a time of remarkable spiritual, moral, and civic instability in America. But out of that instability came a social transformation that provides valuable lessons about both the dangers and opportunities for social change inspired by religious activism. What happened in early nineteenth-century America is commonly known as the Second Great Awakening, which refers to a series of evangelical revivals that started in the northeast but ultimately spread to the western frontier.[6] And

3. For a discussion of Jefferson's religious beliefs, see John G. West Jr., *The Politics of Revelation and Reason: Religion and Civic Life in the New Nation* (Lawrence, Kans.: University Press of Kansas, 1996), pp. 56-67, 79-80.

4. See Don C. Setz, *Famous American Duels* (New York: Thomas Crowell, 1929).

5. James Q. Wilson and Richard J. Herrnstein, *Crime and Human Nature* (New York: Simon and Schuster, 1985), p. 434.

6. For coverage and discussion of the Second Great Awakening and its various revivals, see Nelson R. Burr, *A Critical Bibliography of Religion in America* (Princeton: Princeton University Press, 1961), IV: 155-56; John B. Boles, *The Great Revival, 1787-1805: The Origins of the Southern Evangelical Mind* (Lexington, Ky.: University Press of Kentucky, 1972); Whitney R. Cross, *The Burned-Over District: The Social and Intellectual History of Enthusiastic Religion in Western New York, 1800-1850* (New York: Harper Torchbooks, 1965); Garth M. Rosell, "Charles G. Finney: His Place in the Stream of American Evangelicalism," in *The Evangelical Tradition in America,* ed. Leonard I. Sweet (Macon, Ga.: Mercer University Press, 1984), pp. 131-47; Paul E. Johnson, *A Shopkeeper's Millennium: Society and Revivals in Rochester, New York, 1815-1837* (New York: Hill and Wang, 1978); Mary P. Ryan, *Cradle of the Middle Class: The Family in Oneida County, New York, 1790-1865* (New York: Cambridge University Press, 1981); William G. McLoughlin, *Modern Revivalism: Charles Grandison Finney to Billy Graham* (New York: Ronald Press, 1959); Timothy L. Smith, *Revivalism and Social Reform in Mid-Nineteenth Century America* (New York: Abingdon

these revivals tell only part of the story. They were paralleled by a mass infusion of evangelical Christians into the public arena, where they organized scores of voluntary associations to preach the gospel, diminish poverty, curb practices such as dueling, and reduce alcoholism.[7]

Visiting the United States during the early 1830s, Alexis de Tocqueville saw these efforts firsthand and later wrote that Americans were "forever forming associations."[8] The far-reaching network of voluntary associations established by evangelicals helped re-shape both the manners and the morals of American society before the Civil War and enthroned evangelical Protestantism as the de facto religion of American culture.[9] Three of the most influential reform efforts were Sunday schools, temperance societies, and anti-poverty programs.

Sunday Schools

During a time when public education was virtually nonexistent in many areas (particularly on the western frontier), Sunday schools formed the backbone of education in many communities, teaching both children and adults to read and instructing them in the principles of morality and religion. In 1828, an estimated 127,000 pupils attended Sunday classes; by 1835 that figure had expanded to one million. To accommodate such large numbers required an extensive infrastructure of 16,000 Sunday schools and more than 130,000 teachers, all of whom volunteered their time without remuneration. Some of the more prominent Sunday school teachers in antebellum America included President William Henry Harrison and U.S. Attorney General Benjamin Butler.[10] The vast majority of Sunday schools were affiliated with the American Sunday School Union, which spearheaded an aggressive program to spread the classes into new areas of the country and published vast quantities of reading material in the hope of reforming the character of American children's literature. By 1830, the Union

---

Press, 1957); Charles Roy Keller, *The Second Great Awakening in Connecticut* (Hamden, Conn.: Archon Books, 1968); Donald G. Mathews, *Religion in the Old South* (Chicago: University of Chicago Press, 1977). See also the final chapter in Alan Heimert, *Religion and the American Mind: From the Great Awakening to the Revolution* (Cambridge, Mass.: Harvard University Press, 1966), especially pp. 540-52.

7. See West, *Politics of Revelation and Reason*, ch. 2.

8. Alexis de Tocqueville, *Democracy in America*, ed. J. P. Mayer (Garden City, N.Y.: Doubleday, 1969), p. 513.

9. See charts in Roger Finke and Rodney Stark, *The Churching of America, 1776-1990: Winners and Losers in Our Religious Economy* (New Brunswick: Rutgers University Press, 1992), pp. 16, 55.

10. *First Report of the American Sunday School Union* (Philadelphia: I. Ashmead and Co., 1825), pp. 21-22; Baird, *Religion in America*, pp. 313-14.

had produced at least 250 separate works; 46 of these were released in 1829 alone, adding over six thousand pages of new reading material.[11]

Temperance Societies

By 1828, more than four hundred temperance societies had been established across the United States, including statewide societies in New Hampshire, Vermont, Pennsylvania, Virginia, and Illinois.[12] These societies sought to educate the public about the extent of the alcohol problem and to pressure retailers not to deal in alcoholic beverages. Sometimes pressure was exerted through a boycott of recalcitrant retailers. In other cases citizens urged elected officials to deny liquor licenses to retailers. The temperance society in North Stonington, Connecticut, employed the latter approach with considerable success. As a result of its efforts, only three of the town's eleven dealers in spirited liquors even sought renewal of their licenses, and none of the three that sought a new license succeeded in obtaining one. Many local societies pointed to significant drops in liquor consumption as proof of their effectiveness.[13]

Anti-poverty Programs

A number of local groups focused on helping and educating the poor, but these explicit efforts to help the hard-core poor were only a small part of the evangelical anti-poverty agenda.[14] More informally, workingmen who were drawn into

11. Baird, *Religion in America,* p. 314; *Sixth Report of the American Sunday-School Union* (Philadelphia, 1830), pp. 13-15; *Seventh Annual Report of the American Sunday School Union,* 2nd ed. (Philadelphia: American Sunday School Union, 1831), pp. 17-24.

12. E. C. Tracy, *Memoir of the Life of Jeremiah Evarts* (Boston: Crocker and Brewster, 1845), p. 75; Lyman Beecher, *The Autobiography of Lyman Beecher,* ed. Barbara M. Cross (Cambridge, Mass.: Belknap Press, 1961), I:179-84; II:22-25; Beecher, "Lectures on Intemperance," in *Works of Lyman Beecher* (Boston: Jewett, 1852), I:347-425; Anson Phelps Stokes, *Church and State in the United States* (New York: Harper and Brothers, 1950), II:40-41; *Second Annual Report of the Executive Committee of the American Society for the Promotion of Temperance* (Andover: Flagg and Gould, 1829), p. 9.

13. *Second Annual Report of the American Society for the Promotion of Temperance,* pp. 12, 15.

14. Charles Foster, *An Errand of Mercy: The Evangelical United Front, 1790-1837* (Chapel Hill, N.C.: University of North Carolina Press, 1960), pp. 275-79; Theodore Frelinghuysen, *Address Delivered . . . Before the Meeting of the Society for the Education of Poor and Indigent Children of the Parish of Orange* (Newark, N.J.: W. Tuttle and Co., 1827); Beecher, *Autobiography,* I:253-56.

evangelical churches found they now had access to a variety of resources that could help them improve their economic status, as a study of the revivals in Rochester has shown. Wealthy church members in Rochester organized a savings bank for the benefit of the working classes, and they provided capital for budding entrepreneurs among Christian workingmen by forming business partnerships with them.[15] As a result of these measures (and the personal discipline and industry instilled by evangelical theology), converts from the working classes experienced a profound upward mobility.[16] "Of the clerks who joined churches during the revivals and who remained in Rochester in 1837, 72 percent became merchants, professionals, or shopkeepers. Most non-churchgoing clerks left Rochester. Of those who stayed, half skidded into blue-collar jobs."[17] Similar efforts were made to assist poor women. Key associations in this area included New York's Association for the Relief of Respectable, Aged, Indigent Females (1814-), the Society for Employing the Female Poor in Cambridge, Massachusetts (1825-), and the Magdalen societies in both New York and Philadelphia which sought to rescue women from prostitution.[18] Female reform societies served as a kind of "informal employment agency" for needy young women. Wealthy female members of the societies sought to find positions for young girls in the households of their friends.[19]

Participation in evangelical voluntary associations reached phenomenal levels before the Civil War in major population centers such as New York City. By 1829, more than "40 percent of the children in New York City between the ages of four and fourteen were said to attend Sunday schools" and "by 1860 . . . nearly *half* of all adult Protestant males in the city were members of at least one church-related voluntary association."[20] The impact of this wave of reform efforts could also be seen in Americans' consumption of alcohol, which had risen dramatically early in the 1800s and had fostered brawling and other forms of civil disorder in America's cities. By 1850, after decades of temperance efforts, per capita consumption of alcohol in America had plummeted by 80 percent.[21]

Though far from perfect, evangelical reformers in the early 1800s were remarkably successful in bringing about cultural change, and their efforts offer several practical lessons for those seeking to revitalize American culture in the new millennium.

15. Johnson, *Shopkeeper's Millennium*, pp. 118, 124-25.
16. Johnson, *Shopkeeper's Millennium*, p. 123.
17. Johnson, *Shopkeeper's Millennium*, p. 123.
18. Foster, *Errand of Mercy*, pp. 188-89, 275-79.
19. Ryan, *Cradle of the Middle Class*, pp. 118-19.
20. Wilson and Herrnstein, *Crime and Human Nature*, p. 432; emphasis in the original.
21. Wilson and Herrnstein, *Crime and Human Nature*, p. 433.

Lesson 1: Use Private Associations to Provide Public Goods

The first lesson concerns the importance of using private associations to deliver public goods. Prior to the Second Great Awakening, many American evangelicals looked to government to promote both piety and morality. They thought that in order for religion to flourish, government had to promote it through public days of fasting and thanksgiving, strict laws against Sabbath-breaking, and the use of tax dollars to pay the salaries of ministers. Congregationalist evangelicals in New England were the fiercest supporters of the view that piety had to be promoted through law. They almost seemed to think that vibrant religion depended on government. Thomas Jefferson and his political party disagreed, and they advocated an end to state subsidies to churches. When the Jeffersonians began to triumph in state and local elections in New England, disestablishment — the ending of official government support for churches — finally came even to such Congregationalist bastions as Connecticut and New Hampshire in 1818 and 1819.

Congregationalist evangelicals first thought disestablishment was the end of the world. The Reverend Lyman Beecher recalled in his autobiography that the day state support of religion was voted down in Connecticut he had "the worst attack [of depression] I ever met in my life. . . . It was as dark a day as ever I saw. . . . The injury done to the cause of Christ, as we then supposed, was irreparable."[22] Or was it? Beecher continued: "For several days I suffered what no tongue can tell *for the best thing that ever happened to the State of Connecticut*."[23] Disestablishment, said Beecher, "cut the churches loose from dependence on state support. It threw them wholly on their own resources and on God."[24]

State support had been a crutch that had kept the churches crippled. While Congregationalists in New England looked to government as their savior, they had little incentive do much on their own. As a result, their churches dwindled and Unitarianism won the hearts and minds of the people. When state support was removed, however, New England evangelicals finally realized that they had to go out and hustle. They had to try to persuade people that their religious beliefs were right. They could no longer depend on government subsidies or government compulsion. Of course, some evangelicals had known this truth all along, especially Baptists. That's why many of them supported Jefferson. But for Congregationalists and Presbyterians from New England, the free enterprise system in religion was a radical innovation. Once they accepted it, they prospered. And so did evangelicalism in general. The scores of voluntary associations orga-

22. Beecher, *Autobiography*, I:252.

23. Beecher, *Autobiography*, I:252 (Beecher's emphasis).

24. Beecher, *Autobiography*, I:252-53.

nized for evangelism, missions, and social and political reform transformed American society in a way that few government programs ever could.

Beecher became one of the chief theoreticians of this movement, delivering a series of sermons articulating a system that one historian has dubbed America's "'voluntary establishment' of religion."[25] In the past, government had promoted civic virtue by compelling people to "support the gospel and attend the public worship of God," Beecher told legislators in Connecticut. "But these means of moral influence of the law can no longer apply; and there is no substitute but the voluntary energies of the nation itself, in associations for charitable contributions and efforts, patronized by all denominations of Christians, and by all classes of the community who love their country."[26]

Beecher advocated replacing government support for religion and morality with a network of voluntary societies that would spread the gospel, inculcate moral habits in the young, and reclaim the dissolute. In those cases where government action might still be necessary, the associations would seek to create a public consensus through educational efforts — because in a free society, Beecher realized, persuasion should precede enforcement.

"They say ministers have lost their influence," Beecher wrote years later. "The fact is, they have gained. By voluntary efforts, societies, missions, and revivals, they exert a deeper influence than ever they could" have by state support.[27]

There are obvious ways in which this lesson can be applied today to such areas as welfare and education. During the past decade, there has been increased recognition of the importance of private welfare initiatives, especially those tied to churches and other religious organizations. As Marvin Olasky has shown in his pathbreaking books, private faith-based efforts are often far more effective than government programs in moving people out of poverty.[28] The success of faith-based welfare efforts has encouraged initiatives such as the charitable choice provisions of the 1996 federal welfare reform act which encourage the use of private associations to deliver public welfare services. Similarly, many people are advocating ending the government school monopoly and increasing the ability of middle-class and poor parents to send their children to privately run educational institutions that are free to fully incorporate religious and moral instruction into their curricula.

25. Elwyn A. Smith, "The Voluntary Establishment of Religion," in *The Religion of the Republic*, ed. Elwyn A. Smith (Philadelphia: Fortress Press, 1971), p. 155.

26. Lyman Beecher, *A Sermon Addressed to the Legislature of Connecticut* (New Haven, Conn.: I. Bunce, 1826).

27. Beecher, *Autobiography*, I:253.

28. See, for example, Marvin Olasky, *The Tragedy of American Compassion* (Washington, D.C.: Regnery Publishing, 1992), and *Renewing American Compassion* (New York: Simon and Schuster, 1996).

But welfare and education are not the only areas where private associations might be able to help reinvigorate public life. Civic religion is another area. For much of American history, most Americans accepted the idea that religion is a public good because its holidays and rituals help tie citizens together into a common culture. From prayers in public schools to nativity scenes on the courthouse steps, public expressions of religion were regarded as part of the community-building process. Many of these public expressions of religion have been curtailed by Supreme Court decisions since the 1960s, however, and a great deal of political energy has been expended trying to overturn these decisions without much success.

Private associations supply a fresh way to recapture some of the community-building activities of the past. Many civic rituals involving religion can be reconstituted merely by changing the sponsorship of the event from government to a private association. If a community would like to celebrate the religious aspects of a holiday such as Christmas, or hold a Thanksgiving parade down Main Street that gives thanks to God, or even stage a prayer service for its public schools, it can do so by having these events sponsored by local business or community groups (including churches) rather than the government.

An example of this approach was a back-to-school prayer rally held in 1998 in the city of Federal Way, Washington. The event was publicized by stories in local newspapers, and it was promoted by the superintendent of the school district, who spoke at the event. There were no legal threats over this event, yet it took place in the public high school stadium, was a community event, and was promoted by a government official.[29] For all practical purposes, this was a civic ceremony. But its official sponsor was a group of community — primarily church — leaders rather than the government. In short, the event was what might be called privately sponsored public speech — speech and activities that are in the public square but are not officially sponsored by the government.

If citizens wish to encourage religion in their community's civic life, they can sponsor public ceremonies that include the religious segments of their community. The possible variations on this principle are endless. High school baccalaureate ceremonies can be reconstituted by making them privately sponsored. Crèches, crosses, and menorahs can be displayed on public property by private groups when the public property is open to private displays.[30] Holiday parades can incorporate religious elements (and keep out certain groups that

29. Sally Macdonald, "Back to school prayer rally has approval of state officials," *The Seattle Times,* 11 September 1998.

30. See *Capitol Square v. Pinette,* 515 U.S. 753 (1995), where the Supreme Court ruled that a cross placed in the Statehouse plaza of Columbus, Ohio, by a private group did not violate the Establishment Clause.

run counter to the traditional moral views of a community) if they are sponsored by private associations.[31]

In modern America, public goods are too often thought to be the exclusive domain of government, and public life is routinely equated with activities of the government. But as nineteenth-century evangelicals came to realize, the public square encompasses far more than government, and private associations can often provide public goods when government cannot.

Lesson 2: Cultivate Common Ground

A second lesson that can be taken from nineteenth-century evangelical reform is the importance of cultivating common ground and building coalitions. One reason for the success of evangelical initiatives in the 1800s was the conscious effort to forge coalitions across denominational lines and mount an "evangelical united front" on social issues. Overlooking their differences on such issues as church governance and liturgy, members of America's Protestant churches became increasingly willing during the nineteenth century to join together on behalf of common social objectives. They came to understand that they could retain their theological differences even while working together to bring about reforms based on their shared morality.

Such interdenominational cooperation was key to the development of associations at the national level that focused on particular issues.[32] These national associations included the American Bible Society, the American Tract Society, the American Colonization Society, the American Temperance Society, and the American Sunday School Union. A nonsectarian spirit prevailed among most of these groups, and the boards of many of them boasted members from all the major Protestant denominations. Evangelical unity became so marked at the national level that several of the major associations began holding their annual meetings together each May in New York City.[33]

31. See *Hurley v. Irish-American Gay, Lesbian and Bisexual Group of Boston*, 515 U.S. 557 (1995), where the Supreme Court allowed the private sponsor of Boston's St. Patrick's Day Parade to exclude a homosexual group from the parade.

32. Beecher laid the groundwork for these larger single-issue groups by noting that they could serve a vital coordination function by "collect[ing] facts, and extend[ing] information, and, in a thousand nameless ways . . . exert[ing] a salutary general influence. . . . Associations of this general nature, for the promotion of the arts and sciences, have exerted a powerful influence; and no reason, it is presumed, can be given, why the cause of morals may not be equally benefited by similar associations." Beecher, "Reformation of Morals," in *Works*, II:96.

33. Foster, *Errand of Mercy*, pp. 130-31, 146-54; Clifford Griffin, *Their Brothers' Keepers: Moral Stewardship in the United States, 1800-1865* (New Brunswick, N.J.: Rutgers University Press, 1960), p. 66.

The same kind of interdenominational cooperation could be seen at the local level. The membership rolls of the Moral Society of East Haddam, Connecticut, for example, included Baptists, Presbyterians, and Episcopalians.[34] During a revival in Rochester, New York, meanwhile, "Baptist, Methodist, Presbyterian, and Episcopal ministers preached from the same pulpit, and the place of meeting shifted indiscriminately between churches."[35]

Making all of these joint efforts between Christians possible was the adherence to a common moral framework supported by reason as well as religious authority. Evangelicals of the period had a firm belief in God's general revelation — that God revealed his moral laws to all human beings by writing them on their hearts. This belief in general revelation can be seen most clearly at evangelical colleges, which had a long history of offering courses in moral philosophy. During the eighteenth century, the Reverend John Witherspoon told his students at Princeton that moral philosophy by definition was "an inquiry into the nature and grounds of moral obligation by reason, as distinct from revelation," and they should have no problem with using it to that end.[36] According to Witherspoon, Christians who wondered whether it was dangerous to study morality by reason should not worry. "If the Scripture is true, the discoveries of reason cannot be contrary to it; and therefore, it has nothing to fear from that quarter."[37] Indeed, said Witherspoon, moral philosophy might strengthen belief in Christianity by confirming the moral teachings of the Bible.

Witherspoon's lectures on moral philosophy were dutifully transcribed by his students and later used at a number of colleges where Princeton graduates taught. The lectures were also repeatedly published in the early 1800s.[38] As the nineteenth century progressed, other evangelical scholars wrote complete textbooks on moral philosophy, including Presbyterian Samuel Stanhope Smith (Witherspoon's son-in-law), Baptist Francis Wayland, and Episcopalian Jasper Adams. Despite their differences in theology and politics, all three men firmly agreed with the proposition that morality could be known apart from special divine revelation.[39] Even die-hard Congregationalists like Timothy

34. Foster, *Errand of Mercy*, p. 134.

35. Johnson, *Shopkeeper's Millennium*, pp. 118-19.

36. John Witherspoon, *An Annotated Edition of Lectures on Moral Philosophy*, ed. Jack Scott (Newark, Del.: University of Delaware Press, 1982), Lecture I, p. 64.

37. Witherspoon, *An Annotated Edition*, p. 64.

38. Witherspoon, *An Annotated Edition*, p. 52.

39. See Samuel Stanhope Smith, *A Comprehensive View of the Leading and Most Important Principles of Natural and Revealed Religion*, 2nd ed. with additions (New Brunswick, N.J.: Deare and Myer, 1816), pp. 11-71; Samuel Stanhope Smith, *Lectures . . . on the Subjects of Moral and Political Philosophy* (Trenton, N.J.: Daniel Fenton, 1812), I:184-88, 300-321, II:10-116; Francis Wayland, *The Elements of Moral Science*, ed. Joseph Blau (Cam-

Dwight and Nathanael Emmons — who espoused a fairly bleak view of human nature — acknowledged that men retained a natural capacity to understand the basic principles of morality.[40]

Nineteenth-century evangelicals' belief in general revelation meant that they had no problem in articulating political and social objectives on secular grounds. Because of this, when they fought the practice of dueling, or objected to slavery, or promoted prison reform, they were able to join together with people from different theological traditions, sometimes including Unitarians. None of this is to suggest that nineteenth-century evangelicals were perfect in cultivating common ground. They were not, of course. According to today's standards, their efforts to build coalitions were rather parochial. While evangelicals promoted interdenominational efforts among Protestants, for example, they remained strongly opposed to any sort of coalition with Roman Catholics.[41] Moreover, some evangelicals tried to frame policy issues in specifically religious terms.[42] But these exceptions do not disprove that evangelicals on the whole tried to forge a united front based on a common morality.

Nineteenth-century evangelicals' belief in a moral common ground has important implications for contemporary efforts to reform culture. One of the most significant challenges facing those who wish to influence public life today is the need for a common moral vocabulary that can be accepted by both religious adherents and secularists. For too long much of American public life has been based on the assumption that traditional morality is based only on personal religious preferences, and that it therefore cannot be used as a standard for public policy. In this frame of reference, cultural conflicts are almost invariably seen as religious wars, which raise the rhetorical stakes to dangerous levels and balkanize citizens based on their religious affiliations. America's nineteenth-century experience shows the importance of articulating moral positions in a way that is understandable to the broadest number of citizens. The recent revival of interest in the concept of natural law among both Protestants

---

bridge, Mass.: Belknap Press, 1963), pp. 39, 42-75; Jaspar Adams, *Elements of Moral Philosophy* (Cambridge, Mass.: Folsom, Wells, and Thurston, 1837), pp. 1-37.

40. See Nathanael Emmons, "Dignity of Man," in *Works of Nathanael Emmons,* ed. Jacob Ide (Boston: Crocker and Brewster, 1842), II:27-28; Dwight, as transcribed in Theodore Dwight Jr., *President Dwight's Decisions and Questions Discussed by the Senior Class in Yale College, in 1813 and 1814* (New York: Jonathan Leavitt, 1833), p. 347; Timothy Dwight, "The Nature and Danger of Infidel Philosophy. Sermon I," in *Sermons by Timothy Dwight* (New Haven, Conn.: Hezekiah Howe and Urie and Peck, 1828), I:334; also see comments on p. 317.

41. For a discussion of evangelical anti-Catholicism, see West, *Politics of Revelation and Reason,* pp. 104-6.

42. West, *Politics of Revelation and Reason,* pp. 133-34, 209-10.

and Catholics is a step in the right direction,[43] as is "Evangelicals and Catholics Together," a declaration seeking common ground between traditional Protestants and Catholics on cultural issues.[44]

Lesson 3: Employ the Constitution as a Defense

A third lesson from nineteenth-century evangelical reform concerns how to handle criticism. By the 1820s, evangelical voluntary associations had come under harsh attack from critics ranging from Unitarians and freethinkers to pietist evangelicals who did not believe in social reform. Though by this time disestablishment had taken place in every state except Massachusetts, critics regularly accused evangelical reformers of intolerance and seeking a "union of church and state."[45] Even Sunday schools were not immune from allegations of evildoing. In 1828, the Pennsylvania legislature refused to grant the American Sunday School Union a charter of incorporation, fearing that it was part of a conspiracy to unify church and state, destroy freedom of the press, and exclude nonevangelicals from political power.[46]

Such attacks forced evangelical reformers to defend their actions, and their defense was based squarely on the principles of American constitutionalism. Seizing the moral high ground, evangelical reformers claimed that their efforts were protected by religious liberty and accused their detractors of being intolerant with all their cries of "priestcraft" and "persecution." The Reverend F. Freeman declared that "this cry of persecution is itself the bitterest persecution. This charge of intolerance is the very hand of intolerance itself, stretched forth with unrelenting grasp."[47] Religious liberty encompasses the

43. See J. Budziszewski, *Written on the Heart: The Case for Natural Law* (Downers Grove, Ill: InterVarsity Press, 1997); and Michael Cromartie, ed., *A Preserving Grace: Protestants, Catholics, and Natural Law* (Grand Rapids: Eerdmans, 1997).

44. Richard John Neuhaus and Charles Colson, eds., *Evangelicals and Catholics Together: Toward a Common Mission* (Dallas: Word, 1995).

45. See, for example, *Trumpet and Universalist Magazine,* 30 August 1828, p. 34; Robert L. Jennings, "Religion Necessary to Make and Keep People Virtuous," *Free Enquirer,* 24 December 1828, p. 71; "Orthodox Attack on Congress," *Trumpet and Universalist Magazine,* 4 February 1829, p. 130; Frances Wright, "Address," *Free Enquirer,* 18 October 1829, pp. 3-4; A Layman, "To Any Member of Congress," *Free Enquirer,* 27 February 1830, pp. 138-40; "Plots and Masks," *Working Man's Advocate,* 30 October 1830, p. 3.

46. "Sunday School Union, or Union of Church and State," reprinted in Ezra Stiles Ely, *The Duty of Christian Freemen to Elect Christian Rulers* (Philadelphia: William F. Geddes, 1828), pp. 18-28.

47. F. Freeman, *Religious Liberty: A Discourse* (Plymouth, Mass.: Benjamin Drew Jr., 1832), p. 23.

freedom to speak as well as the freedom to think, said Freeman, and no person has the right to hinder another person from candidly expressing his views. That nation is not free where one group of people cannot express their views about God and morality without subjecting themselves "not only to the jeers and revilings of the debased, but to every unamiable feeling shown by those who profess respectability and would fain be considered liberal . . . ."[48]

When evangelicals were condemned as theocrats for petitioning Congress to shut down post offices on Sundays (so that postal workers would not be compelled to work on the Sabbath), they responded by appealing to the First Amendment's right of petition: "Have not religious persons the same right as others to petition Congress?" asked one pamphleteer. "And when they have done so, are they to be denounced before the nation as a treasonable combination to change the government . . . ?"[49]

Other evangelicals drew implicitly on American constitutional theory to show that evangelical voluntary associations could not credibly lead to a church-state union. In an address titled "On the Misrepresentation of Benevolent Actions," the Reverend David Ogden pointed out that evangelical reform was spearheaded by all major evangelical denominations, and he contended that it was unreasonable to think that these different denominations (each with its own peculiar doctrines and form of worship) would join together on behalf of church-state union. This was true however one defined such a union. Evangelical reformers could not be working toward the establishment of one denomination over the rest, because they could never agree which denomination to establish. They could not even be working together for nonpreferential aid to all sects because "some large [evangelical] sects as a body, and individuals in all [evangelical] sects believe that this is an unchristian way of supporting religion. And then there are innumerable small sects, besides a multitude of infidels and men indifferent to all religion, who would join together on this subject, and defeat such a plan."[50]

In other words, the sheer multiplicity of sects in America discouraged evangelical union on any other grounds than the common good. According to Ogden, this was precisely the motive that had spurred Methodists, Episcopalians, Baptists, and Presbyterians to join together for evangelical reform. They sought to promote the "moral welfare of their species" by distributing the Bible to those who could not afford it, by educating children so they would not be-

48. Freeman, *Religious Liberty,* p. 17.

49. *Review of a Report of the Committee . . . by the Honorable Richard Johnson* (Washington, D.C., 1829), p. 21.

50. David Longworth Ogden, "Second Discourse, On the Misrepresentation of Benevolent Actions," in *Two Discourses* (Hartford, Conn.: Hudson and Skinner, 1830), p. 28.

come delinquents, and by promoting "respect for the Sabbath which they believe to be essential to our political prosperity."[51]

Ogden did not invoke James Madison in his discourse, but his analysis rested squarely on Madisonian principles. Echoing Madison's argument in *Federalist* numbers 10 and 51, Ogden essentially argued that America had such a variety of sects, evangelical and otherwise, that the only successful religious combinations would be those based on the "principles . . . of justice and the general good."[52]

Similar arguments can be made today to deflect the criticism inevitably sparked by religious-based reform efforts. In modern America, the Constitution remains a symbol of moral authority, and cultural reformers should never allow that authority to be ceded to their opponents. For example, when groups such as the ACLU assert that vouchers for private schools violate the Establishment Clause of the First Amendment, supporters of vouchers should not only rebut this claim but make a principled argument for why religious liberty and the rights of conscience actually encourage government policies that accommodate the needs of religious believers. Similarly, when constitutional arguments are offered against government funding for faith-based charities, a positive case for funding can be offered based on the principles of equality and religious liberty.

A good example of the efficacy of positive constitutional arguments can be seen in the "equal access" movement of the 1980s and 1990s. By the late 1970s, religious groups were routinely discriminated against in their access to public facilities. This fact was especially apparent in public schools. High school students who wanted to pray or read the Bible during lunch or before school were frequently denied access to school facilities, even though nonreligious student groups were allowed to meet at the same times. Students were sometimes prevented from distributing religious tracts to classmates, even when the distribution of political leaflets was allowed. Religious groups were also prohibited from renting school facilities after hours, even in school districts that allowed a wide variety of nonreligious community groups to rent school facilities.

These restrictions were usually justified as being mandated by the First Amendment's Establishment Clause. Those who worked to overturn the restrictions, however, decided not only to rebut the Establishment Clause claim but to offer a positive argument against the restrictions. They argued that the First Amendment's free speech clause *required* that religious individuals and groups be accorded the same access to public facilities as nonreligious individu-

51. Ogden, "Second Discourse," pp. 26, 31-32.

52. James Madison, Federalist #51, *The Federalist Papers,* ed. Clinton Rossiter (New York: New American Library, 1963), pp. 322, 325.

als and groups. For example, if a city allowed a community group to stage a rock concert at a public park, it should also have to allow a religious group to hold a worship service there — otherwise it would be discriminating against certain groups on the basis of the content of their speech. Congress eventually guaranteed religious student groups equal access to public high schools in the Equal Access Act of 1984, a law which the Supreme Court upheld in *Board of Education v. Mergens* (1990). The Supreme Court subsequently guaranteed religious groups equal access to the rental of school facilities in *Lamb's Chapel v. Center Moriches Union Free School District* (1993) and to university activity fees in *Rosenberger v. The Rector and Visitors of the University of Virginia* (1995).[53]

Lesson 4: Look to the Future

A fourth lesson from nineteenth-century evangelical reform is the need to focus on the future. Too often reform efforts try to solve current problems simply by turning back the clock. While there was an element of backward looking in evangelical reform during the 1800s, there was also a healthy interest in the future.

Lyman Beecher was one of the ones who understood the importance of looking toward the future. In the 1830s, he left a thriving pastorate in Boston for the much rougher environs of Cincinnati, Ohio. Recognizing that the United States was expanding westward, Beecher saw that the future of the nation was in the west, and that if evangelicals wanted to continue to thrive they would need to be as aggressive in establishing churches and voluntary associations on the frontier as they were in the established cities of the eastern seaboard. With this vision in mind, Beecher helped create Lane Seminary in order to educate clergy who could help spread the gospel in the territories.[54]

Beecher's vision was strategic. He focused on influencing the culture not by recapturing the current power elites but by shaping the leadership of the next generation. Adopting a long-term view, Beecher sought to win over the culture by raising up leaders among the next generation who would impact the nation as it expanded.

53. *Board of Education v. Mergens,* 496 U.S. 226 (1990); *Lamb's Chapel v. Center Moriches Union Free School District,* 508 U.S. 384 (1993); *Rosenberger v. The Rector and Visitors of the University of Virginia,* No. 94-329 (1995). For a more detailed discussion of the background and development of equal access, see John G. West Jr., "The Changing Battle over Religion in the Public Schools," *Wake Forest Law Review* 26, no. 2 (1991): 361-401.

54. See Vincent Harding, *A Certain Magnificence: Lyman Beecher and the Transformation of American Protestantism* (Brooklyn: Carlson Publishing, 1991), pp. 281-302; Lyman Beecher, *A Plea for the West* (Cincinnati: Truman and Smith, 1835).

Beecher's long-term outlook is particularly relevant for today. Rather than simply dousing the cultural brushfires of the moment, those interested in genuine cultural revival need to start thinking in terms of the next generation, not just the next election. Money and resources should be directed to long-term intergenerational change, not just short-term battles. Those concerned about the negative cultural effects of TV and film, for example, should spend less time trying to influence current members of the entertainment industry and more time seeking to mold the artists, writers, musicians, and executives of the next generation. Similarly, those worried about the lack of high-caliber leaders in politics should devote resources to training young people who will be political leaders a decade from now. Long-term cultural investments can be a hard sell in an age of immediate gratification, and philanthropists, policy makers, and citizen activists all tend to demand quick results for their actions and donations. But long-term efforts are the only credible way to bring about sustained reform.

Lesson 5: Embody Integrity

A fifth lesson from nineteenth-century evangelical reform is the importance of personal integrity. During the 1790s and through the first years of the new century, many conservative Protestants had allied themselves with the Federalist Party against the Jeffersonians. During these years, some ministers virtually became party hacks, demonizing members of the other political party and using the pulpit to generate support for the political agenda of the Federalist Party. Eventually there was a backlash against this harsh partisanship among Christians and an increasing recognition among many religious leaders that Christians in politics had not lived up to the requirements of their faith and had to do better. They had to guard against the dangers of pride and hatred even while striving to stand up for the truth.

Timothy Dwight was one of the people who recognized this. President of Yale, Dwight himself had been one of the fiercest critics of Jefferson and a staunch supporter of the Federalist Party, but he came to realize the dangers of tying Christianity so closely to party politics, and he began trying to counteract this practice. In his commencement address of 1816, he told students that

> the prejudices, the fervour, and the bitterness, of party spirit are incapable of vindication. I may be permitted to think differently from my neighbour; but I am not permitted to hate him, nor to quarrel with him, merely because he thinks differently from me.
>
> . . . Our countrymen have spent a sufficient time in hostilities against each other. We have entertained as many unkind thoughts, uttered as many

> bitter speeches, called each other by as many hard names, and indulged as much unkindness and malignity; as might satisfy our worst enemies, and as certainly ought to satisfy us. From all these efforts of ill will we have not derived the least advantage. . . . Friends and brothers have ceased to be friends and brothers; and professing Christians have dishonoured the religion which they professed.[55]

One of Dwight's students from a few years before was a young man named Jeremiah Evarts. Of all the politically active evangelicals during the early 1800s, perhaps Evarts was the one who displayed most clearly during this period a reconciliation between personal holiness and political action. Evarts was a lawyer, a journalist, and missionary leader. He took a stand on such issues as slavery and alcohol abuse before those issues were popular. But his greatest legacy was his defense of the treaty rights of the Cherokee Indians in Georgia.[56]

The Cherokee had become Christians and adopted a democratic form of government. They had been promised their treaty lands forever by the federal government. But in the late 1820s, a concerted effort was made to take away the Cherokee's land and compel them to move further west. The effort finally succeeded in a tragic episode of American history. But it took years to actually force the Cherokee to move — and that was largely due to the gallant efforts of Jeremiah Evarts and his missionaries. Evarts's activities on behalf of the Cherokee literally drove him to exhaustion and death.[57]

Even most opponents of Evarts respected him. An indication of why they did so can be seen from his daily prayer list found among his papers after his death. Evarts prayed daily that he would "be preserved from rash and imprudent speeches in regard to the government" and pleaded for help with avoiding self-righteousness: "Whenever I hear of sinful actions, before I say a word by way of censure, let me remember how much I find to blame in myself, though under so great advantages."[58]

Evarts was a powerful example of how one can stand up strongly for what one believes to be right and still do it in a responsible manner. He was an example of what St. Paul called "speaking the truth in love."[59] Avoiding the twin wrongs of self-righteousness and unprincipled pragmatism, Evarts showed what it truly means to be a person of faith in politics.

55. Dwight, "On Doing Good," *Sermons,* pp. 540-41.

56. See Tracy, *Memoir of the Life of Jeremiah Evarts;* John A. Andrews, *From Revivals to Removal: Jeremiah Evarts, the Cherokee Nation, and the Search for the Soul of America* (Athens, Ga.: University of Georgia Press, 1992).

57. West, *Politics of Revelation and Reason,* pp. 171-97.

58. Tracy, *Memoir of the Life of Jeremiah Evarts,* p. 429.

59. Ephesians 4:15.

Lesson 6: Act Prudently

A final lesson to be culled from nineteenth-century evangelical activism is the need for the virtue of prudence. Prudence involves selecting the best means to actually achieve noble goals. To be prudent is to be an idealist about goals but a realist about methods. Prudence is of particular relevance to religious activists in public life because they are susceptible to disillusionment if they cannot immediately reach their goals. Religion is usually idealistic, and as a consequence religious people in public life can be moralistic and uncompromising. That is their great strength, but it is also their weakness. The danger of religious idealism in public life is that when the idealists don't get their way they will give up on the system, perhaps even work to undermine it.

Evangelicals faced this problem after the failure to save the Cherokee Indians in the 1830s. After every legal and political remedy to prevent Cherokee deportation had been exhausted, the evangelical missionaries were faced with the question of whether to counsel the Cherokee to continue to resist or to seek the most favorable removal agreement possible. Most evangelicals urged the Cherokee to conclude a new treaty with the federal government, realizing that outright resistance would now be futile. The only prudent course was to try to make the best of an admittedly bad situation. A few evangelicals, however, supported continued resistance by the Cherokee.[60]

The debate over Cherokee resistance was predictive. It underscored the difficulties religious reformers sometimes have in dealing with the hard realities of politics, and it foreshadowed a much larger debate that would take place in the 1840s and 1850s about slavery. The question then was how far Christians should go to oppose slavery in a country where its existence was constitutionally protected. Some abolitionists sought to work within the system to stop the spread of slavery and ultimately make it unsustainable. Others attacked the Constitution itself as a corrupt document and advocated going beyond the law to dismantle slavery.

Civil disobedience has a long and honored pedigree in America, and anyone who accepts the idea of a higher law ought to accept at least a theoretical right to sometimes disobey unjust laws. Nevertheless, this is perilous territory, as Abraham Lincoln suggested in his justly famous Lyceum Address.[61] The danger of taking the law into one's own hands is that in the process one may destroy the very foundations that make law itself possible. If one is seeking to es-

60. West, *Politics of Revelation and Reason,* p. 203.

61. Abraham Lincoln, "Address to the Young Men's Lyceum of Springfield, Illinois" (1838), in *Abraham Lincoln, Speeches and Writings, 1832-1858* (New York: Library of America, 1989), pp. 28-36.

tablish a legal right for someone, it is problematic to undermine the legal system in order to assert it.

Unless religious idealists have a firm grasp of the idea of prudence, religious idealism in politics has the tendency to be overzealous and even politically destabilizing. What is needed to counteract this tendency is a heavy dose of realism. Unsurprisingly, Lyman Beecher was someone who understood this. In one of his earliest sermons on reform, he discussed the possibility that the reformers would not achieve all their goals, and he warned his listeners about adopting an all-or-nothing approach toward reform.

"We are not angels, but men," he declared. "If we can gradually improve ourselves, and improve the society in which we live, though in a small degree, it is an object not to be despised."[62] In this era when the wonders of technology lead many Americans to expect almost instantaneous changes, Beecher's words supply a healthy caution for would-be cultural reformers.

62. Beecher, *The Practicality of Suppressing Vice by Means of Societies Instituted for that Purpose* (New London, Conn.: Samuel Green, 1804), p. 17.

Antonio Gramsci and the Transformation of Institutions

JOHN FONTE

Many observers have declared that America's cultural crisis is rooted in the problems that have inevitably arisen as our society moves from an industrial to an information-based economy. Others have emphasized the destructive growth of relativist and nihilist attitudes among both elites and the population at large. In addition to the very real problems associated with both technological-economic change and the spread of relativism and nihilism, however, there remain further normative issues at the center of our cultural crisis.

This essay will argue that one of the greatest challenges to American cultural renewal is normative. At the heart of this challenge are philosophical, intellectual, and moral arguments about what our culture is, and what it should be. Foremost is this question: should American culture — its first principles, primary values, habits, customs, and institutions — be *transmitted* or be *transformed?*

The cultural renewalists (Tocquevillians) believe that the decline of American culture must be reversed and that our culture's core mores and first principles need to be revitalized and restored. The ultimate goal of this movement is to transmit a renewed culture to future generations of Americans. These cultural renewalists are opposed by cultural transformationists (Gramscians), whose goal is to transform rather than to transmit America's core mores and first principles. The terms "Tocquevillian" and "Gramscian" were chosen because, while the nineteenth-century Frenchman Alexis de Tocqueville is the intellectual and spiritual godfather of the cultural renewalist movement, the twentieth-century Italian thinker Antonio Gramsci is the great theorist for the cultural transformationist argument. This essay will (1) examine Antonio Gramsci's core ideas relating to cultural transformation; (2) explore the influence of Gramscian and Hegelian Marxist arguments in today's debates; (3) describe the neo-Tocquevillian assumptions behind the American cultural renewal movement; and (4) analyze the nature of the clash between Gramscians and Tocquevillians.

Antonio Gramsci's Theories

Antonio Gramsci (1891-1937), an Italian Marxist intellectual and politician, has exerted a broad influence on contemporary thinking about cultural and ideological conflict. Although he was one of the founding fathers of the now defunct Italian Communist Party, his innovative writing has had a global impact across the political spectrum, influencing Chilean communists and Polish anti-communists, British leftists and Argentine rightists, Italian Catholic Democrats and French New Right pagans, as well as liberals and conservatives in American academic and intellectual circles. What follows is a brief overview of Gramsci's thinking on cultural transformation.

Throughout History the World Has Been Divided between Two Types of Groups: Dominant and Subordinate

Gramsci writes that all societies in human history have been divided into two basic groups: the privileged and the marginalized, the oppressor and the oppressed, the dominant and the subordinate, the rulers and the ruled. Dante Germino, a leading Gramsci scholar, notes that Gramsci broadened Karl Marx's analysis of class struggle to include a wide range of groups excluded from the center of power on other than economic grounds.[1] Gramsci writes in his famous *Prison Notebooks,* for example, that "The marginalized groups of history include not only the economically oppressed but also women, racial minorities and many 'criminals'."[2] What has historically been described as "the people," Gramsci describes as an "ensemble" of subordinate groups and classes in every society that has ever existed until now.[3] This collection of oppressed and marginalized groups, "the people," lack unity and, often, even

1. Dante Germino, *Antonio Gramsci: Architect of a New Politics* (Baton Rouge: Louisiana State University Press, 1990), p. 250.
2. Germino, *Antonio Gramsci,* p. 250.
3. Germino, *Antonio Gramsci,* p. 262.

consciousness of their own oppression. To reverse the correlation of power from the privileged to the marginalized is the goal of Gramsci's cultural project. Thus, for Gramsci, "In its most realistic and concrete significance, the word *democracy* means the molecular passage [transformation] of ruled groups into the ruling groups."[4]

Hegemony

Power, Gramsci writes, is exercised by privileged groups or classes in two ways: (1) through domination, force, or coercion and (2) through "intellectual and moral leadership," consent, or "hegemony." Domination is exercised through coercive state power. Hegemony is the ideological supremacy of a system of values, beliefs, morality, and habits that supports the class or group interests of the predominant classes or groups and, thus, of the established order. This hegemony or "intellectual and moral leadership" is exercised through the institutions and associations of civil society such as schools, churches, trade unions, and civic associations, which serve to "legitimize" the rule of the predominant groups. In the institutions of civil society the subordinate groups are influenced to internalize the value systems and worldviews of the privileged groups and, thus, to consent to their own marginalization. Gramsci believed that a privileged group that is merely "dominant" (i.e., relies only on force) and not "leading" or "directing" (i.e., relies upon hegemony or implied consent) is inherently weak. He insists that even the most authoritarian regime needs some degree of popular consent, some degree of hegemony, to survive in the long run. It is important to note that although Gramsci puts great emphasis on the intellectual and moral spheres, he still, as a Marxist, considers economic-material factors primary in the sense that hegemonic values are not simply independent of material conditions, but are built upon an understanding of the empirical economic relationships existing in a specific historical situation.[5]

Civil Society and the War of Position

The Soviet Revolution of 1917, Gramsci noted, was a direct frontal assault upon the state (a "war of movement or maneuver"). This was possible because civil society in Russia was "primordial" and the ruling classes had not established an

4. Germino, *Antonio Gramsci,* p. 232.

5. Antonio Gramsci, *Selections from the Prison Notebooks,* ed. and trans. by Q. Hoare and G. Nowell Smith (London: Lawrence and Wishart, 1971), pp. 12-13, 55-58.

effective ideological and cultural hegemony. In the West, however, "The state was only an outer ditch, behind which there stood a powerful system of fortresses and earthworks" (civil society).[6] In the West, therefore, revolutionary strategy would first entail a "war of position" which, as scholar Joseph Femia notes, would not be "simply aimed at the conquest of state power ('the outer trench') but [would focus] on the gradual capture and possession of the 'powerful chain of fortresses' behind" — civil society or what we are calling in this book "the culture."[7] Hence the initial task of the revolutionary was ideological and cultural struggle. It was necessary first to delegitimize the dominant belief systems of the predominant groups and create a "counter-hegemony" (a new system of values for the subordinate groups) before the actual conquest of state power could proceed. Moreover, because hegemonic values permeate all spheres of civil society — schools, churches, the media, high culture, labor unions, voluntary associations — it is the great battleground in the struggle for ideological and cultural hegemony.[8]

"Everything Is Political"

Gramsci states that "all life is political."[9] Thus, private life, the workplace, religion, philosophy, art, and literature — and, as we have seen, civil society in general — are contested battlegrounds in the revolutionary struggle to achieve cultural and societal transformation. In contrast to more classical Italian Marxists, Gramsci originally considered the avant-garde futurist movement a de facto ally in the hegemonic struggle against bourgeois-Catholic civilization, because, as Gramsci scholar Carl Boggs notes, the futurists called "into question a broad realm of cherished values (notably religion itself), as expressed through poetry, drama, painting, ballet, literature, etc."[10] Likewise, Gramsci praises the playwright Luigi Pirandello for helping to subvert the Aristotelian-Catholic philosophical core of the ruling classes' hegemonic worldview by undermining the concept of metaphysical reality with the concept that human reality is a social construction.[11]

Gramsci characterized his approach to the connection between politics and all aspects of life as "totalist" in the sense of a unity of theory and practice and

6. Gramsci, *Prison Notebooks,* p. 238.

7. Joseph V. Femia, *Gramsci's Political Thought: Hegemony, Consciousness, and the Revolutionary Process* (Oxford: Oxford University Press, 1981), p. 191.

8. Femia, *Gramsci's Political Thought,* p. 191.

9. Germino, *Antonio Gramsci,* p. 253.

10. Carl Boggs, *Gramsci's Marxism* (London: Pluto Press, 1976), p. 60.

11. Germino, *Antonio Gramsci,* p. 226.

philosophy and politics. Thus, he states, "Everything is political including philosophy or the philosophers . . . and the only philosophy is history in the act — that is, life itself."[12] It is significant, Germino notes, that Gramsci's last entry in the *Prison Notebooks* argues "that even the choice of grammar was a political act," because Gramsci placed the study of grammar within a world comparative (thus, internationalist) context instead of a merely national or provincial context.[13]

Consciousness

Classical Marxists implied that a revolutionary working-class consciousness would simply develop from the objective (and oppressive) material conditions of working-class life. Gramsci disagreed, noting that "there have always been exploiters and exploited" but very few revolutions, because subordinate groups usually lack the "clear theoretical consciousness"[14] necessary to convert the "structure of repression into one of rebellion and social reconstruction."[15] It is this revolutionary "consciousness" that is crucial because, as Gramsci put it, "Man is above all else mind, consciousness — that is, he is a product of history, not nature."[16] Unfortunately, the subordinate groups possess "contradictory" or "false" consciousness; that is to say, they accept the conventional assumptions, the "common sense," the ideological worldview of the dominant groups as "legitimate," or as a fair approximation of the way things ought to be. Gramsci makes it clear that real change can come about only through an intellectual and moral transformation of consciousness.

The Modern Prince and the Role of the Intellectuals

In order to achieve revolutionary transformation, the struggle for hegemony needs an organism to develop consciousness and direct the ideological-cultural struggle. For Gramsci, the revolutionary party serves as this institution. He called it the "modern Prince," a counterpart to Niccolo Machiavelli's classic work *The Prince*. According to Gramsci, Machiavelli's object in *The Prince* was to develop consciousness of the need for political action to forge Italian unity. The party or modern Prince would assist in developing a new counter-hegemonic worldview of the subordinate groups to challenge the ideologies of

12. Gramsci, *Prison Notebooks*, p. 357.
13. Germino, *Antonio Gramsci*, p. 253.
14. Femia, *Gramsci's Political Thought*, p. 44.
15. Boggs, *Gramsci's Marxism*, p. 59.
16. Quoted in Boggs, *Gramsci's Marxism*, p. 59.

the dominant groups. It would also direct a three-way interrelated struggle (economic, political, and ideological-culture) against the ruling classes.[17]

Clearly, as Marx himself had argued, if revolutionary social transformation is to be successful, the ideologies and worldviews of the predominant groups must be unmasked as instruments of domination. This crucial task of demystifying and delegitimizing the ideological hegemony of the dominant classes or groups is performed by intellectuals, because they are the purveyors of consciousness. Great intellectuals develop overarching worldviews that are transmitted by lesser intellectuals (teachers, activists, journalists, local clergymen) and these visions eventually become the "common sense" of society. Since intellectuals are the group most responsible for stability (if they work to sustain the status quo) they could also be, Gramsci notes, the group most responsible for change, if they would work to alter modes of thinking and behavior. Gramsci distinguishes between two types of intellectuals: traditional and organic. Traditional intellectuals are the creative artists and scholars who are usually thought of by society as intellectuals. Although traditional intellectuals are often considered autonomous and independent of the dominant social groups, Gramsci insists that this is not the case: traditional intellectuals, whether consciously or not, promote for the most part ideas that serve the interests of the dominant groups. Even those traditional intellectuals who do not share the worldviews of the ruling groups eventually effect a compromise with them, because of institutional or financial pressures.[18]

What subordinate groups need, Gramsci maintains, are "organic intellectuals," intellectuals who are integrated into the fabric of their oppositional subcultures. This would constitute a "new type of intellectual" who is "constructor, organizer, permanent persuader."[19] At the same time, the defection of traditional intellectuals to the subordinate groups is important in the cultural struggle, because traditional intellectuals who have "changed sides" are well positioned within established institutions. In the final analysis, however, the revolutionary impetus and the power of the oppressed groups will be greatly enhanced by the strength of their own organic intellectuals. Thus, Gramsci writes:

> One of the most important characteristics of any group that develops towards power is its struggle to assimilate and conquer "ideologically" the traditional intellectuals. Assimilations and conquests are more rapid and

17. Antonio Gramsci, *The Modern Prince and Other Writings*, trans. Louis Marks (New York: International Publishers, 1957), pp. 135-40.

18. Gramsci, *The Modern Prince*, pp. 118-25; Femia, *Gramsci's Political Thought*, pp. 131-35.

19. Gramsci, *The Modern Prince*, p. 122.

> effective the more the given social group puts forward simultaneously its own organic intellectuals.[20]

Historicism and the Rejection of all Forms of Transcendence

Gramsci declares that of all worldviews only the philosophy of praxis (Marxism) is "liberated from every residue of transcendence and theology."[21] He strongly rejects both religious and secular or philosophical forms of transcendence such as the concept of metaphysical realism, that there is an objective reality beyond man's creation. He also rejects the concept that there are universal moral standards evident to all men with normal moral vision. Gramsci describes his position as "absolute historicism," meaning that morals, values, truths, standards, and human nature itself are products of different historical epochs.[22] There are no absolute moral standards that are universally true for all human beings outside of a particular historical context.

Gramsci specifically rejects the morality of both religion and Kant's categorical imperative (to act as if the substance of one's action could become a universal law). He notes that morality is socially constructed and should be examined in relationship to the political power of dominant and subordinate groups. Gramsci writes:

> The modern Prince, as it develops, revolutionizes the whole system of intellectual and moral relationships, in that its development means precisely that every action is conceived as useful or harmful, virtuous or vicious, only insofar as it is referring to the modern Prince itself and contributes to increasing or opposing its power. The Prince takes the place in the consciousness (of its members) of the divinity or the categorical imperative and becomes the basis for a modern secularism and a complete secularization of all life and of all customary relationships.[23]

That argument of Gramsci's has ignited controversy among Gramsci scholars, with one group (particularly Catholics and anti-Communists) accusing Gramsci of making the Communist party a God and of advocating the extreme relativist stance that truth is whatever serves the party. On the other hand, academics more sympathetic to Gramsci's politics (including most Gramsci experts in the West) such as Joseph Femia, Carl Boggs, Mario Finocchiaro, and Dante

20. Gramsci, *The Modern Prince,* p. 122; Gramsci, *Prison Notebooks,* p. 10.
21. Gramsci, *Prison Notebooks,* p. 402.
22. Femia, *Gramsci's Political Thought,* p. 245.
23. Gramsci, *Prison Notebooks,* p. 133.

Germino interpret this passage differently.[24] Germino, for example, responds, "Gramsci's assertion that the party takes the place both of God and of Kant's categorical imperative in the minds of its members does not mean that he is deifying the party." Instead, Germino insists that Gramsci is essentially saying that "there is no heaven beyond the earth and that there can be none within the world either." Further, Germino states that according to Gramsci the revolutionary party (the instrument of "intellectual and spiritual reformation") should be the "touchstone of men's consciences." Therefore, Gramsci is "calling on those who support the new politics of inclusion to discipline their selfish individual interests in the name of advancing the cause of the marginalized majority."[25]

The Goal of a New Culture and a New Man

Gramsci declared that he was not a "utopian." He defined utopianism as the attempt by a ruling elite to secure economic equality through force of will and arbitrary legislation. He stated that there could be no political equality without economic equality and that economic inequality would exist as long as there were dominant and marginalized classes and groups.[26] While the core of all politics was the division between the rulers and the ruled, the eventual goal for Gramsci was to somehow "attenuate this fact and make it disappear."[27] Whether there would always be this division would be worked out in historical practice. He foresaw the Marxist era of class struggle as lasting several hundred years, with the eventual possibility of the disappearance of political society (the State) and its transformation into a "regulated society," a new type of regime in which civil society would absorb political society or government.[28] Thus, Gramsci wrote that "one can imagine . . . state coercion exhausting itself" and that this transition would "probably" take centuries.[29] Since human nature is historically conditioned, this new type of "regulated society" would see a new type of human being and a new "integral" culture. Even in the new society, however, Marxism would not be a "stagnant doctrine" but, as Germino puts it, "will be in perpetual struggle with lethargic elements."[30]

24. See Maurice A. Finocchiaro, *Beyond Right and Left: Democratic Elitism in Mosca and Gramsci* (New Haven, Conn.: Yale University Press, 1999), pp. 175-76; see also Boggs, *Gramsci's Marxism;* Femia, *Gramsci's Political Thought;* Germino, *Antonio Gramsci.*

25. Germino, *Antonio Gramsci,* p. 261.

26. Germino, *Antonio Gramsci,* p. 258.

27. Germino, *Antonio Gramsci,* p. 243.

28. Gramsci, *Prison Notebooks,* p. 382.

29. Gramsci, in Germino, *Antonio Gramsci,* p. 257.

30. Germino, *Antonio Gramsci,* p. 239.

Gramsci and the Hegelian Marxist Tradition

Antonio Gramsci's theories have had a global impact in the examination of the way culture is captured and transformed. His thought is often lumped together with other writers who are classified as "Hegelian Marxists."[31] While there is some debate whether Gramsci or the Hungarian Marxist Georg Lukacs, author of *History and Class Consciousness* (1923),[32] is more deserving of the title "founder of Hegelian Marxism," there is little debate that Gramsci's thought has been greatly influential among Western elites. Besides Gramsci and Lukacs, leading Hegelian Marxists include the German thinker Karl Korsch and members of the "Frankfurt School" (such as Theodor Adorno and Herbert Marcuse), a group of theorists associated with the Institute for Social Research founded in Frankfurt, Germany, in the 1920s, some of whom attempted to synthesize the thinking of Marx and Freud.

These intellectuals developed a form of Marxism that rejected economic determinism and the immutable materialist laws of history. They were inspired by the idealist philosophical concepts put forth by Hegel such as the role of will and consciousness in human history. What Gramsci and the other Hegelian Marxists emphasized more than anything else was that the decisive struggle to overthrow the bourgeois regime (middle-class, liberal democracy) would be fought out at the level of consciousness. That is, the old order had to be rejected by its citizens intellectually and morally before there would be a physical transformation of power to the subordinate groups.

Gramscianism and Hegelian Marxism Today

Intellectual historians have long noted that at certain periods in a nation's history particular ideas are "in the air." In the America of the past few decades Gramscian and Hegelian Marxist concepts have been, clearly, "in the air," and they have been influential in cultural and moral arguments about the most important questions facing the nation. This is not to say that contemporary cultural transformationists have consciously studied Gramsci or that large numbers of people involved in American cultural debates have read (or even heard of) him; nor do I mean to ignore the great influence that other (and non-Marxist) critical thinkers, such as Dewey, Nietzsche, and Heidegger, have had on

31. See Femia, *Gramsci's Political Thought,* pp. 1-2, 128-29; Boggs, *Gramsci's Marxism,* pp. 12, 18, 21-22, 46-47, 57-59, 67-69, 119-26.

32. Georg Lukacs, *History and Class Consciousness,* trans. Rodney Livingstone (London: Merlin Press and Cambridge, Mass: MIT Press, 1971).

transforming cultural values. Nevertheless, Gramscian and Hegelian Marxist ideas are prominent in today's cultural conflicts in different forms and combinations, without necessarily any conscious reference to their origins or implications (in the same way that seminal and complex ideas have always been popularized, vulgarized, and synthesized throughout intellectual history). What is significant is that many of these ideas — for example, that dominant and subordinate groups based on race, ethnicity, and gender are engaged in struggles over power; that the "personal is political"; and that all knowledge and morality are social constructions — are assumptions and presuppositions at the center of today's Zeitgeist which determine how moral and political issues are framed.

At the core of the Gramscian-Hegelian Marxist worldview is the concept of permanent struggle between dominant and subordinate groups. In this conflict, the subordinate groups represent the positive advance of history, whereas the dominant groups represent the oppressive status quo. Morality is group-based; it is what serves the interests of the subordinate classes. As noted earlier, Gramsci wrote that in the system of moral and intellectual relationships "every action is conceived as useful or harmful, virtuous or vicious, only insofar as" it "contributes to increasing or opposing" the "power" of the revolutionary party that embodies the interests of the subordinate groups. Hegelian Marxist group-based morality challenges the central tenets of the Judeo-Christian and Kantian-Enlightenment ethical framework which holds that (1) individuals are responsible for their own actions and (2) humans should be treated as "ends" in themselves, not as simply "means" to an "end" such as the creation of a new and better society. Today, group-based morality, the idea that what is moral is what serves the interests of "oppressed" or "marginalized" ethnic, racial, and gender groups, is widespread among American elites.

Law professors at leading American universities, for example, have endorsed the concept of "jury nullification." Building on the Hegelian Marxist concepts of group power and group-based morality, advocates of jury nullification argue that minorities serving on juries should use their "power" as jurors to refuse to convict minority defendants regardless of the evidence presented in court, because the minority defendants have been "powerless" or lifelong victims of an oppressive system that is skewed in favor of dominant groups, such as white males.[33] Indeed, "critical theory," a direct descendant of Gramscian and Hegelian Marxist thinking, is widely influential in both law (including race and feminist legal studies) and education. The critical legal studies movement seeks to "deconstruct" bourgeois legal ideas that serve as instruments of power

33. See Clay S. Conrad, *Jury Nullification: The Evolution of a Doctrine* (Durham, N.C.: Carolina Academic Press, 1998); Joan Biskupic, "In Jury Rooms, A Form of Civil Protest Grows," *Washington Post,* 8 February 1999.

for the dominant groups and to "reconstruct" them to serve the interests of the subordinate groups.[34]

This is what Michigan law professor Catharine MacKinnon has successfully accomplished in her writing and public advocacy. Professor MacKinnon writes, "The rule of law and the rule of men are one thing, indivisible," because "State power, embodied in law, exists throughout society as male power. . . ." Furthermore, "Male power is systemic. Coercive, legitimated, and epistemic, it *is* the regime."[35] Therefore, MacKinnon notes, "a rape is not an isolated event or moral transgression or individual interchange gone wrong but an act of terrorism and torture within a systemic context of group subjection, like lynching."[36] Professor MacKinnon has argued that sexual harassment is essentially an issue of power exercised by the dominant over the subordinate groups rather than a transgression based on sexual desire, and the United States Supreme Court has adopted MacKinnon's theories as the basis for its interpretation of sexual harassment law.[37] Thus, today we have major social policy based not on Judeo-Christian precepts or on Kantian-Enlightenment ethics, but on Gramscian and Hegelian Marxist concepts of group power.

Likewise in education, concepts of group-based power are widespread. During the past decade multicultural education has become a major influence in American schools. Many multicultural educators have defined democracy in terms of group power. That is to say, a democratic society is one in which various ethnic and racial groups share power as groups more or less proportionally. Professor James Banks of the University of Washington is a major textbook writer and one of the leading theorists of social-studies and multicultural education. Banks writes that American democracy needs to be transformed: "To create an authentic democratic unum with moral authority and perceived legitimacy, the pluribus (diverse peoples) must negotiate and share power."[38]

The clear message of the neo-Gramscian Hegelian Marxist critique is that the American regime itself is illegitimate. After all, in a truly legitimate regime legal and educational norms would aim toward justice for all citizens. These

34. See James W. Ceaser, *Liberal Democracy and Political Science* (Baltimore: Johns Hopkins University Press, 1990), p. 117; Katherine T. Bartlett and Rosanne Kennedy, eds., *Feminist Legal Theory: Readings in Law and Gender* (Boulder: Westview Press, 1991).

35. Catharine MacKinnon, *Toward a Feminist Theory of the State* (Cambridge, Mass.: Harvard University Press, 1989), p. 170.

36. MacKinnon, *Toward a Feminist Theory,* p. 172.

37. See *Meritor Savings Bank v Vinson,* 477 U.S. 57 (1986); Richard A. Epstein, *Forbidden Grounds: The Case Against Employment Discrimination Laws* (Cambridge, Mass.: Harvard University Press, 1992), pp. 350-66.

38. James A. Banks, "Transforming the Mainstream Curriculum," *Educational Leadership* (May 1994), p. 4.

norms would not simply be "instruments" used by the dominant groups to exercise power over subordinate groups. If, as Professor MacKinnon puts it, "male power" is "coercive" and "systemic" and "is the regime," then the "regime" — that is to say, the American liberal democratic system, its dominant value structure, and its way of life — must be, by definition, illegitimate. And if, as Professor Banks insists, negotiation and power sharing among "diverse peoples" (not political parties and democratic citizens) are necessary to "create" a democratic order "with moral authority and perceived legitimacy," then it is clear that contemporary American liberal democracy does not possess either "moral authority" or "legitimacy," and that, therefore, a legitimate American regime has yet to be created. Obviously, if the regime is illegitimate its culture should not be renewed and transmitted to future generations, but should be transformed instead.

MacKinnon in law and Banks in education are examples of the success of the Gramscianization of American intellectual and moral argument. As leading "organic intellectuals" in key institutions of civil society they are performing the Gramscian task of demystifying bourgeois ideology and creating counter-ideologies (radical feminism, multiculturalism) that aim to establish intellectual and moral dominance or "hegemony." The issues they raise of group-based morality and group consciousness are central to what Joseph Femia describes as the "core feature of Gramsci's proposed strategy — the long march through the institutions of civil society in order to subvert and replace bourgeois hegemony."[39] Indeed, Professor MacKinnon often sounds as if she is reading directly from Gramsci. Thus, she states that "the pursuit of consciousness" is crucial: "The key to feminist theory consists in its way of knowing. Consciousness raising is that way. . . . An oppressed group must at once shatter the self-reflecting world which encircles it and, at the same time, project its own image onto history. In order to discover its own identity as distinct from that of the oppressor, it has to become visible to itself. All revolutionary movements create their own way of seeing."[40]

All of this suggests that the movement to renew American culture faces normative — as well as techno-economic, relativist, and nihilist — challenges. Certainly, human agency and will are as significant as technological transformation and nihilist malaise. There is a struggle for hegemony going on in American culture today in the Gramscian sense of that term. That is, an adversarial intelligentsia is challenging and attempting to transform the dominant value structure of the American regime. This is an intellectual and moral struggle over the major principles, values, and concepts that shape the culture and, therefore, the regime in general.

39. Femia, *Gramsci's Political Thought,* p. 235.
40. MacKinnon, *Toward a Feminist Theory,* p. 84.

The Neo-Tocquevillian Assumptions of the American Cultural Renewal Movement

Facing this Gramscian-Hegelian Marxist challenge to transform American culture stands a cultural renewal movement based on neo-Tocquevillian assumptions and presuppositions. Probably more than that of any other single theorist, the American cultural renewal movement embraces the thought of Alexis de Tocqueville as its exemplar. Writing in *Policy Review*, editor Adam Myerson described the task of cultural renewal as "applied Tocquevillianism."[41] In explaining one of his key points, Tocqueville writes in *Democracy in America* that "mores" are central to the "Maintenance of a Democratic Republic in the United States." He defines "mores" as not only "the habits of the heart," but also the "different notions possessed by men, the various opinions current among them, and the sum of ideas that shape mental habits." In short, Tocqueville declares, "I use the word to cover the whole moral and intellectual state of a people."[42]

One of the leading manifestos of the cultural renewal movement, "A Call to Civil Society: Why Democracy Needs Moral Truths," published by the Council on Civil Society, outlines the traditional civic and moral values (Tocqueville's "mores") that buttress the American democratic republic.[43] The document (endorsed by, among others, Dan Coats, Don Eberly, Jean Bethke Elshtain, Francis Fukuyama, William Galston, Glenn Loury, Joseph Lieberman, Cornel West, James Q. Wilson, and Daniel Yankelovitch) states that the "civic truths" of the American regime are "those of Western constitutionalism, rooted in both classical understandings of natural law and natural right and in the Judeo-Christian religious tradition." It continues that "our founding idea is liberty, guided by the proposition that people are created equal" and that the "briefest expressions" of our civic creed are "inscribed on our coins": "Liberty" and "E Pluribus Unum." "The moral truths that make possible our experiment in self-government are in large part biblical and religious," informed by the "classical natural law tradition" and the "ideas of the Enlightenment." The "most eloquent expressions" of these truths are "found in the Declaration of Independence, Washington's Farewell Address, Lincoln's Gettysburg Address and Second Inaugural Address, and King's Letter from the Birmingham Jail." The "briefest expression" of these truths is "inscribed in our coins: 'In God We Trust.'"[44]

41. *Policy Review* (January-February 1996).

42. Alexis de Tocqueville, *Democracy in America,* ed. J. P. Mayer, trans. George Lawrence (New York: Harper Perennial, 1988), p. 287.

43. Don E. Eberly, *America's Promise: Civil Society and the Renewal of America's Culture* (Lanham, Md.: Rowman & Littlefield Publishers, Inc., 1998), pp. 217-47.

44. Eberly, *America's Promise,* p. 227.

The statement declares that "our civilizational values" include a "reliance on reason and the scientific method" and "a belief in the objectivity of truth and knowledge."[45] At the climax of the twenty-page statement the authors declare that their final (and most important) goal is to "revitalize a shared civic story informed by moral truth." In regard to our "civic faith," the statement insists that "our main challenge is to rediscover the democratic bonds that, amidst and because of our differences, unite us as one people." In regard to our "public moral philosophy," the statement declares that "our main challenge is to rediscover the existence of transmittable moral truth."[46]

Throughout this document and throughout the writings of the cultural renewalists generally, the prefix "re" is predominant. Thus, American culture is to be "renewed"; our shared civic story is to be "revitalized"; civic faith and moral philosophy are to "rediscovered"; our civic and moral resources are to be "replenished"; personal responsibility is to be "restored"; society is to "remoralized"; and values are to be "renormed."

An emphasis on "renewing" and "rediscovering" American mores, of course, suggests that there is in fact a healthy civic and moral core to the American regime, which can now be brought back to life. Moreover, if the first task is cultural renewal, the second task is cultural transmission. Thus, the "Call to Civil Society" declares that the "central task of every generation is moral transmission." Religion, in particular, the statement posits, "has probably been the primary force" that "transmits from one generation to another the moral understandings that are essential to liberal democratic institutions." Moreover, "at their best . . . our houses of worship foster values that are essential to human flourishing and democratic civil society: personal responsibility, respect for moral law, and neighbor-love or concern for others."[47] In addition, the statement declares that a "basic responsibility of the school is cultural transmission"[48] and recommends that current educational practices be changed to focus on "transmitting to students a knowledge of their country's constitutional heritage, an understanding of what constitutes good citizenship, and an appreciation of their society's common civic faith and shared moral philosophy."[49]

45. Eberly, *America's Promise,* pp. 225-26.
46. Eberly, *America's Promise,* p. 233.
47. Eberly, *America's Promise,* p. 223.
48. Eberly, *America's Promise,* p. 225.
49. Eberly, *America's Promise,* p. 241.

The Nature of the Conflict between Tocquevillians and Gramscians

As we have seen, Tocquevillians and Gramscians clash on almost everything that matters. Tocquevillians believe in transcendence, Gramscians in immanence.[50] Tocquevillians believe that there are objective moral truths applicable to all people at all times; Gramscians believe that moral "truths" are subjective and depend upon historical circumstances. Tocquevillians believe that these civic and moral truths must be revitalized in order to remoralize society; Gramscians believe that civic and moral "truths" must be socially constructed by subordinate groups in order to achieve political and cultural liberation. Tocquevillians believe that functionaries such as teachers and police officers represent legitimate authority (except when they abuse this authority); Gramscians believe that teachers and police officers "objectively" represent power (not legitimacy), that is, the group interests of the dominant groups (although they would concede that individual teachers and police officers often act decently). Tocquevillians believe in personal responsibility; Gramscians believe that "the personal is political." For Tocquevillians "consciousness" means having an individual conscience and applying the Judeo-Christian-Kantian ethic to all human beings, particularly to the most vulnerable members of society; for Gramscians, "consciousness" means awareness of how subordinate groups are oppressed by dominant groups. In the final analysis, Tocquevillians favor the transmission of American culture, Gramscians the transformation of American culture.

What exists in America today is a major values conflict on two cultural fronts: the civic and the moral. In both the civic and moral realms the Gramscian challenge is a normative phenomenon that, if successful, will result in the transformation of the traditional Tocquevillian core of American culture and, thus, of the American regime itself. The cultural renewalists (or contemporary Tocquevillians) are well positioned to compete with the cultural transformationists (contemporary Gramscians) in the moral realm. On this front, the Tocquevillians are prepared. They understand the "big picture," that is, the revolutionary nature of the transformationist challenge. They know on what ground to engage; they know where to stand and fight. They are not ready to abandon transcendence, objective truth, and concepts of right and wrong to

50. Immanence in the Gramscian sense means that all moral values are human constructions, created within human activity and human history. Transcendence means that moral values are trans-historical and based on metaphysical objectivity, which could be religious (God-based morality) and/or secular (e.g., classical natural law), which is "discovered" but not "created" by human reason and true for all men in all historical epochs. The contemporary Tocquevillians, whom we are discussing, usually combine faith and reason and view God-based morality as consistent with a natural law discovered by right reason.

historicism, subjectivity, and situational ethics. This is not to say that the Tocquevillians will ultimately triumph over the Gramscians, but they are prepared to do so, and that is the first step.

On the civic front, however, the situation is different. Here there is confusion because the nature of the challenge is not as fully understood and, thus, the ideas and infrastructure for meeting this challenge are underdeveloped. In analyzing civic revival initiatives (as opposed to those of moral renewal) leading contemporary Tocquevillians have rightly criticized the shallowness and "softness" of much of what passes for civic renewal, such as an emphasis merely on "participation" and "volunteering" and a reluctance to confront negative behavior with moral criteria.[51]

A closer look at the arguments of many "civic revivalists," however, reveals that they are often civic transformationists in renewalist clothing — more Gramscian than Tocquevillian. Interestingly, both Gertrude Himmelfarb and Don Eberly have specifically mentioned political scientist Benjamin Barber as an example of a civic revivalist who eschews any connection between the civic and the moral.[52] Professor Barber, an enthusiast for Swiss-style participatory democracy, is not in favor of "renewing" the traditional liberal democratic norms of American civic life. "American democracy," he tells us, "is a thin incomplete version of what any good democratic theorist will mean by democracy."[53] He explicitly prefers "social democracy" to "liberal democracy";[54] rejects the Founding Fathers' realistic view of human nature ("Whig skeptics and their American imitators like James Madison asked too little of humanity's better side and surrendered too much to its worse side");[55] and insists that all genuine citizenship involves human "transformation."[56]

Indeed, a good part of the debate in the civic arena is more concerned with cultural transformation than cultural renewal. Transformationist arguments dominated a major colloquy in *Boston Review* on "patriotism and cosmopolitanism" set off by philosopher Martha Nussbaum's reply to Richard Rorty's comments on patriotism several years ago. Since then numerous books by some of the intellectual participants in that colloquium, including Todd Gitlin, Richard Rorty, Martha Nussbaum, and Benjamin Barber, have further

51. See Don Eberly, "Civic Renewal vs. Moral Renewal," *Policy Review* (September-October 1998), pp. 44-47; Gertrude Himmelfarb, *One Nation, Two Cultures* (New York: Alfred A. Knopf, 1999), p. 38.

52. Eberly, "Civic Renewal," pp. 44-47, and Himmelfarb, *One Nation*, p. 38.

53. Benjamin R. Barber, *A Passion for Democracy: American Essays* (Princeton, N.J.: Princeton University Press, 1998), p. 37.

54. Barber, *A Passion*, pp. 38-40.

55. Barber, *A Passion*, p. 35.

56. Barber, *A Passion*, p. 34.

developed the transformationist paradigm in both the civic and moral spheres, and the transformationist ideology emerging from this discourse is challenging traditional American mores in a number of ways.

Martha Nussbaum began the symposium by criticizing Richard Rorty's argument that patriotism should not be disdained as a value. She declared that "patriotism is very close to jingoism."[57] In point of fact, Rorty's advocacy of patriotism was purely instrumental. He would prefer, he declares in his new book *Achieving Our Country,* that "the United States of America . . . someday yield up sovereignty to what Tennyson called 'the Parliament of Man, the Federation of the World,'" but for the time being the American nation-state is useful in achieving certain progressive political ends.[58] In a similar vein, a leading civic theorist, Princeton professor Amy Gutmann, wrote in the same symposium that it is "repugnant" that American students should "learn that they are above all citizens of the United States."[59]

Even when many of the intellectuals involved in the ongoing dialogue embrace American civic identity, they interpret this identity in a way that ignores America's constitutional liberal democratic tradition. Thus, Todd Gitlin sees the American experiment as closely paralleling the French revolutionary project — a utopian Enlightenment experiment that "seriously aims to bring about understandings that do not yet exist."[60] For Richard Rorty there are no enduring or permanent American principles; instead, our "tradition" is best understood as constant change, flux, and transformation.[61]

Significantly, many civic intellectuals of the cultural transformationist bent active during the past decade — including Benjamin Barber, Lawrence Levine, Amy Gutmann, Martha Nussbaum, and Todd Gitlin — adhere in varying degrees to a worldview in which struggle between dominant and subordinate groups is crucial. Indeed, Lawrence Levine, the author of *The Opening of the American Mind,* declares that the "culture wars" are "a small price to pay" for increasing "diversity,"[62] and he states that American universities should be "representative of the diverse peoples" that "comprise America."[63]

57. Martha Nussbaum, "Patriotism and Cosmopolitanism," *Boston Review* (Fall 1994).

58. Richard Rorty, *Achieving Our Country* (Cambridge, Mass.: Harvard University Press, 1998), p. 3.

59. Amy Gutmann, "Democratic Citizenship," *Boston Review* (Fall 1994).

60. Todd Gitlin, *The Twilight of Common Dreams* (New York: Metropolitan Books, Henry Holt and Company, 1995), p. 218.

61. Wilfred M. McClay, "Is America an Experiment?" *The Public Interest* (Fall 1998), pp. 13-15.

62. Lawrence W. Levine, "Struggles Are a Small Price to Pay for Diverse Universities," from the symposium "Have the Culture Wars Ended?" *Chronicle of Higher Education,* 6 March 1998, opinion section, B5.

Affirmed by these intellectuals in the name of the "civic" are group-based ideologies, a generic a-patriotic civic ethos that is essentially post-American, and vaguely utopian impulses and sentiments. What is not affirmed is the concrete heritage of American constitutionalism, ordered liberty, and *e pluribus unum*. Under the rubric of "diversity," this worldview is implemented by what Gramsci called "lesser intellectuals" in administrative positions in government agencies, corporations, churches, universities, and schools.

Cultural renewalists should be particularly concerned with the "diversity" message that is being forwarded to the children of immigrants. While there is no doubt that acculturation of the young (both the children of native-born and the children of immigrants) will occur in some form, the major question is whether America's children will be assimilated into a Gramscian framework of group ideologies or into more traditional Tocquevillian mores. Public schools today often affirm anti-assimilationist messages like the theories of James Banks (noted earlier) that describe American civic life as an arena in a struggle for power among the different "peoples" that comprise the United States. Moreover, there is evidence that anti-assimilation ideologies are influencing first generation American students. A longitudinal study (the first of its kind) for the Russell Sage Foundation in 1997 revealed that after four years of American high school the children of Mexican and Filipino immigrants were 50 percent more likely to consider themselves Mexicans or Filipinos than Mexican-Americans or Filipino-Americans (or plain Americans). This study, the most extensive conducted to date, highlights a process of de-assimilation.[64] The "Call to Civil Society" document has rightly suggested that the American civic creed is expressed in the concepts of "Liberty" and "E Pluribus Unum," and it is precisely this message that needs to be articulated by cultural renewalists all across the culture with vigorous intellectual and moral arguments.[65]

At the end of the day, the transformationist assault on personal responsibility in the name of group consciousness and on the American *unum* in the name of multiculturalism threatens our moral truths as well as our civic truths. The civic front represents the "soft underbelly" of the ongoing cultural struggle and needs to be vigorously defended. Tocquevillians need to combine the patriotic and "vigorous" virtues of courage, honor, heroism, and patriotism with the more "caring" virtues of respect, trustworthiness, fairness, decency, and compassion. As Gertrude Himmelfarb has noted, the "two kinds of

63. Lawrence W. Levine, *The Opening of the American Mind* (Boston: Beacon Press, 1996), p. iii.

64. Ruben G. Rimbaut, "Passages to Adulthood: The Adaptation of Children of Immigrants in Southern California," Report to the Russell Sage Foundation Board of Trustees, 16 June 1997, New York.

65. Eberly, *America's Promise*, p. 227.

virtues are not mutually exclusive, for they pertain to different aspects of life."[66]

In general, the Tocquevillians could strengthen their position by emphasizing patriotism or what is "American" in American cultural renewal. They should take the offensive and seize new ground in the culture conflict — by promoting the civic assimilation of immigrants and welcoming them into our *common* American culture; by advocating the restoration of our federally funded museums as institutions whose primary goal is to affirm (not deconstruct or "problematize") America's *common* cultural heritage; and by recognizing that those young people who proudly serve in our nation's military are performing an important cultural function. Currently, there is little in the cultural renewal literature on the positive contribution of military service to our nation's well-being. Yet to risk one's life for one's fellow Americans in the armed forces of the United States is, clearly, as important to our nation's cultural health as participation in any of the many worthy associations of civil society. In the final analysis, if the renewal of American culture is ultimately to be successful, Tocquevillians will have to engage in a comprehensive strategy. They must address what is specifically American, as well as what is universal, in cultural renewal; and they must envision the civic and moral realms as two closely related fronts in the continuing (and perhaps perpetual) normative conflict over the future of American culture and, thus, over the future of the American Idea.

66. Himmelfarb, *One Nation,* p. 81.

Oasis Strategies

HERBERT LONDON

In *Slouching Towards Gomorrah,* Robert Bork makes the claim that "Decline runs across our entire culture." Having described a book burning at Yale, Bork concludes with the comment that "the charred books on the sidewalk in New Haven were a metaphor, a symbol of the coming torching of America's intellectual and moral capital by the barbarians of modern liberalism."[1] Alas, the barbarians are at the gates, and, despite an occasional cultural victory by the Right, any realistic assessment of American cultural life today must acknowledge that the Left has utterly triumphed in the *kulturkampf.*

Richard Goldstein recognizes this when he exults in the pages of the *Village Voice,* "The Culture War is Over! We Won!" There is no question about the "we" to whom he refers. As Goldstein notes, "in the other America . . . the nation of home entertainment centers — the Republicans have no legs. Their roiling attacks on Hollywood and gangsta rap, their crusade against the evil empires of Levin and Eisner . . . their jeremiads against Jenny Jones, have all but fallen on deaf ears."[2]

Among conservatives and liberals, there is consensus on this one point, that the Left has won the culture war. A 1960s generation weaned on polymorphous perversity is different from its ancestors. Believing that the self is the

1. Robert H. Bork, *Slouching Towards Gomorrah: Modern Liberalism and American Decline* (New York: Regan Books, 1996), pp. 342-43.

2. Richard Goldstein, "The Culture War Is Over! We Won! (For Now)," The *Village Voice,* 19 November 1996, p. 51.

measure of all meaning and the arbiter of what is right, the 1960s generation arrived at adulthood worshipping the great demiurge solipsism. In its rejection of tradition, of all that came before, this generation assumed a societal tabula rasa that could be imprinted with self-expression. In this so-called postmodern period, what *I* feel or think is all that counts; "responsibility" and "duty" are obsolete words from an increasingly anachronistic age.

Against this backdrop of self-expression is a technological revolution in which every individual is encouraged to express himself without restraint. Thus the virtual superhighway leads directly to the Tower of Babel. Standards are impossible when radical egalitarianism demands that everyone is heard, and, amid the din, taste and probity are drowned out. A cultural Gresham's Law is at work: the tasteless driving the tasteful out of existence. If this seems exaggerated, compare the popularity of gangsta rap to the financial struggles of most symphony orchestras.

The unfortunate truth is that traditionalists are inept at engaging their adversary in the culture war, conservatives with money and power are too often co-opted by media panjandrums, and most conservatives are unwilling or unable to recognize the influence of culture on politics. Thus traditional viewpoints in the media have been easily supplanted by radicalism over the last four decades. A direct assault on cultural pollution is therefore unlikely to succeed. For those who determine programming, a moment of retreat today is worth a dramatic lunge forward sometime in the future. There is a growing recognition that the virtuecrats (this is not a term of derision) do not have staying power. And surely any cultural influence they do have pales before the growing market for the hedonistic, violent, and pornographic.

The Decline of Our Institutions

Even the institutions that once stood as guardians of the good, true, and beautiful have succumbed to the baneful influence of popular taste. A recent poll of twenty-two major colleges and universities revealed that thirteen English departments had dropped their "great books" requirement. Shakespeare has been downgraded in the contemporary curriculum. English majors at Georgetown University are no longer required to study Shakespeare, Milton, or Chaucer.

Compounding these egregious cases are the many examples of conservative newspapers stolen or destroyed by those who dislike their arguments. At the University of Pennsylvania, University of Texas, and George Washington University, student newspapers have been stolen with scarcely a murmur from the administration. These targeted raids on conservative student newspapers violate the very intellectual standards a university should seek to protect and preserve.

When the university is in thrall to the symbolic and ephemeral and freedom is denied to those with views in disfavor, there can be little doubt that a cultural shift has occurred. Relativism is the handmaiden of complacency with any belief system, and vitiating standards have been the catalyst for the dumbing-down of American students. If students rarely read good books, how will they know what is good? If they are told that truth is an illusion designed to reinforce the status quo, why should they pursue truth, and if they are led to believe that beauty is only in the eye of the beholder, why should they accept the judgment of the past?

The modern museum, presumptively the repository of cultural artifacts that should be preserved, has become a center for the storage of detritus. Instead of offering what may be uplifting, the modern museum provides a menu of the shocking, degrading, and politically correct, and its myrmidons defend its shows as manifestations of "anti-art" or as a critique of the bourgeois sensibility. Curators don't defend shows as another form of beauty, but as intentionally ugly and deformative.

Similarly, language has slid down the rabbit hole of deconstruction. Words are now whatever you want them to mean, and every form of language, even the most crude, is accepted in this era of democratization. Coarse language has been accompanied by coarse behavior, its natural outcome. As a consequence, manners have been relegated to the ash heap of a bygone age.

This litany of cultural deterioration merely confirms that the culture war is over for the time being, and that refinement, taste, and aesthetics are missing in action. For those who lament this outcome, little in the way of solace is available. Judge Bork, for one, says we should hope for the best, but he prescribes little besides hope.

A Counterrevolution Based on "Parallel Structures"

Suppose, however, that the ambiance of freedom, converted by radicals into license, were to be turned into a cultural instrument for rejuvenation. In Ray Bradbury's classic novel *Fahrenheit 451,* a group of outcasts defeated in a culture war retains a sense of the worthy by assigning to memory every one of the classic texts. They form a community of moral archivists, with each person assuming responsibility for memorizing a text. In this way, they prevent the book burners from destroying the culture of the past.

It seems to me that the Bradbury approach has much to recommend it. With Shakespeare increasingly out of fashion at college campuses and Dante replaced on Stanford's classic reading list by an Ecuadorian indigene (Rigoberta Menchu, an admitted dissimulator), and with Milton and Chaucer denigrated as irrelevant, dead, white, European males, the time may be swiftly approaching when reading the classics of Western civilization will be an act of rebellion, a guerrilla action in the face of the prevailing culture.

Museums, colleges, films, magazines, newspapers, television, radio, book publishers, and music companies have already been conquered by the radical sensibility. There is no sense in discussing containment or rollbacks, nor is there any point in taking too much satisfaction from a Rush Limbaugh, *Apollo 13,* or any other occasional nod to conservatism. Although hesitant to use Trotskyite language, I am calling for a counterrevolution based on "parallel structures."

The Oasis Strategy

As prisoners of the culture war, cultural traditionalists, like all prisoners of war, have few options available. We can leave this nation, but there are few places inoculated against American popular culture. We can surrender, but this is acceptable only for those who do not understand culture. We can fight back, but the odds against success are formidable. What can be done — in my judgment — is somewhere between retreat and resistance. I call it an oasis strategy.

In this cultural desert, those with a traditionalist stance must assert it in modest but meaningful ways. A museum should be created devoted to the best that has been achieved in artistic forms. (By the "best" I am referring to that which is spiritually enriching, aesthetically pleasing, and technically uncompromised.) A college should be established without any concessions to the *zeitgeist,* where students would meet rigorous requirements without electives, read the great works of our civilization, be literate in two foreign languages, have numerical skill, and be familiar with scientific laws and methods. A film company should be designed around family entertainment that neither patronizes nor depreciates the human experience. These films will not indulge the vulgar with coarse language, but instead teach and edify through great storytelling and inspiring myth.

In some respects the oasis strategy recreates the approach of Antonio Gramsci's progeny who "infiltrated" institutions until their numbers represented a critical mass. Wherever there are openings, traditionalists today should try to advance their agenda by "leavening" institutions now dominated by the Left. For example, if affirmative action judgments militate against fair play and the pursuit of excellence, these arguments should be emphasized and perhaps fictionalized into film and television programs. How can a society with our legacy resist appeals to fair play?

As cultural consumers, traditionalists should shun the bad and embrace the good, pointing out — for those who care — what is meant by true, good, and beautiful. When there is a sound adaptation of a Henry James novel into film, one that avoids the gratuitous sex and vulgarity James himself would have deplored, traditionalists should go out of their way to praise it as a hopeful cultural indicator.

There are many other possible illustrations. My point is simply that edifying cultural examples do exist, and that they must be the traditionalists' response to cultural degradation. Just as Bradbury's characters roamed the forest primeval reciting their assigned books, traditionalists must resist sensate culture within the oasis where their culture flourishes. They should be immune to the charge that their institutions are elitist. Affirmative action and radical egalitarianism have no place in the oases; these are institutions where merit and excellence count and are rewarded.

The best response to a degrading culture is its opposite, forcefully defended within a psychological island of like-minded adherents. Occasionally, unlikely visitors may find succor in the oasis — and may even be converted. But the most likely scenario is that the traditional culture oases will remain isolated and bereft of widespread support. A lack of popular support, however, does not suggest a lack of moral victories. As long as there remain a few hardy souls who recognize greatness, all is not lost. Being the last defenders of superior culture is an admirable calling to which some noble people will unquestionably respond. Now we must build the institutions to which these people can gravitate.

Building the Institutions

How we build these institutions isn't obvious. Even if like-minded people congregate that in itself won't change the barren landscape of culture. What is necessary are models.

A few faculty members devoted to the restoration of Great Books can forge a new department without an enormous financial investment. All that is needed is evidence that students will embrace the idea. Surely if radical faculties can influence students, moderate faculty members should be able to do so as well.

Based on all the audio tapes of superb books now available in the Blackstone catalogue, it would not be difficult to syndicate a series of radio programs that give audiences a chance to hear several of Jane Austen's novels in a given week and perhaps *The Iliad* and *The Odyssey* the following week. As a refreshing change from the many culturally-degrading stations in the country, this could be a commercial success in addition to being a cultural breakthrough.

In the Internet age there are virtually no impediments for establishing a "chat room" devoted to the serious exchange of ideas. Assignments could be given and papers "delivered."

A catalogue of national museums devoted to aesthetically pleasing and uplifting works could be created. How many cultural sophisticates are aware of the extraordinary Hudson River collection housed in the Hastings-on-Hudson Newington Cropsey museum?

If the *Blair Witch Project* could become an overnight box office sensation by relying on cheap thrills, it seems that films can be made inexpensively and still find an audience. Perhaps more edifying films could also be made inexpensively; a film based on the life of Teddy Roosevelt as a child, for example, would have visual appeal and powerful moral lessons.

The purpose of such projects is to create a beachhead on the hostile cultural landscape, a safe place for experimentation with worthy artifacts and wholesome ideas. Naturally critics will decry such efforts as the *cri de coeur* of Babbits. But that's okay; they don't have to participate.

My suspicion, however, is that in time skeptics will become converts. When the Goodspeed Opera House in Connecticut first opened, audiences couldn't be found for the musical theatre productions of yesteryear. That has changed. Today there are sellout crowds for virtually every performance.

Moreover, the projects to which I refer need not be stolid or boring. What is culturally uplifting is often surprisingly enjoyable even for audiences weaned on violence and sexual perversion. As I see it, shifting the culture is not unlike turning a battleship in mid-ocean. It's hard, it requires seamanship skills, and it demands determination. Recognizing the goal, of course, is ultimately what is critical, and the goal is producing what is worthy for those who will appreciate it and developing models for those who can be converted.

Can an Oasis Strategy Be Successful?

Whether the oasis strategy can be successful is not clear. Despite my ardent belief that it is worth trying — what else can a traditionalist do? — the strategy has its weaknesses.

For one thing, there is the argument that these tactics cut traditionalists out of the so-called mainstream. That stream, of course, is polluted and it doesn't welcome anti-toxins, but it is what Americans consume and that cannot be taken lightly. While I would welcome an elitist label, it should be noted that in a radical egalitarian environment, elitism is a pejorative. As a consequence, even popular culture that attempts to be uplifting is swimming upstream.

Second, in our morally indeterminate climate, judgment about what is worthwhile and what is degrading is relativistic. The contagion of moral libertinism has turned the public's passion against truth and coarsened the culture to such a degree that the Nike ad to "Just do it" is the existential calling card for the entire society.

Furthermore, the nihilism of our capitalist culture makes it difficult to even attempt an oasis strategy. Unless you can demonstrate beyond a shadow of a doubt that there is a commercial market for an uplifting cultural product, financial investment will not be forthcoming.

Last, the assault on moral indeterminacy and cultural suicide by the virtuecrats has not resulted in a cultural retreat. On the contrary, appealing to shame in a shameless environment doesn't work, and appeals to religious principle in an increasingly nonreligious climate are regarded as mere superstition.

The dawn of a new era catalyzed by oases of renaissance culture faces formidable obstacles that cannot be overlooked. The key to this struggle — which is both moral and aesthetic — can perhaps be found in religious institutions. If they can reclaim the terrain once appropriately held, culture might go through an efflorescence. If not, oases might be trapped by isolation in an increasingly hostile climate.

The struggle in which traditionalists are engaged requires moral regeneration, which, although very hard, is not impossible. Working for cultural change won't be easy, but it is certainly better than merely hoping for the best. As I see it, cultivating little gardens of cultural beauty in the vast contemporary desert is a worthwhile activity despite the impediments that stand in the way of successful cultivation. Rejecting what is demeaning, and restoring what is uplifting, may be a Sisyphean task; nonetheless, in a nation with increasingly fat wallets and hollow souls, it is the right thing to do.

Radical Vision: Christopher Lasch and the Quest for Community

ERIC MILLER

Among Christendom's vestiges is the longing for what we somewhat prosaically, somewhat romantically, call "community." The offspring of a Protestant civilization, we seem damned to remember wistfully at least this one dimension of the old world that joined household, church, and state to create a "culture," another notion scented with medieval romance. While inhabitants of nations with Catholic roots seem actually still to practice "community" in some fashion — at least according to scholars such as Claudio Veliz — we, the prototypical moderns, know "community" best as a theoretical construct.[1] Our myriad historical explications and sociological typologies have not led to the filling of our perceived political and cultural void. The communitarian ideal remains as elusive as ever — seen most concretely in our past, tellingly, rather than in our present.

This broad and noble vision of a public world unified by common morality and political purpose persists, though, and Christopher Lasch (1932-1994), the American historian and social critic, stands among those who most ably and passionately tended to its upkeep. When he longingly (and frequently) spoke of a "decent society," he meant it. He moved toward this deceptively simple ideal — a "decent society" — with an intensity born of the deep conviction that some sort of social reality beyond the status quo was possible, indeed, was necessary.[2] Critics caricatured him as a gloomy moralist due to his consistently

1. See Claudio Veliz's brilliant *The New World of the Gothic Fox: Culture and Economy in English and Spanish America* (Berkeley: University of California Press, 1994).

2. In a 1978 letter Lasch defined his understanding of a "decent society" as "a society

harsh analysis of contemporary American life, but it was his hopeful political vision that impelled him to spend so much time surfacing the dross of the past and present. A "restless shade," Wilfred McClay once tagged Lasch, an apt description. He was in continuous uneasy motion, probing, seeking insight, searching for ways to harness his ideals to history.[3]

The historian John Patrick Diggins points out that "How one interprets existing conditions is largely determined by whether one believes they can be fundamentally changed."[4] While Lasch's understanding of what in the world should and could be changed shifted over the course of his career, his confidence that *something* more — *much* more — was necessary did not. People should live together for the common good. "Commonwealth" should not be merely a linguistic artifact of a distant civilization. Politics has to mean more than procedural, interest-driven governance by elites. With ire he attacked those whom he perceived to be militating against this necessary, possible America. There was, surely, another way.

One of Lasch's long-standing formulations of his political and social ideal was to call it, simply, democracy. "Most of my recent work," he wrote near the end of his life, "comes back in one way or another to the question of whether democracy has a future." This was democracy as a way of life, not merely as a political system. Real democracy required "democratic habits," including "self-reliance, responsibility, initiative." Put differently, democracy, the "decent society," was a cultural phenomenon, and as such it needed a certain kind of intellectual, economic, and moral framework in order to survive, let alone thrive. This framework, in turn, must be maintained by the self-conscious actions of real people: citizens. "Democracy works best," he contended, "when men and women do things for themselves, with the help of their friends and neighbors, instead of depending on the state." His hope, steady throughout his career, centered on "self-governing communities" whose members would aggressively take responsibility for the well-being of their own corner of the world.[5]

---

that would make concern for the future its central preoccupation, merge work and nurture, and do everything possible to assure that new generations will inherit a more hospitable environment." Christopher Lasch (hereafter CL) to Wini Breines, typewritten letter (TL), 16 January 1978, Christopher Lasch Papers, Rare Books and Special Collections, Rush Rhees Library, University of Rochester, Rochester, New York. All letters cited in this essay are from this collection. Uses of "decent society" in Lasch's published writings can be found in works including *The Agony of the American Left* (New York: Knopf, 1969), p. 201; and *The Culture of Narcissism* (New York: Norton, 1978), pp. xv, 235.

3. Wilfred McClay, review of Lasch's *The Revolt of the Elites and the Betrayal of Democracy, Commentary* 99, no. 5 (May 1995): 79.

4. John Patrick Diggins, *The Rise and Fall of the American Left* (New York: Norton, 1992), p. 42.

5. Christopher Lasch, *The Revolt of the Elites and the Betrayal of Democracy* (New York: Norton, 1994), pp. 3, 7, 7-8, 8.

For Lasch, history itself, finally, was a moral affair, and wherever there was human willing there went he, sorting through the fall-out of decisions, exposing fulsome trajectories, dissecting pathologies, highlighting visions of the possible; what he found he broadcast widely. The beacon of a "decent society" remained before him throughout his life, and he moved with fervor in its palpable, elusive direction.

Leaving Liberalism

At a frustrating moment in 1962, a young "Kit" Lasch admitted to his friend and fellow historian Staughton Lynd that his recently released first book, *American Liberals and the Russian Revolution,* gave little hint of his "general point of view." There was a good reason for this, and he put it bluntly: "I don't have one." Admittedly attracted to but not convinced of the merits of pacifism and anarchism, he also knew that he was by no means a "new conservative" or a "realist." "Probably," he concluded, bemusedly, "it will turn out that all along I've been a mugwump, or something equally deplorable."[6]

Most specifically the term for those aristocratic politicos who bolted the GOP in 1884, "Mugwump" has come to connote high-minded independence, along with a moralizing public spirit. Throughout his career of more than thirty years as a leading American historian and social critic, Lasch consistently displayed both of these tendencies, and with good reason: his father, an editorial writer for several big-city newspapers, and his mother, a social worker and a philosophy Ph.D., created for Lasch a home in which politics was central and argument about it continual. And this was public argument, as a matter of course; too much was at stake not to enter the public square with purpose and verve, in whatever capacities possible. Lasch's parents incarnated the aged republican ideal of vital, connected citizenship. Young Kit followed eagerly and easily in their traces.

In a 1993 interview Lasch recalled that as a teenager he had "made impassioned speeches" for Progressive Party candidate Henry Wallace in high school assemblies in 1948, which gives a good indication of the variety of politics he imbibed from his parents.[7] Robert Lasch was at that time an editorial writer for the *Chicago Sun,* a position he had taken because he was certain that at the *Sun* he could earn a living "as a working liberal."[8] Both Robert and his wife, Zora

6. CL to Staughton Lynd, TL, 28 November 1962.

7. Casey Blake and Christopher Phelps, "History as Social Criticism: Conversations with Christopher Lasch," *Journal of American History* 80, no. 4, pp. 1311-13.

8. Robert Lasch, "What I Remember," written between 1982-1987, personal manuscript, Box 69, folders 26, 27 of Christopher Lasch Papers, University of Rochester. The quotation is from page 94.

Schaupp Lasch, found a political home on the leftward wing of FDR's New Deal, giving young Kit's childhood a distinctively Democratic shape. Not until he was twenty did he see a Republican in the White House, and both he and his parents shared a sense of consternation when the earth trembled and Dwight Eisenhower defeated Adlai Stevenson in 1952. "For me," Kit wrote to his parents the day after Ike's victory, "the hardest thing to realize is that the Democrats will no longer be in the White House, that the long journey is at last finished, that the last of the New Dealers are passing from the scene. It was inevitable that it should end," he knew, "but it seems impossible."[9]

As a young man Lasch's life was indiscernible to himself apart from the all-pervading political dimension. At an uncertain moment during his senior year at Harvard he wrote movingly to a friend about "the unforgettable heritage of a liberal upbringing," revealing the reverence with which he as a child had absorbed the public, political world. He recalled

> the voice of Roosevelt which made you not afraid, and you never really believed that he could hardly walk; and the death of Roosevelt with the radio commentator having to stop and you realized suddenly that he could not go on because he was crying, and [you] knew that even radio announcers cried when a Man died, and you were crying too, for a man you didn't even know, whom you had never met and whose hand you had never shaken — although your father had shaken his hand and would tell you about it if you asked him . . . and the Sunday afterward you were in a hotel lobby in Lincoln, Nebraska and in honor of the President they played Beethoven's *Heroica* with the roll of muffled drums . . .

He recalled, too, how his mother "always said They, the unknown forces which were trying to drag the whole world to rack and ruin and must somehow be resisted and fought and beaten so the world would be a place you could fall in love in; and how you remembered hearing that Justice Holmes also referred to They, and how you choked when you heard it . . . " He perceived, in this poignant moment, that he, despite intense feelings of aloneness, was "a part of America whatever that means." Having been formed in a home infused with civic consciousness, Lasch sensed that whatever it meant to be "a part of America," it most certainly meant that, as he put it, "wherever I go I cannot not be a part of it."[10] Born and raised a citizen, civic identity — American identity — charged his soul and limned his horizons.

For all of their remarkable success in forging in their son an abiding polit-

9. CL to Zora and Robert Lasch, typed letter signed (TLS), 5 November 1952.
10. CL to Naomi Dagen, autographed letter signed (ALS), 22 January 1954.

ical consciousness, Zora and Robert Lasch were less successful in keeping him in the general vicinity of their own liberal, Democratic politics. Kit's departure from the fold began while he was completing graduate studies at Columbia. As his political perspective matured he grew increasingly disaffected with liberal thought and conduct during the Cold War; gradually he became convinced that the "new realism," which was championed by leading postwar liberals (and Republicans, of course), and which he as a graduate student had also embraced, held little promise for loosening, let alone resolving, the potentially catastrophic impasse at which the USSR and the USA had arrived. Realism's pessimism about human political possibilities seemed, the longer the Cold War continued, to pile self-fulfilling prophecy upon self-fulfilling prophecy.

It was the U-2 incident of May 1960, and the subsequent collapse of what was to have been the first summit of the Cold War, that sparked Lasch's rejection of Cold War liberalism; his movement away from it, tellingly, was rooted in a fundamental sense of moral outrage. "The U-2 affair abounded in revelations," he wrote in a *Nation* essay that underscored the moral concerns that were propelling him toward a more radical politics.[11] He had found himself most incensed that leading realists like George F. Kennan and key members of the Eisenhower administration had not even bothered to condemn on pragmatic grounds the risky practice of conducting espionage flights right up to the eve of the summit, let alone called the general practice of this sort of spying into question. Worse, in response to the crisis Kennan drew "only the familiar lesson about the futility of summit diplomacy." Rather than backing the hopeful pursuit of a thaw in the Cold War, Lasch could now see that the realists had "embraced the Cold War as a way of life."[12] He found this repugnant, a politics of hopelessness and an abdication of moral responsibility.

Lasch, like so many coming of age in the postwar years, became convinced that he must help to articulate and embody a more bracing moral vision, one that might give a more sane and hopeful shape to American politics and culture. His received vision of America had been punctured, damaged beyond repair. He now could see that his was a nation bloated with self-regard and blind to its own pathologies; the "realism" of many leading intellectuals had, as he remarked later to the sociologist Daniel Bell, "congealed into a passive political dogma supportive of many of the worst tendencies in American life."[13] He no longer knew where he fit on the political spectrum, as he confided to Lynd in 1962, but he did know where he did not belong: liberalism's moral

11. CL, "The Historian as Diplomat," *The Nation*, 24 November 1962, p. 349. Lasch also discusses the U-2 incident as a turning point in Blake and Phelps, "History as Social Criticism," pp. 1314-15.

12. CL, "The Historian as Diplomat," p. 351.

13. CL to Daniel Bell, TL, 12 November 1978.

bankruptcy and inability to lead toward the fulfillment of axiomatic American ideals was now painfully apparent. Another way of achieving America must be discovered.[14]

Lasch's brief embrace of "realism," ironically, pushed him toward a political stance that seemed to him to be more realistic and idealistic at once. "By the end of the sixties," Lasch wrote in 1991, "I thought of myself as a socialist." If widely embraced, a Marxian politics, he had come to believe, might lead to "the gradual preparation of a new culture," one that could begin to embody the ideals that his heritage of what he once termed "Middle Western Progressivism" had instilled in him. His vision of the "decent society" gained intensity, became more vivid in his mind.[15]

A New Radical

Lasch became a firm presence in American intellectual life following the 1965 publication of *The New Radicalism in America, 1889-1963: The Intellectual as a Social Type;* he was just turning thirty-three. In a series of deft portraits of American radicals, ranging from Jane Addams to Norman Mailer, Lasch attempted to purify a political tradition that he believed to be besmirched by moral and political compromise. Radicals, he argued, had traded in their birthright of "detached," "critical" inquiry for the pottage of political influence. Intellectuals, argued Lasch, should not forsake "the role of criticism" but should conscientiously and single-mindedly pursue it, fostering radical political change by means of their activities in the cultural sphere. Far-reaching solutions to the mayhem of modern life could be realized only if intellectuals resolved to "pursue a life of reason in a world in which the irrational has come to appear not the exception but the rule." The way of reason might eventually lead to deliverance if intellectuals would only stop their politicking and pining for "experience" (at the expense of more rational, ethical pursuits) long enough to pursue it.[16]

The New Radicalism's broad reception was the stuff of fantasy, including reviews in most major journals of opinion; a glowing review by Alfred Kazin in the *New York Review of Books* especially boosted Lasch's standing.[17] Lasch's po-

14. For Lasch's immediate reaction to the U-2 affair, see his letter to the editor: "Our Spy," *The New Republic,* 30 May 1960, p. 24.

15. CL, *The True and Only Heaven: Progress and Its Critics* (New York: Norton, 1991), pp. 28, 29 25.

16. CL, *The New Radicalism in America, 1889-1963: The Intellectual as a Social Type* (New York: Knopf, 1965), pp. xv, xvii.

17. See Alfred Kazin, "Radicals and Intellectuals," *New York Review of Books* 4, no. 8 (20 May 1965): 3-4.

litical intent in *The New Radicalism,* however, was vague and inchoate, as more than one reader noticed. Lasch himself knew that he had not yet satisfactorily solved the problem of a "general point of view," and he referred to the book in later years as "over-praised."[18] Nevertheless, after the publication of *The New Radicalism,* Lasch's engagement with the Left took a decidedly more committed and sophisticated turn. Young but already veteran Lefties like Staughton Lynd, James Weinstein, and Eugene Genovese espied in Lasch a promising player for their early efforts to mobilize an intellectually rigorous counterpart to the less thoughtful, often thoughtless student radical groups that had begun to proliferate following Johnson's 1964 troops-escalation policy. Lasch began to write with a political edge that invariably provoked response.

With the sort of intellectual vigor that was becoming his hallmark, Lasch moved beyond the writings of leftist American critics such as C. Wright Mills and Dwight Macdonald, influential for him in the early 1960s, to more substantive theorists of the Marxist tradition. "Somewhat belatedly," recalled Lasch, "I plowed through the works of Marx and Engels. I read Gramsci and Lukacs, the founders of 'Western Marxism.' I immersed myself in the work of the Frankfurt school," whose "synthesis of Marx and Freud . . . struck me as enormously fruitful, providing Marxism for the first time with a serious theory of culture."[19] A vision of a more moral, more human society gained solidity, and he employed more than just his pen in its service. Lasch became an active participant at the early teach-ins at the University of Iowa, where he was a faculty member, as well as at Wisconsin, Michigan, and other universities with large student movements. In both his writings and his political agitating he tried to spawn hope for a day when the most abhorrent features of American life — economic inequality, crass consumerism, racial animosities, destruction of the earth, imperial pretensions — would be overcome.[20]

It was a *new culture,* recall, that he was after. He ended *The Agony of the American Left,* his 1968 *cri di coeur,* by articulating the hope that a "humane and democratic socialism" might come about as the result of a "struggle . . . not merely for equality and justice but for a new culture, absorbing but transcending the old." Forging a new culture was the highest political end: he wrote sympathetically of the advance of the civil rights movement in the South in the 1950s and early 1960s, which, he argued, was made possible by the establishment of an "American Negro culture" that had been established based on strong families and churches with "strict standards of sexual morality." These

18. Richard Wightman Fox, "An Interview with Christopher Lasch," *Intellectual History Newsletter* 16 (1994): 9.

19. CL, *True and Only Heaven,* pp. 28-29.

20. Lasch covered a teach-in for the *Nation* in 1965. See CL, "New Curriculum for Teach-Ins," *Nation,* 18 October 1965, pp. 239-41.

institutions led to the "accumulation of talents, skills and leadership" which had made the civil rights movement successful in the south. A culture, he underscored, had taken root among African Americans in the South, one whose commitment to community basics — solid families and religious institutions — enabled it to move in healthy, life-generating political directions.[21]

Tragically, he judged, America as a whole was far from achieving this end, and Marxian perspectives helped him to see why: the existing power structures — sanctioned by a soulless liberal political framework — ensured that the sorry status quo would be maintained. The triumph of corporate capitalism, he contended, "has created a society characterized by a high degree of uniformity, which nevertheless lacks the cohesiveness and sense of shared experience that distinguish a truly integrated community from an atomistic society . . . the United States of the mid-twentieth century might better be described as an empire than as a community."[22]

Lasch now placed his hope for a way out of this mayhem in socialism, but this raised a troubling question: was there reason to believe that a socialist society, given the twentieth-century track record, would be any different than the sort of mechanized, atomistic mass-America that Lasch so deplored? He acknowledged that socialism, to most Americans, rightly "has ugly overtones of bureaucracy, centralization, and forcible repression." The approach that he and his coterie were advancing, though, had more explicitly communitarian means and ends that bore the flavor of the era. Lasch credited the student radicals, whom he often criticized harshly, for "espousing decentralization, local control, and a generally antibureaucratic outlook." These "values," he wrote, were "the heart of radicalism," and essential for the reversal of the "dehumanizing effects of bureaucratic control."[23] But Lasch also insisted, tellingly, that although economic and bureaucratic decentralization were necessary components of the realization of the radical ideal, they were not sufficient. It was an "illusion," he wrote in 1970, echoing the French sociologist Jacques Ellul, that "a change in political structures, without attendant spiritual or cultural transformation, will bring about a genuinely democratic society." "Culture," intrinsically moral and even "spiritual," must somehow be infused with dynamic, salubrious energies that could elevate human experience to a higher plane — toward becoming what Lasch called "a genuinely civilized society."[24]

An earlier American, or a different precinct of contemporary American society, might have looked to religion to provide this sort of morally trans-

21. CL, *Agony of the American Left,* pp. 212, 122.

22. CL, *Agony of the American Left,* p. 27.

23. CL, *Agony of the American Left,* pp. 210, 211.

24. CL, *The World of Nations: Reflections on American History, Politics, and Culture* (New York: Knopf, 1973), pp. 274, 292.

formative dynamic — might, indeed, have perceived Lasch's desire for a "culture" to be a diminished secular variant of "religion." But Lasch, by this time nearing the end of his fourth decade, had little personal proclivity or intellectual affinity for the sphere of formal religion. Raised by parents whom he later regarded as "militant secularists," he had had little exposure to religion of any variety before arriving at Harvard College in 1950.[25] The "moral" concerns that were so central to his political vision in the late 1960s and 1970s were only distantly connected to actual religious traditions, and were modified and flattened by the distinctively modern channels through which he had received them. When he underscored the need for "cultural regeneration" in 1970, he was hopeful that the sort of public and personal morality that his "decent society" required could be fostered through altered social structures in which a more "rational" formation of the human being could take place.[26]

Throughout all of his heady experiences of the late 1960s — being solicited regularly to contribute to leading journals of opinion, collaborating with various groups of intellectuals on a number of political projects, addressing student and civic groups — Lasch himself continued to yearn for participation in the sort of community that he hoped could be realized throughout the nation. To a member of his cohort, the political scientist Gar Alperovitz, he described his situation at Northwestern University in the late 1960s as "increasingly dispiriting" due to his "isolation" from others of like political purpose. He confided that he and Eugene Genovese, a leading socialist historian, had resolved to "try to get positions at the same university," signaling the lengths to which he was willing to go to realize his political-cultural ideals.[27] Politics, the means of achieving "community," stood at the center of his hopes.

But by 1970, after joining Genovese at the University of Rochester, he was looking back on his activities of the previous five years with a sense of despondency. In a reflective letter to Richard Hofstadter, Lasch sarcastically described a number of the recent "projects, all abortive" that had occupied so much time, including "new political parties (which turned out to consist of about 15 people, none of whom could agree on anything), a proposed journal that would be purely political (and would immediately rally the whole country behind it), and others of a similarly fantastic nature."[28] After the collapse of yet another journal project in 1971 he described his situation to his parents in deflated tones: "I have returned to my own work sadder but I hope wiser. From now on I am resolving to let nothing interfere with it."[29]

25. Blake and Phelps, "History as Social Criticism," p. 1313.

26. CL, *World of Nations,* p. 292.

27. CL to Gar Alperovitz, TL, 7 April 1969.

28. CL to Richard Hofstadter, TL, 22 October 1970.

29. CL to Zora and Robert Lasch, TL, 2 July 1971.

Nationally, Lasch sensed, the political energies of the 1960s were dissipating. "The campus is quiet," he wrote to his parents in the fall of 1971. "Even a visit from Jerry Rubin did not arouse the students from their torpor." The hopes that had fired his imagination and many others' for a radically altered politics and culture were dying, painfully. "There's no life in the student movement," he reported to his parents that winter, "and none in the black movement either." He sensed a sea change in attitude and focus: "Most people give the impression of being too overwhelmed with private difficulties to listen, anyway. . . ."[30] Hopes for a "new culture" would give way to visions of, as the title of his best-selling 1979 volume proclaimed, a *Culture of Narcissism.*

Leaving the Left

Lasch appeared to have little sense that he was leaving the Left in the mid-1970s. It seemed to him, rather, that the Left was leaving him. *Haven in a Heartless World: The Family Besieged* appeared in 1977, his first book since a 1973 collection of essays, and the antagonistic reaction to it by many on the Left opened his eyes to see "how far we had traveled down different roads."[31] Just as many radicals were more stridently championing the abandonment of traditional understandings of marriage and the family, Lasch began vociferously to argue that the family as traditionally conceived — father, mother, children, and attached kinship network — was central to democratic hopes, an argument rooted in the premise that only parents (preferably, both parents) are capable of providing the conditions for proper character formation in children. "Without struggling with the ambivalent emotions aroused by the union of love and discipline," he argued, in a Freudian vein, "the child never masters his inner rage or his fear of authority," making him or her more likely to develop "personality traits more compatible with totalitarian regimes than with democracy."[32] Lasch's (now) controversial thesis, with its Huxleyan cast, generated much attention, but it also began to alienate him from the leftist constituency of which he had been a leading light for more than a decade. "Cultural conservatism," in short, had begun by the late 1970s to develop a vital political and intellectual presence, an eventuality Lasch, somewhat unwittingly, was helping to establish.

His inquiry into the family had begun in the early 1960s, but it was not until the aftermath of that decade that he had begun earnestly to pursue this

30. CL to Zora and Robert Lasch, TL, 19 October 1971; CL to Zora and Robert Lasch, TL, 21 December 1971.

31. CL, *Haven in a Heartless World: The Family Besieged* (New York: Basic Books, 1977); Blake and Phelps, "History as Social Criticism," p. 1328.

32. CL, *Haven in a Heartless World,* pp. 123, xv.

line of research and writing. Long interested in the connection between culture and personality, Lasch was also spurred to pursue this topic as a result of his own experiences at home. "The unexpectedly rigorous business of bringing up children exposed me," he recalled, "to our 'child-centered' society's icy indifference to everything that makes it possible for children to flourish and grow up to be responsible adults. To see the modern world from the point of view of a parent is to see it in the worst possible light." From this vantage a vast "moral collapse" was evident, making for less than ideal cultural conditions in which to form human beings.[33] *Haven in a Heartless World* was his early attempt to wrestle with this unsavory historical development. The driving questions of his study were simple but piercing: "Why has family life become so painful, marriage so fragile, relations between parents and children so full of hostility and recrimination?"[34]

Lest anyone mistakenly think he had departed, like other erstwhile leftists, to the political right in his defense of what many radicals supposed to be an outmoded, repressive institution, Lasch made it clear that he believed the fundamental social and economic structures of American society were militating against healthy family life in America. Corporate capitalism, he maintained, was ravaging the family's all-important political and cultural fruit with its extraction of work from the home and its relentless advertising campaigns. Living under the aegis of the market, citizens had become "full-fledged consumers, perpetually restless and dissatisfied" and plagued by the attendant psychological disorders such conditions helped to advance. Moreover, the "helping professions" — culturally powerful groups of medical, sociological, and psychological "experts" on matters pertaining to the family — had developed as adjuncts of the corporate state, making what was "formerly the business of the family" their own province and so diminishing the authority of parents and shrinking the precinct of family life. In the end, charged Lasch, the "managerial and professional classes" had "eroded the capacity for self-help and social invention," both essential for democratic life. If "community" in America was faltering, it was due in part to the absence of the sustained experience of family life. To be sure, families had always "passed along the dominant values of a society," but they had also "unavoidably provided the child with a glimpse of a world that transcended them, crystallized in the rich imagery of maternal love." Without this sort of experience, human pursuits, not surprisingly, had devolved into individualistic, narcissistic modes of behavior, diminishing American prospects for community, for the "new culture."[35]

33. CL, *True and Only Heaven,* pp. 33, 34.
34. CL, *Haven in a Heartless World,* p. xvi.
35. CL, *Haven in a Heartless World,* pp. 20, xv, xvii.

The Culture of Narcissism: American Life in an Age of Diminishing Expectations followed *Haven in a Heartless World*, emerging from the same body of research less than two years later. If in *Haven* Lasch attempted to tell the story of the recent past from a sociological point of view, *Narcissism* unveiled the psychological angle: the toll of what he called "the wreckage of capitalism" on the individual. He based his study on the premise that "Every society reproduces its culture — its norms, its underlying assumptions, its modes of organizing experience — in the individual, in the form of personality." America's "current malaise," in this light, was etched out in the dominant personality type of the day: the narcissist. Not simply a pleasure-seeking hedonist, the narcissist's condition was much more grave. Capitalism's "new kind of paternalism," he contended, had by the 1970s weakened dramatically the ability of Americans to act as individuals; lacking the "inner resources" that could be nurtured only in the family, the typical American looked outward to others to prop up his or her own deeply inadequate sense of selfhood. Insecurities of colossal dimensions increasingly guided behavior, and instead of cultivating the virtues of "character and probity" — virtues essential for democracy — Americans focused on "style" and appearance in feeble efforts to make up for the inner dearth. The misshaping influence of narcissism was everywhere — in sports, politics, education, and the "sex war." Perniciously, the narcissistic tendency quashed the very elements democratic renewal required: the inner strength and clarity of vision required to mount an attack against these destructive social structures.[36]

The strong reception of a Lasch *New York Review of Books* essay on narcissism in 1976 had signaled to him that the issues he intended to raise in the book "seem to be on a lot of people's minds at the moment," as he put it in a 1977 letter.[37] But when the book appeared two years later he was completely unprepared for the overwhelming public response. Not only did leading journals of opinion feature it prominently, *Time* and *Newsweek* covered it as well; even *People* featured an interview with Lasch. Letters poured in from around the nation, from schoolteachers, urban professionals, artists, fellow academics. President Carter himself took note of the book and in the summer of 1979 invited Lasch to the White House to discuss with a small group of other intellectuals and activists the current cultural and political state of affairs. Surprisingly, though, when the dust settled Lasch looked more and more like a pariah — a popular pariah, to be sure, but isolated, an uneasy fit in the existing political framework.[38]

36. CL, *Culture of Narcissism*, pp. xv, 34, 218, 210, 53; chapter eight was entitled "The Flight from Feeling: Sociopsychology of the Sex War," pp. 187-206.

37. CL to Robert Silvers, TL, 5 February 1977.

38. Lasch recounts his experience at the White House in Fox, "An Interview with Christopher Lasch," pp. 12-13.

One reviewer noted that following the publication of *Haven* and *Narcissism* Lasch's "old readership, the veteran radicals of the 1960s," had in the main "mourned the old Lasch" and had "tried to bury his new arguments about the need for order and authority within the family and, by extension, within society at large."[39] Lasch felt this general rejection acutely and sensed that the political landscape was undergoing rapid, tectonic change. "The lines of political and cultural debate grow progressively more fuzzy," he observed in a letter to his former colleague at Northwestern, the literary critic Gerald Graff, in December of 1977. "You never know who your friends are going to be from one minute to the next, and one hardly knows how to conduct himself except to adopt a surly demeanor toward one and all in the hope of offending *everybody*." He confessed to being nonplused to find himself agreeing with neoconservatives like Midge Decter and Norman Podhoretz on issues like "the importance of kids having parents instead of professional day-care sitters."[40] He was particularly troubled by attacks from feminists: "If you talk about the growing tensions that so often seem to characterize relations between men and women, it's assumed that you want women to return to the kitchen," he complained to friends living in France, lamenting that "only two positions are recognized, 'progressive' and 'traditional.'"[41] Lasch's virulent opposition to capitalism in (at least partial) defense of traditional conceptions of society made him a lonely soul. "The danger of my becoming a hero of any political group seems pretty remote," he remarked to a friend in 1979.[42]

Just how Lasch fit into the current political framework bedeviled many. Michael Kammen, in a review of *Narcissism*, conjectured that Lasch "so far as I can tell, is a conservative radical."[43] These terms, awkwardly juxtaposed in the last third of the twentieth century, did point to twin impulses present in Lasch's work from the outset. All along Lasch had been anchoring a good deal of his cultural hopes in the inheritance of a pre-capitalist past that antedated "progressive," "liberal" conceptions of human relations. He once explained his early attraction to "the tradition of English Marxism" in the 1960s as stemming in part from its ability to "absorb the insights of cultural conservatives and provide a sympathetic account, not just of the economic hardships imposed by capitalism, but the way in which capitalism thwarted the need for joy in work, stable connections, family life, a sense of place, and a sense of historical conti-

39. Fred Siegel, "The Agony of Christopher Lasch," *Reviews in American History* 8, no. 3 (September 1980): 285.

40. CL to Gerald Graff, TL, 15 December 1977.

41. CL to Ed and Cheryl Berenson, TL, 19 December 1977.

42. CL to Ed and Cheryl Berenson, 16 October 1979.

43. Michael Kammen, "A Whiplash of Contradictory Expectations," *Reviews in American History* 7, no. 4 (December 1979): 452.

nuity" — all key elements in his "decent society."[44] In this spirit Lasch had decried in *The New Radicalism* "the renunciation of culture, of the past, of history itself" that was "so characteristically American."[45] A few years later in an essay entitled "Is Revolution Obsolete?" he stated what was by then a foundational premise for him, that "Revolutionary movements articulate new ideas of liberty and equality, but these ideas are rooted in traditional, pre-industrial ways of life."[46] When a feminist friend took issue with his dour perspective on contemporary radical prospects in 1978, he wondered, along similar lines: "Can anyone deny that the prospects for socialism were much brighter a hundred years ago than they are today?" He certainly could not, and his reasoning gave ample insight into some of the reasons for his distance from self-styled "progressives" of the 1970s: one hundred years ago, he explained, "the memory of communal traditions antedating capitalism kept alive the vision of a post-capitalist society. . . ."[47] While many radicals in the 1970s admired what they perceived to be the communal nature of pre-industrial societies, most did so while shucking as repressive and outmoded the very ethical and theological distinctives which caused those societies to cohere. Lasch's failure to share their understanding of "repression" and "progress" made him a "conservative" to these radicals, despite his harsh view of capitalism and his generally egalitarian views on gender issues.[48]

For one so attracted to fraternal ideals, the pain of parting with the intellectual community of the Left, where he had gained hard-won intellectual and political rooting in the mid-1960s, was considerable. At the height of his popularity, Lasch found himself in a difficult and lonely place politically and intellectually. "Forced by the hostile reception of *Haven* to think about what had happened both to me and the Left," he recalled in a 1993 interview, "I began to rethink issues that I thought I had more or less resolved to my satisfaction."[49] His primary concerns and ideals had not changed; his archetypal vision of robust, locally governed communities comprised of strong families remained firmly in place. But the Marxian and Freudian foundations that he had developed to support his political edifice in the late 1960s and 1970s had begun to crack and erode, forcing him to search for more firm footing to ensure its survival. He made no quick and easy discoveries. He later recalled being "very

44. CL, *True and Only Heaven,* p. 29.

45. CL, *New Radicalism,* p. 28.

46. CL, *World of Nations,* pp. 107-8.

47. CL to Wini Breines, TL, 21 September 1978.

48. A posthumously published collection of Lasch's essays that profile his various stances on these matters is *Women and the Common Life: Love, Marriage, and Feminism,* ed. Elisabeth Lasch-Quinn (New York: Norton, 1997).

49. Blake and Phelps, "History as Social Criticism," p. 1328.

troubled" and feeling "intellectually and politically completely at sea" during these years.[50] But journey on he did, following the moral imperatives that had guided him thus far. Hopes for a "new culture," though, had been severely tempered, if not abandoned.

A Populist's Protest

Lasch in the 1980s continued his long quest for a political and intellectual home, all the while seeking companions with whom he could journey and make common cause. The psychologist Robert Coles and political theorist Jean Bethke Elshtain were two of the more prominent intellectuals who discovered in Lasch a like mind on matters related to family and politics. For the most part, though, Lasch found alliances difficult to come by, and became increasingly dissatisfied with current political options.[51]

In the midst of the *Culture of Narcissism* phenomenon, Lasch had commented to one sympathetic reader that "The whole point of my two recent books was to begin a new debate, not to take sides in an old one, and it's a source of deep chagrin to me that so many readers persist in trying to pigeonhole the argument into one or another of the available political positions, all of which, it seems to me, exhausted themselves a long time ago."[52] Twelve years later he had done enough thinking about this historical problem to develop his premise into a book-length argument. He began 1991's *The True and Only Heaven: Progress and Its Critics* with the contention that "old political ideologies have exhausted their capacity either to explain events or to inspire men and women to constructive action." He called on recent history as his witness. In the intervening decade the United States, and much of the world, had seen "the unexpected resurgence of the right," which had "thrown the left into confusion and called into question all its old assumptions about the future." Despite its success at the polls, though, the Right had not succeeded in its stated aim of restoring "moral order and collective purpose to Western nations. . . . [S]piritual disrepair," he concluded, "is just as evident today as it was in the 1970s."[53] What

50. Fox, "An Interview with Christopher Lasch," p. 13.

51. See Coles's lengthy review of *Culture of Narcissism*: "Unreflecting Egoism," *New Yorker*, 27 August 1979, pp. 98-105. Elshtain pays tribute to Lasch in "The Life and Work of Christopher Lasch: An American Story," *Salmagundi* 106-107 (Spring-Summer 1995): 146-61. Coles wrote about his relationship with Lasch (and the relationship Lasch, Elshtain, and he had) in "Remembering Christopher Lasch," *New Oxford Review*, September 1994, pp. 16-19.

52. CL to David Marr, TL, 6 August 1979.

53. CL, *True and Only Heaven*, pp. 21, 22.

he wished for culturally and politically, in short, did not seem to be within the grasp of late twentieth-century American politics. He took this as a challenge not to quit, but to keep working harder.

In his search for allies and for ways of understanding and combating the "spiritual disrepair" that he felt, Lasch's hopes were raised in the early 1980s by the launching of *democracy,* a quarterly journal of opinion that, as he defined it to one potential contributor, was "devoted to a radical but non-Marxist politics, if that isn't a contradiction in terms." *democracy* had a "stated determination not to be content with received political answers," a position Lasch warmly embraced.[54] With enthusiasm he accepted a post on the editorial board, describing the launching of the new magazine as "the most encouraging news I've heard in a long time"; he had, he explained, "pretty much reached the end of what it seems possible to do in political and intellectual isolation."[55]

Sadly, his enthusiasm was short-lived. At the end of 1983 the magazine folded, after reaching a peak circulation of around ten thousand subscribers. Lasch's disappointment ran deep, rooted as it was in his sense that *democracy* had begun to carve out the sort of niche on the political spectrum he had long been seeking; no other publication was positioned to take its place. But despite its failure, the journal did last long enough to enable Lasch and others to create a forum in which to think together about connections between politics, morality, history, and community outside of the dominant leftist strictures. Assessing *democracy*'s complexion as it was folding, Lasch pegged it as "just about the only journal on the left that showed much interest in the small-is-beautiful tradition on the left (if it is even correct to identify it as a left-wing tradition)." The journal had succeeded, he thought, in making a fairly "rigorous case for localism and 'soft' technology," without the "metaphysical mumbo-jumbo and mysticism . . . that so often seems to go along with this kind of politics."[56] *democracy*'s journalistic and political achievement, despite its brief lifespan, was considerable, and in the case of Lasch bore much fruit. In helping to give *democracy* this shape Lasch himself started down the path upon which he would remain until his death in 1994.

It was a path that the historian Jackson Lears had seen in formation in the late 1970s. "The most powerful critics of capitalism have often looked backward rather than forward," wrote Lears. Lasch, he suggested, belonged in this company, alongside those "cultural conservatives" who had "arraigned capitalist 'progress' for promoting untrammeled individualism and eroding loyalties to family, craft, community or faith." Lears was prescient: Lasch, with poet and

54. CL to Henry Davis, TLS, 17 August 1980 — a letter apparently never sent.

55. CL to Sheldon Wolin, TL, 13 November 1979.

56. CL to Jean-Christophe Agnew, TL, 16 October 1983.

essayist Wendell Berry, would become in the last twenty years of his life arguably the most compelling American critic in the last half of twentieth-century American history to engage and invigorate a political tradition that in America had by then lapsed into quiescence.[57]

Influenced by such books as Alasdair MacIntyre's *After Virtue,* the historical dimension of Lasch's social criticism, surprisingly (but tellingly) weak in the 1970s, grew more rich in his later work; he gradually abandoned his Marxian-Freudian framework, which had been sophisticated, to be sure, but also flat and faintly formulaic.[58] From trying to envision the altered social conditions that might make possible a "new culture," he moved to a search for existing embodiments of the "decent society" that he so prized. His critical vision gained a human thickness that had been noticeably lacking before.

He discovered one historical trajectory of the "decent society" in what he termed, in *The True and Only Heaven,* the "populist tradition," which was "most simply described, perhaps, as the sensibility of the petty bourgeoisie." Despite its "characteristic vices of envy, resentment, and servility," the lower middle class, he averred, had tended to understand that life should be lived with a profound awareness of "a sense of limits," a sensibility that consumer capitalism and the "progress" that it underwrote needed to eradicate in order to triumph. "Populism," then, went well beyond the political movement of the late nineteenth century to include among its denizens thinkers and movements that had paid heed, with the previous century's agrarian opponents of "improvement," to

> The habits of responsibility associated with property ownership; the self-forgetfulness that comes with immersion in some all-absorbing piece of work; the danger that material comforts will extinguish a more demanding

57. Jackson Lears, "Therapy's Triumph," *The Nation,* 27 January 1979, p. 91. Lasch himself in *The True and Only Heaven* and *The Revolt of the Elites* referenced two Wendell Berry books: *The Unsettling of America: Culture and Agriculture* (New York: Avon, 1977) and *Sex, Economy, Freedom, and Community* (New York: Pantheon, 1993). A brief and succinct statement of Lasch's anti-capitalist cultural conservatism is "Conservatism Against Itself," *First Things* 2 (April 1990): 17-23.

58. *After Virtue* was published in 1981 (Notre Dame: University of Notre Dame Press); Lasch had been sent an advance copy. To Wolin, *democracy*'s editor, Lasch wrote: "Although I can't claim fully to have assimilated the argument, it's clearly an important book we should pay attention to. It's a critique of liberal individualism. . . . He is equally critical of Rawls and of Nozick, liberalism and 'conservatism.' I find it extremely suggestive on a whole range of issues, and I wish I could think of someone who could review it for us." (CL to Sheldon Wolin, TL, 10 August 1981.) Lasch was a part of a University of Rochester faculty study group that together read MacIntyre's volume, and he hosted a MacIntyre lecture at the university in the spring of 1983.

> ideal of the good life; and the dependence of happiness on the recognition that humans are not made for happiness. . . .[59]

Anchoring his hope in what he thought of as an embodied historical tradition, rather than in theoretical frameworks worked up in the European context, he absorbed himself in the stories of Americans who "had grappled with the same issues that preoccupied European thinkers in the nineteenth century — secularization, industrialism, the division of labor — and worked out positions that," he came to think, "should not be dismissed simply because they couldn't be reconciled with Marxism, liberalism, or social democracy."[60] Jonathan Edwards, Ralph Waldo Emerson, Orestes Brownson, Reinhold Niebuhr, and Martin Luther King Jr. all made appearances in Lasch's unfolding of populism, a "distinctive tradition of moral speculation" that, he underscored, was "drawn from everyday experience (as well as from the heightened experience of spiritual fervor). . . ."[61]

Religion, then, figured quietly but centrally in Lasch's later political thinking. This was a big departure. In the early 1980s his confidence in purely secular, social-scientific ways of explaining and inculcating morality (and thus the "decent society") had begun to wane, a direction first evident in his 1984 sequel to *Narcissism, The Minimal Self: Psychic Survival in Troubled Times.* He had begun in those years, as he later stated, to believe that "it was a mistake to write off this whole realm of experience as if it didn't matter."[62] By the time he wrote *The Revolt of the Elites and the Betrayal of Democracy,* which was posthumously published in 1994, Lasch could affirm, with Augustinian overtones, that "Alienation is the normal condition of human existence. Rebellion against God is the natural reaction to the discovery that the world was not made for our personal convenience."[63] If he had not gotten religion, he had certainly gotten serious about it. His searing moral vision, anchored more overtly in religious formulations, in the last years of his life dictated the direction of his thought and politics with, if possible, even more intensity than it had before. The historian David Chappell, one of his former students, poignantly evoked the personal dimension of Lasch's moral stance in a letter recommending him for a teaching award: "One of the most helpful things I learned from studying with Lasch is something I do not think I could have learned from just reading Lasch: When Lasch criticizes modern society, he criticizes his own self, which he sees as irretrievably and lovingly bound to

59. CL, *True and Only Heaven,* pp. 532, 17, 16.

60. Blake and Phelps, "History as Social Criticism," p. 1328.

61. CL, *True and Only Heaven,* p. 532.

62. Fox, "An Interview with Christopher Lasch," p. 13.

63. CL, *Revolt of the Elites,* p. 244.

modern society. That explains the depth of his insight and the urgency of his criticism."[64]

Chappell sensed correctly that as much as Lasch came to appreciate religion and admire the religious, he lived with a sense of tension. He felt deeply "bound to modern society," with its sometimes ambivalent, often antagonistic, relationship to religion. As if torn between two worlds, Lasch at the end of his life orbited often the religious sphere, touching down occasionally, but never landing in any particular religious communion. ("I certainly hadn't undergone some kind of religious conversion," he emphasized when asked in 1993 about his recent interest in religion.) Throughout the last decade of his life his public use of categories like "religion" and "morality" seemed to be grounded in social scientific perspectives as much as in a particular theology; the doctrinal particularity which gives any religious faith its identity and historical force tended to be missing from his formulations. Raise "moral concerns" he did, but always in a way that was at least somewhat amenable to the pluralistic audiences he usually addressed.[65]

Some evidence, though, indicates that the nature of his encounter with the Christian faith was more than intellectual. Dale Vree, a close friend and the editor of *The New Oxford Review* (a Catholic journal of opinion to which Lasch contributed), wrote following Lasch's death of his own confidence, based on many conversations, that "Kit was 'one of us,' that he had died 'a holy death.'"[66] Another Catholic editor and friend, Richard John Neuhaus of *First Things*, disclosed Lasch's diffident encounter with the Christian faith, or at least Catholicism, when he remarked to a very ill Lasch that "Jean Elshtain says she's not sure you're actually praying the rosary, but you have it near at hand." Know, Neuhaus intoned, "that you are very much in my thoughts and prayers."[67]

Lasch's resolute commitment to judge all dimensions of culture, society, and politics by high moral criteria, in the end, lies at the center of the rich legacy he left for us. In carrying out this commitment, though, Lasch inevitably was forced to reckon with the bedeviling problem of particularity: whose morality, in the end, should be our standard? Forced to confront this question, Lasch wrestled seriously with embracing the particularity of a religious com-

64. David Chappell to David W. Beach, TLS, 3 November 1993, box 7c, folder 4.

65. Fox, "An Interview with Christopher Lasch," p. 13. For a good example of Lasch's use of "religion" in a general way see his review of recent literature on the topic of shame: "For Shame: Why Americans Should Be Wary of Self-Esteem," *The New Republic,* 10 August 1992, pp. 29-34; this essay is included in his *The Revolt of the Elites* as "The Abolition of Shame," pp. 197-212.

66. Dale Vree, "Christopher Lasch: A Memoir," *New Oxford Review,* April 1994, pp. 2, 5.

67. Richard John Neuhaus to CL, ALS, n.d., box 7c, folder 4.

munion over against possessing a mere respect for "religion" and its social utility. How, and if, he resolved these matters is something we may never know.

But the integrity of his example in addressing these concerns may, in the end, spur us to grapple with what may be the most decisive question confronting us today. Lasch's many books and essays — indeed, his life itself — compel us to ask whether "community," whether the "decent society," is possible apart from the thickness of connection and the singleness of mind and action that are at the center of the most robust religious traditions? Is respect for "religion" and "morality," apart from the distinctive forms of living that actual membership in religious communions engenders, sufficient to eliminate the cultural pathologies that have so devastated our country?

The life of Christopher Lasch leaves us nodding in both directions. His undeniable integrity enlarges the hope that improved cultural conditions can indeed be obtained apart from widespread religious renewal. But his trek in the direction of religious and theological particularity seems to express his own sense that his received secular framework was not enough, that more was needed — *much* more. Humans, he seemed to intuit, were designed for a level of personal and social experience far more rich than our history as a race, at least most of the time, tells us is possible. He left us with an honest sense of ambiguity — and, no doubt, the implicit charge to keep furrowing where he, sadly, had to leave off far too early.

The Communitarian Model

AMITAI ETZIONI

Communitarianism is a social philosophy that maintains that societal formulations of the good are both needed and legitimate. It is often contrasted with classical liberalism, a philosophical position holding that each individual should formulate the good. Communitarians examine the ways shared conceptions of the good (values) are formed, transmitted, enforced, and justified — hence their interest in communities (and moral dialogues within them), historically transmitted values and mores, and the societal units that transmit and enforce values, such as the family, schools, and voluntary associations from social clubs to independent churches.

While laissez-faire conservatives and welfare liberals differ mainly with regard to the respective roles of the private sector and the state, communitarians are especially concerned with the third sector, civil society. They pay special attention to the way social responsibilities are fostered by informal communal processes of persuasion and peer pressure.

While the term "communitarian" was coined only in the mid-nineteenth century, ideas that are communitarian in nature can be found in the Old and New Testaments, in Catholic theology (e.g., the emphasis on the Church as community, and more recently on subsidiarity), and in socialist doctrine (e.g., writings about the early commune and about workers' solidarity).

While all communitarians uphold the importance of the social realm, and in particular of community, they differ in the extent to which their conceptions are attentive to liberty and individual rights. Early communitarians like Ferdinand Tönnies and Robert Nisbet stressed the importance of closely knit social fabric and authority. Asian communitarians are especially concerned about the values of social order. In the 1980s, Robert Bellah and his associates Charles Taylor, Michael Sandel, and Michael Walzer criticized the excessive individualism of classical liberalism, America under President Ronald Reagan, and Britain under Prime Minister Margaret Thatcher. Most recently, Alan Ehrenhalt's book *The Lost City: The Forgotten Virtues of Community in America* questioned the value of enhancing choice at the cost of maintaining community and authority.

In the 1990s, responsive communitarians such as Robert Bellah, Jean Bethke Elshtain, William A. Galston, Mary Ann Glendon, Philip Selznick, and I emphasized the need to balance commitment to the social good with respect for individual rights, and to reconcile the promotion of social virtue with liberty. These individuals were among those who issued a platform endorsed by a wide range of leading Americans, published a quarterly *(The Responsive Community),* and formed a communitarian network. They have often been credited with having influenced leaders of different persuasions in a number of Western countries.[1]

Responsive communitarians have developed several specific concepts and policies, drawing on their philosophy. They favor shoring up families, but advocate peer marriages (in which mothers and fathers have equal rights and responsibilities) rather than the traditional authoritarian family structure. They have fostered schools that provide character education rather than merely teaching academics, but oppose religious indoctrinization. They have developed notions of community justice in which offenders, victims, and members of the community work together to find appropriate punishments and meaningful reconciliation. Responsive communitarians favor devolution of state power and the formation of communities of communities (within national societies and among nations), among many other policies.

The Moral Voice

Audiences who are quite enthusiastic about the communitarian message cringe when someone introduces the term "moral voice," the idea that in order to make society better than it would be otherwise, people must speak up for the values they believe in. They say that the term reminds them of the Moral Majority and maintain that "nobody should tell us what to do." *Time* magazine, in an otherwise highly favorable cover story on communitarian thinking, warned

1. For more information and a comprehensive communitarian bibliography, see http://www.gwu.edu/~ccps.

against busybodies "humorlessly imposing on others arbitrary [meaning their own] standards of behavior, health and thought." Studies of an American suburb by sociologist M. P. Baumgartner found a disturbing unwillingness of people to make moral claims on one another. Most people did not feel it was their place to express their convictions when someone did something that was wrong.

At the same time, the overwhelming majority of Americans, public opinion polls show, recognize that the nation's moral fabric has worn rather thin. Why are people who recognize the full measure of the moral deficit the nation faces at the same time so reluctant to lay moral claims on one another? One reason is that they see immorality not in their friends and neighborhoods, but practically every place else. (In the same way that they find Congress members in general to be corrupt but often re-elect "their" representative because he or she is "OK," and complain frequently about physicians but find their doctor above reproach.) This phenomena may be referred to as moral myopia, and there seems to be no ready cure.

In addition, many Americans seem to have internalized the writings of Dale Carnegie on how to win friends and influence in society: you are supposed to work hard at flattering the other person and never chastise anyone. Otherwise, generations of Americans have been told by their parents, you might lose a "friend" and set back your networking. A study found that when college co-eds were asked whether or not they would tell their best friend if, in their eyes, the person the friend had chosen to wed was utterly unsuitable, most said they would refrain. They feared losing the friend. They would rather she go ahead and hurt herself rather than take the risk of endangering the friendship. This clearly indicates that they ranked their fear of losing a friend above the commitment to help that friend. Daniel Patrick Moynihan has argued convincingly in his recent article in *The American Scholar,* "Defining Deviance Down," that people have been so bombarded with evidence of social ills that they have developed moral calluses, which make them relatively inured to immorality.

When Americans do contemplate moral reform, many are rather a-sociological: they believe that the problem is primarily one of individual conscience. If youngsters would be taught again to tell right from wrong by their families and schools, if churches could reach them again, our moral and social order would be on the mend. They focus on what is only one, albeit one important, component of the moral equation: the inner voice. In the process, many Americans disregard the crucial role of the community in reinforcing the individual's moral commitments. To document the importance of the community, one must ask what constitutes a moral person.

I build here on the writings of Harry Frankfurt, Albert O. Hirschman, and others who have argued that humans differ from animals in that, while both species experience impulses, humans have the capacity to pass judgments upon their impulses. These authorities do not suggest that humans can "control" their impulses, but that they can defer responding to them long enough to evaluate the behavior toward which they feel inclined. Once this evaluation takes place, sometimes the judgments win, sometimes the impulses. If the judgments always took precedence, we would be saintly; if the impulses always won, we would be psychopaths or animals. The human fate is a constant struggle between the noble and the debased parts of human nature.

It is to the struggle between judgments and impulses that the moral voice of the community speaks. The never-ending struggle within the human soul over which course to follow is not limited to intra-individual dialogues between the impulses that tempt us to disregard our marital vows, be deceitful, and be selfish, and the values we previously internalized, which warn us against yielding to those temptations. In making moral choices (to be precise, choices between moral and immoral conduct rather than among moral claims) we are influenced by the approbation and censure of others, especially of those with whom we have close relations — family members, friends, neighbors — in short, our communities.

It may not flatter our view of ourselves, but human nature is such that if these community voices speak in unison and with clarity (without being shrill), we are much more likely to follow our inner judgments than if these voices are silent, conflicted, or speak too softly. Hence, the pivotal import of the voice of communities in raising the moral level of their members.

Various challenges have been posed to this line of argument. Some argue that the reliance on community points to conformism, to "other-directed" individuals who merely seek to satisfy whatever pleases their community. This is not the vision evoked here. The community voice as depicted here is not the only voice that lays claims on individuals as to the course they ought to follow, but rather is a voice that speaks in addition to their inner one. When the community's voice and the inner one are in harmony, this is not a case of conformism, of one "party" yielding to the other, but one of two tributaries flowing into the same channel. (For example, if I firmly believe that it is wrong to leave my children unattended and so do my neighbors, and if I then stay home, this is hardly an instance of conformism.) If these two voices conflict, I must pass judgment not only *vis-a-vis* my impulses (should I yield or follow the dictates of my conscience?), but also on whether or not I shall heed my fellow community members or follow my own inclination.

In short, the mere existence of a community moral voice does not necessarily spell conformism. Conformism occurs only if and when one automatically or routinely sets aside personal judgments to grant supremacy to the community. That happens when personal voices are weak — far from a necessary condition for the existence of a community voice. To put it differently, while conformism is a danger so is the absence of the reinforcing effects of the communal voice. The antidote to conformism is thus not to undermine the community's voice but to seek to ensure that the personal voice is also firmly instilled.

Above all, it must be noted that while the moral voice urges and counsels us, it is congenitally unable to force us. Whatever friends, neighbors, ministers, or community leaders say, the ultimate judgment call is up to the acting person. (True, under some limited situations, when a community excommunicates or hounds someone, the pressure can be quite intense. This rarely happens in modern-day communities, however, because individuals are able to move to other communities when they are unduly pressured, since they often are members of two or more communities — of residence and of work, for example. Individuals thus are able psychologically to draw on one community to ward off excessive pressure from the other.)

Others argue that the community voice is largely lost because of American pluralism. Individuals are subject to the voices of numerous communities, each pulling in a different direction and thus neutralizing the others, or together creating such a cacophony that no clear voice can be heard. The notion that no community is right and all claims have equal standing, championed especially by multiculturalists, further diminishes the claim of the moral voice.

While all this is true, there is no way to return to the days of simple, homogenous communities. And those quite often were rather oppressive. The contemporary solution, if not salvation, lies in seeking and developing an evolving framework of shared values, which all subcultures will be expected to endorse and support without losing their distinct identities and subcultures. Thus, Muslim-Americans can be free to follow the dictates of their religion, cherish their music and cuisine, and be proud of select parts of their history (no group should be encouraged to embrace all of its history). But at the same time they (and all other communities that make up the American society) need to accept the dignity of the individual, the basic value of liberty, the democratic form of government, and other such core values. On these matters we should expect and encourage all communities to speak in one voice.

Other critics argue that the essence of individual freedom is that every person follows his own course and that social institutions leave us alone. (More technically, economists write about the primacy of our preferences and scoff at intellectuals and ideologues who want to impose their "tastes" on others.) These critics confuse allusions to freedom from the state, its coercion and controls, with freedom from the moral urging of our fellow community members. One can be as opposed to state intervention and regulation as a diehard libertarian and still see a great deal of merit in people encouraging one another to do what is right. This need not involve frustrating people and preventing them from acting on their preferences, which is what the coercive state does, but rather should focus on appealing to people's better selves to change or reorder their preferences.

Indeed, a strong case can be made that it is precisely the bonding together of community members that enables us to remain independent of the state. The anchoring of individuals in viable families, webs of friendships, faith communities, and neighborhoods — in short, in communities — best sustains their ability to resist the pressures of the state. The absence of these social foundations opens isolated individuals to totalitarian pressures. (This, of course, is the point Tocqueville makes in *Democracy in America.*)

In deliberating on these matters one may borrow a leaf from Joel Feinberg's seminal work *Offense to Others.* In his book, Feinberg asks us to imagine that we are riding on a full bus we cannot readily leave. He then presents a series of hypothetical scenes which would cause offense, such as someone playing loud music, scratching a metallic surface, handling what looks like a real grenade, engaging in sexual behavior, and so on.

Here the issue is not so much what the members of a community find tolerable versus unbearable, but what will make them speak up. I hence asked students and colleagues, "imagine you are in a supermarket and a mother beats the daylights out of a three year old child — would you speak up?" (I say "mother" because I learned that if I just say "someone" most of my respondents state that they would not react because they would be afraid the other person would clobber them.) Practically everyone I asked responded that they would not speak up. They would at most try to "distract" the mother, "find out what the child really did," and so on. I also asked, "imagine you are resting on the shore of a pristine lake; a picnicking family, about to depart, leaves behind a trail of trash — would you suggest they clean up after themselves?" Here again, many demurred, but a fair number were in this scenario willing to consider saying something.

It is possible that my informal sample is skewed. It seems to me, however, that something else is at work: that we had a consensus-building grand dialogue about the environment. While there are still sharp disagreements about numerous details (for instance, the relative standing of spotted owls vs. loggers), there is a basic consensus that we must be mindful of the environment and cannot trash it. We have had neither a grand dialogue nor a new consensus about the way to treat children, however. This would suggest one more reason our moral voice is so feeble and reluctant: too many of us, too often, are no longer sure on behalf of what to speak.

A return to a firmer moral voice thus will require a major town hall meeting of sorts, the kind we have when Americans spend billions of hours in bowling alleys, next to water coolers, and on call-in shows forming a new consensus. The kind we have already had about the environment, civil rights, and excessive general regulation, and which we are now beginning to have about gay rights. This time we need to agree with one another that the common good requires that we speak up while also enunciating the values for which we speak. To reiterate, heeding such consensus should never be automatic; we need to examine the values the community urges upon us to determine whether or not they square with our conscience and the basic values that we sense no person or community has a right to violate. Here, however, the focus is on the other side of the coin: it is not enough to individually be able to tell right from wrong, as crucial as this is. We must also be willing to encourage others to attend to values we as a community share and ought to actively seek to uphold.

Deliberations, Culture Wars, and Moral Dialogues

Communitarians tend to argue that democratic societies require a core of shared values; that if democracy is merely a procedure that allows individuals who have different ultimate normative commitments to work out shared policies, then that polity will lack in legitimacy. As I see it, reasoned deliberations are not sufficient if a community seeks to collectively formulate shared values, and I will explore here the additional processes that are needed, which I call moral dialogues.

The literature that explores the ways collectives formulate their course is deeply influenced by the liberal way of thinking. Liberal thought maintains that typically the way people ought to proceed (or/and do proceed) is for them to assemble and dispassionately discuss the facts of the situation, explore their logical implications, examine the alternative responses that might be undertaken, and choose the one that is the most appropriate based on empirical evidence and logical conclusions. The process is often referred to as one of *deliberation.* The overarching image that is reflected in this concept is that of a New England town meeting or of the ancient Greek polis.

James Kuklinski and his associates put it well: "From Kant to Rawls, intellectuals have unabashedly placed a high premium on deliberative, rational thought and by implication, rejected emotions and feelings as legitimate (although unavoidable) elements of politics."[2] Jack Knight and James Johnson write that "Democratic legitimacy accrues to political outcomes insofar as

2. James Kuklinski et al., "The Cognitive and Affective Bases of Political Tolerance Judgments," *American Journal of Political Science* 35, no. 1 (1991): 22.

they survive a process of reasoned debate sustained by fair procedures."[3] They elaborate:

> Deliberation involves reasoned argument. Proposals must be defended or criticized with reasons. The objective is to frame pressing problems, to identify attractive, feasible solutions to them, and to persuade rather than compel those who may be otherwise inclined to recognize their attractiveness and feasibility. Here the crucial point is that parties to deliberation rely only on what Habermas calls the "force of the better argument"; other forms of influence are explicitly excluded so that interlocutors are free to remain unconvinced so long as they withhold agreement with reasons.[4]

Deliberation and civility (or democratic polity) are often closely associated in such discussions. A civil society is one that deals with its problems in a deliberative manner. As James Kuklinski and his associates sum up this view,

> In a democratic society, reasonable decisions are preferable to unreasonable ones; considered thought leads to the former, emotions to the latter; therefore deliberation is preferable to visceral reaction as a basis for democratic decision making. The preceding words summarize a normative view that has dominated thinking at least since the Enlightenment. It prescribes that citizens are to approach the subject of politics with temperate consideration and objective analysis, that is, to use their heads when making judgement about public affairs. Conversely, people are not to react emotionally to political phenomena. A democracy in which citizens evaluate politics affectively, to use the current language of social psychology, presumably leaves much to be desired.[5]

To round off the picture, deliberations are contrasted with an irrational, harmful, if not dangerous, way of attempting to chart a new course. As James Q. Wilson writes, "The belief in deliberation is implied not only by the argument for an extended republic but also by the contrast Madison draws between opinions and passion, since opinion implies a belief amenable to reason whereas passion implies a disposition beyond reason's reach."[6]

3. Jack Knight and James Johnson, "Aggregation and Deliberation: On the Possibility of Democratic Legitimacy," *Political Theory* 22, no. 2 (1994): 289.

4. Knight and Johnson, "Aggregation and Deliberation," p. 286.

5. Kuklinski, "The Cognitive and Affective Bases," p. 1.

6. James Q. Wilson, "Interests and Deliberation in the American Republic; or, Why James Madison Would Have Never Received the James Madison Award," *PS: Political Science and Politics,* December 1990, p. 559.

Deliberations are often implicitly if not explicitly contrasted with culture wars, a term used to suggest that the people are profoundly divided in their commitments to basic values, and that segments of the public confront one another in unproductive manners instead of dealing with the issues at hand. In culture wars two or more groups within the same community or society confront one another in a highly charged way, demonizing one another, turning differences into total opposition. Such culture wars tend to make reaching a shared course more difficult and they often invite violence (from the bombing of abortion clinics to outright civil war). James Hunter writes that "Culture wars always precede shooting wars. . . . Indeed, the last time this country 'debated' the issues of human life, personhood, liberty, and the rights of citizenship all together, the result was the bloodiest war ever to take place on this continent, the Civil War."[7]

Given such sharp contrast between deliberations and culture wars, reason and passion, amicable resolutions and emotional deadlock (or war), it stands to reason that many political scientists strongly favor the deliberative model. To argue, in contrast, that deliberations of the relatively pure kind are almost impossible to achieve, or even to approximate under most circumstances, invites the response that they are still normatively superior to culture wars, and that they provide a positive normative model to which one ought to aspire even if it is not attainable. The question remains if one can find a model that is more realistic than deliberations *and* much more compelling morally than culture wars. I suggest that an examination of the actual processes of sorting out values that take place in well-functioning societies shows that rather different processes are taking place, which neither qualify as rational deliberations nor constitute culture wars. Furthermore, these "other" processes are fully legitimate — at least in the eyes of those who approve social formulations of the good. I refer to these processes as moral dialogues. In these, the participants combine working out normative differences among themselves, in a nonconfrontational manner, with limited but not insignificant use of facts and logic, of rational reasoning.

There are at least two powerful reasons the purely deliberative model needs to be replaced with one that includes moral dialogues:

(1) In charting a shared communal course, participants are not two-legged computers, stuffed with information and analytic software; they are members of the community who must earn a living, attend to their children, and so on. Hence, unlike privileged males in ancient Athens, these citizens must study matters of public policy in their rather limited spare time. Moreover, even if all deliberants did come equipped with a mind full of information and statis-

7. Wilson, "Interests and Deliberation," pp. 4-5.

tical techniques, and a super computer, they still would not be able rationally to complete the analysis of the kind of issues they typically face — a problem widely recognized by the champions of artificial intelligence, not to mention of the human kind. It is common to point out that it is impossible to decide in a chess game what the optimal (most rational) move is because the permutations are too numerous. And compared to real-life decisions, the choices in chess are very simple. In chess, there are only two players, immutable rules, all the necessary information is right in front of the actors, power relations among the pieces are fixed, and the rules of engagement are fully established. In communities and societies, the number of players is large and changing, rules are modified as the action unfolds, information is always much more meager than what is needed, the relative power of those involved and those affected changes frequently, and the rules of engagement are in flux. As a result, participating in all decision-making must rely on much humbler processes than the rational decision-making school, at the heart of the deliberation model, assumes.[8]

(2) Most important, the issues that are subjects of discussion are to a significant extent normative and not empirical or logical matters, yet the deliberation model rests on assumptions akin to those of the scientific approach. Even consideration of many issues that seem technical is often deeply influenced by normative factors. For instance, the question of whether or not to put fluoride into a town's water brings into play values of those who oppose government "paternalism";[9] the importation of tomatoes from Mexico evokes values associated with questions such as the extent to which we should absorb real or imaginary health risks for the sake of free trade and better neighbor relations; and questions concerning the best way to teach English to immigrant children raise value questions concerning the commitment to one's heritage versus that to one's new nation. There seem to be few if any norm-free decisions of any significance. And hence most, if not all, communal conclusions require processes through which shared normative foundations can be found or, at least, through which normative differences can be narrowed.

I am not arguing that information and reason play no role when public policies are examined by communities and societies. Rather, I am pointing out that they play a much smaller role than the deliberation model assumes, and that other factors play a much larger role. I turn now to explore these "other" processes that are not deliberative in the usual sense of this term.

8. For further discussion, see Amitai Etzioni, *The Moral Dimension* (New York: The Free Press, 1988), pp. 136-50; Charles Lindbolm, *The Intelligence of Democracy* (New York: The Free Press, 1965); Kenneth E. Boulding, "Review of a Strategy of Decision: Policy Evaluation as a Social Process," *American Sociological Review* 29 (1962): 930-31.

9. Bette Hileman, "Fluoridation of Water," *Chemical and Engineering News* 66, no. 31 (1988): 26, 27, 42.

Moral dialogues occur when a group of people engage in a process of sorting the values that will guide their lives. For example, in the United States there is an intense dialogue over the question of whether or not the virtue of a color-blind (nondiscriminating) society or of affirmative action (to correct for past and current injustices) should guide employment and college admission policies. And there is a moral dialogue over the extent to which we should curtail public expenditures in order not to burden future generations with the debt we have been accumulating.

Such dialogues take place constantly in well-formed societies — which most democracies are — and they frequently result in the affirmation of a new direction for the respective societies (albeit sometimes only after prolonged and messy discourse). For instance, moral dialogues led in the 1960s to a shared normative understanding that legal segregation had to be abolished, and in the 1970s to the understanding that as a society we must be much more responsible in our conduct toward the environment than we used to be.

Society-wide moral dialogues come in two basic forms: first, through the piecing together of a myriad of local dialogues through organizations that have local chapters (including numerous ethnic, religious, and political associations); and, second, through national media such as call-in shows, televised town meetings, and panel discussions.

Moral dialogues have their own procedures which are distinct from those of the deliberative model. One often-used procedure in moral dialogues is to *appeal to an overarching value that the various parties to the sorting-out process share.* Robert Goodin is in effect using this rule when he seeks to pave the road for a community that must sort out a course between the rights of nonsmokers and those of smokers.[10] At first, this may seem a typical clash between two values: the rights of one group versus those of another. Goodin points out, however, that *both* groups are committed to the value that one's liberty does not allow that person to violate the "space" of the other. In popular terms, my right to extend my arm stops when my fist reaches your nose. (Actually, quite a bit before that.) Goodin argues that because nonsmokers, in their nonsmoking, do not penetrate the smokers' space, while smokers do violate nonsmokers' space in public situations, nonsmokers' rights should take priority. Using such arguments, American communities reached the normatively compelling shared understanding that lies at the foundation of the new restrictions on smoking in numerous public spaces. (The fact that these new regulations met very little opposition shows that they were based on a thoroughly shared moral understanding, unlike Prohibition.)

10. See Robert E. Goodin, *No Smoking: The Ethical Issues* (Chicago: The University of Chicago Press, 1989).

While the particular way Goodin developed his argument may not be employed often, it is more frequently used in another form. Members of communities often argue that this or that measure under consideration is not compatible with a free society, a self-respecting society, or a caring people. These, as a rule, are not empirical arguments. Take, for example, the argument that there is evidence that if a community engages in a given measure, liberty will be seriously endangered. This is a way of arguing that if the community proceeds in a given manner, this is incompatible with an important value it seeks to uphold. I suggest that an empirical examination of values-sorting will show that in communitarian societies much of this sorting takes place by evoking a higher order, more general values to sort out the ranking among other values.

Another procedure is to *bring a third value into play when two diverge or clash.* For instance, those who recently tried to restore the black-Jewish coalition of the 1960s in the United States argue that both groups share a commitment to liberal causes. And, as the participants struggled to work out a joint statement, those attempting to create an interfaith coalition pointed to the shared commitment to fight poverty.[11]

In effect, most of the considerations ethics bring to bear are discussions of the relative merit of various values rather than conflicts between the good and its corresponding evil. Values-talk is not composed of various people coming and declaring their values the way some individuals state that they do not like broccoli without feeling any need or inclination to explain their taste. *(De gustibus non est disputandum.)* Values require an accounting. And those accounts can be examined and challenged, for instance, by arguments that they are inconsistent with other values the party holds or would lead to normative conclusions the party could not possibly seek, and so on. Using such arguments, members of communities convince one another, when moral dialogues are successfully advanced, to reach new shared normative understandings.

To protect values-talks from deteriorating into culture wars, rules of engagement can be and are being applied. They basically reflect a tenet that one should act on the recognition that the conflicting parties are members of one and the same community, and that they should therefore fight with one hand tied behind their back rather than go at it whole-hog. This issue has come to the fore in recent years in discussions of what makes for a civil dialogue.

It is widely agreed that the contesting parties should not "demonize" one another, that they should refrain from depicting the other side's values as completely negative — as those who characterize Iran as "satanic" or those who portray Israel as a betrayer of the Jewish people do. Another case in point: after the

11. See Michael Lerner and Cornel West, *Jews and Blacks: Let the Healing Begin* (New York: G. P. Putnam's Sons, 1995).

GOP won the 1994 elections in a landslide, the ebullient new Speaker of the House, Newt Gingrich, referred to his side being supported by "God-fearing" Americans who were opposed by "Godless" people.[12] This and other such exclamations were widely regarded as a violation of civil values and discourse, and not only by Democrats, and were one factor leading to a high negative rating of the Speaker in public opinion polls.[13] The Speaker used such phrases less often in the following months, bowing to the norms of values-talk. In Israel, it was widely believed that the comparison of Prime Minister Rabin to Hitler and the characterization of him as a traitor by several religious groups egged on those who assassinated him. Such verbiage also fed the culture war between extreme religious groups and secular ones. Civility is a vital element of moral dialogues.

Another rule of values-talk is *not to affront the deepest moral commitments of the other groups.* The assumption must be made that each group is committed to some particular values that are especially sacrosanct to that group, and that each group has some dark moments in its history upon which members would rather not dwell. Thus, to throw into the face of a German, whenever one discusses a specific normative difference, the horror of the Holocaust, or to tell Jews that it did not happen, hinders values-talk while refraining from doing so enhances it.

Closely related is *drawing a line between the legal right to free speech,* which allows one to say most things however offensive, *and the merit of not voicing whatever offensive thoughts come to mind.*[14] Several of the leading hosts of radio call-in shows were blamed for ignoring this distinction and undermining values discourse as a result.

More generally, communitarian and Harvard law professor Mary Ann Glendon makes a strong case that using less the language of rights and more that of needs, wants, and even interests helps make dialogues more conducive to truly shared resolutions. As Glendon puts it, "For in its simplest American form, the language of rights is the language of no compromise. The winner takes all and the loser has to get out of town. The conversation is over."[15] She adds:

12. Sidney Blumenthal, "The Newt Testament," *The New Yorker,* 21 November 1994, p. 7.

13. "[T]he more people see and hear Mr. Gingrich, the more some seem uncomfortable with him. The share of Americans holding a negative impression of him is up to 41 percent, compared with 27 percent who report positive feelings" (Michael K. Frisby, "Politics and Policy: Americans, Polled on GOP and 'Contract,' Like Big Picture But Have Trouble with the Small Print," *The Wall Street Journal,* 9 March 1995, A20).

14. See William Galston, "Rights Do Not Equal Rightness," *The Responsive Community* 1, no. 4 (1991): 7-8. See also Amitai Etzioni, *Spirit of Community* (New York: Simon and Schuster, 1993), pp. 192-206, 201-4.

15. Mary Ann Glendon, *Rights Talk: The Impoverishment of Political Discourse* (New York: The Free Press, 1991), p. 9.

> The most distinctive features of our American rights dialect [are] its penchant for absolute, extravagant formulations, its near-aphasia concerning responsibilities, its excessive homage to individual independence and self-sufficiency, its habitual concentration on the individual and the state at the expense of the intermediate groups of civil society, and its unapologetic insularity . . . each of these traits make it difficult to give voice to common sense or moral political discourse. . . .[16]

I do not attempt here to develop a full list of rules of engagement, but only to illustrate that just because values-talk does not proceed by the canons of deliberation (which are surprisingly close to those of science), this does not mean that it does not have a canon.

Conclusion

Understanding the ways values-talk takes place and can be enhanced is a subject of great importance to democratic societies because such dialogue sustains one of the key elements required for the social order. It is a subject that requires much more study and is likely to intensify once the notion of relying on deliberations is set aside and the importance of values-talk as distinct from culture wars is more widely recognized.

In sum, new or responsive communitarian thinking, building upon previous works, is concerned with the social processes and structures that make people and societies virtuous. It asks how this can be achieved by minimizing the role of the state rather than making it a major moral agent, as it is in theocracies. Raising the moral voice and drawing on moral dialogues are two key components of a communitarian society, one that formulates *and* fosters shared meanings of the good.

16. Glendon, *Rights Talk,* p. 14.

Minister to Freedom: The Legacy of John Witherspoon

JOSEPH LOCONTE

There are few things that seem to be less understood than the nature, extent and obligation of visible religion.[1]

John Witherspoon

On July 30, 1776, British troops, flush with bravado as they prepared to run George Washington's ragtag army off of Long Island, burned the general in effigy. Alongside Washington they torched the figure of a minister, the Reverend John Witherspoon. One English officer denounced him as a "political firebrand, who perhaps had not a less share in the Revolution than Washington himself."[2]

That wasn't just sour grapes. As much as any figure in the colonial era, Witherspoon embodied the potent alliance between faith and freedom that would radically distinguish America from her European cousins. Religious wars, after all, had bloodied the Continent since the Reformation. In the years leading up to the French Revolution, the air was thick with anti-religious venom. "We will strangle the last king," was the cry, "with the guts of the last priest."

1. John Witherspoon, Sermon XIV, "The Nature and Extent of Visible Religion," in *The Works of John Witherspoon* (Edinburgh: n.p., 1815), vol. II, p. 324.

2. Varnum Lansing Collins, *President Witherspoon* (New York: Arno Press, 1969), p. 133.

It was not so in America, and John Witherspoon's career was part of the reason. As a member of the Continental Congress, he signed the Declaration of Independence — the only minister to do so — and lost a son in the Revolutionary War. As a leader of the American Presbyterian Church, he argued that robust religion depended not on government sponsorship, but on freedom of conscience. And as president of the College of New Jersey (later Princeton), he not only made the campus a "seminary of sedition," but prepared a generation of men — including James Madison — for leadership roles in the new nation. John Adams called him "as high a son of liberty as any man in America."[3]

The example of Witherspoon is especially important now, when many Americans seem deeply ambivalent about the role of religion in society. Yale law professor Stephen Carter bemoans a "culture of disbelief," while activists agitate for a return to "Christian America." Others seem ready to retreat altogether into enclaves of isolation. At a time when American society is perhaps most in need of widespread renewal, people of religious conviction seem ill prepared to lead the way.

By contrast, Witherspoon offers people of faith a stiff tonic for civic and political engagement. A confirmed Calvinist, Witherspoon applied some of the best ideas of the Protestant tradition to each of the institutions in which he toiled — the church, the academy, and politics. His emphasis on human corruption and sin, for example, made him advocate a government with checks and balances on its power. While some effused idealistic verbiage about their social and political objectives, Witherspoon made prudence a judge over his own. While other clerics thoughtlessly linked the Bible to political issues, Witherspoon appealed to conscience and common sense, convinced that God had stamped his moral law on every man's heart. And in an age of declining attention to morals, he made character the touchstone of religious truth and the requisite for effective public service. Historian Garry Wills has called him "probably the most influential teacher in the entire history of American education."[4]

Preamble to Liberty

A native of Scotland, Witherspoon was born in 1723 to the Reverend James Witherspoon, a Presbyterian pastor, and Anne Walker, a minister's daughter.

3. Charles Francis Adams, ed., *The Works of John Adams, Second President of the United States* (Boston: Little, Brown, and Company, 1850-1856), vol. II, p. 356.

4. Garry Wills, *Explaining America: The Middle and Southern States, 1783-1837* (University, Ala.: University of Alabama Press, 1980), p. 2.

John was reading from the Bible by the time he was four and soon could recite large portions of the New Testament. He seemed destined for the pulpit.

His career in politics, however, would have been much harder to predict. As pastor at Paisley Abbey in Scotland, he counseled against ministers getting entangled with public affairs. It was sinful and reckless for them, he said, "to desire or claim the direction of such matters as fall within the province of the civil magistrates." Witherspoon delivered that warning in a sermon in September 1758. Twenty years later he was in the American Continental Congress and would help ratify the U.S. Constitution.[5]

Nevertheless, Witherspoon's experience in the embattled Church of Scotland would shape his approach to church and political reform in his adopted country. He ministered at a time when Scottish Presbyterianism was in schism: theological Moderates, with the help of British party politics, had gained advantage over the more conservative Popular Party, or Evangelicals. Active in the church's General Assembly, Witherspoon battled the more liberal wing at every opportunity.

Under contention, however, were not only matters of faith, but those of church governance. Witherspoon and the Evangelicals clung to the traditional system in which the entire congregation elected both the clergy and the elders and shared in authority over church affairs. Moderates championed the patronage law, which gave aristocrats — their natural allies — leverage over congregational matters. Many Evangelicals simply voted with their feet: thousands bolted from the Church of Scotland. It is estimated that in 1765, more than 120 churches had joined the Secessionists.[6] The breach was getting out of hand, and some of Witherspoon's closest friends joined the exodus.

Yet Witherspoon was no schismatic. Instead, he became a leader of Evangelicals who wished to remain within the church despite their minority status. His strategy was to focus on doctrines all could accept, and his aim was to create a common ground of agreement while guarding the fundamentals of the faith. "The reason of my doing so," he wrote in his *Essay on Justification,* "is that I would willingly rather reconcile, than widen these differences."[7]

Witherspoon's prestige as a conciliator and leading Evangelical eventually caught the attention of American Presbyterians, trying to quiet their own doctrinal squabbles. They needed a new president at the College of New Jersey, an incubator for Presbyterian ministers, and the Scottish doctor seemed an excellent choice. He accepted the post and landed in Philadelphia harbor on August

5. Collins, *President Witherspoon,* p. 55.

6. William Law Mathieson, *The Awakening of Scotland* (Glasgow: Jams Machelhose and Sons, 1910), pp. 160-68.

7. John Witherspoon, *The Works of John Witherspoon* (9 vols.; Edinburgh: John Turnbull, 1805), vol. I, p. 49.

7, 1768, with his wife and five children. When he arrived in Princeton, he found the college building, Nassau Hall, lit from top to bottom with candles to greet him. Few could have guessed that he would help set the campus ablaze with revolutionary fervor. Indeed, within a decade he would become "America's foremost academic propagandist for independence."[8]

Faith and Freedom

The immediate task before President Witherspoon was to restructure the college curriculum, and for the first several years of his tenure he was busily involved in administration, preaching, and teaching. He designed mandatory, extensive courses in rhetoric and moral philosophy. He purchased state-of-the-art scientific equipment, and he greatly expanded the college's library. His grammar school soon became one of the best in the colonies.

Nevertheless, not even the studious halls at Princeton were soundproofed from the clamor of political dissent. By July 1774, Witherspoon had joined seventy-two representatives from the state to help elect New Jersey delegates to the First Continental Congress. In June 1775, shortly after fighting broke out at Lexington, Reverend Witherspoon drafted a letter for the Synod of New York and Philadelphia urging ministers to back the war effort. His recommendations, to be read to all congregations, "changed the role of the Presbyterian clergy from uncommitted observers to active supporters of the revolution."[9] A year later he was appointed as a representative to the Second Continental Congress and led the movement in New Jersey to depose the royal governor.

As a politically engaged minister, Witherspoon certainly was no oddity. James Hutson, Chief of the Manuscript Division of the Library of Congress, says, "it would be difficult to count the number of ministers who served in civil capacities during the revolutionary period." Religious leaders served in state legislatures and constitutional conventions. Parson Peter Muhlenberg, after delivering a sermon to his congregation in Woodstock, Virginia, tossed off his clerical robes only to reveal the uniform of an officer in the Virginia militia. Such was the climate on the eve of independence.[10]

8. James L. McAllister, "John Witherspoon: Academic Advocate for American Freedom," in *A Miscellany of American Christianity: Essays in Honor of H. Shelton Smith*, ed. Stuart C. Henry (Durham, N.C.: Duke University Press, 1963), p. 183.

9. Thomas Miller, ed., *The Selected Writings of John Witherspoon* (Carbondale, Ill.: Southern Illinois University Press, 1990), p. 29.

10. James H. Hutson, *Religion and the Founding of the American Republic* (Washington: The Library of Congress, 1998), p. 46.

Yet Witherspoon's patriotic impulses had a somewhat different footing. In 1776, two months before the Declaration, Witherspoon preached a sermon on the political crisis called "The Dominion of Providence Over the Passions of Men." Its purpose was not so much to attach God's blessing to the American cause, but to underscore the importance of religious conviction to both personal and public life. "Unless you are united to [Christ] by a lively faith," he told his Princeton congregation, "not the resentment of a haughty monarch, but the sword of divine justice hangs over you."[11] While acknowledging the "singular interposition of Providence" in behalf of the colonies, the minister sternly warned against misplaced pride. Finally, in language that was both plain and powerful, he joined political and religious freedom at the hip. "There is not a single instance in history in which civil liberty was lost, and religious liberty preserved entire," he said. "If therefore we yield up our temporal property, we at the same time deliver the conscience into bondage."[12] The sermon perfectly captured the mood of the colonies. Widely distributed, it carried the weight of one of the nation's most respected educators and clerics. William Warren Sweet, dean of American church historians, calls it "one of the most influential pulpit utterances during the whole course of the war."[13] The Scottish preacher had become an American patriot.

How Democracy Nourishes Religion

One of Witherspoon's major arguments for democratic government was that it ultimately would promote religious conviction. In "Dominion of Providence," he cited historical precedent to insist that political freedom would aid religious freedom. "The knowledge of God and his truths have from the beginning of the world been chiefly, if not entirely, confined to those parts of the earth where some degree of liberty and political justice were to be seen."[14] This, however, would happen not on the European model — with a nationally established church — but mostly through indirect means.

Limited governments, Witherspoon said, allow for the greatest civic freedom; they make room for the political, commercial, and social relations that both require and nurture the virtues all citizens should desire. During a debate at Nassau Hall just months before signing the Declaration of Independence, Witherspoon explained what he considered the "essential benefit" of liberty:

11. Miller, *Selected Writings,* pp. 137-38.

12. Miller, *Selected Writings,* pp. 140-41.

13. William Warren Sweet, *Religion in the Development of American Culture, 1765-1840* (New York: Scribner, 1952), p. 8.

14. Miller, *Selected Writings,* p. 140.

"its tendency to put in motion and encourage the exertion of all the human powers. It must therefore evidently improve the human mind, and bring with it, in highest perfection, all the advantages of the social state. It is the parent or the nurse of industry, opulence, knowledge, virtue, and heroism."[15]

Witherspoon joined a growing number of religious leaders who argued that religion would not be secure until it was officially separated from the state. Here he followed in the steps of Protestant thinkers from Martin Luther to Oliver Cromwell to Roger Williams, who stressed the primacy of individual judgment in the act of faith. The lesson from Europe was clear enough: established churches always trampled the consciences of dissenters. This helps explain why Witherspoon joined with other Presbyterian and Congregational clergymen to prevent the establishment of an Anglican episcopate in America. "His taste of arbitrary civil authority wielded by the Moderates in the patronage controversies," according to historian Douglas Sloan, "strengthened his conviction that true religion wins its way by persuasion, not coercion."[16]

The best help the state could give religion was to refrain from imposing any faith on its citizens. "The greatest service which magistrates or persons in authority can do with respect to the religion or morals of the people," Witherspoon said, "is to defend and secure the rights of conscience in the most equal and impartial manner."[17] Though he never expected government to be neutral about religion or irreligion, he cleanly rejected the idea that any church, even his own American Presbyterian Church, should receive privileged legal status. If the state were to aid religion, it must do so even-handedly. In his "Address to the Inhabitants of Jamaica," he assured prospective students — many, no doubt, belonging to minority faiths — that he was "a passionate admirer of the equal and impartial support of every religious denomination."[18] When the Presbyterians reorganized after the war under the General Assembly, Witherspoon drafted the preface to their statement on religious liberty:

> Therefore they consider the rights of private judgment, in all matters that respect religion, as universal and inalienable: *they do not even wish to see any religious constitution aided by the civil power,* further than may be nec-

15. "Dialogue on Civil Liberty," delivered at a Public Exhibition in Nassau Hall, January 1776, reprinted in *Pennsylvania Magazine,* April 1776, p. 167.

16. Douglas Sloan, *The Scottish Enlightenment and the American College Ideal* (Columbia University, New York City: Teachers College Press, 1971), p. 142.

17. "Pastoral Letter," in *The Works of the Rev. John Witherspoon,* 2nd ed., 4 vols. (Philadelphia: William W. Woodward, 1802), 3:14, quoted in John G. West Jr.'s *The Politics of Revelation and Reason: Religion and Civic Life in the New Nation* (Lawrence, Kans.: University Press of Kansas, 1996), p. 28.

18. Miller, *Selected Writings,* p. 114.

> essary for protection and security, and, at the same time, be equal and common to all others.[19] (emphasis added)

The American Presbyterian Church, while adopting the Westminster Confession of Faith in 1729, had departed from the confession on this very point: Civil magistrates would have no authority over church affairs, not even in the suppression of heresies. Thus, Witherspoon was not an innovator in this regard, but his formulation — asserting a universal right of conscience, while rejecting special government support for churches — foreshadowed the two clauses of the First Amendment (penned several years later by former student James Madison). Witherspoon's preface remains the official position of American Presbyterianism to this day.

How Religion Sustains Democracy

Witherspoon's commitment to freedom of conscience comports with his view of religion as a leavening influence in society. That is, as people gain the civic and political freedom to practice their faith, they will live lives of exemplary citizenship. As scholar John West notes, Witherspoon agreed with skeptic Benjamin Franklin that this was one of the obligations of religious communities. Churches "are well secured in their religious liberty," Witherspoon said. "The return which is expected from them to the community, is . . . [that] their people may be the more regular citizens, and the more useful members of society."[20]

Before unpacking this view, however, it is vital to appreciate the minister's understanding of human nature. He firmly upheld traditional Protestant beliefs about the corrupting influence of sin, both on individuals and on society. In his college *Lectures on Moral Philosophy,* the first sermon in his series on the Christian gospel begins thus: "The whole revelation of the will of God to mankind, both in the Old Testament and the New, proceeds upon the supposition that they are sinners." Even in one of Witherspoon's most political sermons — at the outbreak of hostilities with Britain — he feels obliged to insist that "nothing can be more absolutely necessary to true religion, than a clear conviction of the sinfulness of our nature and state."[21]

19. Quoted by James Hastings Nichols in "John Witherspoon on Church and State," in *Calvinism and the Political Order,* ed. George L. Hunt (Philadelphia: The Westminster Press, 1965), p. 133.

20. John Witherspoon, "[Sermon] Delivered at a Publick Thanksgiving," *The Works of the Rev. John Witherspoon,* 3:81, quoted in John G. West Jr., *The Politics of Revelation and Reason,* p. 27.

21. Miller, *Selected Writings,* p. 128.

The Christian doctrine of man's sinfulness, however, is often mistaken for a despising of human life and human striving. The tragedy of man's guilt is that it represents a "fall from grace" — men and women are no longer what God intended them to be and remain alienated from him and his holiness. Yet here is the Christian corollary to human sin: human dignity. Man, even fallen man, retains inestimable dignity and worth in that he continues to bear the image of his creator. This makes the pursuit of virtue possible. "But as the scripture points out our original dignity and the true glory of our nature," Witherspoon said, "so every true penitent is there taught to aspire after the noblest character and to entertain the most exalted hopes."[22]

From this biblical dualism — man's greatness and man's shame — flow several political implications. First, because sin and vice are the natural drift of every human being, any government that fails to reckon with this fact is doomed to collapse. This is critical for the health of democracies, which maintain order not through authoritarian rule but by the self-regulating behavior of their citizens. "Nothing is more certain than that a general profligacy and corruption of manners make a people ripe for destruction," he said. "A good form of government may hold the rotten materials together for some time, but beyond a certain pitch, even the best constitution will be ineffectual, and slavery must ensue."[23] Consequently, political leaders have an interest in promoting virtue whenever possible.

Second, the problem of sin requires not only that government be limited (because of the temptation to abuse power), but that it also be balanced by competing institutions. "It is folly to expect that a state should be upheld by integrity in all who have a share in managing it," he said. "They must be so balanced, that when every one draws to his own interest or inclination, there may be an even poise upon the whole."[24] To be sure, Witherspoon drew from Scottish Whiggism and John Locke's republicanism to argue for independent branches of government. But his understanding of man's essential selfishness undergirded his own theory of a separation of powers — and almost certainly influenced those of his student, Madison, the main architect of the U.S. Constitution.

Third, the doctrine of original sin makes the democratic impulse plausible, because all stand under the judgment of God. A just government is one that recognizes, especially in its legal system, this essential equality of all persons. "The magistrate with his robes, the scholar with his learning, and the day la-

22. Miller, *Selected Writings,* p. 117.

23. Miller, *Selected Writings,* p. 144.

24. Quoted by James H. Smylie, "Madison and Witherspoon: Theological Roots of American Political Thought," in *Ideas in America's Cultures,* ed. Hamilton Cravens (Ames: Iowa State University Press), p. 123.

borer that stands unnoticed are all upon the same footing," Witherspoon concluded, "for we must all appear before the judgment seat of Christ."[25]

The practical conclusion: A self-governing republic demands self-governing citizens. Self-governing citizens need "republican" virtues that are hardly sustainable without religion. But real religion must be uncoerced, meaning government may not impose one of its own. Thus: freedom requires virtue, which requires faith, which requires freedom.

This forms the heart of Witherspoon's argument for "the public interest of religion." Whatever their actual convictions, virtually all the Founders publicly praised the social utility of religion. Even Franklin once chided Thomas Paine for dismissing religious belief: "He who spits in the wind spits in his own face. . . . If men are wicked with religion, what would they be without it?" As historian Paul Johnson puts it, the Founders agreed that education was essential to a functioning republic, and who else would supply moral education but the churches? The Northwest Ordinance of 1787 was unambiguous: "Religion, morality and knowledge, being necessary to good government and the happiness of mankind, Schools and the means of education shall forever be encouraged."[26]

Nevertheless, few argued as strenuously as Witherspoon for an indissoluble link between faith and social stability. "He is the best friend of American liberty who is most sincere and active in promoting true and undefiled religion," he said, "and who sets himself with the greatest firmness to bear down profanity and immorality of every kind."[27] "True religion" for Witherspoon, a Protestant minister, naturally meant Christianity. Yet his arguments were devoid of any denominational bias, respecting the religious pluralism that already existed in the colonies. Thus, three times Congress turned to the minister to help author national religious proclamations. In the national Thanksgiving Day Proclamation of 1782, he called the sincere practice of religion "the great foundation" of public prosperity and national happiness.[28] He concluded his most famous political sermon, "The Dominion of Providence," with this appeal: "God grant in America true religion and civil liberty may be inseparable and the unjust attempts to destroy the one, may in the issue tend to the support and establishment of both."[29]

25. Quoted in "Christian Magnanimity," in Miller, *Selected Writings,* p. 125.

26. Paul Johnson, *A History of the American People* (New York: HarperCollins, 1997), pp. 208-9.

27. Miller, *Selected Writings,* p. 144.

28. Matthew F. Rose, *John Witherspoon: An American Leader* (Washington, D.C.: The Family Research Council, 1999), p 85.

29. Miller, *Selected Writings,* p. 147.

The Politics of Persuasion

One of the most striking features of Witherspoon's approach to civic life was the way he grappled with the leading political and philosophical challenges of his era. As he himself admitted, his "chief comfort" was teaching the Christian gospel and training men for religious duties. Nevertheless, in his roles as educator and politician, he called for direct engagement with the public issues of the day — from philosophical skepticism to the federalist debates of the 1780s. For him, the faithful citizen bore an obligation not merely to proclaim, but to persuade: to use all the intellectual tools available to win over one's adversaries. "Military skill and political wisdom have their admirers," he told his students, "but far inferior in number to those who admire, envy, or would wish to imitate him that has the power of persuasion."

Essential to persuasion is the discipline of rhetoric. Witherspoon launched the most extensive program of oratorical study in revolutionary America. He reinstituted student philosophical societies squelched by a previous administration. Students gathered nearly every night for speeches and debates in the main college building, Nassau Hall. Witherspoon himself delivered commencement addresses heavy with political themes. "The purpose of combining classroom instruction with extensive public practice was to prepare students to speak to the practical problems of public life," concludes Thomas Miller.[30] And speak they did. Witherspoon and his students delivered orations on free trade, civil discord, the rights of women, immigration policy, and the horrors of war.

In contemporary culture, in which so much of our political rhetoric seems impoverished, it is easy to overlook the importance of public debate in revolutionary America. Rhetoric was a political art of no mean influence, especially as Americans began to embrace a national political state. Witherspoon clearly understood the importance of the discipline, calling it "one of the most admired and envied talents."

In his opening address in *Lectures on Eloquence*, he warned his students not to dismiss the practice of rhetoric either for social reasons (evil men abuse it) or religious reasons (it may lead to pride). Along the way he delivered a stinging rebuke against anti-intellectualism: "Learning in general possessed by a bad man is unspeakably pernicious, and that very thing has sometimes made weak people speak against learning; but it is just as absurd . . . [to say] we will use no arms for defense, for if the enemy take them from us, they will be turned against us."[31]

30. Miller, *Selected Writings*, p. 21.
31. Miller, *Selected Writings*, pp. 231-32.

The warning would appear often in his lectures. Witherspoon seemed especially mindful of the unfortunate impulse to elevate "spiritual" knowledge while neglecting tough intellectual labor. The result, he feared, would be to damage the public reputation of Christianity. "We see sometimes the pride of unsanctified knowledge do great injury to religion," he said in his "Address to the Senior Class." "On the other hand, we find some persons of real piety, despising human learning, and disgracing the most glorious truths, by a meanness and indecency hardly sufferable in their manner of handling them."[32] As few other educators of his day dared, Witherspoon connected current affairs to academic learning. As historian Wilbur Samuel Howell puts it, he "made his students see that eloquence was a part of the concern of mankind for liberty, national welfare, the rule of law, and moral truth."[33]

A Common Sense Philosophy

The intellectual foundation for Witherspoon was Common Sense Philosophy, or Scottish Realism, an attempt to use natural reason to support the claims of religion. It was a philosophy developed by Thomas Reid at the University of Glasgow, who argued that the truths of Christianity were based on "common sense" and "self-evident axioms." Witherspoon borrowed heavily from the Scottish Realists for his *Lectures on Moral Philosophy* — a required course for every Princeton graduate — to challenge the Deism of his day and articulate a system of social and political ethics.

He had his right-wing critics. Many ministers were deeply suspicious of arguments from reason; one notable New England divine once dismissed moral philosophy as "infidelity reduced to a system."[34] Nevertheless, thanks in large part to Witherspoon's influence at Princeton, Scottish Realism became the most important philosophical tradition shaping American Protestantism — and had no small effect on the formation of the American constitutional order.

Several themes emerge from Witherspoon's application of these ideas to education and political life:

32. Quoted in Collins, *President Witherspoon,* vol. 2, p. 198.

33. Wilbur Samuel Howell, *Eighteenth-Century British Logic and Rhetoric* (Princeton: Princeton University Press, 1971), p. 687.

34. Miller, *Selected Writings,* p. 35.

Reason and Revelation

First, Witherspoon united reason and revelation. As an evangelical Protestant, he considered Scripture the ultimate source of truth and moral authority. It was not, however, the only source: Scripture itself taught that God made man as a rational, purposeful being. Man is certainly more than a thinking creature, but he is not less. To bear God's image, even as fallen man, is to possess the capacity to think and discover truths apart from an understanding of Scripture; for God has built his truths into the fabric of the natural world. "If the Scripture is true, the discoveries of reason cannot be contrary to it; and therefore, it has nothing to fear from that quarter."[35]

Consider how he exhorted his students to cultivate self-restraint in his lecture on "Christian Magnanimity":

> The importance and difficulty of this struggle appear not only from the Holy Scriptures, but also from the experience and testimony of mankind in every age. What cautions are given by Solomon upon this subject? "He that is slow to anger is better than the mighty, and he that ruleth his spirit, than he that taketh a city." *The wisest heathens have inculcated the necessity of self-government* and the dangers of surrounding temptation by many instructive images.[36]

It is true, he said, that those who scoff at religion misuse argument for their own ends. But that's no reason to abandon reason. "The best way is to meet them upon their own ground and to show from reason itself the fallacy of their principles."[37] Or, as C. S. Lewis once put it, "good philosophy must exist, if for no other reason than that bad philosophy needs to be answered." Moreover, reason had its limits. Witherspoon attacked the Deists for believing reason was a sufficient guide to life and right living. On this he never budged: reason could never by itself produce a repentant heart or saving faith; it must always be tested by the claims of revealed religion.

Yet one of the fruits of recognizing a legitimate role for reason was that it helped Witherspoon show charity toward those with whom he disagreed. If the Scriptures were not the only source of wisdom, then other thinkers — even Enlightenment figures — could be studied and appreciated. He exposed his students to Shakespeare, Pope, Swift, and Locke. Though he called Hume "an infidel in opinion," nevertheless he said he possessed "great reach and ac-

35. Miller, *Selected Writings,* p. 152.
36. Miller, *Selected Writings,* p. 121 (emphasis added).
37. Miller, *Selected Writings,* p. 152.

curacy of judgment in matters of criticism."[38] Another benefit of reason was that it made conversation — and debate — possible between believers and skeptics. If reason was indeed a universal faculty, then there was no need to constantly invoke the Bible to make philosophical or political arguments. "This is not the language of religion only," he warned in a sermon against self-seeking ambition. "It is the language of reason and the dictate of the human heart."[39]

The Appeal to Moral Instincts

Second, Witherspoon appealed to man's moral instincts. He followed Francis Hutcheson and other eighteenth-century philosophers who equated the moral sense with what the Bible calls "conscience." Man's understanding of good and evil, Witherspoon said, was as much a part of his nature as his love of beauty. He regarded it as man's noblest attribute, but never divorced it from the Divine will. "It is the law which our Maker has written upon our hearts, and both intimates and enforces duty, previous to all reasoning."[40]

In this Witherspoon again avoided two extremes: those to his theological left who glibly imagined human nature ripening inexorably to perfection; and those to his right, who saw little possibility of virtue among free men. "It pleased God to write his law upon the heart of man at first," he told his Glasgow congregation in 1759. "And the great lines of duty, *however obscured by our original apostasy, are still visible,* as to afford an opportunity of judging, what conduct and practice is, or is not agreeable to its dictates."[41]

Confidence in the dictates of conscience would buttress Witherspoon's teaching and political activity for the next forty years. Indeed, the purpose of political philosophy was to elucidate societal norms consistent with basic moral convictions — ideas not only about natural rights but moral obligations. The job of the legislator was to craft civil laws based on the moral law wherever practical. "Political law," he said, "is the authority of any society stamped on moral duty."[42] As historian Roger Fechner describes it, for Witherspoon, "du-

38. Sloan, *Scottish Enlightenment,* p. 133.

39. Miller, *Selected Writings,* p. 120.

40. John Witherspoon, *Lectures on Moral Philosophy and Eloquence* (Philadelphia, 1810), pp. 12-13, quoted in "The Influence of Princeton on Higher Education in the South Before 1825," by Donald Robert Come, *William and Mary Quarterly,* vol. II (1945): 364.

41. John Witherspoon, "The Trial of Religious Truth by Its Moral Influence," Sermon 38, in *The Works of the Rev. John Witherspoon,* 4 vols., 2:391.

42. Quoted in McAllister, "John Witherspoon: Academic Advocate for American Freedom," p. 198.

ties and rights were the exact moral counterparts of each other."[43] Much of his public debate would reflect that relationship.

Politics involves the art of persuasion, of course, and for Witherspoon persuasion carried intellectual and moral freight. His persuasive power depended not on the force of his personality — he never was considered a charismatic speaker — but on the logic of his arguments, upheld largely by an appeal to people's moral instincts.

In November 1779, for example, Congress was debating whether it should recommend a plan for fixing the prices of labor, manufactured goods, and imports. Witherspoon vigorously opposed the plan, not only because it was impractical but also because it coerced private busnessmen. If prices seemed unreasonably high, "this will fix of itself by the consent of the buyer and seller better than it can be done by any politician upon earth." Lawmakers, he insisted, must "carefully distinguish between what is effected by force and what by persuasion, and never preposterously mix these opposite principles and defeat the operation of both."[44] Though not wholly consistent, Witherspoon employed a morally grounded — though not necessarily moralizing — approach to politics that today is in short supply.

The Discipline of Prudence

Third, Witherspoon practiced the discipline of prudence. Moral principles are fine, but in politics they must be carefully applied to achieve the desired ends. Reason, common sense, a knowledge of history, a sense of the current moment — Witherspoon used all these qualities to arrive at arguments that were both principled and prudent.

At the outbreak of hostilities with Britain, in his first political sermon in America, it is noteworthy what Witherspoon did not do: he did not invoke America as the "New Israel," desperate to break free from the Egyptian-like grip of Great Britain. Recall that clergymen at this time were virtuosi in finding biblical analogues to current political events; they painted the war with England as a cosmic struggle between good and evil.[45] Not Witherspoon. "I do not refuse submission to their unjust claims because they are corrupt," he insisted. The real problem was that Britain — separated from America by an ocean — had no right, or ability, to restrict the freedoms of Americans. "A wise and prudent

43. Roger J. Fechner, "The Godly and Virtuous Republic of John Witherspoon," in *Ideas in America's Cultures,* ed. Hamilton Cravens, p. 16.

44. Collins, *President Witherspoon,* p. 24.

45. Hutson, *Religion and the Founding,* p. 42.

administration of our affairs is as impossible as the claim of authority is unjust."[46]

In the debate over the Articles of Confederation he opposed his friend Benjamin Franklin, who objected to the document because he thought a confederacy based on equal votes would not last long. Witherspoon countered that the fate of Sparta and the Roman provinces suggested that weaker states inevitably succumb to the more powerful. More importantly, Witherspoon said, it was imperative that the union be agreed to now, when all the states faced a common enemy; otherwise, as the conflict deepened, they easily could lose heart. If agreement could not be reached now, "what madness is it to suppose that there will ever be a time, or that circumstances will so change, as to make it even probable that it will be done at an after season?"[47]

He possessed a keen sense of the importance of the cultural moment. And that helped him argue for appropriate political action — especially when inaction could prove fatal. "Shall we establish nothing good, because it cannot be eternal? Shall we live without government because every constitution has its old age and its period?" He implored the other Founders instead to exercise their best judgments: "It only requires the more watchful attention to settle government upon the best principles and in the wisest manner that it may last as long as the nature of things will admit."[48] In other words, do the best you can, and don't let the perfect be the enemy of the good.

The Academy as Incubator

If politics was the most important crucible for Witherspoon's public philosophy, the academy was its cradle, which in eighteenth-century America was still tightly bound to religion. Virtually all the early colleges and universities were founded as religious schools; nearly half the signers of the Declaration had seminary degrees or training. Outside the church, Witherspoon could hardly imagine a more important institution for forging the souls of young men — or the future of a young nation.

"The importance of the presidents in giving shape to the influence which the college exercised cannot be overestimated," asserts Donald Robert Come.[49] Part of the reason was the direct involvement that presidents had in the lives of their students. Witherspoon taught them grammar, history, geography, moral

46. Miller, *Selected Writings,* p. 141.

47. Collins, *President Witherspoon,* p. 9.

48. Collins, *President Witherspoon,* p. 9.

49. Donald Robert Come, "The Influence of Princeton on Higher Education in the South Before 1825," *William and Mary Quarterly,* vol. II (1945): 362.

philosophy, and divinity. He set up student philosophic societies and approved most of the public speeches they delivered. He knew personally the family of nearly every boy under his charge.

Witherspoon served as president of the College of New Jersey from 1768 to 1794, and they proved to be twenty-five years of immense change. As a professor of divinity, he lectured candidates for the ministry, one of the major aims of the college at its founding. Yet even before he arrived, the school was giving less attention than Harvard to religious and classical studies, and more to moral philosophy. It was still considered a "public seminary of learning,"[50] but under Witherspoon that mission would be greatly transformed.

Indeed, as tensions with Britain heightened, Witherspoon would help turn the campus into what English detractors called "a seminary of sedition." One British officer complained that the president "poisons the minds of his young Students and through them the Continent."[51] That's a bit overheated, but it's clear the campus became a center of revolutionary fervor and a refuge for freedom fighters. By 1770, students angrily burned a letter from New York merchants who ignored the Non-Importation Agreement. Four years later, they staged their own "tea party" after patriots in Boston led the way. That same year the entire student body burned in effigy the reviled British sympathizer, Governor Thomas Hutchinson of Massachusetts. There is no evidence the president, an otherwise rigid disciplinarian, offered a whisper of protest. Meanwhile, at every commencement seniors waxed eloquent on liberty and the rights of free men.[52]

As the political crisis deepened, there was mounting pressure for leaders who could write and speak for public debate. The cultural landscape was shifting; a new social leader was required, a well-educated political leader who could speak to the issues of the day. Witherspoon understood the moment. He groomed his students to address the most important political audiences imaginable: signers of the Declaration of Independence, future U.S. presidents, Supreme Court justices, delegates to the Constitutional Convention.

The Faithful Statesman

There are few better expressions of the religious ideal of the citizen-statesman than Witherspoon's sermon "Christian Magnanimity." First delivered at com-

50. Quoted in Miller, *Selected Writings,* p. 20.

51. Collins, *President Witherspoon,* p. 133.

52. Francis L. Broderick, "Pulpit, Physics, and Politics: The Curriculum of the College of New Jersey, 1746-1794," *William and Mary Quarterly,* vol. VI (1949): 64.

mencement in 1775, it would be repeated every year for a decade, and later made mandatory reading by successor Ashbel Green. Witherspoon sought to show that, contrary to critics who dismissed Christian virtue as lacking nobility, real greatness was inseparable from sincere piety. This is because only genuine faith can keep the heart set on right ambitions. "The object of our desires must be just as well as great," he warned. "Some of the noblest powers of the human mind have often been exerted in invading the right instead of promoting the interest and happiness of mankind."[53]

Promotion of the common good was an important theme for Witherspoon. Only a small number of men would ever be called into the ministry; the vast majority would take up occupations outside the church. All the more important, he reasoned, to "fit young Gentlemen for serving their Country in public Stations."[54] Their Christian influence would come from within their chosen professions, depending on the sincerity of their faith, the constancy of their character, and the wise application of their God-given talents:

> In a public view, every good man is called to live and act for the glory of God and the good of others. Here he has as extensive a scene of activity as he can possibly desire. He is not indeed permitted to glory or to build an altar to his own vanity, but he is both permitted and obliged to exert his talents, to improve his time, to employ his substance and to hazard his life in his Maker's service or his country's cause. Nor am I able to conceive any character more truly great than that of one, whatever be his station or profession, who is devoted to the public good under immediate order of Providence.[55]

If Witherspoon's frequent encouragement from the lectern failed to fling his students into public service, his personal example would do the job. "In 1740 America's leading intellectuals were clergymen and thought about theology," writes historian Edmunds Morgan. "In 1790 they were statesmen and thought about politics."[56] Witherspoon somehow managed to think about both. His mailing list included the likes of James Madison, Alexander Hamilton, John Adams, Benjamin Rush, and George Washington. While holding his post at Princeton, he shuttled back and forth to Philadelphia to serve as a member of the Continental Congress. He personally delivered assistance to General

53. "Christian Magnanimity," in Miller, *Selected Writings*, p. 120.

54. Quoted in Miller, *Selected Writings*, p. 21.

55. "Christian Magnanimity," in Miller, *Selected Writings*, pp. 121-22.

56. Edmunds Morgan, "The American Revolution Considered as an Intellectual Movement," in *Paths of American Thought*, ed. Arthur M. Schlesinger Jr. and Morton White (Boston: Houghton Mifflin, 1963), pp. 11-33.

Washington and his troops in New Jersey and argued vigorously for support of the army. President Woodrow Wilson, another Princeton man, once remarked that "it was as if Washington himself spoke in council for the things which Washington in the field needed, when John Witherspoon stood upon his feet in the Continental Congress."[57]

Witherspoon spent more time practicing rhetoric than teaching it. When other delegates wanted to delay passage of the Declaration of Independence because it seemed the colonies were not "ripe" for independence, he argued that they were "not only ripe for the measure but in danger of becoming rotten for the want of it." As a delegate to the Continental Congress (1776-1782), he served on no fewer than 126 committees. He signed the Articles of Confederation, helped ratify the federal Constitution, and helped pass three of the first four organic laws of the United States.

Ultimately, it seems, Witherspoon's vision of the engaged Christian citizen was contagious. As a leading minister he exerted significant influence on the American Presbyterian Church, where he served as the first moderator of its General Assembly. As a teacher of theology and ethics he extended that influence through his students. According to the church's *Minutes* for 1789, 52 of the 188 ministers on the roster had been trained under him. Of the 469 graduates of the college during his presidency, 114 became pastors in churches throughout the colonies.

Yet equally significant is what became of the rest. During his tenure, the proportion of students who pursued professions outside the church steadily increased. Prior to his arrival, nearly 50 percent of all graduates went into the ministry; only half that many would so during his administration.[58] The political crisis surely had much to do with this. Nevertheless, Witherspoon helped shift the mission of the college from training ministers to preparing men for leadership — in politics, education, and law.

The result was that this evangelical minister presided over the foremost school for statesmen in the new American republic.[59] Among his graduates were one U.S. president (James Madison, B.A., 1771); a vice president (Aaron Burr, B.A., 1772); twelve members of the Continental Congress; five delegates to the Constitutional Convention; forty-nine U.S. representatives; twenty-eight U.S. senators; three Supreme Court justices; eight U.S. district judges; one secretary of state; three attorneys general; and two foreign ministers. Another

57. Quoted in Teresa O. de Prevost, *John Witherspoon: George Washington's Close Friend and Sponsor* (1932 pamphlet), p. 21. (She reports that Wilson delivered these remarks at dedication ceremonies for the Witherspoon statue in Washington, D.C.)

58. Collins, *President Witherspoon*, p. 222.

59. McAllister, "John Witherspoon: Academic Advocate for American Freedom," p. 193.

twenty-six served as state judges, seventeen as members of their state conventions that ratified the proposed Constitution. Though Witherspoon's own political career was considerable, his greatest influence in public life was mediated through his students.[60] In this sense, he became a pivotal figure in America's transition from clerical to political leadership.

The Demands of Leadership

Though Witherspoon was strenuously involved in public affairs, he repeatedly emphasized the private side — the person of character and faith. What force is it, he once asked, that carries the greatest influence over the opinions of men? It is the power of example. "What is it that first begins, establishes, or perpetuates their influence? Nothing else, but the real or apparent sanctity of their character."[61] Reason and argument are important, he said, "but example seizes and keeps possession of the heart."[62]

As a pastor and teacher of divinity, Witherspoon vigorously defended the importance of right doctrine. Yet he did not do so as an academic or intellectual exercise. For Witherspoon, faith that failed to produce a moral life was, quite simply, no faith at all: "Moral influence is the proper touchstone and trial of religious truth." Conversely, there were few things more damaging to the public witness of faith than religious charlatans — those who "assume the form, while they are strangers to the power of it."[63] Unlike many of his Calvinist colleagues, he stressed the inner transformation of heart and mind that faith in Christ produced. His was not a theology primarily of judgment or of "sin management," but, rather, one of grace. "The leading principle of true holiness, according to the gospel, is a deep and grateful sense of redeeming love."[64]

Surely this helps explain how Witherspoon, never a lax disciplinarian, elicited genuine affection from his students. James Madison called him "the good doctor." John Chavis, a black man sent to Princeton as "an experiment," became famous as a schoolmaster and preacher in North Carolina.[65] Ashbel Green, another graduate, who later served as president of the college, remarked:

60. Jeffry Hays Morrison, "John Witherspoon and 'The Public Interest of Religion,'" *Journal of Church and State* 41, no. 3 (Summer 1999): 553.

61. John Witherspoon, "The Trial of Religious Truth by Its Moral Influence," in *The Works of the Rev. John Witherspoon,* 2:397.

62. Witherspoon, *The Works of the Rev. John Witherspoon,* 2:398.

63. Witherspoon, *The Works of the Rev. John Witherspoon,* 2:395.

64. Witherspoon, *The Works of the Rev. John Witherspoon,* 2:406.

65. Collins, *President Witherspoon,* p. 217.

"To Dr. Witherspoon more than to any other human being, I am indebted for whatever of influence or success has attended me in life."[66]

Such influence cannot be separated from Witherspoon's own example. As historian Roger Fechner concludes: "He persuaded his listeners by the accuracy of his learning and the force of his personal piety."[67] Yet it was more than piety that commended Witherspoon to his generation; it was moral courage. In May of 1776 he argued that "when liberty, prosperity, and life are at stake, we must not think of being scholars but soldiers." At fifty-four, Witherspoon was too old to be much of a soldier, but he was a son of liberty. In July he signed the Declaration of Independence, pledging with his compatriots "our Lives, our Fortunes, and our sacred Honor." By November the vow was put to the test: Witherspoon was forced to cut the term short, dismiss the college, and flee with his wife and family for their lives. Washington and his battered army marched through Princeton on December 2. Within a week a brigade of British troops arrived, quartered themselves in the empty college building, and staged the battle of Princeton.

Witherspoon would return to the college within a few months to carry on his duties — academic and political. Even in his *Lectures on Eloquence* he drove home the connection between private virtue and public action: "There can be no doubt that integrity is the first and most important character of a man. . . . This integrity should show itself in undertaking causes."[68] And undertake them he did. In addition to his contribution to the cause for American independence, he launched numerous humanitarian efforts — securing better treatment for prisoners, improving military hospitals, arranging for the printing and distribution of Bibles.

Here is a vision for cultural influence which avoids the excesses of much of our contemporary debates about religion and politics. Witherspoon embodied the man of faith as citizen-statesman. He warned his listeners, almost to excess, of the need for personal piety and exemplary character; yet he never eluded the call to public action. A favorite text from the gospels — "let your light shine before men, that they may see your good works, and glorify your Father in heaven" — precluded for him the life of a cloistered cleric. He would reject not only religious triumphalism in politics, but pseudo-spiritual withdrawal from culture.

Writing on the eve of Independence, John Adams feared that "we have not Men, fit for the Times." Those men would appear, thanks in no small measure to the preacher-cum-politician. Combatants in today's culture wars, religious or secular, could learn much from this forgotten son of liberty.

66. Joseph H. Jones, *The Life of Ashbel Green* (New York: R. Carter and Bros., 1849), p. 146; also quoted in "The Influence of Princeton on Higher Education in the South Before 1825," by Donald Robert Come, 365.

67. Fechner, "The Godly and Virtuous Republic," p. 10.

68. Miller, *Selected Writings*, p. 301.

Catholic Moral Teachings: Subsidiarity

T. WILLIAM BOXX

The term "order" in social order indicates the absence of chaos and the presence of principles of cohesion. It refers to the condition of all the parts of society working harmoniously for the good of the whole in service to the members of society. Society itself may be broadly understood as being comprised of three interrelated macro systems of organization — political, economic, and cultural — within each of which various institutions facilitate the satisfaction of the diverse material and intangible needs and desires of the members. The question of social order, then, is how social relations are most satisfactorily governed among individuals and the institutions that make up society.

Social order, however, cannot be properly conceived of as only the structure of the sociological units. Most fundamentally, what gives order is the collective sense of the norms and values of the people, rooted in the interaction of beliefs and the practices of everyday life. The principles by which people live in society, whether articulated or not, are absolutes in the sense that they are assumed to be universal — everyone more or less lives by them and they are accepted as both true and useful. Otherwise, to the extent that social principles are widely violated, disorder prevails. Thus, social order is, metaphorically, the spirit that animates the societal body or the public philosophy that arises from tried and true social relationships. When the validity of values and norms weaken, and when the presumptive truth and utility of certain fundamental social institutions are swallowed by the encroachments of others, the harmony and ordered balance of society dissipates.

Social Order and Culture

It should be clear that much of the social order depends upon the cultural sphere. Social order and particular cultural foundations are not invented per se (though they obviously reflect human choices), but rather evolve over long periods of time in complex and innumerable interrelationships. Culture cannot be successfully constructed whole overnight or in one or two generations. Tragically, it can deteriorate in a short period of time, but rebuilding it is no simple matter. As T. S. Eliot put it, when culture decays "you must start painfully again, and you cannot put on a new culture ready made. You must wait for the grass to grow to feed the sheep to give wool out of which your new coat will be made."[1] As the old order declines, there follows a deepening twilight of uncertainty and confusion, the signs of which a growing number now detect. Our practical task, then, must be one of renewal and rejuvenation, not *creatio ex nihilo,* to push back the approaching long dark night if we can.

The social order falls when the culture becomes discredited and the people no longer have confidence in the formerly presumed norms according to which decisions were made and public life progressed. Many sense such decline, and the nightly pictures of social dissolution incrementally reinforce the prophecies of inevitability. We fear that a destiny of ruin awaits us as surely as the biblical writing on the wall: "you are weighed in the balance and found wanting." As fell Babylon to the Persians, we wonder about our fall, not to an external force but to the self-destructive tendencies of postmodernism. Thus, like Scrooge's desperately hopeful inquiry of the spirit of the future, we also are led to ask: "Are these the shadows of the things that will be, or are they shadows of the things that may be only?"[2]

The heart of culture is morality, so that at its essence ours is a moral crisis. Will Herberg observed more than twenty-five years ago that it is not only that moral standards are too often violated — thus has it always been. The far more distressing fact is that "the very notion of morality or a moral code seems to be itself losing its meaning for increasing numbers of men and women in our society."[3] Herberg saw the pervasiveness of relativism as leading toward a "nonmoral, normless culture" where the idea of truth is denied and with it any sense of natural or divine law.

1. T. S. Eliot, *Christianity and Culture: The Idea of a Christian Society and Notes Towards the Definition of Culture* (New York & London: Harcourt Brace Jovanovich, 1949), p. 157.

2. Charles Dickens, "A Christmas Carol," in *Christmas Books and Stories,* vol. 1 (London: The Hawarden Press, 1899), p. 160.

3. Will Herberg, "What Is the Moral Crisis of Our Time?" *The Intercollegiate Review,* Fall 1986, p. 7.

The validity of morality itself rests upon it being transcendent of mere human invention, either by virtue of the natural order or by divine design or both. The moral order is discovered (and to the theologically committed, also revealed) and while changing circumstances engender new insights and interpretations, these do not alter the conviction that the essence of the moral life is rooted in nature and its Creator. It is hard to fathom how morality conceived of as mere preferences of lifestyle and variable personal values, constrained only by isolated individual choices, could sustain a civil and humane order. Yet that is the prevailing elite paradigm. Fortunately, the mass of people, although less confident than in the past perhaps, have not as yet lost hold of their common sense notion that moral habits and the qualities of good character are defined and compelled by less arbitrary authority. Almost everyone in American society believes in God, and the renewal of social order fails if it does not take our civil heritage of belief into account.

Moral norms fundamentally restrain negative, selfish tendencies and promote a vision of the good and meaningful life. It is obvious that those who have little or no moral discipline — who are not restrained in private life — will not be restrained in public life either. Moral relativism simply does not work and cannot inspire a vital culture or effective social order. In challenging moments, weakly formed moral sentiments will too easily give way to expediency and selfishness or to passion and appetite. Michael Novak puts it this way: "For how can a people profess to be capable of self-government, of government of, by and for the people, if they cannot govern their own passions? How can a people govern a whole society who cannot, each of them, govern themselves?"[4] It is senseless to speak of political freedom without moral standards. In a democratic polity such moral laxity translates into accelerating demands for government provision and diminishing expectations of personal responsibility.

We are made to be moral-cultural beings, both by biological necessity and, if you will, by our transcendent nature. Particular human behavior is largely learned — it is not instinctive. Through natural processes our predecessors emerged as creatures of culture whose very survival was dependent upon learned behavioral patterns of culture. Those who exhibited moral-like qualities, which were perhaps grounded in affection for the young and familial attachment and which led to mutual cooperation and social affiliation, were more successful.[5] We have the capacity and necessity for culture, including moral judgment. Although the mechanisms for moral-cultural judgment are

4. Michael Novak, "Virtue and the City," (Public Arguments) in *Crisis: A Journal of Lay Catholic Opinion,* May 1994, p. 9.

5. See James Q. Wilson, "What is Moral, and How Do We Know It?" *Commentary* 95, no. 6 (June 1993): 37; and his *The Moral Sense* (New York: The Free Press, 1993) for a fuller study.

ingrained, the surety of their expression is not. It is important to emphasize that the moral capacity is one of the only predispositions with no guarantee of ongoing effective manifestation. Successful and stable patterns of culture are required for proper nurturance and encouragement. Social policy that works against this nature, however well intended, is bound to be dysfunctional in the end.

The human person is part of nature and its natural processes, but also transcends nature. We are self-aware with a unique consciousness and rational capacity that sets us apart from the rest of creation. Particular biological developments are the necessary conditions for the existence of our transcendent qualities but ultimately, I would affirm, we owe their emergence to the transcendent Creator and they cannot be satisfactorily explained otherwise. As rational beings we discover the moral order in creation, and as creatures of the Creator we are called to likewise be responsibly creative within that natural order. Thus, morality and creativity are in our nature as potentialities and our cultural arrangements and social institutions must reflect and facilitate the manifestation of that nature.

Because we are transcendent creatures and biocultural beings, personal moral responsibility and a concomitant societal moral consensus are requisite conditions of our existence. Our human nature is such that cultural arrangements cannot be subject to limitless reconstructions, which might, for example, present a false dichotomy between the individual and society, or which would tend to blur the distinctions or diminish the validity of moral life. Individualism in its extreme form, on the one hand, and socialism, on the other, are errors of some magnitude because they have a distorted view of human nature — a nature which entails both personal moral responsibility and social cooperation.

Responsible Freedom

Moral responsibility presumes the freedom to make moral judgments, so freedom is a necessary condition of moral life. We must be free to choose, but because human life in its fullest is not possible absent social cooperation — which requires the presumption of established norms — individual choice cannot in all cases be the ultimate standard for social resolution or organization. Society must be ordered so as to encourage the exercise of responsible freedom, for both personal and social well-being. It is necessary, for the sake of freedom, to leave many life decisions to individual preferences, but the institutions of society must have the vigor and presumption of rightness to confidently uphold certain standards of behavior and social order. In other words, there must be a strong sense of what is normal and good, in spite of deviations which may be freely chosen by some individuals. Radical individual freedom cannot be established as the super-value that automatically overwhelms the normative institutions of society whenever conflicting claims are pressed; this has too often been the legal and political tendency in the moral-cultural field of our time. (In the economic sphere, on the other hand, freedom has tended to be overrun by the lopsided demands of the state.)

The question then is, how do we best promote responsible freedom through culture and the social order? Social order must be rooted in human nature if it is to be successful — that is, if it is to call forth the best potentialities in the people and assure the propagation of civil society. The good society presumes that some measure of what was classically known as virtue must exist in the people. The ancient Greeks recognized four cardinal virtues — prudence, fortitude, temperance, and justice, to which Christian theology would add faith, hope, and love. Plato understood that the human person was by nature oriented to the Good, but that virtuous character must be vigorously inculcated in the young until they come to love the Good on their own. And Aristotle recognized that one acquires virtuous habits by the practice of virtue. You learn moral habits by doing, which requires examples to follow and social reinforcement. If the precepts of the virtuous or moral life are not widely held and affirmed by key institutions, society collapses. And then what is freedom when everyday life is a struggle and basic security becomes precarious? The late Dr. Russell Kirk insightfully expressed the contingencies of freedom: "Out of faith arises order; and once order prevails, freedom becomes possible. When the faith that nurtured the order fades away, the order disintegrates; and freedom no more can survive the disappearance of order than the branch of a tree can outlast the fall of the trunk."[6] As we lose our moral foundations, we will hardly be able to hold onto civic freedom in any meaningful sense.

The American Order

The founders of the American regime, themselves students of the classics, presumed a republican citizenry possessing the characteristics of virtue. As James Madison rhetorically inquired: "Is there no virtue among us? If there be not, we are in a wretched situation. . . . To suppose that any form of government will secure liberty or happiness without any virtue in the people is a chimerical idea."[7]

6. Russell Kirk, *The Wise Men Know Wicked Things Are Written on the Sky* (Washington, D.C.: Regnery Gateway, Inc., 1987), p. 110.

7. James Madison quoted in the introduction to *The Federalist Papers by Alexander Hamilton, James Madison and John Jay,* ed. Garry Wills (Toronto: Bantam Books, 1982), p. xxi.

He knew that the political order must comport with human nature and called government "the greatest of all reflections on human nature."[8]

The American republic was founded upon the presupposition that there are such things as "truths" about the human endowment and a rightness of order derived from "nature and nature's God." Political organization and public life in general cannot be established upon relativistic assertions about human nature, and it is foolishness beyond hubris to think any civilization can be sustained by such.

The new American political order was not cut from completely new cloth. Americans were accustomed to political freedom and largely unimpeded commerce as a result of the ideas and social arrangements of the British civilization to which they belonged. That is what made the hardening restrictions and disdainful behavior of King George's government so intolerable. They certainly established a "new order for the ages," a new political order, but it was founded upon the widely held "rights of Englishmen" and the philosophy and beliefs of the European culture to which they were heir. It was not a radical revolution along the lines of the near contemporary French revolution of 1789 or the Russian communist revolution of 1917. They did not create from nothing but rather built upon the deeply rooted values of the people and the best of their culture. Thus their social history was the social history of Europe, and therefore of Rome, of Athens, and of Jerusalem.

The American social order was constituted of Judeo-Christian religious traditions as well as the philosophical insights of Enlightenment thinking. That is how the Founders could presume a certain degree of virtue in the people and how they could speak of "self-evident truths." And that is how they could propose a system of government that was, as John Adams said, "made only for moral and religious people."[9] In this sentiment the Founders shared the thought of their British contemporary Edmund Burke: "We know and what is better, we feel inwardly, that religion is the basis of civil society, and the source of all good and of all comfort."[10] A well-ordered American society requires the renewal of political culture, along with its moral and philosophical presuppositions, as envisioned by the Founders and statesmen like Burke. And, I might add, citizen-statesmen who can put the common good above narrow and special interests and self-interest. Yet in the last several decades especially, decades

8. James Madison, *Federalist 51,* p. 261.

9. John Adams quoted in John Eidsmoe, "The Religious Roots of the Constitution," *The New Federalist Papers,* ed. J. Jackson Barlow, Dennis J. Mahoney, and John G. West Jr. (Lanham: University Press of America, 1988), p. 274.

10. Edmund Burke, *The Speeches of the Right Hon. Edmund Burke, with Memoir and Historical Introduction by James Burke, Esq., A.B.* (Dublin: James Duffy and Co., Ltd., 1858), p. 445.

of accelerating social dysfunction, our political order — through the courts and legislated policy — has pushed the religious foundations of morality out of the public square and fostered an environment of hostility toward traditional values. During the very time when the anomic influences of postmodernism most needed countering by confident public moral reaffirmation, the leadership of key societal institutions gave over to the false dualistic rationalism of secular extremism. What is needed today is a renewed understanding of the indispensable connection of morality to social order and to freedom.

Subsidiarity and Mediating Structures

The "well-ordered society" means that the key spheres and institutions of society work harmoniously and effectively in concert with the highest qualities of human nature, promoting, among other things, responsible freedom. It follows that no one part can be allowed to encroach upon and diminish the other parts and that the principles and norms behind public life be transmitted and upheld in a vigorous fashion. This the concept of subsidiarity proposes and a vital system of mediating structures presumes.

The term "subsidiarity" was originally formulated in Roman Catholic social teaching. Derived from the Latin, it describes the principle according to which the purpose of higher political and social organizations or communities in relation to lower ones is that of *helping*. Those functions that can be performed by smaller structures should be performed by them, and mediating structures — those institutions or communities within society that mediate, or stand between, the individual and the state, such as families, neighborhoods, local communities, churches, and voluntary associations — are therefore very important. As a system of thought, these concepts put the emphasis on the institutions and communities closest to the individual. For instance, the vitality of the family as the closest mediating institution to the individual should not be weakened by, say, the policy of the federal government; rather, the federal government as a higher community should help to maintain that vitality.

Subsidiarity first became prominent public discourse in 1931 through Pope Pius XI's encyclical *Quadragesimo Anno,* which was written as a commemoration of the fortieth anniversary (hence the title) of Pope Leo XIII's landmark social encyclical *Rerum Novarum* (New Things). The theme of Pius's encyclical was, appropriately, "On Reconstructing the Social Order," a phrase contained in the fuller title.

Pius XI led the Roman Catholic Church from 1922 until his death in 1939. During his pontificate, he faced the social and political disruptions which followed in the aftermath of the first World War: the Great Depression, the rise of fascism and Nazism, the expanding influence of communism, and the looming threat of the second World War. Human society itself seemed threatened in this time, with dehumanizing regimes in the ascendancy and economic systems in turmoil or out of balance. He saw that the world needed true peace and a return to moral law with the principles of justice and charity at the heart of right social order.[11]

Pius objected both to what he called liberalism, which today might more appropriately be called a type of libertarianism, and to socialism — that is, to radical individualism and collectivism. Liberalism was seen as an error because it failed to take into account the social character of private property and denied public authority any control over economic life. Great concentrations of wealth were the result, to the detriment of the mass of working people. Furthermore, it was thought, those few in control of the wealth tended to inordinately influence the state, thus becoming an economic oligarchy and denying the state its proper function.

Collectivism, either in the form of socialism or communism, on the other hand, was in error (in contrast to liberalism) by its denial of the individual character of the right of property. The themes of class warfare and abolition of private property were recognized by Pius as damaging to human society whether variously tempered or not. Socialism's emphasis on production and the material was such that the higher goods of the human person, including freedom, were relegated to secondary importance. It implied a level of unacceptable coercion and made no place for true social authority, which rests on the Creator and not on temporal and material advantages. Thus Pius emphatically affirmed that true socialism is incompatible with Christianity. He also warned against those who downplayed the dangers of the brutal and inhumane communist regimes then in power. His warnings were vindicated when the inhumanity of those regimes led to their downfall, beginning in 1989.

Quadragesimo Anno has three major parts. The first division (paragraphs 16-40) comments on the contributions of Leo XIII's *Rerum Novarum,* which focused on the conditions of workers. The second division (paragraphs 41-98) elaborates on certain aspects of Leo's encyclical and applies its teaching to modern conditions. The final part (paragraphs 98-110) deals with the changes in economic life since Leo, the development of socialism, and the causes of socioeconomic evils and the necessity of moral reform.

It is in the second part that the concept of subsidiarity, which builds upon Leo's political economy as interpreted by Pius in the first part of the encyclical,

11. Terrance P. McLaughlin, "Introduction," in *The Church and the Reconstruction of the Modern World: The Social Encyclicals of Pope Pius XI* (Garden City, N.Y.: Image Books, Doubleday and Co., 1957), pp. 1-23.

is offered. Pius calls for the reform of institutions and morals, with the state the most prominent of the institutions to be considered. He qualifies the importance of the state by denying it the ability to create "universal well-being" by its activities. He perceives that the "rich social life which was once highly developed through associations of various kinds" has become nearly extinct with only individuals and the state remaining. This situation he wishes to correct with a right understanding of how the state ought to function within society.

With the moribundity of this former "structure of social governance" the state has assumed the burdens formerly borne by associations, such that it has become overwhelmed by "almost infinite tasks and duties," causing great harm to the state itself. In other words, there is a limit to what the state should be expected to do. Even recognizing the changing conditions of history, Pius nevertheless affirms what he calls "that most weighty principle, which cannot be set aside or changed," and which must remain a "fixed and unshaken" social philosophy. This social philosophy, placing the state in the context of the overall society, he describes as follows:

> Just as it is gravely wrong to take from individuals what they can accomplish by their own initiative and industry and give it to the community, so also it is an injustice and at the same time a grave evil and disturbance of right order to assign to a greater and higher association what lesser and subordinate organizations can do. For every social activity ought of its very nature to furnish help to the members of the body social, and never destroy and absorb them. (79)

Thus, the state should not absorb the roles of the various other institutions and associations in society, in the same way that individuals should not be relieved of their responsibilities. The state, according to Pius, should "let subordinate groups handle matters and concerns of lesser importance," leaving to it the things only it can do, those functions characterized by "directing, watching, urging, restraining, as occasion requires and necessity demands." Those in authority should assure that "a graduated order is kept among the various associations" of society. This above described social philosophy and order he terms the principle of "subsidiarity function," an order of helping relationships that respects the proper function of each social unit (80).

Quite clearly, the state is conceived of as an important part of society but only a part, not synonymous with society. Most particularly, Pius presumes that the state is not superior to the natural rights of individuals (elsewhere discussed in the context of the right of private property) because the human person is "older than the state" and families are "prior both in thought and in fact to uniting into a polity" (49). The fundamental function of the state is to preserve the common good. To be sure, Pius can be interpreted as allowing quite vigorous action by the state in carrying out this duty; nevertheless, his rule is for the state to help maintain the vitality of all the parts of society and not to absorb them or abolish the inherent freedom of the human person. The inference is that society is built upon human nature — upon the human person as one who is simultaneously a free, morally responsible, and social creature.

Pope Pius's current successor, John Paul II, reaffirmed the importance of subsidiarity as the organizing principle for social teaching in his 1991 encyclical *Centesimus Annus,* written for the one hundredth anniversary of *Rerum Novarum.* Building upon Pius, John Paul interprets the implications of subsidiarity as requiring that "A community of a higher order should not interfere in the internal life of a lower order, depriving the latter of its functions, but rather should support it in case of need and help to coordinate its activity with the activities of the rest of society, always with a view to the common good" (*Centesimus Annus* 48). The viability of mediating institutions must be affirmed and supported by the state, which is subsidiary, that is, a help to society. This is so because the social nature of the human person is such that it is "realized in various intermediary groups, beginning with the family and including economic, social, political, and cultural groups that stem from human nature itself and have their own autonomy, always with a view to the common good" (13).

For these reasons, John Paul is particularly critical of the contemporary welfare state or what he calls the social assistance state. He employs the concept of subsidiarity to define the state's proper role, which would avoid "enlarging excessively the sphere of state intervention." Such a misunderstanding of the state creates the "malfunctions and defects" of "bureaucratic ways of thinking" leading to an "inordinate increase of public agencies" and enormous increases in spending as well as misspent human energies. He affirms that needs are best understood and satisfied by those closest to them, which obviously assumes a prominent role for mediating institutions in providing support (48).

Like Pius, John Paul recognizes the family (founded upon marriage) as the primary mediating institution of society, which he calls "the first and fundamental structure for human ecology." In the family, the human person receives his or her "first formative ideas about truth and goodness and learns what it means to love and to be loved, and thus what it actually means to be a person." John Paul reveres the family "as the sanctuary of life" (39). The state cannot truly provide or replace these functions without totalitarian pretensions, although it can support or hinder the social environment necessary for family vitality.

In the context of limited state intervention, one of the most widely discussed concepts in *Centesimus Annus,* and something of a watershed in contemporary Catholic social teaching, is John Paul's strong affirmation of the free economy. Whereas Leo's and Pius's criticisms of both liberalism (imprecisely assumed to apply to American capitalism) and socialism led many Catholic thinkers to look for a "third way" in political economy, John Paul seeks to put that quest to rest. He supports capitalism, understood as "an economic system which recognizes the fundamental and positive role of business, the market, private property, and the resulting responsibility for the means of production as well as free human creativity in the economic sector" (42). Perhaps because the term "capitalism" has a pejorative connotation in some circles where human failings and precapitalistic political economics have been mistakenly judged as indicating the inherent fallacy of the capitalistic system, he prefers the terms "business economy, market economy or simply free economy." In any event, the free economy is rooted in human freedom, which is a requirement of human dignity.

The state has strong and decisive limitations in terms of interventions but John Paul is not proposing a strictly libertarian political economy. His teaching on capitalism entails a free economic sector "circumscribed within a strong juridical framework which places it at the service of human freedom in its totality and which sees it as a particular aspect of that freedom, the core of which is ethical and religious" (42). The economic system must function within a moral-cultural context and the rule of law. The state serves society by watching over the common good and intervening in limited ways when necessary (especially on behalf of the weakest) and in a manner that is supportive of intermediary groups and individual responsibility.

One sees in Catholic social teaching a recognition that society must be organized on the basis of human nature, a nature that is inherently free and social. It is also a nature that tends toward the good but is capable of evil. Therefore, right social order must especially respect the family as the primary social unit wherein the moral life and highest values of humanity are irreplaceably first nurtured. Likewise the fuller social nature of the human person presumes a network of various other affiliations, which the state is bound to respect, along with human freedom, in its service to civil society. The concept of subsidiarity is conceived of as harmoniously balancing the individual and social aspects of the human person and orienting human activity toward the common good.

Mediating Structures and Public Policy

The indispensability of healthy mediating structures for a well-balanced society has steadily gained broad recognition among social scientists and policy experts during the last couple of decades. A pivotal point for greater attention to the subject was a 1977 monograph by Peter Berger and Richard John Neuhaus sponsored by the American Enterprise Institute and partially funded by the National Endowment for the Humanities.[12]

In *To Empower People: The Role of Mediating Structures in Public Policy,* Berger and Neuhaus examined the welfare state in light of two apparently contradictory tendencies in American public opinion. One tendency is the desire for a high level of provided services and the other is distrust of big government. Given the continuing need for a welfare state in modern society, they proposed "alternative mechanisms" in providing welfare state services so as to address both tendencies. Their concern was not, however, merely for efficiency of delivery, but more significantly for a recognition in public policy of the necessary "meaning and identity" bestowing functions of mediating structures. The premise of this social vision is that mediating structures can more humanely serve the purposes of the welfare state and bridge the meaning gap between the isolated individual and the "megastructures" (most notably, the state) of modern society.[13]

Berger and Neuhaus chose to focus on four mediating structures that most people could relate to and which were relevant to problems of the welfare state. Those mediating structures — the neighborhood, family, church, and voluntary associations — are the kind of key institutions that relate the political order to the "values and realities of individual life" and, thus, provide its moral foundation.[14]

The crippling risk of cynicism when political life becomes detached from the foundational values of individual and community life was recognized by Berger and Neuhaus. Although promising political and social movements have transpired since the time of their writing, the credibility of the political order, to say the least, remains a serious problem. A majority of the population believes that most federal representatives are corrupt, and sizable portions of the electorate do not see much point in voting. It is exceedingly unhealthy in a democratic republic for politics to be held in such disrepute as it is today. While one could examine a number of causal possibilities, the continuing breach between the life and work of ordinary citizens and that of the political leadership is no small consideration. The term limits movement is one understandable reaction to this detachment between ordinary life and its values and a political system perceived as unresponsive and irresponsible.

A significant step toward amelioration of denigrated political life is a renewed emphasis upon, as Berger and Neuhaus phrased it, "the value-generating

12. Peter L. Berger and Richard John Neuhaus, *To Empower People: The Role of Mediating Structures in Public Policy* (Washington, D.C.: American Enterprise Institute, 1977).

13. Berger and Neuhaus, *To Empower People,* p. 3.

14. Berger and Neuhaus, *To Empower People,* p. 3.

and value-maintaining agencies in society."[15] To help implement this effect, *To Empower People* presents three propositions for government that would enhance the legitimacy of domestic public policy and, therefore, of the political order: (1) mediating structures are essential for a vital democratic society; (2) public policy should protect and foster mediating structures; and (3) wherever possible, public policy should utilize mediating structures for the realization of social purposes.[16]

Government concern for mediating structures does not necessarily presuppose a particular set of policies (though that needs to be offered as well) but it does entail taking into account the effect of proposed and existing public policies upon, especially, the family and local community affiliations, wherein real people really live. It also means that mediating institutions and nongovernmental associations should be (with all responsible considerations) favored mechanisms for public policy implementation over bureaucratic systems. Along the lines of cost-benefit analysis, there should be a mediating structures analysis and impact statement with social welfare programs.

To effectively involve religious institutions, the current political system will need to modify the prevailing radical church-state separation ideology and return to something more resembling the founding intent of the First Amendment, which was simply to prevent the establishment of a state church (as in England) and the state persecution of religious diversity, rather than to begin a wholesale exclusion of religion from the public square. To suppose that, as Richard John Neuhaus has disparagingly put it, "wherever the writ and coin of government run, religion must retreat" is to abuse one of civil society's most valuable institutions and to disturb the balance of social order in favor of the voracious state.[17] True civic pluralism and freedom requires no less. Religion's unnatural exclusion (for example, in education) and limitation through counter-productive or denuding regulatory conditions perpetuates the perverse identification of all things public with governmental exclusivity.

Renewed emphasis on the significance of mediating institutions (whether the exact terminology is used or not) has arisen through various sociopolitical themes in recent years. Much of their animating force stems from the social deconstruction undeniably progressing, as starkly enumerated by William Bennett in *The Index of Leading Cultural Indicators.* The data reveals that over the last thirty years there has been more than a 500 percent increase in violent crime, an over 400 percent increase in illegitimate births, a tripling of the per-

15. Berger and Neuhaus, *To Empower People,* p. 6.

16. Berger and Neuhaus, *To Empower People,* p. 6.

17. Richard John Neuhaus, *Doing Well and Doing Good: The Challenge to the Christian Capitalist* (New York: Doubleday, 1992), p. 273.

centage of children living in single parent households, a tripling in the teenage suicide rate, a doubling in the divorce rate, and a seventy-five point drop in SAT scores. All of this has been accompanied by tremendous increases in government spending including inflation-adjusted increases on welfare of 630 percent and on education of over 200 percent.[18]

Such sociopolitical orientations as the communitarian perspective, empowerment strategies, family-values initiatives, volunteerism, character and virtue education, and cultural renewal projects — all of these intellectual and civic endeavors — seek, in one way or another, to restore a lost balance between the individual and social nature of the human person for the sake of civil society. Two such sociopolitical approaches, communitarianism and the empowerment movement, will be briefly sketched to exemplify these common chords of concern for institutional well-being.

Communitarianism

A salient feature of the communitarian perspective is that it recognizes that the "preservation of liberty depends upon the active maintenance of the institutions of civil society."[19] Institutions such as the family, education, and local communities are the spheres in which shared values and responsible citizenship are fostered. The family, as the primary socializing institution, requires special attention. Generally, the communitarian perspective recognizes that the best interests of children are served by stable, two-parent families and that social policy should encourage this mother-father child-raising pattern as normative. Schools also should support the role of the family in the moral education of children, teaching basic values that Americans share (for example, honesty, thrift, respect, responsibility, an appreciation of democracy) and creating an environment where good character and civil behavior are normative. The raising and educating of children is of first level importance for, among others, the reason David Popenoe identifies: "Successful civilizations heretofore have been based on a family foundation, one that assured that children were taught the values, attitudes, and habits of the culture and became, as adults, reasonably well integrated into society."[20]

18. William J. Bennett, *The Index of Leading Cultural Indicators: Facts and Figures on the State of American Society* (New York: A Touchstone Book, Simon and Schuster, 1994), p. 8.

19. *The Responsive Communitarian Platform: Rights and Responsibilities* (Washington, D.C.: The Communitarian Network, undated), p. 1.

20. David Popenoe, "The Family Condition of America: Cultural Change and Public Policy," in *Values and Public Policy,* ed. Henry J. Aaron, Thomas E. Mann, and Timothy Taylor (Washington, D.C.: The Brookings Institution, 1993), p. 82.

The balancing of rights and responsibilities is also an important aspect of communitarian thinking. It aims, as Amitai Etzioni has said, for "a judicious mix of self-interest, self-expression, and commitment to the commons — of rights and responsibilities, of I and we."[21] By its nature, communitarian thought obviously perceives that the current imbalance is weighed in favor of the rights side and that community commitments need to be added to the equation to balance it, not to tilt it to the other side.

The principles of sociopolitical organization that follow from a communitarian perspective echo the basic tenets of subsidiarity. In general, social responsibilities should not be assumed by a higher level or larger institution than necessary. This applies to social groups as well as governments so that, to the extent possible, many typical welfare functions are best handled by those closest to the need rather than by the state. A preference for viable local communities means that higher levels of government should be involved only when "other social subsystems fail, rather than seek to replace them." There may be roles for government and private partnerships but government must not, in effect, replace local communities.[22]

As would be suspected, there are many and varied facets within communitarian thought, and since views about social policy and political economy are diverse, all of them cannot be reviewed here. What is important is that common threads and connections across sociopolitical orientations can be identified which lead toward the revivification of social order.

Empowerment Movement

The empowerment movement is another important development for sociopolitical reform that seeks to reorder domestic policy in favor of individual, familial, and communal responsibility. Its approach is to empower individuals and communities through grassroots organization and public policy reform. Empowerment strategies are oriented toward helping individuals and local communities take charge of their lives and put to an end to dysfunctional social conditions. Empowerment is a practical and real-life application of the movement to restore civil society.

Policy initiatives focus on housing, welfare, education, economic development, and crime and other social problems. An empowerment approach to public housing, for example, is to turn management over to tenants and to pro-

21. Amitai Etzioni, *The Spirit of Community: The Reinvention of American Society* (New York: A Touchstone Book, Simon and Schuster, 1993), p. 26.

22. *The Responsive Communitarian Platform*, p. 6.

mote private ownership. Housing controlled by tenants themselves or owned by individuals is more efficaciously maintained, and social pathologies (for example, crime, drugs, prostitution) are less present in that environment. When people are systematically empowered to accept responsibility through self-management and ownership they tend to accept it, having more incentives to do so.

People need to be allowed the dignity of responsibility, the freedom to make individual choices, and the opportunity to change their lives for the better. That should be the overarching paradigm of all welfare state policies. In welfare assistance programs, this approach favors initiatives that promote two-parent families, savings and ownership, and work opportunities. In other words, it works to bring the poor and marginalized into mainstream society rather than perpetuating dependence. The perverse incentives of the current system are a scandal to the good intentions of most Americans and are ruinous to the citizens and communities they are designed to help.

Empowerment means better and greater choices in life and that is nowhere more applicable than the education of one's children. Education, as most parents realize, is the key to the future. Parents should have the opportunity to send their children to the schools that best meet their goals and needs. In many places, especially in economically depressed urban areas and predominantly minority communities, parochial and independent schools clearly provide a superior learning and social environment. The monopolistic and centralized approach to education has most dramatically failed people who are poor and they, above all, know it. A voucher system empowers parents and their children and would help spur the educational revival the country as a whole increasingly needs to compete in the world and to provide a better quality of life.

We have to overcome the notion that public education necessarily means government-run education. The principle of subsidiarity, recognition of mediating structures, and communitarian principles, as well as the failing level of achievement at many government schools, all logically compel a revamping of the way education has come to be primarily delivered. One of the crucial misjudgments in the history of education was the trend of centralization and the consolidation of schools away from their natural communities, which has been combined with increasing political control. Education is fundamentally parental and communal in nature and the dominant political system has largely absorbed and displaced these qualities — sometimes in service to special interests — rather than helping to support them.

Other empowerment approaches focus on economic development and job opportunities through such programs as enterprise zones, investment assistance, technical assistance, and so forth. Efforts to restore community security through crime watch and other neighborhood programs are also important. Fundamentally, the empowerment approach seeks to eliminate barriers to individual and community betterment and to inspire citizens and policymakers to do the same.

Conclusion

Across the spectrum of responsible and pioneering sociopolitical thought, the common principles of social governance that emerge involve a recognition of four things:

- The practical and moral indispensability of reinvigorated mediating institutions, especially the family, for a free and civil society.
- The vital necessity of moral renewal and social reinforcement of responsible behavior.
- The understanding of government as a help to and not a master of individuals and mediating institutions — government as a servant of civil society.
- The fundamental duality of freedom and responsibility, and the individual and social nature of the human person, which are at the heart of each of the above.

Building the well-ordered society, or restoring the social order, entails reinvigorating the mediating institutions of society that transmit and reinforce personal and social responsibility and moral constraint. It also entails restoring public (including state) recognition of normative values that bind citizens and their institutional affiliations into a truly civil society. In a country where the state has incrementally absorbed many social functions and where the political system has become so debased as to have largely lost its moral and philosophical moorings, the renewal of political culture needs to be among the high priorities in rebuilding a well-ordered society.

American society is in trouble and almost everyone knows it. We are in trouble because too many of us and our intellectual, social, and political leaders have forgotten or denied that society is not endlessly malleable just as individuals are not. We must return to the understanding that there is a created human nature out of which a moral order and "self evident truths" flow. A democratic republic is an experiment in ordered liberty and cannot be grounded on less than the presumption of enduring principles and the rightly formed character of its citizens.

The shaken Scrooge asked if the dark shadows of the future which were shown to him might yet be changed. And from the innate wellspring of hope of a converted man he answers his own question: "if the courses be departed from, the ends will change. Say it is thus with what you show me!"[23] Say it is thus.

23. Dickens, "A Christmas Carol," p. 160.

III. STRATEGIES FOR CULTURAL RENEWAL

Mass Social Movements:
Essays by Movement Organizers and Scholars

Fatherhood

WADE F. HORN

Fatherlessness today is an unprecedented reality with profound consequences for children. In 1960, the total number of children in the United States living in father-absent families was less than ten million. Today, that number stands at over twenty-four million.[1] This means that nearly four out of ten children in America do not live in the same home as their father. By some estimates, this figure is likely to rise to 60 percent of children born in the 1990s.[2]

For nearly one million children each year, the pathway to a fatherless family is divorce.[3] The divorce rate nearly tripled from 1960 to 1980 before leveling off and declining slightly in the 1980s.[4] Today, 40 out of every 100 first marriages now end in divorce, compared to 16 out of every 100 first marriages in 1960. No other industrialized nation has a higher divorce rate.[5]

The second pathway to a fatherless home is out-of-wedlock fathering. In

1. Wade F. Horn, *Father Facts* (Lancaster, Penn.: National Fatherhood Initiative, 1995), p. 15.

2. Frank F. Furstenberg Jr. and Andrew J. Cherlin, *Divided Families: What Happens to Children When Parents Part* (Cambridge, Mass.: Harvard University Press, 1991), p. 11.

3. U.S. Department of Health & Human Services, National Center for Health Statistics, *Advance Report of Final Divorce Statistics, 1988,* Monthly Vital Statistics Report, vol. 39, 1991.

4. U.S. Department of Commerce, Bureau of the Census, *Statistical Abstract of the United States, 1993* (Washington, D.C.: Government Printing Office, 1993).

5. National Commission on Children, *Just the Facts: A Summary of Recent Information on America's Children and Their Families* (Washington, D.C.: National Commission on Children, 1993).

1960, about 5 percent of all births were out of wedlock. That number increased to 10.7 percent in 1970, 18.4 percent in 1980, 28 percent in 1990, and nearly 33 percent today.[6] In the United States, the number of children fathered out of wedlock each year (approximately 1.3 million annually) now surpasses the number of children whose parents divorce (approximately 1 million annually).

Father absence has profound consequences for the well-being of children. Almost 75 percent of American children living in single-parent families will experience poverty before they reach the age of eleven, compared to only 20 percent of children in two-parent families.[7] Violent criminals are overwhelmingly males who grew up without fathers, including up to 60 percent of rapists,[8] 75 percent of adolescents charged with murder,[9] and 70 percent of juveniles in state reform institutions.[10]

Children who grow up absent their fathers are also more likely to fail at school or to drop out,[11] experience behavioral or emotional problems requiring psychiatric treatment,[12] engage in early sexual activity,[13] develop drug and alcohol problems,[14] commit suicide as adolescents,[15] and be victims of child abuse or neglect.[16] On nearly every measure of child well-being one can imag-

6. Congress, House Committee on Ways and Means, *1991 Green Book* (Washington, D.C.: Government Printing Office, 1991).

7. National Commission on Children, *Just the Facts.*

8. Nicholas Davidson, "Life Without Father: America's Greatest Social Catastrophe," *Policy Review,* no. 51 (1990): 40-44.

9. Dewey Cornell et al., "Characteristics of Adolescents Charged with Homicide," *Behavioral Sciences and the Law,* no. 5 (1987): 11-23.

10. M. Eileen Matlock et al., "Family Correlates of Social Skills Deficits in Incarcerated and Nonincarcerated Adolescents," *Adolescence,* no. 29 (1994): 119-30.

11. Debra Dawson, "Family Structure and Children's Well-Being: Data from the 1988 National Health Survey," *Journal of Marriage and Family,* no. 53, 1991; U.S. Department of Health and Human Services, National Center for Health Statistics, *Survey on Child Health* (Washington, D.C., 1993).

12. U.S. Department of Health and Human Services, National Center for Health Statistics, *National Health Interview Survey* (Hyattsville, Md., 1988).

13. Irwin Garfinkel and Sara McLanahan, *Single Mothers and Their Children* (Washington, D.C.: Urban Institute Press, 1986); Susan Newcomer and J. Richard Udry, "Parental Marital Status Effects on Adolescent Sexual Behavior," *Journal of Marriage and the Family,* May 1987, pp. 235-40.

14. U.S. Department of Health and Human Services, National Center for Health Statistics, *Survey on Child Health* (Washington, D.C., 1993).

15. Patricia L. McCall and Kenneth C. Land, "Trends in White Male Adolescent Young-Adults and Elderly Suicide: Are There Common Underlying Structural Factors?" *Social Science Research,* no. 23 (1994): 57-81; U.S. Department of Health and Human Services, National Center for Health Statistics, *Survey on Child Health* (Washington, D.C., 1993).

16. Catherine M. Malkin and Michael E. Lamb, "Child Maltreatment: A Test of Sociobiological Theory," *Journal of Comparative Family Studies,* no. 25 (1994): 121-30.

ine, children who grow up absent their fathers do worse compared to those who grow up with an involved, committed, and responsible dad.

In addition to the physical absence of fathers from the home, it is also apparent that many physically present fathers are nonetheless psychologically absent from the lives of their children. Overall, parents today spend roughly 40 percent less time with their children than did parents a generation ago.[17] One study found that almost 20 percent of sixth through twelfth graders had not had a good conversation lasting for at least ten minutes with at least one of their parents in more than a month.[18] In regard to fathers, a 1992 Gallup Poll found that 50 percent of all adults agreed that "fathers today spend less time with their children than their fathers did with them."[19]

If ever there was an institution in need of broad-based cultural renewal, it is fatherhood, for the evidence suggests that we can expect little improvement in the well-being of children without reversing a nearly four-decade decline in the number of children growing up with a responsible, committed, and involved father. The question is: How?

Child Support Enforcement

The historic answer to the problem of father absence is child support enforcement. This has not been without some merit. Any man who fathers a child ought to be held financially responsible for that child. Moreover, research generally substantiates that child well-being is improved when nonresident fathers pay child support.[20] Nevertheless, child support enforcement is unlikely, by itself, to be the solution to the problem of fatherlessness for several reasons.

First, while receipt of child support has been found to be associated with improvements in child outcomes, the magnitude of the effects tends to be quite small. That's because the average level of child support is quite modest, only about $3,000 per year.[21] This amount of additional income, although cer-

17. William R. Mattox, "The Parent Trap: So Many Bills, So Little Time," *Policy Review*, Winter 1991, pp. 6-13.

18. Peter L. Benson, *The Troubled Journey: A Portrait of 6th-12th Grade Youth* (Minneapolis: Search Institute, 1993), p. 84.

19. Gallup Poll for the National Center for Fathering, "The Role of Fathers in America: Attitudes and Behavior" (Shawnee Mission, Kans.: April 1992).

20. For a review of this literature see Irwin Garfinkel, Sara S. McLanahan, Daniel R. Meyer, and Judith A. Seltzer, eds., *Fathers Under Fire: The Revolution in Child Support Enforcement* (New York: Russell Sage Foundation, 1998).

21. Congress, House Committee on Ways and Means, *1996 Green Book* (Washington, D.C.: Government Printing Office, 1996), p. 578.

tainly helpful, is unlikely to substantially improve the life trajectory of most children.

Second, many noncustodial fathers are under-educated and under-employed themselves, and as such may lack the resources to provide meaningful economic support for their children.[22] Moreover, as word circulates in low-income communities that failure to comply with child support may result in imprisonment or revocation of one's driver's license, many of these marginally-employed fathers may simply choose to disappear rather than face the possibility of such harsh consequences. It is hard to be an involved father when one is in hiding from the law. Thus, the unintended consequence of such policies may be to decrease, not increase, the number of children growing up with an actively involved father, proving once again that no good policy goes unpunished.

Third, child support enforcement ignores the many noneconomic contributions that fathers make to the well-being of their children. Fathers are more than just cash machines to their children. They are also nurturers, disciplinarians, mentors, moral instructors, and skill coaches. Reducing fatherhood to merely an economic function is to downgrade fathers to, in the words of noted author Barbara Dafoe Whitehead, "paper dads."

Indeed, what troubles fatherhood most is not that some men do not fulfill their financial responsibilities to their children, but that our culture increasingly has come to view fathers' presence as relatively superfluous to the well-being of children. In this sense, our culture has lost the very idea of fatherhood — the notion that fathers provide unique and irreplaceable contributions to the well-being of children. As a result, we have come to believe that a child's father is easily replaced by a welfare or child support check, and, as the president of the Institute for American Values, David Blankenhorn, has stated, any "nearby guy."

There is, however, simply no precedent in human history to support the supposition that millions of men will commit to raising other men's children. Moreover, what children need from their fathers is not their money, but their time. Renewing fatherhood must be about more than male mentors and child support enforcement, as important as male mentors and child support enforcement may be. What is needed is a cultural recapturing of the very idea of fatherhood.

22. According to Garfinkel et al., 20 percent of all nonresident fathers earn less than $6000 annually.

Recapturing the Fatherhood Idea

It was with the task of recapturing the fatherhood idea in mind that the National Fatherhood Initiative (NFI) was launched in March of 1994. The mission of the NFI, which was founded by Don Eberly, is to build a society-wide movement on behalf of responsible fatherhood and, in so doing, improve the well-being of children by increasing the number of children growing up with involved, committed, and responsible fathers. With the support and involvement of such notable Americans as the actor James Earl Jones, former U.S. Health and Human Services Secretary Louis W. Sullivan, and pollster George Gallup, NFI developed a two-part strategy for restoring fatherhood as a national priority.

The first part of this strategy is to send a more compelling message both to men and to the broader culture as to the unique and irreplaceable role fathers play in the lives of their children. Working in conjunction with the Ad Council and others, the NFI develops and distributes, both nationally and within individual states, television, radio, and print public service announcements (PSAs) intended to raise the awareness of every American that fathers matter and that collectively we need to do more to encourage and support men to be good and responsible fathers. To bring added attention to these messages, NFI enlisted the participation of a number of prominent Americans, including Colin Powell, then Vice President Al Gore, actors James Earl Jones and Tom Selleck, golfer Tiger Woods and his father Earl, former Housing and Urban Development Secretary Jack Kemp, former U.S. Senators Dan Coats and Bill Bradley, U.S. Representatives J. C. Watts and Steve Largent, and Penn State football coach Joe Paterno.

Indications are the NFI's public education campaigns are having an effect. In its first four years, NFI's television and radio PSAs have garnered in excess of $110 million in donated broadcasting time. Furthermore, nearly seventy-five thousand phone calls requesting additional information have been made to NFI as a consequence of these PSA campaigns. Although most phone calls are from individual men requesting information on how to be a more effective father, thousands of phone calls also have been received from representatives of community-based organizations seeking assistance in starting local fatherhood outreach, support, and skill-building programs. Moreover, an independent evaluation by researchers at the University of Virginia of a statewide public awareness campaign developed by NFI and implemented in Virginia determined that 40,000 fathers were spending more time with their children and 100,000 non-fathers had reached out to support or encourage a father in their community as a result of the campaign.

NFI has also begun to challenge the negative portrayals of fatherhood by the media. In the spring of 1999, NFI released the first-ever analysis of television's portrayal of fatherhood. This analysis revealed that across the five major networks, only 15 of 102 prime-time, entertainment-oriented shows depicted a father as a central, recurring character with children under the age of eighteen years. Of these 15 shows, only 5 depicted the father as both competent and involved. The typical portrayal was one of incompetence. A similar analysis will be conducted annually to determine whether or not television is responding to NFI's challenge to provide more positive portrayals of fatherhood.

While promoting the idea of involved fathering is certainly important, it is not sufficient for renewing fatherhood in America. In order to accomplish this, every important mediating institution — churches, synagogues, schools, and civic organizations — needs to encourage, support, and honor responsible and committed fatherhood by sponsoring outreach and skill-building initiatives for fathers.

Hence, the second part of NFI's strategy is to mobilize and equip as many sectors of American society as possible to help address the issue of fatherlessness. To this end, in October of 1994 NFI convened the first ever National Summit on Fatherhood in Dallas, Texas, at which several hundred of our nation's civic, business, and philanthropic leaders gathered to begin building a national consensus that something must be done to combat father absence. Since then, NFI has organized a series of follow-up summits focusing on faith communities, urban programming, and community-based organizations, and has been working with such national civic organizations as United Way of America and the Boys and Girls Clubs of America to utilize their existing networks to stimulate local voluntary efforts at making our communities more father-friendly.

In addition, NFI has organized bipartisan task forces involving the nation's governors, mayors, U.S. representatives, and U.S. senators. Each of these task forces is exploring ways in which federal, state, and local government can help to promote responsible and involved fathering. The NFI assists each task force by disseminating materials describing "best practices" in fatherhood programming, hosting meetings of the task forces, and providing individual members with direct consultation. As one measure of the impact of these efforts, numerous states and an increasing number of municipalities, often with NFI's direct assistance, are implementing state or local fatherhood initiatives, often incorporating NFI's core dual strategy of raising awareness and mobilizing communities to action.

To help equip community-based organizations to promote and support responsible fatherhood, NFI has also established a national fatherhood resource center. NFI's resource center provides training, technical assistance, and consultation to organizations interested in making existing services more father-friendly, in establishing an outreach, support, or skill-building program for fathers, or in evaluating efforts to promote responsible fatherhood.

NFI's resource center also takes its pro-fatherhood message directly to individual men. Through the development of skill-building information and community resource materials, NFI helps individual men become better fathers, encourages employers to institute workplace practices that allow their employees time to be better fathers, and assists local communities in developing father-friendly neighborhoods.

The NFI does not, of course, operate in isolation of other efforts. Today, there are literally dozens of national groups advocating responsible fatherhood and thousands more providing local support, encouragement, and skill-building programs targeted to fathers. One of the most promising of these programs is run by the National Center for Responsible Fathering and Child Development headquartered in Washington, D.C. The strength of this program, which focuses on outreach to low-income fathers, lies in its focus on enhancing father-child ties first, and paternity establishment and child support second. Experience from this program suggests that as the father increases his attachment to the child, his desire to claim the child as his own and to take care of his child also increases, including an increased desire to provide economic support.

Other important efforts include the National Center for Fathering headquartered in Kansas City, which conducts seminars for men on how to be more effective dads and provides training to help social service agencies meet the needs of fathers; the National Center on Father and Families, based at the University of Pennsylvania, which conducts research on ways programs can facilitate the effective involvement of fathers; and the Fatherhood Project of the Families and Work Institute, located in New York City, which provides information to employers on how they can make their workplaces more father-friendly.

Supplementing these national efforts are a growing array of community-based fatherhood initiatives. Indeed, when NFI was founded in March of 1994, there were barely two hundred local fatherhood programs operating in the U.S. Today, the best estimate is that there are several thousand operational community-based organizations promoting, supporting, and encouraging responsible fatherhood. Some of these programs are based in civic organizations, some in faith-based institutions, and others are freestanding efforts. Some of these efforts focus on enhancing fathering skills, and others on raising community awareness of the issue. The central defining characteristic of each is that they share the idea that fathers do matter, and that more needs to be done to support and encourage involved, committed, and responsible fatherhood.

Evidence of Renewal

There is evidence that all of this activity is starting to make a difference. Since the mid-1980s, the divorce rate has been decreasing. Moreover, the out-of-wedlock birth rate, after increasing every year since 1960, has recently leveled off, and has actually declined for African-Americans. Furthermore, a 1996 Gallup Poll found that 79 percent of Americans believe "the most significant family or social problem facing America is the physical absence of the father from the home," up from 69 percent in 1992.[23] Another recent survey found that 84 percent of men in their 30s and 40s agree that the definition of success is being a good father.[24]

The U.S. Congress remains poised to support the growing responsible fatherhood movement by passing legislation which would provide funds to local community-based organizations to improve the fathering skills of men, increase the employment skills of fathers so that they are better able to financially support their children, and promote married fatherhood as the ideal. Introduced by Representatives Nancy Johnson (R-CT) and Ben Cardin (D-MD), this bipartisan legislation passed by an overwhelming 328-92 vote in October of 1999. Similar bipartisan legislation has been proposed in the U.S. Senate by Evan Bayh (D-IN) and Pete Dominici (R-NM).

Challenges Remain

But more needs to be done. Tonight, nearly 40 percent of all children in America will still be going to bed in a home without their father present. Many millions more live with disconnected, neglectful, and sometimes even abusive fathers.

Furthermore, while it is becoming increasingly popular to speak of the importance of fathers to the well-being of children, it is still out of fashion to speak of the importance of marriage to the well-being of fatherhood. Yet research has consistently found that unmarried fathers, whether through divorce or out-of-wedlock fathering, tend over time to become disconnected, both financially and psychologically, from their children. About 40 percent of children in father-absent homes have not seen their father in at least a year. Of the remaining 60 percent, only one in five sleeps even one night per month in the fa-

23. Gallup Poll conducted for the National Center on Fathering, as reported in "Father Figures," *Today's Father,* vol. 4, no. 1 (1996): 8.

24. Ross Goldstein, *The New American Adulthood* (Half Moon Bay, Calif.: Consumer Survey Center, 1996).

ther's home. Overall, only one in six sees their father an average of once or more per week.[25] More than half of all children who don't live with their fathers have never even been in their father's home.[26]

Unwed fathers are particularly unlikely to stay connected to their children over time. Whereas 57 percent of unwed fathers are visiting their child at least once per week during the first two years of their child's life, by the time their child reaches 7 1/2 years of age, that percentage drops to less than 25 percent.[27] Approximately 75 percent of men who are not living with their children at the time of their birth never subsequently live with them.[28]

Even more importantly, there is a substantial and growing empirical literature attesting to the fact that children do best when they grow up with their two, continuously married parents. The empirical literature also is quite clear that adults — women as well as men — are happier, healthier, and wealthier than their single counterparts.[29]

Consequently, there is a growing chorus of voices within the fatherhood movement singing the praises of marriage as an indispensable part of the solution to the fatherhood problem. The National Fatherhood Initiative in particular is a strong advocate for emphasizing married fatherhood as the ideal, for while married fatherhood is by no means a certain pathway to a responsible, committed, and involved father, it is a more certain pathway than any other.

Another challenge is to prevent the fatherhood movement from overly focusing on the expansion of service delivery to fathers. While increasing support and skill-building services to fathers is certainly important, too strong a focus on this aspect of fatherhood renewal could threaten the most important goal: recapturing the fatherhood idea. If the fatherhood movement becomes just another categorical funding stream, competing with every other categorical funding stream, rather than helping to renew fatherhood as an institution, it will only serve to reduce the fatherhood renewal movement into just another self-serving interest group.

25. Frank F. Furstenberg Jr. and Christine Winquist Nord, "Parenting Apart: Patterns of Child Rearing After Marital Disruption," *Journal of Marriage and the Family*, November 1985, p. 896.

26. Furstenberg and Andrew Cherlin, *Divided Families*.

27. Robert Lerman and Theodora Ooms, *Young Unwed Fathers: Changing Roles and Emerging Policies* (Philadelphia: Temple University Press, 1993).

28. Lerman and Ooms, *Young Unwed Fathers*.

29. Steven Stack and J. Ross Eshleman, "Marital Status and Happiness: A 17-Nation Study," *Journal of Marriage and the Family*, 60 (May 1998): 527-36; see also Maggie Gallagher, *The Abolition of Marriage* (Washington, D.C.: Regnery, 1996); and Linda J. Waite, "Does Marriage Matter?" *Demography*, no. 32 (1995): 483-501.

WADE F. HORN

The End of the Beginning

The good news is that our culture is re-awakening to the idea that fathers are important to the well-being of their children. Men are increasingly likely to aspire to be loving, committed, and responsible fathers. And there does seem to be a fatherhood renewal movement emerging in America. But, at the same time, millions of children still live absent their fathers or with dads who might as well be. And many persist in a cultural illusion that marriage and involved fatherhood have little to do with each other.

The battle for fatherhood, therefore, while encouraging, is far from over. In 1942 after the allies had won the battle of North Africa Winston Churchill cautioned his countrymen, "Now this is not the end. It is not even the beginning of the end. But it is, perhaps, the end of the beginning." So it may be with fatherhood renewal in America.

Character and Ethics

THOMAS LICKONA

In the early 1980s, the Developmental Studies Center in San Ramon, California, secured foundation funding to launch an unprecedented study of character education known as the Child Development Project (CDP). Would a multifaceted character education program begun in kindergarten and sustained through sixth grade make a significant difference in the moral thinking, attitudes, and behavior of students — and would the differences still be evident in the middle school years after the program was over?[1]

The CDP program consisted of five complementary components: (1) a values-rich reading and language arts curriculum; (2) frequent use of cooperative learning; (3) developmental discipline that engaged students in solving social problems and building a caring classroom community; (4) activities that fostered a schoolwide sense of community; and (5) parent involvement strategies, including values-centered "family homework" and a school leadership team made up of parents and teachers.

The CDP program was initially implemented in three K-6 San Ramon elementary schools, with three equivalent, nonprogram schools serving as the comparison group. The second phase of the research replicated the original program in six diverse sites: three in California, one in Kentucky, one in Florida, and one in White Plains, New York. In each of these replication sites, two ele-

1. For a copy of the research report on the Child Development Project, write to : Developmental Studies Center, 2000 Embarcadero, Suite 305, Oakland, CA 94606.

mentary program schools and two comparison schools were selected. Here are the findings of this ambitious study:

Teacher implementation of the CDP program varied considerably from school to school. Greater teacher implementation was associated with a combination of supportive conditions: an atmosphere that encouraged faculty to look critically at their teaching; professional development to help teachers acquire new skills; ready access to teaching strategies and materials; positive pressure for change from colleagues and supervisors; and administrators who placed a high priority on character education.

In CDP schools where the program was well implemented, students were significantly superior to their peers in nonprogram schools in four areas:

- interpersonal attitudes and behavior such as conflict resolution skills, trust in and respect for teachers, altruistic behavior, and commitment to democratic values;
- self-related attitudes such as sense of personal efficacy and reduced loneliness in school;
- school-related attitudes and behavior such as liking for school and active engagement in class;
- reduced participation in problematic behavior such as marijuana and alcohol use.

The CDP program ended in sixth grade. Middle school follow-up studies found that some of the previously significant effects favoring program students, such as greater altruistic behavior and lower use of marijuana and alcohol, had faded to statistical nonsignificance. This weakening over time of some program effects points to the importance of continuing a character education program in order to sustain gains. However, other positive outcomes favoring program students, such as greater trust in teachers, sense of personal efficacy, and liking for school, were still evident two years later. Moreover, some new differences favoring program students emerged: higher middle school grades, higher standardized achievement, and, unexpectedly, more frequent attendance at religious services, even though nothing in the character education program had touched on religion. Here, then, was empirical evidence that a comprehensive elementary school character development program could make a measurable and enduring difference in children's character development.

The Example of Jefferson Junior High School

Shortly after the Child Development Project got underway, I began to gather other examples of schools that were making an intentional effort to foster character development. Jefferson Junior High in Washington, D.C., was one. Ninety percent of Jefferson's students come from single-parent families. "When I arrived," says principal Vera White, "parents and the community felt they were losing the children." Theft and fighting were common. Academic achievement was near the bottom in the district. Twelve to fifteen girls got pregnant each year.

Principal White met with faculty, parents, students, clergy, and other members of the community. They decided they needed a long-range plan. Year 1 would focus on setting objectives and strategies; developing students' "sense of responsibility for their own behavior" became the primary goal. Year 2 would have the theme "attitude counts." Year 3 would focus on conflict resolution training, while Year 4 would focus on community service.

Personal responsibility is now the theme of daily morning meetings in Jefferson's homerooms and in weekly grade-level assemblies. All students are expected to have assignment notebooks, to use them in every class, and to take their schoolbooks home with them each day. Strengthening Jefferson's academic curriculum has been aided by a partnership with a nearby corporation, which has helped to develop a strong, state-of-the-art program in math, science, and technology. Jefferson's character-building effort has also included three sexuality education programs, including Elayne Glover Bennett's Best Friends curriculum, all of which teach students the value and skills of abstaining from sexual activity.

The school has also sharply raised expectations for parents. "Our parents," Vera White says, "must come to school for Back to School Night and for teacher-parent conferences during the year. Every parent is also asked to volunteer 20 hours of service to the school each year."

Since implementing these changes, Jefferson has experienced a marked decline in thefts and fighting. In the city of Washington, D.C., it has been recognized for having the highest student academic achievement, the greatest academic improvement, and the highest attendance rate. It has won two U.S. Department of Education awards and has a waiting list of four hundred to five hundred students. Student pregnancies are now rare.[2]

2. See *Character Education in U.S. Schools: The New Consensus* (Washington, D.C.: The Character Education Partnership, 1996), pp. 13-14. Principal White's quoted comments come from a meeting with the CEP Board of Directors, January 1995.

The Return of Character Education

What happened at Child Development Project schools and at Jefferson Junior High is now happening all across the country. In the 1990s, character education became a national movement. That decade saw a spate of books on character and character education (such as *The Book of Virtues,*[3] *Why Johnny Can't Tell Right from Wrong,*[4] and *Building Character in Schools*[5]); the emergence of several national organizations dedicated to promoting character education (the Character Education Partnership, the Character Counts Coalition, and the Communitarian Network among them); million-dollar grants by the U.S. Department of Education to more than a score of states for character-education activity; state mandates requiring public schools to spend time on character education; national reports on how schools of education can better prepare teachers to be character educators;[6] an explosion of grassroots character initiatives by schools and communities; and a flurry of media attention to the movement. In a 1996 national survey, the National School Boards Association reported that 45 percent of responding school districts (about 10 percent returned the survey) said they had begun some sort of character education initiative and another 38 percent said they were considering doing so in the near future.[7]

Character education in the schools reflects a renewed societal concern for character. Scholarly inquiry, media attention, and everyday conversation have all focused attention on the character of our elected leaders, the character of our fellow citizens, and the character of our children. The psychiatrist Frank Pittman reminds us, "The stability of our lives depends upon our character. It is character, not passion, that keeps marriages together long enough to do their work of raising children into mature, responsible, productive citizens. In this imperfect world, it is character that enables people to survive, to endure, and to transcend their misfortunes."[8] The Greek philosopher Heraclitus captured this truth concisely: "Character is destiny."

3. William J. Bennett, *The Book of Virtues* (New York: Simon and Schuster, 1993).

4. William Kilpatrick, *Why Johnny Can't Tell Right from Wrong* (New York: Simon and Schuster, 1992).

5. Kevin Ryan and Karen Bohlin, *Building Character in Schools* (San Francisco: Jossey-Bass, 1998).

6. See, for example, *Teachers as Educators of Character: Are the Nation's Schools of Education Coming Up Short?* (1999) and the Association of Teacher Educators' report, *Character Education: The Foundation for Teacher Education* (1999), both published by the Character Education Partnership (Washington, D.C.).

7. Judith B. Saks, *Character Education in America's Classrooms: How America's School Boards Are Promoting Values and Virtues* (Alexandria, Va.: National School Boards Association, 1996).

8. Frank Pittman, "On Character," *Networking* (newsletter), 1992, p. 63.

Character education, of course, is not a new idea. Throughout history, in countries all over the world, education has had two great goals: to help students become smart and to help them become good. The American Founders argued that educating for character was essential to the success of our democratic government. Democracy, they maintained, requires a virtuous citizenry, one committed to the moral underpinnings of democracy such as respect for individual rights, voluntary compliance with the law, participation in public life, and concern for the common good.

For most of American history, character education was a central part of the school's mission. Character education declined, however, in the second half of the twentieth century, when much of society began to think of morality as private and relative and not something public schools should try to teach in an increasingly pluralistic age. The 1963 Supreme Court decision banning school prayer contributed to educators' increasing wariness of teaching moral values, as they feared being perceived as promoting religion.

The current resurgence of character education is driven by at least six factors: the breakdown of the family as a moral socializer, with the result that growing numbers of children arrive at school with little sense of right or wrong; the rise of the mass media as a negative influence on youth values; the public perception that the country is in a period of moral and spiritual decline; troubling youth trends showing high levels of juvenile violence, dishonesty, disrespect, self-centeredness, substance abuse, and sexual activity;[9] a disenchantment with nondirective values education such as values clarification emphasizing process rather than moral content; and, finally, the recovery of the idea that there are objective moral standards that are the basis of good character and a civil and just society.

The Nature of Character Education

The premise of the growing character education movement is that behaviors such as violence, dishonesty, incivility, sexual promiscuity, drug abuse, and a poor work ethic have a common core: the absence of good character. Unlike educational reforms that focus on symptoms, character education, by addressing the root problem, offers the hope of progress in all these areas. Since character is formed by many social influences, not just by schools, all those groups that

9. For documentation of these trends, see Thomas Lickona, *Educating for Character* (New York: Bantam Books, 1991); William Kilpatrick, *Why Johnny Can't Tell Right from Wrong;* and *Report on Youth Ethics* (Marina del Rey, Calif.: The Josephson Institute for Ethics, 1996).

touch the values of the young — families, schools, religious institutions, sports leagues, youth groups, businesses, government, and the media — bear a responsibility for modeling and promoting good character.

Character education has three goals: good people, good schools, and a good society. We need good character — strength of mind, heart, and will — to be fully human, to be capable of love and work, two of the hallmarks of human maturity. We need character education in order to have good schools. Schools are much more conducive to teaching and learning when they are civil, caring, and purposeful communities. Finally, character education is essential to the task of building a moral society. Societal problems such as greed, family disintegration, growing numbers of children living in poverty, and violence toward life born and preborn have deep roots and require systemic solutions. But it is not possible to build a virtuous society if virtue does not exist in the minds, hearts, and souls of individual human beings.

Character education is the deliberate effort to develop virtue. Virtues are objectively good human qualities. Chief among them are the cardinal virtues named by the ancient Greeks: prudence, or practical wisdom, which enables us to judge what we ought to do; justice, which enables us to give other persons their due; fortitude, which enables us to do what is right in the face of difficulties; and temperance, or self-mastery, which enables us to control our desires and to avoid abuse of even legitimate pleasures. Other virtues are aspects of these four; for example, perseverance, patience, and courage are all aspects of fortitude. Virtues are good for the individual in that they help us lead a fulfilling life and good for the whole human community in that they enable us to live together harmoniously and productively. Because they have intrinsic worth, virtues don't change; prudence, justice, fortitude, and temperance always have been and always will be virtues. Virtues transcend time and culture.

Every virtue, like character as a whole, has three parts: moral knowledge, moral feeling, and moral behavior. To possess the virtue of justice, for example, I must understand what justice is and what justice requires of me in human relations (moral knowledge). I must also care about justice — be emotionally committed to it, have the capacity for appropriate guilt when I behave unjustly, and be capable of moral indignation when I see others suffer unjustly (moral feeling). Finally, I must practice justice — acting fairly in my personal relations and carrying out my obligation as a citizen to help advance social justice (moral behavior). Thus, in order to develop virtuous character, we must come to know what the virtues are, appreciate their importance and want to possess them, and practice them in their day-to-day conduct. Character education thus conceived seeks to develop habits of the mind, habits of the heart, and habits of action.

In its underlying philosophy, character education reasserts the idea of objective moral truth: the notion that some things are truly right and others wrong. Objective truth — whether scientific, historical, or moral truth — is independent of the knower. That Lincoln was president during the Civil War is objectively true, even if someone doesn't know it. That adultery is wrong, torture wrong, rape wrong, racism wrong, cheating wrong, and the taking of innocent life wrong are objective moral truths — even if many people do not realize it. Objective moral truths have a claim on our conscience and behavior. We are obliged to honor them — to be honest, respectful, and responsible — whether we want to or not. Our task in developing our characters — a lifelong project — is therefore to learn what is true and right and conform our consciences and conduct to that high standard. It is a cultural cliché that we must "follow our own conscience" but there is a prior duty: to form our conscience correctly, in accord with what is truly good and right. All of this obviously runs counter to the postmodern subjectivism that denies objective truth and still dominates much, if not most, of the academy.

Character education, in short, does not mean letting students decide for themselves what's right and wrong; rather, the school must stand for virtues and promote them explicitly at every turn. It's not just talk; thinking and discussing are important, but the bottom line is behavior. Character education seeks to have students perform positive actions repeatedly, until it becomes relatively natural for them to do so and relatively unnatural for them to do the opposite.

Character education is not a separate course, though a published character education curriculum (there are now hundreds) can be a useful component. Some high schools now have a home-grown course in character development, typically for freshmen, that includes elements such as study skills, communication skills, goal-setting, and service learning. In its essence, character education is the proactive, systematic, and schoolwide effort to cultivate virtue by creating a community of virtue, one where virtuous behaviors such as respect, honesty, kindness, and diligent work are modeled, expected, studied, discussed, upheld, celebrated, and continuously practiced in classroom interactions and in every other part of the school environment.

A Comprehensive Approach to Character Education

In order to develop character in its cognitive, emotional, and behavioral dimensions, schools need a comprehensive approach. At the State University of New York at Cortland, our Center for the 4th and 5th Rs (Respect and Responsibility) defines a comprehensive approach in terms of twelve research-based strategies, nine for the classroom and three that are schoolwide.

These twelve strategies are both direct and explicit (e.g., explaining the virtues, studying them, and intentionally practicing them) and indirect and implicit (e.g., being a good example, treating students with respect and love, and developing a good moral environment that enables students to experience the virtues in their peer relationships). A comprehensive approach regards adults' moral authority and leadership as an essential part of character education, but also values students' taking responsibility for setting character goals and building their own characters. There is an effort to transmit a moral heritage of tested virtues but also to equip students to think critically about how to apply the virtues to difficult moral challenges (such as combating the destruction of the environment, or solving the problem of abortion in a way that both respects preborn life and supports women). Let me briefly define each of the twelve strategies in this comprehensive model.[10]

Classroom Strategies

In classroom practice, a comprehensive approach to character-building calls upon the individual teacher to:

1. *Act as caregiver, model, and mentor* — to treat students with love and respect, set a good example, supporting pro-social behavior, and correct hurtful actions through one-on-one guidance and whole-class discussion.
2. *Create a moral community* — to help students know each other as persons, respect and care about each other, and feel valued membership in, and responsibility to, the group.
3. *Practice moral discipline* — to use the creation and enforcement of rules as opportunities to foster moral reasoning, voluntary compliance with rules, and a generalized respect for the rights of others.
4. *Create a democratic classroom environment* — to involve students in collaborative decision-making and shared responsibility for making the classroom a good place to be and learn.
5. *Teach character through the curriculum* — to use the ethically rich content of academic subjects (such as literature, history, and science) as a vehicle for studying the virtues; and to ensure that the sex, drugs, and alcohol education programs promote self-control and the same high character standards taught elsewhere in the curriculum.
6. *Use cooperative learning* — to develop, through collaborative work, students' appreciation of others, perspective-taking, and ability to work toward common goals.

10. See Lickona, *Educating for Character,* for a fuller discussion.

7. *Develop the "conscience of craft"* — to foster students' valuing of learning, commitment to excellence, and public sense of work as affecting the lives of others.
8. *Encourage moral reflection* — to foster moral thinking and thoughtful decision-making through reading, research, essay writing, journaling, discussion, and debate.
9. *Teach conflict resolution* — to help students acquire the moral skills of solving conflicts fairly and without force.

Schoolwide Strategies

Besides making full use of the moral life of classrooms, a comprehensive approach calls upon the school *as a whole* to:

10. *Foster caring beyond the classroom* — to use positive role models to inspire altruistic behavior and provide opportunities at every grade level for service in the school and in the community.
11. *Create a positive moral culture in the school* — to develop a total moral environment (through the leadership of the principal, schoolwide discipline, a schoolwide sense of community, meaningful student government, a moral community among adults, and making time for discussing moral concerns) that supports and amplifies the virtues taught in classrooms.
12. *Recruit parents and the community as partners in character education* — to inform parents that the school considers them their child's first and most important moral teacher, to give parents specific ways they can reinforce the character expectations the school is trying to promote, and to seek the help of the wider community in promoting the core virtues.

The Role of Religion in Character Education

What is the proper role of religion in a character education effort? If a school is religious rather than secular, its religious vision can and should inform the whole character education effort. For example, in Catholic and other Christian schools that take their faith mission seriously, the goal of character education is to develop the character of Christ. That includes the moral virtues that can be taught in public schools but also spiritual virtues that public schools can't teach: prayer, sacrificial love of others, faith in God, gratitude for God's blessings, and total obedience to God's will. From a faith perspective, union with

God is the goal of life and the most important reason to lead a moral life, and, moreover, the power to live a moral life comes not just from our will but from God's grace.

Does religion have a place in public schools? Currently, at least in the United States, the character education movement is only just beginning to ask, how might religion be integrated into public school character education in a constitutionally permissible way? A number of ways have been proposed that would honor the First Amendment, respect pluralism, and support students' character development: (1) We can show students that great moral principles such as the Golden Rule and core moral virtues such as honesty, generosity, and forgiveness are not only central in the Judeo-Christian heritage, but are taught by all the major world religions; (2) we can make students aware that the American Founders considered our human rights "unalienable" because they are "endowed by our Creator," not given out by the government; (3) we can study the role (often ignored) that religion has played in providing the leadership and moral energy for our nation's social reform movements; (4) we can examine the motivation, including religious motives (commonly neglected), in the lives of exemplars of altruism or justice such as Mother Teresa and Martin Luther King Jr.; (5) we can include, where appropriate, religious perspectives in the curriculum;[11] (6) we can encourage students to bring their faith traditions, if they have one, to bear on personal moral decisions in areas such as social justice (e.g., "What is my obligation to the less fortunate?") and sexual behavior (e.g., "Should I have sex before marriage?"); (7) we can examine religious perspectives on whether there are objectively true, universally binding moral standards (religion has historically asserted that right and wrong do exist); and (8) we can challenge students to develop a vision of life that addresses ultimate questions (e.g., "What is the purpose of my life?," "What is my ultimate destiny?"). In the final analysis, if character development is not grounded in a worldview that gives life meaning and direction, the quest for character lacks a spiritual rudder.

The Community's Role

A basic belief of the character education movement is that all groups that affect the lives of the young must come together in common cause. Every social institution must be held accountable for how well it nurtures the core virtues that foster personal fulfillment and a healthy democracy.

11. See, for example, Warren Nord and Charles Haynes, *Taking Religion Seriously Across the Curriculum* (Alexandria, Va.: Association for Supervision and Curriculum Development, 1998).

For that reason, it's good news that a growing number of villages, towns, and cities across the nation are making a formal effort to become communities of character. To cite just one example: Eight years ago, the Board of Aldermen of Nashua, New Hampshire (population 80,000), passed a resolution calling upon the schools and the entire community to promote character education. That resolution led to the formation of a 25-member Character Education Council including Mayor Donald Davidson, two members of the Board of Aldermen, business representatives, members of the police and fire departments, representatives of sports leagues and service organizations, school administrators, teachers, parents, and youth. The Council began to meet monthly to plan how to promote character education.

The Character Education Council recommended that Nashua promote the following character traits, which were then adopted by the schools:

September	RESPONSIBILITY
October	RESPECT
November/December	CARING AND COMPASSION
January	PERSEVERANCE AND EFFORT
February	TRUSTWORTHINESS
March	FAIRNESS AND TOLERANCE
April	COURAGE
May/June	CITIZENSHIP

Training was conducted in the schools, with the Board of Aldermen and various government departments. Businesses agreed to display the *Word of the Month* and related quotes in their storefronts. Company newsletters and billboards also promoted the Word of the Month. The community Cable TV station launched a series of shows on character.

Mayor Davidson says his role has been mainly public relations: promoting the character initiative through talks, dedications, visits to schools, and media interviews. He comments: "Character education is a no-brainer; why wouldn't every community get involved in this? It's also opened the eyes of parents to what they have not been doing." Alderwoman Claire McGrath comments: "After implementing character education, one of our schools saw suspensions drop from 32 a year to not a single child. Theft and vandalism also went down. But the real benefits have been with the adult community. It's made people stop and take account of their own behavior."[12]

12. Kevin Conlon, "Nashua, New Hampshire's Community-Wide Character Initiative," *The Fourth and Fifth Rs* (newsletter) (Cortland, N.Y.: Center for the 4th and 5th Rs, Spring 1999), p. 6.

Conclusion

The character education movement faces many challenges: How to ensure that schools do not trivialize character education by reducing it to posters, slogans, and announcements? How to help schools envision and implement the kind of character education that has the power to transform school culture and change lives? How to keep the nation's academic standards movement from pressuring schools into a narrow focus on test scores that neglects deeper learning and character development? How to help schools reach out to stabilize and strengthen the family, a child's most powerful moral teacher and the present source of so many character problems? How to promote abstinence education as a logical and necessary part of character education, so that students learn to practice genuine respect, authentic responsibility, and self-mastery in this crucial and vulnerable area of their lives?[13]

"Character is higher than intellect," Emerson once said in a lecture at Harvard. His words echo those of an anonymous sage: "When wealth is lost, nothing is lost. When health is lost, something is lost. When character is lost, all is lost." A revitalized concern for character is one of the most important ethical developments of our time. As we face the challenges of a new millennium and a world in moral disarray, a focus on character is hope on the horizon.

13. See the chapters in this book by Elayne Bennett (pp. 357-367) and Joe McIlhaney (pp. 380-393) for accounts of efforts to help young people understand that abstinence is the only medically safe, emotionally healthy, and morally responsible choice for unmarried teens.

Marriage

DAVID POPENOE

There can be no doubt that popular culture in America and in other modern nations has become increasingly anti-marriage, and has thus helped to generate the continuous weakening of marriage as a central social institution. In television and films, popular music, and leading newspapers and magazines, marriage has been undercut in recent years by such themes as the glories of single life, the joys of nonmarital sex, the self-fulfillment that divorce can bring, and the special strengths of nonmarital families. In contrast, the theme of building and staying in a committed marital relationship for the good of children and society as well as an enriching lifelong partnership has been all but forgotten. Partly as a result, the marriage rate has dropped by more than a third since 1970 and the out-of-wedlock birth ratio remains fixed at about one third of all births. Long-term marriages have become especially decimated, with a divorce rate holding at close to 50 percent compared to about 20 percent in the 1950s.

At the same time, because cultural values are at issue there is some hope for reversing the decline of marriage. Unlike most technological changes, cultural changes are more open to modification by concerted social action. We have seen dramatic changes in the twentieth century in the areas of race, women's roles, gay rights, and even peace and environmental issues. Indeed, the value changes in these areas over a short period of historical time have been quite remarkable. Although many social and economic trends in place made some of these changes inevitable in the long run, surely the changes were encouraged and advanced by strong, well-organized social movements. This essay explores the possibilities for a movement designed to reverse the decline of marriage.

The Marriage Problem

Throughout most of human history, sex, reproduction, and marriage have been culturally interlocked. Yet today — especially since the 1960s — the separation of these three activities has become marked. One no longer needs to marry to have children, much less to have sex. Marriages are now based mainly on love alone, and because love is considered a personal matter the larger institutions and forces that used to help hold marriages together — religion, economics, and the law — have become less involved. Moreover, love is a feeling, and feelings can change over time. As a consequence, the divorce rate has risen steeply and more people realistically question the possibility of committing to one person for a lifetime, thus contributing to the high rate of nonmarital births.

The separation of sex, reproduction, and marriage, in turn, has been strongly shaped by the larger forces of modernity. These forces and trends include the growing affluence and commercialization of life together with the continuing movement toward self-aggrandizing individualism; high personal and social mobility; secularization, cultural relativism, and the withering of moral standards; and the loss of child-centeredness stemming from radically reduced fertility and the mesmerizing attractions of the new workplace. All of these have tended to corrode personal and family relationships and pull people in directions from which neither they nor the larger society ultimately will benefit.

A Marriage Movement?

To counteract some of the anti-social consequences of these forces and trends of modernity, specifically to bring sex and children back into the sanctuary of long-term marriage, would indeed require a social and cultural movement of massive proportions. Such a movement would be possible if there were a strong latent interest in society for the revitalization of marriage. Does such an interest exist at the present time?

There is some evidence that the nation might be ready for a return to marriage. According to public opinion polls, there has been a growing awareness among Americans in the past decade that something has gone wrong with the family. As compared to their parents at the same age, today's generation of young people puts family life slightly higher on its agenda for the future, perhaps because of having had less of it during the growing-up years. Many people have observed that the topic of marriage recently has become somewhat more tolerated in public and professional debate.

Such opinion shifts may already have influenced a change in behavior. For example, the out-of-wedlock birthrate has leveled off and the divorce rate has dropped a little. Teen pregnancies are down. For several years in a row the percentage of children living in single-parent families has not increased.

Building on these few rays of hope, a number of recently organized efforts have been attempting to encourage and advance the cause of marriage. An Internet-based network called the Coalition for Marriage, Family, and Couples Education, founded by a former official of the American Association for Marriage and Family Therapy, focuses on helping people stay in relationships through skills training; it has had highly successful national conferences with mostly pro-marriage themes. The Marriage Savers group, founded by a religion and ethics newspaper columnist and headquartered in Maryland, has had an impact in many communities and a number of states, focusing on getting churches to better educate people for marriage. One branch of the fatherhood movement, the National Fatherhood Initiative, has made the revitalization of marriage a central focus. An academic group called The Religion, Culture, and Family Project, based at the Divinity School of the University of Chicago, is working to make marriage revitalization a concern of the mainline Protestant churches. And groups on the so-called religious right such as Focus on the Family, the Family Research Council, and a loose alliance of family policy organizations in many states, have made marriage central in their activities.

The National Marriage Project was established in 1997 at Rutgers University in New Jersey, and was designed to provide research and education to the American public about what has been happening to marriage, why this is a problem, and the ways in which the institution might be revitalized. Research and public education on marriage are also being conducted at such nonacademic, conservative-leaning groups as The Heritage Foundation, based in Washington, D.C., and The Manhattan Institute and The Institute for American Values with its Council on Families, based in New York City.

In several states, notably Oklahoma, Arkansas, Utah, and Florida, governors have embarked on broad-based campaigns to make marriage an issue in an effort to cut the nonmarital birth and divorce rates. Two states, Louisiana and Arizona, have instituted "covenant marriage" laws, designed for couples who want to express an extra level of commitment to their marriage. Many other states are considering various marriage-improvement proposals as well as legal changes.

Do these varied activities add up to a marriage movement? Social and cultural movements typically proceed through several discrete stages. First is a general but unarticulated discontent with a social condition. This is followed by a second stage consisting of efforts to articulate the discontent and bring people together who share a common awareness that something needs to be done. The third stage involves the emergence of formal organizations at the national level with leaders, policies, and programs, all directed to social and cultural change. In the fourth and final stage the movement becomes institutionalized in the culture and, where relevant, in the law. To the degree that one exists, the marriage movement in America today could be said to rest mostly at stage two, articulating the discontent and bringing like-minded professionals together. No national, broad-based, formal organizations focused principally on marriage yet exist (stage three), and obviously the movement is a long way from becoming institutionalized (stage four).

The marriage-movement activities just noted are important and they provide much hope, but unfortunately their effect on our national life so far has been limited. There is surely across the country a general feeling of social discontent about the family, providing the interest necessary for a social movement. But this discontent has not yet been well articulated and the possible remedies remain cloudy. In particular, there has not yet emerged any national agreement that the strengthening of marriage — as distinct, for example, from more day care centers, better divorces, more help for single-parent families, or pursuing dead-beat dads — is what is needed to solve the problems of the family.

In the political arena, neither major political party and no major political figure at the national level has taken up the issue of marriage in more than episodic fashion. Indeed, most politicians studiously seem to be avoiding it, a reason being perhaps that too many constituents — including the divorced, single parents, gays and lesbians, and radical feminists, not to mention young people who have become wary of what they interpret as "moralizing" — are allied against any serious discussion of marriage. Also, there is a belief that marriage trends are something about which governments can — and perhaps even should — do little. In the cultural sphere, marriage revitalization has not yet been taken up seriously by the academic community, by any of the major national periodicals, or by the mainline religious communities. Most importantly, there is no sign of any grassroots movement for marriage, especially on the part of those who count — the young adults.

Thus, and sadly in the face of a marriage rate that continues to drop rapidly, it is fair to say that the nation as a whole remains mostly uninterested in this issue. The marriage movement today seems not nearly as advanced as, say, the environmental movement, with which it shares some similarities. Even at the basic level of public education — articulating the general social discontent about family trends in a way that makes clear that revitalization of marriage is essential — much remains to be accomplished.

Revitalizing Marriage

In thinking about the future direction of a marriage movement, one's thoughts turn immediately to today's popular culture and its effects on marriage. Can anything be done to generate a more marriage-friendly Hollywood? Unfortunately, the answer is probably not very much.

Through extensive organization and commercialization, popular culture has become highly attuned to meeting the desires of its audience. If there were no market for sex and violence, a popular culture that features these themes would not exist. But of course there is an enormous market for such themes, especially among young adults. In the affluent age of "do everything, try everything," the normal desires and fascination with sex and violence are prime subjects for attention. And, with much of popular culture now driven by advertising, advertisers regard still-impressionable young adults as primary targets.

Moreover, young adulthood today lasts an unusually long time. If measured from puberty to marriage, in fact, the time period is between fifteen and twenty years. By every indicator we have, this period will only lengthen in the coming decades.

In assessing what can be done about popular culture it is also important to consider the place of children in modern life. In previous generations most households contained children, and the adults in such households surely must have had a strong child-consciousness that entered into their behavior and views of life. Today, less than a third of households contain children — down from more than three quarters in the mid-1800s — and one gets the strong impression that adult needs, desires, and fantasies are often molded quite apart from what is best for children. According to every indicator we have, even fewer households in the future will contain children.

In modern times, then, a situation has developed in which unattached and childless young adults, catered to by an ever more powerful and influential popular culture, have come to dominate much of our national life. This is the same group that, if marriage is to be revived, must somehow change its behavior and outlook. The members of this group must take a longer view of life, realize that committed marital relationships would be highly beneficial for themselves, their children, and their society, and begin to think and act in ways that would be more rather than less likely to lead to such relationships. This would mean such things as avoiding promiscuous sex; educating themselves for wiser mate-selection, marriage and parenthood; and planning and organizing their careers much more around family life.

It is possible that some short-run modifications could be made in popular culture to make it more marriage-friendly. For example, the worst of violence and perverted sex might be withdrawn or at least restricted to later time slots when young children would be less likely to be watching. But popular culture will change only when popular demand changes. To have real success, a movement to reverse the decline of marriage would probably have to bypass popular culture and focus directly on young adults and their parents.

The most likely scenario for a marriage movement is one where popular culture remains about the same but becomes increasingly less influential over the minds of the young because other forces such as family and religion become more influential. At least a strong minority of young people could over time consciously come to reject the popular culture around them, as has already happened to some extent in strongly religious communities and in strong families that seek to protect their children from what they consider to be pernicious cultural elements. From this perspective, a marriage movement would have to start as a countercultural movement among the young, and then spread to ever-larger groups.

How could a countercultural marriage movement among the young be actively supported and encouraged? Such a movement could stem from a religious base, as it already has in the world of evangelicals. But to have society-wide success the movement would need strong secular as well as religious roots. The four main secular possibilities are governments, schools, parents, and voluntary associations.

Our national government has limited influence over family issues because, unlike in most European nations, American family law and most family concerns reside at the state level. But moral and political presidential leadership could be important, along with White House conferences, as could marriage-friendly policies enacted by Congress. In a few Western and Sun Belt states, as noted above, state-level political leadership has recently developed pro-marriage agendas. Indeed, these are currently the most promising developments in the budding marriage movement. Yet it is by no means clear how many other states will follow their lead; possibly not very many.

Our society places a high premium on education as the solution of many of its problems. Many of the state-level efforts, for example, are directed through the educational system, where marriage education courses could prove to be successful in getting students to think more about, and plan for, eventual marriage. Yet the public schools are probably not a reliable source for any kind of countercultural movement. Teachers are typically tied to the dominant liberal culture, and in any event they do not usually find themselves in situations where they can promote controversial topics.

The ultimate success of a marriage movement probably depends on enlisting the support of large numbers of parents. Parents have a very large stake in positive outcomes for such a movement. They want their own children to have stable relationships in adulthood and they desire grandchildren. Even when their own marriages were not successful or lasting, they usually hope their grandchildren will be raised within long-term marriages. Although adolescence and young adulthood are intrinsically times when young people break away from their families of origin and seek to move on, the young during these periods are probably more influenced by their parents than by anyone else. For a return to a marriage-based culture, parents would need to spend more time with their children stressing the benefits of married life and helping them to prepare for marriage, including the wise selection of a mate. In other words, parents would need to do what many of them used to do in times past.

The problem is that parents have been notoriously difficult to combine into a common "interest group." Attempts to organize parents for political and social purposes the way the elderly, for example, have been organized have so far largely been failures. Still, the possibility remains open, and this is where voluntary associations fit in. Voluntary associations that deal with parents as well as youth, ranging from local Scout troops to professional organizations, must be encouraged to make the revitalization of marriage a major part of their activities.

For those parents and organization leaders who are reluctant to support marriage strongly, these key points should be remembered:

- To be healthy and happy we all need warm, intimate relationships with others. People without such relationships are at a distinct disadvantage in life. Throughout most of history this need for intimate relationships has been met through living not only in families but also in larger, close-knit groupings. In modern life, with the growth of both individualism and affluence, such larger groupings are either weak or they no longer exist. The one residual group from the past that still does still exist is the nuclear family based on the long-term union of a man and a woman. Indeed, because the larger groupings have tended to fade away, the marriage-based nuclear family is more important than ever for human well-being. People in strong marriages and families gain substantial health and emotional as well as economic benefits.
- The alternative to the modern nuclear family is the voluntary friendship group. But we should not expect friendship groups to have the same lasting power as married nuclear families because the latter are more strongly rooted in human biology. The human species has always been a "pair-bonding" species in which man and woman mated and together

raised their children, and our inherited biological predispositions for this presumably have not changed.

- What has changed is the nature of marriage, which at one time was a functional link in the struggle for survival but consists today of an emotional tie in the struggle for happiness. This emotional tie is often fragile and problematic, not only because our standards of happiness have gone up but because marriage now has to carry the emotional load once carried by a wide complex of intimate family and community groupings. This suggests two requirements for the success of modern marriage: adequate premarital preparation, especially training in relationship skills, and a level of personal commitment to the partner, and to the institution, going well beyond that of ordinary friendships.
- By all the evidence at our disposal, the married, two-parent nuclear family is much better for raising children than any alternative. Compared to children from intact families, children from single-parent and stepfamilies run two to three times the risk of having serious, long-term problems in life. If marriage continues to decline, children will pay a heavy psychological price.

Based on this line of thinking, here is the general message for parents to give to their children: *A good marriage today is more difficult to achieve than ever, but it is also more important because there are no longer many real alternatives either for personal fulfillment or for child well-being. This means that you should be preparing for and working at marriage with at least the same amount of focus and attention that you currently give to your career.*

Conclusion

In recent decades modern societies have developed an increasingly laissez-faire attitude toward marriage. Unwed pregnancies have been almost completely destigmatized, divorce has become fully accepted, and nonmarital cohabitation and alternative family forms are viewed with little concern and even approbation. In order to turn these marriage-related trends around and revitalize the institution of marriage we need to find ways to make society more aware of the profound benefits of married living. These benefits — for personal happiness, child development, and the overall success of our society — have been seriously overlooked in recent years.

Compared to other recent and successful social movements, the movement for marriage is still in the early stages. To move forward, it will have to develop a strong countercultural base of operations in the secular society. A massive public education campaign is required to shift public opinion, especially that of young people and their parents, more in favor of actively revitalizing marriage. Whether such a movement can ultimately be successful in changing the culture, of course, remains an open question.

Faith-based Charities

AMY L. SHERMAN

The considerable applause faith-based charities have received the last few years from people across the political spectrum is legitimate, welcome, and overdue. After all, these groups quietly, for years, have been transforming broken lives and renewing distressed neighborhoods among people and places many had given up as lost. Little quantitative analysis has been performed (the existing evidence suggests religious groups are more successful and cost-effective than their secular counterparts), but the anecdotal reports of these groups' efficacy are considerable. This, combined with widespread acknowledgment that the welfare state had failed, aided the passage of the "Charitable Choice" section of the 1996 welfare reform law. In the spirit of devolution (shifting increasing responsibility for public welfare from the federal government to state and local levels), Charitable Choice encourages government entities to partner with local faith-based organizations (FBOs) and churches in the fight against poverty. Since 1996, unlikely voices in politics and the media have highlighted the faith community's social work, relating the stories of crack addicts healed, gang members and ex-cons turned into model citizens, formerly welfare-reliant women achieving self-sufficiency through work, neighborhoods cleaned up from decay and violence, and teens dissuaded from sexual promiscuity.

Growth in Faith-based Social Service

While FBOs represent individual "points of light" in society, their scope is by no means trivial. A third of all day care programs in the United States are housed in religious buildings.[1] A 1991 national survey of congregations found that 92 percent reported operating at least one human service or welfare program; these congregations also spent $4.4 billion annually for human services and $4 billion annually on health and hospitals.[2] Based on findings from a 1997 study of the outreach efforts of congregations in six cities, researcher Ram Cnaan estimates that nationally congregations contribute some $36 billion annually to social services.[3] In addition to church-based efforts, religious nonprofits are highly active. A 1985 study of faith-based nonprofits by the Council on Foundations estimated that such agencies spend between $7.5 and $8.5 billion annually in grants, loans, and services to individuals and communities in need.

Recent enthusiasm over the contributions made by FBOs and churches has fueled considerable discussion of how to expand even further the scope, scale, and effectiveness of faith-based action. Groups within the faith community itself are vigorously pursuing these goals. Since 1996, the Call to Renewal, the Interfaith Community Ministry Network, and World Vision–USA have all hosted national training conferences; the Center for Public Justice (in Maryland), Project One (in Kentucky), Common Heart (in Washington), Twin Cities Urban Reconciliation Network (in Minnesota), the Center for Renewal (in Texas), and a variety of denominational organizations have sponsored similar, regional events. Attendance at these conventions has often exceeded the organizers' projections, and participation in the most important annual gathering on this topic — the autumn conference of the Christian Community Development Association (CCDA) — has risen from a few hundred to over three thousand in just a few years.

The faith community is also producing a variety of practical, educational materials on effective ministry among the poor. The conservative Family Research Council, for example, published *The Welfare of My Neighbor: Living Out Christ's Love for the Poor,* accompanied by a detailed "how-to" workbook, while a more liberal group, Evangelicals for Social Action, has launched "Network

1. Ram A. Cnaan, *The Newer Deal: Social Work and Religion in Partnership* (New York: Columbia University Press, 1999), p. 176.

2. Cnann, *The Newer Deal,* p. 180.

3. Cnann, *The Newer Deal,* p. 181. It should be noted that Professor Mark Chaves, director of the National Congregations Survey of 1998, believes this estimate is too high. See Chaves, "Congregations' Social Service Activities" (The Urban Institute, Center on Nonprofits and Philanthropy Policy Brief #6, Dec. 1999).

9:35," an initiative to get training "resource kits" quickly and cheaply into the hands of pastors and church leaders.

Government social service departments have also engaged in a flurry of activity to empower the faith community to serve families affected by welfare reform. Virginia, New Jersey, and Texas have all sponsored statewide education and training conventions while many more states (Alabama, California, Michigan, North Carolina, Wisconsin) have held regional or city-wide gatherings. Illinois has launched a statewide effort called "Partners in Hope" to encourage cooperation between local Departments of Social Services, churches, and FBOs. Indiana is pursuing a similar approach through its new "Faithworks" organization. North Carolina and Texas have assigned regional Department of Human Services staff members to serve as "faith community liaisons." In 1999, Texas also granted approximately $7.5 million in new "local projects innovations grants" aimed at supporting the work of small community-based and faith-based organizations fighting poverty. A study by the Center for Public Justice, based on research in nine states, identified eighty-four examples of new (post–welfare-reform) financial collaboration between government and FBOs, with contracts ranging from $5,000 to over $350,000.[4]

All this talk about and training in faith-based action is resulting in new programs and organizations. Through just four new initiatives in church-based welfare-to-work mentoring — Mississippi's Faith and Families, Michigan's "Project Zero," South Carolina's "Putting Families First," and Texas's Family Pathfinders — an estimated 1,400 congregations are engaged in new, face-to-face friendships with needy families. They join another 1,100 congregations doing similar work through smaller programs in seventeen other states. The Jobs Partnership, a model of three-way collaboration among churches, businesses, and government to serve welfare-reliant and working poor families, was launched in 1996 in Raleigh, North Carolina. Already it has been (or is now being) replicated in twenty-two additional cities, involving hundreds of churches and putting hundreds of unemployed people into new jobs. Today, approximately 20 percent of the 3,600 member organizations of the National Congress for Community Economic Development label themselves "faith-based." Membership in the CCDA has grown from 37 to over 300 groups in just ten years. The Interfaith Community Ministry Network, established in 1995, represents approximately 1,200 umbrella groups of churches and religious nonprofits, representing 24,000 congregations and hundreds of individual FBOs. In short, the faith-based charities movement is blossoming.

4. Amy L. Sherman, *The Growing Impact of Charitable Choice* (Annapolis, Md.: Center for Public Justice, 2000).

Wider Ripples

The growth of faith-based social action is surely good news for the individual poor people served by religious charities. And it is good news for government agencies that know they need help from civic organizations to fulfill their new, ambitious mandate of moving families from dependency to self-sufficiency through stable employment. But the beneficial ripple effects of faith-based charities go wider and deeper. FBOs' successes in lifting people, one by one, out of poverty are readily visible and valuable. The contributions FBOs make toward cultural renewal are less obvious, but at least as important in the long run. At least four such contributions can be identified, and will be summarized here. (Readers should note that I limit my discussion primarily to Christian FBOs, though many of the same points can be made about Jewish and Muslim FBOs.)

It is also important to note that not *all* FBOs make these contributions to cultural renewal. FBOs that do are characterized by certain common features: a commitment to relational, holistic ministry; an ecclesiology that exalts the local church; a "theology of place"; and a philosophy of ministry that emphasizes mutual transformation of giver and receiver. Even some FBOs marked by these features make the kinds of contributions discussed below *unselfconsciously*, rather than as part of a deliberate strategy. Thus, FBOs could do their work of cultural renewal even more vigorously and effectively if they became more intentional in assessing their ministries according to their long-term cultural influence (rather than evaluating themselves exclusively in terms of their "service delivery"). It is hoped that this listing of four specific contributions to cultural renewal being made by certain FBOs will help all members of the faith-based charities movement recognize the "unintended good" they may sometimes perform. With a better understanding of this, leaders of FBOs can think more deliberately and strategically about how their programs can be shaped so as to offer the most powerful, long-term, cultural "seasonings" to produce social reformation. So what are these contributions?

1. FBOs Defend a Humane View of Human Nature

FBOs animated by historic Judeo-Christian values can be understood as "Christian humanists" — at least as Protestant scholar and cultural analyst Ken Myers has defined the term. Myers asserts that in our present "post-Christian" age, the task of the Christian humanist is to assert that "being human means something rather than nothing, and something rather than anything. *Christian humanism involves a deliberate effort to understand and live out the fullest consequences of the meaning of our divinely-given humanity, and the rejection of cul-*

tural forms that fail to do justice to who we are as embodied image-bearers of our Creator."[5] There are indeed contemporary cultural forms that "fail to do justice" to who humans really are. As sociologist Craig Gay has observed, "Modern worldliness is every bit as hard on the belief in humanity as it is on the belief in God. . . . Indeed, the importance in establishing the connection between the secularization of modern life and culture, and the impersonality of modern social and cultural life cannot be overemphasized today."[6] The "impersonality" of modern cultural life is expressed in multiple ways, such as the (technologically driven) denial of a "fixed essence" to human nature,[7] the reduction of "person" to "consumer," and the nihilistic belief in the ultimate meaninglessness of existence.

FBOs deeply grounded in the Hebrew and Christian scriptures counter these degradations of the human person in several ways. First, they teach that individuals are immensely precious, made in the image of God. They assert that human beings possess *inherent* dignity. These FBOs see the *image Deo* as the basic foundation of a healthy self-image. (FBOs that buy into pop psychology, however — precariously basing "self-esteem" on how people subjectively feel about themselves — do not make this contribution.)

FBOs also undergird a humane definition of human nature when they exalt the high calling of life — to delight in God and find ultimate joy and meaning through worshipping and serving him. This teaching intensifies people's sense of purpose, as against the culture's nihilism that urges only present-day consumption and exclusively self-oriented "personal fulfillment."

Highly dysfunctional people, such as drug addicts, are particularly susceptible to anti-human assertions that persons have no real contribution to make, no meaningful purpose to pursue. These people are self-aware of their extreme limits; they live with the nagging torment that "I'm worthless and can't do 'nuthin for nobody." But effective FBOs working with drug users combat this aggressively. They insist that addicts even a short way down the road to recovery take responsibility for assisting others worse off than themselves. This allows them to see themselves as contributors, as givers — and stimulates a beneficial "other-regardingness." Juan Rivera, an ex-heroine addict who now works for the faith-based Victory Fellowship, explains the phenomenon in these words:

5. "Christian Humanism in a Post-Christian Age," four lectures by Kenneth A. Myers (Charlottesville, Va.: Mars Hill Audio, 1999).

6. Craig M. Gay, *The Way of the (Modern) World; or, Why It's Tempting to Live As If God Doesn't Exist* (Grand Rapids: Eerdmans, 1998), p. 15.

7. Myers, "Christian Humanism." Cf. also Sherry Turkle, *Life on the Screen: Identity in the Age of the Internet* (New York: Simon and Schuster, 1995).

> When these guys were addicts, they saw everything and everyone — even their wives and children — only in terms of how they could feed their addictions. Part of their recovery involves a commitment to others who are trying to end their addictions. They keep a vigil of prayer and caregiving over the cots of newcomers who are breaking their hard-core addictions. In that process . . . a part of their heart opens and they have, for the first time in years, a sensitivity to the condition of another person.[8]

Relatedly, culturally-influential FBOs offer people both hope and challenge: hope that they can change and challenge that they must accept personal responsibility for their lives. This contrasts with the "victim mentality" prevalent in our culture which, in the end, is both hopeless and enervating. Hopeless because if others are to blame for my circumstances, I am dependent on them to change the conditions of my oppression. Enervating because there is no incentive for me to work to change myself and my circumstances (since a better life is contingent on others' actions). Rivera is eloquent on this point too:

> The problem is not in the economy, or housing, or racism. Those are only byproducts and symptoms of a greater problem that exists, *and that problem is in you.* Now, once that problem has been taken care of, then you can be successful in anything.[9]

FBOs assert that even those society considers irredeemable can be transformed by the power of God into decent, contributing citizens. I call this the "oaks of righteousness" view, from an inspiring portion of the Hebrew scriptures (Isaiah 61). In this passage, the prophet Isaiah describes the work that God will do in reclaiming and healing broken people. He then announces that these very people — once burdened with sin, oppression, and despair — will be "oaks of righteousness" who will rebuild ruined cities. The disheveled homeless drunk, the crack-addicted prostitute who beats her kids, the hardened, fourteen-year-old gun-slinging "super predator," the convict doing time for his third drug bust — all may appear initially as anything but "oaks of righteousness" (or even seedlings!). But workers in faith-based charities I've known sincerely believe that "with God all things are possible" and that his transforming power is limitless.

Consider the case of Luis Osoy, a notorious Guatemalan gang member and drug dealer who became a "street minister" through the love shown to him

8. Quoted in Robert L. Woodson Sr., *The Triumphs of Joseph: How Today's Community Healers Are Reviving Our Streets and Neighborhoods* (New York: The Free Press, 1998), p. 87.

9. Woodson, *Triumphs of Joseph*, p. 86.

by Jeff Kanner and other volunteers from Neighborhood Ministries, an urban outreach to poor Hispanics in Phoenix. "I used to hate Kanner," Osoy admits now. "He was always inviting me over to eat; always trying to be nice, and I got tired of his invitations." Eventually, though, Kanner's persistent friendliness in the face of Osoy's hostility piqued Osoy's curiosity. "I kept thinking, 'Why is that guy like that? Why is he different? What is different about these church people?' And I began to cry."

Though he was beginning to want to change, Osoy was doubtful he could break away from his drug-dealing partners. "You can't just say, 'Okay, I'm not going to sell drugs any more — Bye,'" Osoy explains. "You do that and, wow, something terrible is going to happen to you. I'm talking about death. So I thought, well, selling drugs is going to be the end of my life."

But one night after police captured all the members of Osoy's drug-selling clan and put them in jail, Osoy saw a way out. He began spending more time with Kanner and others from Neighborhood Ministries who offered their friendship. "They talked a lot about God's love," Osoy recalls, "but, to a gangster, 'love' is a gross word." Eventually, though, Osoy was "won over" and committed his life to serving God. "Now I'm a church volunteer with the younger boys," Osoy professes proudly. "I try to give the kids the advice I didn't have growing up. Also, I like to hang out with gangsters — not as a gangster any more — but to get them to see the reality beyond gangster life." Osoy is enrolled in college, is a budding artist, and has future plans to be involved in a counseling ministry.

2. FBOs Keep Congregations Accountable

In addition to defending humane understandings of human nature in the face of our culture's attacks on the human personality, some FBOs also contribute to cultural renewal by the way they influence religious congregations. Since many faith-based charities are directly or indirectly linked with congregations (or have many volunteers from churches), they influence not only the needy people they serve but the "helpers" as well. Sometimes simply by their existence, and other times by their direct exhortations, FBOs challenge congregations to remain true to their best convictions about the Church's role in society. Put differently, FBOs with a high view of the Church remind congregations of their essential role in cultural renewal and then help them carry out that task.

But a caveat is needed here. In the midst of increasingly loud conversations about the public utility of religious congregations (i.e., what can they *do* to serve society, such as offering their facilities as daycare centers), it is important to remember that churches also make a crucial contribution to the public welfare simply by *being* the Church. Against the culture's materialism, the Church inculcates in its members a transcendent perspective, arguing that there is more to being human than merely consuming. Congregations can often succeed in inculcating in their members, through worship and religious education, a basic decency — honesty, thrift, responsibility, accountability, respect, tolerance — without which a democratic-capitalist society cannot long flourish. Thoughtful FBOs understand the primacy of these "functions" of the Church, and thus do not ask congregations to abandon those tasks in favor of community activism.

Nonetheless, while reminding congregations of their "first order of business," culturally influential FBOs also exhort churches to avoid becoming exclusively inward-oriented. They remind churches to be "salt" in the world — penetrating the culture.

One example of this is that certain FBOs are providing well-off congregations with tangible opportunities to truly engage the culture by overcoming the increasing sense of separation between the rich and poor in American society (where the poor remain in isolated inner-city neighborhoods while the rich retreat to gated communities in the suburbs). Through their relational ministries that link churchgoers to people distanced from themselves (by geography, race, or social status), effective FBOs stimulate the reinvigoration of civic connectedness that must necessarily accompany a viable shift of welfare responsibilities from the state to society. Through the Mississippi Faith and Families initiative, for example, many white, middle-class, suburban church volunteers are befriending low-income, African-American women from the inner city. And these new relationships build bridges between rich and poor. Mississippi Department of Human Services staffer Kim Turberville illustrates this point through a story about one friendship between a church member and a former welfare recipient.

"Tamia" (not her real name) was working on her GED and living with an abusive boyfriend when she volunteered to be mentored through the Faith and Families program. Tamia had no family support and was an emotional wreck. She was matched with a church and linked with "Ellen," a retired schoolteacher. "Ellen talked with Tamia and helped her work through many of her emotional problems; she was like a caring aunt," Turberville relates. As the friendship grew, Tamia severed the abusive relationship, sailed through the GED program, and, with some help from Ellen, learned about various financial aid programs and enrolled in community college. Meanwhile, Ellen was introduced to the "other side" of her hometown of Jackson, Mississippi.

When one of Tamia's aged neighbors needed eyeglasses, Ellen called Turberville to learn whether there was a community program that might help. There was. "So the church became interested in that program — which they saw help someone they knew — and then church members started supporting it with their money and their volunteer time," Turberville relates. What started out as a single friendship became a bridge between Ellen's church and Tamia's neighborhood. This is the key, Turberville argues, for changing the prevailing "it's *their* problem, not *my* problem" attitude toward the poor. Since the elderly neighbor's problem affected Tamia, it touched Ellen's life too — and by extension, the lives of Ellen's co-congregants.

3. FBOs Overcome Oppositional Culture and Create Alternative Communities

A related way some FBOs contribute to cultural renewal is by providing "alternative communities" in distressed, highly dysfunctional neighborhoods. The urban anthropologist Elijah Anderson, and various other social scientists, have noted the presence in many inner-city communities of a highly destructive "oppositional" or "street" culture.[10] It is hedonistic and nihilistic, quick to use violence (without remorse), and scornful of "decent" cultural values (hard work, thrift, self-improvement, sexual responsibility).

The ghetto's oppositional culture is further fortified by what sociologist William Julius Wilson calls "concentration effects":

> The social transformation of the inner city has resulted in a disproportionate concentration of the most disadvantaged segments of the urban black population, creating a social milieu significantly different than the environment that existed in these communities several decades ago.[11]

That is, urban neighborhoods that formerly included families from varying economic classes are now home only to the poorest and most disadvantaged. This creates a "radical isolation" that is expressed in multiple ways. Socioeconomically, these are communities without jobs, banks, libraries, theaters, or restaurants. With disproportionate numbers of addicts, school dropouts, pregnant teens, gang members, and the chronically unemployed, and with an extremely high concentration of poverty-stricken, dysfunctional, single-parent families, concepts like marriage, work, and fatherhood lose plausibility. As Richard John Neuhaus has lamented, in the inner cities "millions of children do not know, and will never know, what it means to have a father. More poignantly, they do not know what a father is. They do not know anyone who has a father

10. Elijah Anderson, "The Code of the Streets," *Atlantic Monthly,* May 1994.

11. William Julius Wilson, *The Truly Disadvantaged: The Inner City, the Underclass, and Public Policy* (Chicago: University of Chicago Press, 1987), p. 58.

or is a father."[12] In such an environment, street culture reigns and those individuals trying hard to a live a "decent" life feel besieged. Into these settings, FBOs introduce alternative communities.

Sometimes this takes the form of sponsoring youth clubs with strong identity rituals and intense meeting schedules. These clubs attempt to replace the destructive gangs lonely, loveless kids are otherwise drawn to.

Other times it involves the creation of networks that legitimate those who strive. A notorious "crayfish syndrome" can plague distressed communities. Folk wisdom has it that if you put a bunch of crayfish in a bucket and one starts to climb out, the others will pull him down. A similar phenomenon sometimes confronts impoverished individuals who seek to improve themselves. For example, when Virginia public housing resident and welfare recipient Clarissa Crews set out to get her GED in the early 1990s, her neighbors harassed her. "Who do you think you are? You think you're better than us?" they asked. Sheila Ford, staff member at Minneapolis's "Hopemakers Jobs Partnership," has witnessed the same thing among women involved in their job training program. Ford reports that the people closest to the woman — family, boyfriend, children, neighbors — will not necessarily cheer her decision to get her degree or enroll in an internship. "In some cases, we're fighting the 'significant other' or spouse or kids," Ford laments. "They're not comfortable with the changes. I've seen the boyfriend get livid that the woman is going back to work or preparing her resume or going out on an interview," she reports. "We have to help the women work through that." FBOs aware of this crayfish syndrome intentionally enfold strivers in a supportive fellowship where they can encourage one another and receive affirmation for their efforts. This may take the form of job clubs, regular alumni gatherings for graduates of training programs, or monthly community dinners for individuals engaged in the FBOs' various programs.

Still other times alternative communities are built by an intentional "re-neighboring" of distressed communities. One of the most impressive expressions of this approach is the East Lake Community Foundation's work in Atlanta.

In the 1960s, the East Lake Meadows Federal Housing Project — some 650 small, low-rise apartments — was crammed onto fifty-five acres of land five miles east of downtown Atlanta and right next to the East Lake Golf Club, home of famous amateur golfer Bobby Jones. Within the next two decades, East Lake was transformed into "Little Vietnam" — a shooting gallery filled with crack cocaine, long-term welfare dependency, and hopelessness — and the golf course died. As resident Eva Davis once put it, "There's no peace of mind here.

12. Richard John Neuhaus, *America Against Itself: Moral Vision and the Public Order* (Notre Dame: University of Notre Dame Press, 1992), p. 83.

There's no safety. There's no recreation — you're afraid for your children to go out and play. And this environment is all they see, all they know. This is what they're growing up into."[13]

All that's changed now. The East Lake Community Foundation, in an ambitious partnership with major corporations and the federal department of Housing and Urban Development, has demolished the housing project and begun building "The Villages of East Lake" — a community of over 540 quality mixed-income townhomes and garden apartments (50 percent are market-rate rent, 50 percent are subsidized public housing). Bobby Jones's golf course has been completely renovated; crime has decreased 58 percent; over four hundred teens from the neighborhood have been employed at the golf course, many earning college scholarships; East Lake has enjoyed the highest home resale price appreciation in the entire seventeen county metro Atlanta area; a new charter school and a state-of-the-art YMCA are under construction; the East Lake Golf Academy is ministering to over 115 kids after school through tutoring, mentoring, and sports programs; and Christian "community chaplains" have settled in "The Villages" to serve as bridge builders between the low-income and middle-class residents.

This re-neighboring model is pursued by many members of the CCDA. Relocation of stable, middle-class families into distressed communities provides comradeship for the besieged, "decent" families already there and places additional positive role models before young people.

The Reverend Carey Casey, co-pastor of Lawndale Community Church in south Chicago, remembers speaking with some local kids after he and his wife moved in to the area. "We came out of the house and were talking to some little children," Casey recalls. "They asked my wife, 'What's this ring on your finger?' And my wife said, 'That's my wedding ring. I'm married to Pastor Casey.' And they said, 'You're *married?* He's your husband?' It's as though we'd told them we'd come from the moon." Ann Gordon, wife of the church's founder, Wayne "Coach" Gordon, tells similar stories. "One woman who is about our age . . . who grew up in the neighborhood came to our house one night at dinnertime. When she knocked on the door, we were all sitting around the dinner table eating, and she said, 'Do you do this every night?' It was such a weird thing to her. It seemed like a big event, whereas to us it was just part of family life and very normal." Because church families are now sprinkled throughout the Lawndale neighborhood, local kids are seeing more daddies getting up every morning to go to work and families sitting down to meals and homeowners caring for their lawns. And this simple, visible witness of living "normal" lives influences impressionable kids.

13. Quoted in "The Vision of East Lake: Golf with a Purpose," brochure produced by the East Lake Community Foundation.

William Little is a recent college graduate who grew up in Lawndale and has returned to work with the church's economic development corporation. He remembers the Gordon family's "alternative role models" and considered Coach a hero. "It was cool to play ball, be in the Bible studies, hang out with Coach. That was cool and I wanted to be like that," Little recalls.

4. FBOs Embody Authority

Finally, many FBOs contribute to cultural renewal by legitimizing the concept of authority. To function well, a free society must respect properly constituted and limited authority. FBOs often find themselves in places where, especially among young people, there is little respect for authority. But through their commitment to "being there," religious community activists can gain positions of considerable moral authority and influence.

In his penetrating analysis of the sense of community enjoyed in certain Chicago neighborhoods in the 1950s — and lost in our time — commentator Alan Ehrenhalt writes: "Stable relationships, civil classrooms, safe streets — the ingredients of what we call community — all come at a price. The price is . . . rules and authorities who can enforce them."[14] Ehrenhalt describes how moral authority was effectively exercised in one working-class community in Chicago, called St. Nick's parish, by the senior priest, Father Fennessy:

> For decades Fennessy had walked the neighborhood day and night, dressed in a black cassock that reached down to his shoe tops. He greeted people on their front stoops and handed out dimes to children. . . . "He glided around like a ghost," one child of the parish remembers. "He would appear everywhere. It was his personal fiefdom. He was in the playground, in the hallway, in class. He appeared on the playground, and the grab-ass would stop. He had that effect. He was the lord of the manor, and there was no mistaking who was in charge." *Fennessy represented authority of the most natural and unaffected kind, based neither on persuasion nor coercion, but simply on the identity and credibility of the person exercising it.*[15]

FBO and church staff who live in distressed communities (or work there seemingly "24-7-365") are frequent fixtures, known by residents. They are considered neighbors. They have earned the respect and trust of the commu-

14. Alan Ehrenhalt, *The Lost City: Discovering the Virtues of Community in the Chicago of the 1950s* (New York: Basic Books, 1995), p. 2.

15. Ehrenhalt, *The Lost City* (emphasis mine).

nity simply by being there. Prince Couisnard, who moved with his wife Sheila into Houston's distressed third ward in 1992, is a modern-day Father Fennessy. A former professional baseball player, Prince uses the power of sports to build discipling relationships with neighborhood kids. "The basketball court is where manhood is taught in the ghetto," says Prince. "It's the most fertile ground to get them out of this world of drugs and violence and into the kingdom of Christ."[16] Neighborhood kids tromp through the Couisnards' home so often that the door handles wear out and the plumbing breaks down. But Prince's "being-there" availability has won him the ear of teens — who are even willing to listen to his old-fashioned ideas about dating. Girls involved in the ministry's programs know they have to bring their prom dates to Prince for a "screening." He sits the couple down in front of his battered desk, eyeballs the young man grimly, and informs him that his date is a "precious jewel of God" and that he'll hold the fellow personally responsible if he doesn't return her in exactly the same state as she is then — in other words, not pregnant![17]

Being there is not only essential for developing moral character in inner-city youth, it's an irreducible part of winning the battle for safer streets in urban America. An article in *Newsweek* about the Reverend Eugene Rivers, leader of a Christian community development ministry in Boston that targets urban at-risk youth and gang members, related the following story about a conversation Rivers had shortly after he had moved into the neighborhood:

> Rivers sought out a local drug dealer and gangbanger named Selvin Brown — "a sassy, smartass, tough-talking, gunslinging mother shut your mouth," he says, not without some appreciation. Brown took the Reverend into crackhouses, introduced him to the neighborhood. And he gave Rivers, a Pentecostal, a lesson in why God was losing to gangs in the battle for the souls of inner-city kids. "Selvin explained to us, 'I'm there when Johnny goes out for a loaf of bread for Mama. I'm there, you're not. I win, you lose. It's all about being there.'"[18]

Rivers' 10-Point Coalition has gathered together clergy and laity who regularly patrol the streets of their neighborhoods, getting personally involved in the lives of troubled youth, being on-call at all times. All this being there grants them respect, and it has contributed to an unprecedented drop in youth crime

16. Quoted in Barbara J. Elliott, "Inner City Youth: Training Young Leaders" (Houston: Center for Renewal, 1998).

17. Author's interview with Prince Couisnard, 11 November 1999, Houston, Tex.

18. Quoted in John Leland, "Savior of the Streets," *Newsweek,* 1 June 1999.

in the city (in one twenty-nine-month stretch there was not a single gun-related youth homicide in Boston).[19]

As more and more people of faith accept the challenge to "be there," they become agents of credible authority who can stimulate a revitalization of true community in ravaged inner cities.

Areas for Improvement

That many FBOs have achieved much in transforming broken people and places and nurturing cultural renewal is obvious to anyone who looks closely at their work. Nonetheless, as mentioned earlier, not every FBO is doing such things, and some FBOs could be doing them much better. The majority of American congregations are still engaged in short-term "commodified benevolence" rather than life-transforming relational mercy ministry (with its attendant moral-cultural benefits). Plenty of FBOs satisfy themselves with mile-wide, inch-deep ministry programs that provide short-term, unsustainable, "relief-oriented" help to large numbers of individuals instead of "going deep" and nurturing permanent change among a few families at a time. These FBOs do not connect people of faith in vibrant friendships with poor people — relationships through which lamentable racial and class divides could be bridged. In addition, outside of the CCDA, few churches in evangelical America have a strong theology of place or theology of neighbor that causes them to be "parish-minded," investing significant financial and human resources in the communities in which they are located. Put differently, often white middle-class suburban churches don't accept responsibility for renewing blighted urban areas, and black middle-class congregants — though their churches may be physically located in poor urban neighborhoods — simply commute in for Sunday services and have no vibrant local ministry to their underclass neighbors. Moreover, faith-based "para-church" organizations that do their work without a philosophy of partnering with and serving the local church do not positively influence, teach, and exhort congregations.

Other FBOs are making important cultural contributions through their work, but without a defined strategy for doing so. And even where there is intentionality about playing a "prophetic" role in society (as in Call to Renewal), there is sometimes too much focus on politics and not enough on moral-cultural reformation. Simply put, there are areas for improvement within the faith-based charities movement. To achieve its full potential, the

19. Ronald J. Sider, *Just Generosity: A New Vision for Overcoming Poverty in America* (Grand Rapids: Baker Books, 1999), p. 198.

movement needs leaders who can articulate the public contributions — beyond service delivery — that FBOs can make, and should attempt deliberately to make, as part of their stated mission.

The Reformation of Manners

DON EBERLY

The abolishment of the British slave trade in 1807 is widely regarded as one of the great turning points in world history. Few, however, know the remarkable details of how it came about, much less what lessons it might hold for today. The campaign to abolish the slave trade lasted from 1787 until 1807, a nineteen-year period during which William Wilberforce introduced the same bill to repeal the trade every year. It would take yet another twenty-six years, until 1833, to fully eradicate slavery from the British empire.

How does abolishing the British slave trade relate to manners? The answer is that the two are inextricably linked. Wilberforce knew that government action against slavery was impossible short of a massive shift in the moral attitudes and habits of the people themselves. On October 28, 1787, Wilberforce wrote in his journal words that would radically alter the course of human affairs, first in Britain and later in America: "God Almighty has set before me two great objects, the suppression of the Slave Trade and the Reformation of Manners."

As impossible as the job of abolishing the slave trade appeared, the remaking of a decadent English society seemed even more daunting. The times were characterized by high rates of crime, drunkenness, and general disregard for moral standards. Public confidence in the laws was at an all time low, and there was widespread economic and political corruption. The sophisticated classes mocked religion and embraced skepticism toward moral truth as the fashionable outlook, while malicious and lewd behavior was commonplace.

Slavery, according to Wilberforce, could not be understood in isolation from these debauched conditions. Moral indifference toward the evil of slavery, he discerned, was nourished in a cultural environment of coarseness and crudeness. The "systematic misery" of slaves was but one or two steps removed from the "habitual immorality and degradation" that characterized the masses in society at the time.

By recognizing this linkage, Wilberforce was merely reflecting what others from different places and times in history had observed: that laws are, to a very large extent, a reflection of the culture. Perhaps Edmund Burke offered the most famous encapsulation of this: "Manners are more important than laws. Upon them, in a great measure, the laws depend." Manners, Burke continued, are "what vex or soothe, corrupt or purify, exalt or debase, barbarize or refine us, by a constant, steady, uniform, sensible operation, like that of the air we breathe in."

This being the case, Wilberforce concluded that to change the law he had to go "upstream" to the tributaries of moral beliefs and conduct. He had to confront the moral ethos in which the slave trade was nourished. Uprooting a corrupt law required reforming the debased culture that legitimated it.

Wilberforce also recognized that, unlike passing anti-slavery legislation, the work of reforming manners and morals was not the work of the state; such a task would have to be carried out by various voluntary associations within civil society. Over the course of three decades, Wilberforce personally founded, led, or participated in as many as sixty-seven voluntary associations aimed at the reform of manners and morals, resulting in one of the most dynamic chapters in the history of voluntary reform societies. His success at achieving the twin goals — reforming manners and, in turn, eradicating slavery — stands as a monument to the power of voluntary associations and reform societies in bringing social and moral uplift to a debauched culture.

America's Moribund Manners

Whether America has, in its current ill-mannered state, reached the same low-water mark as Britain at the turn of the nineteenth century is open to debate. Judging from the assessment that Americans themselves make of their current condition, it would appear that this is so. A survey by *U.S. News and World Report* and Bozell Worldwide indicates that many people believe that the behavior of Americans is deteriorating. Large majorities of Americans feel their country has reached an ill-mannered watershed. Nine out of ten Americans think incivility is a serious problem, and nearly half think it is extremely serious. Seventy-eight percent say the problem has worsened in the past ten years.[1]

1. John Marks, "The American Uncivil Wars," *U.S. News and World Report,* 22 April 1996, pp. 67-68.

Americans do not see rudeness merely as a private irritant. They see in disrespectful behavior the portent of a more worrisome social disintegration. More than 90 percent of those polled believe incivility and rudeness contribute to the increase of violence in the country; 85 percent believe they divide the national community, and the same number see them as eroding healthy values like respect for others.[2]

In other words, the abandonment of responsible behavior is no longer seen as isolated in an occasional episode, nor is it viewed as a matter of merely private concern with no social consequences; it is thought to be both pervasive and to be affecting the nation's social health.

Pollster George Gallup, who has long tracked American attitudes about values, has "a sinking feeling" when he looks over surveys. A recent Gallup poll showed a large majority of Americans believe that society has "a harsh and mean edge," Gallup says, noting that the United States has become "a society in which the very notion of a good person is often ridiculed," where "retribution is the operative word."[3]

Columnist Michael Kelly describes a "Gresham's law in aesthetics" that operates in our manners just as in economics, which he says works with "breathtaking, ruthless rapidity." Nothing, he says, "is not fit to print," not even the act of the nation's highest leader and the chief living symbol of democracy soiling the dress of his adulteress. Kelly proclaims: "The Marxist ideal is at last reached. We live, finally, in a classless society: No one has any class at all."

Kelly cites as evidence of his "classless society" thesis a number of cultural trends adopted by the demographic mainstream, including those in the areas of popular fashions and the use of vulgarity. What is remarkable about this, he says, is not that deviance is being used to offend the sensibilities of the refined, which has occurred for centuries, but that deviancy may no longer exist as a category. The offenders are not cultural rebels; they are the mainstream culture. "The horror," he says, "is that we are fast approaching a culture where it is impossible to offend."[4]

Stories of America's slipping manners are regularly captured in our headlines and decried by columnists. Language and behavior standards on film, television, and popular music have eroded to an unprecedented degree. Nearly every community in America has witnessed increased anger and rudeness in public places and road rage occasionally turning violent.[5]

Soccer moms and dads have become so loudmouthed and ill-mannered

2. Marks, "The American Uncivil Wars," pp. 67-68.

3. Don E. Eberly, "Civil Society: The Paradox of American Progress," *Essays on Civil Society* 1, no. 2 (January 1996), p. 2.

4. Michael Kelly, "The Age of No Class," *Washington Post,* 11 August 1999, p. A19.

5. Associated Press, "Man Dies After Road Rage Attack," 23 November 1999.

on the sidelines that one youth soccer league in West Palm Beach has adopted a policy requiring the parents of all kids who suit up for the game to complete an ethics class. The Juniper-Tequesta Athletic Association, which serves six thousand kids ages five to eighteen, is now requiring parents to take an hour-long class in ethical conduct, including training in how to show positive support and good sportsmanship. "We just want to try to de-escalate the intensity that's being shown by the parents at these games," says the volunteer athletic league president.[6]

Few public spaces are not seen as suitable for broadcasting ideas and images once widely thought of as reflecting bad manners. Bumper stickers, for example, have always been around, advertising one's favorite politician or rock band or promoting a charity or social cause. It has been commonplace to broadcast offbeat ideas and causes via this medium. Today, however, bumper sticker messages carry sexual references and insults, the "F" word, and cartoon characters urinating on anything they find unacceptable.[7]

In an article entitled "A Small Plea to Delete a Ubiquitous Expletive" in *U.S. News and World Report,* Elizabeth Austin plaintively suggests that if American society can agree on nothing else, perhaps establishing the modest goal of removing the now common use of the "F" word from polite circles might be a modest start. Virtually all individuals, including people who never use bad language, are now forced to hear it frequently used "on the street, on the job, at the health club, at the movies — anywhere two or three disgruntled citizens might gather." Austin adds that the need to work for the elimination of the English language's most vulgar word would have been seen as preposterous a couple of generations ago since neither it nor any comparable word would ever have been used in polite company.[8]

More than anything, America is deeply confused and divided over what should be permissible under what circumstances. It's not that Americans aren't dismayed — the polls themselves show that they are. It is more the case that, as Lee Bockhorn puts it, "Americans have become schizophrenic about manners." We flock by the millions, he says, "to scatological comedies from the toilet-mouthed *South Park* to the masturbatory *American Pie.*" "At the same time," however, "polls reveal that a huge majority believe American manners and morals have undergone a precipitous and deplorable decline."[9] In other words,

6. Associated Press, "Loudmouth Parents Must Take Ethics Course for Kids' Games," 18 November 1999.

7. Gil Smart, "Bumper Sticker Shock," *Lancaster Sunday News,* Lancaster, Penn., 11 November 1999.

8. Elizabeth Austin, "A Small Plea to Delete a Ubiquitous Expletive," *U.S. News and World Report,* 6 April 1988, p. 58.

9. Lee Bockhorn, "Do Manners Matter?" *The Weekly Standard,* 16 August 1999, p. 36.

programming that large majorities of Americans privately report finding deplorable — be it shock radio, soft porn on television, or vulgar language and shockingly degraded movies — is being consumed by sizable numbers of Americans, including many of those who report finding it offensive.

Manners as Voluntary Rules of Behavior

What Wilberforce understood in his day, and what growing numbers of Americans are coming to appreciate in our own time, is that there is an unbroken link between uncivil and ill-mannered behavior of the milder variety and tolerance for the more barbaric treatment of human beings, illustrated in Wilberforce's time by the slave trade. The corruption of superficial and seemingly harmless behavior can have a far deeper corrupting effect. The attempts by some organizations and movements today to restore civility and recover manners should be seen as an attempt to renew the linkage between freedom and its responsible use with the aid of social rules and restraints. Manners, it is becoming increasingly clear, serve important purposes in maintaining an ordered freedom in democratic society.

Manners have a unique history as an informal and voluntary tool for shaping individual behavior and social standards. In 1530 the philosopher Erasmus wrote in his etiquette book, *de Civitate*, that a young person's training should consist of four important areas: religion, study, duty, and manners. Another book on manners from the same era, written by French Jesuits in 1595, was translated into English and was adopted by George Washington two centuries later.

John Moulton, a noted English judge, speaking in 1912 on the subject of "law and manners," divided human action into three domains. The domain of law essentially compels people to obey, without much choice in the matter, while the domain of free choice grants the individual unconstrained freedom. Between these two domains lies a third domain that is neither regulated by the law nor free from constraint. This "domain of obedience to the unenforceable" was what Moulton termed manners. Manners were about proper behavior, of course, but they also entailed a larger concept of moral duty and social responsibility. They involved "doing right where there is no one to make you do it but yourself," where the individual is "the enforcer of the law upon himself."[10]

What Moulton understood was that cultural conditions could not be reversed by government action or changes in the law alone, but only by a recovery

10. John Silber, "The Media and Our Children: Who Is Responsible?" *Windgate Journal,* from Boston University Commencement Address (May 1995), pp. 11-13.

of manners. Moulton saw the domain of manners as "the whole realm which recognizes the sway of duty, fairness, sympathy, taste, and all others things that make life beautiful and society possible," things which can be easily corrupted but not so easily corrected, at least not by laws.[11]

While the state is in no position to restore manners, the quality of public life and of government is inextricably linked to them. Government is forced to deal with the consequences of the breakdown of manners and moral norms. The erosion of cultural norms practically ensures that the state becomes the arbiter of conflict, and will thus continually expand.

Manners: Small Morals, Limited Government

Every society, to function as a society, must settle on some basic notion of right behavior that is regarded as important and legitimate enough to enforce. Societies have basically two means to enforce right behavior. One is the law, which is a clumsy, heavy-handed, and often inappropriate tool. The second, as Lord Moulton pointed out, is manners. As many observers have pointed out, there is an inverse relationship between the widespread practice of manners and the intrusiveness of law.

When the rules for determining what conduct is proper are no longer set by custom, morality, and religion, the rules of society become decided through politics alone. Judith Martin, leading etiquette expert, sees manners fulfilling a "regulative" function, similar to that of the law. Where manners function properly, the conscience is informed and behavior is constrained without having to resort to policy or the courts. Martin says that manners work to "soften personal antagonisms, and thus to avert conflicts," so that the law may be restricted to "serious violations of morality."[12] Social rules bring respect and harmony to daily situations.

The wide practice of manners can make the job of governance easier. Political philosopher Thomas Hobbes understood manners as "small morals," and no small protection for a society against what he famously described as the "state of nature." Manners are part of the routine of an ordered society, where civility and respect are practiced voluntarily apart from the compulsion of law. They are the bridges between private freedom and public duty.

A system of manners is a way for a free society to induce people to act respectfully by voluntary means. As Hobbes pointed out, manners contribute to

11. Roger Kimball, "You Are Not Excused," *The Wall Street Journal,* 13 July 1999.

12. Judith Martin and Gunther S. Stent, "I Think; Therefore I Thank: A Philosophy of Etiquette," *American Scholar* 59 (Spring 1990): 245.

the maintenance of order and balance in society, safeguarding society from the nasty, brutish conditions that characterized man in his uncivilized state while minimizing the need for a highly intrusive state.

As individuals make their decisions less and less in accordance with either private conscience or widely accepted moral standards and more on the basis of the law, society becomes legalistic in its approach to behavior; the law, not morality, guides behavior. Under this law-based system of regulating conduct, many are prone both to resort to the law in sorting out differences and to assume that whatever the law does not formally forbid must therefore be permissible. In other words, when the law is the principal arbiter, other gentler forms of regulation — such as ethics and manners — tend to recede.

Judith Martin explains it this way: On the one hand, she says, many Americans have come to believe and to put into practice "the idea that any behavior not prohibited by law ought to be tolerated." On the other hand, she says, people resort to the law to correct minor offenses that should be socially regulated by manners: "people who found rude but legally permitted behavior intolerable have attempted to expand the law to outlaw rudeness." Ultimately, says Martin, attempts to eradicate rudeness or obnoxiousness through the law pose a threat "to the freedoms guaranteed by the constitution."[13]

Social regulations such as manners not only govern more softly than the law, they are more flexible. Social regulation leaves room for nonconformity, which the law does not, and requires no costly governmental apparatus. The state's rules are absolute and binding, enforceable through arrest and imprisonment. Thus, when conflicts arise in a society governed by a pervasive law rather than social constraints, these conflicts — whether on highways, school playgrounds, or in malls — quickly escalate and must be resolved by external authorities. An illustration of this phenomenon at work is the increased number of security personnel serving in locations where they were never needed before, such as in schools and at sporting events.

The founders of the American democratic system were attuned to manners and related topics. While they contributed some of our most profound political theory in such documents as the Federalist Papers, many of their private writings were filled with references to such things as habits, sentiments, mores, dispositions, and manners. These were the ingredients of a well-ordered society in which individuals took it upon themselves to govern themselves.

At least two founders, George Washington and Benjamin Franklin, contributed their own original thoughts and writings on manners. Washington

13. Judith Martin, "The Oldest Virtue," in *Seedbeds of Virtue: Source of Competence, Character and Citizenship in American Society,* ed. Mary Ann Glendon and David Blankenhorn (Lanham, Md.: Madison Books, 1995), p. 67.

translated onto a small plain notebook 110 "Rules of Civility and Decent Behavior in Company and Conversation." In Washington's day, civility was furthered through a set of voluntary rules whereby a person seeking social advancement and distinction learned to display deference to the interests and feelings of others.

Rules of civility were consciously adopted by Washington to win the respect of his fellows and to advance in leadership.[14] By means of a strict code of courteous behavior, Washington established a towering command as a leader on the battlefield. The first principle of manners, according to Washington's rules, had to do with public leadership and conduct: "Every action done in public ought to be done with some sign of respect for those who are present." Manners and simple courtesy added grace to Washington's natural gift for iron-willed leadership. Manners were also the means by which he imposed upon himself self-regulation, ultimately mastering what was widely known to be a severe temper.

Renewal Movements

Periodically throughout American history, society has realized the importance of "the unenforceable" social rules and embraced renewal movements to revive them. In nineteenth-century America, for example, books and manuals for the application of manners to every aspect of life flourished. One bibliography assembled during this period counted 236 separate titles on manners.[15] When Emily Post's famous book *Etiquette* was published in 1922, it became such a publishing success that it rivaled Sinclair Lewis's *Babbitt,* also published that year.

Today's manners movement has arisen in very much the same fashion. Manners are offered as at least a partial corrective to the excesses of a generation that spent its youth determined to throw off social conventions and constraints. A growing interest in manners is reflected in the popularity of books on the subject and a widening network of civility advocates. These contemporary authors carefully avoid appearing stiff or Victorian, and instead link manners to a widely expressed desire for greater social harmony and mutual respect.

Modern day manners philosopher Judith Martin, who has written extensively on the subject, says manners are defined as that "part of our fundamental

14. Richard Brookhiser, *Rules of Civility: The 110 Precepts That Guided Our First President in War and Peace* (New York: Free Press, 1997), p. 12.

15. James Morris, "Democracy Beguiled," *Wilson Quarterly,* August-September 1996, p. 24.

beliefs or wants that include such notions as communal harmony, dignity of the person, a need for cultural coherence, and an aesthetic sense."[16] Etiquette is the set of rules that emerges from these fundamental beliefs.

Evidence that a search is on for more civilized social customs can be found in the popularity of films, such as those based on the novels of Jane Austen, set in highly mannered societies where the characters suppress their emotions and urges and express fastidious regard for others. Further evidence can be found in the astonishing success of *The Rules,* a runaway best-seller which establishes for women new (actually old) rules of conduct in courtship in order to secure the respect and fidelity of one's suitor. *The Rules,* says Maggie Gallagher, "violate the most sacred precepts of the 1960s about sex and love: that men and women are the same; that love means letting it all hang out; that people shouldn't play games." By games, she meant essentially the rules of polite romantic encounter, grounded in mutual respect and mannerly conduct.

The return to manners reflects a growing awareness that the loss of standards in courtship has been costly, especially to women. In her book *A Return to Modesty,* Wendy Shalit describes the dreadful consequences of declining respect for women in areas of courtship and sex and predicts a counterrevolution in women's attitudes: "In the face of all the cultural messages that bark at them that promiscuity and exhibitionism are liberation, they are slowly but surely coming to think the opposite."

Promoting the rules of respect may also be good for commerce. Sensing that courtesy might strengthen the city's tourism industry, New York City civic leaders launched a campaign to encourage its citizens to be nicer to the twenty-five million visitors who visit the city each year. "Instead of Making a Wise Crack, Smile" the campaign encourages, and another slogan warns, "Turn your Back on Tourists and They'll Turn Their Backs on New York." Thanks to the program, cabbies get a new supply of air fresheners, while cops, airport personnel, and subway workers get sensitivity training.

The history of manners suggests that they inevitably rebound when conditions require, as if by some law of nature. Mark Caldwell describes an "innate and unconscious human law" that seems to conserve manners, even against the odds. He observes that as the Internet has already begun to demonstrate, "even a social space created with conscious lawlessness quickly demonstrates a need for order and generates a rough code of manners."[17]

16. Martin and Stent, "I Think," p. 245.
17. Bockhorn, "Do Manners Matter?" p. 36.

Conclusion

Examples such as these show that interest in a much-needed renewal of manners exists in America. If this reformation is to succeed, however, much remains to be done, for too many Americans fail to understand the insidious cultural effects of our deteriorating manners, and still others admit the problem but continue to consume and support the culture that exemplifies it. It is important to remember that Wilberforce devoted nineteen years of his life to the reformation of manners and abolition of the slave trade before slavery was abolished in England; our own struggle for renewal may take equally long. Such a thought might seem discouraging if one did not also remember the successful outcome of Wilberforce's struggle against slavery, and the amazing impact of his attempts to reform manners. If one man could accomplish so much, surely a concerted effort by the legions of concerned Americans today can prove equally successful.

Teen Abstinence

ELAYNE GLOVER BENNETT

Unwed motherhood, especially in the preteen and teenage years, is a virtual catastrophe. Economically and psychologically, in terms of parenting, education, and social stability, it is ruinous. One could hardly design a more effective plan for damaging the life of a mother and a child. The widespread existence of teen pregnancy has become a pervasive influence on the success and financial stability of women in today's society. If current trends continue, it is possible that in the year 2015, one of every two babies in the United States will be born out of wedlock. For a young girl, the effects of an unwed pregnancy extend beyond her teenage years to influence her potential for achievement and empowerment in later life. Statistics show that 82 percent of babies born out of wedlock have mothers with a high school education or less, while only 4 percent are born to mothers who have obtained a college degree. A recent U.S. Census report found that married black Americans make nearly four times more than black single-parent households. The median income for a single mother regardless of race is less than $20,000 a year.

Furthermore, the cycle of poverty is likely to repeat itself in a new generation. Girls born to teenage mothers are 83 percent more likely than those born to older mothers to become pregnant in their teens. In addition to the financial and educational limitations for teenagers who have babies, this issue provides a significant burden for taxpayers and government funding. Teen childbearing costs U.S. taxpayers $6.9 billion per year, and the cost to the economy in lost productivity equals $29 billion annually.

Increased sexual activity during the last three decades has not only brought about a 32 percent rate of out-of-wedlock births, but also dramatic increases in sexually transmitted diseases. An estimated three million teens are infected with an STD (sexually transmitted disease) each year. This is especially alarming because today many STDs that can lead to infertility, such as human papilloma virus (often called genital warts), are untreatable with antibiotics. Oral sex is the latest fad among middle school students, especially in middle class and upper middle class areas. They fail to realize that oral sex is highly dangerous because of the risk of contracting STDs, including AIDS. According to the 1998 report of the Allan Guttmacher Institute, in a single act of unprotected sex with an infected partner, a teenage girl has a 1 percent risk of acquiring HIV, a 30 percent risk of infection with genital herpes, and a 50 percent chance of contracting gonorrhea.

It is not surprising that when The American Association of University Women Foundation surveyed two thousand girls ages eleven–seventeen about their foremost concerns they discovered that the vast majority of girls said that sex and how to say "no" in emotionally charged relationships was their number one concern. Girls said that the pressure to have sex comes not just from boys, but also from other girls, from friends, and from the media. In a September 15, 1999, *USA Today* article the Foundation's president remarked, "This report is a warning flag to America's parents and teachers. Besides test scores and vouchers, educators must also address the difficult issues teens face."

Providing Guidance to Help Girls Say "No"

Adolescent girls truly want to know how to say "no" and we — our schools and our communities — have not been providing them with the guidance they need. Considering the pressure adolescent girls feel to have sex and the limitations placed on those who bear children in their teenage years, it is vital to support programs that address this issue and are designed to change attitudes and behavior. We must support the 51 percent of adolescents who have decided to postpone sex.

After thirteen years of working with adolescent girls, I know that they want to hear the abstinence message and will respond when it is offered in a developmentally sound program in an educational setting that provides fun, companionship, and caring. Since 1987, thousands of adolescent girls in the Washington, D.C., area and across the country are responding to the abstinence message and gaining self-respect through the practice of self-restraint. They are making positive decisions and supporting one another in postponing sex and rejecting illegal drug and alcohol use. The Best Friends Program has helped to accomplish all this.

The Origin of the Best Friends Program

Best Friends has its genesis in 1987, when I was a faculty member at Georgetown University's Child Development Center. I began to realize that something had to be done to provide guidance to our adolescent girls. Premature, underweight babies born to younger and younger mothers caused concern among the staff. Many adolescent girls referred for counseling seemed to have emotional problems that evolved from sexual promiscuity. I began to wonder if anyone was telling girls not to have sex.

I thought girls would benefit from being part of a positive peer support group guided by responsible women. With the encouragement of Dr. Phyllis Magrab, director of the Child Development Center, I began to develop an educational curriculum based on the concept of girls supporting one another in waiting to have sex. The support of friends is a very important part of a girl's self-image and self-worth. As Aristotle taught his students, the best kind of friend to have is one who encourages you to be a better person. So our program's name, Best Friends, speaks for itself.

We first tested the Best Friends concept and our curriculum chapter on "Love and Dating" with tenth graders at Langley High School in Virginia. More than 73 percent of the students said they would like to belong to a group whose members supported each other in waiting to have sex until at least after high school graduation. From the girls' evaluation questionnaires we learned two very important things that guided the development of our program. The girls advised us to exclude the boys from their sessions and to begin with younger girls. One girl wrote: "It is too late for me. I wish someone had told me I could say 'no.' Start with my younger sister, who is 12. She is already receiving pressure."

Best Friends was introduced to a class of sixth grade girls at Amidon Elementary School in southwest Washington, D.C., who were followed to junior high and senior high school. Since then more than a thousand girls in D.C. public schools have participated in the program.

Today, Best Friends has grown into a national program of nearly 5,000 girls attending 90 public schools in 26 cities in 14 states, the District of Columbia, and the U.S. Virgin Islands. The Washington, D.C., area program, and its replications in other school districts, is conducted by the Best Friends Foundation, a 501(c)(3) nonprofit organization located in Washington, D.C., with funding from private foundations, corporations, and individuals.

What Is Best Friends?

Best Friends is a youth development program with a character-building curriculum for girls in grades 4-12 with messages encouraging abstinence from sex, drugs, and alcohol. It provides a developmentally-sound curriculum in an educational setting that promotes fun, companionship, and caring. Through a cohesive peer support group and one-on-one mentoring, Best Friends helps girls set personal goals, develop positive self-worth, and achieve academically with skills that will benefit them throughout life.

A girl enters the program as part of the school curriculum in the fourth, fifth, or sixth grade, when her attitudes toward life are forming, and continues to participate through middle and high school. The program is delivered by educators during the school day as part of the school curriculum, and is provided to all the girls in a class or to a cross-section of girls randomly selected from three categories: school leaders/high achievers, average students, and students considered "at risk." Parental permission must be received for a girl to participate in the program. Each year each girl receives at least 110 hours of guidance and activities. Girls learn to resist pressure to engage in sex, drugs, and alcohol and to make informed, sound decisions. They learn to counter arguments, such as "everyone is doing it," with the skills to make the decision to wait.

Best Friends fosters self-respect by promoting achievement and self-restraint. Low self-concept has been cited often as a cause of adolescent pregnancy and substance abuse. According to researcher Erik Erikson, the most important lesson of adolescence is the establishment of a positive self-concept or identity. He asserts that successful intimate relationships are not possible until a sense of self has been firmly established. Best Friends helps girls to define themselves as individuals and as part of their peer group.

This program is based on the true spirit of friendship — on adolescent girls discussing their problems, desires, and dreams with each other and helping each other make sound decisions. Through a seven-part curriculum, we provide hours of personal attention, guidance, and help with skills that adolescent girls need to lead happy and healthy lives. We do not employ scare tactics and are positive and upbeat in our message.

The long-term commitment and intensity of Best Friends sets it apart from most teenage risk reduction and pregnancy prevention programs. In 1997, it was recognized as one of the nation's most effective programs with an award from The National Campaign to Prevent Teen Pregnancy.

Annually, the Best Friends Foundation administers an anonymous pre- and post-program survey to each participant. From the 1999 post survey we found these facts from 2,600 Best Friends girls attending 74 schools in 24 public school districts who had completed one or more years in the program:

A boy has asked her on a date	59%
Understands the difference between love and sex	95%
Had sexual intercourse this year	3%
Was sexually abused this year	4%
Wants to wait until at least after high school graduation to have sex	77%
Wants to wait until marriage to have sex	75%
Was pregnant this year	1%
Has friends or family who use illegal drugs	24%
Has been offered illegal drugs this year	14%
Used illegal drugs this year	14%
Drank beer, liquor, wine coolers, or other alcoholic beverages this year	22%
Smoked cigarettes this year	11%
Someone has been violent toward her this year	21%

Dr. Stan Weed of the Institute for Research and Evaluation examined the data, comparing girls' reported behavior prior to Best Friends to that after one or more years in the program. He found that

- Best Friends has a national sexual abuse reduction rate of 66 percent. Of the 235 (9 percent) girls who said they had been sexually abused, 155 (5 percent) reported no sexual abuse this year in Best Friends.
- Best Friends has a national sexual intercourse discontinuation rate of 46.3 percent. Of the 136 (5 percent) Best Friends girls who reported having sexual intercourse, 83 (3 percent) said they did not have sexual intercourse this year in Best Friends.
- Best Friends has a national drug exposure reduction rate of 38 percent. Of the 534 (21 percent) Best Friends girls who said that they had been offered drugs, 358 (14 percent) reported they were not offered drugs this year.
- Best Friends has a national drug refusal rate of 81 percent. Of the 358 (14 percent) Best Friends girls who said they were offered drugs this year, 289 refused them, 69 (2 percent) used them.

Why Is the Best Friends Approach to Abstinence Education Proving Effective?

Recent research findings from The National Longitudinal Study on Adolescent Health, The National Center on Addiction and Substance Abuse at Columbia

University, and the Institute for Research and Evaluation, as well as other studies, are illuminating why the Best Friends approach to abstinence education is proving effective. We believe that Best Friends works because it provides four important things:

1. A Clear Abstinence-Only Message from Sex, Drugs, and Alcohol

Thousands of Best Friends girls from all socioeconomic and racial backgrounds have responded well to the message of abstinence from sex, drugs, and alcohol. Best Friends makes the standards high and the commitment clear. We review with the girls their commitment to abstinence at least until after high school graduation and at best until marriage.

The Best Friends curriculum also focuses on the dangers of drug use and how experimenting with drugs can destroy dreams and harm family and friends. Alcohol use impairs judgment, making you more vulnerable. A recent study by CASA (The National Center on Addiction and Substance Abuse) found a significant relationship between substance abuse and sexual activity among adolescents. Dr. Weed's research reveals that a girl is more likely to be sexually active if she has a boyfriend, has been sexually abused, or has used drugs. These findings further confirm that to be effective intervention programs must address the broad set of cultural and social factors contributing to adolescent high-risk behavior.

Best Friends does not provide a sex education curriculum or present the mechanics of sex or teach contraceptive techniques. It presents a prevention strategy that addresses high-risk behavior by emphasizing the joys of preteen and teenage years free of the complications of early sexual activity. Our message is pro-active, upbeat, and honest: "You will succeed in life if you set your goals and maintain your self-respect." We focus on friendship and the importance of friends supporting one another in postponing sex.

Unfortunately, not all women's first sexual experience is voluntary. The Alan Guttmacher Institute reports that two-thirds of teen mothers said that they had had sex forced upon them earlier by adult men. The National Center for Health Statistics reported in 1992 that of 185,000 births to girls aged ten to eighteen in 1992, 70 percent were fathered by adult men. In many states adult men having sex with underage girls constitutes statutory rape. During the past decade, however, statutory rape laws have been rarely enforced. Knowledge of contraceptive techniques is not going to help these girls either since the adult men are "hitting on" these young girls because they don't want to use protection. They know young, inexperienced girls are less likely to have an STD, and they are often unconcerned about impregnating them.

When young girls have been used for sexual gratification by these "father figures" — and I use "father" very reluctantly — the girls feel used, with little sense of self-worth. They have been set up for the destructive dependent cycle of love-hate that leads often to a woman becoming another sad statistic in the growing domestic violence in our country.

We know that at least 10 percent of girls entering our program have been sexually abused and we address this sexual abuse through our videos and discussions, which emphasize that sexual abuse is wrong and never the victim's fault. We talk about common-sense safety rules, which, unfortunately, many children don't hear these days. We encourage the girls to never go anywhere alone, to never hitchhike or accept rides from strangers, to leave the room when pornography is present, and to never keep a secret that makes them feel uncomfortable. We are certain that Best Friends girls are far more capable of determining what is acceptable or unacceptable behavior in their boyfriends. And because they have this ability we believe they are far less likely to become victims of abuse and physical violence.

2. An Intensive Peer Support Structure That Builds a Sense of Belonging and Connectedness to School

The selection of friends is a very important part of a girl's self-image and self-worth. The Carnegie Council on Adolescent Development in its report "Preparing America's Youth for the Twenty-first Century" states: "Young adolescents need to see themselves as valued members of a group that offers mutual support and trusting relationships. They need to be able to succeed at something and to be praised and rewarded for their success."

Best Friends provides girls with a sense of belonging to a status group and with opportunities to create low-risk friendships with girls who share their values and are fun. We emphasize that friends must help each other make good decisions and that they sometimes must intervene in each other's lives. Good judgment is necessary to resist the pressures of intimate relationships. Best Friends provides a positive peer support structure in which girls can discuss their concerns and dreams and learn sound decision-making skills. By making good decisions and helping each other, they enhance their self-respect, leading to the development of confidence and good judgment. Our messages include the following:

- Friends help each other make good decisions;
- Boys and girls often have different agendas in their romantic relationships;

- Without self-respect it is difficult to say no to anyone or anything;
- Tomorrow is the first day of the rest of your life, so past mistakes do not mean that a person must continue in the same pattern; and
- Sex is never a test of love.

This approach has been successful. As one girl commented to an independent researcher:

> It was hard to say "no" until I became a Best Friends girl. I have all these friends in Best Friends that check on me and say, "how you doin'?" One time I was going to go with this guy who had this great "line" but they wouldn't let me. I'm really glad. He got another friend of mine pregnant and left her alone. She's sad. We watch out for each other at Best Friends. I can say "no" in seven different ways.

The National Longitudinal Study on Adolescent Health found that one of the factors most protecting an adolescent girl from engaging in early sex is having a group of friends and acquaintances who exhibit low-risk behavior — who do not skip school, smoke, or drink alcohol.

By providing the Best Friends curriculum as part of the school curriculum and having teachers as Best Friends mentors, the program becomes an established part of the school environment. Girls feel connected to their school, a protective factor against early sexual activity according to the National Longitudinal Study on Adolescent Health. Best Friends girls become peer counselors and school leaders. Other students see them as role models and the benefits of the program spread beyond the Best Friends group to the school at large.

3. A Multi-faceted Curriculum with Long-term Adult Involvement

Best Friends provides a long-term intervention of seven to nine years. Girls enter the program in elementary or middle school and continue the curriculum through high school.

The Best Friends curriculum utilizes Albert Bandura's social learning theory, which explains human behavior in terms of continuous reciprocal interaction between cognitive, behavioral, and environmental influences. As was mentioned earlier, each program participant receives each year at least 110 hours of guidance and fun activities through the program's seven components:

- *Group discussions held every three weeks during the school day on curriculum topics important to adolescents:* friendship, love and dating, self-respect, decision-making, alcohol abuse, drug abuse, physical fitness and nutrition, AIDS and STDs. Guidance is provided by teaching effective problem-solving skills, which develop character.

- *Role model presentations by women from the community.*
- *Weekly mentor meetings.* Each Best Friends girl is matched with a female mentor at her school with whom she meets for 30-45 minutes a week.
- *Weekly fitness and nutrition classes,* usually held after school, that are fun and lively.
- *Participation in cultural enrichment activities* that broaden the girls' horizons as to the possibilities in life.
- *Participation in community service projects* to learn to give to others in the community.
- *End-of-year recognition ceremony.* The community honors the girls, their teachers, and their parents for their commitment and achievements, and the girls demonstrate what they have learned through the year.

Obviously, Best Friends is not a one-time assembly. We provide a full curriculum that relies on the commitment of teachers who give freely of their time to serve as Best Friends coordinators, instructors, and mentors.

Best Friends makes abstinence fun and cool. As Barbara Dafoe Whitehead wrote in a 1994 *Atlantic Monthly* article entitled "The Failure of Sex Education":

> Changes in economic incentives . . . may not be enough to reduce unwed teenage childbearing. It may be necessary to alter the psychological-incentive structure as well, including "prettifying" the unglamorous business of going to school, doing homework, and earning respectable grades. The process may also include fostering strong relationships with adult women mentors who can exercise firm guidance and give direction as well as support.

Best Friends accomplishes these goals. Through the program, women of achievement, such as Mrs. Colin Powell and news anchors Barbara Harrison and Lark McCarthy, meet with the girls and talk about their own lives and the decisions they made that led to their success. At the end of each year, the girls are honored at a fun performance in which they are recognized in a printed program and on stage, where they receive a heart-shaped silver or gold pendant. Sometimes the events are covered on the evening news and they learn the rewards of commitment and achievement.

Best Friends makes the benefits of abstinence obvious. We encourage participants to set goals and to create short- and long-term plans to achieve them. We help with academic tutoring and mentors. The girls wear "cool" T-shirts and baseball caps, and in fitness class they learn "cool" dances choreographed by professional dancers, and dance to current music selected for its positive message. Girls throughout the country are proud that they are part of a national program.

Our girls also participate in cultural enrichment activities. In Washington, Best Friends girls attend plays and ballets at Ford's Theater and the Kennedy Center for the Performing Arts and have been guests for tea at the British, French, and Japanese embassies. Best Friends girls from our Wilmington, Delaware, program have attended Broadway shows in New York. Our program in Minneapolis features social etiquette classes provided by Touche Ross executives. The Charlotte and Milwaukee Best Friends utilize local college facilities, introducing girls and parents to a college campus, and our Houston program concludes each year with a recognition ceremony hosted at the Houston Museum of Fine Arts.

We provide many incentives for our girls to succeed, including college scholarships. At present we have twenty-seven girls on college scholarships funded by several generous donors. Seven classes of girls who began as sixth graders have graduated from high school with more than thirty receiving Best Friends college scholarships. Nine scholarship girls have graduated from college and two are attending medical school.

The Best Friends messages are reinforced by our school coordinators, teachers, and mentors and through the student's own awareness of her progress as she completes each year and earns her heart pendant. Smaller steps are reinforced with heart stickers and items desired by adolescents (such as Best Friends back packs, water bottles, and baseball caps).

The Best Friends theme song is the most appealing and repetitive way of ensuring that our message is retained. The song, which is sung at the end of every session, provides messages: that you shouldn't have a crowd mentality; that love starts with self-respect; that sex is not the same as love; that the teen years are special; and that you should reach out to friends who share your goals and dreams. These are the messages we know adolescents need and want to hear and they are effectively presented within our program.

4. A Requirement of Commitment from the Local Community Where the Program Is Initiated, Operated, and Funded

Finally, operating a Best Friends program requires the strong commitment of the Superintendent of Schools and the active involvement of school principals. The most important person in making the Best Friends program work is an enthusiastic and committed school principal who believes in the messages of abstinence from sex, drugs, and alcohol for adolescents. The principal's enthusiasm will motivate teachers to volunteer as curriculum instructors and mentors. Schoolteachers have responded enthusiastically to the invitation to participate in Best Friends because it provides a needed vehicle to help children.

With a tremendous demand for the program, the Best Friends Foundation has not sought out school districts for expansion. We have responded to inquiries from parents, funders, community leaders, and educators, working closely with them to build community coalitions to support the program. The school superintendent must formally request the program and enter into a licensing and participation agreement with the Best Friends Foundation. The agreement requires the school system to operate the program according to the program model and to have their educators trained by the Foundation. National training conferences are conducted twice a year using copyrighted curriculum materials that are developed and published by the Foundation. Adherence to the program model is monitored by the Foundation.

Generally, the cost of providing each Best Friends girl annually with at least 110 hours of guidance, materials, and activities is $600 per girl. Some school districts do it on less. School districts are responsible for funding their Best Friends program. The majority of Best Friends programs are supported by grants from private foundations and corporations. Some school districts receive health and drug prevention grants from their city, county, and state governments. At present, nine of the twenty-six school districts with Best Friends programs receive some support from the federal Title V abstinence education grants awarded by state health departments.

The metropolitan Washington, D.C., Best Friends program, consisting of 700 girls attending 13 public schools and 30 area high schools, is operated and supported entirely by the Best Friends Foundation with funds raised from private foundations, corporations, and individuals. Over the years, the major supporters we are indebted to are The Lynde and Harry Bradley Foundation, The Robert Wood Johnson Foundation, and the American Standard Foundation.

Conclusion

We know that abstinence is a message that young people want to hear and that they need our support. As adults, parents, educators, and role models, it is our responsibility to set high standards and guide them so they can reach their potential free from the dangers of sex, drug, and alcohol. As adults, we must give our children our best. If we do, they will respond with their best. This is the essence of Best Friends.

Courtship

LEON KASS

Many people are distressed over the record-high rates of divorce, illegitimacy, teenage pregnancy, marital infidelity, and premarital promiscuity. On some issues, there is even an emerging consensus that something is drastically wrong. Though they may differ on what is to be done, people on both the left and the right have come to regard the breakup of marriage as a leading cause of the neglect, indeed, of the psychic and moral maiming, of America's children.

But while various people are talking about tracking down "dead-beat dads" or about doing something to slow the rate of divorce — remedies for marital failure — very little attention is being paid to what makes for marital success. Still less are we attending to the ways and mores of entering into marriage, that is, to wooing or courtship.

There is, of course, good reason for this neglect. The very terms — "wooing," "courting," "suitors" — are archaic; and if the words barely exist, it is because the phenomena have all but disappeared. Today, there are no socially prescribed forms of conduct that help guide young men and women in the direction of matrimony. This is true not just for the lower or under classes. Even — indeed especially — the elite, those who in previous generations would have defined the conventions in these matters, lack a cultural script whose denouement is marriage.

To be sure, there are still exceptions to be found in closed religious communities or among new immigrants from parts of the world that still practice arranged marriage. But for most of America's middle- and upper-class youth — the privileged college-educated and graduated — there are no known explicit, or even tacit, social paths directed at marriage. People still get married — though later, less frequently, more hesitantly, and, by and large, less successfully. People still get married in churches and synagogues — though often with ceremonies of their own creation.

Things were not always like this; in fact, one suspects things were never like this, not here, not anywhere. We live, in this respect as in so many others, in utterly novel and unprecedented times. Until what seems like only yesterday, young people were groomed for marriage, and the paths leading to it were culturally well set out, at least in rough outline.

In polite society, at the beginning of this century, our grandfathers came a-calling and a-wooing at the homes of our grandmothers, under conditions set by the woman, operating from strength on her own turf. A generation later, courting couples began to go out on "dates," in public and increasingly on the man's terms, given that he had the income to pay for dinner and dancing. To be sure, some people "played the field," and, in the pre-war years, dating on college campuses became a matter more of proving popularity than of proving suitability for marriage. But, especially after the war, "going-steady" was a regular feature of high school and college life; the age of marriage dropped considerably, and high-school or college sweethearts often married right after, or even before, graduation. Finding a mate, no less than getting an education that would enable him to support her, was at least a tacit goal of many a male undergraduate; many a young woman, so the joke had it, went to college mainly for her MRS. degree, a charge whose truth was proof against libel for legions of college coeds well into the 1960s.[1]

Now the vast majority goes to college, but very few — women or men — go with the hope, or even the wish, of finding a marriage partner. Many do not expect to find there even a path to a career; they often require several years of post-graduate "time off" to figure out what they are going to do with themselves. Sexually active — in truth, hyperactive — they flop about from one relationship to another; to the bewildered eye of this admittedly much-too-old but still romantic observer, they manage to appear all at once casual, carefree, grim, and humorless about getting along with the opposite sex. The young men, nervous predators, act as if any woman is equally good: they are given not to falling in love with one, but to scoring in bed with many. And in this sporting attitude they are now matched by some female trophy hunters.

But most young women strike me as sad, lonely, and confused; hoping for something more, they are not enjoying their hard-won sexual liberation as

1. A fine history of these transformations has been written by Beth L. Bailey, *From Front Porch to Back Seat: Courtship in Twentieth Century America* (Baltimore: Johns Hopkins University Press, 1988).

much as liberation theory says they should.[2] Never mind wooing, today's collegians do not even make dates or other forward-looking commitments to see one another; in this, as in so many other ways, they reveal their blindness to the meaning of the passing of time. Those very few who couple off seriously and get married upon graduation as we, their parents, once did are looked upon as freaks.

After college, the scene is even more remarkable and bizarre: singles bars, personal "partner wanted" ads (almost never mentioning marriage as a goal), men practicing serial monogamy (or what someone has aptly renamed "rotating polygamy"), women chronically disappointed in the failure of men "to commit." For the first time in human history, mature women by the tens of thousands live the entire decade of their twenties — their most fertile years — neither in the homes of their fathers nor in the homes of their husbands: unprotected, lonely, and out of sync with their inborn nature. Some women positively welcome this state of affairs, but most do not. Resenting the personal price they pay for their worldly independence, they nevertheless try to put a good face on things and take refuge in work or feminist ideology. As age thirty comes and goes, they begin to allow themselves to hear their biological clock ticking, and, if husbands continue to be lacking, single motherhood by the hand of science is now an option. Meanwhile, the bachelor herd continues its youthful prowl, with real life in suspended animation, living out what Kay Hymowitz, a contributing editor of *City Journal,* has called a "postmodern postadolescence."

Anyone who seriously contemplates the present scene is — or should be — filled with profound sadness, all the more so if he or she knows the profound satisfactions of a successful marriage. Our hearts go out not only to the children of failed marriages or non-marriages — to those betrayed by their parents' divorce and to those deliberately brought into the world as bastards — but also to the lonely, disappointed, cynical, misguided, or despondent people who are missing out on one of life's greatest adventures and, through it, on many of life's deepest experiences, insights, and joys. We watch our sons and daughters, our friends' children, and our students bumble along from one unsatisfactory relationship to the next, wishing we could help.

Public policy and social decision can undermine inherited cultural forms, but once fractured, they are hard to repair by rational and self-conscious design. Besides, the causes of the present state of affairs are multiple, powerful,

2. Readers removed from the college scene should revisit Allan Bloom's profound analysis of relationships in his *The Closing of the American Mind* (New York: Simon & Schuster, 1987). Bloom was concerned with the effect of the new arrangements on the possibility for liberal education, not for marriage, my current concern.

and, I fear, largely irreversible. Anyone who thinks courtship can make a comeback must at least try to understand what one is up against.

Obstacles to Marriage

Some of the obstacles in the way of getting married are of very recent origin; indeed, they have occurred during the adult lifetime of those over fifty. For this reason, one suspects, they may seem to some people to be reversible, a spasm connected with the "abnormal" 1960s. But, when they are rightly understood, one can see that they spring from the very heart of liberal democratic society and of modernity altogether.

Here is a (partial) list of the recent changes that hamper courtship and marriage: the sexual revolution, made possible especially by effective female contraception; the ideology of feminism and the changing educational and occupational status of women; the destigmatization of bastardy, divorce, infidelity, and abortion; the general erosion of shame and awe regarding sexual matters, exemplified most vividly in the ubiquitous and voyeuristic presentation of sexual activity in movies and on television; widespread morally neutral sex education in schools; the explosive increase in the numbers of young people whose parents have been divorced (and in those born out of wedlock, who have never known their father); great increases in geographic mobility, with a resulting loosening of ties to place and extended family of origin; and, harder to describe precisely, a popular culture that celebrates youth and independence not as a transient stage en route to adulthood but as "the time of our lives," imitable at all ages, and an ethos that lacks transcendent aspirations and asks of us no devotion to family, God, or country, encouraging us simply to soak up the pleasures of the present.

The change most immediately devastating for wooing is probably the sexual revolution. For why would a man court a woman for marriage when she may be sexually enjoyed, and regularly, without it? Contrary to what the youth of the 1960s believed, they were not the first to feel the power of sexual desire. Many, perhaps even most, men in earlier times avidly sought sexual pleasure prior to and outside of marriage. But they usually distinguished, as did the culture generally, between women one fooled around with and women one married, between a woman of easy virtue and a woman of virtue simply.

The supreme virtue of the virtuous woman was modesty, a form of sexual self-control, manifested not only in chastity, but in decorous dress and manner, speech and deed, and in reticence in the display of her well-banked affections. A virtue, as it were, made for courtship, it served simultaneously as a source of attraction and a spur to manly ardor, a guard against a woman's own desires, as well as a defense against unworthy suitors.

Once female modesty became a first casualty of the sexual revolution, even women eager for marriage lost their greatest power to hold and to discipline their prospective mates. For it is a woman's refusal of sexual importunings, coupled with hints or promises of later gratification, that is generally a necessary condition of transforming a man's lust into love.

Sex education in our elementary and secondary schools is an independent yet related obstacle to courtship and marriage. Taking for granted, and thereby ratifying, precocious sexual activity among teenagers (and even preteens), most programs of sex education in public schools have a twofold aim: the prevention of teenage pregnancy and the prevention of venereal disease, especially AIDS. While some programs also encourage abstinence or non-coital sex, most are concerned with teaching techniques for "safe sex"; offspring and disease are thus treated as (equally) avoidable side effects of sexuality, whose true purpose is only individual pleasure.

But perhaps still worse than such amorality — and amorality on this subject is itself morally culpable — is the failure of sex education to attempt to inform and elevate the erotic imagination of the young. On the contrary, the very attention to physiology and technique is deadly to the imagination. True sex education is an education of the heart; it concerns itself with beautiful and worthy beloveds, with elevating transports of the soul. The energy of sexual desire, if properly sublimated, is transformable into genuine and lofty longings — not only for love and romance, but for all the other higher human yearnings. The sonnets and plays of Shakespeare, the poetry of Keats and Shelley, and the novels of Jane Austen can incline a heart to woo, and even show one whom and how. What kind of wooers can one hope to cultivate from reading the sex manuals — or from watching the unsublimated and unsublime sexual athleticism of the popular culture?

Crippled by Divorce

The ubiquitous experience of divorce is also deadly for courtship and marriage. Some people try to argue, wishfully against the empirical evidence, that children of divorce will marry better than their parents because they know how important it is to choose well. But the deck is stacked against them. Not only are many of them frightened of marriage, in whose likely permanence they simply do not believe, but they are often maimed for love and intimacy. They have had no successful models to imitate; worse, their capacity for trust and love has been severely crippled by the betrayal of the primal trust all children naturally repose in their parents, to provide that durable, reliable, and absolutely trustworthy haven of permanent and unconditional love in an otherwise often unloving and undependable world.

It is surely the fear of making a mistake in marriage, and the desire to avoid a later divorce, that leads some people to undertake cohabitation, sometimes understood by the couple to be a "trial marriage" — although they are often one or both of them self-deceived (or other-deceiving). It is far easier, so the argument goes, to get to know one another by cohabiting than by the artificial systems of courting or dating of yesteryear. But such arrangements, even when they eventuate in matrimony, are, precisely because they are a trial, not a trial of marriage. Marriage is not something one tries on for size, and then decides whether to keep; it is rather something one decides with a promise, and then bends every effort to keep.

Lacking the formalized and public ritual, and especially the vows or promises of permanence (or "commitment") that subtly but surely shape all aspects of genuine marital life, cohabitation is an arrangement of convenience, with each partner taken on approval and returnable at will. Many are, in fact, just playing house — sex and meals shared with the rent. When long-cohabiting couples do later marry, whether to legitimate prospective offspring, satisfy parental wishes, or just because "it now seems right," post-marital life is generally regarded and experienced as a continuation of the same, not as a true change of estate. The formal rite of passage that is the wedding ceremony is, however welcome and joyous, also something of a mockery: Everyone, not only the youngest child present, wonders, if only in embarrassed silence, "Why is this night different from all other nights?" Given that they have more or less drifted into marriage, it should come as no great surprise that couples who have lived together before marriage have a higher, not lower, rate of divorce than those who have not.

Feminism against Marriage

Even in the absence of the love-poisoning doctrines of radical feminism, the otherwise welcome changes in women's education and employment have also been problematic for courtship. True, better educated women can, other things being equal, be more interesting and engaging partners for better educated men; and the possibility of genuine friendship between husband and wife — one that could survive the end of the child-rearing years — is, at least in principle, much more likely now that women have equal access to higher education. But everything depends on the spirit and the purpose of such education, and whether it makes and keeps a high place for private life.

Most young people in our better colleges today do not esteem the choice for marriage as equal to the choice for career, not for themselves, not for anyone. Students reading *The Tempest,* for example, are almost universally appalled that Miranda would fall in love at first sight with Ferdinand, thus sealing her fate and precluding "making something of herself" — say, by going to graduate school. Even her prospects as future Queen of Naples lack all appeal, presumably because they depend on her husband and on marriage. At least officially, virtually no young woman will admit to dreaming of meeting her prince; better a position, a salary, and a room of her own.

The problem is not woman's desire for meaningful work. It is rather the ordering of one's loves. Many women have managed to combine work and family; the difficulty is finally not work but careers, or, rather, careerism. Careerism, now an equal opportunity affliction, is surely no friend to love or marriage; and the careerist character of higher education is greater than ever. Women are under special pressures to prove they can be as dedicated to their work as men. Likewise, in the work place, they must do man's work like a man, and for man's pay and perquisites. Consequently, they are compelled to regard private life, and especially marriage, homemaking, and family, as lesser goods, to be pursued only by those lesser women who can aspire no higher than "baking cookies."

Not Ready for Adulthood

Couples today face subtler yet more profound impediments to wooing and marriage: deep uncertainty about what marriage is and means, and what purpose it serves. In previous generations, people chose to marry, but they were not compelled also to choose what marriage meant. Is it a sacrament, a covenant, or a contract based on calculation of mutual advantage? Is it properly founded on eros, friendship, or economic advantage? Is marriage a vehicle for personal fulfillment and private happiness, a vocation of mutual service, or a task to love the one whom it has been given me to love? Are marital vows still to be regarded as binding promises that both are duty-bound to keep or, rather, as quaint expressions of current hopes and predictions that, should they be mistaken, can easily be nullified?

This leads to what is probably the deepest and most intractable obstacle to courtship and marriage: a set of cultural attitudes and sensibilities that obscure and even deny the fundamental difference between youth and adulthood. Marriage, especially when seen as the institution designed to provide for the next generation, is most definitely the business of adults, by which I mean people who are serious about life, people who aspire to go outward and forward to embrace and to assume responsibility for the future. To be sure, most college graduates do go out, find jobs, and become self-supporting (though, astonishingly, a great many do return to live at home). But, though out of the nest, they don't have a course to fly. They do not experience their lives as a trajectory, with an inner meaning partly given by the life cycle itself. The carefreeness and independence of youth they do not see as a stage on the way to maturity, in which they then take responsibility for the world and especially, as parents, for the new lives that will replace them. The necessities of aging and mortality are out of sight; few feel the call to serve a higher goal or some transcendent purpose.

The view of life as play has often characterized the young. But, remarkably, today this is not something regrettable, to be outgrown as soon as possible; for their narcissistic absorption in themselves and in immediate pleasures and present experiences, the young are not condemned but are even envied by many of their elders. Parents and children wear the same cool clothes, speak the same lingo, listen to the same music. Youth, not adulthood, is the cultural ideal, at least as celebrated in the popular culture.

Deeper Cultural Causes

So this is our situation. But just because it is novel and of recent origin does not mean that it is reversible or even that it was avoidable. Indeed, virtually all of the social changes we have so recently experienced are the bittersweet fruits of the success of our modern democratic, liberal, enlightened society — celebrating equality, freedom, and universal secularized education, and featuring prosperity, mobility, and astonishing progress in science and technology. Even brief reflection shows how the dominant features of the American way of life are finally inhospitable to the stability of marriage and family life and to the mores that lead people self-consciously to marry.

Tocqueville already observed the unsettling implications of American individualism, each person seeking only in himself for the reasons for things. The celebration of equality gradually undermines the authority of religion, tradition, and custom, and, within families, of husbands over wives and fathers over sons. A nation dedicated to safeguarding individual rights to liberty and the privately defined pursuit of happiness is, willy-nilly, preparing the way for the "liberation" of women; in the absence of powerful nonliberal cultural forces, such as traditional biblical religion, that defend sex-linked social roles, androgyny in education and employment is the most likely outcome. Further, our liberal approach to important moral issues in terms of the rights of individuals — e.g., contraception as part of a right to privacy, or abortion as belonging to a woman's right over her own body, or procreation as governed by a right to reproduce — flies in the face of the necessarily social character of sexuality and marriage. The courtship and marriage of people who see themselves as self-sufficient, rights-bearing individuals will be decisively different from the courtship and marriage of people who understand themselves as, say, unavoidably incomplete and dependent children of the Lord who have been enjoined to be fruitful and multiply.

The Natural Obstacle

Not all the obstacles to courtship and marriage are cultural. At bottom, there is also the deeply ingrained, natural waywardness and unruliness of the human male. Sociobiologists were not the first to discover that males have a penchant for promiscuity and polygyny — this was well known to biblical religion. Men are also naturally more restless and ambitious than women; lacking woman's powerful and immediate link to life's generative answer to mortality, men flee from the fear of death into heroic deed, great quests, or sheer distraction after distraction. One can make a good case that biblical religion is, not least, an attempt to domesticate male sexuality and male erotic longings, and to put them in the service of transmitting a righteous and holy way of life through countless generations.

For as long as American society kept strong its uneasy union between modern liberal political principles and Judeo-Christian moral and social beliefs, marriage and the family could be sustained and could even prosper. But the gender-neutral individualism of our political teaching has, it seems, at last won the day, and the result has been male "liberation" — from domestication, from civility, from responsible self-command. Contemporary liberals and conservatives alike are trying to figure out how to get men "to commit" to marriage, or to keep their marital vows, or to stay home with the children, but their own androgynous view of humankind prevents them from seeing how hard it has always been to make a monogamous husband and devoted father out of the human male.

Why It Matters

Given the enormous new social impediments to courtship and marriage, and given also that they are firmly and deeply rooted in the cultural soil of modernity, not to say human nature itself, one might simply decide to declare the cause lost. In fact, many people would be only too glad to do so, for they condemn the old ways as repressive, inegalitarian, sexist, patriarchal, boring, artificial, and unnecessary. Some urge us to go with the flow; others hopefully believe that new modes and orders will emerge, well-suited to our new conditions of liberation and equality. Just as new cultural meanings are today being "constructed" for sexuality and gender, so too new cultural definitions can be invented for "marriage," "paternity and maternity," and "family." Nothing truly important, so the argument goes, will be lost.

This view is simply mistaken. Things of great importance have already been lost and no one should be surprised. For the belief in the dispensability of courtship rests on serious errors about the meaning of sex, the nature of marriage, and the character of a fully human life.

Sexual desire, in human beings as in animals, points to an end that is partly hidden from, and finally at odds with, the self-serving individual: sexuality as such means perishability and serves replication. The salmon swimming upstream to spawn and die tell the universal story: sex is bound up with death, to which it holds a partial answer in procreation. This truth the salmon and the other animals practice blindly; only the human being can understand what it means. According to the story of the Garden of Eden, our humanization is in fact coincident with the recognition of our sexual nakedness and all that it implies: shame at our needy incompleteness, unruly self-division, and finitude; awe before the eternal; hope in the self-transcending possibilities of children and a relationship to the divine.[3] For a human being to treat sex as a desire like hunger — not to mention as sport — is then to live a deception.

Thus how shallow an understanding of sexuality is embodied in our current clamoring for "safe sex." Sex is by its nature unsafe. All interpersonal relations are necessarily risky, and serious ones especially so. And to give oneself to another, body and soul, is hardly playing it safe. Sexuality is at its core profoundly "unsafe," and it is only thanks to contraception that we are encouraged to forget its inherent "dangers."

Procreation remains at the core of a proper understanding of marriage. Mutual pleasure and mutual service between husband and wife are, of course, part of the story. So too are mutual admiration and esteem, especially where the partners are deserving. A friendship of shared pursuits and pastimes enhances any marriage, all the more so when the joint activities exercise deeper human capacities. But it is precisely the common project of procreation that holds together what sexual differentiation sometimes threatens to drive apart. Through children, a good common to both husband and wife, male and female achieve some genuine unification (beyond the mere sexual "union" that fails to truly unite): the two become one through sharing generous (not needy) love for this third being as good. It is as the supreme institution devoted to this renewal of human possibility that marriage finds its deepest meaning and highest function.

3. See my "Man and Woman: An Old Story," *First Things*, November 1991.

Marriage and procreation are, therefore, at the heart of a serious and flourishing human life, if not for everyone at least for the vast majority. Most of us know from our own experience that life becomes truly serious when we become responsible for the lives of others in the world when we have said "I do" to one another. It is fatherhood and motherhood that teach most of us what it took to bring us into our own adulthood. And it is the desire to give not only life but a good way of life to our children that opens us toward a serious concern for the true, the good, and even the holy. Parental love of children leads once wayward sheep back into the fold of church and synagogue. In the best case, it can even be the beginning of the sanctification of life — yes, even in modern times.

The earlier forms of courtship, leading men and women to the altar, understood these deeper truths about human sexuality, marriage, and the higher possibilities for human life. Courtship provided rituals of growing up, for making clear the meaning of one's own human sexual nature, and for entering into the ceremonial and customary world of ritual and sanctification. Courtship disciplined sexual desire and romantic attraction, provided opportunities for mutual learning about one another's character, fostered salutary illusions that inspired admiration and devotion, and, by locating wooer and wooed in their familial settings, taught the inter-generational meaning of erotic activity. It pointed the way to the answers to life's biggest questions: Where are you going? Who is going with you? How — in what manner — are you both going to go?

The practices of today's men and women do not accomplish these purposes, and they and their marriages, when they get around to them, are weaker as a result. There may be no going back to the earlier forms of courtship, but no one should be rejoicing over this fact. Anyone serious about "designing" new cultural forms to replace those now defunct must bear the burden of finding some alternative means of serving all these necessary goals.

Is the situation hopeless? One would like to be able to offer more encouraging news than the great popularity — and not only among those fifty or older — of the recent Jane Austen movies, *Sense and Sensibility, Persuasion,* and *Emma,* and on public television the splendid BBC version of *Pride and Prejudice.* But, though at best a small ray of hope, the renewed interest in Jane Austen reflects, I believe, a dissatisfaction with the unromantic and amarital present and a wish, on the part of many twenty- and thirty-somethings, that they too might find their equivalent of Elizabeth Bennet or Mr. Darcy (even without his Pemberly). The return of successful professional matchmaking services — I do not mean the innumerable "self-matching" services that fill pages of "personal" ads in our newspapers and magazines — is a further bit of good news. So too is the revival of explicit courtship practices among certain religious groups; young men are told by young women that they need their father's permission to come courting, and marriage alone is clearly the name of the game. Various groups, including David Blankenhorn's Institute for American Values, have put marriage — and not only divorce — in the national spotlight. And — if I may grasp at straws — one can even take a small bit of comfort from those who steadfastly refuse to marry, insofar as they do so because they recognize that marriage is too serious, too demanding, too audacious an adventure for their immature, irresponsible, and cowardly selves.

Frail reeds indeed — probably not enough to save even a couple of courting water bugs. Real reform in the direction of sanity would require a restoration of cultural gravity about sex, marriage, and the life cycle. The restigmatization of illegitimacy and promiscuity would help. A reversal of recent anti-natalist prejudices, implicit in the practice of abortion, and a correction of current anti-generative sex education, would also help, as would the revalorization of marriage as a personal, as well as a cultural, ideal. Parents of pubescent children could contribute to a truly humanizing sex education by elevating their erotic imagination, through exposure to an older and more edifying literature. Parents of college-bound young people, especially those with strong religious and family values, could direct their children to religiously affiliated colleges that attract like-minded people.

Even in deracinated and cosmopolitan universities like my own, faculty could legitimate the importance of courtship and marriage by offering courses on the subject, aimed at making the students more thoughtful about their own life-shaping choices. Even better, they could teach without ideological or methodological preoccupations the world's great literature, elevating the longings and refining the sensibilities of their students and furnishing their souls with numerous examples of lives seriously led and loves faithfully followed. Religious institutions could provide earlier and better instruction for adolescents on the meaning of sex and marriage, as well as suitable opportunities for coreligionists to mix and, God willing, match. Absent newly discovered congregational and communal support, individual parents will generally be helpless before the onslaught of the popular culture.

As Tocqueville rightly noted, it is women who are the teachers of mores; it is largely through the purity of her morals, self-regulated, that woman wields her influence, both before and after marriage. Men, as Rousseau put it, will always do what is pleasing to women, but only if women suitably control and channel their own considerable sexual power. Is there perhaps some nascent young feminist out there who would like to make her name great and who will seize the golden opportunity for advancing the truest interest of women (and men and children) by raising (again) the radical banner, "Not until you marry me"? And, while I'm dreaming, why not also, "Not without my parents' blessings"?

Sexual Ethics

JOE McILHANEY

Alex Comfort, author of *The Joy of Sex — A Gourmet Guide to Lovemaking*, died in March of 2000. In his obituary, the *Wall Street Journal* noted that his book had been an international sensation, selling twelve million copies, and pointed out that rather than incorporating notions of propriety into his discussion of sexual mechanics he "blasted away all these antique conventions." His book helped shape the new American sexual ethic that began in the 1960s, the ethic of "radical personal autonomy." This new ethic provided license for the change in accepted sexual practice in America, change that has become known as the sexual revolution.

The Sexual Revolution of the 1960s

The roots of the "sexual revolution" that began in the 1960s date back to the early twentieth century. Two women of that era were, without doubt, among the individuals most influential in initiating this cataclysmic social change. Margaret Sanger, in addition to founding the first birth control clinic in America, wrote articles about eugenics such as one entitled "Birth Control: To Create a Race of Thoroughbreds." Sanger, an avowed bisexual, wrote, "The marriage bed is the most degenerating influence in the social order." She founded the American Birth Control League, the precursor of Planned Parenthood, in 1922.

Margaret Mead contributed to the fermenting ideas of the 1920s with the

1928 publication of *Coming of Age in Samoa.* This book, which received wide public acceptance, was published as scientific proof that unrestrained sex is the healthiest sex. Martin Orans and other scholarly anthropologists discredited Mead, and showed that a twenty-three-year-old graduate student who spent a total of nine months in Samoa and had a very poor grasp of the language published findings that were, at best, naïve, and, at worst, dishonest. These criticisms of her work were not widely known of until after her death and have never affected her continued popularity.

Mead was at the peak of her acclaim in the 1950s and Sanger died in 1966. At the same time, two monumental events occurred. The first of these was the advent of television. Prior to television the family could screen the child from the world, selecting what it deemed worthy of exposure to the child. As children watched more and more television, the family's ability to filter information diminished. The second event was the FDA's approval of the first birth control pill in 1960. Oral contraceptives have many health benefits and are prescribed by many physicians, but the availability of "the pill" moved society in the direction of Mead's ideal ("unrestrained sexuality") and Sanger's feminist freedom. Viewed retrospectively, it is clear that a number of uncoordinated energy forces converged and became "laser focused" in the early 1960s, setting fire to new philosophies that had been smoldering for many years and giving birth to the sexual ethic.

The Sexual Ethic of the Sexual Revolution

The new sexual ethic — born in the 1960s and continuing even today — is one of unrestrained personal autonomy. This ethic of radical personal autonomy tore ferociously and successfully through the fabric of the prevailing American sexual ethic of personal restraint for individual and societal good. Individuals such as Comfort, Sanger, and Mead, as well as many modern authorities, seem unable to appreciate what profound protection the traditional sexual ethic had provided society, particularly its younger women. Though society has not yet experienced the state of total sexual anarchy which radical sexual autonomy, when completely accepted, is destined to produce, the societal shift that has occurred is substantial. The change has been both sufficiently dramatic and has existed for a long enough period to enable society to measure and report some of the most shocking and disheartening results. This sexual ethic has given root to the following suppositions:

- People are not meant to be monogamous; therefore, it is not healthy for an individual to limit sexual activity to only one person for life.

- Young people should develop their own values.
- Children are sexual beings and will be hurt if restrained from sexual gratification. If a young person is psychosocially mature, it is appropriate for him or her to engage in sexual activity.
- Sex is a private matter between consenting individuals. Whatever they choose to do is acceptable behavior.
- If an individual is not going to be monogamous for life he or she should be "responsible." "Responsible" in this context means using available means to reduce the risks of sexually transmitted disease or unintended pregnancy. Therefore, this implies, it must be the female who bears the responsibility of protecting herself from pregnancy and it must be the HIV negative person who must protect him/herself from an HIV infected person. If someone gets hurt — physically or emotionally — as the result of "consensual sex," it is the victim's own fault.
- Sex is a recreational activity, and need not be linked to intimacy or even warmth, let alone procreation.

Change in Sexual Practices during the Latter Twentieth Century

The clearest description of changing sexual practices during the twentieth century comes from the report *Sex in America — A Definitive Survey* by the National Opinion Research Center at the University of Chicago. Based on data from the National Health and Social Life Survey (NHSLS), this report is the most comprehensive study done of sexual behavior in America. Included in the report are comparisons of the sexual histories collected from older people with those collected from younger people. The report describes the first sexual relationship of women born from 1933 to 1942 by saying, "practically none of the women in that age group first lived with a sex partner — they almost all married when they entered their first live-in partnership." In comparing these older women to women born from 1963 to 1974, the researchers found both similarities and differences. "[T]he average age at which people first move in with a partner — either by marrying or living together — has remained nearly constant, around age 22 for men and 20 for women. The difference is that now that first union is increasingly likely to be a cohabitation." Only 35.3 percent of these younger women experienced their first partnerships within marriages. This striking decrease — from almost 100 percent to only 35.3 percent — graphically illustrates a monumental result of the change in America's sexual ethic.

This study also reports the number of sexual partners in different age groups. "The oldest people in our study, those aged 55-59, were most likely to have had just one sexual partner in their life-times — 40 percent said they had only one. This reflects the earlier age of marriage in previous generations and the low rate of divorce among these older couples. Many of the men were married by age 22 and the women by age 20." But, the researchers continue, "With the increase in cohabitation, people are marrying later, on average. The longer they wait, however, the more likely they are to live with a sexual partner in the meantime. Since many couples who live together break up within a short time and seek a new partner, the result has been an increase in the average number of partners that people have before they marry."[1]

The Contrast of Sexual Health Associated with the Two Sexual Paradigms

The predominant sexual ethic prior to 1960 resulted in most individuals avoiding sexual intercourse until marriage, practicing sexual fidelity in marriage, and divorcing infrequently. As a result, rates of sexually transmitted disease and nonmarital pregnancy were quite low.

Statistics of STDs and Nonmarital Pregnancy Prior to the Sexual Revolution

Sexually Transmitted Diseases

- Only two common diseases were found, syphilis and gonorrhea, and both were curable with penicillin.
- HIV had not yet appeared, and genital herpes and human papillomavirus (HPV) were yet to be recognized as substantial risks of sexual activity.

Nonmarital Pregnancy

- From 1950 to 1954, only 7.9 percent of first births in fifteen to twenty-nine-year-old women took place out of wedlock, and only 9.3 percent were conceived prior to marriage but born within marriage.
- The proportion of first births taking place out of wedlock during this

1. R. T. Michael, J. H. Gagnon, E. O. Laumann, and G. Kolat, *Sex in America* (Boston: Little, Brown, and Company, 1994).

time period was 5 percent among white women and 32.6 percent among black women.[2]

Statistics of STDs since the Sexual Revolution

The harmful impact of the new sexual ethic of personal autonomy upon American society has been enormous. It has impacted rates of sexually transmitted disease, rates of nonmarital pregnancy, and rates of sexual abuse. It has impacted the family, the health system, the welfare system, the penal system, and the economy. Here is some of the data:

Sexually Transmitted Diseases

- Human Papillomavirus — Approximately 60 percent of sexually active female students at Rutgers University were found to be infected with human papillomavirus (HPV) at some time during a three-year study.[3] HPV causes more than 93 percent of all cervical dysplasia (precancer) and cervical cancer in women.[4] This cancer is causing the deaths of approximately five thousand American women yearly,[5] about the same number of women who die of AIDS annually in America. In all, approximately thirteen thousand women acquire cervical cancer each year. This disease typically requires a hysterectomy or radiation therapy,[6] procedures that eliminate the possibility of future childbearing. Many women who develop cervical intraepithelial neoplasia (CIN or precancer) require surgery for diagnosis and/or treatment. Since HPV does not usually confer immunity, some of these women develop CIN again and may require additional cervical surgery. The more surgery a woman has done on her cervix the more likely she is to experience in-

2. A. Bachu, *Trends in Premarital Childbearing: 1930-1994* (Washington, D.C.: U.S. Census Bureau, Current Population Reports, 1999), pp. 23-197.

3. G. Y. F. Ho, R. Bierman, L. Beardsley, C. J. Chang, and R. D. Burk, "Natural History of Cervicovaginal Papillomavirus Infection in Young Women," *New England Journal of Medicine* 338 (1998): 739-44.

4. F. X. Bosch, N. M. Manos, et al., for the International Biological Study on Cervical Cancer (IBSCC) Study Group, "Prevalence of Human Papillomavirus in Cervical Cancer: A Worldwide Perspective," *Journal of the National Cancer Institute* 87 (1995): 796-802.

5. American Cancer Society, *2000 Facts and Figures:* Selected Cancers. Available at www.cancer.org/statistics/cff2000selectedcancers. Accessed 6 April 2000.

6. American Cancer Society, *2000 Facts.*

fertility or, if she does become pregnant, to experience premature delivery.

- Genital Herpes — A recent study showed that the prevalence of genital herpes in white teens has quintupled in the past twenty years.[7] The same major study showed that approximately 46 percent of all African-Americans twelve years old or older show evidence of this infection.[8] Approximately one in five Americans age twelve or over is herpes infected.[9] Also, individuals with active herpes lesions are at increased risk of HIV.[10] Studies now show that many individuals become infected with genital herpes from a sexual partner who does not have a detectable herpes sore at the time of infection.[11]
- Chlamydia Genital Infection — Chlamydia genital infection is the most commonly reported infectious disease in the United States. It infects more individuals than other commonly recognized diseases such as measles, mumps, or gonorrhea. Chlamydia is important because it is such a common disease. Approximately 6-10 percent of sexually active adolescents are infected with chlamydia.[12] In fact, as many as 85 percent of females who are infected have no symptoms and cannot ascertain whether they are infected without testing.[13] The discomfort, expense, and inconvenience of this procedure discourage many young, single, sexually active females from going for testing. Untreated, chlamydia can cause pelvic inflammatory disease (PID), which can result in both tubal ectopic pregnancy and infertility. Tubal infertility (caused by either gonorrhea or chlamydia) accounts for approximately 27 percent of the infertility in American women who require in-vitro fertilization to achieve pregnancy.[14]

7. D. T. Fleming, G. M. McQuillan, R. E. Johnson, et al., "Herpes Simplex Virus Type 2 in the United States, 1976-1994," *New England Journal of Medicine* 337 (1997): 1105-11.

8. Fleming, "Herpes simplex."

9. Fleming, "Herpes simplex."

10. C. Y. Chen, R. C. Ballard, C. M. Beck-Sague, et al., "Human Immunodeficiency Virus Infection and Genital Ulcer Disease in South Africa: The Herpetic Connection," *Sex Transm Dis* 27 (2000): 21-29.

11. A. Wald, J. Zeh, S. Selke, et al., "Reactivation of Genital Herpes Simplex Virus Type 2 Infection in Asymptomatic Seropositive Persons," *New England Journal of Medicine* 342 (2000): 844-50.

12. Centers for Disease Control and Prevention, *HIV/AIDS Surveillance Report* 11 (1999): 1-43; C. A. Gaydos, M. R. Howell, B. Pare, et al., "Chlamydia Trachomatis Infections in Female Military Recruits," *New England Journal of Medicine* 339 (1998): 739-44.

13. T. R. Eng, W. T. Butler, Institute of Medicine, eds., *The Hidden Epidemic: Confronting Sexually Transmitted Disease* (Washington, D.C.: National Academy Press, 1997).

14. Centers for Disease Control, *HIV/AIDS Surveillance Report.*

- HIV/AIDS — HIV infection will almost always result in AIDS, and AIDS is fatal unless death from some other cause intervenes. Though, in the United States, this infection is less common than other sexually transmitted diseases, it is still an important disease because it has no known cure. To date, more than 400,000 Americans have died of AIDS,[15] which is approximately the same as the total of all Americans who died in World War II. It is estimated that another 560,000 individuals in this country are presently HIV infected.[16]

Financial Cost of the Sexual Revolution

The financial cost of these problems to individuals and to the healthcare system is great. A study by the Institute of Medicine published as a report titled "The Hidden Epidemic" estimates that the total cost of STDs excluding HIV/AIDS is $12 billion per year. When HIV/AIDS is included, the cost increases to $17 billion.[17] Furthermore, the direct annual financial cost of adolescent pregnancies was estimated in a report by the Robin Hood Foundation entitled "Kids Having Kids" to be $6 billion. They estimate total annual costs to be $29 billion.[18]

The Situation Today: Further Effects of the Sexual Revolution

Adolescent Pregnancy

Approximately 900,000 American teenagers become pregnant each year.[19] It is estimated that only 20 percent of these teens are married,[20] and approximately one-third of these pregnancies end in abortion.[21] These pregnancies lead to enormously costly problems, not only for the mothers and fathers involved, but also for the children born and for society itself:

15. Centers for Disease Control, *HIV/AIDS Surveillance Report.*

16. American Social Health Association, *Sexually Transmitted Diseases in America: How Many Cases and at What Cost?* (Menlo Park, Calif.: Kaiser Family Foundation, 1998).

17. Eng, *Hidden Epidemic.*

18. R. A. Maynard, ed., *Kids Having Kids: A Robin Hood Foundation Special Report on the Cost of Adolescent Childbearing* (New York: Robin Hood Foundation, 1996).

19. Alan Guttmacher Institute, *Facts in Brief: Teen Sex and Pregnancy,* available at www.agi-usa.org/pubs/fb teen sex. Accessed April 6, 2000.

20. Alan Guttmacher Institute, *Facts in Brief.*

21. Alan Guttmacher Institute, *Facts in Brief.*

- Seven out of ten adolescent mothers drop out of high school.
- The long-term wage earning power of adolescent fathers is substantially reduced.
- The teenage sons of adolescent mothers are 2.7 times more likely to spend time in prison than are the sons of mothers who delay childbearing until their early 20s.
- The teenage daughters of adolescent mothers are 50 percent more likely to bear children out of wedlock.[22]

Sexual Coercion

Sexual coercion is an often overlooked topic in discussions of sexual ethics, but it is extremely important that this issue be considered. Some recent surveys have demonstrated that many male teens believe that by buying a meal for a girl or paying for her participation in other recreational activities, they are entitled to sexual favors, even if forced. Studies show that many young female teens feel the same way. This unfortunate understanding of the sexual relationship between male and female may partially explain why the Centers for Disease Control found in its Youth Risk Behavior Survey of college students that 20 percent of college females have been forced to engage in sexual intercourse against their will.[23]

Men older than twenty father most teen pregnancies.[24] While most of these pregnancies result from sex between men who are twenty or over and females who are eighteen- or nineteen-year-olds, the study also reveals the chilling finding that the younger a pregnant girl is, the greater the age difference is likely to be. The average age difference between junior high students who give birth and the fathers of their babies is over six years.[25] Though these young women commonly state that their sexual activity was consensual, one might ask if such a sexual relationship, involving an older and probably more sexually experienced male and a much younger and probably less experienced female, can be truly consensual.

In a study of adolescents at a family planning clinic conducted by a researcher at Emory University, the most common desire among sexually active

22. Maynard, *Kids Having Kids.*

23. Centers for Disease Control and Prevention, American Society for Reproductive Medicine, *1997 Assisted Reproductive Technology Success Rates; National Summary and Fertility Clinic Reports* (U.S. Department of Health and Human Services, 1999), p. 41.

24. M. Males, K. S. Chew, "The Ages of Fathers in California Adolescent Births, 1993," *American Journal of Public Health* 86 (1996): 565-68.

25. Males and Chew, "The Ages of Fathers."

youth was for information on "how to say no without hurting the other person's feelings."[26] Though the sexual activity these young women were engaged in was not overtly coercive, at a deeper level it may have been. A recent *Talk Magazine* article titled "The Sex Lives of Your Children" reports a conversation with a teenager. "'Roberta,' (15), a public school student in New York: 'I was in seventh grade and a 34D. . . . I looked like a freak. I got teased a lot. Then these guys in ninth grade kind of adopted me; they were African-American and they loved my boobs. I have sex with them but a lot of the time I start crying. Inside (me) there's sadness because I don't love them. I'm, like, sick of it. But I can't stop. I mean, they are so nice . . . they saved my life. Otherwise I might have ended up being a ho.'"

Sexual Abuse

Sexual abuse is very common among young people in the United States. Twenty percent of college women and 4 percent of college men have at some time been forced to have sexual intercourse.[27] Sexual abuse has been linked to a number of adverse outcomes, affecting both individuals' attitudes and their actions. Studies have shown, for example, that sexual abuse and rape have vast psychological impacts. They are associated with suicide,[28] depression,[29] smoking,[30] and perhaps eating disorders.[31]

Adolescents who have been raped or sexually abused are also more likely to have permissive attitudes toward adolescent sexual activity, become sexually active at a young age, have multiple sexual partners, and become pregnant.[32]

26. M. Howard, "Delaying the Start of Intercourse among Adolescents," *Adolescent Medicine: State of the Art Reviews* 3 (Philadelphia: Hanley and Belfus, 1992): 181-93.

27. Centers for Disease Control, *1997 Assisted Reproductive Technology.*

28. D. M. Fergusson, L. J. Woodward, and L. J. Horwood, "Risk Factors and Life Processes Associated with the Onset of Suicidal Behaviour during Adolescence and Early Adulthood," *Psychol Med* 30 (2000): 23-39.

29. B. C. Miller, B. H. Monson, and M. C. Norton, "The Effects of Forced Sexual Intercourse on White Female Adolescents," *Child Abuse Neglect* 19 (1995): 1289-1301.

30. R. F. Anda, J. B. Croft, V. J. Felitti, et al., "Adverse Childhood Experiences and Smoking during Adolescence and Adulthood," *Journal of the American Medical Association* 282 (1999): 1652-58.

31. L. Brown, J. Russell, C. Thornton, and S. Dunn, "Experiences of Physical and Sexual Abuse in Australian General Practice Attenders and an Eating Disordered Population," *Aust N Z J Psychiatry* 31 (1997): 398-404.

32. B. C. Miler, *Families Matter: A Research Synthesis of Family Influences on Adolescent Pregnancy* (Washington, D.C.: The National Campaign to Prevent Teen Pregnancy, 1998).

Marriage and Family

The family is the most important societal unit for the transfer of societal traditions, and it must be maintained and strengthened so it can perform its important work of transmitting healthy values. Studies clearly show that children do better by almost every measure if a mother and father raise them. The following are statistics from only a few of the many studies indicating that an erosion of the American family has resulted from today's sexual ethics.

- Approximately two-thirds of first unions of both men and women who were born between 1963 and 1974 were cohabitation rather than marriage. By contrast, very few (approximately one in ten) of those born between 1933 and 1942 cohabited prior to their first marriage.[33]
- Couples who cohabit are less likely to stay together than couples who are married.[34]
- Couples who cohabit are more likely to divorce if they do marry after a period of cohabitation.[35]
- From 1990 to 1994, 40.5 percent of first births in women aged fifteen to twenty-nine occurred out of wedlock, and another 12.3 percent were conceived prior to marriage, but born after marriage.[36]
- From 1990 to 1994, among black women fifteen to twenty-nine years of age, 76.9 percent of first births occurred out of wedlock and an additional 8.7 percent were conceived prior to marriage but born within marriage. Therefore, only 14.4 percent were conceived within marriage. Among whites, 32.4 percent were born out of wedlock and an additional 12.9 percent were conceived out of wedlock but born within marriage.[37]
- Thirty-three percent of children are born out of wedlock.[38]
- According to the National Fatherhood Initiative, half of all children will spend a portion of their childhood apart from their fathers.

33. R. T. Michael, J. H. Gagnon, E. O. Laumann, and G. Kolat, *Sex in America.*

34. David Popenoe and Barbara Dafoe Whitehead, *Should We Live Together? What Young Adults Need to Know About Cohabitation Before Marriage: A Comprehensive Review of Recent Research* (New Brunswick, N.J.: Rutgers, The State University of New Jersey, National Marriage Project, 1999).

35. Popenoe and Whitehead, *Should We Live Together?*

36. Bachu, *Trends.*

37. Bachu, *Trends.*

38. J. A. Martin, B. L. Smith, T. J. Mathews, and S. J. Ventura, "Births and deaths: Preliminary data from 1998," *National Vital Statistics Reports* 47 (Hyattsville, Md.: National Center for Health Statistics, 1999).

JOE McILHANEY

The Medical Institute for Sexual Health and Its Role in the Birth of a Modern Healthy Sexual Ethic

In the mid 1980s, I became concerned about the increasing number of single people infected with STDs and the increasing number of nonmarital pregnancies. I began gathering information about these problems and attempts to solve them, and found that the most dominant efforts followed the "safer-sex" model. The message of these programs is that "abstinence is appropriate, but most individuals will have sexual intercourse while they are still single. Because this is true, all single people need to be constantly ready to protect themselves with condoms and other contraceptives." As I studied this issue, I found that despite these programs, the problems had grown much worse. STDs and nonmarital pregnancies had become more common. Because these problems are, at one level, medical issues, it seemed compelling that a new medical and educational organization be established. The purpose of this organization would be to study these issues as objectively as possible and then, with the guidance of this research, confront the problems with initiatives that promised the best chance of success. The Medical Institute for Sexual Health was founded in 1992. A number of outstanding physicians and educators became members of the National Advisory Board of the organization.

A guiding principle for the organization has been a commitment to pursue solutions until dramatic reductions in STD and nonmarital pregnancy rates are achieved. Those involved with The Medical Institute have found that for individuals to make the right decisions about the healthiest use of their sexuality, they need to be guided by a strong and salubrious societal sexual ethic.

Those who advocate the message that sexual abstinence and sexual intercourse with contraceptive use are equally acceptable choices appear to ignore the fact that the problems of STD and nonmarital pregnancy demand a solution founded on a new sexual ethic. One of the primary goals of The Medical Institute is to learn from the mistakes of the past. The organization desires to show those involved in these issues that the change in America's sexual ethic is responsible for problems of STDs and nonmarital pregnancy, and that only the acceptance of a new and healthier sexual ethic will solve these problems.

The New Sexual Ethic

The Medical Institute does not advocate a return to the world of the 1950s. The world today is a much different place and, in many ways, much better. There is, for example, much more openness and honesty about sexual facts and issues. Many of the statements made in this paper would not have been appropriate prior to 1960. We do, however, advocate adoption of some of the timeless ethical principles that were commonly held in the 1950s and before. This new paradigm requires that children be taught to exhibit good character — the capacity to distinguish between right and wrong. The fundamental ethic we advocate, therefore, is "accept personal limitations for personal and societal good." We believe the adoption of this ethic in the sexual realm will support healthy choices by individuals and society.

Presuppositions of the Sexual Ethic of "Personal Limitations for Personal and Societal Good"

Sexual activity certainly should be practiced in private, but it is not exclusively a private matter. We have seen how the sexual decisions of individuals affect society as a whole. This impact includes a financial cost, epidemics of disease, and unhealthy influence on others including children. When we are considering our own personal sexual choices, therefore, we must consider how those choices will impact not only ourselves, but also the world we live in. The new sexual ethic we are advocating gives individuals and society the best opportunity for that impact to be for good. It will lead to recognition of the following standards.

For Individuals

- Marriage is the only safe and appropriate environment for sexual activity — an individual should have sex, therefore, only when married. Society will assist those who are married in maintaining their marriages.
- Sexual faithfulness in marriage will be maintained.
- If sexual activity has occurred before marriage, the individual will return to sexual abstinence until married.
- Individuals must have a commitment to sexual integrity. If there is the possibility that a STD has been transmitted, the potentially infected individual will so inform the person who may have been a victim. Every individual will always inform a potential sexual partner of any known or suspected STD or HIV infection before sexual activity.
- Sexual abuse is not permitted. No form of sexual involvement is appropriate other than that between consenting husbands and wives. Therefore, every individual will avoid forcing such contact on another individual, including a marriage partner.
- Statistics show that children born out of wedlock are themselves more likely to experience or cause a nonmarital pregnancy. Therefore, unmar-

ried individuals who become parents will seek the most reasonable and effective means available to enable the child to be raised in an appropriate two-parent home.

- Individuals who are people of faith will be obedient to the teachings of their faith in the area of sexual ethics.
- Pornography is commonly associated with improper and unhealthy sexual behavior. If pornography addiction develops, counseling will be obtained to solve that problem.
- Parents will train all children in their home to follow this ethic.
- Parents will be appropriately open about sexual issues and be able to discuss them with children when wisdom dictates.

For Society

A new sexual ethic for America would result in a number of changes in the public discourse about sexual issues. Sexuality education legislation and funding, public health initiatives, and many other areas of life would be affected. As a result of a new and healthier sexual ethic, America would do the following.

- Teach our youth that good character can and should be developed. Show them that people do not automatically become "good," but that it is a trait that is developed.
- Teach our youth that character is the foundation for making right choices in the future — choices about sex, drugs, alcohol, violence, and other behaviors.
- Teach that the control of most impulses and desires, including those that are sexual, is healthy.
- Support marriage as the only acceptable and healthy relationship for any sexual activity.
- Teach that, except in marriage, sexual activity between an "older person" and a "young person" (as defined by statutory rape legislation) is wrong. Prosecute individuals who violate this.
- Discourage pornography in all its forms and remove it from public display whenever legally possible. Find legal means for controlling Internet pornography and use it to control that problem.
- Support faith communities when they encourage abstinence for single individuals.
- Create welfare and income tax laws that encourage marriage.
- Hold the media accountable for their role in encouraging a healthy sexual ethic throughout society and encourage them to strive to accomplish this.

- Educate parents about the dangers STDs and nonmarital pregnancy pose for their children. They will then be encouraged and supported in efforts to guide their children to sexual abstinence or secondary virginity.
- Refuse to take the fatalistic approach that "teenagers are going to be sexually active no matter what," and instead clearly direct our children toward abstinence not only from sexual activity, but also from other risky behavior.
- Develop and support, with both governmental and private funding sources, new and innovative abstinence programs. Encourage schools to emphasize in all sexuality education that adolescents should abstain from sexual activity until marriage.

Conclusion

The human sexual drive is clearly an integral aspect of our genetic matrix and exists for an important reason. Without sex the human race would die out. The ethical drama is evident; sexual activity is a function in which most married adults should be involved and yet when used inappropriately it can cause harm.

A sexual ethic that is fundamentally flawed can lead an unsuspecting society into this harm. Sexual chaos can result and where sexual chaos reigns, instability in almost every element of society soon follows. Throughout history when cultures have experienced deterioration, that deterioration has often first been preceded by deterioration in the commonly accepted sexual ethic of that society.

The data presented demonstrates to what degree this deterioration has happened in America. The problems are now so severe that we must accept the need for adopting a sexual ethic of personal responsibility, an ethic of rules, one of right and wrong. This ethic encourages, even urges, "personal limits for the good of individuals and society." This ethic is the ideal and will not be adopted by everyone, but it is an appropriate and healthy ethic, one that can lead to cultural renewal in this country and throughout the world. We must strive for it to be accepted as widely as possible.

Sexual ethics affects all of our lives whether we realize it or not. Sexual issues, therefore, are among the most important issues of life for individuals and society to consider. The practical impact of the sexual ethic of both individuals and society has enormous and virtually constant effect for good or for harm. A sexual ethic that is strong, robust, commonly understood, and consistently followed is a vital element upon which a healthy society is built. On that foundation, families can prosper and children can grow with greater opportunities for health, hope, and happiness.

Community Revitalization

STEPHEN GOLDSMITH

Successful cities require effective governance, but government alone cannot create successful cities. Flourishing societies are built on a foundation of healthy families, faith, shared community standards, and active civic involvement — all things that government can neither create nor impose. The long-term health of American society depends upon the strength of the ties that exist between individual citizens and the institutions that instill character and create order.

Government's role in this endeavor is deceptively simple. First, government must do a better job providing the fundamentals of public safety and infrastructure, including streets, sidewalks, and housing. While government has spent millions providing services better provided by churches and community members, it has neglected the few but important services that citizens rely on government to deliver. Failure to demonstrate a firm commitment to core responsibilities such as public safety and infrastructure discourages neighborhood residents from becoming involved in their communities because it sends the message that the government is unwilling to live up to its end of the bargain.

Second, we must abolish welfare policies that erode families and replace them with a new approach that discourages teen pregnancy and encourages responsible fatherhood. Nothing government can do will produce vibrant neigh-

---

This essay was written while Stephen Goldsmith was mayor of Indianapolis, Indiana, a position in which he served from 1992-1999.

borhoods if the number of children born to teenage parents in fatherless homes continues to climb. Government must put an end to policies that discourage two-parent families. It must hold fathers accountable for their children, and send a clear message that teen pregnancy is simply wrong. Public officials can also play a constructive role by supporting families and by reaffirming the virtues that are the foundation of any successful society.

Third, government must acknowledge the vital role that religion and religious organizations play in the life of a community and support the involvement of churches and other religious institutions in their communities. Many people are moved by religious commitment to reach out to struggling individuals and distressed communities. Faith is a stabilizing element in society, and by encouraging reverence and affirming religion public officials can help to strengthen the moral foundations of their communities. Government must also take better advantage of faith-based efforts at assistance that strengthen communities and connect people to the positive influence of churches and other religious institutions.

Finally, government must energize neighborhood-level associations by giving residents of troubled neighborhoods more authority over the way government services are provided. Struggling neighborhoods often lack the active grassroots involvement that can unify communities. Government can accomplish more by promoting the creation of neighborhood associations in troubled areas and listening to and supporting existing groups than it could ever hope to accomplish through big government programs.

These are the critical areas that local governments must address if we are to revitalize America's blighted urban centers. We know that just as government cannot create morality, it cannot cause people to form families, rejoin churches, and participate in community groups. But government can create the environment necessary for these institutions to thrive. This is our challenge over the next thirty years.

Getting the Fundamentals Right

Civil societies are built on a strong foundation of safe streets and a sound infrastructure. Unfortunately, as government attempts to be all things to all people, public officials often lose sight of these basic responsibilities. Across America, rampant crime and crumbling streets and sidewalks plague inner cities, leaving many community members isolated and disempowered. As one Indianapolis neighborhood leader described the problem, "the communities that are dying are the communities that you drive through and see bars on windows and doors — where the people have had to resort to a private solution to a public problem." Absent safe streets and solid sidewalks and sewers, it is unrealistic to expect community members to become involved in public solutions to the problems that afflict their neighborhoods.

Rather than attempting to provide a wide range of services, and often providing them poorly, government must focus on providing a few core services well. An unwavering commitment to these fundamental obligations creates a foothold for neighborhood residents from which they can reach out and become actively involved in working toward creating thriving communities.

Public Safety

Above all, government exists to protect the safety of citizens. As any inner-city resident can attest, however, government consistently fails to provide this critical service in the areas that need it most.

Even as the crime rate exploded over the last thirty years, enforcement diminished and the penalties for criminal conduct steadily declined. For example, the National Center for Policy Analysis estimates that currently only 7 percent of burglaries committed in the United States result in an arrest. Worse, the chance that any given burglary will result in imprisonment is a mere 1.2 percent. With odds like those, it is no wonder that crime proliferates. The real wonder is that crime is not more prevalent than it is.

Before becoming Mayor, I was the prosecutor in Indianapolis, and I learned from first-hand experience what a failure our criminal justice system is, especially with regard to juvenile offenders. In Indiana, a young gang member convicted of his first or second robbery may not be sentenced at all. For his third conviction, he may be sent to Boys School for ninety days. If he is really bad, he may get six months for his third offense, only to be released to prey again on innocent victims.

High rates of criminality send the wrong messages, both encouraging law breaking and repressing the efforts of private citizens to improve their communities. Lack of effective enforcement causes people to lose faith in the criminal justice system and condemns them to being prisoners in their own homes. Under these circumstances, we cannot expect residents to provide a good example of involvement in their communities. In order for our most challenged communities to thrive, government must put an end to years of resignation in the fight against crime and make protecting public safety its number one obligation.

Sidewalks and Sewers

While public officials spend countless taxpayer dollars on big government programs like welfare, few are willing to make the kind of real investments in troubled communities that can help residents to help themselves. Forging sound infrastructure in inner-city neighborhoods can help attract businesses and jobs to areas in which both have been absent for years. More importantly, meaningful and visible investment in troubled communities can restore confidence among neighborhood residents who have long felt abandoned by city government.

One of the biggest challenges I faced when I took office was the city's physical deterioration. The Indianapolis Chamber of Commerce had recently completed a report entitled "Getting Indianapolis Fit for Tomorrow" that identified a $1 billion infrastructure deficit for the city. Seven inner-city neighborhoods had deteriorated particularly badly. Following decades of neglect from City Hall, houses in these neighborhoods were often boarded-up and economic conditions were the worst in the city.

In 1992, we launched the *Building Better Neighborhoods* initiative — a $530 million program to repair and upgrade the city's streets, sewers, sidewalks, and parks, with an emphasis on the seven targeted neighborhoods. Although we reduced the City budget each of the last five years in Indianapolis, we tripled our infrastructure spending under the *Building Better Neighborhoods* program.

Through the program we repaired dilapidated thoroughfares, bridges, and sidewalks for the first time in decades, renovated sewers a century old, and established several new parks. Vacant lots now have thriving businesses or new housing, and local residents are employed in the new construction. Our commitment to strong infrastructure has helped create a vibrancy in these communities that residents had not experienced in fifty years.

Encouraging Families

The family is the fundamental unit of every successful society. But for the past thirty years, government has consistently undermined this bastion of good values. It has taken money away from families through ever-increasing taxes and then perversely used some of the revenues on programs that actively discourage poor Americans from forming families — rewarding teenage and out-of-wedlock pregnancies, discouraging fathers from living with the mothers of their children, and failing to hold those fathers accountable for even the smallest amount of support.

The negative effects of single, teenage parenthood on our society are difficult to overstate, and nothing that government can do will restore civility to our neighborhoods if illegitimacy continues to rise. Government can, however, battle this trend by promoting abstinence among teenage men and women, by ensuring that irresponsible fatherhood yields consequences, and by supporting vulnerable families.

In 1992, federal, state, and local governments spent $305 billion on welfare programs — more than eight times as much as in 1965 in constant dollars.[1] Over the last thirty years, more than $5 trillion has been spent on welfare.[2] Yet this enormous expenditure represents a fraction of the true cost of America's welfare policies. The real tragedy of this system lies in its perverse incentives and the human dysfunction they have fostered.

For example, for twenty years state and federal governments prohibited an intact family from staying together if either spouse sought to collect welfare. This policy, intended to limit assistance to widows and abandoned mothers, in fact rewarded the absence of fathers and aggravated one of the most disastrous trends in modern society: out-of-wedlock births.

From 1960 to 1990 the percentage of babies born outside of marriage in the United States increased from 5.3 percent to 29.5 percent, and today the United States has the highest proportion of fatherless households in the world.[3] The numbers in Indianapolis are even more discouraging. Indianapolis suffers an out-of-wedlock birth rate of 40 percent — well above the national average. Fully a quarter of our children live in a home with no father. And the numbers for teens, whose birth rates increased by more than 40 percent over the last decade, are even more astounding. Eighty-nine percent of Indianapolis teenagers who gave birth last year were not married.[4]

The negative consequences of out-of-wedlock childbearing reach far beyond single mothers and their children. One obvious consequence is the proliferation of juvenile crime. According to social researchers William Galston and Elaine Kamarck, the relationship between crime and family structure is so strong "that controlling for family configuration erases the relationship between race and crime and between low income and crime."[5]

1. U.S. House of Representatives, Committee on Ways and Means, *1993 Green Book: Background Material and Data on Programs Within the Jurisdiction of the Committee on Ways and Means* (Washington, D.C.: U.S. Government Printing Office, 1993), p. 688.

2. Robert Rector, "Combating Family Disintegration, Crime, and Dependence: Welfare Reform and Beyond," *Heritage Foundation Backgrounder* No. 983 (8 April 1994): 6.

3. Alisa Burns, "Mother-Headed Families: An International Perspective and the Case of Australia," Social Policy Report 6, Spring 1992. Cited in Wade F. Horn, *Father Facts* (Lancaster, Penn.: National Fatherhood Initiative, 1996), p. 4.

4. Marion County Department of Health, Vital Statistics, 1996.

5. Horn, *Father Facts 2,* p. 33.

This observation is confirmed by experience, both in Indianapolis and across the country. Nationally, three-quarters of adolescent murderers, nearly two-thirds of all rapists, and 70 percent of all prison and reform-school inmates grew up without fathers in their homes.[6] In Indianapolis, while the overall crime rate has remained stable for the past ten years, the juvenile crime rate has increased dramatically. Juvenile Court Judge James Payne estimates that 75 percent of the delinquents he adjudicates come from homes without fathers.

And it doesn't stop with crime. Children without fathers face a wide range of serious problems, including twice the risk of dropping out of high school and five times the risk of being poor.[7] In 1961, long before he became a United States Senator, Daniel Patrick Moynihan described the effects of single-parenthood on American society in words that were grimly prophetic:

> From the wild Irish slums of the 19th-century Eastern seaboard, to the riot-torn suburbs of Los Angeles, there is one unmistakable lesson in American history: a community that allows a large number of young men to grow up in broken families, dominated by women, never acquiring any stable relationship to male authority, never acquiring any set of rational expectations about the future — that community asks for and gets chaos. Crime, violence, unrest, disorder — most particularly the furious, unrestrained lashing out at the whole social structure — that is not only to be expected, it is very near to inevitable. And it is richly deserved.[8]

Government cannot create two-parent families, but there are things that government can do — and stop doing — that would discourage teen pregnancy and single parenthood and promote responsible fatherhood. In September of 1995, the City of Indianapolis launched a series of initiatives to confront directly and comprehensively the problem of family breakdown. The *Rebuilding Families* program, established with the support and encouragement of Indianapolis's leading religious, nonprofit, and social service organizations, employs a wide range of strategies to reduce single-parenthood and improve the support and economic opportunities available to vulnerable families.

6. Philip Lawler, "The New Counterculture," *Wall Street Journal,* 13 August 1993. Cited in Bill Bennett, *The Index of Leading Cultural Indicators* (New York: Simon and Schuster, 1994), p. 32.

7. Horn, *Father Facts 2,* p. 35.

8. Daniel Patrick Moynihan, *The Negro Family: The Case for National Action* (Washington, D.C.: Office of Planning and Research, U.S. Department of Labor, 1965). Cited in Bill Bennett, *The Index of Leading Cultural Indicators,* p. 53.

Standards and Stigma

Sadly, most public officials accept teenage pregnancy. Too often their efforts to help teen mothers end up encouraging the very behavior that is at the root of the problem. Schools committed to mainstreaming pregnant teens, for example, convey the message that public institutions will go to great lengths to ensure that those who engage in irresponsible behavior will suffer no consequences for their actions. This tacit acceptance, coupled with the permissive attitude toward sex that pervades popular culture, helps create an environment in which teens, and even their adult role models, ridicule the very notion of abstinence.

The *Rebuilding Families* initiative aims to combat this "normalization" of teen pregnancy and to reinforce the understanding that teen pregnancy is wrong. The prevalence of cultural messages condoning premarital sex and strong peer group acceptance of teen parenthood convinced us that no single response would be sufficient to address the problem. We therefore undertook a number of activities designed to shift the balance of the messages our young people receive in favor of abstinence and responsible behavior.

Before deciding on program content, we sought firsthand information, especially the views of teenagers themselves. As we visited high schools and middle schools and talked to students in focus groups about these issues, young people consistently told us they relied heavily on information given to them by their friends. Even preteens expressed feeling overwhelming pressure from their peers to engage in sexual conduct.

This discovery led us to champion the successful peer-mentoring program *A Promise to Keep.* The program, originally developed through a collaboration between St. Vincent Hospitals and Indianapolis's Office of Catholic Education, uses the power of peer pressure to promote abstinence among teenage youth. It operates under the principle that adults other than parents are too far removed from teen culture to compel young people to choose to be chaste. Older, self-confident teens serve as powerful messengers for promoting chastity and compete with teen idols in the media who endorse premarital sex. Similar programs in other cities have helped reduce teen pregnancy by as much as 30 percent,[9] and these successes inspired Indianapolis's Methodist Hospital to implement a secular version in Indianapolis Public Schools, which have an intolerably high teenage pregnancy rate.

We also targeted school policies that failed to discourage teen parenthood. For instance, most public schools have adopted standards for student

9. Marion Howard and Judith Blamey McCabe, "Helping Teenagers Postpone Sexual Involvement," *Family Planning Perspectives* 22 (1990): 24.

athletes requiring them to refrain from drinking or using drugs and to maintain a certain grade point average and attendance record. Conspicuously absent from these requirements is a standard against fathering a child. We called upon school officials to send a clear message that adult behavior nets adult responsibility by precluding teen parents from participating in school athletic activities. School officials, virtually all of whom share the view that they should not set standards about sexual behavior, thus far remain firmly against the policy. The city attempted to bring parental pressure and teacher concern to bear by releasing the number of births by school from information compiled from birth records. Although school administrators have yet to budge, it is our hope that focusing attention on the comparative data will eventually yield a more forceful response.

Finally, we attempted to balance the flood of messages in popular culture that implicitly endorse premarital sexual activity. Local sports figures, in cooperation with the Indiana Pacers, the Marion County Health Department, and USA Group, Inc., produced advertisements encouraging abstinence that ran on local television stations, on video kiosks in malls, and in movie theaters throughout the city.

There is nothing inconsistent with stigmatizing irresponsible behavior while maintaining a firm commitment to helping young women who need support. Research indicates that 31 percent of young women who give birth under the age of seventeen give birth to an additional child within two years of their first.[10] We can reduce the teen pregnancy rate dramatically by targeting prevention efforts at these at-risk young women and by providing them with the support and incentives necessary to keep them in school, while remaining steadfastly and vocally committed to the proposition that their behavior is wrong.

Accountability and Consequences

Single motherhood is a challenge even when fathers are responsible and live up to their child support obligations. Without support payments it is virtually impossible for low-income mothers to raise their children without assistance — usually from taxpayers. One of the few services government can provide that private citizens cannot is enforcement. Unfortunately, in most states virtually nothing happens to a young father who chooses to ignore his child.

Holding fathers accountable for their children improves the financial sit-

10. Debra Kalmuss and Pearila Brickner Namerow, "Subsequent Childbearing Among Teenage Mothers: The Determinants of a Closely Spaced Second Birth," *Family Planning Perspectives* 26 (1994): 149.

uation of mothers and children, encourages fathers to be active in their children's lives, and may even reduce out-of-wedlock births. Research indicates that government can make a significant, positive impact on the behavior of would-be fathers simply by ensuring that they will face the consequences of irresponsible action.

Unfortunately, although federal law requires mothers to cooperate in establishing paternity as a condition of receiving welfare benefits, the degree of enforcement varies widely. Georgia led all states in 1995 with a paternity establishment rate of 91 percent; in contrast, Oklahoma registered a scant 16 percent the same year (up from 3 percent in 1992). Nationally, the average paternity establishment rate in 1995 was 50 percent.[11] Vigorous action begun while the mother is still in the hospital can improve these results. In Ohio, for example, a policy that pays hospitals a mere $5.20 for each birthing mother they assist in establishing paternity yielded an increase of nearly 30 percent in that state's paternity establishment rate.[12]

Establishing paternity alone will accomplish little, however, as long as a young man can easily escape any real consequence for his action. Delinquent fathers ordered to court on contempt charges often claim inability to pay. Because of limited jail space, judges often order those fathers to find work, only to have them return a month later with the same story and the same result.

In many parts of the country, including Indianapolis, prosecutors have the duty of collecting child support. In my twelve years as prosecutor we made child support enforcement a priority, increasing collections from $900,000 a year to $36 million and improving paternity establishment by a like percentage. I was flattered some years ago when an appreciative welfare recipient confided that she used my name as a verb to threaten a would-be father — as a sort of action she would take against him if he refused to pay support. Stories like these led me to consider enforcement not just as a revenue mechanism but as a way to alter conduct.

Toward that end, we created the *Job or Jail* program in order to give judges an alternative that would enable unemployed parents, who would be connected with private sector employers through the program, to fulfill their financial obligations. Judges refer fathers not immediately employable to a job-readiness program run by the Indianapolis Private Industry Council. The court orders parents who do not take advantage of this opportunity into community service. They work for city departments picking up trash, cleaning garages, and main-

11. U.S. Department of Health and Human Services, Office of Child Support Enforcement, *Report to Congress for FY95* (Washington, D.C., 1995), p. 114.

12. U.S. Department of Health and Human Services, Office of Child Support Enforcement, *Child Support Report,* vol. XV, no. 6 (Washington, D.C., June 1996), pp. 1-4.

taining parks and greenways. In other words, fathers who will not work to support their children work to support the taxpayers who are supporting their children. Once a parent secures employment, the court suspends the sentence of community work. Fathers who refuse to get a job or enroll in job readiness training under this arrangement are jailed and made to do community work as trustees of the jail.

Even when fathers do pay child support, however, those payments do little to help the situation of an AFDC mother, who does not see much of it. Virtually all of the support a father pays actually goes to the welfare department to repay it for AFDC payments previously made to the mother. The proper destination for child support payments is the mother herself, not the government. Making this simple and obvious change to the child support system could have a dramatic positive impact on the ability of welfare mothers to achieve self-sufficiency and would further encourage responsibility on the part of fathers.

Government can also play a constructive role simply by enforcing previously ignored existing laws. National estimates suggest that 30 to 50 percent of men who impregnate teenage girls are more than five years older than the young mothers,[13] and that on average the fathers are 3.5 years older.[14] Similarly, 74 percent of women who had intercourse before age fourteen and 60 percent of those who had sex before age fifteen report having had sex involuntarily.[15] The Indianapolis prosecutor and a few others around the country recently began actively to pursue violators of statutory rape laws, laws which were previously dormant. In 1996, we convicted five men, and we have fifteen cases pending. All of the girls involved were fifteen or younger. We are hopeful that consistent prosecution under statutory rape laws will change the attitudes of young men and protect the girls who might otherwise be affected.

Again, our commitment to consequences for fathers does not preclude us from supporting these young men. On the contrary, programs like the Father Resource Center teach these fathers parenting and job skills and connect them with work. This combination of assistance and enforcement helps fathers to provide for their children while demonstrating in no uncertain terms a commitment to holding them accountable.

13. Editorial, "Adult Sexual Predators and Teen-Age Moms," *Washington Times*, 21 April 1996.

14. R. A. Maynard, ed., *Kids Having Kids: A Robin Hood Foundation Special Report on the Costs of Adolescent Childbearing* (New York: The Robin Hood Foundation, 1996), p. 18.

15. K. A. Moore, C. W. Nord, and J. L. Peterson, "Nonvoluntary Sexual Activity Among Adolescents," *Family Planning Perspectives* 21 (1989): 110-14.

Faith and Families

Religious institutions are in an ideal position to intervene in the lives of challenged families. Communities of faith can do more to help strengthen families than any government agency can hope to accomplish. A little over a year ago, we asked religious leaders to advise city officials and to elevate our discussion of illegitimacy, marriage, and teenage pregnancy. Pastors and rabbis not only sermonized on the subject, they helped to develop the *Faith and Families* program of Indiana.

Inspired by the *Faith and Families* program in Mississippi, leaders from the religious community came together to develop a model that links vulnerable families with congregations in order to help single parents achieve and maintain employment. For teenage parents, the program offers the support they need to complete school and find employment and encourages them to delay having additional children until they are married and self-sufficient. The program also links congregations with each other to enhance available resources, which has resulted in the formation of a number of effective urban-suburban partnerships.

Faith and Families operates without any public support. Instead, it is funded entirely by grants from private charitable organizations. Since the program's inception a year ago, twenty-three congregations in Indianapolis have assisted nearly fifty families.

One person helped by the program is Tanya, a nineteen-year-old single mother of two young daughters. Tanya grew up in a home headed by an alcoholic mother, resided in a group home for some time, and was eventually emancipated by juvenile court. She was fortunate to escape an abusive relationship with the father of her second child, and she receives some child support and SSI for her older daughter. But by the time Tanya entered the *Faith and Families* program she was homeless and living in a church-based shelter for destitute families.

Through the program Tanya was linked with members of St. Luke's United Methodist Church, who helped her find her own apartment. One of the church members also trained Tanya in computer graphics and helped her secure $10-12/hour employment at his firm. Today, Tanya has plans to attend college at night. She also worships at St. Luke's and attends a service for young singles there. She has found the congregation to be warm and supportive and believes this opportunity has given her and her children a new lease on life.

Faith and Families has had an equally transforming effect in the lives of church members, who are enriched by their efforts to improve the lives of the less fortunate. Such efforts, which lie at the heart of the ethic that pervades

American communities of faith, provide clear evidence of the vital role religion can and must play in the effort to restore civil society.

Supporting Religion

Theodore Roosevelt's vision of the social role of our churches is as relevant today as it was when he spoke in a church in 1902, saying,

> The forces for evil, as our cities grow, become more concentrated, more menacing to the community, and if the community is to go forward and not backward they must be met and overcome by forces for good that have grown in corresponding degree. More and more in the future our churches must . . . take the lead in shaping those forces for good.[16]

Sadly, many of those in government today seem to have lost Roosevelt's vision. Elected leaders often shy away from religion because of its political volatility and because they don't want to interfere in personal decisions. Far worse, government is in some cases openly antagonistic to religion, creating unnecessary obstacles to the involvement of religious groups in assisting those in need. By adopting this perverse stance, government not only discourages those who would seek to introduce the constructive influence of religious faith into the lives of vulnerable individuals, it also squanders valuable opportunities to strengthen the role of religious institutions in addressing social problems.

Only hardened skeptics have trouble accepting that widespread belief in a Supreme Being improves the strength and health of our communities. Those who possess strongly-held religious convictions conduct themselves with civility because of their beliefs, not simply because a police officer is on the opposite corner. A Heritage Foundation *Backgrounder* summarized fascinating research showing the connection between religion and healthy families and communities. Among other things, it reported that consistent religious practice

- predicts marital stability;
- helps poor persons, especially young inner-city residents, move out of poverty;
- contributes substantially to the formation of personal character and sound moral judgment;

16. *The Roosevelt Policy* (New York: Current Literature Publishing Co., 1928), p. 28. From an address at an overflow meeting on the occasion of the centennial of Presbyterian Home Missions, New York City, 20 May 1902.

- inoculates individuals against a host of social problems, including suicide, drug abuse, crime, out-of-wedlock births, and divorce; and
- improves mental health and self-esteem.[17]

Religion and religious institutions must play a critical role in the future of our cities, and government can assist in establishing this role in two ways. First, public officials should use the bully pulpit to celebrate and encourage religious commitment without favoring one religious tradition over another. Second, cities can undertake initiatives with churches, like those discussed below, that strengthen communities while encouraging connections that promote religious involvement.

Churches and Parks

When inner-city youths form relationships with churches around nonspiritual concerns, positive by-products of these relationships develop. In Indianapolis, crime and decay haunted many of our two hundred parks. Near a fair number of these troubled parks stood a church. Often the church represented the most important mediating force in the community, yet it lacked adequate resources to program youth activities. At the same time, the community viewed the park not as theirs, but as the city's, and therefore did not reach out in a possessive way to protect and preserve the green and play areas.

My administration worked to generate interest among these churches in maintaining parks in their neighborhoods. Two church deacons, both city employees, led the effort to create city-church park relationships, inquiring whether church-affiliated groups were willing to help reclaim nearby parks. We determined the real cost of maintaining the park and offered small neighborhood-based contracts to churches and other groups to see if they could provide better quality services for the money.

Indianapolis now contracts with ten churches to maintain twenty-nine city parks. Maintenance includes mowing the grass, sweeping the walks and driveways, picking up litter, and keeping athletic areas free of glass and debris. The city continues to maintain equipment, make capital improvements, and accept liability on park property.

These partnerships tend to drive away alcoholics and drug addicts and allow families to return. For example, one local church recently organized a community cleanup of a nearby park and painted a picnic shelter once defaced with

17. "Why Religion Matters: The Impact of Religious Practice on Social Stability," *Heritage Foundation Backgrounder No. 1064,* January 1996.

gang graffiti. The park area that residents fearfully avoided now houses a church-based children's summer camp.

Another church organized a trash patrol for children after school. Children who participate and who cannot afford the cost of park amenities (pools, for example) receive vouchers for free admission to these facilities. One participating church hired residents from its homeless shelter to cut the grass in the parks. Now local businesses pay these individuals to cut their lawns as well and an area bank provides materials and trash can liners for all of the parks involved.

Today in Indianapolis, church leaders and neighborhood residents work together in the parks developing a sense of ownership. They cost the city no more money than previous maintenance, take better care of the parks than the city did, and make the parks safer for general use. The city placed signs in each of these parks with the name and phone number of the involved church and the name of the pastor. Reinvigorated churches now provide services that support neighborhood-driven employment and training, social services, recreation, and housing revitalization. These partnerships not only serve to build up the economic fabric of a neighborhood, but also refocus attention on the importance of churches as sources of moral renewal.[18]

Churches, Religion, and Troubled Youth

Connecting juvenile offenders to local churches provides a stable connection for troubled young people. More importantly, religion can help these youngsters in ways that government cannot. While the criminal justice system can only punish, churches can rehabilitate troubled youth by instilling in them respect, obedience, and hope.

The Indianapolis Training Center provides a remarkable example of how government can work with faith-based organizations. The Center was established by Bill Gothard, the founder of a Christian ministry to youth which conducts teaching seminars across the country. Gothard proposed to purchase a closed hotel in the city and convert it into a training facility for young men and women, where they would participate in a biblically-based program designed

18. Contracts between government and faith-based organizations to provide services can pose problems for government and private charities alike. Some of these pitfalls are touched upon in an article by Joe Loconte in the March/April 1997 issue of *Policy Review* entitled "The Seven Deadly Sins of Government Funding for Private Charities." Churches must also be careful that in cooperating with government they are not subtly transformed into social service agencies, thereby diluting their deeper spiritual purpose and negating many of the positive benefits sought from such cooperation.

to instill character. We encouraged this participation and Gothard expanded to Indianapolis, bringing in young people and their families and adopting urban neighborhoods to assist.

Eventually, Gothard suggested that the Center might use its strong religious and moral base to work with troubled teenage boys and girls. Today the juvenile court uses the Center as an alternative to Girls School and Boys School. The program works not only with troubled adolescents, but also with their families, reflecting the belief that the child who resists his parents is likely to resist the constraints of law and society as well.

The program's emphasis on parental involvement and the values of responsibility, obedience, and respect has proved an enormous success. Eighty-four percent of the juveniles assigned to the Center since it opened in 1993 were offenders who have run afoul of the law multiple times. Yet in four years, more than 71 percent of all juveniles sent to the Center have not re-offended since their release.

Now other courts refer youths to the Center. One young man sent to the program by a court in Jacksonville, Florida, had been convicted of robbery and stayed at the Center for six months. Before being discharged, he called all the people he had robbed to ask their forgiveness.

The DuPage County court system of Illinois sentenced a young woman named Minnie to the Center after she had been arrested more than seventy times. When Minnie and her parents first arrived at the Center, she was violently opposed to joining the program. After speaking with two young graduates of the Center, however, she decided to give it a try. Over the next several months, her attitude changed dramatically, thrilling her parents and amazing the judge overseeing her case. Minnie decided to stay at the Indianapolis Training Center to complete her training to become a cosmetologist. Like the young women who convinced her to give the program a try, Minnie wants to serve other young people at juvenile detention centers in order to help them make the right choices.

These are not the kinds of stories one generally hears about the traditional juvenile justice system, from which most kids emerge more estranged and disaffected than when they entered. While reducing crime among juveniles requires that we consistently punish criminal activity, delinquent youth need more than punishment — they need guidance. Connecting troubled youth to programs that can communicate and instill good values can be a powerful tool in reducing recidivism and can help stem the tide of juvenile crime.

Faith-based Assistance

Church-based groups are better suited than government to help vulnerable individuals. For example, government is typically unable to discriminate between the truly needy and those simply seeking a handout. Government programs are also prevented from instructing those on assistance about the need to exercise proper judgment in their decision-making.

In contrast, when church congregations assist needy individuals, they do more than merely pass out checks to case numbers — they help their neighbors, thereby strengthening the bonds of community. And by making faith an integral part of that assistance, church-based efforts provide needy individuals with a source of strength and a moral impetus for personal change that government simply cannot.

Too often government has usurped the role of churches in helping struggling community members. Worse, increasingly bizarre interpretations of the constitutional separation of church and state have in some cases produced overt government antagonism toward religion. The proper role for government is to support, not supplant, the involvement of churches in their communities. Government can accomplish more by working with faith-based efforts than it can ever achieve by circumventing them.

In Indianapolis, suburban and urban religious leaders regularly work with city officials to look for ways to reach out to communities in need. For example, in 1995 the city provided grants to twelve churches to run summer programs to develop skills, prevent violence, and provide evening recreation. Nearly fifteen hundred inner-city children participated. One of the churches runs a summer day camp in the park it maintains and a local bank is setting up educational accounts for each camper.

Other faith-based groups provide assistance without the involvement of the city. The Care Center, for example, affiliated with Englewood Christian Church, provides shelter to the homeless and victims of domestic violence, food and clothes to the destitute, and moral support to the poor in spirit. Before free, hot lunches are served at the Center, a prayer is said. During the meal, a woman sings religious songs. The Center furnishes medical and dental services and runs a camp program for children. In return, the Center encourages (and in some cases requires) patrons to help on the grounds and attend religious services.

The Salvation Army also combines physical assistance with religion in a way that profoundly affects the lives of many in need. Like the Care Center, the Army makes religious instruction and self-responsibility conditions of assistance. Every person housed in the group's Adult Rehabilitation Center must participate in religious services and work in some capacity for the good of the

Center. For the Salvation Army, there is a close connection between religious observance and self-sufficiency. As the director of the Center expresses it, the Army believes that "if you make a man spiritually right, he can handle most of his problems on his own."

Twelve years ago, Becky Khan arrived at one of the Army's domestic violence shelters with three young children in tow. The Army provided her with comfort, aid, support, and encouragement, and enrolled her in a support group for battered women. Becky often left the shelter through a back door that exited through a church, providing her first exposure to the Salvation Army's religious underpinnings. Slowly she became active in worship services. She later went on to earn her Graduate Equivalence Degree and become a teacher, and she now directs one of the Army's community facilities.

Other faith-based rehabilitation efforts show equally impressive results. Consider the example of Teen Challenge, a worldwide Christian organization that helps people of all ages escape from drug addiction. Formal studies have found that the group has long-term cure rates of 67 to 85 percent.[19] These remarkable results are achieved at a fraction of the cost of secular programs having far lower success rates. Reverend Phil McClain, who directs Teen Challenge of Michigan, attributes this success to prayer and Bible study, noting that "when a student gets right with God, that is the starting point for progress."[20] As Pastor Sidney Watson says, "I've referred people to secular counseling, but that usually accomplishes only a drying-out. This changes lives."[21]

Ironically, despite the success of programs like those run by the Salvation Army and Teen Challenge, these groups have at times met with government interference and antagonism. In an editorial for the *Wall Street Journal* entitled "Addicted to Bureaucracy," Marvin Olasky describes how Texas bureaucrats opposed to the religious emphasis of the Teen Challenge program attempted to put it out of business in that state. Good results were irrelevant to state officials, who cited the program for not using state-licensed substance abuse counselors and proposed a fine of $4000 a day.[22]

The Salvation Army has also encountered government interference, initiated by officials opposed to government support of faith-based nonprofits. A decade ago a county court judge in Indianapolis prohibited the county from providing homeless care through the Salvation Army because of its religious

19. Dr. Roger D. Thompson, *Teen Challenge Alumni Survey Report* (Chattanooga: University of Tennessee, September 1994).

20. Quoted in Burton Folson, "Teen Challenge: Kicking Two Bad Habits," *Viewpoint on Public Issues* (Michigan: Mackinac Center for Public Policy, 5 August 1996), p. 1.

21. Quoted in Marvin Olasky, "Addicted to Bureaucracy," *Wall Street Journal,* 15 August 1996, p. A14.

22. Olasky, "Addicted to Bureaucracy."

base. According to the judge, acceptance of government funds by the Army, amounting to 15 percent of its revenues, required the cessation of mandatory church services in return for assistance.[23]

Laws and regulations that prevent the government from using religious institutions to provide services have the ultimate if unintended effect of favoring homelessness over shelter with religion, and preferring addiction over treatment by unlicensed counselors. Tragically, in some cases government aversion to religion is now so pronounced that bureaucrats actively discourage prayer and religious worship.

This aversion is something we have experienced firsthand in Indianapolis. Each year the federal government grants dollars to cities to fund summer jobs for youth. Although mayors appreciate the opportunity to be associated with any sort of job creation, the programs provide little, if any, lasting value. In the summer of 1994, we asked church groups to become involved in our job training program in hopes that linkages would be created between underemployed urban youths looking for jobs and value-promoting institutions in their neighborhoods.

At the end of the summer, the State of Indiana cited the city as "out of compliance" with a state law barring the use of funds for promoting religious activities. The State complained that participants voluntarily prayed before eating meals and going on field trips. Voluntary cursing, of course, did not create an offense, but praying violated the rules.

Every day, churches and faith-based organizations across America undertake extraordinary efforts to improve their communities and the lives of challenged individuals. Many people are motivated by their faith to help the less fortunate by introducing others to what has been a source of strength and guidance for them. Faith "works" for a lot of people, and to the extent that government precludes groups from using this potent tool for positive change it does a great injustice.

The issue is not partisan. While at a conference about juvenile crime, John Norquist, the Democratic mayor of Milwaukee, scribbled me a note which read, "There are far greater threats to inner-city kids than religion." What the federal government has yet to figure out, mayors of both parties have long known: the values associated with civility and reverence are far more essential to helping the inner cities than bigger government.

23. Kimberly Dennis, "The Place of the Businessman in the Free Society," Philadelphia Society remarks, November 1995, p. 4.

Bolstering Community Organizations

Tight-knit, active neighborhoods are the building blocks of successful cities. Common purpose, cohesiveness, and shared hopes and values enhance the success of neighborhoods, and active grassroots community involvement fortifies them. Wherever these ties are lacking, communities degenerate. If residents with strong values view escape as the only possible route to success — and, tragically, many do — the degenerative process accelerates. In recent decades, changes in technology and the marketplace facilitated this escape, and the federal government subsidized these centrifugal forces by using tax money to reduce the costs of urban sprawl. Highway trust funds paid for expensive road improvements that allowed massive suburban development, in effect using the gas tax dollars paid by urban residents to subsidize the escape of their neighbors. Likewise, grants and low-interest loans allowed for the below-market-cost expansion of sewer and wastewater treatment systems.

As city governments raised taxes, those who were wealthy enough to take advantage of this increased mobility did so, moving out to suburban areas and leaving behind a smaller inner-city tax base. Predictably, mayors responded to revenue shortfalls by further raising taxes on the remaining population, providing increasingly larger incentives for urban flight and imposing greater financial strain on those who could not afford to leave. Worse still, governments used some of these tax revenues to further undermine communities by usurping the traditional role of neighborhood groups and religious institutions, discouraging the formation of two-parent families, and subsidizing joblessness.

Across America, many city governments send inner-city residents a clear message that City Hall does not care about their neighborhoods. Too often, government neglects fundamental obligations such as infrastructure maintenance and repair and ignores concerned community members trying to make a difference in their neighborhoods. When government investment in inner-city communities takes the form of welfare checks instead of real community development, neighborhood residents rightly feel abandoned. Government can do more to help revive inner-city neighborhoods by living up to its core responsibilities and by helping community members help themselves than it could ever accomplish through big government programs.

Neighborhood Empowerment

Thriving neighborhoods tend to yield active local organizations that reinforce shared community standards and goals and address issues that affect the community. Challenged neighborhoods, often characterized by low levels of organization, are denied the benefits of these neighborhood associations and their leadership. That is why in Indianapolis we actively encourage the creation of neighborhood associations in areas where they are lacking and support these associations where they exist by ensuring that they are equipped with the skills and the knowledge they need to be effective.

The Indianapolis Neighborhood Resource Center (INRC) is a nonprofit organization that provides information and assistance to neighborhood associations, churches, and community development corporations to assist them in addressing the problems facing their neighborhoods. The INRC, which receives a third of its funding from the city, informs neighborhood leaders about such topics as starting neighborhood organizations, managing finances, understanding legal issues, recruiting volunteers, and designing action plans. The Center also teaches neighborhood organizations and leaders how to communicate with the government on such issues as zoning, the use of public resources, and how to be effective advocates. In addition, the INRC makes computers and printing equipment available for use by community groups.

Since 1994, the Neighborhood Resource Center has helped create eighty new neighborhood and homeowner associations, and worked with more than two hundred existing groups in 1996 alone. Last year, the INRC provided twenty-one countywide training sessions, with an average attendance of twenty-six neighborhood leaders at each session. Through the program, participating organizations and individuals have made an immediate impact on their neighborhoods — from playing an active role in the financial management of their communities to winning zoning cases.

Of course, many community members do not need training in order to become leaders in their communities. Committed neighbors like Carolyn Hooks see a need in their communities and feel impelled to act. The leader of a near Southside neighborhood, Carolyn showed up at my office one day with other residents demanding the city do a better job of abating nuisances, such as health and zoning violations. She pinpointed on a map every crack house and identified the associated violation.

Next she organized anti-drug marches in front of high crack areas. One night I visited them as they set up just before midnight to picket a crack house, demonstrating their outrage and condemnation. Citizens, once intimidated by criminals, stood up to them, and sent a strong signal to their fellow residents. Now every Friday night, neighbors hold pitch-in dinners at one of these spots. In the first six months, twenty-five drug houses closed and violent crime plummeted. Fifty-eight weeks of marches emboldened other residents to use their public spaces and parks more openly. Anti-litter and cleanup efforts followed.

Thousands of small daily examples occur in every city where individuals in tough communities reach out positively to help. These efforts stabilize and socialize a community, reinforcing the positive values that allow cities to thrive. In order to encourage these efforts we created the Mayor's Partnership Award, a recognition program that celebrates the wonderful accomplishments of these unsung neighborhood heroes in order to bolster community pressure for positive values. Judges review nominations from around the city on a quarterly basis, selecting exceptionally dedicated individuals for public recognition.

Vonda O'Neil, for example, is a quiet leader who has lived all her life on the near Eastside of Indianapolis. In addition to raising seven children as a single parent, Vonda has maintained a constant involvement in her community. She first became involved in her neighborhood more than twenty years ago, when she led an effort to rid the area of a local gang and transform its headquarters into housing — an effort which grew to become the Holy Cross/Westminster Neighborhood Association. Ever since, she has been a leader in her community in many ways, leading trash pick-ups, organizing picnics for neighborhood youth and police who patrol the neighborhood, and bringing the community together to combat crime. Vonda was a founding member of Metro Advocate Ministries, which provides assistance to the poor and the homebound, and through her church she helped create an after-school program that provides tutoring and youth activities for neighborhood children. She was also a founding member of the Indianapolis Neighborhood Resource Center.

Vonda O'Neil embodies all the qualities of a good neighbor and citizen, yet the impact she has on her community is far less likely to receive media attention than the story of an individual who impacts his community through the commission of a criminal act. It is our hope that by publicly recognizing positive efforts like Vonda's, we may at the least combat some of the cynicism and indifference that pervades contemporary society, and at best inspire others to follow her example.

Helping neighborhood groups rally and publicly demonstrate their support for order and decency also sets an important example. Open and visible disrespect for the law greatly undermines efforts to communicate positive messages to young people and reinforces the acceptance of negative conduct. Open-air drug markets or alcoholism and public intoxication around commercial liquor stores clearly send the message that neither public officials nor community leaders consider the conduct bad enough to stop it.

We set out to increase the number of individuals and groups in inner-city neighborhoods willing to stand up and fight for positive conduct. We have rallied citizens in opposition to renewals of liquor licenses in problem locations, furnishing the groups with legal assistance and changing the law to force neighbors to be notified and included in the process.

Late last year I stood surrounded by cheering neighbors at an inner-city liquor store, long a serious neighborhood nuisance. The store, abutting a residential area, attracted crime, public intoxication, and drug dealing and loudly proclaimed that criminals, not citizens with positive values, ruled the area. On that December day, surrounded by inner-city residents, community development leaders, pastors, and children, we announced the closure of the store. It represented just one nuisance in a large area, but it symbolized publicly the battle between irresponsibility and criminal indulgence on the one hand, and sobriety, self-respect, and hard work on the other. Before his friends and television cameras, the Reverend Jim Harrington, one of the leaders, praised God and thanked his friends that good had triumphed.

Even simple clean-ups can inspire confidence. A grandmother from out of town wrote to me about her daughter who lived with a fourteen-month-old baby in a difficult area. Her letter described a visit after some storm damage when she "saw 10 young people with rakes and shovels. . . . They were cleaning our area of that debris! We asked and found out that they were from the International Church of God. Praise the Lord for such community service! They even invited us to their church and to an upcoming home-cooked dinner."

Conclusion

No community can thrive when crime is pervasive and goes unpunished and roads, sewers, and sidewalks are in disrepair. In order for our neighborhoods to succeed, government must demonstrate a firm commitment to its core responsibilities of public safety and infrastructure maintenance and deliver these services well.

But strong neighborhoods are not built with bricks alone. Successful communities are built on the character, concern, and active, coordinated involvement of community members, and government does more harm than good when it attempts to replace these concrete moral obligations with impersonal programs.

Government can and should play a role in revitalizing our communities, but it can only do so by supporting the institutions that create and nurture values, not by supplanting them. Neighborhood-based, grassroots organizations deserve government's support, as it is only through their efforts that our communities can be renewed. Likewise, government aversion to religion and religious institutions must end. Elected officials should not shun contact with religious leaders, but nurture it and assist religious institutions in reaching out to their communities. No number of government good deeds will produce as much benefit to our communities as simply supporting the institutions, organizations, and individuals who possess a clear vision of a civil society and who are resolutely committed to making that vision a reality.

The Demand Side of Television

MICHAEL MEDVED

Americans invest an inordinate amount of time in fights over the content of television — as if relatively minor adjustments in programming could fundamentally alter the medium's impact on our society. In 1999, for instance, the NAACP threatened boycotts and legal action unless the major networks took immediate and drastic steps to create more minority characters in major programs. After a seemingly endless series of summit conferences and discussions with the press, the networks buckled: three of the four agreed to appoint new executives in charge of "diversity," while CBS agreed to hire one new minority writer for every major series. With much fanfare, the activist groups celebrated this "progress," while the broadcast executives congratulated themselves on their progressive values.

In the midst of this festival of warm, fuzzy feelings, no one paused to ask what, if anything, had actually been accomplished. Assuming that the vulgar, brain-dead nature of TV programming remains essentially unchanged, how would adjusting the skin color of some of its characters help any segment of this society? Even with an under-representation of African-Americans on current TV series, blacks already watch 40 percent more TV each week than the national average. If more black characters mean even more TV viewing by the African-American community, will this development help — or hurt — that community's children?

Coming to Terms with Television's Overriding Impact

It's not just politically correct "civil rights" organizations that fail to come to terms with the overriding impact of television — and the sad reality of TV addiction among our children. Conservative activists also misstate the basic challenge the medium poses for our society and its values. A worthy and well-intentioned organization called the Parents Television Council, for instance, has been running the same full-page ad for years, featuring a photograph of the legendary comedian Steve Allen. "TV Is Leading Our Kids Down a Moral Sewer!" the text proclaims, and suggests that sponsor boycotts could lead to a new sense of responsibility, which could lead in turn to new content restrictions among broadcasters. This entire agenda presumes that at some point in the past television enjoyed a golden age (represented in the ad by Steve Allen) and was a wholesome force in our society; it thus connects with the fond recollections of better, more family-friendly fare in the infancy of the new medium. Polls show that overwhelming majorities of our fellow citizens believe that current TV offerings, despite the astonishing increase in variety (and occasionally even in quality) made possible by cable and the new broadcast networks, provide less valuable entertainment than forty years ago.

Again, the public, and groups like the Parents Television Council, seem to miss the most important point: the essential problem with the TV we all watch isn't so much its low quality as it is its high quantity. Most Americans who fret over television focus on its seedy content, often waxing nostalgic for the innocent fare of yesteryear. If only "The Beaver" hadn't transmogrified into "Beavis," they sigh, then TV might still function as a source of harmless diversion and even reassuring uplift.

But this argument crashes head-on into a wall of contradictory history. The generation nourished on such wholesome family fare as *Ozzie and Harriet, Make Room for Daddy, The Mickey Mouse Club, The Real McCoys, Father Knows Best,* and, of course, *Leave It to Beaver* did not grow up to be well-adjusted, optimistic, family-affirming solid citizens. Instead, children of the 1960s went more or less directly from *The Donna Reed Show* to campus riots, psychedelic experimentation, love-ins, long hair, and all-purpose looniness. Could it be that TV itself, rather than the specific content of its programs, erodes American virtues?

The most significant fact about the 1960s kids is not that they were the offspring of specific shows like *Howdy Doody* or *Captain Kangaroo* but that they were the first TV generation. The boob tube arrived in most American homes in the 1950s, just as baby boomers turned old enough to watch in earnest, which suggests that TV's destructive force lies in the medium, not the message. This insight should force us to reconsider our approach to the battles over television content, the new ratings system, the abandoned family hour, and the rest. If the family-friendly programs of the 1950s and 1960s led a generation directly to Woodstock, Abbie Hoffman, and the illegitimacy explosion, why try to reproduce those shows' conservative themes today?

Consider a simple thought experiment. Imagine that the cultural conservatives manage to install Bill Bennett or Robert Bork as national TV "czar." Henceforth, every show must pass some rigorous virtue test before airing. Sure, TV would thereafter exert a less harmful influence on our children, but would it suddenly become a force for sanity and character-building? If children continued to watch the tube for dozens of hours each week, should their parents be entirely reassured by the programs' improved quality? Or does the sheer quantity of TV viewing represent a deeper, more intractable problem for this society?

These questions are uncomfortable precisely because the answers are so apparent. It is the inescapable essence of television, rather than a few dozen incidentally destructive shows, which undermines the principles most parents strive to pass on to their kids. When consumed in the American pattern of several hours each day, TV inevitability promotes impatience, self-pity, and superficiality.

Impatience

The most recent analyses reveal that the major cable and broadcast networks titillate viewers with a new image every nine seconds on average. This quick editing contributes in an obvious and unmistakable manner to the alarming decline in the American attention span. Andy Warhol's "15 minutes of fame" seems to have shrunk to perhaps fifty seconds.

The effect of TV's rapidly flashing images is most obvious in preschool classrooms. America's three- and four-year-olds seem less able than ever before to sit still for a teacher — in part because no teacher can reproduce the manic energy or protean transformations of the tube. But those teachers can easily identify the children in class who watch the most TV. Please note that when it comes to this crucial issue of attention span, the admired *Sesame Street* exerts the same worrisome influence as the universally reviled *Power Rangers.* Even sympathetic studies of *Sesame Street* worry over the way that breathlessly fast-paced show encourages restlessness in its young viewers.

Television promotes impatience in other ways for older audience members. The very structure of televised entertainment — packed half-hours — undercuts habits of deferred gratification and long-term perspective. In the world of TV, every problem can be solved within thirty minutes — or, if it's a particularly formidable and complex one, then sixty will suffice. It's hardly surprising that many Americans feel frustrated when their personal projects — in romance, weight loss, or career advancement — fail to produce results as neat and immediate as those they witness on TV.

The commercials that consume so much of each broadcast day also foster the peevishness and unfulfilled desire suffered by many viewers. The purpose of these cunningly crafted messages is to stimulate impatience — to nurture an intense, immediate desire for a hamburger, an electronic toy, a beer, or a luxury car. If advertising does its job effectively, it will leave the mass audience with a perpetual attitude of unquenchable yearning for a never-ending succession of alluring new products.

Self-Pity

The inevitable inability to acquire enough of these products helps to produce self-pity and insecurity, an attitude reinforced by even the most acclaimed and purportedly constructive "public affairs" programming. That programming, like all other "reality-based" television, offers a wildly distorted vision of the contemporary world: TV doesn't broadcast the news, it broadcasts the bad news. A 1996 report in *USA Today* determined that 72 percent of that year's local news shows from around the country led off with stories of violence or disaster, living up to the rule of broadcast journalism, "If it bleeds, it leads."

Contrary to popular belief, this obsession can't be blamed on the blood, lust, and ratings hunger of unscrupulous news directors. It is a built-in, unavoidable aspect of the medium. If a father comes home after a long day at work and lovingly tucks in each of his five children, asking God's blessing on their slumber, that's not news. But if the same father comes home and goes from bedroom to bedroom shooting each child, it is news.

Television has an especially intense effect because of the medium's affinity for portraying horror and pain. Depicting love or heroism usually requires some sort of background or explanation, and visual media can't easily explain anything. Their strength is immediacy, especially in the impatient, rapid-fire world of contemporary TV. Even if a news broadcast were determined to balance its footage of mutilated bodies and burning buildings with equal time for noble parents and dedicated teachers, which images would make the more visceral impression, or remain longer in the public memory?

The same preference for the dangerous and the bizarre inevitably shows up in "entertainment" television as well, reflecting an age-old tradition. After all, Shakespeare focused on murders and witches and scheming villains and transsexual masquerades, not functional families and upstanding individuals. Nevertheless, the disturbing behavior in novels and plays and even radio shows of the past never enveloped an audience in the way that television does today, when an average American family owns multiple TV sets and keeps them on for hours a day. One pioneering Chicago station, WTTW, based its call letters on its chosen designation as a "Window To The World." For many viewers, that's the function the tube still performs.

The vast number of vivid images that pour through that window enter our consciousness with little distinction between the factual and the fictional. Whether it's the evening news, a sitcom, a daytime talk show, a docudrama, a cop show, or *60 Minutes,* TV blurs the dividing line between the real and the imaginary and shapes our notions of the wider reality and prevailing behaviors that exist beyond our homes. Producers of soap operas report that they regularly receive letters from devoted viewers who address comments to their favorite characters. And literally tens of millions of Americans will instantaneously (and often unconsciously) imitate catchy phrases or gestures from popular TV shows.

This tension between televised "reality" and the actual lives of ordinary Americans prompts self-pity. The impression people take away from regular viewing is that the world is unpredictable, menacing, violent, and full of deviant, exciting, and compelling chaos. Decades of research at the University of Pennsylvania's Annenberg School of Communication suggests that the principal legacy of TV's emphasis on violence is a "mean world syndrome" in which people become more fearful about the present and future. This helps answer the question posed in a celebrated *Forbes* cover story: "Why Do We Feel So Bad When We Have It So Good?" Real-life trends have recently been improving in numerous areas, including unemployment, the deficit, crime, air quality, and even teen pregnancy and AIDS affliction. Have you noticed a comparable brightening in the public?

If TV's dangerous world leaves people needlessly frightened and insecure, it also makes them resentful that their personal lives are vastly more "boring" than what they see on the tube. Our national epidemic of whining is aided not only by TV's natural emphasis on bad news, but by the way most citizens remain relatively untouched by these disasters — and so their quiet lives can't live up to the excitement, drama, and sexual adventure that television advances as a new American entitlement.

Superficiality

In television, there is only the thrill of the moment, with no sense of the past and scant concern for the future. Venal programmers hardly deserve the blame for this tendency; it's a given in a medium that by its nature emphasizes immediacy and visceral visual impact. Flashbacks in a TV drama, no matter how artfully constructed, can never compete with the power of a live broadcast, no matter how insipid. How else can one explain the embarrassing fact that millions of Americans interrupted their lives to watch long-distance shots of a certain white Bronco lumbering down a Los Angeles freeway?

The O.J. idiocy illustrates another aspect of TV's superficiality: the all-consuming concern with physical appearance. Those who believe our fascination with Simpson's murder case stems from his sports-star status miss the point: does anyone honestly suppose that the trials would have generated equal interest if O.J. and his murdered wife had resembled, say, Mike Tyson and Janet Reno? The preoccupation with glamour and good looks is nowhere more painfully apparent than in TV news, where the overwhelming majority of these supposedly brilliant and dedicated professional journalists just coincidentally happen to be exceptionally attractive physical specimens.

In real life, we rightly associate "air heads" with an abiding obsession with looks and grooming, but TV doth make airheads of us all. Currently, the most popular show in the world is that profound and probing melodrama, *Baywatch.* Its appeal can hardly be explained by the vividness of its characterizations; it has everything to do with gorgeous bodies abundantly displayed. TV trains us to feel satisfied with surfaces, to focus our adoration on characters who make the most appealing visual presentation, without examination of their ethics or accomplishments. Given the lifelong television training of most Americans, it's no surprise many voters readily forgive the misdeeds of political leaders who look cute and compassionate when they emote on the tube.

Beyond bad politics, beyond misleading glamour, television emphasizes another form of destructive superficiality: setting fun as the highest human priority. As my friend Dennis Prager points out, fun is fleeting and unearned — a thrill ride at a theme park, an engaging video game, a diverting half-hour sitcom on TV. Happiness, on the other hand, requires considerable effort and commitment, and in most cases proves durable and long lasting. Fun can never be counted upon to produce happiness, but happiness almost always involves fun. Casual sex, for instance, may (occasionally) provide a few hours of fun, but it will never lead to the long-term happiness that a permanent marriage can provide. Similarly, watching professional sports on TV can be fun, but it hardly compares to the benefits of actually playing on a team yourself.

Television viewing represents the most empty-headed, superficial sort of fun in an increasingly fun-addicted society. It is meaningless precisely because it demands so little of its viewers; in fact, physiological examination of TV-watchers suggests they are three-quarters asleep.

Sleepers, Awake!

It is high time we all woke up, especially those families who attempt to honor Jewish and Christian teachings. In each of the areas described above, TV contradicts the fundamentals of faith-based civilizations. While TV promotes impatience, restlessness, and a short-term horizon, our religious traditions command a serene, steady spirit and a view toward eternal consequences. Where television encourages self-pity and fear, religious teachings emphasize gratitude and rejoicing in our portion. And while electronic media inspire superficiality and shallowness, believers know to look below the surface at the cause lying beneath the confusing effects. Instead of transient, unearned fun, Judaism and Christianity stress the permanent good of achieving happiness through a full and virtuous life.

The increasingly unmistakable conflict between investing time in television and the religious priorities that most parents hope to pass on to their children brings us to a potentially historic crossroads. The current situation of TV addiction resembles the situation of nicotine addiction thirty-five years ago. Shortly after the surgeon general reported that cigarettes are a health hazard, the initial impulse from the tobacco industry and the public was to make the "cancer sticks" safer by improving filters or reducing tar and nicotine. Of course, such measures probably succeeded in saving a few lives, but they were hardly a long-term solution.

Today, efforts to reduce televised levels of shock and stupidity resemble those old attempts to reduce tar and nicotine in tobacco. They may be worth doing, but they're hardly the ultimate solution. The most important response to the dangers of cigarettes was a long-term, overall decline in the number of smokers, even though millions of Americans continue to smoke to their own detriment. Similarly, the most significant reply to TV's malign influence will involve exhortations that lead to a long-term overall decline in the rate of TV-viewing — even though many millions will be free to continue in their television addictions.

This is not a pipe dream. A recent *Wall Street Journal*/NBC News poll found that an astonishing 65 percent of Americans say they are "watching less television altogether" than they were five years ago, despite the explosion of entertainment choices and cable and satellite-dish technologies. Nielsen ratings and other studies confirm the encouraging news that Americans are spending a bit less time with the tube than they did ten years ago.

In fact, today's wide array of televised possibilities has done nothing to inspire public appreciation of TV. When asked whether "TV has changed for the better or for the worse over the past ten years," 59 percent thought it had worsened; only 30 percent said it had improved.

There just may be a receptive audience for a new campaign to reduce TV-viewing — to give back a few years of life to the average American who will currently spend an uninterrupted 13 years (24-hour days, 7-day weeks) of his life in front of the tube. After all, no one would consciously choose as an epitaph, "Here lies our beloved husband and father, who selflessly devoted 13 years of his life to his television set."

Fortunately, one of the most respected moral philosophers of our time has courageously stepped forward to enlighten humanity about TV's danger to our children. "Television is pure poison," she declares. "To be plopped in front of a TV instead of being read to, talked to, or encouraged to interact with other human beings is a huge mistake, and that's what happens to a lot of children."

So says Madonna, in an interview with the British magazine *She.* When even the most publicized princess of pop culture appreciates the pitfalls of television, surely more conventional parents will consider pulling the plug and liberating their families from the tyranny of too much TV.

The Supply Side of Television and Film

DAVID G. MYERS

Few things these days evoke more parental outrage than images of third graders watching MTV, sixth graders listening to rap lyrics glamorizing "f— —ing the bitch," ninth graders learning human relations from *Rambo* and *Robocop,* or twelfth graders getting their sex and intimacy education from *The Young and the Restless,* Jerry Springer trash talk, and *Freshman Fantasies* pornography. That outrage became a national obsession after Eric Harris and Dylan Klebold reportedly spent hours playing splatter games such as Doom and watching two crazy kids commit carnage in *Natural Born Killers* prior to committing carnage at Littleton's Columbine High School. "All our children," says a palpably angry Marian Wright Edelman, "are growing up today in an ethically polluted nation where instant sex without responsibility, instant gratification without effort, instant solutions without sacrifice, getting rather than giving, and hoarding rather than sharing are the too-frequent signals of our mass media."

Psychologist James Garbarino illustrated this vulgarization by asking children to close their eyes and tell him what came to mind when he said "Mister Rogers." With smiling faces, the images spilled out: "Kind." "Gentle." "Cares about you." "King Friday." "Nice." Then he asked them to do the same with Beavis and Butthead. The looks and words change: "Nasty." "Mean." "Rude." "Hurts people." For them, Mister Rogers was history — "from our childhood,"

This essay has been adapted, with permission, from *The American Paradox: Spiritual Hunger in an Age of Plenty* (Yale University Press, 2000). Documentation for research and quotes may be found in *The American Paradox.*

said one eight-year-old. Beavis and Butthead were the present. "This experience crystallized for me," Garbarino reflected, "the fact that one important feature of the social toxicity of the environment for children is the nastiness to which they are exposed so early in life . . . and nastiness is the last thing children need."

"Father Knows Squat," reported the *Washington Post* on how the media regularly ridicule, caricature, and marginalize parents. "Lately, I can't seem to even look at my mother without wanting to stab her repeatedly," said the lead character in the opening episode of *My So-Called Life.* Although *Father Knows Best* and *Ozzie and Harriet* were patriarchal, they did honor the parental role. "Here on prime time television were loving, hardworking parents raising their children with wisdom and humor — solving problems, teaching values, and providing an all-important protective shield," Sylvia Hewlett and Cornell West recall with a touch of nostalgia. "Themes such as family togetherness, respect for one's elders, commitment to one's spouse, and devotion to children reverberated like drumbeats through the culture of the day." By the century's end, however, parenting had become "a countercultural activity," they say. "It feels as though we are swimming upstream" against the cultural currents.

Are today's parents rightly concerned? With most children now arriving at an empty home after school, does late-afternoon television fare matter? Does it matter if, instead of leaving our children to Beaver, we leave them to Beavis? Does viewing prime-time crime influence their thinking and acting? Does onscreen sex shape their (and our) sexual perceptions, expectations, and behavior? Do the media mold us? Mirror us? Or both?

By analyzing program content, by correlating media viewing habits with behavior, and by experiments that manipulate media exposure to discern cause and effect, social science research provides some clear and credible answers. Let's allow these answers to inform our national dialogue. And then let's see if there might be a path toward America's renewal that weaves between the rock of repressive censorship and the hard place of shameless greed.

Does Hollywood Mirror Reality?

In 1961 President Kennedy's newly appointed federal communications commissioner Newton Minow challenged members of the National Association of Broadcasters to "sit down in front of your television set when your station goes on the air and stay there without a book, magazine, newspaper, profit and loss sheet, or rating book to distract you — and keep your eyes glued to that set until the station signs you off. I can assure you that you will observe a vast wasteland."

Repeating the exercise in the mid-1990s, what would broadcasters observe on their stations? Would they see social reality as in a mirror? Do today's entertainment media simply reflect the big, bad world? The answer is most definitely not. On evening dramas broadcast in the United States during the 1980s and early 1990s, and often exported to the more than one billion television sets around the world, only one-third of the characters were women. Fewer than three percent were visibly old. One percent were Hispanic. Only one in ten was married.

Network programs offer about three violent acts per hour — and six times as many (eighteen per hour) during children's Saturday morning programs. From 1994 to 1997, the National Television Violence Study analyzed some ten thousand programs from the major networks and cable channels. Six in ten contained violence ("physically compelling action that threatens to hurt or kill, or actual hurting or killing"). During fistfights, people who go down usually shake it off and come back stronger — unlike most real fistfights that last one punch (often resulting in a broken jaw or hand). In 73 percent of violent scenes, the aggressors go unpunished. In 58 percent, the victim is not shown to experience pain. In children's programs, only 5 percent of violence is shown to have any long-term consequence; two-thirds depict violence as funny.

What does this add up to? By the end of elementary school, the average child views some 8,000 TV murders and 100,000 other violent acts. If one includes cable programming, movies, and video rentals — which together provide the biggest media change of the past decade — the violence numbers escalate, because the major networks are the relative nice guys. Premium cable channels like HBO and Showtime, offering popular films like *Die Hard 2* with its 264 deaths, are much more violent than major network programs. So is MTV. So are new Hollywood films, 65 percent of which were R-rated in 1998. Reflecting on his twenty-two years of cruelty counting, University of Pennsylvania media researcher George Gerbner lamented, "Humankind has had more bloodthirsty eras but none as filled with images of violence as the present. We are awash in a tide of violent representations the world has never seen, . . . drenching every home with graphic scenes of expertly choreographed brutality." This is indeed life as rendered by a rather peculiar storyteller, one that reflects our culture's mythology but not its reality.

Hollywood's sexual mythology is hardly a better mirror of reality. In the real world, intercourse occurs mostly among married people (because most people are married, married people have sex more often, and extramarital sex is rarer than commonly believed). In the entertainment world, implied acts of sexual intercourse overwhelmingly occur between unmarried people. In soap operas, for example, unmarried partners have outnumbered married partners 24 to 1. In the first four weeks of one recent year, seven sitcom women, including Murphy Brown, were pregnant or considering it; "only one was married — and she didn't want a child," the *New York Times* reported.

In an average prime-time hour, the three major networks offer some fifteen sexual acts, words, and innuendoes — one every four minutes, nearly all involving unmarried persons with nary an expressed concern for birth control or sexually transmitted disease. (Those numbers are not inflated by MTV's videos or the Fox Network's sexual modeling through such programs as *Melrose Place.*) On television, impulsive couples seldom hesitate over their first deep kiss and passionate aftermath. When "they" (the young and unmarried) "do it" 20,000 times a year on television and no one gets pregnant, says Planned Parenthood, that is massive sex *dis*information. In reality, most relationships progress more awkwardly and tentatively. Through network television and MTV, Walkmans, and VCRs, the incessant sexual message, Planned Parenthood frets, is "Go for it now. . . . Don't worry about anything."

The unreality extends beyond violence and sex. In television's world, 6 percent of people have a religious identity; in America, 88 percent do. In television's world, 25 percent of people have blue-collar jobs; in America, 67 percent do. In television's world, 45 percent of beverages consumed are alcoholic; in America, 16 percent are. Hollywood may reflect our culture's mythology, but it radically distorts its reality.

Media Effects on Thinking: From Screen Images to Cerebral Scripts?

In 1945, Gallup pollsters asked Americans, "Do you know what television is?" Today, 98 percent of American homes (and a similar percentage in other industrialized nations) have a TV set. That's more than have telephones. With the average house now having 2.2 sets, America alone among the world's countries has nearly as many televisions as people. But MTV and CNN span the globe, and *Baywatch* is seen in 142 countries, so television also is creating a global pop culture.

In the average American home the set is on more than seven hours a day, with individual household members averaging three to four hours. All told, television beams its electromagnetic waves into children's eyeballs for more growing-up hours than they spend in school. More hours, in fact, than they spend in any other waking activity. From these hours — 20,000 hours diverted from talking, playing, reading, and so forth — what do children learn?

Viewing Violence

Psychologists study media effects the way geologists study erosion, with experiments that discern small effects that, over time, could cumulate to create big effects. By showing brutality to some children or adults but not others, they have identified two cognitive effects of viewing even a short stream of violent acts, much less a hundred thousand plus.

Viewing Violence Desensitizes People to Cruelty

Take some emotion-arousing stimulus, perhaps an obscene word, and repeat it over and over. Over time, what will happen to your emotional arousal? Gradually, it will extinguish. What initially bothered you will bother you less and less.

After witnessing thousands of cruel acts, there is good reason to expect a similar emotional numbing. The response might well become, "I don't see why it's such a big deal. It doesn't bother me at all." This is precisely what University of Utah researcher Victor Cline and his colleagues observed when they measured the physiological arousal of 121 boys who watched a brutal boxing match. Compared with boys who watched little television, the responses of those who watched habitually were hardly more than a shrug.

Of course, these boys might differ in ways other than viewing habits. But experiments reveal that watching violence breeds a more blasé reaction when later viewing the film of a brawl or when actually monitoring two children who begin fighting (as seen on supposed closed-circuit TV from an adjacent room). Further experiments reveal a similar desensitization — a sort of psychic numbness — that grows as young men view slasher films. In one such study, researchers Charles Mullin and Daniel Linz showed University of Wisconsin men a sexually violent movie, such as *Friday the 13th,* every other day for a week. After they had viewed two such films, the third film provoked less physiological arousal and seemed less violent to the inured men. And compared with men who didn't see the films, the viewers expressed less sympathy for actual domestic violence victims (shown from a PBS documentary) and rated their injuries as less severe. Ergo, watching cruelty fosters later indifference to cruelty.

Viewing Violence Molds Our Perceived Reality

In their surveys of both adolescents and adults, Gerbner and his associates found that those who watch television more than four hours a day are more likely than those who watch two hours or less to exaggerate the frequency of violence in the world around them and to fear being personally assaulted. Television, Gerbner said, fosters a perception of a "mean world."

Adults can distinguish television crime from neighborhood events. Viewers of crime dramas may not be more fearful of their own neighborhood than those who don't watch these shows, but they tend to see New York, or even their own city, as a more dangerous place. Among children, television colors perceptions of more immediate surroundings. One national survey of seven- to eleven-year-old children found that heavy viewers more than light viewers admitted fears "that somebody bad might get into your house" or that "when you go outside, somebody might hurt you." To one who views the world through the screen of television, the world seems more menacing.

Viewing Erotic and Sexual Images

Summing up many experiments on the cognitive effects of media images, we can say this: repeatedly viewing violence desensitizes people to violence and shapes their perceived reality. As I document in *The American Paradox,* erotic images likewise tend to

- distort people's perceptions of sexual reality,
- decrease the attractiveness of their own partners,
- prime men to perceive women in sexual terms,
- make sexual coercion seem more trivial, and
- provide mental scripts for how to act in sexual situations.

In such ways, "All of us who make motion pictures are teachers," George Lucas reminded the 1992 Academy Award audience, "teachers with very loud voices." "Those who tell stories hold the power in society," echoes Gerbner. "It's incumbent on [filmmakers] to realize that the films they choose to make have an effect on the workaday lives of the audience and their ability to deal with the world they inhabit," producer David Puttnam writes, reflecting on what motivated him to immortalize idealism and commitment in *Chariots of Fire* — values that have been "almost obliterated by the insidious spread of contemporary cynicism." The popular arts are not ineffectual; they color consciousness and teach us how to act.

Curiously, most folks agree that media affect the culture but deny the effect on themselves. Many parents will recall hearing this from their children: "Don't worry, Mom. Watching this doesn't affect me." This phenomenon is so robust that researchers have given it a name — "the third-person effect." Others more than us, we think, are affected by ads, political information, media violence, and social scripts. The research, however, disarms our hubris; we have met the "others" and they are us.

Media Effects on Behavior

By providing scripts and models, do the media stimulate the behaviors they depict? Or do they do the opposite — by enabling people to cathartically vent their pent-up aggressive and sexual impulses? "Seeing a murder on television can be good therapy," Alfred Hitchcock once remarked. "It can help work off one's antagonisms."

Viewing Violence and Actual Violence

Examples abound of copycat crimes. In Utah, two men murdered three people by forcing them to drink Drano. Earlier that month the men had seen the movie *Magnum Force,* depicting murder by Drano, three times in one day. Such stories may not be aberrations. In one informal survey of 208 prison convicts, 9 of 10 acknowledged learning new criminal tricks by watching crime programs, and 4 of 10 said they had attempted specific crimes seen on television. As Yogi Berra once said, "You can observe a lot just by watching."

Informal crime reports are not, however, persuasive scientific evidence. Hoping to slice the fog of contradictory claims by media critics and defenders, researchers have correlated viewing habits with behavior, and then experimentally manipulated media exposure.

Correlating Viewing and Behavior

To some extent, children's viewing does predict their aggressiveness. The more violent a child's television diet, the more aggressive the child. Though modest, the relationship consistently appears in studies in the United States, Europe, and Australia.

Does this indicate that watching violence increases aggressiveness? Perhaps, but it could also mean that aggressive children prefer aggressive programs. Or perhaps some underlying third factor, such as lower intelligence, predisposes some children both to prefer viewing violence and to act aggressively.

To test the "third factor" possibility, British researcher William Belson statistically pulled out such complicating influences in a study of 1,565 London boys. Compared with those who watched little violence, those who watched a great deal (especially realistic rather than cartoon violence) admitted to 50 percent more violent acts during the preceding six months (for example, "I busted the telephone in a telephone box"). When Belson extracted the influence of twenty-two likely third factors, such as family size, the heavy and light violence viewers still differed. He therefore surmised that the heavy viewers were indeed more violent because of their TV diet.

In a pioneering American study, Leonard Eron and Rowell Huesmann found that violence viewing predicted aggressiveness among 875 eight-year-olds even after equating the children on several possible third factors. When they restudied the subjects as nineteen-year-olds they discovered that viewing violence at age eight modestly predicted aggressiveness at nineteen, but that earlier aggressiveness did *not* predict violence viewing later. Aggression followed viewing, not the reverse. Eron and Huesmann and their colleagues confirmed these findings in follow-up studies of 758 Chicago-area and 220 Finnish youngsters. The researchers also examined the later criminal conviction records of their initial sample of eight-year-olds. At thirty, those who had watched a great deal of violence as children had more often been convicted of a serious crime.

Even murder rates increase where television goes. In Canada and the United States, the homicide rate doubled between 1957 and 1974 as the first TV generation was growing up. In census regions where television came later, the homicide rate jumped later. In white South Africa, where television was not introduced until 1975, a similar near doubling of the homicide rate did not begin until after 1975. From such data University of Washington epidemiologist Brandon Centerwall surmises that, without television, violent crime today would be half what it is. This doubling of violence extends beyond crime. In one closely studied rural town where television came late, playground aggression doubled.

With such data in hand, a scientific consensus has emerged: across time and across people, watching violence predicts aggression. In 1993, the American Psychological Association's Commission on Violence and Youth declared that there is now "absolutely no doubt that higher levels of viewing violence on television are correlated with increased acceptance of aggressive attitudes and increased aggressive behavior." Eron, the commission's chairman, explains: "As a child, you see a Dirty Harry movie, where the heroic policeman is shooting people right and left. Even years later, the right kind of scene can trigger that script and suggest a way to behave that follows it. Our studies have come up with a lot of evidence that suggests that's possible." All in all, "the evidence is overwhelming," he concludes. The viewing-aggression relation "is about the same as that between smoking and lung cancer." Many who smoke don't die of lung cancer, and many who absorb countless hours playing Mortal Kombat or watching Rambo reruns will live gentle lives. (The viewing effect is most noticeable with angered or characteristically hostile individuals.) Still, the correlation is undeniable.

Sexual Violence and Behavior

Similar results come from studies that correlate men's viewing of sexual violence with their aggression against women. It's not enough, of course, to verify that men who rape have experienced pornography. (Nearly all convicted rapists are habitual bread eaters, and some 9 in 10 consumed bread in the 24 hours before committing their violence.) So what shall we make of the finding that across the world reported rape rates increased as pornography became more widely available during the 1960s and 1970s? Is it a coincidence, researcher John Court wonders, that in places that controlled pornography, rape rates tended not to jump? In Hawaii, for example, the number of reported rapes rose ninefold between 1960 and 1974, dropped when restraints on pornography were temporarily imposed, and rose again when the restraints were lifted. (Japan, which has experienced an increase in available pornography and a decrease in sexual crimes over the past twenty-five years, is a notable exception to the pornography-crime correlation.)

In another correlational study, Larry Baron and Murray Straus discovered that sexually explicit magazine sales in the fifty states correlated with state rape rates. After controlling for other factors, such as the percentage of young males in each state, the correlation remained. Alaska ranked first in sales of magazines like *Hustler* and first in rape. Nevada was second on both measures.

When interviewed, Canadian and American sex offenders commonly acknowledge pornography use (although not greater exposure during childhood and adolescence). Compared with men who are not sexual offenders, Ontario rapists and child molesters have been big customers of the pornography industry. The chief U.S. postal inspector, Kenneth Hunter, reports that "approximately 30 percent of the individuals we investigate for using the mails to traffic in child pornography are or have been involved in the sexual abuse of children." The Los Angeles Police Department reports that pornography was "conspicuously present" or used in 62 percent of its extrafamilial child sexual abuse cases during the 1980s. An FBI study also reports disproportionate pornography exposure among serial killers. Tragic examples abound, such as Milwaukee mass murder Jeffrey Dahmer — in whose apartment police found pornographic tapes.

Experiments reveal that it's the violence more than the sex (whether in R-rated or X-rated films) which immediately increases men's aggression against women. Based on such findings, the surgeon general's conference of twenty-one social scientists agreed that "in laboratory studies measuring short-term effects, exposure to violent pornography increases punitive behavior toward women." Nonviolent erotica between consenting partners has multiple other effects, but in the short run it seems not to make a man more violent or hurtful.

Television Viewing Experiments

Defenders of the cigarette and entertainment industries object that "mere correlations" can only *suggest* cause and effect. If you get sick after eating oysters, the oysters may or may not be responsible. No correlational study can eliminate the endless list of possible third factors that could conceivably create a merely coincidental relation between viewing violence and aggression (or between smoking and lung cancer). Fortunately, there is a simple way to control for extraneous factors. Randomly assign some children to watch violence and others nonviolence. Then observe their aggressiveness. If the two groups differ, it must be due to their one difference: what they watched.

Picture this scene from a trailblazing midcentury experiment by Stanford psychologist Albert Bandura. A nursery school child is at work on a picture. An adult in another part of the room is working with some Tinker Toys. The adult then gets up and for nearly ten minutes pounds, kicks, and throws a large inflated doll around the room, yelling, "Sock him in the nose . . . Hit him down . . . Kick him."

After observing this outburst, the child is taken to another room where there are many appealing toys. Soon the experimenter interrupts the child's play and explains that she has decided to save these good toys "for the other children." She now takes the frustrated child to an adjacent room containing a few toys, including a similar doll. When left alone, compared with children not exposed to the adult model, children who observed the aggressive outburst were much more likely to lash out at the doll.

Soon after this experiment, social psychologists Leonard Berkowitz and Russell Geen extended the findings to university students. Angered students who had viewed a violent film acted more aggressively than similarly angered students who had viewed nonaggressive films. Such experiments, coupled with growing public concern about media mayhem, prompted the surgeon general to commission fifty new studies during the early 1970s. In congressional testimony, political scientist Ithiel de Sola Pool, a onetime critic of broadcast regulation, summed up the findings: "Twelve scientists of widely different views unanimously agreed that scientific evidence indicates that the viewing of television violence by young people causes them to behave more aggressively."

Skepticism nevertheless lingered, especially among media advocates who persisted in believing that people can purge their hostilities through viewing violence. "Watching action shows cannot only be cathartic, but can encourage play," offered Margaret Loesch, Fox Children's Network president. So psychologists ran more experiments. Chris Boyatzis and his colleagues showed television's most popular — and violent — children's program, *Power Rangers,* to some elementary school children but not others. Immediately after viewing an episode, the viewers committed seven times as many aggressive acts per two-minute interval as the nonviewers. As in Bandura's pioneering studies, the boy viewers often precisely duplicated the characters' acts, including their flying karate kicks. Like geologic erosion, such little effects can eventually produce big results. In Norway in 1994 a five-year-old girl was stoned, kicked, and left to freeze in the snow by playmates imitating acts seen on the show — causing it to be banned by three Scandinavian countries. Informed by such experiments, a 1982 National Institute of Mental Health report echoed the surgeon general's 1972 report: "The consensus among most of the research community is that violence on television does lead to aggressive behavior by children and teenagers who watch the programs." Later statements by the American Psychological Association, American Medical Association, and American Pediatric Association concurred. To be sure, the aggression provoked in these brief experiments is not assault and battery. No one alleges that folks watch movies then grab their guns. The effect is more on the scale of a shove in the dinner line, a cruel comment, a threatening gesture. And, like the gradual toxic contamination of air and water, it accumulates to create a cultural climate that fosters violence. "The irrefutable conclusion," said the American Psychological Association's 1993 youth violence report, "is that viewing violence increases violence."

Why Watching Violence Affects Behavior

Researchers now believe these effects stem from a combination of factors — from violence-related ideas (the social scripts mentioned earlier), from excitement and arousal, from the erosion of inhibitions, and from imitation.

Arousal can heighten aggression just as it heightens all forms of social behavior. Parents see the "emotional spillover" effect as their hyped-up children sometimes waver between anger, tears, and laughter. Dozens of experiments show that adults, too, can experience a stirred-up state as one emotion or another very different one, depending on how they interpret and label it; arousal from emotions as diverse as anger, fear, and sexual excitement can spill from one to another. The arousal that lingers after an intense argument or a frightening experience may intensify sexual passion. Insult people who have just been aroused by pedaling an exercise bike or watching an exciting film and they will find it easy to misattribute their arousal to the provocation. Their feelings of anger will then be greater than those of similarly provoked people who were not previously aroused.

Viewing violence also causes disinhibition. In Bandura's experiment, the adult's punching the doll seemed to legitimize such outbursts and to lower the children's inhibitions. As television primes violence-related thoughts, inner restraints dwindle.

As dramatically evident in the *Power Rangers* experiment, the media also evoke imitation, a phenomenon familiar to elementary and junior high teachers. We look and we learn.

By looking at the media, children may "learn" that physical intimidation is an effective way to control others, that free and easy sex brings pleasure without the misery of unwanted pregnancy or disease, or that men are supposed to be macho and women gentle and seductive. The television industry can hardly dispute such influence when it persuades advertisers to fork over $29 billion a year — much of it enticing our behavior with models who eat, drink, and drive these products.

Erotica and Sexual Behavior

Social scientists have focused mainly on Hollywood's violence, not its sex. So what about the sex? We noted earlier that saturation viewing of uncommitted sex alters people's perceptions of sexual reality, diminishes their attraction to comparatively less exciting partners, primes men's perception of women in sexual terms, makes sexual aggression seem less serious, and teaches "social scripts" that may later influence their behavior in real life situations.

But does it influence behavior? Does it play any part in the decline of marriage, the corruption of childhood, and the expansion of social chaos? Except for possible spillover from sexual arousal to hostility, explicit portrayals of impulsive sex seem not to directly cause violence. But do they help foster the social conditions, such as nonmarital childbearing and family fragmentation, that breed violence?

Sexual Modeling

In 1896, a film called *The Kiss* outraged moral guardians by showing a couple stealing a quick kiss. "Absolutely disgusting," said one critic. "Such things call for police action." By the 1990s, prime-time network entertainment offered sexual remarks or behavior every four minutes. From their monitoring of network programs for Planned Parenthood, Louis Harris and Associates estimated that the average viewer witnesses fourteen thousand sexual events annually. Nearly all involve unmarried people. An analysis of one week of network prime-time TV found that intercourse was mentioned or intimated by unmarried couples ninety times and by married couples once. Rarely are there any consequences. No one gets herpes or AIDS. No one gets pregnant. No one has to change diapers, get up in the middle of the night, or heroically struggle to socialize a fatherless child. In fact, more than two-thirds of the time (in another analysis of 220 scenes of unmarried sex) the activity is portrayed as desirable, less than 10 percent of the time as undesirable.

Developmental psychologist David Elkind wonders also about teens' "constant exposure to sexually explicit rock lyrics." He illustrates with his eleven-year-old niece and a friend, who easily listed sexual songs they were familiar with, including "Let's Talk About Sex," "I Wanna Sex You Up," "I Want Your Sex." If imagination is insufficient, MTV visualizes such images with Janet Jackson, Madonna, Robert Kelly, and others gyrating simulated sex acts. So, also, do readily accessible R-rated movies featuring teens — in which unmarried sex partners outnumber the married by a 32 to 1 ratio.

In seeking to explain today's early age of first intercourse — which most women look back on with regret — one New Zealand research team points to media depictions "of sex as glamorous, pleasurable and adult, while negative consequences and the responsibilities involved in sexual relationships are seldom portrayed." "That's putting it mildly," reflected Jane Brody. "In a currently popular movie, *Slums of Beverly Hills,* a precocious 13-year-old decides to have sex with an older boy 'just to get it over with.' Is this the message we want to convey to American youth," the normally dispassionate *New York Times* columnist wondered, " — that sex is something you try, like rollerblading or water skiing, to see what it's like or to add to your roster of achievements?"

With 68 percent of video rental shops offering sexually explicit tapes and with 9.8 million XXX Web pages to be found through Alta Vista, pornography also has become more accessible to all ages in all places. If you've ever wondered what these X-rated films depict, curious social scientists have sampled the fare and counted the behaviors. Some titles leave little room for wondering — *Kill the Bitch, Raped School Girls, Black Bitches in Bondage.* But others are more ambiguous. So Illinois psychologist David Duncan and his associates rented and watched fifty randomly selected "adult" videos from a local video store. The average video offered eighteen scenes (activity sequences in a given context), ten containing explicit sex, one-fifth of which also contained violence and 30 percent of which contained acts of degradation.

Hans-Bernd Brosius and his colleagues did a similar but more detailed content analysis of fifty pornographic videos randomly drawn from an archive of all such materials targeted to German heterosexuals during the 1980s (most were produced in the United States). Four student coders counted everything you've ever wanted to know about such films. Two-thirds of scenes were devoted to sexual activity, usually involving nude partners, lasting an average 5.28 minutes. Like TV's population of sexually active people, only 6 percent were portrayed in a committed relationship such as marriage. Intercourse occurred in 61 percent of sex scenes, fellatio in 54 percent, and cunnilingus in 40 percent. Nearly always the scene ended with the male orgasm, which usually was displayed with semen ejaculated onto the woman's body or into her mouth. Only one percent of women and none of the men mentioned any use of contraceptives.

Catharsis?

"Viewing a porno movie could have a beneficial effect that results in releasing the pent-up energy in a harmless manner," contends a letter writer to my local paper during a controversy over neighborhood pornography peddlers. Under Freud's lingering influence, he has much company. By nearly a two to one margin, Americans during the 1980s felt that "sexual materials provide an outlet for bottled-up impulses." As ACLU president Nadine Strossen explains, "Erotic publications and videos offer an alternative sexual outlet for people who otherwise would be driven to engage in psychologically or physically risky sexual relations" and thus "serve a positive public health function."

If Strossen's pop psychology idea is right, then Nevada, with its sex industries and high consumption of sex magazines, should have a low rape rate. And viewing pornography should at least temporarily lessen sexual arousal. But the opposite is plainly so. Sexually explicit videos are an aphrodisiac; they feed sexual fantasies that fuel a variety of sexual behaviors. In the hours after watching erotic films, people become more likely to engage in masturbation and intercourse. Moreover, reports William Griffitt, studies show "increases in the frequency of sex conversations, sex fantasies, sexual desires, and sexual dreams following exposure." This result perfectly parallels the finding that theater patrons interviewed after a violent action film express greater hostility than those interviewed beforehand. Viewing aggression and sex arouses rather than discharges pent-up impulses. Still, the catharsis legend persists. As John F. Kennedy said, the "great enemy of truth" is often not the deliberate lie but the persistent, persuasive myth.

The Sexual Climate

Social psychologists who have studied the recipe for sexual aggression identify two key ingredients, which Neil Malamuth calls *hostile masculinity* and *promiscuous-impersonal sex.* What makes a man sexually aggressive is not a strong sex drive or abundant sexual fantasies; a man can have strong sexual urges yet restrain their expression in celibacy or a committed, loving relationship. What's explosive is a history of unrestricted sex with many different partners — a behavior pattern that threatens an ongoing relationship — combined with a defensive, hostile attitude toward women.

Many sexually aggressive men acquire their hostility growing up in macho cultures or a home marked by parental fights and child abuse. Where do they acquire their scripts for promiscuous, impersonal sex? We decry impersonal or exploitative sex, unprotected sex, and teen pregnancy and its associated social pathologies. Yet these are exactly what our current media fare gives us.

Film critic Michael Medved, for twelve years the host of *Sneak Previews* on PBS, says it is "appallingly illogical" to contend "that intensely sexual material does nothing to encourage promiscuity." Child advocate Edelman agrees: "Parents alone are not responsible for the perversions of family and community values today. . . . Telling our children to 'just say no' is hypocritical and useless while parent and other adult role models send cultural messages and provide examples that 'say yes.'" "Americans once expected parents to raise their children in accordance with the dominant cultural messages," reflects Ellen Goodman. "Today they are expected to raise their children in opposition."

Studies of children's capacity for "observational learning" make such concerns understandable. Moreover, the repeated, vivid, consistent portrayal of casual sexuality, uncontested by equally potent alternative sources of sexual information, make television an ideal medium for scripting children's future sexual behaviors. MTV understands this. MTV "is a cultural force," it declared in an *Adweek* advertisement. "People don't watch it. They live it. MTV has affected the way an entire generation thinks, talks and buys." MTV's former chairman Bob Pittman explained, "At MTV, we don't shoot for the 14-year-olds, we own them."

Where Do We Go from Here?

In 1992, an upset Texas dentist, Richard Neill, orchestrated a campaign to draw attention to the social deviance on after-school talk shows hosted by Phil Donahue and others. In response to the criticism, Donahue called Neill a censor and a zealot. Pressed by Dan Rather, Donahue asked rhetorically, "What kind of country do we want?"

"That *is* the question, all right," emphasized Newton Minow and Craig LaMay in *Abandoned in the Wasteland*. "Do we want to be the kind of nation, the kind of people, who abandon their children to a state of subhuman exploitation and regard them only as customers . . . ? Americans have never debated this question; rather, they have defaulted on it." We would never allow strangers to walk into our homes and parade antisocial behavior before our children and excite their avarice for three hours a day, Minow and LaMay argue. Yet when such strangers come via television we resign ourselves to what we feel helpless to control.

Minow and LaMay speak for countless outraged parents. When *USA Weekend* invited readers to call in their agreement or disagreement with the statement "Hollywood no longer reflects — or even respects — the values of most American families," 21,221 callers called to register disagreement, and a record 54,453 callers registered agreement, not to mention 400,000 unsuccessful attempts to call the jammed "agree" line (as counted by phone company computers). In President Clinton's State of the Union address in 1995, the most applauded line was the one about the damage that "comes from the incessant, repetitive, mindless violence and irresponsible conduct that permeate our media all the time."

Although Phil Donahue acknowledges that "we've got a culture in decay" and trash talk pioneer Geraldo Rivera now is "sick of the garbage that is on," media executives and apologists typically respond by advising parents simply to press the off button. "If you don't like it, don't watch it — and don't interfere with my rights to watch it." "It is vitally important that we not interfere with the rights of those who like [trash television]," counseled Ann Landers.

Such advice is either naive or disingenuous. It overestimates parental influence and underestimates the power of the cultural winds. It is equivalent to saying, "If you don't like the air pollution, don't breathe." Even if one were willing to rebuff children's pleas to watch what their friends are watching, one cannot control what they see in their friends' homes, nor the promos they see hyping off-limits programs, nor the media effect — akin to secondhand smoke — transmitted through peer values and behavior. "Very few people can sustain values at a personal level when they are continually contradicted at work, at the store, in the government, and on television," observes Stephanie Coontz. "To call their failure to do so a family crisis is much like calling pneumonia a breathing crisis. Certainly, pneumonia affects people's ability to breathe easily, but telling them to start breathing properly again, or even instructing them in breathing techniques, is not going to cure the disease."

Indeed, it just doesn't do for cynical executives to lecture parents about family viewing policies while continuing to pollute the cultural atmosphere. "When Hollywood markets the worst and tells parents to do their best, it's like shooting holes in the family boat and telling us to keep plugging," writes Ellen Goodman. "There's a point at which you just sink." And that is why the new social ecology movement expects more.

Reforming the Media

My aim as a social psychologist is not to write laws, propose regulations, or set media policies but to inform the public debate. I do, however, recoil at three tired arguments opposing efforts at media reform.

Witless argument number one is to label critics as censors. Robert Dole may have been hypocritical in excluding Republican actors like Bruce Willis and Arnold Schwarzenegger from his list of those who "poison the minds of our young people . . . for the sake of corporate profits." But his hypocrisy is exceeded by the producers and actors who, rather than engage the debate, dismiss critics as McCarthyite censors. In 1992, when a group of women organized Turn Off the TV Day, National Television Association president Peter Chrisanthopoulos objected, "Participating in national boycotts is an infringement on the networks' First Amendment rights." What lovely irony, note Minow and LaMay, "that the networks, having long insisted that a parent's only constitutional recourse was to turn off the set, now view even that act as unconstitutional." When media defenders "use the First Amendment to stop debate rather than to enhance it," they reduce "our first freedom to the logical equivalent of a suicide pact."

Critics who heap shame on producers and broadcasters also have been called censors. For advocating voluntary warning labels on rock albums, Tipper Gore was vilified and accused of supporting censorship. Ice Cube granted that "the editor of *Billboard* has a right to give his opinions" about misogynist, racist, violent rap lyrics. "But when he says . . . think twice before you buy this, that's a form of censorship." The CEO of Time Warner labeled public disgust at a cop-killing rap song an attack on free speech. But whenever critics find a book or film worthless or odious, they implicitly tell us, "Skip it." And they ask the producer, who can choose from 27,000 scripts registered each year with the Writer's Guild and from countless demo tapes offered by aspiring music groups, "Why did you pick this one?" "I don't know what a critic is supposed to be doing if he or she does not write in strong terms about strong dislikes," critic Roger Rosenblatt explains. "And if that's censorship, I'll eat my hat."

Witless reaction number two is to recycle the domino theory: if we give an inch, they'll take a mile. We heard this often during the Vietnam War: "If we don't stop Communism there, it may soon spread like cancer." Well, we didn't, and it hasn't. Libertarians of left and right also wing the theory with clichés about allowing in the thin edge of the wedge, admitting the camel's nose into the tent, and descending down a slippery slope. Pass a law curtailing TV violence, warned People for the American Way, and "curfews, newspaper censorship, book burning," and the suspension of the Constitution are not far behind. Let the government require commercial Internet sites to block access to pornography by children (as under the 1998 Child On-Line Protection Act signed into law by President Clinton, though later struck down by the Supreme Court) and soon a police state will be censoring the free flow of ideas.

But reasonable laws — all of which restrain our freedom — seldom cascade us down a slippery slope or trip a line of dominoes. "Not every young woman who allows herself to be kissed before marriage ends up a hooker," Amitai Etzioni chides. Credit the American people with enough sense to draw lines that respect important rights while affirming social responsibilities. Censoring slander, false advertising, cigarette ads, and pornography from network TV has not threatened *Catcher in the Rye*'s place on my library's bookshelf, much less threatened what the First Amendment was intended to protect (the expression of ideas — what Justice Oliver Wendell Holmes called "freedom for the thought that we hate"). What has curtailing the rights of child pornographers done except make it more difficult to sell child pornography?

As these examples suggest, "censorship" is a red herring. In a 1995 *Time*/CNN poll only 27 percent of Americans favored "government censorship" of sex and violence, though 66 percent approved of "more restrictions on what is shown on television." Actually, nearly all Americans favor some forms of censorship, such as on child pornography or X-rated films on prime-time TV, while supporting the free press envisioned by Thomas Jefferson. Pornography has nothing to do "with the free speech intended by the Founding Fathers," Elizabeth Fox-Genovese argues. Rather than shut off debate with cries of "slippery slope" or "censorship," let's engage the debate — as we have with gun control, environmental legislation, and drug laws.

Witless argument number three implies that if a problem has multiple causes, there's no warrant for doing anything. Cancer is mostly caused by things other than cyclamates or secondhand smoke, so why control these? The cultural crisis is not mostly the media's fault, so don't imagine that a television world featuring nonviolent conflict resolution and committed love will suddenly reduce assaults and teen births.

The parallels between libertarians who favor a broad First Amendment interpretation (called liberals) and libertarians who favor a broad Second Amendment interpretation (called conservatives) are striking. Communitarians respect the First Amendment but want it balanced with the Fourteenth

Amendment's guarantee of equal protection for all (women and children included) and with the Constitution's priority on our general welfare: "We the People of the United States, in Order to . . . promote the general Welfare . . . establish this Constitution for the United States of America."

Although many conservatives decry current media fare, they have the vigorous deregulation policies of the Reagan administration to thank for today's profit-driven schlock. "The marketplace will take care of children," said Mark Fowler, President Reagan's FCC chair. If children would rather watch Jerry Springer than do homework, so be it. From an average eleven hours per week of educational programming in 1980, ABC, CBS, and NBC descended to one hour a week in 1992. "Virtually overnight," report Minow and LaMay, deregulation transformed broadcasting "from a public trust into one of the hottest businesses on Wall Street. In their celebration of the bottom line and their open contempt for traditional public-interest values, broadcasters began to restructure, dismantle, or simply abandon many of the features for which the public had admired them most — news divisions, children's programs, standards-and-practices departments. The number and volume of commercials increased, and broadcasters adopted an anything-goes programming policy."

Adam Smith would not have been astonished. He described profit-motivated businesspeople much as Bob Dole described Hollywood's corporate profiteers — as "an order of men, whose interest is never exactly the same with that of the public, who have generally an interest to deceive and even to oppress the public." *Christian Century* editor James Wall put it more bluntly: "The market is a monster without values, and it will do whatever is needed to make profits." We recognize that when we impose public interest obligations on the tobacco industry, the automobile industry, and to a lesser extent the entertainment industry. Civic-minded industrialists often welcome such obligations, which enable them to add air pollution controls knowing that their competitors must bear the same costs. Lacking a mandated level playing field, those who exploit the lowest common denominator can defeat their more benevolent corporate rivals.

In considering restraints on either air or airwave pollution, we weigh the harm to corporate and personal rights against the harm to societal health. Most Americans give greater weight to First Amendment freedoms than to Fourteenth Amendment equal protection, to individual rights than to social responsibilities. But at some point on the perniciousness scale most of us become accepting of restraints on our freedom. We accept the restrictions of open housing laws that provide equal protection to people of all races. We accept some restrictions on hate speech or on gang members' rights to roam in packs carrying chains and tire irons.

Not all morality should be legislated, but sometimes communities do affirm morality with laws. Laws help "convince citizens that the community is serious about its professed standards of responsibility," William Galston urges. "From drunk driving to racial discrimination, vigorous enforcement backed by sanctions has proved essential in changing behavior." Etzioni concurs: "Without punishing those who do serious injury to our commonly held values — child abusers, toxic polluters, fathers who renege on child support, corporations who market unsafe drugs — no moral order can be sustained. We do not have to love the coercive side of the law, but we cannot fail to recognize its place as a last resort."

Should we then enact laws to prohibit violent programming when children are a large part of the viewership? Should we require broadcasters to label violent programs? Should we require the FCC to establish violence standards that would be enforced as a condition of license renewal? Should we require the FCC to issue quarterly TV violence reports, identifying sponsors of violent shows? Does it make sense, asks Harvard child psychiatrist Robert Coles, to tell the tobacco companies, "Don't poison people," and then to tolerate television's poisoning of our children's minds?

Content warnings clearly are an anemic response. Alerting teens to graphic programming tends, in fact, to tantalize them, Iowa State University researchers Brad Bushman and Angela Stack report; suggest parental or viewer discretion and they will be *more* likely to watch a movie. And a national survey in 1998 showed that most adults — even in homes with children — pay little attention to ratings like "TV-PG."

Short of censorship, there is another controversial policy option: empower citizens to hold the media legally responsible for their products' effects, just as citizens can hold drug or toy companies responsible. State lawsuits against tobacco companies and city lawsuits against firearms manufacturers — seeking recompense for the medical and law-enforcement costs of cigarettes and "unreasonably dangerous" weapons — illustrate efforts to hold corporations responsible for marketing products known to be harmful. If you produce and profit from, say, a sexually violent video — an illustrated how-to manual on sexual abuse — then anyone who believes she was victimized as a result of your product could try to prove a claim against you in court.

Lawyer-writer John Grisham agrees that product liability laws should extend to media merchants. After an acquaintance of his was gunned down by two people who had watched Oliver Stone's *Natural Born Killers* for the umpteenth time before the shooting, Grisham castigated Stone: "He's an *artist* and he can't be bothered with the effects of what he produces." But let him lose a product liability suit, "and the party will be over." Civil libertarians disagree.

"I do not believe, for example, that publishers of how-to-books for murderers, kidnappers and thieves should be held liable for the crimes of people who read them," says Wendy Kaminer. "And, when a woman is raped I would not impose any liability on the publisher of a violent, sexually explicit magazine enjoyed by her rapist. In order to protect the right to express unpopular, provocative views and political freedom, the First Amendment should effectively prohibit third-party liability in cases involving speech."

Empowering Parents

Another debated idea — now becoming a reality — is the violence-chip requirement incorporated into the 1996 telecommunications bill. When installed in every new set, the chip will allow parents to block programs carrying designated ratings. Although the networks have, for now, elected a movie-style rating system, the Electronic Industries Association, representing television manufacturers, promises a technology that could block shows with violence, sex, or profanity at various levels, perhaps rated 0 to 5. By dialing their V-chip to numbers of their choice, parents could admit only shows that meet their criteria. The technology is cheap — adding about a dollar to the cost of a new TV. It can be as kid-proof as a pin-numbered ATM card. And it involves no government censorship — no prior restraint.

The chip is no panacea. It doesn't directly modify programming. And most parents won't use it. But some will — enough, backers suspect, to make blocked programs less appealing to advertisers (some of whom will not wish to be associated with such programs), and enough, one infers from network reactions, to make the chip a perceived threat. For NBC general counsel Richard Cotton, "This legislation turns the FCC into Big Brother." CBS Broadcast Group's former president Howard Stringer worried that "the V chip is the thin end of a wedge. If you start putting chips in the television set to exclude things, it becomes an all-purpose hidden censor." "We see [a ratings system] as beginning down the slippery slope of censorship," said Marty Franks of CBS. "Quite frankly," fretted Fox Television chairwoman Lucie Salhany, "the very idea of a V-chip scares me. I'm also very concerned about setting a precedent. Will we have an 'S-chip' [for sex]?"

These reactions expose what Adam Smith, Bob Dole, and Newton Minow warned us to expect: that corporate concern for profits exceeds concern for the public interest. The cable industry, much of whose $38 billion income in 1996 came from viewer subscriptions, supported the V-chip. The major networks, whose money comes from advertisers, resisted the chip — despite its empowering parents to do more effectively just what the networks have long advised: use the off button. For that's all the chip is — an automated off switch, an intelligent remote control. If parents want to program their chip to block gratuitous sex — or sports or news, for that matter — why should they not be free to do so? When parental control over reception gets called "censorship," then we must wonder with Lewis Carroll's Alice about the wisdom of making a word "mean so many different things."

Awakening Public Awareness: The Gauche Factor

The state has *some* power to sway individuals' moral behavior. As the civil rights era (and countless social psychological experiments) have taught us, we can, to some extent, legislate morality. After the Supreme Court's school desegregation decision in 1954, the percentage of white Americans favoring integrated schools more than doubled, and now includes nearly everyone. In the decade following the Civil Rights Act of 1964, the number of white Americans who described their neighbors, friends, co-workers, or fellow students as all-white declined by about 20 percent each. During this period of increasing interracial behavior, the proportion of whites who said that blacks should be allowed to live in any neighborhood increased from 65 percent to 87 percent. Racial morality has been noticeably legislated. This illustrates why we are "a government of laws" and not just of individuals. Valuing our freedom, we want limits on the laws and regulations that constrain us. Valuing civility and order, we also welcome some agreed-upon rules.

But our great need today is much less for government censorship than for corporate citizenship. Morality cannot depend primarily on government decree. Mostly, it grows from the culture's moral voice. Prohibition failed because it lacked a cultural mandate. Restrictions on smoking in public places are succeeding because a long period of conversation and education helped transform public consciousness.

Pleas to Hollywood have largely fallen on deaf ears. In a *U.S. News and World Report* poll, 83 percent of the public, but only 38 percent of the Hollywood elite, expressed concern about televised portrayals of premarital sex. The media culture that American parents want piped into their homes is not what the corporate world provides. But let's not discount the power of an awakened public consciousness. In the 1940s, movies often depicted African-Americans as childlike, superstitious buffoons. Today such images are not illegal, they are just gauche. An informed and aroused public voice gets heard.

The successes of the public health campaigns to reduce drug and cigarette use suggest a two-pronged effort. First, parents, schools, and churches can offer children media awareness education. Second, we can all work to increase public consciousness of the media's part in the cultural crisis, with the aim of making barbarism and impulsive promiscuity as gauche tomorrow as racial degradation is today. Better yet, we can hope for a new generation of creative artists who will do as Joan Baez, Pete Seeger, and Peter, Paul, and Mary did in their music for the civil rights movement — give us soul-stirring songs that challenge lovelessness, greed, exploitation, and degradation and offer images of a more nurturing, selfless, spiritually sensitive, and joyful world.

Media Awareness Education

Parents can increase their children's media literacy. The American Psychological Association advises parents to limit their children's TV watching. Step one for any parent should be to end — right now — the increasingly common but irresponsible practice of placing televisions in children's bedrooms. Second, parents can watch programs with their children and discuss the social scripts. The cable television industry's "Voices Against Violence" initiative urges parents to "kick the glamour out of violence" by talking about it. Ask children: How would you feel if that happened to you? Could this stuff really happen — no blood on the floor, no problem jumping back up after being clobbered with a two-by-four or beaten with fists? Could this problem have been solved in some other way?

Of course, the cable industry telling us to take the glamour out of the violence they pipe into our homes is like the water department sending us polluted water with instructions on how to detoxify it. Doubting that the networks would ever "face the facts and change their programming," Eron and Huesmann taught Chicago-area children that television portrays an unreal world, that aggression is less common and effective than TV makes it seem, and that violence is wrong. When restudied two years later, these children were less influenced by violence they watched than were untrained children.

Researchers have also studied how to immunize young children so they can more effectively analyze and evaluate television commercials. This research was prompted partly by studies showing that children, especially those under eight, have trouble distinguishing commercials from programs and fail to grasp their persuasive intent, trust television advertising rather indiscriminately, and desire and badger their parents for advertised products — findings that will astonish few parents. Children, it seems, are an advertiser's dream: gullible, vulnerable, an easy sell. Moreover, half the twenty thousand ads the typical child sees in a year are for low-nutrition, often sugary foods.

Armed with such data, citizens' groups have given the advertisers of such products a chewing out: "When a sophisticated advertiser spends millions to sell unsophisticated, trusting children an unhealthy product, this can only be called exploitation. No wonder the consumption of dairy products has declined since the start of television, while soft-drink consumption has almost doubled." On the other side are the commercial interests, who claim that such ads allow parents to teach their children consumer skills and, more important, finance children's television programs. In the United States, the Federal Trade Commission has been in the middle, pushed by research findings and political pressures while trying to decide whether to place new constraints on TV ads aimed at young children.

Meanwhile, researchers have wondered whether children can be taught to resist deceptive ads. In one such effort, a team of investigators led by Norma Feshbach gave small groups of Los Angeles-area elementary school children three half-hour lessons in analyzing commercials. The children were inoculated by viewing ads and discussing them. After watching a toy ad, for example, they were immediately given the toy and challenged to make it do what they had just seen in the commercial. Such experiences helped breed a more realistic understanding of commercials.

Encouraged by such findings, a report of the Carnegie Council on Adolescent Development in 1995 urged schools "to introduce instruction and activities that contribute to media literacy." Britain, Canada, Australia, and Spain already require media literacy as part of their language arts programs. In the United States, media literacy education — supported by such organizations as the Center for Media Literacy — is in its infancy. But already New Mexico and North Carolina have included it as a basic skill in their curricula, as has the Girl Scouts, which offers three media literacy and communications badges.

Spurring a Cultural Shift

The fundamental question for our time is what kind of culture do we want? Is it the culture we have — and were moving toward from 1960 to the early 1990s?

Of all the world's creatures, we humans are the most impressionable — the most capable of learning. That breeds hope, for what is learnable we can potentially teach. And it breeds concern, for the same potential puts us at risk for learning evil. The media's power is not intrinsically good or bad. It is like nuclear power, which can light up homes or wipe out cities. It is like persuasive power that enables us to enlighten or deceive. So how can we harness media power for good rather than evil, to create a culture we will love rather than loathe?

The answer surely will involve waving some cultural sticks. TV networks and film producers are legally free to recreate a racist Amos 'n Andy for the new century, or to display anti-semitism or celebrate gay bashing or animal torture. But they know that any bigot who did so would face moral outrage, advertiser boycott, and ultimate financial ruin. We the people are not powerless. When the revolted revolt, their voices get heard. "For 30 years, our families have been under assault," President Clinton declared in a talk to five hundred Hollywood executives, producers, directors, and stars. "We have to have the help of the people who determine our culture." That needn't mean projecting an unvarying image of the middle-class average to small, sleepy audiences. The successes of the *Cosby Show* in the 1980s and *Home Improvement* in the 1990s demonstrate that profits and principles can coexist.

The cultural shift must also involve an offering of carrots. These carrots include not only patronage of prosocial entertainment but resources that support positive programming. The presidents of the American Psychological Association, American Academy of Pediatrics, and American Psychiatric Association have written to 125 entertainment industry leaders offering assistance in understanding and reducing the harmful effects of media violence. Mediascope, an outgrowth of meetings sponsored by the Carnegie Council on Adolescent Development, offers curricular materials for workshops and courses that can be taken by moviemaking students.

In C. S. Lewis's *Screwtape Letters,* senior devil Screwtape counsels junior devil Wormwood, "The safest road to hell is the gradual one." As so many social psychology experiments demonstrate, succumbing to little evils paves the way for bigger ones. In complex societies, too, big evils are built of little evils. Nazi leaders were surprised at how easily they got German civil servants to handle the paperwork of the Holocaust. They were not killing Jews, of course. They were merely pushing paper. And so it is in our daily lives: the drift toward evil occurs in small steps, without any conscious intent and even without perceiving ourselves as cogs in an evil process. So it happens that nice people, good people, enable the social recession that, in the end, devastates so many lives. Can we awaken from their moral slumber those who, whether celebrities or clerks, film producers or ticket takers, conspire to define the popular culture? Must we wait, asks commentator Gregg Easterbrook, until a teenager guns down the children of studio executives in a Bel Air or Westwood high school?

Could we agree on a voluntary code declaring: "Broadcasters have a special responsibility toward children. Programs should contribute to the sound, balanced development of children. Programs involving violence should present the consequences of it to its victims and perpetrators." We have done it before. Those words are excerpted from the National Association of Broadcasters' voluntary code, abandoned in 1983 — "a powerful statement of citizenship and community responsibility," according to U.S. Senator Joseph Lieberman, D-Conn.

And can we humanize the next generation's awareness of the real human costs of violence and impulsive or coercive sex? Can we create a culture that values kindness and civility, attachment and fidelity — a culture of commitment? "Our utopian and perhaps naive hope," say media researchers Edward Donnerstein, Daniel Linz, and Steven Penrod, "is that in the end the truth revealed through good science will prevail and the public will be convinced that these images not only demean those portrayed but also those who view them."

Technology and the Internet

ELIZABETH L. HAYNES

Early in the year 2000 the United States entered its tenth year of sustained economic growth.[1] The dramatic gains since 1996 can be attributed to the strategic force of information technology and the digital economy. "To understand the post-1999 economy without acknowledging the revolutionary impact of the Internet," argues Alan Reynolds, "is impossible."[2] The continued expansion of the Internet will be the most far-reaching political and economic development of the technology revolution.[3]

The Internet evolved from a network of university and research lab super-computers developed in the 1960s.[4] In the early 1970s engineers began to

1. Robert Kuttner, "Boom Box," *The American Prospect,* 2 February 2000, p. 4.

2. Alan Reynolds, "Thank You New Technology," *The American Enterprise* 11 (March 2000): 29.

3. Donald Lambro, *Future Forces: Ten Trends That Will Shape American Politics and Policies in 2000 and Beyond,* Heritage Lectures 637, 5 May 1999 (Washington, D.C.: The Heritage Foundation, 15 June 1999), p. 4.

4. Barry M. Leiner et al., *A Brief History of the Internet,* available from www.isoc.org/internet/history/brief.html, accessed 19 March 2000; Robert Hobbes Zakon, *Hobbes Internet Timeline v 5.0,* available from www.isoc.org/guest/zakon/Internet/History/HIT.html, accessed 19 March 2000; *PBS Life on the Internet — Timeline,* available from http://www.pbs.org/internet/timeline/index.html, accessed 22 March 2000; *History of the Web,* available from http://www.hitmill.com/internet/web_history.html, accessed 22 March 2000; Tim Berners-Lee, *Answers to Frequently Asked Questions by the Press,* available from http://www.w3.org/People/Berners-Lee/FAQ.html, accessed 22 March 2000; and National Science Foundation, *Science and Engineering Indicators —*

formulate the protocols to handle communication between multiple, independent, open-design computer networks; the Internet was introduced in 1983. The year 1991 was a pivotal one in the history of the Internet, because it was then that the National Science Foundation permitted commercial use of the networks it managed, and by 1995 it relinquished the Internet to the commercial entities. A physicist developed the World Wide Web — computer code that permitted users to easily create a set of computerized documents that could be cross-referenced to each other across remote computers through hypertext links embedded in the documents. And a group of university students introduced the first graphical user interface (GUI) browser (software used to access the Internet) called Mosaic, which evolved into the first version of Netscape Navigator in 1995.

The Internet is now a variety of computer sub-networks and applications such as the World Wide Web, electronic bulletin boards, topical message forums, electronic mail, scientific data exchange, and more. As it stands today, "the Internet is as much a collection of communities as a collection of technologies, and its success is largely attributable to both satisfying basic community needs [and] utilizing the community in an effective way to push the infrastructure forward."[5] It is an example of the benefits of sustained investment, commitment to research, innovation, and collaboration.

The Internet's potential as a technology has been only partially realized in the last five years — the Internet is well known and commonplace, but not yet as pervasive as the television. "According to the research firm Jupiter Communications, only 37 percent of U.S. households were connected to the Net in 1998; by 2003 this figure will have risen to 63 percent — and that's a conservative estimate."[6] With regard to electronic commerce, the Internet is still in the experimentation and capitalization stages — an era of false promises, pipe dreams, and denial — but soon it will be entering the management and hypercompetition stages wherein a great deal of fallout will occur.[7] According to Jim Clark, founder of Netscape, the growth of the Internet over the next ten years will be due to new applications, services, and industries barely conceivable today.[8]

1998, available from http://www.nsf.gov/sbe/srs/seind98/start.htm, accessed 23 March 2000.

5. Leiner et al., *A Brief History of the Internet.*

6. Glenn McDonald and Cameron Crotty, "The Digital Future," *PC World* 18 (January 2000): 132.

7. Eric W. Pfeiffer, "Where Are We in the Revolution?" *Forbes ASAP*, 21 February 2000, pp. 68-70.

8. Rodes Fishburne et al., "Voices of the Revolution," *Forbes ASAP*, 21 February 2000, p. 80.

The original (and current) "hot" application for the Internet was electronic mail (e-mail); other early major uses included the ability to transfer computer files between computers and the ability to emulate a terminal on a remote computer. Today there are over 9.6 million web servers worldwide (which may host multiple web sites) and over 92 million people sixteen years of age and older using the Internet in the United States.[9] People use the Internet to obtain information for work, personal use, or education, to review current events, to purchase goods and services, to engage in discussion groups, and to pursue entertainment-related activities.[10] According to the Pew Research Center,

> Fully 75 percent of those who go online say the Internet is a good thing because it brings together people with similar interests, while just 14 percent say the Internet is bad because it can bring together small groups of people with dangerous ideas. Among Americans who do not go online, just 42 percent say the Internet is a good thing, while 37 percent worry that it is bad.[11]

On the negative side, Internet users worry about the unauthorized use or modification of their computer files and software (i.e., hackers), harassment through derogatory messages ("flame") and unsolicited commercial e-mail (also know as "spam" — the flooding of the Internet with many copies of the same message), computer viruses (programs that are intended to harm another computer system, application, or data), message interception, electronic commerce fraud, and copyright violation. To many, the Internet is social anarchy.[12] It reflects what Don Eberly viewed as the problem with today's American culture: "the steady replacement of an ordered liberty with the libertarianism of John Stuart Mill, in which freedom is absolute, the self is unbounded by even private morality and convention, and one's actions are protected even from social disapproval."[13] The Internet has redefined some old societal problems, such

9. *Internet Usage Around the World*, available from www.headcount.com/count/datafind.htm?choice=country&choiceV%5B%5D=The+US&submit=Submit, accessed 19 March 2000; and Hobbes Zakon, *Hobbes Internet Timeline.*

10. James A. Dewar, *The Information Age and the Printing Press: Looking Backward to See Ahead* (Santa Monica, Calif.: Rand, 1998), also available from www.rand.org/publications/P/P8014/index.html, accessed 19 March 2000; and The Pew Research Center for the People and the Press, *Technology 1998: Sections I-IV,* available from http://www.people-press.org/tech98mor.htm, accessed 19 March 2000.

11. The Pew Research Center for the People and the Press, *Technology 1998: Sections I-IV.*

12. Douglas Rushkoff, *Media Virus! Hidden Agendas in Popular Culture* (New York: Ballantine Books, 1996), p. 238.

13. Don Eberly, "What Chills Me About the Future," *American Outlook,* Fall 1999, pp. 20-21.

as pornography, "hate" speech, and the invasion of privacy, and raised some new ones, such as equal access to the Internet, the regulation and taxation of electronic commerce, encryption of computerized data and software, and the definition of community. All of these issues are important. Due to the topic of this essay and space limitations, however, I will briefly investigate only a few of these issues that are pertinent to civil society.

Internet-based Strategies for Renewing Civil Society

As Don Eberly explains, a civil society is, minimally, "the entire web of voluntary associations that dot our social landscape: families, neighborhoods, civic associations, charitable enterprises, and local networks of a thousand kinds. . . . These institutions are important because they perform innumerable functions . . . and generate individual character and democratic habits."[14] To renew civil society, the civic revivalists support civic participation by individuals, whereas the moral revivalists support restoring the moral foundations of this country.

Both sides of the civil society renewal debate agree that economic progress does not ensure social progress. Since the Internet is fueling economic progress, and since it is now part of the social and cultural fabric of this nation, it can and should be used constructively to advance the tenets of a civil society. Of the four strategies presented below, the first three stress using private means, as opposed to government mandates and interventions, to deal with Internet problems, and the fourth presents a method by which a civil society can be actively promoted.

Use Private Means to Censor the Internet; Do Not Permit Government Interventions to Prevail

The low cost and ease of entry onto the Internet, as either a "publisher" or a "reader," has resulted in a proliferation of "negative" web sites and Internet-based activities. According to a recent survey, Americans are concerned about pedophiles contacting their children via the Internet, pornographic web sites, and "hate-speech" and violence-oriented web sites (e.g., "how to build a bomb"), and they want the government to protect them.[15] In 1997 the U.S. Su-

14. Don Eberly, "Civic Renewal vs. Moral Renewal," *Policy Review*, September-October 1998, p. 44.

15. NPR Online, *Survey Shows Widespread Enthusiasm for High Technology*, available from http://www.npr.org/programs/specials/poll/technology, accessed 3 March 2000.

preme Court overturned the Communications Decency Act, which would have criminalized "indecency" on the Internet, because it restricted free speech.[16] The Court pointed out that there were less restrictive technologies available, such as filtering software and rating systems. The fight against "The Child Protection Act of 1999," which would have required that libraries receiving federal funds install filtering software, used the same interference-with-free-speech argument. From a different perspective, the Free Congress Foundation argued that filtering software blocks whatever the filterer wants, and "in the case of public school teachers and librarians, who by and large share the liberal establishment's viewpoint on many issues, filtering software harms conservative organizations as well as anyone with a website carrying a conservative message."[17]

To address the problem of access to inappropriate web sites, organizations such as public libraries with public-access computers should voluntarily institute a two-tiered system. First, a set of computers open to any user should have filtering software installed; although the software is not foolproof, it is better than nothing. The vendor of the software should publish on its own web site the criteria it uses to block sites. (This is where organizations such as the Free Congress Foundation should challenge the inappropriate criteria.) Second, a set of computers open to adults and to children with signed parental permission slips should not have the filtering software. These computers could be placed either in totally private cubicles or in plain view of passersby, especially in places where those in charge can see them. Private institutions such as universities (who own the equipment and the services) should develop policies appropriate for the institution and require that subscribers sign user agreements. For home use, parents could install their own filtering software, or parents could sign up with an Internet Service Provider (ISP) that provides this service. Of course, nothing is better than full parental oversight of children's activities on the Internet. Finally, there should be a movement to have ISPs voluntarily agree to not accept objectionable material on their subscribers' web sites, delete the material once it was reported (via a system that permits users to e-mail the objectionable site's host server), and have personnel eavesdrop on discussion groups (chat rooms) and messaging systems. These ISPs could receive and display a "seal of approval" from a sponsoring organization. Objectors could always find another ISP.

16. Daniel J. Weitzner, *Blocking and Filtering Content on the Internet after the CDA: Empowering Users and Families Without Chilling the Free Flow of Information Online*, Center for Democracy and Technology, available from www.cdt.org/speech/rating-issues.html, accessed 21 March 2000.

17. Free Congress Foundation et al., *Memorandum to House and Senate Conferees to Appropriations Subcommittee on Labor, Health & Human Services and Education re HR2560 "The Child Protection Act of 1999,"* 18 October 1999, available from www.freecongress.org/centers/technology/memo991018.htm, accessed 21 March 2000.

Use Private Means to Protect Privacy; Do Not Permit Government Interventions to Prevail

Privacy issues include "intrusion on one's seclusion, publicity that places one in a false light, misappropriation of one's name or likeness and public disclosure of private facts."[18] Sophisticated Internet users are aware that the web sites they contact can obtain information about them from their own computers, but these methods are not truly an invasion of privacy. Small programs called "cookies" are files placed on a user's computer by a web site to track the user's movement on the Internet. Cookies enable the vendor to conduct targeted marketing, most often in the form of advertisements specific to the user's interests or a personalized "welcome back" screen, but also by the selling of users' activity lists to other companies. Spam (unsolicited electronic mail) is very annoying, but it goes out to groups of users indiscriminately and without knowledge of their identities, beyond their e-mail addresses. The most obvious collection of user data comes when the user is required to complete a registration form, really no different than the warranty registration form for a product purchased at a store.

The movement to protect Internet privacy is gathering momentum. Since it went into effect in May 2000, the 1998 Children's Online Privacy Protection Act (COPPA) has required that child-oriented web sites obtain parental permission before collecting information on children under age thirteen. Recently, more than fifty privacy-related bills have been introduced in Congress, most imposing either "mandatory opt-in" (requiring an individual's consent before collecting the data) or "mandatory opt-out" (permitting a user to use a web site without providing data — a requirement on commercial web sites).[19]

Those people who want the government to regulate the way in which online companies gather information about their customers start with several false assumptions: that a person owns his or her "identity," that web sites abuse their power to collect information, and that the profit motive overcomes a respect for privacy.[20] First, whenever a user enters a web site there is often a "price" to pay, ranging from a full fee-based subscription to the simple provision of information, whether obvious through registration screens or unobvious through cookies. These web sites do not look through the user's computer files for private information. In other words, an implied contract has been established, and current contract laws are quite sufficient to protect the

18. John C. Dvorak, "The Privacy Pinch," *Forbes*, 7 February 2000, p. 138.

19. Justin Matlick, *Governing Internet Privacy: A Free-Market Primer* (San Francisco: Pacific Research Institute, 1999), p. 13.

20. Virginia Postrel, "No Telling," *Reason* 30 (June 1998): 5; and Justin Matlick, *Governing Internet Privacy*, p. 5.

contractual relationship, as are other rules and laws governing the conduct of business in general. Second, market forces are already driving businesses to alleviate privacy concerns because, to keep their customers who value privacy, these businesses know that privacy must be protected.

The solutions to stopping unwanted "invasions" of privacy are relatively simple. First, Internet Service Providers and web browsers should provide clear instructions about the use of cookies and spam and how to control them. Also available are "informediaries" who provide software that permits users to send their privacy preferences to a web site and to avoid sites that do not comply with these preferences. Second, people already have the choice of "opting-out" if a site requires personal information in exchange for entry into the site; there are thousands of other sites that do not require personal information. Third, users should share information on which sites honor their privacy and which sites do not. Finally, there is always legal action to remedy breaches of contract. Government intervention would smother the dynamic self-regulatory process, harm consumers by giving them a false sense of security, hinder electronic commerce by increasing start-up costs, and erode protections provided in the U.S. Constitution.[21]

Provide Points of Access to the Internet through Community-based Organizations

The source for alarm over a "digital divide" (between those people who have computers and/or Internet access and those who do not) was a December 1998 Commerce Department study, *Falling Through the Net: Part II — Internet Access and Usage*, which stated that

> more than one-third of Americans go online from any point, either at home or outside the home. . . . While Americans are becoming increasingly connected, there are still significant discrepancies in access: Blacks and Hispanics, for example, are less connected than Whites are at home.[22]

People with lower incomes, less education, and the unemployed are also less connected. While one set of numbers may support these contentions, the Commerce study exaggerated the gap by excluding computer usage outside

21. Matlick, *Governing Internet Privacy*, p. 5.

22. U.S. Department of Commerce, *Falling Through the Net: Part II — Internet Access and Usage*, available from www.ntia.doc.gov/ntiahome/fttn99/part2.html, accessed 19 March 2000.

the home in many of its comparisons. A survey by the Pew Research Center for the People and the Press, done in the same period as the Commerce study, found that 41 percent of the adults went online, and that "increasingly people without college training, those with modest incomes, and women are joining the ranks of Internet users."[23] According to more recent surveys the gap is closing. A Forrester Research Report stated that, because of the rapid decline of computer prices, the increasing availability of free Internet access, and the surge of first-time computer buying in the 1988 and 1999 Christmas gift seasons, "40 percent of black households will be online at some point this year [2000], while 44 percent of whites will — hardly a 'racial ravine.'"[24] The founder of BlackPlanet.com has stated that

> the critical statistic is not what are the current rates of usage but rather what are the current rates of adoption. . . . Over time, most advanced technologies that are available only to an elite few become widely dispersed among the broader population (e.g., television). . . . With dropping prices the data do indeed show that every American who wants one is getting a PC (personal computer.)[25]

A late 1999 poll by National Public Radio, the Kaiser Family Foundation, and Harvard's Kennedy School of Government indicated that income and education (not race) are the keys to the Internet, and that Americans over age sixty are the major group left out of the loop.[26]

In order to increase access to the Internet, organizations should fund computers, networks, and Internet access services (*and* the support personnel), not at the public schools (since that is already being done), but at places where the community gathers — churches, meeting halls, senior centers, and support organizations such as "soup kitchens." Trainers and support personnel are essential to fostering the proper and continuing use of the equipment. The purpose of this type of program is obvious: the reduction of the digital divide in whatever form it takes and the building of communities — people coming together as real communities to access the "virtual" communities.

23. The Pew Research Center for the People and the Press, *Technology 1998: Summary,* available from http://www.people-press.org/tech98sum.htm, accessed 19 March 2000.

24. Eric Cohen, "United We Surf," *The Weekly Standard,* 28 February 2000, pp. 27-28.

25. Adam Clayton Powell III, "Falling for the Gap," *Reason,* November 1999, p. 44.

26. NPR Online, *Survey Shows Widespread Enthusiasm.*

Create Local, Regional, and National Portals That Support the Values of the Civil Society

Currently organizations such as the Heritage Foundation provide hypertext links to member or related sites (see their townhall.com). This concept could be taken much further if conservative organizations banded together and funded local, regional, and national portals. Portals, such as America Online, Microsoft Internet Start, and Yahoo! are web sites that act as starting points for Internet access by creating channels (categories for information on the Internet) and by providing electronic mail and instant messaging services, discussion forums (chat rooms), shopping guides, games and software, and Internet search programs.[27] Portals could also provide filtering services and software, web site rating systems, and "seals of approval" for member organizations and businesses. A channel or set of channels on a portal could be personalized by the subscriber for quick access to the web sites of local, regional, or statewide public and private organizations and governmental agencies.

By creating a kids' market, the engineers of consumer culture created a kids' culture, what we now call Generation X — "the first generation of Americans fully engaged in a symbiotic relationship with the media."[28] Perhaps the creation of a civil-society market could create a civil-society culture. The appeal would be to those people already online who tend to be slightly more politically conservative than the general population.[29] This appeal would be to self-interest (especially ease of use), and the desire for community standards and shared values, not authority.[30] In his article "Beyond the Digital Divide," Neal Peirce writes that

> What's rare, so far, is using the Internet to strengthen a local community. The shared personal, business, religious, and environmental issues of the places we live *are* critical, and the Internet should let us work on them in new, highly effective ways. A good community net should also strengthen local merchants and craftsmen against the Wal-Martization of the world. . . . The withering of the Digital Divide, if true, is exciting news. But

27. PC Magazine Online, *Home on the Web,* available from http://www.zdnet.com/pcmag/features/webportals, accessed 29 March 2000.

28. Rushkoff, *Media Virus,* pp. 30-31.

29. The Pew Research Center for the People and the Press, *Technology 1998: Sections I-IV.*

30. *The Network Observer,* March 1994, available from http://dlis.gseis.ucla.edu/people/pagre/tno/march-1994.html, accessed 19 March 2000.

> there's a huge leap still to be made — to harness the power of digital connectivity so it enhances the life of our communities.[31]

According to Jupiter Communications, "the key to creating successful community is interaction — communication or collaboration, with a common intent and the reciprocal exchange of information and ideas."[32] First generation community-building web-site models target participants by sex, interest, or age; the next generation models will target participants by level and type of interaction.

Conclusion

James A. Dewar of the Rand Corporation has likened the Information Age to the printing press era because (1) changes in the Information Age will be as dramatic as those in the Middle Ages in Europe, (2) the future of the Information Age will be dominated by unintended consequences, and (3) it will be decades before we see the full effects of the Information Age. Because of these factors, Dewar argued for keeping the Internet unregulated and taking a much more experimental approach to information policy.[33] Providing alternative and private means for censorship and consumer protection are examples of unregulated approaches; providing new community-based points of Internet access and portals are examples of experimental approaches.

The Internet can become an important tool for the civil society movement, no matter what strand one follows.[34] For the followers of Adam Smith, who argue for an economy guided by individual choices, restricted government role in civil society, and the acceptance of responsibility for one's actions, the freedom of the Internet is compatible. For the Tocquevillians, who strongly believe that, in addition to family and work, voluntary associations are the "third place" to enhance and create the fabric of civil society, the Internet can become a "fourth place." For the Victorians, who believe that the problem today "is the moral decay of American society, the widespread loss of the fundamental knowledge of right and wrong, and the degradation and coarsening of American culture," the Internet can be used to strengthen moral values.[35]

31. Neal Peirce, "Beyond the Digital Divide," *Asheville Citizen-Times,* 2 March 2000, p. A7.

32. NUA Internet Surveys, *Jupiter Communications, January 4, 1999,* available from www.nua.ie/surveys/?f=VS&art_id=905354601&rel=true, accessed 20 March 2000.

33. Dewar, *The Information Age and the Printing Press,* pp. 1-2.

34. John Clark, "Conflicts, Coalitions, and the Civil Society Movement," *American Outlook,* Winter 2000, pp. 50-52.

35. Clark, "Conflicts, Coalitions," p. 51.

The two cultures that exist in the United States are essentially based on different worldviews. Within cultural orthodoxy there is an adherence to an external, definable, and transcendent moral authority; "within cultural progressivism (the dominant culture), by contrast, moral authority tends to be defined by the spirit of the modern age, a spirit of rationalism and subjectivism."[36] Even though we may not be able to see a reunion of the two cultures in the near future, writes Gertrude Himmelfarb, "we may look forward to more modest achievements — at the very least to an abatement of the diseases incident to democratic society," including poverty, racism, unemployment, inequality, "the collapse of ethical principles and habits, the loss of respect for authorities and institutions, the breakdown of the family, the decline of civility, the vulgarization of high culture, and the degradation of popular culture."[37] "Civil society has been described as an 'immune system against cultural disease,'"[38] former U.S. Senator Dan Coats has said. The Internet can be a booster shot.

36. James Davison Hunter, *Culture Wars: The Struggle to Define America* (New York: Basic Books, 1991), p. 44.

37. Gertrude Himmelfarb, *One Nation, Two Cultures* (New York: Alfred A. Knopf, 1999), pp. 146, 20.

38. Dan Coats, as quoted in Gertrude Himmelfarb, *One Nation,* p. 37.

Fashion

CHERIE S. HARDER

Clothes possess an influence more powerful over many than the worth of character or the magic of manners.

Louisa May Alcott

The fashion industry is at once the most visible and overlooked of cultural institutions. Malls, streets, magazine racks, television shows, and runways are filled with people making fashion statements — some angry, some extreme, some incoherent. Established rules of style have virtually all been discarded, even disdained by fashion magazines, designers, and devotees. Where fashion historically celebrated beauty and vitality, recent fads have glamorized death and degradation. Clothes are marketed, even in mainstream fashion magazines, in a manner designed to shock the reader rather than flatter the wearer. A brave new world of fashion has been ushered in — one that cultural critics have been largely blind to, and whose fashion statements they have allowed to go unanswered.

Fashion has always afforded self-expression, but in times of prosperity and peace the influence of the fashion industry and importance placed on style spikes upward. Over the last couple decades, the cultural import and impact of the fashion industry has reached possibly unprecedented levels. The power and profitability of fashion have grown steadily as its co-dependency with other forms of popular culture intensifies and its marketing opportunities extend into the world of music, television, movies, toys, and even video and computer games. Clothing sales in the United States alone exceeded $120 billion in the last few years and are steadily rising. Celebrities compete to make memorable fashion statements, confident that the louder or stronger the statement, the more publicity they generate for themselves. (Hence Jennifer Lopez and Cher generate more coverage of their Oscar-night attire than, say, Jodie Foster and Julia Roberts, despite Foster's and Robert's greater box-office popularity and critical acclaim.)

But while celebrities, entertainers, designers, and most young people in America understand the persuasive power of a fashion statement, most cultural critics and reformers have avoided contact with, much less a response to, the often pathological and destructive messages that fashion trends and fads market. Unlike virtually every other leading indicator of popular culture, fashion has received little attention, analysis, or critique from cultural reformers; no social movement has yet emerged to challenge its agenda. This essay will argue that this is a colossal mistake: fashion statements are often both influential and philosophy-laden and, therefore, often need to be challenged and rebutted. Until they are, the "march through the institutions" will be stymied.

The Message Fashion Sends

One does not need to be a fashion expert to understand that fashion statements are so-called because they are intended to send a message. The content of those messages is an increasingly important component of the state of our culture. There are several reasons why this is so.

First, fashion helps define and shape popular culture, which, in turn, drives much of American culture writ large. The last few years have provided numerous examples of the influence fashion wields in shaping popular culture. Television and movies have, since their beginning, spawned fashion trends, but are increasingly institutionalizing their fashion influence. "Supermodels" have begun hosting television shows, opening restaurants, and starring in movies. All-fashion programs are making their appearance on cable stations: E! Television network launched an all-fashion channel called *Style,* as well as hosting its own fashion program *Fashion Emergency.* CNN offers *Style with Elsa Klensch,* while the American Movie Classics channel (AMC) has started a program entitled the *Hollywood Fashion Machines.* Show business is now in the clothes business.

Fashion has also become intertwined with the newest and fastest-growing popular culture entertainment sector: video games. As the video game industry skyrockets in pervasiveness and popularity (it is expected to surpass the movie industry in revenues in 2000), it is only natural that its icons should both reflect and affect fashion trends. And so they do. Indeed, one of the more famous video game characters, Lara Croft, has been featured in various publications sporting designer fashions. As the crossover between video games, movies, and television accelerates, so will this trend.

Similarly, the music and fashion industries are growing ever more intertwined. Music magazines — *Rolling Stone, Spin, Vibe,* and others — often feature fashion spreads, in addition to the fashion-conscious musicians they profile. VH1 now offers the yearly *VH1 Vogue Fashion Awards;* MTV boasts the *House of Style* program. As far back as 1985, the Council of Fashion Designers of America gave MTV a special award for its influence on fashion. That influence has steadily and significantly grown. Many of the most widespread teen fashion fads have been launched by musicians — Madonna, Michael Jackson, Marilyn Manson, Nirvana, Courtney Love, and others have all popularized a distinct look, imitated by countless young people. Fashion becomes an integral part of what young people consider cool, attractive, stylish, and entertaining. Even *Newsweek* admitted that "Style counts: Teen cliques are more fluid than adults think, but each has its own distinctive tribal markings, from hippie chic to body art to buttoned down prep."[1] Indeed, virtually all pop culture trends have a fashion component; one cannot adopt a role without looking the part.

As fashion has grown more intertwined with popular culture, its reach and influence have extended to younger consumers. Children provide an emerging market for the fashion world, and prove an increasingly lucrative one. According to some studies, direct spending by teens and preteens has tripled since 1990; in 1998, children under twelve alone spent over $28 billion, much of it on clothes.[2] Children are more susceptible to peer pressure and fashion fads than adults; their increasing purchasing power is a sure sign that fashion advertising — and its institutionalized presence in much of popular culture — will target more and more marketing efforts toward children. As fashion grows more influential, it will direct its statements toward the more easily influenced.

But if fashion has grown more powerful, it is also less monolithic. No longer do a handful of designers dictate the parameters of fashion; designers increasingly cater to subcultures, and trends now start in the street and spread upward as well as being initiated by celebrities. Thanks to the development of the Internet, new teen fads can spread far and fast and later be picked up by the fashion establishment.

Fashion not only helps shape and define popular culture, however; the growing influence of the fashion industry has also led to the increasing politicization of fashion. Pop culture celebrities have long sought the *gravitas* of

1. Sharon Begley, "A World of Their Own," *Newsweek,* 8 May 2000.
2. Cited in "Having Them for Life," *Propositions,* No. 8, Spring 2000.

political involvement, so the dabbling of designers and dress-makers in (almost always left-leaning) politics is not new. Many clothing advertisements carry overtly political slogans and images that have nothing to do with clothing, such as the recent Benetton sweater ads featuring a series of photographs of death row inmates — but no sweaters. Previous ad campaigns included images of starving children and AIDS patients — none of whom had donned Benetton apparel. Exactly what the link is between Benetton sweaters and the death penalty or AIDS policy is unclear, but Benetton's disdain for both is not.

The increasing clout and celebrity of those within the fashion industry has also yielded political access. A generation ago, it would have been difficult to imagine a model being invited to testify on Capitol Hill; today, models have been asked to do everything from advise Congress on foreign affairs (as when the model Iman testified about slavery in Sudan) to lead public health campaigns (Lauren Hutton's campaign for hormone therapy). Nor is the fashion industry's political access limited to the United States. In 1998, when models Naomi Campbell and Kate Moss finished their photo shoot in Havana, on a lark they sent a note to Castro requesting a meeting. Castro met with them for a full ninety minutes — half an hour longer than he spared for the Pope. In addition, Cuba's chief revolutionary showed himself to be fairly well acquainted with fashion trends, congratulating Miss Moss on starting the "revolution" toward smaller models.[3]

A third factor is that fashion is significant in its capacity to both reflect and affect larger historical trends. "Fashion is a mirror of history," declared Louis IV. And David Wolfe, creative director of the fashion consulting Doneger Group, has stated that "Fashion is both predecessor of what has taken place in the larger society, and a predictor of what will take place."[4]

There are numerous examples to prove their point: the end of the first World War and subsequent expansion of economic wealth and opportunity unleashed daring and expensive new fashions. The passage of the nineteenth amendment, extending the right to vote to women, coincided with the advent of pants, shorter skirts, looser-fitting clothing for women, bobbed hair, and flapper fashions — clothing that made it far easier for women to participate in activities (dancing, riding, exercising, etc.) that yesteryear's confining clothing and social norms restricted. The departure of flapper fashion from previously accepted norms was radical in and of itself, as well as reflective of seismic changes underway in the status and treatment of women. The shortening of women's hemlines and advent of the dropped-waist dress (which eliminated

3. "Marxist Models," *Washington Times,* 21 August 1998.

4. Quoted by Catherine Fitzpatrick, "Countdown to 2000," *Milwaukee Journal Sentinel,* 6 June 1999.

the need for corsets) were vehemently criticized for being "unfeminine," with the result that social concepts of femininity underwent alterations along with hemlines and haircuts. Fashion accelerated the movement of history — and not only by enabling women to walk faster. The adoption of new fashions became a social, even philosophical statement, in some ways. Indeed, the most renowned author of the time, F. Scott Fitzgerald, penned his most famous short story "Bernice Bobs Her Hair" in a book entitled *Flappers and Philosophers.* In some cases, fashions, such as the bikini swimsuit, even acquired their name from current events. The bikini — declared by fashion doyenne Diana Vreeland to be "the most important invention since the atomic bomb" — owes its name to that device. This was exactly the effect designer Louis Reard was looking for. Four days before he was to unveil his design, he was still searching for a name — something to express the explosive impact he hoped his itsy-bitsy teeny-weeny creation would spark. He found it when the Army detonated a nuclear bomb near the South Pacific Islands known as the Bikini Atoll. History was made, a new fashion born, and our assumptions about national security and personal modesty underwent alteration.

Finally, and most importantly, fashion statements are significant because they purport to define what an individual and/or a society believes is and should be attractive, desired, and emulated. The fashion industry's primary purpose is to glamorize a particular "look" and hold it up as something to be admired, purchased, and adopted. It is about endowing a certain appearance with glamor and encouraging others to aspire toward its emulation. As one critic noted, "In virtually all forms of fashion photography, there is a patina of glamor. Once anything is touched by the hand of fashion, it takes on an enticing glow and a secular and commercial appeal."[5]

Feminists have long been hip to this fact. At one Columbia University conference on "Standards of Beauty," Betty Friedan shouted to the fashion editors, "The images in the mass media are important, for God's sake!" She later denounced waif models as "prepubescent invitations to pedophilia."[6]

But if fashion statements are worth taking seriously, many such statements of the last few years have been angry, pathological, and destructive. Consider just a few recent trends.

5. Robin Givhan, "Ghoulish Spin on Fashion," *Washington Post,* 12 August 1998.

6. Quoted by Phil McCombs, "One Person's Beauty: The Media's Message and Its Effects on the Beholder's Eyes," *Washington Post,* 23 February 1995.

"Junkie Chic"

The mid-1990s saw the sudden glamorization of the heroin-addict look, an appearance the *Washington Post* described as a "nihilistic vision of beauty that includes torn clothes and the wasted silhouettes and pinched faces of drug addicts."[7] Fashion's "hippest" photographers posed emaciated, stoned-looking models sprawled in front of toilets, evoking the image of a junkie coming off a heroin high. Designer Jil Sander released a catalog featuring strung-out women with one sleeve pushed up. *New York Times* reporter Amy Spindler observed that "The 1990s may well be remembered as the decade when fashion served as pusher . . . of what appeared to be the best-dressed heroin addicts in history."[8] Or, as former model Zoe Fleischauer recounted in an interview with *Newsweek:* "They [the fashion industry] wanted models that looked like junkies. The more skinny and f— —d up you look, the more everybody thinks you're fabulous."[9]

In their effort to push the envelope, fashion photographers had, in the minds of many, pushed the bounds of decency by glamorizing a lethal addiction. Drug Enforcement Agency (DEA) head Thomas Constantine testified before Congress that the single greatest reason for the resurging popularity of heroin in the mid-1990s was the popularizing of "heroin chic" by the fashion and entertainment industry. It proved one of the few fashion trends to prompt cultural critics into commentary. Columnists, magazines, and critics skewered and satirized the trend. Even President Clinton felt compelled to denounce fashion's new trend, declaring: "The glorification of heroin is not creative, it's destructive. It is not beautiful, it is ugly. And this is not about art, it's about life and death. And glorifying death is not good for any society."[10]

Abuse Allure

Some purveyors of junkie chic went a step further: their models looked not only strung out, but beat up. Mainstream fashion magazines featured models who stared at the camera with the angry, frightened look of a battered woman, deep circles under their eyes, cowering from an unseen figure. Fashion standard-bearers such as *Vogue* and *W* included shots of formal dresses modeled by

7. Robin Givhan, "Fashion Smack in the Face," *Washington Post,* 21 July 1996.

8. Amy Spindle, "A Death Tarnishes Fashion's Heroin Look," *The New York Times,* 20 May 1997.

9. Gregory Beals et al., "Rockers, Models, and the New Allure of Heroin," *Newsweek,* 26 August 1996.

10. Quoted by Peter Baker, "Clinton Blasts 'Glorification of Heroin' in Magazine Fashion Photo Spreads," *Washington Post,* 22 May 1997.

women whose eyes have been blackened to the point of looking bruised. At several runway shows during the late 1990s, models stalked down the runways with a fearful glare, hair mussed and clothes torn open, as if they had just escaped from a beating.

Fashion magazines were not alone in presenting a victimized look as sexually alluring. *Rolling Stone* featured "The Girls of Scream 2" and the "Pleasures of Terror" as a cover story and featured photographs of the movie's heroine-victims (teen idols, all) bound and gagged, dripping blood, stabbed in the shower, and in the early stages of strangulation.

Fetish Fashion

The 1990s not only brought us the glamorization of lethal drug use and domestic abuse, but an increasing popularization of "fetish fashion" — the incorporation of the trappings of "transgressive" sexual practices in fashion marketing (examples include designer Theiry Mugler's leather corsets, which are often festooned with spikes, and Versace's "bondage" look). Fashion historian Valerie Steele noted that "The emergence of fetish fashion [is] one of the most significant styles of the 1990s. . . . It is important to stress that this is not just a sporadic fad; for the last 30 years, the iconography of sexual 'perversion' has increasingly influenced both high fashion and street style. Sexual fetishing, cross-dressing, and sado-masochism have influenced the work of many designers."[11]

Even *Vogue,* the standard-bearer of fashion magazines, admitted, "These are the days of perversion chic. After a decade in which America often seemed to be gripped by a new Victorianism, kinkiness has abandoned the margins and begun conquering the mainstream, which is increasingly filled with tales of cross-dressing and sodomy, incest and child rape, bondage, bestiality, and necrophilia. The line between art and pornography keeps growing fainter."[12] This trend may be most clearly evident in fashion advertising, which is persistent in its pursuit of racy new images to grab readers' attention. Themes of lesbianism and pedophilia have moved from porn magazines to fashion advertising. *Vogue* and *Bazaar* magazines carry Christian Dior ads featuring two sweaty female models locked in a spread-eagle embrace. And Calvin Klein — well-known for his eagerness to skate the cutting edge of sexual taboos — produced a series of commercials in which children were asked to undress, and an off-screen male voice appraised their bodies. Another Klein series featured

11. Valerie Steele, *Fifty Years of Fashion* (New Haven, Conn.: Yale University Press, 1997).

12. "Perversion Chic," *Vogue,* March 1997.

underaged-looking models posed in crotch shots in a seedy-looking interior. (After escaping any censure for his other racy ads, Klein professed himself surprised that people would read pedophilia into his commercials.)

Gangster Glamor

The 1990s also brought us the glamorization of both gangster gear and prison uniforms. A few designers — most notably Tommy Hilfiger — carved an industry niche in glamorizing and marketing the thug look. Hilfiger, who earned the nickname "hip-hop's favorite haberdasher" (his praises were even sung in a 1995 gangsta rap hit entitled "Criminology"), deliberately copied and marketed the designs of prison clothing and street gangs. As one critic noted:

> Not be outdone, some state prisons have actually allowed inmates to sell clothing to outsiders. Convicts at an Oregon state prison have sold their own designs (dubbed "Prison Blues") to outsiders for over a decade, thus capitalizing on a trend of their own making. According to some cultural observers, fads in rap music, tattoos, and low-riding pants all got their start in prisons around the country, and spread outward. As Richard Stratton, editor of *Prison Life* magazine, observed: "What you're seeing is the prison culture spilling out and becoming the regular culture."[13]

The spillage has extended all the way to the cosmetic counter and juniors department. Hard Candy cosmetics — sold in such tony stores as Saks Fifth Avenue, Burdine's, Nordstrom's, and Marshall Field's — offer nail polish in shades dubbed "gangsta," "booty," "libido." And Urban Decay cosmetics offers polish in shades called "violence," "hostage," "gash," "gangrene," "asphyxia," "Scream" (based on the movie), and "bruise." The outfitter "Boiy Krazi" makes and markets denim "prison suits" printed with inmate numbers. In the space of just a few years, fashion designers and marketers were able to accomplish an amazing feat: the transformation of a prison uniform from a stigma to a fashion statement.

Body-Molding

One of the most recent fads seeks to redesign the body itself. Whereas tattoos or body-piercing used to be the disfiguring fashion of choice, they have now be-

13. Cited by Gary Fields, "Prison Garb Breaks Out as a Fashion Statement," *USA Today*, 2 November 1995.

come almost commonplace. Those seeking an edgier fashion statement have turned to branding (the literal branding of the skin) and body-molding, or "bod-mod." "Bod-mod" aficionados insert plates in their foreheads, file their teeth into fang-like incisors, and alter other body parts; the great promise of bod-mod is that individuals can re-create their own bodies, even alter their identities. Various accounts have cropped up of people attempting to turn themselves into lizards (*Time* reported a young man's attempt to do so by tattooing scales over his body, inserting plates into his head and shoulders, and surgically attaching a tail[14]), tigers (the "tiger-lady" has appeared on late-night talk shows), and various birds. No matter how lovely one believes the animal kingdom to be, the appeal of bod-mod is not merely aesthetic, but philosophical: bod-mod practitioners can fashion for themselves a new body, a new identity, and a new twist on what it means to be human.

Meanwhile, simple tattooing and body piercing have slid into near-respectability. Little girls can even play with "Butterfly Art Barbie," who comes with multiple stick-on tattoos, and with Barbie's friends who boast nose studs.

Death

Perhaps the most disturbing trend in the fashion industry is the growing popularization of death images. Consider just a few recent fashion spreads in *Spin* magazine. *Spin* attempts to sell its issues with the image of a young woman holding a razor blade to the throat of a bound, identically-dressed captive. Behind the razor-wielding trend is an electric saw, an incinerator, and a fire extinguisher. Across the page is splashed: "*Spin* . . . 12 issues, $9.95."

A year earlier, in their September 1998 issue, *Spin* spotlighted the latest fashion trends with the image of a young man, skinny, clammy, and hanging by his belt. His pupils were dilated and mouth agape, as if to suggest autoerotic suffocation. Given that this was a fashion spread, the presumed effect was to sell the pictured clothes — a white shirt, black blazer, and, most prominently featured, a black belt. "The idea there was to really bridge the gap between fashion and music," explained *Spin*'s editorial fashion director Haidee Findley-Levin.[15]

Not to be outdone, the Australian rock/style magazine *Juice* featured a fashion photography spread by Jez Smith entitled "Live Fast . . . Fashion to Die For," which showcased strangled, beaten, drowned, and pummeled models, along with time of death and clothes worn on the occasion. More recently, promotionals for the ultra-violent movie *American Psycho* plugged the "killer

14. Jeffrey Ressner, "Brand New Bodies," *Time,* 12 September 1999.
15. Robin Givhan, "Ghoulish Spin on Fashion."

looks" and fashion tastes of the serial killer protagonist; the movie's website even features a "killer looks" link which describes the murderer's fashion ensembles.

Such advertising has its greatest appeal to young people, not adults. Such ads typically appear in teen and rock magazines, as opposed to fashion magazines aimed at adult women. As such, they are more likely to go unnoticed by adult critics. But the consequences of glorifying death are anything but trivial — particularly in a society where teen suicide has more than tripled over the last three decades. Draping "dead" models in fancy threads is a blatant attempt to glamorize death — an in-your-face urging to "live fast, die young, and have a good-looking corpse."

Consequences and Causes

Each of these trends affects not only a subculture, but the larger culture as well. They shape and define what society in general, and young people in particular, come to regard as cool, socially acceptable, and worthy of emulation. Trends and fads are not always trivial; they reflect what we value and seek to imitate, which, in turn, reveals much about our national character. When the fashion industry and institutions wield their considerable influence to glamorize and peddle nihilism, degradation, and addiction, they can have an immeasurable impact in molding attitudes and assumptions — which, in turn, shape the way we act, relate, and behave.

And yet, while significant and sustained attention has been paid to other forms of popular culture — television, movies, video games, music, advertisements, the Internet, and the like — fashion statements seem to have fallen on deaf ears. The importance of how we look and what we wear may be given ample attention in fashion, music, teen, and women's magazines, but rarely inspires discussion in news magazines or intellectual journals.

Of course, every so often, a particularly offensive ad campaign shocks a few cultural commentators into aggrieved reproach. Calvin Klein's "kiddie porn" ads of the mid-1990s, featuring blank-faced, spread-eagle, underaged models clad only in their undies, managed to ruffle a few feathers, and ultimately resulted in Klein pulling the ads. But such occasions are rare. It is far more common for a fashion statement designed to shock to elicit only interest, approval, or at worst, a yawn.

There are several understandable reasons for this lack of interest. There is a traditional, and religious, aversion to paying undue attention to appearance. Both classical philosophy and religious texts suggest that a focus on outward beauty in general and clothing in particular is a blind spot. One early Platonic dialogue known as the "Great Hippias"[16] links attractive clothes with the pursuit of beauty, but in the context of a deception on the part of those that seek beauty. Similarly, there are religious warnings against an over-interest in beautiful dress or a gullibility in being taken with them. The Old Testament book of Proverbs warns that "charm is deceptive and beauty is fleeting,"[17] and the apostle Paul counsels women to "dress modestly, with decency and propriety, not with braided hair or gold or pearls or expensive clothes, but with good deeds."[18] Fundamentalist Muslims require women to cover themselves head to toe in the unfashionable equivalent of a black pup tent. Buddhists and Hindus downplay interest in the body of man, much less the apparel, the focus of their belief pertaining to the spirit.

Others have equated an interest in fashion with shallowness. Expressing a great deal of concern about one's dress has typically (and with reason) been associated with a lack of more substantial concerns, and in some cases, the absence of a strong mind or sound character. Ralph Waldo Emerson went so far as to say, "It is only when mind and character slumber that the dress can be seen."

And yet, cultural critics' and reformers' uninterest in the world of fashion is a mistake. One does not need to be seduced by fashion to respond to it (indeed, it is far better if one is not). Despite each of the above objections, we should care about fashion, because how we choose to adorn ourselves is perhaps the closest reflection of what we consider attractive, even beautiful — which, in turn, says much about who we are, what we value, even what we wish to become.

An Effective Engagement of the Fashion Industry

If we are to begin reclaiming key aspects of civil society, we cannot detour around this highly influential popular culture industry. An effective engagement of the fashion industry could take various forms, but it would include several elements:

First, it would acknowledge the philosophical import of fashion trends and consider carefully the message being advertised. Instead of standing mum when the fashion industry exalts nihilism, addiction, violence, and pathology, cultural reformers would take these statements seriously enough (millions of young people do) to respond to them — to analyze, critique, and if necessary, rebut them.

16. Authorship is still disputed.
17. Proverbs 31:30 (NIV).
18. 1 Timothy 2:9-10 (NIV).

Of course, this is not to argue for an emerging social movement to critique hemline lengths or palettes, but simply to be cognizant and responsive to fashion trends that undercut human dignity rather than affirm it. One of the most hopeful developments that could occur would be the various fashion designers voluntarily and conscientiously considering the message and potential impact of their advertising campaigns and runway dramas on the larger society. An effective social movement would encourage fashion insiders to do so, and affirm their actions when they did.

Second, an effective engagement of the fashion industry would celebrate life and health over death and degradation. Cultural reformers need to recognize the import and criticize the appearance of death-glorifying and violence-glamorizing ad campaigns. It need not presume to dictate fashion — indeed, it should not. But there is something deeply perverse and potentially tragic when gangster garb and lifestyles are glamorized, when suicide is depicted as chic, and when physical abuse is presented as alluring.

The degradation of the junkie chic look — the slumped posture, stoned expression, despairing eyes, and wasted frame — was described by some fashion critics as "the glorification of having no standards." But of course, there are standards. For all its pretense otherwise, the fashion industry is resolutely and intensely elitist. Even when models emulate cadavers, the corpse is invariably thin and beautiful, with perfect skin and eye-pleasing features. Fashion photography may glamorize addiction over health, death over life, angst over contentment, promiscuity over fidelity, sexual precociousness over innocence, but it never glamorizes cellulite, large noses, or close-set eyes.

The central idea is not that the homely can achieve hipness, but that the young and the beautiful must degrade themselves before doing so. There is nothing stylish in being ugly, only in carelessly neglecting or destroying one's health. It is not that age is glamorized, only the profligate destruction of youth. There is no style in sickness, only in the young deliberately destroying their health with drugs. In short, the essence of style has become destruction — of beauty, of health, of happiness, of life. The standards of beauty that are deliberately flouted are of a moral and cultural, rather than biological, origin.

A successful march through the fashion industry would return a celebration of the healthful and beautiful. Certainly, this is already standard practice in much, even the majority, of fashion photography; most catalogs aim simply to present their clothes in the most attractive light possible, and many women's fitness magazines resolutely affirm health and fitness as the archetype of beauty. Fashion should aim to flatter rather than degrade the wearer.

A third and final necessary component in any effective engagement of the fashion industry would be to seek the end of the premature sexualizing of children's fashion. The precocious sexuality encouraged and glamorized by much of fashion photography is both exploitive and ugly. A culture is defined largely by its boundaries; exploiting children in fashion spreads should be off limits and out-of-bounds. The increasing purchasing power of teens and preteens ensures that they will continue to be the target of edgy and sexually-charged fashion advertising. A successful fashion critique would clearly and decisively oppose the exploitation of children and the commercializing of children's sexuality — whether it is a slickly packaged pedophilia appeal aimed at adults (ala Calvin Klein) or the precocious sexualizing of pre-teenyboppers (such as cosmetics designed for eight-year-old girls).

Fashion statements are worth taking seriously because they have a serious impact on our values, as well as on our aesthetic preferences. What we see as fashionable is closely linked to what we believe acceptable and admirable; fashion adjusts norms as much as hemlines. Certainly there are many creations of the fashion industry worthy of admiration and approval — for their beauty, ingenuity, and craftsmanship. But when fashion's statements glamorize death and degradation, they require a response. It's time to speak up.

III. STRATEGIES FOR CULTURAL RENEWAL

Reform of Professions and Elite Fields

The Professions

CURT SMITH

Just as the three primary colors combine to create every hue and tone of the rainbow, so, too, do the three primary institutions of the created order — the family, government, and the faith community — combine to form a platform for human endeavor. These endeavors, many of which are tied to the professions, involve things as diverse as healing, commerce, the arts, learning, and communication. In the aggregate, some might refer to them as "the economy." A closer examination, however, shows that these pursuits contain — but are not limited to — the activities at the heart of commerce and business. They are thus, in a broader view, thought of not only in relation to the economy but also in relation to civil society, for when healthy they help create civilization and the good society. When dysfunctional, however, there is deterioration or even destruction of culture and society. The professions, then, can be an important retardant against or promoter of healthy culture.

A distinction between civil society and the economy is more than an academic distinction. By separating this platform of civil society or culture-creating pursuits from its institutional underpinnings of the household, state, and church, we more fully understand both the opportunity and the challenge of employing the professions and elite endeavors as a force for cultural and social renewal. Making these critical distinctions between the seminal institutions of culture and the culture-creating professions also helps reveal the strategies needed to unleash the power of cultural renewal inherent in many professions. This essay will explore several strategies for employing the professions and elite disciplines as forces for cultural renewal. These strategies include appealing to the ideal, employing core values of a profession to overcome unhealthy cultural biases, and encouraging creative competition within the existing disciplines.

The Family, Government, and the Faith Community

First, however, these essential distinctions must be further developed. As already noted, the three primary institutions of the created order are the family, government, and the faith community. Virtually all cultures and societies across time have organized in one fashion or another in some amalgam of these institutions. The family births and nurtures new life and, ideally, conveys the sense of significance and worth to each individual. Government restrains evil and promotes justice to create security. The faith community addresses transcendent questions and issues, providing a measure of stability in the midst of a potential sea of doubt and despair. (In this regard, it should be noted the faith community is not always theistic. Some individuals place their faith in the hope of humankind to make progress on the many problems we face. This faith, called humanism, is not a theistic faith, but it is still a faith.) Many promising opportunities to influence culture and society occur among, between, and within these primary institutions, and other essays in this book explore those opportunities. These institutions are not, however, the only means of shaping culture; a closer look at the professions reveals that they too hold an enormous (though often overlooked) power to positively influence culture.

In order to understand this potential, we must first recognize that the diversity and complexity of human activity that occurs on the platform of civil society is dizzying. In an effort to oversimplify it, everything is sometimes lumped together under the broad umbrella of "the economy." But that is too simplistic, and it fails to take into account that many of our pursuits are not motivated by the pursuit of financial gain. Most work to eat, rather than eat to work, to paraphrase one familiar expression. When we distinguish between and among many of these particular pursuits upon this platform we call civil society, we begin to see opportunities to harness them for culture-building activities. Distinguishing between "the economy" and what many do as part of their professions or vocational pursuits suggests ways to employ the professions in ennobling and culture-building pursuits.

Appealing to the Ideal

One helpful place to begin is to consider the very word "professional." Many would say it simply means someone who is paid for his or her work. They might even contrast it with an amateur (a person who is not paid for a pursuit or activity). An example would be an amateur athlete as opposed to a professional athlete. Still others might think of professionals as highly skilled workers with special credentials, suggesting the legal or medical professions as examples. Some might even note that many professions are self-regulating bodies. But the root of the word, of course, is "profess." To profess means to state or believe something. In its deeper sense, to profess means to utter and adhere to a core belief or tenet.

Such an understanding helps us see the professions in their original light, and suggests to us the first strategy for reforming the professions — namely, calling professionals back to the original, historic, or ideal understanding of their profession or discipline. One example from the world of political campaigns shows how journalists could be persuaded to embrace the best traditions of their professions. It is interesting to note this appeal succeeded where coercion and threats had no influence on overturning editorial decisions.

Journalism's Tradition of Truth-Telling

Many Americans would assert that our nation's brand of journalism is defined by the Constitution's First Amendment. (It is interesting to note journalism is the only profession, trade, or commercial activity acknowledged and protected by the United States Constitution.) The Constitution declares that Congress shall pass no law abridging the freedom of the press. But American journalism took its first steps of independence from the Crown of England even earlier, in 1735, during a little-known trial in New York State. That trial, of printer John Peter Zenger, birthed American freedom of the press when a jury was persuaded by a young Alexander Hamilton that truth should be a defense against libel. Zenger wrote an article critical of the Crown, what was known at the time as seditious libel. The law clearly stated that anyone criticizing the King was guilty of such libel, and the Royal judge pointed that out to the jury. But Hamilton succeeded in convincing the jury that a publisher committed no crime if he simply published the truth, even if the facts were critical of the Crown. The jury's finding of innocence was revolutionary, and helped set in motion events that would lead to the Revolutionary War by challenging the Crown's unbridled protection in order to advance freedom of the press. That freedom, however, was forged in the defense of truth, not the press.

More than 270 years later, U.S. Representative John Hostettler, Republican of Indiana, used this knowledge of the history and "professions" of journalists to convince several network television station executives to remove from their stations hard-hitting, negative television ads running against him in his district.

Hostettler, who was elected to Congress in 1994, faced a tough re-election bid in 1996. Many organized labor groups targeted him for defeat, as they did a score or so of the freshman incumbents who wrested control of the House of Representatives away from the Democratic Party after the watershed election of 1994. In district after district, these groups ran ads against incumbents who had supported budget reforms, claiming the vote was actually a cut of Medicare funding. The commercials were designed to arouse opposition from senior citizens, a large portion of the population and the demographic group most likely to turn out to vote.

Hostettler's chief of staff, a former journalist (and the author of this essay), wrote to each station in the district, providing information clearly explaining that the votes did not cut Medicare funding. The reforms simply slowed the rate of growth of Medicare spending. The letter asked the stations to weigh carefully their responsibility to present truthful and accurate information to the public, and expressly appealed to the tradition of truth-telling as the heart of the profession in requesting that the ads be removed from the air. All four national network affiliates in the Congressman's hometown of Evansville, Indiana, stopped running the commercials from third-party organizations, forgoing tens of thousands of dollars of income in the process. Several stations in neighboring regions also took the commercials that targeted Hostettler off the air.

More than twenty other Congressional offices also protested the ads, but not one office anywhere in the country had a similar experience. The appeals they issued took a very different approach. In many instances they threatened legal action, suggested there might be lengthy Congressional hearings detrimental to the station's industry or interests, or indicated that the Federal Communications Commission might look harder at broadcast license renewals because of the station's willingness to air such ads.

Hostettler appealed to the truth-telling traditions of journalism, and the ads came off. In the process, the political dialogue and discourse in one portion of the country was more civil and more issue-oriented than in other regions of the nation. It may not be stretching too much to say that a bit of the cynicism about politics was muted in the process. Furthermore, a new generation of television station executives steeped in the economics of their industry got a history lesson and tutorial on the rich heritage of journalism. Today these executives are in a better position to evaluate all the programming they broadcast, not just the issue-advocacy ads from groups injecting themselves into campaigns, with a more critical eye toward its truth or falsity.

This strategy of appealing to the ideal can work with many professions and businesses, but only if cultural reformers themselves know the history, traditions, and ideals at the heart of the profession they are seeking to reform.

Employing Core Values to Overcome Biases

Another promising strategy is to take advantage of a core value of a profession to move it beyond an unhealthy bias against faith. One example from the medical community highlights this approach. The medical profession in general and psychiatry in particular, in large part because of Sigmund Freud's open hostility toward religion, has long eschewed any link of religious practices, such as prayer or attending worship services, to good physical health. In fact, standard training told medical students that religious practices were harmful to both physical and mental health. But David B. Larson, M.D., M.S.P.H., a psychiatrist who would be the last to call himself a cultural reformer, has changed all that for the medical profession by simply following a core value of his profession — the objectivity of science in medicine.

Larson's 1992 work, *The Forgotten Factor in Physical and Mental Health: What Does the Research Show?*, was the start of this process. He summarized study after study that he encountered in his work as a research doctor with the federal government showing the positive effects of religious commitment and practice on physical and mental health. For example, a three-year study of mortality rates and causes produced this eye-opening finding for the medical community:

> The study found that the risk of dying from arteriosclerotic heart disease was much less for men who attended church weekly or greater. Even after allowing for the effects of smoking, socio-economic status and water hardness, the risk for frequent church attendees was only 60 percent of the men who attended church infrequently.

With a grant from the John Templeton Foundation, he was able to pull these many peer-reviewed, scientifically sound, and carefully verified studies together for his profession. The resulting self-study guide for medical professionals was just the beginning of a sea change in attitude and practice among medical professionals. Today many medical schools across America have made changes to their curricula because of Dr. Larson's refusal to ignore the research's findings.

He did not set out as a cultural reformer, nor could he have predicted the impact his work would have in making his profession — medicine — more civil and more humane as well as more effective for patients. He just followed the data, the science. In fact, one of his more notable quips disarms potential critics who speculate that he has a hidden religious agenda. "I'm not religious," he quickly states, then adds, "I'm an Episcopalian." After the chuckle fades, the truth remains. Medicine, properly practiced, follows the science, even when that science underscores a truth that seemingly strikes at science itself: Faith and religious commitment are not clinically harmful to one's mental or physical health, but beneficial.

The good doctor has a prescription for us all. Do not let the biases or preconceived notions of a profession, even one as established as medicine, stand in the way of the culture-building, life-affirming principles at the heart of the good society. Explore and examine the key beliefs and tenets of that profession to discern the best pathway to culture-enhancing, life-affirming practices. Then go to work, just as Dr. Larson did.

Creative Competition

A third approach is creative competition, where compelling positive models are offered to compete with the best that a profession offers. In other words, rather than retreat to a subcultural ghetto, those concerned with cultural renewal can compete within the existing channels of commerce and communication to provide culture-shaping and society-affirming examples. Two exciting examples include the very different worlds of creative writing and commercial network television.

Creative Writing

Entrepreneur W. James Russell decided to fight discouragement about what he saw as the lack of positive, culture-affirming articles and essays in the public domain. He created an annual award program, providing $34,000 in cash prizes for promising works, including a $10,000 grand prize for the most promising submission. Called the "Amy Awards," the competition is carefully designed to encourage what it believes is the wellspring of healthy culture. "The Amy Foundation believes the historic value system of Western Civilization springs from the Judeo-Christian ethic," the official contest rules state. "We believe the truths of the Old and New Testaments of the Bible breathe life and vitality into this view."

Essays and articles are evaluated on the basis of whether they apply the moral, ethical, and religious teachings at the root of Western Civilization to a contemporary issue or concern. Authors must publish in a secular (nonreligious) publication, and they must identify and quote at least one passage or verse from the Bible. It is this application of enduring truths to contemporary issues or concerns that the Amy Foundation seeks to stimulate. And stimulate it does. In a recent year, the program attracted more than one thousand submissions, no doubt inspiring many authors to more explicitly identify the source of the verities they offer in proposing solutions to our many pressing problems.

The Amy Foundation provides an incentive to create clear alternatives to public policy proposals based on current trends or contemporary social research, some of which identifies deeper truths and some of which misses the mark. But by requiring that submissions be published in secular publications, whether part of the popular press, a trade journal, or a scholarly periodical, the Foundation effectively uses the strategy of stimulating compelling alternatives within the current channels of communication, conversation, and commerce. The fruit of that pursuit produces a very different outcome than creating parallel or even competing channels of communication. Here cultural reformers compete in the marketplace of ideas.

Commercial Network Television

Another effective advocate and practitioner of this strategy was the late Bob Briner, a sports executive and an Emmy-award-winning television producer. In his 1993 book, *Roaring Lambs,* he called on the church community to quit complaining about television programming and to begin to mold young professionals who can enter this endeavor and create quality programming while also reflecting that community's perspective.

"For despite all the fancy buildings, special programs, and highly visible presence, it is my contention that the church is almost a nonentity when it comes to shaping culture," he writes in the book's opening chapter. "In the arts, entertainment, media, education, and other culture-shaping venues of our country, the church has abdicated its role as salt and light. Culturally, we are lambs. Meek, lowly, easily dismissed, cuddly creatures that are fun to watch but never a threat to the status quo. It's time for those lambs to roar."

After pointing out that the religious community he is trying to reach with his book has "created a phenomenal subculture," Briner notes that it is then handily dismissed by the larger culture. He then details promising ideas and initiatives to enhance the arts, the movie industry, literature, television, and the university with the culture-building work of the faith community. He argues consistently that the Christian faith community has no one to blame but itself for its lack of cultural relevance.

Citing his own example as a successful television executive, Briner notes the views he experienced from his nonreligious colleagues. "These people are not anti-Christian. They haven't blacklisted me from their business meetings or social events once they learned I was a Christian. If anything, they are the most spiritually hungry people I've ever met. . . ." He then cites the work of the

Quaker author Elton Trueblood, who wrote in his book *The Company of the Committed* that "The test of the vitality of a religion is to be seen in its effect on culture."

Briner's work lives on in the heart of all professionals committed to mastering the skills needed to be successful within their fields — mastering them so they can earn the right to be heard as to how that profession or endeavor should be used to build up the good society.

Conclusion

These are but three examples of compelling strategies for employing the professions in cultural renewal. Properly carried out, they can have an enormous impact on shaping culture. They can move the moral consensus at the heart of society and culture in the right direction, toward the life-affirming, good-society notions that once were the ideals of the American experience, however far the society may have been from fully practicing them.

These examples and this focus suggest another important aspect to this work, however, which can be simply stated: it is likely that true cultural reform from the elite fields and professions will come from within, from committed practitioners of an art, science, or discipline who long to see their work in the larger context of life-affirming and culture-shaping endeavors.

Here the need is to provide positive models, a type of "best practices," for those seeking to employ their professions for more than just a livelihood. In addition, there is a need for a gathering place — actual or virtual — to coalesce community and precipitate participation from the professionals. Many of these pursuits are at the heart of the dramatic market forces that are reshaping wealth and affluence around the globe. Others of these professions are poised to be able to help humankind deal with the deeper questions of significance, security, and stability in a volatile and accelerated world.

If cultural renewal is to be successful, Americans in all fields will need to mobilize their professions for cultural renewal, even as the issues confronting families, faith communities, and the government are also addressed.

Journalism

TERRY MATTINGLY

The Example of John Grisham

Soon after John Grisham finished law school in 1981, he started hanging out at the DeSoto County Courthouse on the town square in Hernando, Mississippi. He had tried writing a book or two at the University of Mississippi, but nothing came of it. Then one day he overheard the horrifying courtroom testimony of a twelve-year-old girl who had been raped. What would happen, he asked himself, if the girl's father became so outraged that he killed the rapist?

Grisham couldn't get this story out of his head. Soon he was getting up at 5 a.m. with a notepad, writing chapter after chapter of his first courtroom drama. It took three years to finish the manuscript, and another year of rejections by dozens of companies before Wynwood Press published five thousand copies in 1988.

But there was more to this process than telling a story that was in his head and heart.

"While I was writing *A Time to Kill,* I read everything that was on the *New York Times* list," said Grisham, at a Baylor University conference called "Art & Soul" in March 2000. "Most of it, I said to myself, 'I can do better than this.' A lot of it, I said, 'I'll never be that good.'"

Grisham realized that he was not writing the first legal thriller. So he read the competition and he learned the rules — the writing style of the marketplace in which he would have to compete. He created a likable hero and then ensnared him in a dangerous conspiracy. Then he carefully plotted a way to get him out of that mess, creating tension through as many entertaining twists and turns along the way as was possible. "I didn't invent that," said Grisham.

And before that first, highly personal book was off the presses, he started the second one — *The Firm*. Grisham decided to follow the same pattern as his first book, but make it even more exciting if possible. Nevertheless, the Southern Baptist Sunday school teacher refused to heed an agent's advice to "spice this thing up a little" with some sexy subplots.

"I made a calculated decision," said Grisham, "to write a story that was as slick and as compulsive and as commercial as I could possibly make it, without resorting to a lot of things that I don't put in books."

What Grisham did was set out to master a highly specific craft so that he could take a message into the public square. That meant having both the drive and the humility to sit down and learn the rules of the arena in which he wanted to succeed. He had to do his homework. Eventually, he made a few compromises that he felt he could make, while refusing to make other compromises that would violate his own values and faith.

I have a reason for bringing up this story at the start of a discussion of what cultural and even political conservatives need to do in order to have a greater impact in another corner of the public marketplace — the one called mainstream journalism. All writers have to master a specific style and craft while accepting, to a greater or lesser degree, its rules and limitations. This may mean years of hard work just to learn a form of writing that is not precisely the form the writer most yearns to practice. That's the way things work. Piano players have to play scales before they can play Chopin or jazz. Writers must learn the skills they need to survive in order to earn the right to take the messages they most want to share to as many readers as possible.

This is what Grisham was willing to do. He didn't like all of the rules of the legal-thriller game, but he mastered them. He made a conscious decision to compete in a larger arena, playing by as many of its rules as he possibly could. To use an old Southern saying, he didn't settle for preaching to the choir. He dared to court the American marketplace as a whole, not, let's say, the niche for Southern Baptists who like to read cleaned-up crime stories.

This is precisely what we need in journalism and the sooner the better. We need more journalists, not fewer, and we need real journalists from different backgrounds and cultures. This would sound like a politically correct call for diversity, except that the largest gap in the American newsroom is between the journalistic elites and moral and cultural conservatives.

But there's a problem. Conservative Americans have grown far too accustomed to complaining about how they are locked out of the media centers that count. I'm convinced that most "conservative" and "Christian" writers don't want to learn the rules of mainstream journalism. Please note that I am not saying that the rules are perfect, nor am I saying that all the competitors play by the rules all the time. I'm not even saying that the rules are, these days, consistently enforced by the referees.

But rules do exist and journalists must learn them if they want to escape their ideological niches. I fear that one of the main causes of the ideological imbalance that exists in journalism is that conservative institutions, especially America's religious institutions and schools, are doing little or nothing to produce journalists who have mastered the skills required to work in real newsrooms.

Grisham's career offers one more sobering lesson. It was only after he had shown that he could succeed in the marketplace that he could begin focusing his readers' attention on deeper stories and issues that mattered most to him as a writer. It rarely works the other way around. Writers must learn to be craftsmen before they can be pundits or, heaven forbid, preachers. Grisham did write a gritty death-row conversion scene in *The Chamber,* an inspiring plot twist that would seem right at home in a Billy Graham movie. But that followed the runaway commercial success of *The Firm, The Pelican Brief,* and *The Client.* Later, a church project with the homeless led to *The Street Lawyer.* A missionary trip inspired *The Testament.* A writer can get away with plots like that when he has millions of books in print.

It isn't enough to tell good stories, or, for journalists, to have good information, great contacts, and fresh story ideas. The writer has to play by, and respect, the rules. Win a few big games and then you can call some of your own plays. "When I write a legal thriller, that's where I start," Grisham has said. "If I'm lucky, and if the timing is right, I can then take an issue — like homelessness, or tobacco litigation, or insurance fraud, or the death penalty — and wrap the story around that. . . . That's how I do it."

Liberal Media

While I was teaching journalism at a Christian liberal arts college during the 1990s, a conservative think tank inside the Beltway came out with a red bumper sticker that said "I'm fed up with the liberal media."

My students really liked that and one suggested that I would do what most professors do with cartoons, headlines, and posters they like, which is stick them up as quasi-political statements in their offices. After all, one student said, isn't that slogan saying what you have been saying semester after semester? Not exactly.

Before I stuck the sticker on a filing cabinet, I drew a black X over the word "the," so that it said "I'm fed up with liberal media." Marking out that little word made a big difference, I told my students, for the simple, statistical truth is that American media, even the maligned mainstream press, are not all liberal, and some are more liberal than others on specific issues. The reality is more complex than the bumper sticker assumes. Part of the story is that journalists are more likely to be united by a shared cultural and educational background than they are by articulated political or theological dogmas.

In other words, there is no conspiracy to produce THE liberal media. You don't need a conspiracy when so many journalists go to the same schools, work their way up through the same media structures, and respect the same cultural heroes while hating the same enemies. But the divisions are real and they do affect the news, especially on cultural issues.

Journalist Peter Brown demonstrates this through a unique set of statistics he has collected, data that started with the home addresses and zip codes of 3,400 journalists in markets such as Little Rock, Arkansas, and Knoxville, Tennessee, as well as Washington, D.C., and Denver, Colorado. Brown is not a scribe for a conservative think tank or for the Religious Right. He was formerly the chief political writer for the Scripps Howard News Service and he currently edits the Sunday Insight section of the *Orlando (Fla.) Sentinel.*

What Brown learned through his research was that anyone looking for journalists should look in neighborhoods that the marketing experts describe with labels such as "Bohemian mix" and "money and brains." Journalists are much more likely to be single than married with children. They read *Rolling Stone* instead of *Christianity Today.* They go to the theater, not yard sales. They eat sushi rather than Tater Tots. Most journalists simply do not speak the language of people who live in suburbs, and Brown believes they look down their noses at the lives of ordinary Americans.

U.S. News and World Report columnist John Leo is also convinced of the divide: "Reporters tend to be part of a broadly defined social and cultural elite, so their work tends to reflect the conventional values of this elite. The astonishing distrust of the news media isn't rooted in inaccuracy or poor reportorial skills but in the daily clash of worldviews between reporters and their readers." Brown says of journalists: "They simply do not share political, religious, or monetary values with the general population."

Continues Brown:

> This is an explosive situation for any industry, particularly a declining one. Here is a troubled business that keeps hiring employees whose attitudes vastly annoy the customers. Then it sponsors lots of symposiums and a credibility project dedicated to wondering why customers are annoyed and fleeing in large numbers. But it never seems to get around to noticing the cultural and class biases that so many former buyers are complaining

> about. If it did, it would open up its diversity program, now focused narrowly on race and gender, and look for reporters who differ broadly by outlook, values, education, and class.

As Brown once told me when discussing the "disconnect" between mainstream newspapers and cultural conservatives: "Any business that doesn't understand or respect the lives of somewhere between 25 and 40 percent of its potential customers isn't a business that is very serious about growing or even surviving."

Naturally, turnabout is fair play. It isn't surprising that many religious and cultural conservatives have developed their own negative attitudes toward journalists. In his still unpublished book, Brown tells one story that is symbolic, funny, and sobering.

> The Salvation Army headed relief efforts in Waco, Texas, in the spring of 1993 when 80 men, women, and children holed up from federal law enforcement officials for almost two months in a (Branch Davidian) compound before perishing in a conflagration. During that period, it got a few dozen calls from people who saw pictures showing this group distributing coffee, cold drinks, and sandwiches to the hundreds of reporters on hand. One woman from Detroit was so incensed she called the Salvation Army commander there, Maj. Avedis Kasarian. "She said her blood pressure went up about 40 points when she read we were serving the news media," he recalled. "She couldn't understand why anyone would be nice to journalists."

Conservative politicians know that these feelings exist out there and, thus, include attacks on journalists in virtually all of their speeches and writings. In a special pre–2000 election issue of *The American Enterprise,* former Speaker of the House Newt Gingrich bluntly stated that politicians on the left side of the aisle knew they had unique advantages as they navigated the troubled waters of the presidency of Bill Clinton and planned ahead.

"They . . . understood that media bias would save them over and over," said Gingrich, who left office scarred by his own media battles. "I suggest the odds are at least even money that by November, the person the Republicans nominate in March will be almost unrecognizable as the same person to the average American, because the media will subject the nominee to an unending, relentless, hostile redefinition."

What's the solution? Gingrich urges conservatives to buck up and, for the most part, to ignore the press and communicate as directly as possible to the American people. One crucial venue, he stresses, is television entertainment and forms of popular culture that create and break the careers of celebrities and politicians alike. He doesn't have much to say about the fact that the elite leaders of the entertainment media are, culturally, to the left of the news media.

"In the age of the elite media," he concludes, "we must focus on the grassroots and not on Washington. I would say to any presidential candidate, You had better have three or four big ideas, and you had better stick to them, and you had better not answer questions about little things, because one of the little things will become the headline, the lead on the evening news, the cover of the newsmagazine, and you never know which one it is because they will ask you 40 until they get to the one that hurts you the most."

Gingrich knows that journalists control one corner of the infamous Washington, D.C., triangle of media, government, and lobby groups — bolstered by academia think tanks. But for some reason, he thinks that cultural and political conservatives are going to be able to get their messages out and receive fair coverage while competing in only two of the three corners in this interconnected, almost claustrophobic triangle that is American politics.

So get out there, says the former speaker, and preach to the choir. It's inevitable that the journalists who cover your sermons will intentionally distort what you have to say and there is nothing that can be done about that.

Read the speeches of conservative leaders and, day after day, year after year, you will find variations on this same angry theme. It's good for fundraising.

It's true that journalists will be journalists. It is also true that it is unrealistic to think that conservatives could "take over" a few major newsrooms and then balance the marketplace of ideas. It's unrealistic to think that alternative media — talk radio, the Web, and a few tiny news periodicals for true believers — will have a major impact. After all, niche journalists in alternative media spend most of their time commenting on the sins of omission and commission in the real media, the dominant newspapers, wire services, and networks.

At some point, someone needs to talk about finding ways to increase interaction between news consumers and news producers. Someone needs to find a way to produce some real journalists who hail from different zip codes and campuses and pews. The people who run newsrooms are supposed to be committed to putting as much information as possible, and as many viewpoints as possible, into the marketplace of ideas.

What we need is more information, more competition, and more journalists. What we don't need are more writers who settle for preaching to the choir.

Christian Writers and Japanese Tennis Players

Once, tennis fans with cable television occasionally could see Jun Kuki and Jan Kamiwasumi compete in major tournaments in London, Paris, Sidney, or New

York. They didn't win many top matches and they never won one of the majors, but they were fine sportsmen and did a lot to promote and improve tennis back home in Japan. In the end, they helped create a separate professional tour for Japanese players. Today it's rare to see Japanese professionals venture into the tougher competition of the international tour. After all, it is easier and less painful for them to earn their fame and fortune in Japan. This also means that most Japanese players stopped trying to improve their skills by competing, and usually losing, to the world's best players.

"Obviously, with this kind of attitude, no Japanese player will ever win Wimbledon or the U.S. Open," writes the late sports executive and television producer Bob Briner in his book *Roaring Lambs*. "No player from Japan will ever be ranked number one in the world. Japan will almost certainly never win the Davis Cup. . . . Even more sadly, no Kukis or Kamiwasumis will be out there in the great international mix of players, bringing their own special flavor, adding their own special perspective to the sport." Japanese players still compete, but only with each other. "No one knows the names of any of the players. No one knows."

And then Briner nails home his point: "Christian writers are like Japanese tennis players."

I apologize for dragging religion into this, but it is impossible to discuss the conflicts between America's journalistic elites and cultural conservatives without talking about conflicts rooted in religion and morality, especially hot-button issues like abortion, Darwinian orthodoxy, and sex outside of marriage. Numerous research groups — from the Freedom Forum to the Center for Media and Public Affairs — have published data demonstrating that the most dedicated critics of the American press can be found in traditional religious sanctuaries.

But the mainstream media is not going away. No one has been madder, longer, than conservative religious leaders and no one has worked harder to set up a parallel media culture to avoid the mainstream. I have seen this close up because, for the past two decades, I have worked as a journalist who covers religion news in the secular press — including twelve years as the weekly "On Religion" columnist for the Scripps Howard News Service in Washington, D.C. Also, since in the early 1990s I have lectured about media and culture in numerous seminaries and colleges, while teaching at Denver Seminary, Milligan College, and in the nationwide Council for Christian Colleges and Universities.

Briner is right. Peter Brown is right too.

The mainstream press and traditional religious groups are just not getting along and, at times, it seems that no one on either side of this divide wants to improve the situation. This is affecting politics. It is affecting newspaper sales and television ratings. And I am convinced this bitter gap also is affecting who works in newsrooms and who does not. This gap must be addressed, for only after doing so can we begin to come up with strategies for increasing the ideological diversity in American newsrooms.

I learned that this gap existed soon after I became a working journalist, but it really locked into my mind once I started working with students on the campuses of Christian colleges and universities. Let me offer one symbolic story, taken from a visit I made a decade ago to a campus in the Ozarks.

It was a sleepy Saturday morning, but the young journalist who joined me for breakfast was bright-eyed and enthusiastic. The day before I had lectured to a student gathering about the biases that I believe shape the mainstream media's coverage of moral and cultural issues. She was surprised that I thought the biggest problem was not outright prejudice, or even hatred, but the lack of people in newsrooms who had any knowledge of the complicated world of religion or who were even interested in learning more about it.

She said she enjoyed the lecture so much that, afterward, she went to a local convenience store and bought her first newspaper. She was a junior in college, she said, and she had never bought a newspaper before with her own money. I regrouped and asked the obvious question: Why are you majoring in journalism? "I like to write and I want to write for a Christian magazine someday," she said. "Either that, or I'll go into public relations."

I have heard these kinds of remarks for years. This young Christian did not want to be a journalist. Up to this point in her life she had watched some television news and scanned a few newspapers, but she had never really been exposed to the journalism marketplace. And this is crucial: she had not grown up or been educated in an environment in which the craft of journalism was respected or praised.

She said she liked to write, which meant that she liked to write essays about her feelings and beliefs. She thought that she might want to be a "Christian" writer (substitute "conservative" if you wish). She might even consider being a "Christian" journalist (substitute "conservative" if you wish). But she had no real interest in being a journalist. She did not like journalists or journalism and she was convinced there was no place for her in that field of work. If there were "Christian" newspapers, producing news to please an audience of "Christian" consumers, then that might be acceptable.

She is not alone. And she has adult mentors.

Producing Cultural Conservatives Who Like and Respect Journalism

Some people believe that moral and cultural conservatives should strive to find a way to produce more "conservative" or "Christian" journalists, so that the marketplace will include more magazines, more newsletters, more radio shows, and perhaps even more niche cable television networks that can compete with existing journalistic institutions.

That may be good and, in fact, this is almost certain to happen in the age of explosive growth in digital media, not only in print, audio, and video, but also in Internet projects that blend all three. But this will not put new voices in the mainstream media. It will not help repair the "disconnect" that Brown sees between major newsrooms and a large block of suburban readers, people of faith and cultural conservatives. It will not add the kind of ideological diversity in newsrooms that might lead to increased, effective efforts to promote balanced and fair coverage of heated cultural and moral debates.

At some point, cultural conservatives must admit that they will only have an impact on mainstream journalism when they produce more journalists committed to working in mainstream journalism. And this will only happen when cultural conservatives produce more young people who like and respect journalism.

What is preventing this from happening? The answer to that question is a matter of journalism philosophy. Simply stated, conservatives tend to think that the solution to biased journalism on the cultural left is to respond with waves of biased journalism from the right.

Is there any alternative? Yes. Conservatives could — especially in this age of declining newspaper sales and television news ratings — encourage the principalities and powers in news to recommit themselves to traditional journalistic values of accuracy, fairness, and balance. They also could help produce more journalists who have mastered the skills needed to compete in these newsrooms.

Once again, the conflict between these camps can be seen most clearly in a debate taking place among Christian conservatives that focuses on a broader issue about the goals and rules of journalism itself. This is, I am convinced, a debate between two philosophies of journalism — one European and one American. The contrast is especially easy to see in debates about news coverage of religious, moral, and cultural issues.

First of all, there is what historians call the "American" model of the press. This model evolved in the mid-nineteenth century, as American editors used faster printing presses to reach out to mass audiences, promising them that they would be given news that was factually accurate, "fair," "neutral," and, some would even dare to say, "objective." At the very least, this model commits the journalist to seeking a 50-50, balanced approach presenting both sides of controversial issues.

Note that we live in an age when most conservatives — no matter what camp they are in — would welcome the chance to engage in 50-50 debates with opponents. Meanwhile, Christians who work in the secular media often cite this model as a worthy goal for those who humbly work in a sinful, fallen world. I have heard Christian colleagues in journalism voice views such as "God is not afraid of fair debates" or "We're sinners, too. We must strive to be fair to other viewpoints." In other words, "It's journalism, stupid."

But there is another approach. If the American model seeks fairness, or even "objectivity," there are others who openly call for a journalistic approach based on subjectivity, opinion, and analysis. This is often referred to as a "European" model of the press.

This viewpoint argues that all journalists write from highly personal perspectives and that they should confess this worldview right up front. Journalists are, in this model, still expected to be accurate, but they are not expected to hide their biases and in some cases they may not even be expected to be fair to other points of view. In America, this approach can be seen in many political magazines and journals — such as *The New Republic* or *National Review.*

There is, however, a problem. This "European" model is filtering back into mainstream American newsrooms, although rarely embraced openly. It is especially tempting to moral pluralists and progressives who, statistically, dominate elite media. After all, in this postmodern age there are many public figures and thinkers who would claim that the only objective truth is that there are no objective truths. In March of 1999, the *New York Times Magazine* published a profile of an anti-abortion activist who had veered far outside the pro-life movement and, apparently, into deadly violence. As he concluded his article, writer David Samuels made the following observation about public issues of right and wrong, truth and error: "It is a shared if unspoken premise of the world that most of us inhabit that absolutes do not exist and that people who claim to have found them are crazy. . . . Perhaps sacrifice in the name of a higher good — God, Marx, freedom or whatever the good of the moment happens to be — is admirable only as long as you support the cause. Or perhaps, in the absence of absolutes, we must judge beliefs not by their inherent righteousness but by their visible consequences."

Many cultural and religious conservatives are convinced that this is precisely what most journalists think of them — that people who believe in absolute truth are crazy. It's that simple. How are journalists supposed to do fair and balanced coverage of people they believe are crazy?

The closer you get to the gospel of the sexual revolution, the more likely you are to hit statistical evidence of bias in newsrooms. A recent study by the Center for Media and Public Affairs noted that journalists remain paragons of progressive virtues on hot moral issues. In 1980, 90 percent were pro-abortion rights. It was 97 percent in the mid-1990s. Support for gay rights was 76 percent in 1980 and slipped by a statistically insignificant amount, to 73 percent, in the new report.

I am convinced that a high percentage of American journalists morph into European journalists when they cover news stories that have anything to do with sex. And there are strong voices in the marketplace urging journalists to do just this, including lobby groups with chapters operating inside mainstream newsrooms. In October 1999, conservative columnist L. Brent Bozell III of the Media Research Center printed remarks by a leader of the Gay and Lesbian Alliance Against Defamation in which she claimed that it is time for reporters and editors to cut their ties to the journalistic canons of the past.

"One of the most important things you can do is have those tough conversations with journalists about when it is completely inappropriate to run to some radical group like the Family Research Council because of misguided notions of 'balance,'" said spokeswoman Cathy Renna of GLAAD. "We have to offer them more moderate voices, or convince them that there is no other side to these issues. We are now in the position of being able to say, 'We have the high ground, we have the facts and we don't have to go one-on-one with these people.'"

Once again, how are journalists supposed to do "fair" and "balanced" reporting about crazy people, they seem to wonder. Why would any self-respecting, civic-minded journalist want to try?

It's tempting, in such an atmosphere, for moral and cultural conservatives to think that the best way to get ahead is by getting even.

Today, there is another influential voice in these debates between advocates of the American and European models of the press — Dr. Marvin Olasky. Olasky is a journalist who believes God wants him to be a "biased journalist." The University of Texas journalism historian is convinced that if the secular media elites are going to be biased and unbalanced, then "Christian" and alternative conservative journalists must be willing to fight fire with fire. Olasky is best known as a writer whose work on poverty, abortion, and other cultural issues influenced Newt Gingrich during the GOP surge in the 1990s and George W. Bush in the 2000 race for the White House.

Olasky is more than a professor and political strategist, however. He also leads the conservative newsmagazine *World*, which allows him to put many of his journalistic convictions into action. As editor, Olasky openly acknowledges that he encourages his reporters to eschew traditional standards of fairness and objectivity. Instead, he says journalists should write the news stories that God wants them to write, the way God wants them written. The goal is "true objectivity" or the "God's-eye view."

"Biblically, there is no neutrality. . . . Christian reporters should give equal space to a variety of perspectives only when the Bible is unclear," argues Olasky in his book *Telling the Truth: How to Revitalize Christian Journalism.* "A solidly Christian news publication should not be balanced. Its goal should be provocative and evocative, colorful and gripping, Bible-based news analysis." Many people call it journalistic heresy.

Let me stress that Olasky is a journalist. He openly mocks those who, when push comes to shove, revert to a kind of "public relations" model that promotes purely positive coverage of friends and allies. He doesn't want to settle for publishing what one critic called "happy little Christian stories." Olasky likes news and he likes journalism. Nevertheless, Olasky's philosophy of "directed reporting" is, at its heart, a clarion call for Christians and other conservatives to embrace, as their primary journalistic model, a "European" approach to the news. In other words, Olasky wants to respond to the journalistic sins of our age by openly adopting the philosophy that some mainstream journalists have covertly adopted.

Put it this way: How are journalists supposed to do "fair" and "balanced" reporting about immoral, liberal people? Why would any biblical, conservative journalist want to try?

It's impossible to avoid this debate. Ask almost any practical question about media strategies, journalism education, or a host of other issues referred to in this chapter and this philosophical question will present itself.

Should moral and cultural conservatives listen to voices such as Gingrich and write off the mainstream media, in effect waving a bloody white flag and fleeing to talk radio and legions of niche news sites on the World Wide Web?

Should conservative donors make it possible for more students to attend the nation's top journalism schools, using the money currently flowing through organizations that are concerned about traditional views of culture, faith, and other politically incorrect subjects? Or should they continue to emphasize programs that stand apart from the career-shaping world of higher education, offering students short bursts of "conservative journalism" training that emphasize editorial writing and political activism over traditional skills in reporting and editing?

Should conservative campuses — which almost always means Christian colleges and universities — strive to offer traditional journalism degrees or news programs within mass-media departments, rather than continuing to emphasize the less risky subject of public relations? And if they dare to embrace journalism, what kind of journalism will it be? American? European? What does it mean to have a "Christian" journalism program?

Will conservative politicos, donors, church leaders, seminary educators, think-tank directors, denominational bureaucrats, and others who shape opinions and life in morally and culturally conservative circles make attempts to interact with and critique the mainstream press, rather than merely blasting away in public shouting matches? Will they realize that the power of the press is built into the very foundations of America's public life and, thus, is worthy of respect, if not admiration?

The answers, you see, depend on the ultimate goal. They depend on whether the goal is to compete in the marketplace of American journalism or to avoid it, to take part in its debates or to flee to safer ground. How we answer these questions also depends on whether or not we believe that the craft of journalism truly matters — journalism with no adjectives attached.

No one needs to deny that there are major problems in the marketplace of American journalism. Journalistic standards of fairness, balance, and even accuracy are under attack — from the left and from the right. But I, for one, am not willing to say that the journalistic canons are no longer relevant. I am not willing to say that it is time to give up on the American model of journalism.

It is impossible to accuse the news media elites of journalistic heresies if we, too, are journalistic heretics.

Bioethics

WESLEY J. SMITH

The case of *James H. Armstrong, M.D. v. The State of Montana* should have been merely a skirmish in the never-ending national struggle over abortion. Instead, relying on the reasoning of certain "experts" about the moral choices surrounding health care, the Montana Supreme Court issued in October 1999 a sweeping decision that could make huge changes in the way Montanans live — and the way they die.

What happened in Montana is happening across the country, usually less dramatically but nonetheless steadily. The United States has a bad case of "expertitis," and for many years we have been ceding to experts control over our public decisions. Now the most important questions about health care have been added to the list. Decision-making has been quietly co-opted by "bioethics," a genre of philosophical discourse practiced by a self-selected group of academics, philosophers, lawyers, and physicians, many of whom are openly hostile to the sanctity of life and the Hippocratic traditions that most people still take for granted.

Bioethicists spend much of their time arguing with one another, beneath — or, more accurately, above — the public radar, in arcane academic journals, books, university symposia, and government-appointed commissions. This is no empty intellectual enterprise, but a project aimed at changing America. In the course of their arguments, bioethicists are arriving at a consensus about the course of our medical future, and they are slowly succeeding in transforming the laws of public health and the ethics of clinical medicine in the direction they desire.

The Montana Case

At issue in the Montana case was a state law requiring that doctors (as opposed to physician-assistants) perform all abortions. The court unanimously overturned this law, but it didn't stop there. Writing for a 6-2 majority, Justice James C. Nelson went on to impose a radical philosophical imperative on the people of Montana, unwarranted by the facts of the case and unnecessary to its prudent adjudication. Indeed, Nelson's broad opinion will be grist for litigation in Montana for many years to come.

Its essential holding is this: "The Montana Constitution broadly guarantees each individual the right to make medical judgments affecting her or his bodily integrity and health in partnership with a chosen health care provider free from government interference." As the two justices who objected to the scope of the ruling, Karla M. Gray and Chief Justice J. A. Turnage, warned, "the Court's opinion sweeps so broadly as to encompass and decide such issues as the right to physician-assisted suicide and other important health and medical-related issues which simply were not litigated in this case."

Gray and Turnage's trepidation is abundantly warranted. If the ruling means that virtually anything goes medically in Montana so long as a patient requests it and a health care professional is willing to provide it, then patients can ask doctors to kill them for organ-donation purposes, parents or guardians can secure the killing of disabled infants, and people can volunteer to be experimented on in dangerous ways that are currently illegal — all this as a result not of a considered decision by the people of Montana but of a little-noticed ruling by the state supreme court.

As it happens, the Montana Constitutional Convention that created the state right to privacy in 1972 explicitly refused to include abortion and other medical issues in the privacy guarantee. So, to justify its ruling, the court looked to precedents like *Roe v. Wade,* the 1973 U.S. Supreme Court decision that legalized abortion nationwide. Even more than on case law, however, the Montana court relied on philosophical treatises. In particular, the authority the court cited most frequently was the book *Life's Dominion: An Argument About Abortion, Euthanasia, and Individual Freedom,* published in 1993 by the attorney and bioethicist Ronald Dworkin.

The Influence of Bioethics and Ronald Dworkin

Dworkin's thesis is that true adherence to a modern understanding of the sanctity-of-life ethic requires that all of us be permitted to "decide for ourselves" about abortion and euthanasia and that our decisions be accepted by society and tolerated by those who disagree. Otherwise society is "totalitarian." The majority opinion in *Armstrong* cites *Life's Dominion* so many times and applies its reasoning so enthusiastically that Ronald Dworkin's philosophy may now be considered the court-mandated health care creed of the state of Montana.

Dworkin's triumph in *Armstrong v. Montana* illustrates the growing influence of bioethics. How does one become a bioethicist? It isn't hard. No tests have to be passed. Practitioners are not licensed, like attorneys, physicians, real estate agents, and hairdressers. While more than thirty universities offer degrees in bioethics, there are no standards of excellence that generally apply. A Catholic priest may be a bioethicist, as may an atheist college professor. Health care professionals such as nurses and community ombudsmen may get appointed to hospital ethics committees, take a few training courses, and call themselves bioethicists. Indeed, I could say that I am a bioethicist, having written and lectured extensively on the ethics of assisted suicide and the withholding of medical treatment from dying and disabled people.

The mere designation, however, does not give one influence within the bioethics movement. That is to say, there is a very big difference between being a bioethicist and subscribing to the ideology of mainstream bioethics. It is the adherents of the ideology who matter and who hold a steadily increasing sway over the laws of public health, the application of medical ethics, and the protocols that govern hospital care.

This phenomenon is relatively new. It began about thirty years ago as an intellectual exchange among medical ethicists, philosophers, and theologians with widely varying views about how to resolve the dilemmas presented by the growth of technological medicine. In the early years, there was a robust contest for the heart and soul of the movement. Adherents of human equality and the sanctity of life, such as the late Paul Ramsey, were pitted against utilitarians who emphasized the quality of life, such as the late Joseph Fletcher, the patriarch of modern bioethics. Over the years, the Ramsey school made crucial contributions — most notably, helping promote the right to refuse unwanted medical treatment — but steadily lost influence. Today, mainstream bioethics is substantially homogeneous in outlook, and the primary differences among bioethicists concern the proper ways to apply generally agreed-upon values to health care policy and individual medical decisions. It is in this sense that bioethics has become an ideology, albeit one that not every bioethicist shares.

Bioethics: Out of Step with Mainstream American Thinking

In order to have clout within the bioethics movement and seriously affect the discourse that is its hallmark, one must subscribe to its intellectual underpinnings. Pro-lifers have no influence, by definition, and those whose advocacy is rooted in religion are usually ignored. Mainstream bioethics reached a consensus long ago that religious values are divisive in a pluralistic society and thus have little place in the formulation of public policy. Those who believe in abortion rights but also hold that all born humans are equally endowed with moral worth, along with those who subscribe to the "do no harm" ethos of the Hippocratic oath, have little impact, since mainstream bioethics rejects Hippocratic medicine as paternalistic and shrugs off equal human moral worth as a relic of the West's religious past.

In mainstream bioethics, human beings per se have no special rights or moral value. The movement as a whole no longer thinks in that idiom. Instead, it overwhelmingly embraces a so-called "quality-of-life ethic" that requires individual humans to earn their moral and legal rights by displaying certain cognitive capacities. This is usually described as achieving the status of a "person." As we shall see, the criteria for personhood are still a matter of debate among bioethicists. But the notion that personhood rather than humanness is what counts in determining moral worth and legal rights is nearly universally accepted within the mainstream movement and has been taught in American universities and colleges to a whole generation of students. Bioethics ideology rejects person status for newborns, people with severe brain damage, and those with dementia, all of whom it regards as beings of lesser worth than those with more developed frontal lobes. There is serious debate within bioethics, however, whether to extend personhood to some animals ("nonhuman animals," in bioethics parlance), even as it is being stripped from some humans.

Part of what makes this alarming is that the values and presumptions of bioethics ideology are not shared generally throughout society. Unlike adherents to this ideology, most people believe that being human in and of itself confers a special moral status. Most people view a newborn infant as having the same moral worth as all other humans and want their doctors to subscribe to the Hippocratic oath. This means that as the government, the law, and organized medicine rely increasingly on "expert" bioethicists to supply the answers to public policy dilemmas in areas such as cloning, stem cell research, health care rationing, and organ procurement for transplantation, those answers are likely to be based on beliefs not generally shared by the people affected. More and more, public policies and medical protocols are likely to conflict with, rather than reflect, the values of the citizenry.

Bioethics: Consistent with the Mindset of the Elite

If bioethics ideology is out of step with mainstream American thinking, however, it is entirely consistent with the mindset of the elite. As Daniel Callahan, one of the movement's pioneers, wrote in the Hastings Center Report in 1993, the "final factor of great importance" in bioethics' success was the "emergence ideologically of a form of bioethics that dovetailed nicely with the reigning political liberalism of the educated classes in America."

It is not surprising, then, that movement bioethicists have become among society's most powerful members or that their work affects American culture from top to bottom: They serve on federal and state public policy commissions. They write health legislation. They teach the next generation of doctors, lawyers, business executives, and government policy makers in our institutions of higher learning. They are paid by HMOs to consult on issues such as when desired medical treatment can be withheld or withdrawn unilaterally. They direct hospital and nursing-home ethics committees that make or influence decisions ranging from whether to withhold treatment from premature infants to whether to pull feeding tubes from stroke patients who are not dying. They testify as expert witnesses in court cases and submit friend of the court briefs in legal cases of major significance, thereby affecting the evolution of law. They serve on institutional review boards that oversee the ethics of medical experiments using human subjects. They help write protocols governing organ procurement. Occasionally, their work leads to startling lurches in the law, as in Montana. More typically, their advocacy erodes ethical standards and values slowly, as waves transform shorelines, through a succession of subtle changes in public policy and medical ethics — a process known within the movement as "policy creep."

What makes this especially worrisome is that once a policy is formally adopted or embedded in law, it has the power to modify the beliefs of the people it affects. Thus, the patriarch, Joseph Fletcher, viewed the field expansively, as determining how "we are to live and act," a "wisdom" he deemed "specially appropriate to the medical sciences and medical arts." Some bioethicists see themselves as the creators of a new moral paradigm that will replace the archaic Judeo-Christian order as the philosophical underpinning of society.

To appreciate fully the mindset of bioethics and the consequences that will flow from its growing influence on public policy, one need only look to the journals in which its leading thinkers communicate with one another and with their colleagues in the trenches of American medicine — in physicians' offices, on hospital ethics committees, at consultancies advising nursing homes — where bioethics values affect everyday decisions. Two of the most prominent journals devoted exclusively to bioethics are *The Hastings Center*

Report, a bimonthly published by the bioethics think tank the Hastings Center, of Garrison, New York, and *The Kennedy Institute of Ethics Journal*, a quarterly published by Georgetown University. Although not every article in these publications embraces bioethics ideology, the vast majority do. These journals channel the discussion in a definite direction.

Personhood

The December 1999 issue of the *Kennedy Institute of Ethics Journal* is a case in point. It concentrates on the continuing debate over personhood. A person, the journal's introduction says, is "someone morally considerable who is the subject of moral rights and merits moral protection." Most people would say that all human beings qualify. The authors of several articles disagree.

The lead author, John Harris, the Sir David Alliance professor of bioethics at the University of Manchester, in England, claims that it is necessary to establish the criteria for personhood so as to "identify those sorts of individuals who have the 'highest' moral value or importance." It is not life per se that is dispositive, but life of such quality as to "bring individuals into the same moral categories as ourselves." Being human alone does not do the trick: Personhood theory creates castes of "us" and "them," in an explicit hierarchy of human worth.

Harris makes a rather astonishing assertion, considering the brouhaha over abortion. He baldly states that human life begins at conception. This, of course, does not mean he opposes abortion — to the contrary. Remember, it is not human life that matters in personhood theory; human beings do not deserve special status merely because of their species. Harris blandly denigrates unborn human life: "The human embryo and fetus," he writes, "in all stages of its development from conception to birth is no more interesting or complex than the embryos of other creatures and indeed no more interesting than the adult forms of other creatures, for example cats and canaries."

Harris next opines that the exploration of who is a person must include animals, because the exclusion of fauna from personhood deliberations would be arbitrary and an act of "speciesism" — a claim of superiority based on species, which Harris considers as "disreputable" as an assertion of superiority based on "race, gender, nationality, religion, or any other nonmoral characteristic."

So, who (or what) should duly be deemed a person? To Harris, a person is "a being that can value existence." This means "persons might, in principle, be members of any species, or indeed machines." He explicitly states that fetuses and newborn infants are not persons, nor are people with significant cognitive disability or dementia.

The ultimate purpose of personhood analysis is to determine whom we can kill and still get a good night's sleep. Harris writes, "Persons who want to live are wronged by being killed. . . . Nonpersons or potential persons cannot be wronged in this way because death does not deprive them of something they value. If they cannot wish to live, they cannot have that wish frustrated by being killed." So much for the moral wrongness of murdering newborns and throwing them into trash dumpsters.

In the same issue of the *Kennedy Institute of Ethics Journal,* Georgetown's Tom L. Beauchamp, co-author with James F. Childress of one of the most influential bioethics textbooks, *Principles of Biomedical Ethics,* also writes about personhood, taking a different route to essentially the same destination as Harris. Beauchamp asserts that the key to determining personhood is analyzing whether a being enjoys "moral personhood," which he calls both a "cognitive and moral-capacity criterion" for possession of moral rights. He writes, "It is safe to assume that a creature is a moral person if (1) it is capable of making moral judgments about the rightness and wrongness of actions and (2) it has motives that can be judged morally." Beauchamp, like Harris, asserts that under his theory, "unprotected persons would presumably include fetuses, newborns, psychopaths, severely brain-damaged patients, and various demented patients."

Beauchamp does not believe that moral personhood should be the sole basis for moral rights or that animals can be moral persons, but he does assert that humans who are not moral persons may be treated with the same levels of respect or exploitation as animals are now; some humans are "equal or inferior in moral standing to some nonhumans." "If this conclusion is defensible," he writes, "we will need to rethink our traditional view that these unlucky humans cannot be treated in the ways we treat relevantly similar nonhumans. For example, they might be aggressively used as human research subjects and sources of organs." In other words, Beauchamp holds out the prospect that we may someday exploit living infants and cognitively disabled human beings as if they were mere natural resources.

When Is Dead Dead?

The November-December 1999 *Hastings Center Report* focuses on the ethics of expanding organ procurement from "non-heart-beating cadaver donors," that is, people who have died from cardiac arrest instead of "brain death." Much of the discussion has to do with how long doctors should have to wait after a heart stops beating before judging the donor dead for purposes of organ procurement to be in compliance with the "dead donor rule," which requires that donors of vital and non-paired organs be dead before having their organs procured. (Many bioethicists want to discard the dead donor rule, to increase organ availability, but that argument is not made here.) Some organ centers currently wait only two minutes after the cessation of the heartbeat to procure organs; a recent bioethics panel recommended five minutes. The arguments are important, but arcane, and would take too long to explain here.

That said, the ultimately utilitarian approach of mainstream bioethics is much in evidence. John A. Robertson, holder of the Vinson and Elkins chair at the University of Texas Law School, where he teaches criminal law, constitutional law, and bioethics, makes an audacious proposal. He notes that until and unless law and medical ethics discard the dead donor rule, as many bioethicists urge, it will be impossible to use such people as anencephalic infants (babies born with most of their brains missing) or unconscious people as vital-organ donors. Even with the dead donor rule in place, however, Robertson suggests that single kidneys and some other body tissues could be harvested from such people, who "would not be directly harmed by such use." Again, the proposal is to use cognitively disabled people as mere natural resources. One wonders whether the New Mexico woman who recently woke up after being unconscious for sixteen years would have objected had she awakened to learn that one of her kidneys and her corneas had been taken from her on the theory that the loss of them could not harm her.

Like ruminating cows, bioethicists earnestly chew and rechew their ideas until they have explored every nuance and considered every implication, and until the movers and shakers of the movement have achieved consensus about a particular approach. When that point comes, public policy often changes fast: notice the speed with which removing feeding tubes from unconscious, cognitively disabled people became ethical and legal throughout the country once bioethicists agreed it was no different morally than withdrawing antibiotics.

How to Address the Problem

If mainstream bioethicists tread gingerly in pushing their agenda into policy, it is for fear of a public backlash, provoked by what bioethicists jokingly call "the yuck factor." For those of us who believe that bioethics is directing us down immoral and dangerous paths, this fear of the light offers the best hope of an antidote. Since it is almost surely too late to transform the movement's utilitarian assumptions from within, keeping the movement contained inside the academy appears to be the most promising strategy to prevent our society from being remade in bioethics' image. To do this will require heightened media scrutiny and public awareness of what ideological bioethics is, what it stands for, why it matters, and what consequences will befall us all if the "new medicine" becomes our future.

That is easier said than done, of course. But there are ways. The ideology could be engaged vigorously, from the grass roots to the academy to the halls of Congress to the courts. Politicians, devoted to their constituents' welfare, could resist the bioethics tide. For example, to avoid imposing upon people laws and policies that do not reflect their values, when a bioethicist renders an opinion about proposed legislation or testifies before a legislative committee, decision-makers should always "consider the source" and vigorously question the moral presumptions that served as the basis for the opinion. Philanthropists could be persuaded to endow academic chairs dedicated to exploring human equality as the basis for health care law and policy, much as bioethics chairs are used currently to promote the quality-of-life agenda. They could also be induced to fund grants to pay for research into bioethics advocacy trends, and the information gained could serve as the basis for books, magazine articles, and Internet reporting. Nonprofit groups could be formed to follow the bioethics movement, publish journals, engage the proponents in public debate, hold symposia, and alert the media to particularly noxious developments. The popular media, especially television and radio talk shows, could recognize the urgency of covering bioethics as seriously as they cover politics. After all, are not issues like personhood and the harvesting of organs from living people as compelling as tax policy and welfare reform? Experts on the dangers of bioethics could offer themselves as consultants to Hollywood writers and producers, perhaps stimulating motion pictures and television ideas in the tradition of the prophetic *Soylent Green,* and *Coma,* allowing compelling drama and science fiction to warn against the rising bioethics tide.

Beyond the media, a counter-bioethics movement could be created by those who believe that the only truly moral way to resolve the dilemmas with which bioethics grapples is by strict adherence to universal human equality. Perhaps this new, ethical bioethics could be called "human-rights bioethics." It would boldly promote universal human equality as the proper basis for making health-care policy decisions and as the fundamental basis of medical ethics. The proposition would actually be simple but profound: that there is no "them and us" — only us. If any value has the power to unify a diverse society, it is the belief in equality. That being so, surely an abundance of academics, physicians, lawyers, disability rights activists, patient advocates, theologians, and just ordinary people would be willing to stand up proudly for the equal moral worth of all living people.

Much is at stake in how bioethics controversies are resolved in the next decades. Waiting passively for bioethics to decide for us is a prescription for disaster, particularly for the weakest and most vulnerable among us. Health care is just too important to be left to the so-called "experts." There must be no more "Montanas." The time has come for the people to be heard.

The Arts

ELIZABETH LURIE

In all object making, that aspect which relates to its conceptual interpretation is art, that which relates the object to its intended purpose is design, and the quality of its execution is craft.

Hella Basu

The true, the good, and the beautiful.
The false, the evil, and the ugly.

In the so-called postmodern world, we are not used to distinctions such as those in the lines above, the presumption being that all such distinctions are subjective, unknowable externally, the fruits of illusion. Today, the very ideas of objective being (reality) and knowledge (truth) are in question. Be that as it may, the distinctions to which I refer are the foundation of discernment necessary to any understanding of the arts, for they allow us to apprehend and comprehend, and to transmit what we know of the arts from one generation to the next. I leave to the postmodern philosophers their pseudo-rationalism that is actually the end of the lonely, solipsistic, and narcissistic nihilism that eventually emerged from the Enlightenment.

In this essay, I treat "the arts" as visual, and I speak almost exclusively of painting, although sculpture and architecture (and, today, some photography) surely lie within the realm of the visual arts. There are, of course, many other arts — among them music, theatre, dance, and literature (including poetry), as well as today's electronic arts of film, television, and even the creations of (or on) the Internet. But I choose to speak of painting not only because its rich history should inform (even) the postmodernists, but also because the images I refer to are easily located in readily available reference books, or online via any number of sites on the Internet.

Recreation vs. Re-creation

That the arts are now commonly perceived, that is "viewed," both literally and figuratively as a form of recreation, rather than as a form of re-creation, is both deceptive and sad. The terms often used in newspapers to reference sections or pages containing art reviews and announcements, such as "Arts and Leisure" or (worse) "Arts and Entertainment," imply that the arts are not serious or worthy of study directed toward discernment of the excellent, but rather are a form of passive entertainment for the viewer (or of "self-expression" for the artist) comparable with watching Monday night football. This arts-as-entertainment view relegates potential inspiration and its integration into the mind and soul of the viewer to mere pastime, and, in so doing, contravenes the arts' seeking of the true, the good, and the beautiful — or, conversely, the false, the evil, and the ugly. In other words, the notion that the arts are merely to be "appreciated" severely narrows our understanding of their nature and scope. Paradoxically, the current opinion that the arts are, or should be, in and of the realm of popular culture and entirely accessible *prima facie* has only served to further our isolation from their delights and discontents.[1]

Precisely how we arrived at this peculiar and demeaning view of the arts is largely beyond the scope of this essay. Yet some précis is necessary as background. In the nineteenth century, the full emergence of modernity was prepared via the narrowing of truth to encompass only the rational, in the context of the coalescence of the ideas of Marx, Freud, Nietzsche, and Darwin (never mind the numerous contradictions among them). Concurrent with the galloping Industrial Revolution was the ever-expanding development and adoption of the scientific method as the arbiter of "real," proved knowledge.

These currents led artists first to flee from the triumph of rationalism to the nostalgia of Impressionism. Ironically, Impressionism, so dearly beloved today, laid the foundation for the entry, in the early twentieth century, of what is

1. The possible but in my view somewhat doubtful exception is the "blockbuster" art show, examples of which are often featured at the National Gallery of Art in Washington, D.C. While well curated, these shows are often so crowded as to not permit study.

now commonly considered Modern Art. Perhaps the best known relatively early example is Pablo Picasso's *Les Demoiselles D'Avignon* (1906-7).[2] Here we clearly see the break with the representational that began with the early *Fauves'* Expressionism and soon developed into Abstraction and Fantasy:

> The first [Expressionism] stresses the artist's emotional attitude toward himself and the world; the second [Abstraction], the formal structure of the work of art; the third [Fantasy] explores the realm of the imagination, especially its spontaneous and irrational qualities. We must not forget, however, that feeling, order and imagination are all present in every work of art: without imagination, it would be deadly dull; without some degree of order, it would be chaotic; without feeling, it would leave us unmoved. These currents, then, are not mutually exclusive. . . . Moreover, each current embraces a wide range of approaches, from the realistic to the completely non-representational (or non-objective). Thus these currents do not correspond to specific styles, but to general attitudes. The primary concern of the Expressionist is the human community; of the Abstractionist, the structure of reality; and of the artist of Fantasy, the labyrinth of the individual human mind.[3]

By 1930 the pure abstraction of Mondrian (see, for example, *Composition with Red, Blue, and Yellow*) appeared. Even earlier, in the second decade of the century, Kandinsky, Joseph Stella, Léger, and Chagall were experimenting with semi-abstract forms. Chagall and Klee began to play with Fantasy themes, later sometimes turning to themes of hopelessness as World War I loomed and passed. Following in rapid succession were Dada (or Dadaism) and Surrealism. By 1950, *pace* Janson, the distinction between order and chaos collapsed in Pollack's raging self-expressionism ("Action Painting"). To be sure, older influences both persisted and were intermingled with the new, but after World War II "Pop Art" and its successors established that "the rules" regarding and

2. I acknowledge that I am skipping over a great deal here. Just as Neoclassicism and Romanticism (roughly, the period 1750-1850) were reactionary in their own way, neither of these twins of the period could have emerged absent a climate of intellectual individualism (essentially rationalist), while comparatively little of the noted art of this period addresses religious (that is, Christian) themes or subjects. The schooled reader is asked to forgive compression and gross oversimplification in the interest of brevity.

3. H. W. Janson, *History of Art,* 2nd ed. (New York: Harry N. Abrams, Inc., 1977). Note Janson's traditional use of language, which to some readers today will no doubt sound quaint. Janson assumes an objective (knowable) reality with structure; he assumes order vs. chaos, as well as feeling vs. numbness. How far in but twenty-three years have we come!

linking emotion, structure, and imagination had been cast aside in favor of . . . no rules.[4]

Notable throughout the post Second World War period is the continuing, gradual, and now nearly complete disappearance of sacred (Christian) images from the arts of the West, and certainly from the attention of the newly self-appointed *cognoscenti* of critics, curators, and collectors. Also significant is that by 1950 traditional art education — instruction in drawing, perspective, color, form, etc., as well as the study of art history — had all but disappeared from the elementary and secondary schools. What replaced it was a feel-good "self-expression" approach involving the recreational "play" of untutored finger painting, with recognition for participation (effort) rather than accomplishment, and without the teaching of any art history at all.

The net result is that fifty-odd years later, we are more informed by ignorance than anything else insofar as the arts are concerned: anything goes because nobody knows.[5] Indeed, for the postmodernists, anything goes because nobody *can* know. In that event, of course, all art is reduced to the wholly subjective — idiosyncratic, incommunicable, and even incomprehensible. In short, one's individual taste becomes the sole arbiter of what we see:

> "I like that. The yellow is pretty, don't you think?"
> "Well, it's all right, I guess; but the green really turns me off."

How often have you heard this conversation, or its like, when visiting a museum exhibit?

The Arbiter of Art

When taste is the arbiter of art, it is logical that, observing licentiousness or iconoclasm, cultural traditionalists dismiss what they don't like as "not art," which is fruitless in that it is rather like standing under a shower while claiming to be dry. ("What culture? There is no culture!") In parallel fashion, cultural postmoderns embrace every art fad, fashion, and trend as of identical worth. ("What culture? Everything is culture!")

Today, in the absence of any arbiter but taste, these two views intersect — and clash — at the First Amendment to the Constitution. That the amendment

4. I ask readers to once again forgive oversimplification. There is and remains a different set of rules for "breaking the rules." See, for example, Frank Stella's *Empress of India* (1965), in Janson, *History of Art.* Frank Stella knew "the rules" and knew them well. Sadly, many of today's artists do not.

5. I am indebted to sculptor Reed Armstrong for the formulation of this pithy summary.

says something about speech but nothing about the arts seems to escape everyone's attention; but that is not particularly surprising in an environment in which politics informs culture rather than the right way around. Nor should it surprise us that people who "know" nothing but what they like or dislike should attempt to make law the servant of their preferences. Opponents in wars of taste quickly embrace coercion, although one wonders why, being entirely self- or perhaps "socially" constructed, the denizens of the postmodern bother to write, or paint, or war, or do anything at all. (Perhaps it is a matter of keeping occupied, since for them there is no purpose under heaven.) At least some of the cultural traditionalists present their arguments from the perspective of establishing standards; unfortunately they do not know that taste is an opinion, not a standard.

If the foregoing is not surprising, then what is surprising is that we do still see a good deal of art that soars in its aspiration, riveting the attention of our minds and souls, inviting integration and inspiring our engagement of life. Not all of those engaged in producing works of art have forgotten "the rules." Consider, for example, two very recent examples from architecture, both located in Los Angeles: The Getty Museum by Richard Meier and Partners, and the now-under-construction Disney Hall by Frank O. Gehry. Both of these complexes are eminently suited to their purposes, and both convey a sense of awe that admits us into their architects' visions of the nature of aspiration. Both convey a sense of the sacred.

Art: To Communicate the Aspirations of Faith

Distinctions do prevail — even if they are but distinctions of mere taste, *pace* postmodernist philosophers in their self-imposed and rather silly exile. Penultimately, the arts are purposive and they are about the true, the good, and the beautiful, as well as the false, the evil, and the ugly. The arts' purpose is to reveal aspiration in a knowable (true) form derived from a synthesis of the artist's intellect and imagination (and informed by craft), so as to evoke inspiration (also derived from a synthesis of intellect and imagination) on the part of the viewer. Put in religious rather than secular humanist terms, the arts' purpose is to communicate the aspirations of faith, such that the viewer may be inspired in his own commitment to faith.[6] Thus Michelangelo in executing his vision of the Sistine Chapel at the Vatican in Rome.

6. Even the decorative (as opposed to the fine) arts contain these elements. Consider Genesis 1:31: "And God saw every thing that He had made, and behold, it was very good." This verse, of course, appears before man embraced the knowledge of evil.

So then, what are we to make of a similarly religious image, the famous (or infamous) *Piss Christ* by Andres Serrano (1987)? Readers may recall this large (40″ × 60″) cibachrome photograph of a crucifix submerged in the artist's urine.[7] Surely, to a Christian — and even perhaps to anyone of any of the monotheist traditions — the image conveys an aspiration to evil via iconoclasm. It speaks to contamination and even destruction of that which is Other (God), by literal human elimination, and in so doing it asserts that the capacities and power of man are both supreme and absolute (and thus not false). Iconoclasm, the image says, is the means by which the world is to be made beautiful. And with what inspiration is the viewer to come away from this work of art? How does it speak to the viewer's intellect and the soul? It is clearly intended to invite the viewer to reject the sacred, even to abhor it, and to exorcise awareness of the sacred from his life — and by extension, from our community life. Even for a nonreligious person who nevertheless respects the religious among us, the image is evil, it invites doing evil, and hence its "truth" is but falseness and its "beauty" but the epitome of ugliness.[8]

Analysis of a wholly secular image yields parallel conclusions. In 1979, feminist artist Judy Chicago exhibited *The Dinner Party*, a triangular mosaic "table" which depicts each place setting at the "dinner" as a female vagina, representing, according to the artist, thirty-nine "forgotten" women. Reams of twaddle have been written about this piece, nearly all of it feminist polemics regarding the "liberating" nature of the work and its heroines — the women at the table, as well as artist Chicago and her 400-odd collaborators in production (the work was begun in 1974). To what does Chicago aspire? It seems that she defines women exclusively by their unique genitalia, and indeed that these geni-

7. I select this and the other works discussed in this section because they are representational and therefore less difficult to comprehend than non-objective works.

8. Recall that Genesis gives no account of art, only of nature, in the Garden of Eden. Man-made, art *qua* art is first referenced by God in his giving of the Decalogue to Moses. Exodus 20:4: "Thou shalt not make unto thee a graven image, nor any manner of likeness, of any thing that is in heaven above, or that is in the earth beneath, or that is in the water under the earth." While Moses is on Mount Sinai (Exodus 31), the Lord informs Moses that his commandment has been violated by Aaron's construction of what can be considered the first work of art, a golden calf. God is so offended that he asks Moses to leave him alone so that he may "consume" the people. Moses entreats God to spare them on the basis of earlier promises made by God to Abraham. God forbears the intended destruction, and Moses, upon coming down from Sinai, "took the calf which they had made, and burnt it with fire, and ground it to powder, and strewed it upon the water, and made the children of Israel drink of it" (Exodus 31:20).

Until several centuries into the common era, many Christians observed the law against graven images. After much controversy, the matter was settled at the Council of Nicaea (7th Ecumenical) in 787 C.E. Source: http://www.iclnet.org. This site provides a translation of the pertinent text issued by the Council.

talia are to be consumed in some fashion, since they have come together at dinner but no food is in sight. And by whom are these disembodied stone genitalia to be consumed? By men? By women? The (absent) people at the dinner party can be interpreted as offering their vaginas for consumption by entry or other contact with us. Hence the import is that a woman see her identity only in terms of her most intimate orifice, one presumably divorced from any connection with procreation, as there are neither men nor children in evidence. The truth presented here is a truth of lies — that there is nothing to aspire to outside of ourselves, that we have neither minds nor souls with which to engage our existence. In secular terms, *The Dinner Party* is merely bad rather than evil; it does not even admit to the idea of evil, and so must be demoted to simple badness. As to beauty, that too presumes a consciousness which extends beyond the sentient but blind and headless physicality of this work; failing utterly in such consciousness, *The Dinner Party* does not address the beauty-ugliness spectrum.

These well-known if somewhat dated examples are not in the least rare or extreme. Roger Kimball recently previewed the 2000 Whitney Biennial.[9] He notes that, "For years, these exhibitions at New York's Whitney Museum of American Art have been little more than freak shows . . . full of hectoring left-wing political gestures and celebrations of sexual deviance."[10] Describing an installation for the exhibition, *Sanitation* by Hans Haacke, Kimball informs us that this Whitney-commissioned work

> includes a row of garbage cans containing speakers playing a tape of marching soldiers. Above the cans is a copy of the First Amendment . . . [with] six quotations printed in the Gothic script favored by the Third Reich. Three of these come from statements New York Major Rudolph Giuliani made about the infamous "Sensation" last fall at the Brooklyn Museum, which included a depiction of the Virgin Mary covered with pornographic cutouts and clumps of elephant dung. The other quotations come from statements about art and culture by Pat Robertson, Pat Buchanan, and Senator Jesse Helms.[11]

Rightly, Kimball laments that "Trivialization is not an innocuous or morally neutral process. . . . When monstrous evil [the Third Reich] is trivialized . . . it loses its power to horrify and admonish us. It marks a step down the path from civilization toward barbarism."[12] We ignore such trivialization at our

9. Roger Kimball, "Unsanitary 'Art,'" *Wall Street Journal,* 14 March 2000, section A.
10. Kimball, "Unsanitary Art."
11. Kimball, "Unsanitary Art."
12. Kimball, "Unsanitary Art."

peril, and far too often we simply either reject — or, good heavens! — celebrate the barbaric as *avant-garde.* Neither stance reflects what is most needed and what is so sorely missing from the artists themselves as well as from the viewers of their works: objective discernment. Only by remedying our vast ignorance of art's history can we even begin to learn to discern the true, good, and beautiful from the false, evil, and ugly. And the discernment of both is necessary if not sufficient for us to assess art's manifestations within our lives and those of our children.

Teaching Discernment and Judgment

The reason discernment is necessary but not sufficient is that judgment is required to recognize and advocate excellence, as well as to recognize and advocate the rejection of corruption. Art that in its expressions of aspiration inspires us to integrate intuition (feeling), intellect (structure), and imagination (fantasy, in the secular, or faith, in the religious) is *better* than art which aspires to reject, deny, or condemn these aspects of man in his relation to the universe. Art that is whole in the senses that I describe is that art which engages us fully in our humanity, and therefore in our relation to others, our community, our society. Such art provides an added bonus for those of faith, in that it inspires us to affirm the enduring principles of our beliefs.

Ultimately, as I have hinted elsewhere in this chapter, the arts define a view of the worthy or, in religious terms, the sacred. There is a reason that through the ages the arts have served the gods, and God after the arrival of monotheism. The reason is that the artists among us — the painters, sculptors, architects, composers, writers, actors, and dancers — *knew* their place. They did not "know" that anything goes because no one *can* know. And, for many, their place remains to serve the sacred by defining the true, the good, and the beautiful in moral terms going far beyond our observable earthly existence. Put simply, men and women, both artist and viewer, *can* know the difference between hubris and humility. Since many artists and viewers today do not know this difference, we must teach them, first discernment, and then judgment.

An Overview of Academia

STEPHEN H. BALCH

American higher education has many problems. This essay will deal with just one of them, though a very important one: its failure to sustain intellectual pluralism and a climate of healthy debate.

Before real progress can be made toward reviving academic pluralism some habits of thought may have to be changed. Chief among these is the too easy equation of the intellectual world of the natural sciences with that of the social sciences and the humanities, leading many to assume that the latter can sustain open and reasoned discourse as easily as the former. In fact there are real and critical differences. With respect to the problem we're considering, one is paramount: professors in the humanities and social sciences characteristically bring to the analysis of questions in their fields much stronger feelings about the answers they prefer.

This is, to some extent, inescapable. Unlike the questions that occupy physics, chemistry, mathematics, and even biology, those relating to justice and moral truth — the stuff of the humanities and social sciences — are also strenuously contested in the outside world. Factional alignments are thus produced which, early in life, can generate loyalties of a political, religious, or cultural nature. Because emotional involvement, and interest, in the particulars of social controversy go hand in hand, those recruited to their scholarly study usually ar-

---

Parts of this essay were derived from an article on "charter colleges" co-authored by Stephen H. Balch and Michael R. Block that appeared in *The Chronicle of Higher Education,* 24 March 2000.

rive already equipped with strong dispositions toward one or another of the warring sides. Furthermore, the academic continuation of these controversies remains encapsulated within the global ones, reinforcing and being reinforced by them, thus creating interactions that can sustain intense career-long factional loyalties.

The old joke that academic controversies are so bitter because so little is at stake misses a major point. Unlike the larger public realm where most citizens have only a tangential interest in vindicating their opinions, and even political leaders can walk away from conflicts after splitting the difference, in the academy, professional lives, fortunes, and, perhaps most sacred, self-esteem, hang on the outcome of even the most recondite disputes. Under such circumstances, dogmas that preempt debate, and define a comfortable environment of uncontested truth, may carry special appeal, preventing the pain of cognitive dissonance and enhancing career security. But knowing what can safely be thought often leads to suppressing what cannot.

The strong preference problem is compounded by the complex and ambiguous nature of the phenomena filtered through them. Compared to the natural sciences the human domains make do with fuzzy concepts, contested analytic frameworks, a paucity of reliable data, and chronic difficulties in posing decisive tests between rival hypotheses. In such a context, theory stays murky and prediction hazardous. What reigns instead is judgment, at best informed by good sense, relevant learning, and careful observation, but never entirely escaping the suspect realm of opinion. This inherent cloudiness makes it even more tempting to dismiss views with which one disagrees as mere prejudice.

That is not to say that healthy argument and open-minded inquiry in these fields is impossible. Each has canons of good practice that permit intellectual advance. Clarity, consistency, and evidence confer advantages, at least insofar as practitioners value science over comfort. And from time to time events intrude, as in the condemnation inflicted on Marxist theory by communism's collapse, a verdict more psychologically effective than anything the best-controlled experiments could have produced. Still, these fields are too imperfect in their methods of inquiry to be trusted to police themselves in the same reliable way as do the "hard" sciences. An uncomfortable percentage of the time, theoretical ascendancy is determined more by power than by cogency. This is not, as some postmoderns would have it, because power establishes truth, but because power can more easily establish orthodoxy when error is difficult to detect. Strong feelings and messy methods thus lie at root of academe's political correctness problems.

The "City-States" of Colleges and Universities

Considered as constitutional systems, our institutions of higher learning are ill equipped to thwart the power of overbearing intellectual majorities that these strong preferences can mobilize. In fact, their characteristic mode of governance magnifies majoritarian power. As polities, colleges and universities actually bear more than a passing resemblance to federations of ancient city-states, in this case made up of the semi-autonomous departments that comprise their main subdivisions. These departments generally hire, tenure, and promote their teaching staffs; fix major and graduate studies requirements; admit and fund graduate students; award the doctorates that credential new practitioners; and help these journeymen secure their initial jobs. The bigger and more prestigious the institution, the less the department is likely to be subject to serious oversight from above.

Little republics are subject to all the dangers memorably delineated by James Madison in *Federalist Ten.* Being small they easily fall under the sway of compact majorities that persistently monopolize positions of power and grind down opponents. And because the admission of new citizens is subject to the majority's control, as time passes majorities tend to expand inexorably. Swollen majorities, of course, eventually generate their own factions. But subsequent splitting in a context of diminished diversity may leave academic departments little more than a nest of wrangling sectarians.

Not only have departments suffered this fate, it has overtaken whole fields as well through a process somewhat analogous to that which occurs in representative bodies such as the Electoral College, the United States Congress, and the British House of Commons, whose members are elected via a district-by-district or state-by-state winner-take-all system. Such systems characteristically distort voter preferences, exaggerating the representation of any party winning a majority, or even just a plurality, of the vote. Furthermore, in academic disciplines there are few of the external correctives that operate in the public sphere. In politics the electorate often reacts against parties too long at the helm, treating them to the same district-by-district pummeling once visited on their opponents. By contrast, academic departments have both the first and last words. Thus, if the same factional grouping captures the majority in most departments, it can effectively exclude minority views from meaningfully influencing the life of the field overall.

Collegial vs. Adversarial

Again, the first step to reform is to admit the real differences that exist among different fields of inquiry. In some, the classic paradigm of scientific investigation is largely realized and internalized checks can be more or less relied upon to keep things on the straight and narrow. In others, rationalist aspirations are too clouded by passion and prejudice to long prevail without extra reinforcement. Disciplines of the former type are *collegial* in that, though rivalries exist among hypotheses and investigators, there is general agreement on the means of resolving them and a strong sense of shared intellectual mission. Such fields typically have well-established paradigms within which research proceeds, extensive histories of settling theoretical disputes in a manner that restores consensus, and findings that receive unambiguously productive employment in the larger world. Conversely, disciplines of the latter type are *adversarial* in that rivalries shade into enmities, bear heavily on methods of verification as well as the substance of disputes, involve judgments of value as well as of fact, and reveal an absence of shared mission. Adversarial fields are likely to be divided into enduring factions whose partisans often treat their rivals more as foes than colleagues.

Adversarial disciplines occupy something of a twilight zone between plain politics and mature science. To frankly recognize this is not to disparage them. They deal with important questions that demand scholarly answers. But if the university is to assimilate them productively into its life, they must be treated in a manner that acknowledges their distinctive character and problems. Exclusive reliance on the forms of governance serviceable for collegial disciplines is unlikely to preserve a healthy level of intellectual competition in adversarial ones. Hence special efforts must be made to sustain their discursive commitments to evidence, logic, clarity, and civility.

Effective policy should aim at two related goals: encouraging as much rational discourse within an adversarial field as is possible, and inhibiting the formation of intellectual monopolies based purely on organizational clout. Practices should be considered that, on the one hand, draw academic adversaries into sustained reasoned discourse and, on the other hand, afford limited shelter for diverse views. Needless to say, a balance has to be struck between shelter and competition. In the polity we're generally willing to settle for outcomes acceptable to the majority. In the academic world we want progress toward the truth. Simply protecting viewpoint differences will not suffice. Ideas must be able to defend themselves in fair fights to earn their academic keep. But they must also be protected from lynching. Striking this balance will not be easy, and a good deal of institutional experimentation will undoubtedly have to take place if it is to be gained.

Since the process has to begin somewhere, I'll hazard a few proposals under three headings: "top-down" approaches, mainly oversight activities that can be undertaken by governing boards and senior university administration; "lateral" proposals, those that involve modifications in existing modes of faculty self-governance; and "bottom-up" strategies, consisting of devices for reviving intellectual diversity through the initiative of rank-and-file academics. At the very least these may serve to launch a round of productive discussion.

Methods of Reform

Possible Top-Down Approaches

In recent decades university governing boards have generally avoided involvement in purely academic issues on the assumption that laymen cannot render informed judgment about subtle points of scholarly controversy. Memories of trustee efforts to censor and purge dissidents earlier in the century also encouraged self-restraint. But repeated demonstrations of the magnitude of intellectual intolerance within the academic community argue for the trustee role to be revisited. If abuses of academic power are best restrained by distributing it among a variety of sites, one might ask which intellectual powers might usefully be restored to boards.

Undoubtedly, trustees go beyond their competence when they try to adjudicate specific scholarly disputes. Unless decisions are forced upon them by the inability of academic bodies to resolve such differences, they should keep clear. But they do have general competencies that can be constructively exercised, including ensuring that a spirit of reasoned discourse prevails throughout the institutions they govern. The norms of reasoned discourse are not so obscure that trustees cannot grasp them or assess the extent to which they actually prevail in the academic subdivisions they oversee. The degradation that afflicts the humanities in particular often involves obviously fallacious intellectual practices — such as the *ad hominem* attack, special pleading, and inappropriate appeals to authority (especially that of certified "victim groups") — of a type once routinely debunked in freshman logic. Indeed, some of it proceeds from the explicit repudiation of concepts like truth, disinterestedness, and other premises of science-like inquiry.

A first step toward salvaging the adversarial disciplines might thus be a reassertion of legitimate trustee interest in their intellectual health. Governing boards could then proceed to take a number of concrete steps.

First, trustees should make an understanding of, and commitment to, reasoned discourse, the litmus test for hiring presidents and chancellors (who will then, presumably, do the same for their own subordinates). Needless to say, *the courage* to stand up for reasoned discourse should also be an indispensable quality. Hiring academic CEOs is the one remaining, unquestioned trustee prerogative, and few are likely to object to the introduction of such baseline criteria. A president willing to join his trustees in ensuring a climate of reasoned discourse will make the responsible and confident exercise of their other oversight responsibilities much easier. Despite the persistent vetting of academic executives by the partisans of political correctness, brave and principled individuals can still be found if search committees approach their task with resolution.

Second, trustees could join with their presidents to create special academic advisory bodies to evaluate the health and vigor of the spirit of reasoned discourse within their institution and its various subdivisions. These would give boards and presidents an independent perspective on the adequacy of intellectual quality controls, supplementing the opinions received on these matters via existing administrative-faculty channels. The objective would not be the hindrance of intellectual innovation and dissent; subjects of inquiry, lines of theoretical conjecture, or opinions reached would not themselves become issues. Instead, the body's attention would be directed toward matters not-to-be-taken-for-granted (in the adversarial domains) such as respect for evidence, logic and clarity in discourse, commitment to testing and falsifiability, and civility in debate, as well as toward the adequacy of controls against abuses like research fakery and plagiarism (controls equally needed in the collegial fields).

These bodies might be composed of senior scientists and scholars, distinguished for the integrity and fruitfulness of their work, and drawn disproportionately from those fields consistently maintaining high levels of practice. Rotated in office, and nearing the end of their professional lives, the loyalty of these scholars to good practice could be expected to outweigh any self-interested reason for covering-up shoddiness, charlatanism, and inanity, or any temptation to act as ideological enforcers. By way of further safeguard, these bodies might also be entrusted with the selection (subject to board confirmation) of their successors, or even be temporarily enlisted on-leave from other academic institutions through regular programs of exchange. Their conclusions could be fed into tenure and promotion decisions as well as utilized in departmental management and budgetary decisions.

Sharpening trustee understanding of the nature of the scientific mission and good scholarly practice could also be part of the charge of these entities. This might involve, among other things, the organization of orientation programs for incoming trustees and periodic retreats for continuing ones. The same might well be done for the faculty too. Perhaps most important, graduate courses on reasoned discourse and the ideals of scientific inquiry could be developed that would serve as prerequisites for the receipt of a research or teaching degree.

Under such a dispensation, trusteeship would be a rather different proposition than it is now, and probably less attractive to individuals not prepared or equipped to do the intellectual work required. More demanding responsibilities might also prompt governors and legislators to make appointments with greater deliberation and regard for intellectual qualifications than is now often the case. In fact, they would probably be pressed hard to do so by university faculties compelled to take their governing boards more seriously. As a result, more retired scholars, journalists, and scientists from government and the private sector might be enlisted to serve alongside the lawyers, businessmen, and community leaders who now dominate board membership.

This remedy, however, carries a strong caveat. In the hands of the politically correct an academic oversight agency could prove more an inquisitor than a referee. Top-down remedies that rely on lay influence to ensure reason and fairness assume these laymen are sufficiently aware of the Enlightenment heritage to recognize and fight against reason's enemies. Some optimism is thus required. Pessimists may prefer remedies that work through the diffusion of academic powers rather than through their consolidation.

Possible Lateral Approaches

A well-designed academic constitution requires that adversarial fields be governed in a manner ensuring that a broad range of views can flourish. Today's standard forms of academic governance do just the opposite. Defying the wisdom of constitutionalism generally, and the American constitutional tradition in particular, their arrangements typically allow majorities to work their untrammeled will, particularly at the department level where most personnel, and many basic curricular decisions, are made. Chairmen, personnel committees, and curriculum committees are usually elected by a simple majority vote, sometimes of all faculty and sometimes just of tenured ones, permitting the dominant faction to win again and again. Since this process governs new hires, as well as promotions and tenures, dominant factions are positioned to drive their rivals toward extinction. Procedures may therefore be needed that explicitly recognize the value of philosophic pluralism in adversarial fields and provide the institutional means to sustain it.

One relatively straightforward remedy would be to change the voting systems by which key academic decisions are now usually made. Most democracies eschew the winner-takes-all voting systems characteristic of English speaking countries. So too might adversarial departments. Proportional or cumulative voting arrangements might be employed instead to give minority sentiment more weight in hiring and tenuring. Under one possible variant, for instance, faculty members would be allowed to "save their votes," declining to participate in a particular hiring or tenure decision so as to get a double ballot during future go-rounds. Trustees seeking to encourage pluralism might want to consider introducing such procedures.

A more radical idea would allow distinct "schools of thought" within adversarial fields to explicitly organize themselves in a state of partial independence from their rivals. Academics of a multitude of factional persuasions would then be at liberty to develop their positions with a greater sense of freedom from peer coercion than now is often the case. Some Madisonian imagination would be required to get the details right, together with a lot of trial and error, but something like the following could emerge: At large institutions, or within university systems, recognized schools of thought would be allowed to organize around whatever conceptual principles a significant number of scholars most prized. Some might be unified by a worldview like Marxism, feminism, or libertarianism, or a less precisely defined set of philosophic sensibilities. Others might find agreement in a methodological perspective, such as one which separates the more quantitatively from the more normatively and historically oriented practitioners of political scientists, or the analytic from the continental philosophers. Some schools of thought might span a number of disciplines, while others would be confined within one. ("Composite schools," uniting distinct but mutually comfortable outlooks unable on their own to attain the prescribed minima, could also be permitted.) Each, however, would be required to have the minimum number of scholars deemed sufficient to perform the governance roles thereafter expected of them.

These schools of thought would then complement departments in adversarial fields as the basic units of academic governance. While purely housekeeping chores, such as formulating teaching schedules and overseeing clerical staff, could be left to traditional departmental governance, the more intellectually significant functions of hiring, promoting, and tenuring, as well as the development of major and graduate programs, would be shared between them and the schools.

For instance, a school of thought might, at any given moment, be allowed to "own" a proportion of the faculty slots within a department, or across departments within a university system. (The starting share of each school might coincide with the original number of its adherents when these rules first go into operation.) As positions were subsequently vacated they would — normally — be refilled through searches conducted under the auspices of the previous occupant's school. The school and the department would first reach agreement on the subject-matter qualifications of prospective hires. Thereafter the screening of applications, the interviewing of candidates, and the final selection would be in the hands of the school, with other members of the department getting the chance to monitor and comment on all phases of the process. A recommendation to hire would be submitted by the school to the senior administration for final approval, accompanied by supporting, adverse, or mixed comment from the department at large. Seriously contested hires could be rejected by the administration and the searches reopened. So could disagreements over the subject competencies of those hired.

The system would not be static — the fortunes of schools of thought would be allowed to wax and wane. A variety of factors could alter their relative strengths, each, in some sense, reflecting "market mechanisms." Thus, schools that attracted more interest among graduate students, or even undergraduate majors, could be awarded a larger share of faculty slots. So might schools whose members attracted an unusual amount of intellectual, or even financial, support from the outside. And presumably, from time to time purely intellectual considerations would lead some scholars to switch affiliations, carrying slots with them. Senior administration might also retain some discretion, which the process of intellectual oversight already described would help them intelligently exercise.

Essentially, the long-term prospects of different schools of thought would come to depend on the "votes" of constituencies, both inside and outside the academy. Some, of course, would object that this represents an undue intrusion by the external world into what should be the scholar's well-insulated domain. But it might be better understood as a means of placing disciplines in which adversarial politics is an inherent fact of life into a wider and better-balanced nexus of reality checks. The existence of institutionally recognized rival schools of thought, itself the primary check, would bring debate over central methodological and theoretical questions into the clear light of day. (Perhaps the medieval academic institution of the public disputation might be revived to expose them to the broader university community.) The jostling of departments and schools would thereafter provide boards, college councils, and faculty senates, to say nothing of deans, provosts, presidents, and even potential donors, with better information than they presently receive about what is going on inside their institutions. Allowing donors to play some role would also help remove a genuinely scandalous aspect of the current academic scene: that the diversity of sophisticated opinion is immensely greater off campus than on it.

To be sure, such a system would be subject to special dangers of its own. No one wants "affirmative action for ideas." The ultimate safeguard against this would be the intensified competition the coexistence of rival schools of thought would tend to produce. Dominant factions could not suppress their rivals, but would be compelled to attend and answer them. This would not only happen within single institutions, it would also become more likely in adversarial disciplines as a whole, which would inevitably be made more heterogeneous by revived intellectual competition.

Possible Bottom-Up Approaches

Procedures by which rank-and-file faculty members can create new academic programs without recourse to centralized decision-making mechanisms could also work to undercut the power of domineering academic majorities. Allowing faculty groups on large campuses to develop their own general education programs, each broadly conforming to institution-wide norms, but differing from the others in content, difficulty, and philosophic sensibility, represents a relatively modest variant on this idea.

Few academic duties are now as institutionally slighted as that of delivering liberal learning. Here majority rule has had the perverse effect of reducing programs to lowest common denominator pabulum. With individual departments sharing veto rights over curriculum policy, the dynamics of turf protection almost always ensures curricular incoherence, with students left free to cobble together almost any combination of courses they please. This has the benefit of allowing them to escape ideological coercion, but the concomitant drawback of permitting them to graduate without being exposed to fundamental areas of knowledge or leading thinkers — essential ingredients of a good liberal education. Furthermore, their escape from ideology may not be as complete as it first seems. To the extent that anything specific is ingrained in general education requirements, it is typically what the most vociferous campus groups demand: courses on "diversity" and "multiculturalism." Without the overall perspective a serious liberal education brings, students will be deprived of the powers of discernment necessary to recognize indoctrination when it shows its ugly head.

The process would not have to be particularly complicated. Because most existing general education programs specify so little, faculty members could assemble many different sequences of existing courses that satisfy requirements but offer much more. All the college or university would then need to do is advertise their existence and certify their completion. Programs reputed to be rigorous would, presumably, confer a valuable credential on their graduates and thereafter attract more and more of the ablest students.

Academic programs commonly function as important interest groups within the little polities our colleges and universities define. If they have faculty slots assigned them they can hire, promote, and even tenure to their liking. And to the extent that they provide different types of academics secure career tracks they help dissidents speak out with less fear of retaliation. As the history of women's and ethnic studies programs attests, they also often possess a sense of mission relevant to purposes that fall outside their specific educational charge, but which they champion within the wider councils of their institutions. The alternative education programs that could emerge out of this system could therefore help multiply the perspectives brought to bear on a wide range of academic policies.

A more ambitious variant idea would be to open the door to the construction of virtually autonomous, degree granting undergraduate programs — "charter colleges" if you will, analogous to "charter schools" at the primary and secondary education levels. The architects of such programs could devise their own systems of governance, have wide latitude in making personnel decisions and determining teaching loads, and be allowed to get by with as trim an administrative structure as possible. They would also be permitted to craft their own curricula so long as these met the minimum requirements of the host university or system. Each year these programs might receive a per-student payment equal to the average cost of undergraduate education in the conventional institutions. Given the likely operating efficiency of the more successful ones, they might become indispensable baselines against which the cost-effectiveness of other university programming could be measured.

The process of chartering could either be put in the hands of the existing state university system or, to avoid vested-interest vetoes, bestowed on a new statewide agency created for this purpose. Groups of professors would probably comprise the most numerous class of charter applicants, but others, including both not-for-profit and profit-making organizations, could also play a role in founding or managing colleges. Obviously cranky and frivolous programs could be denied charters, threshold enrollments prescribed, basic faculty credentials defined, academic freedom guaranteed, and racial and sex discrimination in admissions and hiring prohibited. Once in operation, any charter college that failed to hold enrollments would be allowed to wither and die (as would existing programming that couldn't compete with the charter colleges).

The curricula of these programs could far exceed the modest requirements typical of the general education curricula of most conventional institutions, affording students enriched encounters with serious subject matter they would otherwise miss. Some charter colleges might only provide the first two years of an undergraduate's education, allowing students to undertake upper-division specialized studies elsewhere. Others might be totally integrated four-year "Great Books Colleges," or be organized around particular intellectual themes, or have a pre-professional focus. Educators emphasizing a multicultural approach could take as much advantage of charters as more traditional educators, but since it is the latter who are now most likely to be shut out of new programming, the opportunities belonging to them would be relatively greater.

The mass of related possibilities involving for-profit post-secondary institutions, and the vast potential of online distance learning, though too numerous to be explored here, are not only already being widely discussed but are actually being put to the test. By introducing a far greater amount of institutional fluidity into a rather ossified environment, they will surely work on pluralism's behalf.

The near monopolization of positions of academic authority by the cultural left came about, in part, through its ability to find ingenious ways to reshape institutions to its advantage. What is required now is the same ingenuity, not in the service of other forms of ideological partisanship, but to promote the robust contest among competing ideas on which the health of the academy ultimately depends.

The Humanities

ROBERT ROYAL

The Humanities are about human beings. It might seem hard to ignore such studies in education. Reasonably humane societies have existed without teaching their members about nuclear physics or astronomy or electronic communications media (however desirable it may be, as an ideal, to pursue all possible human knowledge), but no viable society has ever thought it wise to ignore questions about essential human nature. How can we claim to be full human beings if we have not looked hard at the things that most directly concern us: ourselves and the societies in which, with others, we share the world? And how can we do so without taking seriously the best answers to such questions, which have survived the deaths of their authors, centuries of critics, and even cataclysmic changes in entire cultures?

A vague intuition that such basic questions are widely neglected has given rise during the past few decades to the common lament that the humanities or liberal education or the study of Western Civilization is in serious trouble, indeed in acute crisis and decline. The three terms mark out slightly different subjects: the humanities tell us — or at least we used to think they did so — about the central issues of human life; liberal education, properly understood, focuses on what makes us free and responsible human beings; and the study of Western Civilization arose in the twentieth century as a banner under which to make sense of the kind of society in which we live, after some of its traditional bases had been shaken. Each of these fields might be given separate treatment. But for the sake of the present discussion, we will assume that all three subjects aim at a common goal: the preservation and further development of civilization and the formation of free and virtuous human beings who will both benefit from and contribute to such a civilization.

The Humanities in Crisis

As we well know from frequent complaints, the humanities are in crisis because they have been attacked simultaneously from several sides, including an attack from within by professors and practitioners of the humanities themselves. An internal self-critique has always been one element among many others in the humanistic disciplines. But in the last few decades, intellectuals with varying agendas have succeeded in convincing a large part of the American population, especially young people, that a definable field of the humanities does not exist and that, if it did, it would be dangerous. In this view, a trinity of ideas — race, class, and gender — may be used to explain, and explain away, much of our humanistic heritage. All earlier thought is reducible to struggles to maintain power, usually by white, Western males. Believing that there are core truths about human life, in this perspective, would be to start down the road of intellectual tyranny.

Clearly, this new anti-humanist bent within the humanities represents an even more radical threat to the central human questions than the lamentable fact that students are no longer required to study Shakespeare or U.S. History or some other desirable component of higher education. If the great Western books and issues were given a fair hearing, it would become instantly clear that the claim that they make up a monolithic bid for power is sheer nonsense. One great figure contradicts another, indeed is often spurred to thought by what appear to be the radical errors of some predecessor or contemporary. Aristotle criticizes Plato; Augustine, Aquinas, Luther, and Calvin wrestle with the good and bad among the pagans and their Christian opponents; Descartes and Pascal dispute the bases of earlier knowledge; Rousseau believes that, the Bible notwithstanding, we are born good; and so on.

By comparison, the current anti-humanist orthodoxy, while proclaiming diversity, is actually a quite narrow and monochromatic intellectual straitjacket. Behind the agenda lies the following: a philosophical claim that general truths about human beings do not exist (skepticism); that what one person or culture values another may reject (relativism); and that all valuation is merely subjective, with no basis in reality (nihilism). At the same time — and in complete contrast to the treatment given to the older order — the concepts of race, gender, and class have been elevated in highly politicized and doubtful forms to an absolute truth status, immune to the tools applied to undermine all other truth claims. Skillful analysis of these currents has been done often in recent years and need not be reproduced here.[1]

Science and the Humanities

But this is only one half of the perceived crisis in the humanities. The other half stems from a powerful — perhaps even more potent — challenger: science. Since the middle of the nineteenth century, alongside the erosion of philosophical belief in human truths, a certain type of science has slowly begun to crowd out all alternatives. Science claims to be value-free and, at its best, that is a good thing. But we have recently witnessed an attempt to make the empirical sciences, which are merely one form of human knowing, into all truth. The consequences for human life are devastating. A brilliant scientist such as Edward O. Wilson, for example, dogmatically asserts that neuroscience has now shown us that "human behavior" is the result of genetic inheritance (about 40 percent) and a "complex algorithm" of environmental influences (60 percent).[2] Where human freedom comes into this very precise deterministic cocktail or whether liberty — and therefore a self-governing, free, democratic people — may even be said to exist in such a world does not much trouble Wilson.

This is not merely an abstract argument. It leads to seriously worrisome results. In the early months of the new millennium, for example, two scientists put forward the argument that the tendency for some men to rape could be explained through genes and evolutionary psychology.[3] In their view, rape is a strategy by which certain males are able to assure that their genes will be passed on. The same scientists hastened to say, of course, that rape is wrong. But what the scientific basis for this conclusion might be they cannot say. And since their basic approach, like Wilson's, rules out any realm of authentic liberty where categories of right and wrong, praise or blame, may be assigned to human behavior, this scientific vision is as much of a dead end and a denial of the very possibility of the humanities as the self-immolation of certain practitioners of the old humanistic disciplines themselves.

Of course, neither the scientists nor the nihilistic humanists really believe that, say, rape is just one variant of human evolutionary behavior and,

1. Among many good examinations of the problem, see John M. Ellis, *Literature Lost: Social Agendas and the Corruption of the Humanities* (New Haven: Yale University Press, 1997). Allan Bloom's *Closing of the American Mind,* though now aging, still remains the single most incisive presentation of the problem.

2. Edward O. Wilson, *Consilience: The Unity of Knowledge* (New York: Viking, 1999).

3. See Randy Thornhill and Craig T. Palmer, *A Natural History of Rape: Biological Bases of Sexual Coercion* (Cambridge, Mass.: MIT Press, 2000).

in our sacred diversity, therefore is beyond good and evil. Both would try to preserve, even if only in partial and incoherent form, what the older tradition of the humanities tried to make fully explicit and self-consistent: why there is a difference between human action and the behavior of all other phenomena in the universe, and why we need a different kind of science in our reflection on human nature and in the judgments we make about human action. Science as currently practiced cannot help us here. It can only provide more and more complex explanations that reduce what some of us still insist on calling good and evil to mere physical processes. The deformed versions of the humanities are also of no help: typically they posit a radical individual freedom that should not be interfered with from without, whether by other individuals or by human groups. But on what grounds does a belief in radical individual freedom rest, and why should we prefer it to any number of possible alternatives?

A Misguided Response to the Situation

So the humanities in our day find themselves between two stools. The moral problems that arise from these approaches, grave as they are, are only a sign of even deeper errors that the traditional humanities were intended to guard against.[4] But we need to be careful about what the humanities are capable of doing, lest we destroy their value even as we seek to restore them to their proper place. Many who are upset with what they justifiably regard as the ideological barbarity that has come to be the standard method of teaching the humanities err in their reaction. Because the barbarians show the door to the central principles of the West in general and the United States in particular, those who would recivilize higher learning believe they must impose lessons in the very things those they oppose reject. But this is to fight one ideology with another. The very tradition of humanities in the West — the impartial search for truth — is ill-served in the process. However much the "impartial search for truth" has been used as a cover for nihilism in recent years (how much truth has been discovered by the race-gender-class version of the humanities?), properly reconceptualized and concretely practiced, that search not only teaches *about* the humanities, it embodies their very essence. The impartial search does not mean that the humanities are all search and no truth, as some now believe. It calls on us to make the most strenuous efforts to arrive at the best account we can give of ourselves and our place in the world.

4. For an exposition of the self-contradictions in these views, see Peter Berkowitz, *Nietzsche: The Ethics of an Immoralist* (Cambridge, Mass.: Harvard University Press, 1995).

Many people seem to think that study in the humanities will lead to a revival of religion, public morality, the nuclear family, American principles, or the Western tradition. The humanities *can* lead to such outcomes, and in the present writer's view, it would be a good thing, by and large, if they did. But the humanities are quite different from any of these otherwise worthwhile aims. The relationship between the one and the other has never been better described than by John Henry Newman:

> That perfection of the Intellect, which is the result of Education, and its *beau ideal*, to be imparted to individuals in their respective measures, is the clear, calm, accurate vision and comprehension of all things, as far as the finite mind can embrace them, each in its place, and with its own characteristics upon it. It is almost prophetic from its knowledge of history; it is almost heart searching from its knowledge of human nature; it has almost supernatural charity from its freedom from littleness and prejudice; it has almost the repose of faith, because nothing can startle it; it has almost the beauty and harmony of heavenly contemplation, so intimate it is with the eternal order of things and the music of the spheres.[5]

Amid the many uplifting things said here, which beautifully capture some of the inspiration many have felt as they studied the humanities, we should not overlook the wistful repetition of the "almosts" in Newman's shrewd assessment. Study of the humanities can do a great deal of good in clarifying our understanding of many issues. But what we do with humanistic learning depends on several factors, before and after such study, and not strictly speaking part of the humanities themselves.

How to Restore Study of the Humanities

But let us begin with the question of restoration. How can we restore the study of the humanities? The answer for the foreseeable future may be not to rely overly much on the colleges and universities that constitute formal higher learning. Some resisters to current trends have advocated "home colleging" as a natural sequel to the burgeoning homeschooling movement, and developments such as the Internet and other means of guiding higher studies may make such alternatives possible. But the vast majority of students and parents will have to find a way to make use of the obvious resources available in our institutions of

5. John Henry Newman, *The Idea of a University* (Washington, D.C.: Gateways Edition, 1999), p. 126.

higher learning without falling prey to indifference toward liberal learning or succumbing to self-destructive indoctrination.

This is difficult, but not impossible. The Intercollegiate Studies Institute (ISI) has published a very useful guide to colleges and universities that avoids the simple black-and-white categorization of most humanities-oriented groups. Its editors make the point that it is useful to have some people liberally educated with prestigious degrees from places like Harvard or Princeton, however uncongenial they may be, because it gives them an opportunity for future influence on a wide range of other institutions. Certainly, some institutions are already doing the right thing, others have good departments or programs, and still others have a few professors that students may consult with to make the best of running a difficult minefield. The ISI guide names and sifts the wheat from the chaff for those who want to take the trouble to get a real education.[6]

But as this effort suggests, the whole process of educating students in the humanities requires a much more active role for parents and students than in the past. Most potential college students have no idea what a liberal education is and have to rely on parents and others for guidance. This means parents themselves have to do some homework, not merely continue along the easy path of making sure their children get good grades and then apply to the most prestigious schools. That way lies the decline and death of the humanistic disciplines. Parents and their children have to form an idea of what — other than career advancement — they think college is for. If the answer is becoming a better human being and the available institutions won't do, parents and students will have to demand better — by taking themselves and their tuition payments elsewhere, or by pressuring institutions. Most institutions will claim they can do nothing. But a few deans, department heads, and senior faculty have been known to make quite bold moves when they get the right ammunition from parents and students.

Even where the institutional factor is manageable, however, we need to start much further back. Aristotle remarks in the *Nicomachean Ethics* that the person who is not well brought up will not even be able to see the starting point for ethics. *Mutatis mutandis.* The same might be said for the larger vision on which the humanities depend: we need good early formation to help us recognize that human beings are something special in the world and that failure to recognize the particular nature of human existence and action leads to self-contradictions fatal to good action and, potentially, to outright crimes. In the normal course of things, young people absorb at home, from extended family

6. See the Staff of the Intercollegiate Studies Institute, *Choosing the Right College: The Whole Truth about America's 100 Top Schools,* introduction by William J. Bennett (Grand Rapids: Eerdmans, 1980).

members, from churches and synagogues, and from other early experience with human communities a certain acknowledgment of human specialness and of the obligations this lays on us all to act well. The older term for the habits that arise from such early training is virtue.

Such virtues are always necessary to good order in society. But they are even more necessary in our time to prevent students from being deluded by the false humanism and scientism outlined above. Only people already habituated to recognizing the dangerous consequences of those views can resist and actually confront them when they appear. In most secondary schools and institutions of higher learning today, unfortunately, relativism makes a kind of false peace. People agree — far too quickly — to disagree about their conflicting views. The humanistic discipline of examining various alternatives and their implications in quest of finding the best form of life for individuals and societies consequently never takes place.

But we are coming to recognize more and more that a day of real reckoning cannot be put off forever. One of the things that makes teaching the humanities simple — though never easy — once blinders have been removed is that the material is everywhere around us. We only need to look at things from the right angle to see that we are constantly confronted with classic questions, even in the reductionist approaches of the race-gender-class humanists. If we really believe that human beings of all races, both genders, every ethnic group and economic class, in all times and places, share a unique and sacred quality, for example, questions will arise that can lead us on to basic issues.

By contrast, the usual way of presenting race, gender, and class today has a quite limited horizon. We can confirm this by a thought experiment. Let us say that the current anti-humanists succeed beyond their wildest dreams. Modern societies become utopias of color blindness, gender equality, and classless egalitarianism. Then what? Does the End of History arrive and eliminate the need for the humanities, except to amuse us by helping create the equivalent of Japanese flower arrangements, as Francis Fukuyama has projected?

This outcome is quite doubtful. As anyone who has reflected on human nature will see, no social situation, however ideal, will ever abolish the old human questions. The race-gender-class proponents deal with a set of human *problems*. Whether these are basic or transitory or a fantasy of current scholars is largely unimportant. Problems, as such, can be solved. Beyond the problems that exist at any moment, we have the inescapable *conditions* of human life.

Death always spurs us to reflection. Suffering and injustice raise another set of perennial considerations. In addition, if we have a strong experience of human nature, we cannot believe that any society will abolish the old human tendencies towards envy, lust, ambition, self-promotion — the list could go on without end. They exist as perpetual possibilities in the human soul. Any system that expects to eliminate them will rather soon find that it takes more than some rearrangement of social roles to change human passions.

These conditions will return again and again. How to confront these essentially irresolvable *conditions* of human existence does not admit of many answers. Historically, there have been three or four main positions. We know that there is a spiritual answer: the saint. For Westerners, this means living according to the tradition that originates in the Bible and finds further elaboration in Augustine, Aquinas, Luther, Calvin, and a very small number of other religious thinkers. Even for nonbelievers, knowledge of this set of responses is necessary. Otherwise, they will simply fail to understand what many people in the past and present are all about.

Another answer to the mysteries of the human condition stops short of the theological answer. A rational reflection puts forward the philosopher as another human model. There are several competing traditions even within this kind of rational approach to human conditions. And we may believe that some contemporary thinkers supersede earlier philosophers. But there is no way to know this as a fact without grappling with the pre-Socratics, Plato, Aristotle, the Stoics, Cicero, Augustine and Aquinas (both again), Descartes, Leibniz, Pascal, Hume, Kant, Hegel, and several more recent figures — and comparing their conclusions with our own.

Beyond the heroes of thought, the Western tradition has always recognized heroes of action. The hero occupies an honored place alongside the saint and the philosopher. Some heroes have large, almost eternal echoes. Homer's Achilles, Virgil's Aeneas, and a small number of other figures reveal to us a dimension, neither spiritual nor philosophical, that always deserves human respect and attention. There are modern variations on heroic themes — the heroic scientist or medical researcher, for example. Our challenge is to know how to identify and properly value them.

The usual ways of coming to appreciate these great human types have not been superseded. A very few academic disciplines must bear the weight of humanistic truths. Literature from every age will show us how much of the crucial human concern over ultimate destiny and immediate choice persists in various circumstances and despite all complications. History will illuminate for us those precise differences from one age to the next. Philosophy will lead us into the deeper questions of what these subjects rest on. Politics will expose us to the competition for power but also the pursuit of justice. Theology tells us how much the human may depend on our always precarious intuitions of the divine.

But let us not be naive. The humanities may become a pursuit of immoral power just as much as any other form of human learning. As the great modern political philosopher Leo Strauss has observed, "Karl Marx, the father of communism, and Friedrich Nietzsche, the step grandfather of fascism, were liberally educated on a level to which we cannot even hope to aspire." If the two most murderous and anti-human movements of the past century could grow from such humanistic formation, is there any real use to the humanities at all? The same author continues: "But perhaps one can say that these grandiose failures make it easier for us who have experienced those failures to understand again the old saying that wisdom requires unhesitating loyalty to a decent constitution and even to the cause of constitutionalism. Moderation will protect us against the twin dangers of visionary expectations from politics and unmanly contempt for politics."[7]

Politics and the Restoration of the Humanities

Politics comes into the restoration of the humanities because, like the family, the kind of regime in which people live deeply influences their notions of common decency and public standards. Of course, at the deepest level, the humanities may be studied under any regime, but it may require great genius and heroism to do so. Better, moderate regimes, like better families, make the study easier.

Recognizing this truth, however, may seem discouraging. The United States certainly has a moderate constitutional system and a people ardently devoted to the "cause of constitutionalism," yet these very things — indisputable goods at another time — seem in part to block the way to real humanities study. Many people now think relativism is the natural soil of democracy. This is a view that would have shocked the Founding Fathers, because it seems to rule out all public truth claims in advance. Constitutionalism defined as following the intent of the framers is often decried as a conservative bid for power. Even those who support such constitutionalism may suspect, given its results in our day, that something of its current manifestation was not present at its creation.

Still, the moderate form of democracy, the democracy of Hume, Smith, Burke, Tocqueville, and the Founders, offers rich material for humanistic analysis. One way that the humanities could be reinvigorated at all levels in the United States is quite simple and, for that very reason, would be quite controversial. (Simple is not the same as easy; the most basic truths may take quite Herculean and complex efforts to be appreciated.) Insofar as America has any public beliefs, they are contained in the Declaration of Independence, which was intended to provide a public justification for rebellion against England and

7. Leo Strauss, "Liberal Education and Responsibility," in *Liberalism Ancient & Modern* (Chicago: University of Chicago Press, 1968), p. 24.

the establishment of a free nation. The heart of that founding document is a short phrase: "We hold these truths to be self-evident, that all men are created equal, that they are endowed by their Creator with certain inalienable Rights, that among these are Life, Liberty, and the pursuit of Happiness." What was self-evident to the signers, however, is hardly ever spoken of among us. And what seemed to them constitutional moderation appears almost radical to us because of our peculiar situation.

Yet a whole course in the humanities could be developed from taking this seriously as a proposition to be rejected or defended. For instance, the Declaration asserts that there are truths about human beings. Are there, or is the word "men" that follows a hint that, as many humanities teachers now claim, even America's most cherished principles were merely the attempt of wealthy, white males of European background to secure their own privileges? Of course, a wise teacher will also wish to explore whether, even if this doubtful historical analysis were so, the principle might also be true in a larger sense than the Founders intended.

But the discussion might go much further. Are we really equal, and, if so, in what sense? In every classroom there are obvious inequalities of talent and effort. Do these matter to our respect for others — and, if so, how? Do we have to believe in a Creator who has made us special beings to believe that we have potent natural rights? Are those rights limitless or is there some built-in relationship between rights and responsibilities?

Conclusion

Just outlining the questions that arise from a single pregnant sentence shows what far-ranging issues emerge everywhere when we begin to take matters seriously. There is no guarantee that serious humanistic reflection will lead to assent to any of the Declaration's propositions. In fact, it is quite likely, as we see in every generation, that some people will make serious arguments why they should be denied. But one thing such a global challenge will not allow us to do is to duck questions and the implications of certain answers. When we are reading science or philosophy, for example, we cannot simply write off the notion of free will or human dignity without running the risk of quite serious political repercussions. Reflecting on those repercussions is part and parcel of the philosophic enterprise itself. Similarly, we may come to the conclusion that God-given rights are tenable or that they are not, perhaps because the existence of God is or is not believable to us. But whatever answer we embrace, we will see the need to find some grounding in God or nature (defined differently than the scientists do at present) to allow for our other concerns.

Such an approach would be controversial because it appears to be indoctrinating students in Americanism, or religion, or specific philosophical positions. But teaching less influential — and usually less well thought through — views runs the same risk. Real instruction in the humanities, however, does no such thing. There are a small number of alternative views about the highest things in human affairs. These cannot be avoided except by a prior decision that we will not think about them at all. We have been fortunate in America that our national Founders were also people who had reflected deeply on human nature and history and brought the fruits of their humanistic labors to bear on creating a nation. Some people exposed to their views will reject them. Others will differ in part, agree in part. Ultimately, the humanities are not tied to Americanism or any other national vision. But for us, in our time, professing as we all do that something good, if imperfect, has emerged from the order of the ages in America, we might choose a far worse place to start.

Contributors

Stephen H. Balch is the founder and president of the National Association of Scholars, America's largest and most active academic organization committed to higher education reform. He has written numerous articles on the problems of American higher education and has spoken on many college campuses. He previously spent thirteen years as a member of the Government Department at John Jay College of Criminal Justice in New York City.

Kevin Belmonte is a historian specializing in the study of William Wilberforce and the group of reformers with whom he worked, the Clapham circle. He is the Director of the William Wilberforce Papers Project at Gordon College in Wenham, Massachusetts, and has edited a definitive edition of Wilberforce's magnum opus, *A Practical View of Christianity.*

Elayne Glover Bennett is the founder and president of the Best Friends Foundation, a nondenominational, apolitical organization that helps roughly five thousand adolescent girls (grades 4-12) in schools nationwide find "self-respect through self-restraint." She is the 2000 recipient of the prestigious American Institute of Public Service's "Jefferson Award."

T. William Boxx is chairman and CEO of the Philip M. McKenna Foundation. He is also the co-founder of and a Fellow in Culture and Policy with the Center for Economic and Policy Education at Saint Vincent College, Latrobe, Pennsylvania. Mr. Boxx is co-editor of books on culture and public policy including *Public Morality, Civic Virtue, and the Problem of American Liberalism.*

Zbigniew Brzezinski, a former National Security Advisor to President Carter, is a counselor at the Center for Strategic and International Studies and professor of American foreign policy at the Paul Nitze School of Advanced International Studies, The Johns Hopkins University, Washington, D.C. He is the author of *Out of Control.*

Don Eberly is the author or editor of numerous books on American society and culture, including *Building a Community of Citizens: Civil Society in the 21st Century* and *America's Promise: Civil Society and the Renewal of American Culture.* He has also founded several national civic initiatives, including the Civil Society Project, which he directs, and the National Fatherhood Initiative, of which he is chairman and CEO.

Amitai Etzioni is a professor at George Washington University and a leading contributor to communitarian thought. Among his best-known books are *The Moral Dimension: Toward a New Economics; Public Policy in a New Key;* and *The Essential Communitarian Reader.* He is regarded as a founder of the communitarian movement and directs the Institute for Communitarian Studies at George Washington University.

John Fonte is Senior Fellow and director of the Center for American Common Culture at the Hudson Institute. He has been a visiting scholar at the American Enterprise Institute and served as a senior researcher at the U.S. Department of Education. He has written numerous articles and essays and has testified before Congress on citizenship naturalization and on civil rights issues. He is also co-editor of Education for America's Role in World Affairs.

Mary Ann Glendon is Professor of Law at Harvard University. She writes extensively on issues of law and society and is widely recognized as a leading expert on family law. Her books include *Rights Talk: The Impoverishment of Political Discourse* and *Nations Under Lawyers: How the Crisis in the Legal Profession Is Transforming American Society.*

Stephen Goldsmith was mayor of Indianapolis, Indiana, from 1992-1999. During his tenure, he undertook a number of initiatives designed to organize, energize, and empower the residents of the city's most troubled neighborhoods. Mr. Goldsmith has also contributed to the national public policy debate as chairman of the Center for Civic Innovation and Co-chairman of the National Council for Public-Private Partnerships.

Cherie S. Harder currently works as Policy Director for Senator Sam Brownback (R-KS). She previously served as the Deputy Director of Policy for Empower America. Her professional articles have been published in a variety of magazines and newspapers and her media appearances include CNN, MTV, PBS, and CNBC.

Elizabeth L. Haynes is the Program Officer for the W. H. Brady Foundation. Dr. Haynes has over seventeen years of experience in management, five years of experience in college teaching, and ten years of experience in technical training and writing. She is a member of the advisory board for the Foundation for Individual Rights in Education.

Gertrude Himmelfarb taught for twenty-three years at Brooklyn College and the Graduate School of the City University of New York, and she has written extensively on Victorian history. Her books include *The Demoralization of Society; On Looking into the Abyss; Poverty and Compassion; The Idea of Poverty; On Liberty and Liberalism;* and, most recently, *One Nation, Two Cultures.*

Wade F. Horn is president of the National Fatherhood Initiative. He is currently an adjunct faculty member in the Graduate Public Policy Program at Georgetown University and is an affiliate scholar with the Hudson Institute. He has served as the Commissioner for Children, Youth, and Families, and Chief of the Children's Bureau within the U.S. Department of Health and Human Services.

Leon Kass is Addie Clark Harding Professor in the Committee on Social Thought and the College at the University of Chicago. Dr. Kass has been engaged for thirty years with ethical and philosophical issues raised by biomedical advance, and more recently, with the ethics of everyday life. His works include *The Hungry Soul: Eating and the Perfecting of Our Nature; The Ethics of Human Cloning* (with James Q. Wilson); and *Wing to Wing, Oar to Oar: Readings on Courting and Marrying* (with his wife, Amy A. Kass).

Charles Krauthammer served on staff for the Carter Administration and later became a syndicated columnist, winning the Pulitzer Prize. He is a regular weekly panelist on "Inside Washington" and a contributing editor to *The New Republic* and *The Weekly Standard.* In addition, he also serves on the editorial boards of several journals, including the *National Interest* and *The Public Interest.* A former practitioner of psychiatry, his co-discovery of a form of manic-depressive illness is still frequently cited in the psychiatric literature.

Thomas Lickona is a developmental psychologist and professor of Education at the State University of New York at Cortland, where he directs the Center for the Fourth and Fifth Rs (Respect and Responsibility). Dr. Lickona is an internationally respected authority on moral development and values education, and is the author or editor of five books, including *Educating for Character: How Our Schools Can Teach Respect and Responsibility.*

Joseph Loconte is the William E. Simon Fellow in Religion and a Free Society at the Heritage Foundation. He has written *Seducing the Samaritan: How Government Contracts Are Reshaping Social Services* as well as many articles, and he serves as a regular commentator on religion and culture for National Public Radio's *All Things Considered.* Mr. Loconte has testified before House and Senate subcommittees on federal efforts to expand the role of faith-based poverty-fighting groups.

Herbert London is president of the Hudson Institute. He is also the John M. Olin University Professor of Humanities at New York University. Dr. London is a noted social critic who has authored fourteen books, including *Myths That Rule America; Why Are They Lying to Our Children?; Military Doctrine and the American Character;* and *Armageddon in the Classroom.*

Elizabeth Lurie, a former business owner, has been actively involved in the field of public affairs philanthropy since the mid-1970s, when she began service as an advisor to the W. H. Brady Foundation, an independent charitable corporation. Ms. Lurie currently serves as director, president, and treasurer of the Foundation. In addition, she often writes or edits articles and books on current public affairs issues.

Terry Mattingly writes the nationally syndicated "On Religion" column for the Scripps Howard News Service, and his columns can be found on the World Wide Web at http://tmatt.net. He also is director of the Institute of Journalism at the Council for Christian Colleges and Universities. In addition to his CCCU duties, Mattingly is a frequent lecturer on religion.

Joe McIlhaney is president and founder of The Medical Institute for Sexual Health, a nonprofit medical and educational organization started in 1992 to confront the worldwide epidemics of nonmarital pregnancy and sexually transmitted disease. The organization promotes marriage as a public health issue. A board-certified obstetrician/gynecologist, Dr. McIlhaney was particularly active in the field of reproductive medicine during his twenty-eight years of clinical practice.

Michael Medved is the host of a nationally syndicated daily radio talk show and former chief film critic for the *New York Post.* He served for twelve years as cohost of the PBS weekly movie review show "Sneak Previews" and has written many books including *Hollywood vs. America: Popular Culture and the War on Traditional Values* and, with his wife Diane Medved, *Saving Childhood: Protecting Our Children from the National Assault on Innocence.*

Eric Miller is Assistant Professor of History at Geneva College, Beaver Falls, Pennsylvania. He is currently working on a biography of the American historian and social critic Christopher Lasch. His essays and articles have appeared in

Christianity Today, Books & Culture, The History Teacher, and *Christian Scholar's Review.*

David G. Myers is John Dirk Werkman Professor of Psychology at Hope College. His research and writings have appeared in five dozen periodicals, from *Science* to *Scientific American,* and his textbooks for introductory and social psychology are studied at nearly one thousand colleges and universities. He is the author of *The American Paradox.*

Kenneth A. Myers, a former producer of National Public Radio's *Morning Edition,* is the founding producer of the audio magazine *Mars Hill Audio Journal.* He is the author of *All God's Children and Blue Suede Shoes: Christians and Popular Culture.*

David Popenoe is Professor of Sociology at Rutgers University where he is also co-director of the National Marriage Project. He specializes in the study of family and community life in modern societies and is the author or editor of nine books, including *Life Without Father: Compelling New Evidence that Fatherhood and Marriage Are Indispensable for the Good of Children and Society* and *Promises to Keep: Decline and Renewal of Marriage in America.*

Robert Royal is president of the Faith and Reason Institute in Washington, D.C. His books include *The Virgin and the Dynamo: Use and Abuse of Religion in Environmental Debates; Dante Alighiere: Divine Comedy, Divine Spirituality;* and *The Catholic Martyrs of the Twentieth Century: A Comprehensive Global History.* He is a regular columnist for *Crisis* magazine, and his articles have appeared in a variety of periodicals.

Amy L. Sherman is Senior Fellow at the Welfare Policy Center of the Hudson Institute and Urban Ministries Advisor at Trinity Presbyterian Church in Charlottesville, Virginia. She is also the founder and former executive director of Charlottesville Abundant Life Ministries, a cross-cultural, church-based outreach in an urban neighborhood. Dr. Sherman is the author of several books, including *Restorers of Hope: Reaching the Poor in Your Community with Church-based Ministries that Work* and *The Soul of Development: Biblical Christianity and Economic Transformation in Guatemala.*

Curt Smith is vice president and chief operating officer at the Hudson Institute, under which he led an international team to observe the Indonesian elections. He directs the Institute's efforts to engage the nation in a sustained effort to promote cultural renewal, an enterprise that brought this book to the fore. Before joining the Institute, Mr. Smith was an award-winning journalist and longtime Capitol

Hill political aide. His articles have appeared in such major news outlets as the *New York Times* and the *Washington Times.*

Wesley J. Smith left the full-time practice of law in 1985 to pursue public advocacy and to be an attorney and consultant for the International Anti-Euthanasia Task Force. He is a lecturer and public speaker who has authored numerous books, including *The Senior Citizens' Handbook: A Nuts and Bolts Guide to More Comfortable Living* and *The Culture of Death: The Assault on Medical Ethics in America.* He has also co-authored four books with Ralph Nader, including *No Contest: Corporate Lawyers and the Perversion of Justice in America.*

John G. West Jr. is an Associate Professor of Political Science at Seattle Pacific University and a Senior Fellow at the Seattle-based Discovery Institute, where he directs the program on religion, liberty, and civic life. Dr. West is the author of *The Politics of Revelation and Reason: Religion and Civic Life in the New Nation* and co-editor of *The Encyclopedia of Religion in American Politics* and *The Theology of Welfare: Protestants, Catholics, and Jews in Conversation about Welfare.*

William B. Wichterman is chief of staff to a Pennsylvania Member of Congress and has worked on Capitol Hill for thirteen years. He is active in initiatives to influence culture using both law and other culture-shaping institutions.

Christopher Wolfe is chairman of the Department of Political Science at Marquette University. His primary area of teaching and research has been Constitutional Law and he is the author of several books, including *The Rise of Modern Judicial Review* and *How to Read the Constitution.* Most of his current work is in the area of liberal political theory and legal philosophy. Dr. Wolfe is the founder and president of the American Public Philosophy Institute.